Against the Friars

ALSO BY TIM RAYBORN

*The Violent Pilgrimage: Christians,
Muslims and Holy Conflicts, 850–1150*
(McFarland, 2013)

Against the Friars

Antifraternalism in Medieval France and England

Tim Rayborn

McFarland & Company, Inc., Publishers
Jefferson, North Carolina

Library of Congress Cataloguing-in-Publication Data

Rayborn, Tim, 1968–
Against the friars : antifraternalism in
medieval France and England / Tim Rayborn.
    p.   cm.
Includes bibliographical references and index.

ISBN 978-0-7864-6831-7 (softcover : acid free paper) ∞
ISBN 978-1-4766-1914-9 (ebook)

1. Friars—History.   2. France—Church history—987–1515.
3. England—Church history—1066–1485.   I. Title.
BX2820.R39 2014   271'.06042—dc23   2014032198

British Library cataloguing data are available

© 2014 Tim Rayborn. All rights reserved

*No part of this book may be reproduced or transmitted in any form
or by any means, electronic or mechanical, including photocopying
or recording, or by any information storage and retrieval system,
without permission in writing from the publisher.*

On the cover: Detail of a miniature of Faussemblant (False Seeming or Fraud),
Contrainte Atenance (Abstinence, or Forced Abstinence), and another
speaking to Male Bouche (literally, Foul mouth, or Scandal),
(British Library Catalogue of Illuminated Manuscripts)

Printed in the United States of America

*McFarland & Company, Inc., Publishers
Box 611, Jefferson, North Carolina 28640
www.mcfarlandpub.com*

Table of Contents

Preface 1

Introduction 3

1. Popular Religion, Heresy and Mendicancy   9
2. The University of Paris and the Quarrels   32
3. The Perils of the Last Times: The Writings of Guillaume de Saint-Amour   52
4. Antichrist's Boy: False Seeming, the Apocalypse and the *Roman de la Rose*   63
5. Poetry and Song in 13th-Century France: Rutebeuf, the Trouvères and the Goliards   83
6. Scandalous Fables and Vulgar Animals: Reynard, the Fabliaux and Fauvel   96
7. England: The Turbulent 14th Century, and the Writings of Chaucer, Langland and Gower   117
8. English Religious Criticism: Matthew Paris, Oxford University, Richard FitzRalph and John Wyclif   134

Conclusion 162

Appendix A: Art Bibliography and Resources 165

Appendix B: Music Bibliography and Resources 168

Chapter Notes 172

Bibliography 224

Index 245

Preface

This book is a vastly expanded version of my M.A. dissertation, completed at the University of Leeds more than 20 years ago. I had always found the topic interesting and had intended to revisit it at some time, but my work in the early/medieval music field (as a performer and in other capacities), and other intervening events over the years prevented me from doing so until recently.

As might be expected, scholarship in antifraternalism has continued at a brisk pace over the last two decades, and studies on the topics herein have increased to ever larger numbers. In addition, any early concerns I may have had about being able to find sufficient material on which to write were laid to rest fairly early in my research; this work ended up being more substantial than I had initially imagined, as well as fascinating and quite enjoyable.

The subject of the present work is the varied reactions against the friars (in this study, primarily the Franciscans and Dominicans) in the first two hundred years of their existence, the 13th and 14th centuries. Medieval Europe underwent drastic changes in this period, with not only astonishing social upheavals, but also intellectual conflicts, heretical movements, seemingly endless wars, climate change, famines, the calamities of a devastating plague, and a struggle for the Church itself. The friars were a product of some of these changes, and were caught up in others, but their efforts at giving a voice to popular religious sentiments (in a Church-approved manner) were not always appreciated or wanted. They rather frequently found themselves the targets of attacks, whether theological and complex condemnations, or vernacular and vulgar mockeries. The hostility on occasions could spill over into physical violence. What were the issues involved? Why did these seemingly humble and poor Church servants arouse such anger, resentment, and comic ridicule?

This book is a general survey of medieval antifraternalism in its early manifestations, and is suitable for the newcomer, as well as for those who are familiar with the subject, but might like to investigate specific topics in more detail. Extensive notes and a lengthy bibliography should keep such readers happy and busy for some time. Further, the notes contain a considerable number of excerpts of original texts from various sources, allowing enthusiasts of medieval languages the chance to read these writers in their own words. I hope that this work will give a sufficient window into a fascinating time and subject, and that it will encourage readers to explore its many facets, and perhaps undertake research of their own.

I wish to thank Dr. Marta Cobb (University of Leeds), Stephen O'Shea (author of two excellent books on the Albigensian Crusade and the Inquisition), and Catherine Scholar, who read various chapters and offered their very helpful feedback. I also want to thank Dr. Rosalind Brown Grant, University of Leeds, for her help, and for being the original supervisor of my dissertation those many years ago. I again wish to thank Abby, who understands just how involved these projects can be, given that she's been doing similar levels of intense work of her own. And I would like to acknowledge our felines, who, as any cat owner and lover will understand, continue to come up with creative ways of preventing me from getting books like this finished.

Introduction

> "Friars, friars, woe be to you,
> Ministers of evil!
> For many a man's soul you bring
> To the pains of hell."[1]

This harsh and damning poem addressed to the friars dates from about 1490 in England, but it could easily have been written two centuries earlier in France. Such vitriol from both theologians and vernacular writers, attacking orders created by and answerable only to the pope, is one of the more remarkable aspects of religious debate and controversy in the later Middle Ages. From the mid–13th century, these not-infrequent attacks appeared in a variety of sources and from a number of writers with different backgrounds, both religious and lay. The negative feelings that they evoked have never entirely dissipated.

Indeed, the image of the medieval friar—lazy, corpulent, drunk, jolly, perhaps lecherous or corrupt—is readily called to mind for the modern reader. The Western popular imagination's most famous friar, Tuck of the Robin Hood legends, fits some of these descriptions well enough, though he is an exception, an outlaw of course, but one with a just cause. Few know or care that his very presence among the merry men is an anachronism; Robin Hood and his band of heroes waged a legendary war against Norman oppression in the time of King Richard and his scheming brother, King John, years before Francis of Assisi obtained papal approval for his humble, simply-robed order.[2] The Franciscans, including Tuck, have frequently been mocked and caricatured for their love of good food and alcohol, and the resultant size of their bellies. Today, many images of Franciscan-like friars and monks grace the labels of modern beers, for example, where they are only too happy to raise a glass in toast to the customer.

Others may know of the Dominican order and its involvement in the dreaded Inquisition, ironically through the splendid comic portrayals by Monty Python and Mel Brooks, or perhaps in classic horror movies, where villainous inquisitors extract confessions through torture. Umberto Eco's novel *The Name of the Rose*, and the film based on it, further popularized these orders through a vivid mixture of clever murder mystery, intellectual stimulation, and historical settings. Sean Connery may be the most famous Franciscan, after St. Francis himself.

In each of these examples, the friars are not portrayed in an especially positive manner; there is a lingering sense of mockery, and perhaps some judgement or condemnation. William of Baskerville, Eco's Sherlock-like Franciscan protagonist (even his name recalls the famous Holmes story of the Hound), appeals to us because he differs from so many who held to the prevailing beliefs of his time. He embraces rationalism and rejects superstition. He solves the mystery of the deaths in the abbey through deduction and logic, while the others around him—Franciscans, Dominicans, Benedictines, and heretics alike—all seem foolish and backwards, clinging to fears of devils and the dangers of new ideas.

These unusual fraternal orders stood apart from their contemporaries in many ways. They only appeared in the early 13th century, they were unlike traditional monastic orders (such as the Benedictines or Cistercians) in their organization and mission, and they were often strongly opposed by a number of different factions and groups, both within the Church and outside of it. This book surveys some of that opposition in the first two centuries of the orders' existence in France and England, both from the religious and secular spheres, and looks at why it was so vehement. Sermons, theological tracts, letters, vernacular poetry, music, and art were all used at times to attack the friars, whether through parody, biting satire, or blatant condemnation. What caused this resistance? Why were these orders, theoretically devoted to poverty, humility, service, and preaching, attacked in such ways? There are many answers, as we will see.

The word "friar" derives from the Middle French *frere* and the Latin *frater*, or "brother," which indicates some affinities with monastic orders, though the differences between the friars and more traditional monks were great and a source of much controversy and conflict. Indeed, they presented something of a mid-point between the two extremes of monastic life and that of the laity, but this also put them in competition with the clergy: the bishops, priests, and clerics who would become some of their fiercest critics.

The other commonly-used terms, the "mendicants" or "mendicant orders," derive from the Latin *mendicare*, "to beg," and this became one of the biggest issues for their critics. Friars were expected to live by begging, not by working, even if they were able-bodied. To say that this caused resentment from many around them, both inside the Church and outside of it, would be putting it mildly. "Friar" and "mendicant" are generally used interchangeably throughout this book.

Traditional monasticism called for a personal vow of poverty, but the houses themselves held wealth in common, growing tremendously wealthy and owning enormous amounts of property and land. The friars' poverty, by contrast, was also intended to be reflected in their greater orders, who were not supposed to be seduced by the lure of material wealth. That this ideal soon proved unworkable in the real world, particularly for the Franciscans, was one of the first great issues of conflict for both external critics and for the friars themselves. Many more problems would soon follow, and criticisms which began in earnest by the mid–13th century, would continue and grow over the next several centuries.

For clarity, the term "antifraternal" refers to attitudes and writings against the friars, while the term "anticlerical" generally encompasses a broader scope, and can refer to hostility toward priests, bishops, monks, and others in the traditional Church hierarchy. This book will focus mainly on antifraternal writings, but also include some anticlerical works, to place the former in context. Indeed, in some instances (such as the fabliaux), the friars were merely substituted for monks in new versions of old stories; anticlerical became antifraternal.

In modern scholarship, there are different approaches to medieval writings against the friars. Some, such as Penn Szittya, have labeled the entire phenomenon as an "antifraternal tradition," which began with the "quarrels" at the University of Paris (between the university masters and the friars then present), and extended into the time of Chaucer and then into the Reformation in England.[3] He asserts that these "share a common language, largely derived from the Bible, and a common—theological, symbolic, and prejudicial—perception of the friars."[4]

Others, such as G. Geltner, have more recently called into question the notion of an unbroken and unified tradition, arguing instead that works written against the friars were more haphazard and diverse. They were not part of a single mode of attack, but represented objections to the friars from various areas of society, both religious and lay. The friars were no more singled out for such attacks than any other group, he maintains.[5] Whereas the earliest writers against the friars, such as the Parisian theologian Guillaume de Saint-Amour, sought to abolish them entirely in view of apocalyptic expectations, some later writers were less emphatic, usually seeking the reform or reorganization of what they saw as corruption and hypocrisy.[6] These sins were frequently linked to broader anticlerical themes, such as simony, corruption, and the desire for wealth and power.[7] Further, Geltner states, it would be a mistake to link all such attacks to a common source of anger, resentment, or fear, or to ascribe to them equal historical validity.[8] Indeed, the very presence of the friars at times led to a decrease in anticlerical sentiments among the laity, since they offered a different way of religious life, notably in contrast to the lavish wealth and pomp of bishops and monastic houses.[9]

Both of these views have merit and elements of the truth. In terms of a tradition, it is certain that Guillaume's writings against the friars of Paris circulated relatively widely in England in the 14th century, for example, and may well have influenced the writings of both religious and secular polemicists. Further, he is lauded in the 13th-century *Roman de la Rose*, the most widely read French poem of the Middle Ages, so he was hardly forgotten, even if his calls for the abolition of the friars were not taken up as strongly in succeeding generations.

How guilty were the friars of the various offenses of which they were accused? Certainly some of the criticisms were justified. Any human endeavor, no matter how nobly intended, will have its failures, those who simply cannot live up to its ideals. Geltner notes that "there is no reason not to take satirists and polemicists at their (face-level) word or to dismiss the self-criticism of mendicant reformers as a rhetoric of fallenness. Official deviance among friars was substantial according to both their own administrative accounts and an array of external sources."[10] In England alone, there are 94 recorded cases of mendicant apostasy among the four orders before 1400, as well as additional charges of theft, heresy, and even illegally marrying.[11] This seems a relatively small number, given the proliferation of mendicant convents in the 13th and 14th centuries, though it is not possible to generalize or to know how many additional infractions were not recorded, whether in England or other regions of Europe.[12] Interestingly, records from the 14th century show that those who left the Franciscan order often cited its austerity as the main reason, which contradicts the many accusations about friars living in luxury in defiance of their vows. Further, these "apostates" cited the harsh criticisms and persecutions that they were subjected to from outside the order.[13]

This study will concern itself primarily with the Franciscan and Dominican orders, though two smaller orders, the Carmelites and the Augustinians, were certainly important. For a good study of these and other mendicant orders (which were ultimately suppressed), see the overview by Frances Andrews, *The Other Friars*.[14] As such, "the friars" in this book will generally refer to the Franciscans and Dominicans, with the other orders being specifically named in the instances in which they appear. These two larger orders had some different privileges and standings than their lesser counterparts,[15] and by far they made the biggest impact on events of any of the fraternal orders in the 13th and 14th centuries.

Chapter 1 begins with a brief history of dissent in the 12th century. During a time of spiritual crisis, one common response was the wandering preacher, who addressed the masses and advocated a return to simplicity, often garnering a considerable following. These kinds of figures and movements invariably caused problems for the Church, as their teachings frequently slipped into heresy. Indeed, the greatest threat to the medieval Church, Catharism, became so strong in the south of France that it threatened to eliminate orthodoxy there altogether. From this turbulent situation, the Franciscan and Dominican orders were born, and were seen by the papacy as a perfect solution to the need for popular religious expression. However, new troubles soon followed. The Cathars would not go quietly, and the Dominicans came to prominence during the Inquisition, the reign of terror determined to root out the remaining heretics not exterminated by the Albigensian Crusade.

Chapter 2 examines the first major intellectual conflicts between the secular clergy and friars at the University of Paris in the mid–13th century. Arising over issues of scholarly privilege and masters' rights, the quarrels escalated into a vitriolic war of words. The leader of the university masters in the debate, Guillaume de Saint-Amour, formulated disturbing and elaborate theories about how the friars were precursors to Antichrist and the apocalypse, leading to a showdown involving the papacy and King Louis IX.

Chapter 3 looks at Guillaume's writings in more detail, showing just why he thought the friars represented such a danger not only to the university, but to the Church and the whole world. If his positions seemed strained or improbable now, they were very much of concern at the time, and he had followers who endorsed them wholeheartedly.

Chapter 4 begins the first of four chapters devoted to antifraternal writings in the literary and artistic worlds. The famed French poem, the *Roman de la Rose*, was widely circulated and appreciated for its complex meanings, debates on love, and allegorical imagery. Yet there was a darker side to it. The allegorical character of False Seeming delved deeply into issues about the friars and their supposed corruptions. The author of the longer continuation of the poem, Jean de Meun, was a partisan of Guillaume de Saint-Amour, and two decades after the conflict, Jean used this unusual character to voice some very harsh objections to religious hypocrisy, all in what was supposed to be a lengthy meditation on the varieties of love.

Chapter 5 continues with the French polemicists, looking at the works of the great satirist Rutebeuf, another follower and closer contemporary of Guillaume's, whose satirical writings were directed not only at the friars, but also at Church corruption and even the king, a dangerous path to take. Many of Rutebeuf's fellow poets, who were also musical composers known as trouvères, turned their attention to religious corruption, as did the controversial goliards, the "wandering clerks" who wrote scathing Latin songs celebrating drinking, gambling, women, and a wild lifestyle, while also offering critiques of the hypocrisies of religion.

Chapter 6 looks at the longer literary works of Reynard the Fox, the French beast stories that spare no one in their mockery of literary courtly and social norms, as well as the scandalous fabliaux, frequently obscene stories (even by modern standards) where corrupt and lecherous priests, monks, and friars were never in short supply. Finally, there is a survey of the masterful *Roman de Fauvel*, a remarkable blend of poetry and music from the early 14th-century French court. This cautionary tale of a vice-ridden horse who becomes king satirizes the corruption of power and serves as a warning to all who seek it, whether noble, churchman, monk, or friar.

Chapter 7 looks at the literary life of England in the 14th century, exemplified by its three greatest representatives, Chaucer, Langland, and Gower. All three wrote works in which the friars received considerable abuse, whether comic or serious, but they approached the subject differently from one another.

Finally, chapter 8 reviews the extent of antifraternal writings and attitudes among religious writers in England (clerical and monastic) from the mid–13th century to the end of the 14th, in the writings of the Benedictine monk Matthew Paris (well known for scathing and sarcastic remarks in his chronicles), the conflicts between masters and friars at the University of Oxford, and the writings of England's two most famous antifraternal theologians, Richard FitzRalph and John Wyclif. Wyclif's stances against Church corruption and calls for total reform would have him posthumously condemned, and his followers, the Lollards, burned as heretics. Indeed, the English Protestant reformers of the 16th century looked back to him as the "morning star" of their movement.

No book can give an exhaustive account of all of the instances of antifraternal writings. For each of the examples discussed here, there are dozens more that have been omitted, but it is hoped that this overview will give a sense not only of writings against the friars, but of the larger field of Church criticism which overlapped them. The notes and bibliography can be used as a starting point for more detailed reading and research. Enthusiasts for medieval languages and texts will have many excerpts to peruse in the notes.

Perhaps unfairly, this book does not give the friars a chance to answer their critics. Famous friars such as Bonaventure and Thomas Aquinas (whose large girth may have been one source of the stereotypical obese friar imagery) certainly responded, often vehemently, to the charges leveled against them, defending their way of life with passion and eloquence; this is a topic worthy of study itself. With the exception of Bonaventure's sparring with Guillaume de Saint-Amour, however, space does not permit a proper survey of these responses here, though several are mentioned in the notes and the bibliography. Countless friars were undoubtedly deeply devoted to their calling and accusations against them of hypocrisy and betraying their vows were unfair and misplaced. However, there were always enough friars and convents that deviated from their presumed sanctity to keep the antifraternal hostilities alight, if not always inflamed.

The innovation of the friars initially seemed like a perfect solution to the Church's troubles, and indeed, the orders had considerable enthusiastic support that never wavered, especially from the papacy, to which they answered directly. Their membership grew at an astonishing rate throughout the 13th century, they became counsellors to princes and kings, and they received an almost endless stream of donations and gifts, so they certainly fulfilled a great spiritual need. Yet, there were always those who were not so enamored, who believed that this adulation was misguided or even dangerous, who saw in the friars' actions only hypocrisy and deceit, greed and theft, and worst of all, signs of the end of the world. From outrage at the Inquisition to vulgar animal tales, from harsh theological accusations to fart jokes, these are their stories.

1

Popular Religion, Heresy and Mendicancy

In the early 1130s (possibly 1131), a dramatic event took place in Saint-Gilles-du-Gard, a region between Nimes and Arles, stretching to the southern coast of Languedoc. There, an angry mob seized a priest, Peter of Bruys, and cast him onto a blazing bonfire of burning wooden crosses, crosses that Peter himself had set alight.[1] This horrific death was a reaction to Peter's teachings and his actions against the Church. He embodied the kind of rebellious thinking of popular religious movements that had become numerous and increasingly dangerous to the established order since the "Gregorian" Reform and the First Crusade of the late 11th century. The Reform sought to clarify the authority of the papacy over secular rulers, as well as define the roles of the clergy and laity. Specific corruptions, such as simony, were also targeted.[2] Further, Pope Gregory VII (1073–85) sought the assistance of the laity in helping to curtail clerical abuses. However, this well-intentioned effort at inclusion opened the way to greater criticisms of the Church in general, something that he certainly did not intend. At the same time, there arose an increasing desire to emulate the primitive Church, to follow in the path of the original apostles, renounce possessions and wander the world as preachers.

Given that the Church, and especially the monasteries, owned large areas of land, there began to be a reaction against such extravagance from the 11th century. Views on monasteries as land-holders and rent-collectors aroused suspicion and some resentment among the laity. Why were humble monks wielding such political and economic power? As C.H. Lawrence observes, "The Benedictine abbeys were deeply implicated in the economic and political fabric of society as landlords, territorial rulers, holders of military fiefs and patrons of churches. It is not easy to view one's landlord as a paradigm of sanctity, especially when he raises the rent."[3] In response, new monastic orders such as the Cistercians sought to undo what they viewed as the laxity and extravagance of large, older orders such as the Cluniacs, and adhere to a much stricter observance of the monastic Benedictine Rule.[4]

Individual reactions to perceived Church corruption often came from lone preachers with dangerous ideas, such as Peter of Bruys. Peter, from the Hautes-Alpes region, was dissatisfied with the structure of the Church, and resolved to undertake the life of an itinerant preacher, probably in 1112 or 1113. Like many such figures, he was charismatic enough to attract audiences, and gained a group of followers, dubbed the Petrobrusians, that grew to a sizable number over the next two decades. They engaged in acts of vandalism against churches, threw crosses on bonfires, and assaulted priests and monks.[5] His message was one of returning to simplicity, but it struck at the very heart of some of the principal teachings of the Church, and his movement was one of many that would rock the social structure of Western Europe in the 12th and 13th centuries. The abbot of Cluny, Peter the Venerable, felt compelled to write a lengthy refutation of Petrobrusian beliefs, the *Contra Petrobrusianos*, in which he laid out the various errors in belief and offered his answers to them.[6] Peter the Venerable also wrote against both the Jews and Muslims, and his project to study Islam and refute it as a Christian heresy was the first of its kind in the medieval West.[7]

Peter of Bruys and his followers held certain key beliefs. They rejected the baptizing of infants and children, arguing that salvation was due to one's faith. Infants did not have the knowledge or even the consciousness to make such a decision, and therefore could not willingly enter into that state. He held that places of worship (churches, chapels, etc.) had no special meaning, and that the true Church of God could not be contained in stone buildings; rather it was made up of a community of believers. He detested crosses and crucifix imagery, saying that the cross was nothing more than the vile means by which Christ had been tortured and murdered, and therefore it should not be venerated, but despised.[8] It was this that led the Petrobrusians to gather wooden crosses into piles for bonfires and burn them, which also caused his own ghastly death. He stated that priests had no special divinely granted powers within the sacraments, and therefore the Eucharist had no meaning. There had been only one Eucharist, at the original last supper, and there was no further consuming of the body and blood of Christ (in the 14th century, the reformer John Wyclif would make his own controversial statements about the Eucharist).[9] Peter also insisted that nothing could be done in the service of the dead, as was common practice. This included prayers, masses, and the giving of alms, all common actions performed by those hoping to obtain some benefit for the souls of the departed. Peter felt that the dead would gain only what they had earned in this life, and once dead, no further intercession by the living was possible.[10] Further, he rejected chant and religious music, saying that God did not wish it to be sung; one should address God silently.[11] These assertions essentially denied any power or privilege to priests, monks, or bishops, and undermined the entirety of Church ritual. Some have seen in his views similarities to later Protestant reformers.[12]

After Peter's death, his cause was taken up by Henry of Lausanne, though Peter the Venerable was not certain that the two had ever met. Active in northern France, Henry seems to have distanced himself from the violent reactions to the cross of his predecessor. At one point, he was forced to recant and enter a Cisterican monastery, but was later active again. The records do not give an indication of his final fate.[13] Consensus now holds that neither Peter nor Henry were adherents of the dualist heresies imported from the east, those beliefs held by the Bogomils and Cathars.[14] As such, their beliefs were probably not a coherent heretical system, but rather a reaction to Church authority, and abuses of power.[15]

By the later 1170s, another movement had appeared, and some confused them with a revived gathering of Henry's followers. These were the Waldensians, also known as the Poor Men of Lyons, said to have been founded by one Peter Waldes,[16] a cloth merchant who had grown very rich in his trade, but had become dissatisfied with materialism, not unlike the later Francis of Assisi. He sold his possessions, made provisions for his wife and daughters, and lived the life of an itinerant beggar and preacher. It seems that he possessed a vernacular translation of certain New Testament books, something that was forbidden, as was his desire to preach. As Lawrence notes, "To the ecclesiastical mind, direct study of the Bible by uninstructed lay people was fraught with peril—it was almost bound to engender anti-clericalism and heresy."[17] This fear of losing control over the populace was at the source of many of the fiercest persecutions of heretical ideas and movements, especially the Cathars, as we will see below.

Unlike some other movements, Waldes sought papal approval for his mission, which had attracted a group of followers. In 1181 at a synod in Lyons, he swore before the papal legate allegiance to Church teachings, belief in the sacraments, the truth of infant baptism, the efficacy of the mass and its use for the dead, and the value of confession, all things that Peter of Bruys had vigorously denied. If he hoped that this declaration would gain for his movement Church approval, he was mistaken. At the Council of Verona in 1184, Pope Lucius III declared in his decree *Ad abolendam* that the Waldensians were heretics and thus excommunicated. The result was to split the movement into factions, those that continued to support the Church despite its ruling, and those who rebelled and drifted further away from orthodoxy. Pope Innocent III eventually made efforts to reincorporate those loyal to the Church at the beginning of the 13th century, in part because he realized that such popular movements could be used to help turn the tide against the Cathars.[18] However, heretical branches of the Waldensians continued to exist and be persecuted for several centuries.

At the same time, a similar group arose in Italy, the Humiliati, who also desired a return to apostolic poverty, to live simple and penitential lives, and to preach. The group seems to have consisted of two divisions. The first were those that followed a kind of monastic vocation, practicing celibacy, communal living, and lay preaching. The second consisted of devotees from everyday life who were married, lived in their own homes, and engaged in their professions, but still followed the unofficial rules and guidelines of the movement.[19] This focus on lay members who were not outcasts and continued to live their lives set the movement apart from some others, but it was the act of preaching that once again brought them into conflict with the established Church. Like the Waldensians, they were condemned and excommunicated by Pope Lucius III in 1184, though this did not bring an end to the movement.

Also like the Waldensians, Innocent III saw some potential use in them, and in 1201, he proclaimed that they had been "rehabilitated" and brought into the fold of Mother Church. They were given papal approval and a constitution, and they were further divided into three branches from their original two: an ordained canonical order, a monastic order, and a lay order for the married who wished to partake of the rigorous religious life. This official recognition simply extended how the movement was already organized, but with the significant difference that the ordained were now licensed to preach in a limited manner. This was an extraordinary development that contradicted the traditional role of preaching,[20] one which the friars would also soon be granted and which would cause considerable controversy. Indeed, there were similarities between the Humiliati and the Franciscans, though the latter were more devoted initially to poverty and renunciation. Nevertheless, Innocent's actions opened the door to a new kind of authorized religious order, with rights and privileges of a kind not previously permitted.

While the Humiliati and Waldensians were seeking and gaining some formal acceptance, one group stood out that would never be accepted, the Cathars. Catharism was the quintessential heresy of the High Middle Ages. The name may derive from the Greek for "the pure,"[21] or even the Low German *ketter* ("cat"),[22] though it was not what they called themselves; they were simply "good men" and "good women," or just Christians. Theirs was a belief system so popular that at times in the 12th century, it seemed poised to eradicate and completely replace Catholicism in the region of what is now southern France. Its appeal was enormous, from the lowest peasant to counts and princes, and it directly opposed Catholic teaching and authority, with its own churches and bishops, though in a looser structure than that of the hierarchical Church.[23] Catharism was a dualist heresy, that is, it drew from Eastern concepts about the dual nature of creation. These were various gnostic beliefs that had been common since Roman times and had a variety of names, the most famous being Manichaeism, a heresy to which St. Augustine of Hippo had once belonged.[24] Trying to pinpoint one specific faction of these beliefs as the direct ancestor of Catharism is problematic, but the medieval incarnation certainly shared many of the same tenets, with a Christian gloss. The universe consisted of good and evil, light and dark, spirit and matter. The good that was the spirit was to be embraced, while the darkness of the material world was to be shunned.

As such, Cathars denied the efficacy of and the need for the sacraments, including baptism (water was of the material world), the Eucharist (these objects did not literally become the body and blood of Christ), and marriage (flesh was corrupt and could not be made holy though this action). There was only one sacrament, the *consolamentum* (the "consolation"), which took away the individual's sins and marked them as one of the "perfect" (as they were called by their accusers). This sacrament was often conferred to Cathars who were dying, as those who received it before their deaths thereafter had to live lives of asceticism, renouncing sex, meat (animals came from sexual reproduction), and all worldly things. Cathars also condemned war, capital punishment, and killing, and viewed the cross as nothing but a symbol of Roman torture and death. Intriguingly, they also held a strong belief in reincarnation; souls were condemned to be reborn in the physical world until they had renounced it completely and attained the perfect status, a view that has remarkable similarity to Hindu and Buddhist beliefs and hints at the religion's Eastern ancestry.

This oddly pacifist and egalitarian movement became extremely popular among all social classes, and it grew rapidly throughout the 12th century in the lands from Languedoc to Northern Italy. Early attempts to combat it though preaching and debate failed miserably, for many Cathars were equally learned and educated. This was not the movement of a ragged band of malcontents, but was organized, thoughtful, and importantly, quiet and non-confrontational. Cathars did not send out firebrand itinerant preachers, or engage in mob violence against churches and clergy; this made them far more difficult to detect and counter, much less condemn, for they seemed to be living exemplary lives, and were not at first distinguishable from their Catholic neighbors.[25] Indeed, both groups often lived side-by-side in relative peace. Further, given the territorial aspirations and conflicts in the region, a number of nobles tolerated Cathar beliefs, or even joined the sect themselves, having no desire to be subjected to the dictates of the pope or the French king in the north.

This unusual climate of tolerance of dissenting views and a fierce independence led to great cultural achievements in the region. Perhaps the most famous, the legendary troubadours flourished in Occitania in this relaxed environment, creating their masterful poems and songs for Catholic and Cathar patrons alike, including Eleanor of Aquitaine. Some troubadours were nobles themselves, including Eleanor's grandfather, Guillaume IX.[26]

This culture was to meet an end as a result of the Albigensian Crusade.[27] Innocent III and his predecessors had struggled with how to address the Cathar issue; in 1208, he received the answer, when a papal legate was assassinated (we will examine this below). In retaliation, he declared a crusade against the region of the south, and offered the lands of the heretics and their supporters to the northern knights and nobility, if they would answer his call. This temptation was irresistible, and the north answered with fervor, descending on the rich and fertile southern lands with a mixture of greed and perhaps some genuine religious zeal, though this was not a prerequisite.

In the first years, the northern crusaders had a number of successes (due as much to blunders by the southern forces and sheer luck as by their own military skills), taking several cities and crushing resistance, often with appalling viciousness. The famous, but apocryphal story of Arnaud-Amaury, Abbot of Cîteaux, illustrates this. At the siege of Béziers in 1209, he was asked how the crusaders would know the Cathars from the Catholics in the city once they took it. He is recorded as replying, "Kill them all, the Lord will know his own."[28] Whether these words are true or not, they represent the merciless attitude of the northern crusaders perfectly. The crusaders sacked the city, burning it to the ground. They delighted in massacring some inhabitants, or torturing and mutilating others. Arnaud-Amaury wrote to the pope, boasting that 20,000 had been killed, though this number was likely exaggerated. Still, it was enough to inspire fear and the immediate surrender of some regions.

For a time after 1215, the south was able to strike back, retaking certain cities and lands, and scoring a splendid moral victory by killing Simon de Montfort, the crusade's leader in 1218. Cathar and Catholic were said to have fought alongside one another, united in their hatred of the invading armies and their loyalty to their independence. Ultimately, however, the French forces overwhelmed and defeated the Occitanian armies. The war officially ended with the treaty of Paris in 1229, wherein certain noble families (the House of Toulouse, as well as the Viscounts of Béziers and Carcassonne) were stripped of their independence and most of their fiefs, being brought under the rule of the French crown. Southern independence was at an end.

The peoples of the south were not so ready to capitulate, however, and resistance continued for some time. The Cathars were as stubborn as ever, and so the papacy concluded that only by the setting up of special commissions to root out heresy would the belief ever be exterminated. This plan coalesced from independent tribunals into the dreaded Inquisition from the 1230s onward, whose primary goal was to uncover and exterminate heretics. The relatively tolerant and relaxed culture of the south was replaced by what was in effect a police state, where informants were encouraged, dissidents driven underground, and paranoia reigned. So determined was the Cathar resistance, however, that it was well into the 14th century before it was finally eliminated.[29]

The devastating effects of the crusade (which had been the first against fellow Christians) coincided with upheavals across Europe. Social changes, urbanization, and the growth of learning outside of the monasteries all contributed to creating a new culture and society to which the existing Church structures were having increasing difficulty adapting. Popular religious movements were clearly a threat to the established order, and some exposed issues of corruption and misdeeds that many in the Church hierarchy would rather not have brought to light.

These criticisms extended into the proliferation of vernacular literature. Satires of clerical sins were becoming ever more popular among the laity, both noble and common, and internal criticisms and factional disputes between various branches of the clergy were common.[30] In the century before the establishment of the friars, clergy and monks already had a long-standing tradition of quarrels over issues of preaching and pastoral care.[31] The Church's monopoly over thought and education was being eroded. Previously, learning was nearly the exclusive preserve of the monasteries, but now secular students traveled far from their homes in search of the best teachers at the burgeoning universities. A middle class was emerging, a newly-affluent and better educated group not averse to criticizing what it saw as the failures of Church leadership.[32] One glaring error was the lack of a training program for parish priests, resulting in some being as ignorant and illiterate as their followers, a charge that many friars would later use as a defense of their preaching activities.[33]

In this uncertain and chaotic time, the appearance of the mendicant orders and their charismatic founders must have seemed to be truly a godsend for a beleaguered Church. Though quite different from one another, Francis and Dominic proposed novel and innovative ways of correcting some of the problems they saw besetting their world. For many Church officials, their ideas must have seemed like the perfect solution. Their popularity came in large part from reaching out to the laity in a way which the hierarchical Church had not done (or could not do), especially those in urban areas.[34] They would offer the hope of salvation to the laity in ways that traditional monasticism could not.

The Early Franciscans

Francis of Assisi has retained a hallowed air down the centuries. He is beloved by countless admirers today, both within and outside of the Catholic Church. His name conjures images of saintliness, of a gentle man who preached to animals and showed great care and compassion for all living things, while remaining humble and true to his calling. A cult of personality happily evokes this warm glow, as it did in his lifetime. Indeed, even the most virulent critics of the Franciscan order rarely turned their venom on Francis, though there were some exceptions).[35] Upholding Francis's perceived saintliness was actually a useful tool for the enemies of the order; one of the chief charges levelled against both the Franciscans and Dominicans was how far and how quickly they had fallen from the ideals of their founders.

The truth about Francis is the truth about any saint, or any human being praised by posterity; legends grow up around such an individual, and it can be difficult to disentangle them from the truth. Francis was clearly motivated by an intense devotion to the ideals of a return to apostolic poverty and the simple life. Charity, mercy, love, and compassion were undoubtedly virtues that he held dear. However, he was also quite proud of his friars when they went preaching in Islamic lands and were executed, thus gaining martyrdom, sometimes deliberately so.[36] His famous meeting with Sultan al–Kamil of Egypt, often proclaimed as a kind of early inter-faith dialogue, began as a preaching mission that Francis undertook with the goal of either converting the sultan to Christianity, or dying in the attempt; he failed on both counts, though their meeting certainly was of historic importance.[37]

Keeping in mind that the life of a saint can be as political and subjective as any other topic, perhaps more so, the first life of Francis was written by Thomas of Celano (*ca.* 1200–65), having been commissioned by Pope Gregory IX in 1228. As Lawrence notes, "Although it is couched in the rhetoric of official hagiography, as a historical source it has two important merits: it was begun in 1228, within two years of Francis's death, and it was the work of a friar of the first generation, who had met him."[38] This record would only serve for sixteen years, after which Thomas was commissioned again, this time by the Franciscan general chapter, to expand on his work and flesh it out with more detail and richer content, between 1244 and 1247. Finally, after another sixteen years, the great Franciscan philosopher and theologian Bonaventure (1221–74)[39] was tasked by the chapter of Narbone to write a definitive "official" life of their beloved founder, reconciling conflicting stories, addressing some already-existing political conflicts, and placing Francis at the forefront of holy figures of the time. With the completion of this project, the Franciscans sought to destroy the two earlier lives of Thomas of Celano.[40]

The life of Francis is well-known and does not need to be documented extensively here.[41] He was born in 1181, the son of a wealthy cloth merchant, Pietro Bernadone, in the Umbrian hill town of Assisi. For the first two decades of his life, he was devoted to the affairs of the world, including both business and military activities. He had some education in both Latin and French, and could read and write, skills essential for the merchant's life that he was expected to undertake. In 1205 at the age of 24, he had a dramatic conversion experience to the religious calling, a dream wherein he said that he was called by Christ to abandon his old life and take up a new spirituality. He subsequently renounced his family inheritance and home, and set out on a new path, unsure of where it would lead. Drawn to the solitary and ascetic life, he may have encountered practitioners of these ways in the countryside of Umbria, where they were common enough; these may have included Waldensians and Huliliati.[42] In time, he also became attracted to the apostolic life, the *via apostolica*, of living in poverty and preaching. This was to become the central tenet of the Franciscan order. In 1208, he attended a mass near Assisi which helped him to clarify his mission.[43] Having attracted followers, he made his case to the Curia, and Pope Innocent III granted him permission in 1210 to create his new order. Unlike existing monastic orders, this new brotherhood was modeled entirely on the life of Christ and the apostles; even his primitive rule was based on gospel texts, rather than, for example, the Benedictine Rule. Lawrence notes that "this simple and literal understanding of the Bible was characteristic of Francis. His vision was always direct, literal, and concrete, uncomplicated by the conceptual analysis of the clerk who had been through the schools."[44] This unschooled simplicity by a simple founder would come back to haunt the Franciscans (indeed, Francis did not want his brothers to own books). As we shall see in chapter 2, the secular masters would point to this as proof that the Franciscans should not be seeking prestige and positions at the University of Paris.

Thus, the Franciscan order was born, and set out on its evangelical mission, its brothers adopting a radical voluntary poverty that required them to sell all of their possessions and give the money to the poor before they would be admitted. The early brothers made poverty an absolute, reflected even in their clothing, which was a simple robe tied by a cord at the waist (earning them the name *cordeliers* in later literature). They walked barefoot, no doubt at times a painful and humiliating exercise in itself. They could not hold property in common, as did other monastic houses. They did not assume the title of "monks"; rather, Francis called them his "little brothers," or *fratres minors*, the Friars Minor. With no permanent homes, no possessions, no wealth, and no food, they set out into the world, adopting a mendicant lifestyle and begging for their food, taking shelter where they could, and considering it a badge of honor if they were abused or turned away, living just as they believed the first apostles did. To them, this was a true *imitatio Christi*, one that had papal approval, and thus immediately became appealing to many seeking a withdrawal from the troubled world.

However, it was as obvious to those early brethren as it is to the modern historian that, as the order attracted enthusiastic followers and began to grow, it simply could not sustain this extreme way of life for long, at least not in such an unregulated way. Adjustments to the world of monetary economies and the realities of supporting an ever-growing membership would have to be made, and so the door was open to charges both from within and without of abandoning the order's ideals, of betraying Francis's vision, and of falling back into worldly corruption.[45]

In its early years, the order was already subject to some suspicion and resentment, ironically due to its success in attracting not only good thinkers, but wealthy and aristocratic converts. Aware of Francis's conversion and rejection of his heritage, other wealthy families were less than enthusiastic about their own sons joining such an extreme organization, especially since it reduced all social classes to a state of equality with each other; a knight or prosperous merchant became no better than the poor farmer when they entered the order. Indeed, the Franciscans voluntary adoption of such drastic poverty and squalid living conditions caused them to be associated in the minds of some with outcasts from society, such as lepers and other marginalized groups.[46]

The problem of the use of money became apparent and needed to be addressed. Pope Gregory IX received an appeal from the order in 1230 to help resolve this problem, for money was needed to ensure day-to-day operations, yet Francis had forbidden the brothers even to touch coins. The pope, whether by an ingenious or cynical resolution, decreed in the bull *Quo elongati*[47] that the Franciscans were permitted to appoint a *nuntius*, a special "friend" to the order, who had the power to collect donations of money. These were increasing with the order's popularity, both from living benefactors and from those who left money to the friars in their wills. This "friend" would take care of the worldly affairs so that the brothers would not be tainted. The Franciscans began to house themselves in permanent buildings, rather than barns and shacks, another necessity if their mission was to be successful, and so the problem of ownership arose again. This was solved simply when Pope Innocent IV declared in *Ordinem vestrum* 1245 that said buildings belonged to the Holy See.[48] In effect they were the pope's property, a legalistic trick that allowed the Franciscans to observe their rule in letter, if not in spirit.[49] These changes did not sit well with some brothers, who felt that they betrayed the wishes of Francis, however practical such rulings may have been. These and other accommodations to the secular world would lead to a split in the order, and include heated debates, charges of heresy, suppression of dissent, and persecution.[50] We will examine this conflict in more detail below.

Thus, less than two decades after the death of its founder, the order found itself firmly ensconced in the world that Francis so dearly sought to avoid. The first communities had been in Italy, but already, the order was taking on an international character. However, its initial attempts at missionary work in foreign lands often met with opposition, owing to the unwashed strangeness of the friars, and their lack of language skills in the new countries they visited. There is, for example, the rather comical story of the friars who tried to preach in Germany, but had no knowledge of the language. They could only respond to questions with *ja*, or "yes." When asked in German by suspicious locals if they were heretics from Lombardy, they answered in the affirmative, not knowing what they were answering to, and were beaten, stripped, humiliated, and chased away. Due to this experience, none of the friars dared to return[51]; so much for martyrdom. Such accounts may have been exaggerated somewhat, however, as they wore such humiliation as a badge of honor.[52]

The Franciscans met with suspicion in other lands, including Italy. Salimbene di Adam (1221–90),[53] a noted Italian Franciscan chronicler, was warned by his father Guido not to join the order. Referring to them as "piss-in-tunics," when his son disobeyed him and also took his brother into the order, he cursed them both with great anger, giving them up to devils.[54] This very harsh reaction shows how disliked the friars could be, and this antipathy could extend into wider communities.

The order fared better in France, however, having established a base there at Saint Denis as early as 1219, and soon after received the support of King Louis VIII and Queen Blanche, whose son, the devout Louis IX, would become one of their principal defenders and protectors, much to the chagrin of the secular masters at the University of Paris. More Franciscan houses began to appear in northern France during the 1220s. Unlike their monastic counterparts, the friars (both Franciscans and Dominicans) set up houses primarily in urban environments, though often at the edges of a settlement. This was due to the high costs of procuring buildings, and eventually to resentment by parish clergy.[55] Though this was in line with Francis's wish to preach to the laity and seek to redeem the sinful, it was still a departure from his love of solitude and the natural world. These houses were no longer shacks and huts, but rather began to resemble those of other monastic orders, such as the Benedictines, with stone buildings, a cloister, a permanent church, living quarters, and libraries, all lived in and used safe in the knowledge that the pope owned everything.[56] The buildings began to become larger and grander, as well, perhaps reflecting the new achievements in Gothic architecture in Paris and elsewhere. One consequence of these new urban dwellings was that locals began to rely on the friars for their spiritual needs, rather than consulting the parish priest and the traditional clergy, who had always assumed that this role belonged to them alone. Obviously, this bred resentment and feelings of rivalry.

Some within the order began to get too comfortable with these new arrangements, living in a manner far from their initial calling. A famous early example was the minister general of the order, Brother Elias of Cortona, who in the 1230s aroused considerable criticism for his increasingly lavish lifestyles. Elias had known Francis personally, and had announced his death to the world. He had worked to establish the order in urban settings, with their monastic-like structures, and he also encouraged the friars to travel farther abroad. However, he began to rule too autocratically for the liking of many, and did not consult the brothers though meetings of the general chapter. It was further alleged that he took with him retinues of what were for all intents and purposes servants, and even had a personal cook. In 1238, the pope sent him on a mission to the Holy Roman Emperor Frederick II, long an opponent of the papacy, and then under excommunication. Elias apparently took a great liking to Frederick, who was indeed charismatic; admirers and enemies knew him as *Stupor mundi*, the "wonder of the world." He became a supporter of the emperor, leading to his being deposed at a general chapter in 1239. Elias went on to join Frederick in his military campaigns, though he reconciled with the Church before his death in 1253.[57]

These developments shocked those loyal to Francis's ideals, and Elias became a kind of scapegoat and object of scorn for the *zelanti*, those vehemently opposed to the more worldly direction that the order was taking. Elias' removal was followed by a review of the order's functions and mission, but nothing could stop the direction on which it was now embarked. The transition from a religious movement of the poor to an organization with rules and structures that was well-placed in the hierarchy of the Church was inevitable, despite the protests of the *zelanti* and purists. Burr offers a simple reason that the order had so many supporters for these changes: "The Franciscans should perform the duties because they are so good at them. If that means assuming authority, so be it. Having assumed the duties, they must have the resources to do them well. If that means compromising poverty, so be it. Limiting *minoritas* was the price paid for other benefits gained by the church."[58] Likewise, the generous gifts being offered should be accepted, so that they could be put to good use in assisting the poor, surely as noble a work as maintaining one's own poverty. To reject such gifts undermined the donors' Christian generosity and hopes for their own spiritual well-being.[59]

The order's final constitution and rule were firmly established in 1260 at Narbonne, giving it a permanent structure, but in the decades after Elias's removal, there was still much conflict and disagreement over how it should grow. It was this two-decade time period that corresponded exactly with the conflicts at the University of Paris, as we will see in the next chapter. One result of these quarrels was that the final Franciscan statutes required all potential new postulants to be properly educated with a clerical background, or to be from the laity but with prominence and standing, to have the greatest effect. As Lawrence notes, these strict new requirements ironically would have excluded Francis from joining his own order.[60] One result of this was to create greater inequality among the brethren, as these scholarly recruits were entrusted with the education of their lesser-schooled peers. Such individuals were given leave to study, thus freeing them from some of the duties the others had to undertake, including begging. Often, they had separate lodgings as well, further widening the gap and undermining the egalitarian spirit of the original order. This new educational requirement and the prestige that came with it were akin to such demands that the Dominicans had imposed since their founding, and it is to them that we now turn.

The Early Dominicans

The Order of Friars Preachers was also known as the Dominicans, the Blackfriars, and the Jacobins (so-called in French vernacular literature because their first convent in Paris was attached to the church of Saint-Jacques in the Latin Quarter from 1218). The circumstances of their creation were markedly different than those of the Franciscans, yet the two shared similar goals and both stood outside of the traditional Church hierarchy in their early days. The founder of the order was the Castilian Dominic of Caleruega (1170–1221), who with the assistance of the German Jordan of Saxony created an institution that rapidly became influential and powerful.[61] Unlike Francis, Dominic was educated and came from a clerical background, being one of the Canons Regular of Osma, under the Benedictine Rule, a group of priests who, unusually, followed a monastic practice.

As noted, the creation of the Dominicans came as a response to the spread of Catharism. Dominic had become aware of the pervasiveness of its teachings in the south of France as early as 1203 in Toulouse, and by 1206, he resolved to undertake his own preaching mission after hearing that the Cistercian efforts were not effective.[62] Dominic concluded that since the Cathars were humble in appearance and lifestyle (the "perfect" were famous for their asceticism and devotion to their cause), they could only be fought by the same tactics, if the Church was to win back the hearts and minds of the laity. The Cathars were deceptive, he said, not being truly humble or penitent, but their tactics were successful in leading the innocent astray.[63] Only the genuinely humble and penitent could counter them.

In what seems a striking historical coincidence, Dominic embarked on the task of creating a new order that lived its own version of the *via apostolica*, including the practice of mendicancy. This was apparently done independently of Francis; the two admired one another's efforts, but did not meet before 1217.[64] The idea of these new apostolic orders then, was simply the right one at the right time in response to the changes that the Christian world was experiencing.

The orders differed in that Dominic wanted a highly educated group of brothers, who could effectively counter the heresies of the south. The Cathars were famed for their learning and eloquence, and so the unlearned approach to mendicancy advocated by Francis would not do. Like Francis, he received papal permission for his new order and mission. His proposal was first welcomed by Pope Innocent in 1215,[65] though not without some concerns, and approved by Pope Honorius III in 1216.[66]

Bishop Fulk of Toulouse, formerly the troubadour Folquet de Marselha, had cast off his life as a secular musician around 1195, and turned his attention to the work of exterminating the Cathars, under whose patronage he had once flourished.[67] He viewed Dominic's mission as perhaps the best means of turning the tide against the spread of Catharism in Toulouse and the surrounding areas, and he advocated to the pope strongly on Dominic's behalf. Innocent agreed, but a problem presented itself: preaching and its license were the preserve of bishops; indeed canon law forbade monks from preaching in public. Further, the Fourth Lateran Council (occurring at the same time) had decreed that no new orders were to be created, an attempt to rein in expansion and control popular religious movements. All new orders had to adopt an existing rule. The solution came by having the Dominicans adopt the Rule of St. Augustine, which, as a Canon Regular, Dominic already followed; thus they became an extension of the Canons. Their preaching would be licensed by Bishop Fulk, and they set up their first house in Toulouse.[68]

They did not wish to remain only in this city, however, and by 1217, Dominic already desired to send his friars out into the world. Not content with attempting to convert the Cathars, he wanted his order to undertake a universal preaching mission, like the Franciscans. He may have had a more urgent motive, in that war was clearly coming. Innocent III had placed a ban on Count Raymond VI of Toulouse, for alleged complicity in the assassination of a papal legate, Pierre de Castelnau, in 1208 (who had been feuding with the count). Raymond was also tolerant of Cathar activity, or at least had no desire or the means to exterminate it. Ultimately, he was deprived of his territory by the Fourth Lateran Council, a deliberate act of papal humiliation which transferred lordship to the northern nobility. Determined to win back his city and lands, he reentered Toulouse in September 1217, taking back the city, and defending it against a subsequent siege, which resulted in the shocking death of Simon de Montfort, one of the Albigensian Crusade's great champions.[69]

Prior to this, and sensing the impending danger, Dominic dispersed all but a handful of the brethren, who traveled to Paris, Spain, and other locales, with the endorsement of Pope Honorius. The decision to send them to Paris and Bologna was certainly deliberate, for Dominic had a great interest in education and learning, and he wanted his friars to be immersed in the intellectual lives of these rapidly-growing university cities. He could not have known the consequences of this, as we will see in chapter 2. Once in Paris, they set about recruiting from the nobility, the wealthy, and the educated clerics. Jordan of Saxony (succeeding Dominic as the Master-General in 1222) was at the forefront of promoting education and recruiting new members from the secular students. Monks from other orders were initially prohibited from joining, though this rule was later rescinded. Clerics were especially valuable, and the order required all new postulants to have a certain level of education in grammar before they could join.[70] This draining of secular clerics and university students into the new order would soon lead to resentment and conflict. To enable these friars to continue with their studies, the order did admit, in limited numbers, illiterate lay brothers, whose purpose was to take on essential labors that freed up their learned colleagues to study. While technically "equal" in status, this shows that there was from the start some division and rankings within the order's structure, even if the lay brothers engaged in many of the same activities. They were viewed as equal, but with separate duties.[71]

Dominic died in 1221 in Bologna, the great university city famed for its study of law. He wanted his friars well situated in cities. Urban locations were not only places of great learning, but also the largest potential incubators of heresy, and so they were best suited to the order's preaching mission. Their critics would also be quick to point out that such cities had the most disposable income and property from potential donors and supporters, which the friars were eager to appropriate for themselves.[72] In Paris and Bologna, the Dominicans would achieve great prominence, and in both cities they would make great enemies.

1. Popular Religion, Heresy and Mendicancy

Perhaps most notoriously, the Dominicans are associated with the Inquisition, an outgrowth of the ongoing efforts to purge Languedoc of Catharism in the second half of the 13th century.[73] After decades of failure and a ruinous war, many Cathars still stubbornly held to their beliefs. As scholars and teachers, whose goal was to preach, the Dominicans seemed ideal for the task of rooting out remaining heresies, especially in urban environments like Toulouse, where Catholic and Cathar had lived in such close proximity. Many Dominicans took to the task with relish, such as Robert le Bougre, a convert from Catharism, who was so zealous in condemning the residents of Mont-Aimé in Champagne (most of them innocent) that he had to be relieved of his duties.[74] It is obvious that individuals with similar minds, whether sociopaths or those afflicted with some other mental disorder would be very much attracted to positions where they could wield sadistic power over the accused. Others, such as Humbert of Romans (*d.* 1277, the fifth Master-General), felt that this work was a hindrance to the order's true purpose, namely study and evangelizing.[75] Indeed, some Dominicans were concerned that this duty would ruin their reputation (and rightly so), and that this kind of coercive threatening of heretics was in direct contradiction to their mandate to preach and persuade.[76]

Before the Inquisition was officially established, there were already a considerable number of appalling examples of this new terror. William of Pelhisson was a Dominican friar in Toulouse, whose admittedly biased accounts nevertheless provide important details about the early workings of the Dominican Inquisition. He notes with satisfaction how even those who were dead were not safe. If a suspected heretic was found to be dead, their body was dug up from the consecrated ground where it was buried and promptly burned. Their former property was also destroyed, often regardless of who was currently living in it, even if they were completely faithful to the Roman Church. Living relatives of these desecrated individuals could be further punished by having their own property confiscated, and possibly even being imprisoned.[77] One deceased Waldensian, a certain Galvan, had his house destroyed and made into a garbage pit, and his corpse burned in a field in 1231.[78]

Farther north, the priest Konrad von Marburg (*ca.* 1180–1233) was given a commission by Pope Gregory IX in 1227 to expose and prosecute heretics throughout Germany. Konrad was long thought to be a Dominican, though this is not now scholarly consensus; he was actually a Premonstratensian.[79] He was a zealous crusader for orthodoxy, in the literal sense, having been involved in the Albigensian crusade. Like Robert le Bougre, he was ruthless, exceptionally cruel, and probably paranoid in attempting to uncover suspected heretics; he was not overly concerned with the actual guilt or innocence of the accused. Given leave to use whatever means he deemed necessary, his presence certainly must have evoked fear and hatred from local populations. However, like many with too much power and a lack of wisdom and decency, he overstepped in 1233, when he accused Henry II, Count of Sayn, of heresy, participating in satanic orgies, and bizarrely, of riding large turtles (which may give us some insight into his disturbed mind). The charges were absurd, of course, and Henry was acquitted in Mainz. Konrad refused to accept the verdict, and left the city, indignant. On the road home to Marburg, he and his Franciscan assistant, Gerhard Lutzelkolb, were attacked and murdered, possibly by knights in Henry's service. He was certainly not mourned, being arguably the most despised man in the region. If anything, there were celebrations as news of his violent and fitting death spread; even the pope made no effort to punish his killers.[80]

Such resistance did not prevent the Inquisition from taking shape however, and in 1233, it was formally established, though it was not a centralized program, rather a set of regional jurisdictions. From the start, it attracted those with a penchant for punishing whoever they saw as guilty. The Dominicans were the papacy's first choice for these matters. The Franciscans initially were not called to perform inquisitorial functions, perhaps due to their being comprised of so many brothers originally from the laity. The pope may have feared that they would not have the "backbone" necessary to root out heretics from among those who had once been their own. Pope Innocent IV (1243–54) gave the Franciscans more responsibility in taking on a role in the Inquisition, primarily in Italy.[81] Eventually, the two orders shared the task more or less equally.[82] Pope Innocent IV authorized the extraction of information by torture in 1256, and allowed the friars to absolve each other for using such methods, if they engaged in the torture themselves, rather than employing lay assistants.[83] The Inquisition was uneven in its distribution across Europe, with a strong presence in France, Spain, and Italy. It was never established in England, and was not a major force in Scandinavia.

Despite Humbert's reservations about the practice, Dominican friars who felt a deep calling to rid the world of heresy could resort to some remarkably cruel and macabre actions that to modern readers, are repellent and seem utterly at odds with the professed goals of the order. Moneta of Cremona, an early inquisitor in Lombardy, for example, defended such actions by asserting that it was proper to kill for God, because God killed. If God is free from sin, killing is not sinful if done in the name of God[84] (a similar justification was used for crusading). William of Pelhisson notes some of these practices, and the resistance they met.[85] He records a horrific story wherein an elderly Cathar woman on her deathbed requested the presence of one of the Perfect to see her off, and grant her the *consolamentum*. Guilhabert of Castres, the Cathars' Bishop of Toulouse, had secretly entered the city on other matters at the time and, learning of her situation, agreed to visit her. However, one of her household betrayed her to the Dominicans, whose house was very near to where she lay dying. The Dominican Bishop Raymond du Fauga, hearing of this, entered the woman's house in disguise pretending to be the Cathar bishop. He, with mock concern, coerced her to admit her Cathar loyalties. When she had done so, he revealed himself and condemned her. He had her tied to her bed and carried out beyond the city to a field, where a fire had been lit, and had her thrown on the flames, murdering her in a terrible manner. Afterwards, he and the other Dominicans returned to their house and gladly ate their evening meal, giving thanks to God and Dominic.[86]

As might be expected, the locals did not take kindly to this new quasi-police state being imposed on them, especially since there had previously been at least some form of tolerance and co-existence in the south. Despite the intention to instill fear, the local populations did fight back in their own way. William of Pelhisson notes with derision that if a popular citizen was accused as a heretic, others retaliated, first with words and insults, and then by throwing stones at the friars, and attacking their houses. He accused them of plotting against the friars.[87] Perhaps this was true; the local population certainly had sufficient reasons to do so. Or perhaps he was a victim of the very paranoia he and the brethren were trying to instill. He also notes that in

1234, the inquisitor Arnold Catalan, after rousing the anger of the Cathars in Albi by his condemnations and burnings, was badly beaten and nearly thrown to his death in the river Tarn.[88] William complained that not only the commoners, but the nobility hindered the friars in their work, including having them killed, despite Raymond's assurances of cooperation. Some nobles would protect and hide heretics and injure and kill their pursuers.[89] This also included the planned retaliation and murder of two prominent inquisitors, the Franciscan Stephen of St. Thibéry and the Dominican William Arnald in 1242, whose deaths were apparently widely celebrated.[90]

Such responses were not confined to Languedoc. During an episode in Bologna in 1299, wherein three convicted Cathars were burned, the local population rioted, accusing the Dominicans of convicting innocents for their own gain (i.e., the confiscation of their wealth and property), a charge that was probably true.[91] The people felt that they were avenging good Christians against the true heretics, namely the friars[92]; resentment over the material wealth acquired by the friars was a common theme in many of the attacks against them, as much as retaliation for Inquisition atrocities.[93] Similarly, Peter of Verona, the Dominican inquisitor of Milan, was attacked and killed in 1252 by two assassins, Carino of Balsamo and Manfredo Clitoro, hired by those with Cathar sympathies. Less than a year later, Pope Innocent IV canonized him, the quickest that such a canonization had ever occurred.[94] This event also influenced the pope's decision to authorize torture in carrying out inquisitional activities.[95]

Despite these instances of violent resistance, the friars, were somewhat reluctant to link their self-proclaimed martyrs with the Inquisition in their official lists. As Geltner notes, "their remembrance of anti-inquisitorial aggression was quite measured, especially in the context of the Parisian affair, martyrdom among non–Christians, or altruism during the Black Death.... Such ambiguity is omnipresent in lists of the orders' saints, a genre whose economy of style leaves much to the imagination regarding the circumstances of each death."[96] This vague reckoning of deaths served to show that the friars saw themselves as willing to do whatever was necessary to promote the faith, with the Inquisition being only one of the many duties that exposed them to danger.[97] Further, it may have indicated a certain level of discomfort with the whole task, echoing Humbert's reservations.[98] The promotion of Peter of Verona as a martyr murdered by heretics was an exception to this practice, and was used, among other things, as an ideological weapon in the quarrel with the secular masters at the University of Paris.[99]

The accounts of violence committed against the friars make for an interesting topic, being recently studied in detail by Geltner.[100] They reveal an interesting mix of incidents, certainly not all related to inquisitorial activities, though such attacks are frequent enough. They range from the expected revenge for heretic condemnations to retaliation for successfully recruiting individuals whose families had other plans for them, to rivalries with monastic orders, violence perpetrated by secular powers, or rivalries between the mendicant orders themselves which erupted into violence (the Dominicans, for example, frequently resented the Franciscans implying that they were the superior order who imitated Christ more perfectly).[101] Finally, other clergy tacitly condoned violence against the friars on occasion. Some Franciscans in the 14th century seemed particularly prone to violence; apparently these peaceful friars were not opposed to carrying swords and attacking each other, and this had to be prohibited more than once.¹⁰² Punishments for transgressions were varied, and included fasting, extra masses, whipping, and if more serious, imprisonment, relocation to another convent, or even banishment from the order.¹⁰³

Instances of violence against the friars were not more numerous than other examples of conflict at the time, and it would probably be a mistake to view the friars as being singled out.¹⁰⁴ They do not seem to have been victims of robbery while traveling between urban areas, for example, possibly because they carried little of value. They were more likely to be targeted for violence in towns and cities.¹⁰⁵ Violence in response to the Inquisition may have been directed as much at the papacy as at the friars in particular, who were simply carrying out their duties; sometimes the hostility was simply due to their being strangers in a given area.¹⁰⁶ As we will see in the next chapter, however, the secular masters at the University of Paris did all that they could to make life difficult for the Dominicans at the height of their conflict with each other, including encouraging Parisians to attack them physically. At the same time, the war of words was heating up.

In Languedoc, some troubadours did not take kindly to the intrusions of the friars and the French into their lands, and bravely wrote poems against them.¹⁰⁷ Peire Cardenal (*fl.* 1205–72) was one of the most striking examples. His condemnations of Rome for its actions and his mockery of Dominican indulgence would be echoed in the antifraternal works of his northern counterparts over the next several centuries. A minor nobleman, he was known for his *sirventes* (satirical and moralizing poems), of which 96 survive; three of his works survive with music.¹⁰⁸ In *Ab votz d'angel*, he denounces the Dominicans for their fondness of food and drink, noting that they have arguments over the best wine, and they accuse those that dispute with them of being heretics. They want to be feared.¹⁰⁹ Theirs is not a spiritual poverty; rather they keep everything they have and take what belongs to others. They prefer soft English wool to hair shirts.¹¹⁰ He devotes three more verses to mocking their fine clothing and finer food, ending with how he would not wish for his wife (if he had one) to sit next to such a friar, who does not wear breeches. Indeed, the supposedly sterile Beguines (see below) can miraculously become pregnant through such associations.¹¹¹ These are bold words, but they would be echoed many times by other poets, musicians, and theologians, as we will see.

Peire did not confine his attacks to the friars, but unleashed his venom on the Church that had assaulted his homeland. In *Li clerc si fan pastor*, for example, he writes that clergy pretend to be shepherds, but are actually killers. They act holy when donning their robes, but like Ysengrin the wolf,¹¹² they put on sheep's clothing to go among the sheep and avoid the dogs that would attack them.¹¹³ Kings and nobles used to rule the world, but now the clergy do, by thievery and betrayal, by hypocrisy, doing violence, and preaching (perhaps a reference to the Dominicans).¹¹⁴ Indeed, he has never seen worse people.¹¹⁵

Others went even further. Guilhem Figueira, a troubadour active in the 1230s under the protection of the Holy Roman Emperor Frederick II in southern Italy, wrote a scathing condemnation of Rome and its war against Languedoc. In *D'un sirventes far en est son que m'agenssa*, he blasts the papacy and its corruption in 22 verses. He condemns its deceit and treachery, accusing the Curia of sanctioning murder without cause, committing many felonies and evil deeds, betraying the trust of all, and numerous other crimes.¹¹⁶

The people were also not silent. In 1286, the citizens of Carcassonne appealed directly to the young King Philip IV for some relief from Inquisition abuses. The king was sympathetic and investigated their complaints, concluding in 1291 that the Dominicans were not to be trusted, that only the king's men had the authority to arrest suspected Cathars, and only then with good evidence. The Inquisition would continue, but it would not be given free reign. There was undoubtedly an element of appeasement to a potentially angry populace who saw themselves as being under occupation by a foreign invader, but it is still a striking rebuke of papal and Dominican abuses of power.[117] This naturally did not please the Dominicans, and in 1297, the inquisitor Nicholas d'Abbeville excommunicated the whole city. An accord was reached in 1299, whereby the excommunication was lifted, in exchange for allowing the inquisitors to return to their work.[118] The people were not pleased.

Clearly, there were still those who were willing to resist the Inquisition and its terrorizing practices. The most dramatic of these acts of resistance, perhaps surprisingly, came from a Franciscan friar, Bernard Delicieux.[119] Bernard, the prior of the Franciscans' convent in Carcassonne, was deeply troubled by the abuses of the inquisitors, and made his first stand against them in 1299, defying the Dominicans by sheltering two suspected heretics within the convent walls. When Nicholas' deputy inquisitor and a few dozen soldiers descended on the dwelling, demanding that the suspects be surrendered, they were ambushed by townsmen, assaulted with clubs, swords, and crossbows, and had to make a strategic retreat back to the Inquisition's headquarters. It was a stunning act of defiance and of the hostility that had grown up in some areas between these two orders of friars, and it prompted Nicholas to leave the city for a time.[120]

In the following year, Bernard proved that Inquisition records were fraudulent and contained faked condemnations and information. He showed that accusations of Catharism against one Castel Fabre (a prominent name in the city who had died in 1278) were false; the men who had accused him had never existed, being concoctions with generic names to obtain a conviction that the inquisitors wanted. The Dominicans were unable to provide any proof that these accusers existed, and the case had to be dropped. It was a huge embarrassment for them, leading to even more distrust of their activities, and prompting them to flee the city to avoid the potentially violent consequences of their deception.[121]

Over the next few years, Bernard went from strength to strength, continuing to attract support. He befriended the viceroy of Languedoc, Jean de Picquigny, and together, they were able to convince King Philip of further corruption.[122] The furious king found himself fully in alliance with the dissident friar. As O'Shea notes, "Never before and never again would the inquisition face such overt wrath from a king of France."[123] Bernard was transferred to the convent in Narbonne, perhaps as a peace offering to the Dominicans in Carcassonne, but he was now able to travel about and preach against the Inquisition with impunity; his actions even led to prisoners in the Inquisition's dreaded "Wall," the prison at Carcassonne, being transferred to a more humane jail.[124]

The beginning of Bernard's troubles came from angering the king during a meeting in January 1304, when he suggested that the south was illegally occupied by the French; this resulted in no new policies favorable to Bernard and Languedoc against the inquisitors.[125] Further problems came from the fact that the new pope, Benedict XI (from October 1301), was the Master of the Dominican order (since 1296). In April 1304, in the bull *Ea nobis*, he ordered that Bernard be arrested, though Benedict died in July, before it could be carried out. His untimely death led some to suspect poison or black magic.

At about the same time, Bernard, unsatisfied by the continuing presence of the Dominican inquisitors and with the king's seeming indifference, reached out to young Prince Ferran of Majorca. If he would back a revolt and secession in Languedoc, the consuls of Carcassonne would place the city under his protection, and accept his rule as the region's new king. It must have seemed an irresistible offer to the ambitious and battle-eager young man, but his father, King Jaume II, somehow discovered the plot, and personally beat his son savagely for his recklessness and disobedience.[126] The plan collapsed quickly, and now Bernard was in trouble. In the autumn of 1304, King Philip was made aware of Bernard's treasonous scheme, possibly by King Jaume, or perhaps from multiple sources. Philip summoned Bernard to Paris, and put him under a kind of house arrest, but took no further actions.[127] Thereafter, Bernard was under the watch of the papacy, but again, was not treated like a prisoner. He was eventually allowed to return permanently to Languedoc, probably in 1310.

Once freed, Bernard continued his defiant stance, becoming increasingly associated with the reformist Franciscans known as the Spirituals (who desired a strict return to the order's original poverty, see below),[128] and the women's lay movement, called the Beguines (see also below); both were often suspected of heresy. By associating with them, Bernard seemed to be offering the people "Access to a humane spirituality denied by an authoritarian, sometimes terrifying Church hierarchy."[129]

The Inquisition carried on with its activities and tensions persisted, while the Spirituals also made complaints about Franciscan abuses. In April 1317, a group of Spirituals, including Bernard, were summoned by the unsympathetic Pope John XXII to account for their views. This was in part a trap to capture Bernard, and he was arrested and subsequently tortured.[130] He was brought to trial on four main charges (though he denied that his accusers were qualified or authorized to judge him): disobedience to the Franciscan order by siding with the Spirituals; murdering Pope Benedict XI (of which he was found not guilty); treason against the French king; and attempting to obstruct and hinder the Inquisition. Additionally, the inquisitor Bernard Gui drew up a list of 64 charges in total against him.[131] His guilt was a foregone conclusion, though additional torture proved of limited use in extracting a confession from him. Indeed, he remained defiant, only breaking in November/December 1319, and admitting to obstructing the Inquisition. His accusers had no desire to create a Spiritual martyr by executing him; he confessed and was given absolution, but he would still need to do penance. So he was sentenced to life imprisonment in the notorious Wall in Carcassonne. Initially, they intended only to give him bread and water, but lenience was offered, exempting him from this harsh treatment.[132] However, John XXII was not pleased with this mercy, and ordered the harsh punishment to be reinstated.[133] Bernard may have been dead by the time this order was issued, or this may have finally killed him, but he died at the beginning of 1320, only a short time after being confined.[134] Bernard ultimately failed, and the Spirituals, as we will see, also ran afoul of the Church establishment, but his tenacity in standing up to a fearsome and powerful organization showed that the Inquisition, and by extension the Church, were not invincible, and that the friars themselves could strongly disagree with each other over the proper implementation of religious practice and teaching.

Women as Mendicants

In this study of the friars' early years, we have focused on the thoughts and works of men, but women also formed and took part in their own mendicant orders; Bernard's association with the Beguines was significant, and they became a substantial and controversial movement. Other women took a more orthodox approach. Clare of Assisi (1194–1253) is the most famous example. Born Chiara Offreduccio to a wealthy family in Assisi, her mother was very devout and certainly influenced Clare's later religious vocation. At the age of 18, she heard Francis preach, and desired to follow him, despite her father's objections (he naturally wanted to marry her into another wealthy family). Francis accepted her, and helped her to become settled in a cloistered house near the church of San Damiano (which, according to legend, is where Francis heard Christ speak to him, telling him to rebuild the church, not only the physical structure of that particular building, but the wider Church). Other devoted women soon joined. They were not to wander as the men did, of course, for such a practice would have been impractical and dangerous. Clare's order, first known as the Order of Poor Ladies, and after her death, as the Poor Clares or the Order of Saint Clare, followed the same rigorous Franciscan practices of poverty, begging for alms, and not owning property. Clare was often regarded as a kind of co-founder of the Franciscans. The order spread quickly throughout Italy and then to the rest of Europe.[135]

For the Dominicans, there was also an intake of women and women's orders, some of whom had been cast off by other monastic orders and their nunneries condemned to extinction.[136] Women increasingly had sought out monastic vocations owing to a disparity in numbers between the genders, with many more men having already joined orders, or having been killed on crusade and in other military ventures. In a time with no equality and very little chance of upward social mobility other than marriage, which was increasingly difficult due to this greater lack of marriageable men, women entered convents for protection as much as anything. The Church was once again not fully prepared for this social change. Unfortunately, there was a pervasive misogynist belief among many monastic houses that ministering to women was either not part of their duty, or that bringing monks into such close proximity with women provided unwanted temptations. These nuns and houses that had been cast adrift often found a new home with the friars, though both the Franciscans and Dominicans would try to place their own restrictions on admitting female members.[137]

One intriguing women's movement in Northern Europe merits attention, that of the Beguines.[138] They did not originate with a single founder, though legend would attribute their founding to Lambert le Bègue, a later 12th-century priest with reformist views who was charged with heresy.[139] Rather, they more likely imitated other new apostolic movements. The Beguines were groups of women who created unofficial communities, based on the same ideas of renunciation and celibacy, though interestingly, not poverty. Individual Beguines were expected to provide for themselves through their own labors, or if they were wealthy (a fairly rare situation), from incomes derived from their properties. However, wealth was not celebrated, and the women were encouraged to be charitable and live humbly. They frequently labored as weavers, care-givers in hospitals, and other such service professions.

Mostly concentrated in the Low Countries, France, and Germany, these women did not take monastic vows (they were free to leave the beguinage at any time), but did offer a haven for women who had spiritual yearnings. Some women who joined these groups were simply seeking refuge, perhaps from an unwanted arranged marriage, or an abusive spouse; in effect, they were not unlike women's shelters in modern times. Their spiritual devotion tended toward the mystical (as typified by the writings of the Beguine mystic Mechthild of Madeburg),[140] which naturally aroused suspicions in the established Church; heresy and mysticism made good companions. Further, some of their practices involving the teaching of religious ideals came close to preaching, an activity forbidden to women. At times they also made use of vernacular translations of scripture, which oddly seems to have been tolerated in limited amounts, but naturally led various Church officials to criticize them vehemently. Their close association with the friars both as their confessors and as the directors of their groups would leave them open to a barrage of accusations and insinuations about immoral behavior, particularly from vernacular poets such as Jean de Meun in his continuation of the *Roman de la Rose*, as we will see in chapter 4.

The name itself is derogatory, with *beguina* most likely being derived from an older Indo-European word for "mumble." The Beguines thus were mumblers who spoke deceptively.[141] Viewed with increasing suspicion, some were formally accused of heresy, particularly from the 14th century. As Stoner notes, "Because of the clerics' fear of women as potential sources of sexual immorality and heresy, two dangerous contaminants in religious life, the position of the Beguines as women without the external constraints of male authority, written rules, permanent vows, or enclosure in a cloister presented the men with an almost insurmountable conceptual difficulty."[142]

The Beguines had a male counterpart in the Beghards, communities of men, who were also comprised of the laity, and took no permanent vows, but practiced a voluntary poverty and lived communally. Like the Beguines, they admitted men in poor circumstances, as well as those who wished to profess a greater religious identity, but perhaps were not suitable for the monastic vocations. Prominent in the Low Countries (but also found in France, Germany, and Italy), they were often associated with craft guilds, such as weavers. Initially, they tended to the poor, and lived in poverty, working rather than begging, but their commitment was not life-long if they chose otherwise; they were not required to renounce their possessions, they could return to the greater world, and even marry, if they wished. They were also victims of suspicions about their behavior and intentions, due to being outside of the established Church hierarchy.[143] Both groups increasingly associated with the Spiritual Franciscans, which led to charges of heresy and condemnations from the early 14th century.

Factional Disputes

By the mid- to late 13th century, the Spirituals had become more than just a thorn in the side to the evolving Franciscan order. They were a genuine threat to its unity, and questioned the structure of the Church itself, leaving them open to charges of heresy. Their name derived from their opposition to the "Conventuals," those that lived in established houses or convents. The Spirituals wished to be wandering mendicants, poor and begging, with no home of their own, and adhering to a strict observance to the originals wishes of Francis.[144] Deriving their beliefs from the early *zelanti*, their first great exponent was Peter Olivi (1248–98), from Sérignan on the south coast of Languedoc, an area already torn apart by war and heretical debate before he was born. Olivi argued passionately for poverty in what came to be known as the *usus pauper* controversy, that is, that Franciscans were not only restricted to a lack of personal ownership, they must also practice restriction on the use of any goods in order to truly live a life of poverty.[145] Olivi's arguments were not especially controversial, and probably would have been embraced by Francis, but by the 1280s, the order had shifted enough in its focus that such demands for a return to the simplicity of the early days were no longer possible, and thus had to be suppressed.

Further, his enemies argued, *usus pauper*, though seemingly a simple concept, created a number of problems. Burr notes: "Precisely how limited does such use have to be in order to qualify? How rough or thin must a garment be? What quantity and quality of food is required? With the Franciscans performing a wide variety of tasks in climatic zones from Scotland to Syria, these were not easy things to determine. Olivi's opponents decided that inclusion of *usus pauper* as an essential part of the vow would plunge a good percentage of the order into spiritual crisis."[146] The issue brought the Franciscans into conflict with the Dominicans, as well, who were not subject to the same rule of abject poverty. A dispute arose between them in Oxford in 1269 over the issue of the Franciscans accepting gifts and money. A Dominican named Solomon essentially accused them of hypocrisy, and his attitude can scarcely be distinguished from other religious and secular attacks based on the same concern.[147]

In 1283, Olivi's works were deemed dangerous and in error, and were banned, but he responded with a passionate defense of his position, and in 1287, he was ultimately appointed as lector to a Franciscan school, Santa Croce, in Florence. Eventually, he was sent to Narbonne for similar work, where he died in 1298. Olivi's death was not the end of the matter, however, and the Spirituals, also called the *Fraticelli*, or "little brothers," continued to agitate the Franciscan leadership throughout the 14th century, being charged with heresy and facing severe punishments.[148] Pope John XXII, whose papacy lasted from 1316 to 1334, showed no sympathy to the Spirituals and their secessionist activities. He ordered that their houses be disbanded, and saw that a number of them were charged with heresy, imprisoned, or delivered up to the Inquisition and executed (including four who were burned at the stake in Marseilles in 1318). In 1322, with the bull *Ad conditorem canonum*, he revoked papal ownership of the Franciscans' possessions, and in 1323, he issued *Cum inter nonnullos*, which declared that it was heresy to claim that Christ and his apostles had renounced all private property.[149]

Long before this, other friars had harsh words for their brothers. The Englishman Roger Bacon (*ca.* 1214/20—*ca.* 92/94) was both a university intellectual and a Franciscan friar.[150] Sometimes referred to as the "first" scientist, his interest in optics and light earned him much admiration in the Victorian age, but it now seems that this praise was somewhat overstated. Nineteenth-century historians liked to portray him as an empirical scientist, one of the first to use the scientific method, who was persecuted by a dark and superstitious Church that could not bear to see the results of his experiments. Modern assessments have pulled away from this theory and placed Bacon firmly in the world of medieval scholasticism, whatever his unusual scientific interests might have been.[151] Other spurious legends associated him with ritual magic and alchemy, claiming that he was secretly a master sorcerer who only late in life repented his dealings with the spirit world and burned his grimoires.[152]

The historical Roger was known to be outspoken in his criticisms, as Clegg notes amusingly, "Bacon seemed to expect others to be prepared to take any remark he made, however scathing, as constructive criticism. If you called someone an idiot, he thought, they should be grateful and learn from it. But the world, particularly the medieval world, didn't work like that."[153] His criticisms of fellow Franciscan Richard Rufus of Cornwall, who later took up a chief academic post in England after teaching at the University of Paris, may have caused Bacon to be disciplined.[154] Certainly by 1260, his output seems to have been curtailed somewhat, owing to a prohibition on the writing of new works without the approval of the order.[155] Roger probably had affinities for the Spirituals, and this may also have caused him trouble. In his *Compendium philosophiae*, he has harsh words for his brothers. He laments how the friars have fallen, just as have the other religious vocations, from their original state of dignity. They are now consumed by pride, lechery, and greed. And the clergy were no better, for no matter where they gather, whether in Paris or Oxford, conflict arises and they scandalize the laity with their actions.[156] If these men had proper faith and reverence for the sacrament of the Eucharist, they would never have fallen as they have, beset with errors in belief, vices, and wicked behavior. Rather, they would know the saving truth in this life.[157] He was also a noted critic of the crusades and the military orders.[158]

Bacon was deeply concerned about Franciscan education, and in his *Opus majus*, addressed to Pope Clement IV, he offered solutions for repairing what he saw as a broken system.[159] The sermons of his time were ridiculous, he argued, filled with verbosity and elaborate structures, but no real substance. They should rather concentrate on faith and persuasion, virtue and vice, reward and punishment. These poor sermons were simply the result of poor education.[160] Essentially, one of the very reasons for the Franciscan order existing was now failing miserably, and needed to be rethought, with an emphasis on a broader education for friars, especially in the sciences (of which he was so fond), to produce better preachers. He had caustic remarks for the conflict between the friars and the secular masters in Paris, as well, saying that their debates were nothing more than shouting matches, accusations of heresy, and the throwing about of insults.[161]

There is a tradition that his scientific experiments caused him to be persecuted and imprisoned by his own order. However, if such an imprisonment did occur, it was more likely to be because of his sympathies with the Spirituals. The story of his incarceration at Ancona (a central Italian friary) by the head of the order, Jerome d'Ascoli (later Pope Nicholas IV from 1288 to 1292), for suspected "novelties" dates from about 80 years after his death, making it unreliable.[162]

Hostilities were not limited to words; there are a number of cases of violence committed against friars by other friars, whether over disagreements in doctrine, or more mundane and human reasons, including the striking story of a meeting of the Franciscan chapter in Cork, in 1291. According to the chronicles, the minister general of the Franciscan Order came to Ireland, and in the course of the meeting, fighting broke out between the Anglo-Norman and native Irish brothers, resulting in the deaths of sixteen Franciscans, the injury of others, and the imprisonment of some by King Edward I of England.[163] We do not know whether this was caused by rivalries, differences in religious opinion, or even some kind of nationalism pitting the Irish against their visitors, but it was apparently severe enough for the king to intervene. The veracity of this story has been doubted at times, owing to the argument that the Benedictine chroniclers who recorded it were hostile to the Franciscans and may have wished to portray them negatively,[164] but recent scholarship suggests that it may be true.[165]

In addition to these periodic reports of physical violence, factional disputes and criticism from within the orders were similar to what the friars would face from a variety of outside sources. The Church had a long history of rivalries and hostilities among its various branches, often driven by envy, competition for positions of power, disagreements about authority, and other such causes.[166] The aggrieved were not shy about expressing their opinions and condemnations, as George G. Coulton has shown in his magnificently detailed anthology of fractious inter–Church squabbling.[167] The friars were especially susceptible to this kind of polemic, stepping into an ancient hierarchical system as fully-formed organizations with their own unique privileges. Indeed, Pope Gregory IX issued the bull *Nimis iniqua* in 1231, which ordered bishops to give all friars the freedom to preach without restriction, a situation that would lead to much resentment and hostility from clergy that felt their positions were being threatened.[168] It should have come as no surprise when the invective started. However, it would be incorrect to say that there was a unified "antifraternal" movement, as opposition to the mendicants came, as we have seen, from a variety of sources, religious and lay, many of whom would have been at odds with one another.[169]

Anger toward the friars due to the horrors of the Inquisition notwithstanding, the first major organized attacks against them came not in the form of physical violence, but from the secular masters at the University of Paris, writing polemical tracts. These were intellectual and theological diatribes denouncing mendicant activities and their supposed deceit and duplicity. What started as rivalry over privileged positions at the university became inflated into a conflict of apocalyptic proportions that would involve the papacy and King Louis IX, and would never be fully resolved to anyone's satisfaction.

The University of Paris and the Quarrels

The strong antifraternal sentiments awoken at the University of Paris, the so-called "quarrels," had their origins in the early 13th century. The presence of the mendicant orders in this thriving, cosmopolitan, and uniquely intellectual city was soon to cause serious problems. Their practice of living on alms, and their attempts to secure positions of authority at the university would stir heated debate and bring condemnation from the secular masters, spanning decades of conflict. Beginning with the polemical writings of various university partisans, the mendicants came to symbolize laziness and the willingness to live as freeloaders, accusations that would follow them in one form or another for centuries.[1]

As we have seen, Dominic was a great advocate of education and study. In addition to his other activities, he established a Dominican school in Paris, which he secured with membership in the university in 1217–19; the university helped them to obtain a residence in 1218 at Saint-Jacques. At the same time, the Franciscans set up a school in Paris by 1220, though Francis was less involved with this action than his contemporary.[2] Indeed, Francis referred to himself as *simplex et idiota*, and was not interested in education in the same way as Dominic, opposing his brothers taking an interest in higher learning,[3] since it could lead to vanity and pride in one's accomplishments. This stance would come back to haunt the Franciscans as the conflict escalated, and would be used as an argument against them.

Given that the friars sought to reach as many people as possible, it made sense to establish themselves in cities with large populations. Further, since both desired to recruit the learned, university towns were the perfect place to establish new houses.[4] Initially, both mendicant schools admitted only members of their own orders and they made no attempt to teach others; their religious duties kept them apart from the secular students. Thus, there was no conflict or competition with the university and its faculty. Indeed, some Franciscans and Dominicans were later sent to the university to continue their studies in theology, after completion of work in their own schools. The secular masters welcomed them at first, seeing their presence as good for both the city's spiritual and economic needs.[5]

The masters were not "secular" in the modern sense. Indeed, they are known as the "secular clergy," a term which can be confusing to the modern reader. These masters were also clergy. They were called such because they had earned the degree of that name; at the time "Master" and "Doctor" were not distinct degrees. Becoming a "master" was the true goal of the medieval university student. The degree conferred the ability to teach, and there was no real distinction between having a degree and engaging in the profession of teaching.[6] These secular masters were those who lived in the world (the *saeculum*, or "age"), in contrast to the "regular clergy," those who lived in religious orders under a monastic rule (*regula*), sequestered in communities away from the world, such as the Cistercians or the Benedictines. As we have seen, the friars were a new concept, because they were orders living according to a rule, but they were very much *in saeculum*, in the world. Indeed, it was their duty to go out among the everyday people and interact with them, while remaining poor and apart from them.

In order to understand the relationship and the conflict that would develop between the mendicants and the masters at the university, it is necessary to devote some space to the history, structure, and function of the University of Paris. It was essentially modeled on the Italian universities, such as Bologna, but with a greater focus on theology and spiritual matters in general. It had its origins in the cathedral school of Notre Dame, with a chancellor who represented the Bishop of Paris. Indeed, the masters generally held certain rights and privileges because of their clerical status, including church incomes that were independent of any fees that they might charge their students. Its faculty tended to be more international than those in the universities of Italy, as well, which was part of the appeal for prospective students, though this led to some masters feeling out of place and in greater need of protecting their rights.[7]

However, the university was not solely dependent on its ecclesiastical roots. This new institution had strong ties with the independent schools that had appeared on the Left Bank of the river Seine in the previous century, initially near the church of St. Geneviéve.[8] So important were the 12th-century schools, that later maps of Paris designated the entire Left Bank as simply "the University."[9]

These schools had gained their reputation from the residence of Pierre Abelard (1079–1142) as a lecturer there, widely praised for his brilliant rhetorical skills. Though he ran afoul of the theologian Bernard of Clairvaux over issues of religious doctrine, and would later cause a scandal with his student and secret lover Héloïse d'Argenteuil (leading to his castration and humiliation), his intellect was celebrated in many circles. This, combined with the presence of the abbey of Saint Victor, known not only for its speculative mysticism (Hugh, *d.* 1141, being one of its most famous representatives), but also for its emphasis on the study and knowledge of the wider world, made Paris a center of learning, which attracted eager students from all parts of Europe.[10] Not everyone approved of these new circles of learning; more conservative theologians objected, arguing that the license to teach belonged to bishops and cathedrals, not secular societies.[11] Additionally, there were those in the Church who sought to control what could and could not be taught at universities, and this conflict with secular learning continued for centuries.[12]

Medieval Paris had little in common with its modern counterpart; the wide lanes and open vistas of today date from the 19th century and would have been completely unknown. Instead, the city huddled on both sides of the river Seine, surrounded by a newly-built *enceinte* (wall), constructed at various times between about 1190 and 1220. The wealthier Right Bank was able to complete its portion more quickly than the poorer Left Bank to the south.[13] Within these walls were crammed an astonishing variety of cramped streets and buildings, and a wide cross-section of the population. The medieval city could offer everything from the most exalted to the most despised, from the holiest to the damned. As the city's reputation for learning grew, students (consisting only of young men) arrived in ever greater numbers, and joined the increasingly varied tapestry of Parisian urban life. By the middle of the thirteenth century, some 3,000 may have been residing in the Latin Quarter on the Left Bank.[14] Their background and economic situations were surprisingly diverse, not being limited only to the aristocracy, at least in the 13th and 14th centuries.[15]

The desire for a structured center where this thirst for knowledge could be quenched was realized in the cathedral school of Notre Dame, which would become the birthplace of the university. This was a slow process, however, and in transitioning to a "university," the cathedral school did not disappear. However, it did evolve into a much larger entity, unlike the cathedral schools at Chartres and Rheims in France, or Lincoln and York in England. The reason for the transformation of Notre Dame lies in the many outside influences mentioned above, as well as from papal support, which was ultimately instrumental in the granting of degrees.[16]

The university proper can be said to have originated at the beginning of the 13th century, during the reign of King Philip Augustus.[17] In 1200, he issued a decree specifically granting rights and privileges to students. This arose in response to a conflict between a student and a local, a type of incident that would be replayed often, and would figure strongly in the conflicts of later decades. A noble German student sent a servant to buy wine at a nearby tavern. For whatever reason, a fight broke out and the servant was killed. Various German students were outraged and returned to the tavern as a group to seek retribution. As a result, some Parisians appealed to the provost of Paris, who saw to it that the German students were attacked, and several were killed. Furious, the students appealed directly to the king. Perhaps surprisingly, Philip Augustus took their side against his provost, and gave his backing to their privileges, the *privilegium canonis* and the *privilegium fori* (discussed in more detail below). The king's punishment for the provost and his men was particularly harsh, placing them under permanent arrest, and ordering that they would only be freed if they underwent a trial by water.[18] Most likely this was the ordeal wherein the accused was bound and thrown in water; if they floated they were guilty, if they sank, they were innocent, and freed, provided they could be rescued from drowning. This was not a happy choice for most victims. In any case, it is recorded that the provost died while making an escape attempt.[19]

This was not the first instance of violence, and it certainly would not be the last. The king, in issuing his decree, was hoping that by giving royal assent to clerical privileges, it would set a precedent for resolving any future conflicts. The decree outlined a strict set of procedures for how to deal with quarrels and violence, and it clearly favored the students over the townspeople. From now on, for example, a provost could not use any physical force against a student, unless it was in self-defense.[20] These surprisingly heavy-handed regulations were modified somewhat in later years to be a bit more realistic. Catching a student in the act of committing a violent crime such as rape or murder, for example, justified the use of force. Philip may have been motivated by wider political issues in taking this stance, and was reaching out to the secular clergy for support. He may also have wanted to encourage the growth of scholarship in his realm to increase both its prestige and improve its economy. Guaranteeing a safe environment for the masters and students was an effective way of achieving this.[21] In any case, he noted that he had been advised by his counsel to take these actions, though he must certainly have been aware that not infrequent rowdy violence from students was a continuing problem.[22]

The actual structure of the cathedral school cannot be considered comparable to the modern concept of a "university." In the 13th century, the Latin word *universitas* did not apply specifically to a university. Essentially, it described a group that had independent legal status. It could be formed by as few as three persons in a given profession (which they would call a *collegium*), with the goal of protecting their legal rights. Once they had secured recognition by an authority, or even common law, they were permitted to act in a legal manner, i.e., holding elections for officers, having proper legal representation as a lawful entity, and creating statutes.[23]

A university in the modern sense was more properly known as a *studium*. This designation occurs repeatedly in the documents of universities throughout medieval Europe, and was part of an attempt (established firmly by Pope Innocent IV in 1245) to create a universal standard of degree conference among these institutions. Thus, the possessor of a degree from one *studium universale* (the formal name) could, in theory, be accepted at any other such institute of learning without examinations. In practice, of course, most universities wanted to retain their rights concerning who was admitted. The use of this system was therefore primarily to assist in the control of the founding of new universities, because privileged academic positions were jealously guarded.[24] This protectionist attitude grew to be very prevalent and would greatly contribute to the later tensions in Paris.

The University of Paris was comprised of four faculties, three higher faculties of theology, cannon law, and medicine, and one lower faculty of liberal arts. There were far more teachers in the lower faculty, while the upper three retained only a small number each,[25] an issue which was to become central to the conflict, when the friars began filling these positions with their members, against the wishes of the masters.

Unlike its modern counterpart, the university had no collection of permanent buildings; it was still a poor institution, and needed to borrow buildings for use. Classes were held in the masters' homes, and students took lodging where they could, often not in the best parts of town. Instruction was in the form of lectures using authoritative texts. When questions or disputes arose about them, debates, known as "disputations" were set, over which the master presided, and which were governed by rules and procedures. Each faculty had its own recognized authorities on various texts.[26]

Student life was a curious mixture of rigid discipline and surprising laxity. The daytime activities of a student's life were well-planned, and involved long hours of lectures, disputation, and study. However, at night, students, as in any age, were most happy to find other pursuits more suited to the interests of easily-distracted young men, chief among them gambling, drinking, and whoring.[27] It was not uncommon for students to take lodging next to a tavern of ill repute, where drunken brawls and prostitution flourished. One account recorded how a master taught lessons on a floor above a brothel, which no doubt would have been extremely distracting.[28] The temptation to join in with these activities would have been great, and as we will see, it was just such activities that stoked the first fires of conflict. The friars were not immune from temptation. While some convents tried to enforce "prostitute-free zones" in their surrounding streets, friars were certainly known as clients. Indeed, the terms "monkwhore" and "friarwhore" could refer to both a favorite client from the orders, or even a prostitute who specialized in such clients.[29]

Regardless of their evening activities, students enjoyed many rights and protections, which the university vigorously guarded. Their rents were controlled to prevent gouging by unscrupulous landlords, their books were checked for accuracy and the prices were kept reasonable (a privilege that many modern students would appreciate!), and these books and other possessions could not be seized for failing to pay rent. They also had exemptions from various taxes, tolls, and levies. They benefitted from certain Church decrees, including papal protections against violence, excommunication, and trial in civil courts, among other things. Though they were not ordained clergy, they were expected to have some form of tonsure (a shaved spot on the crown of the head) to identify them. Celibacy, however, was not enforced, and those who did not seek advancement in the Church upon completing their studies were free to marry.[30]

A further consideration in the development of events was the university's relationship to the city, the classic "town-gown" struggle which was to prove instrumental in sparking off conflict in Paris. Universities were in some sense their own worlds, and foreign to the everyday life of a growing and bustling medieval city. They comprised as many as thousands of individuals, most of whom (students and faculty both) came from outside of the given city; many (perhaps most) did not try to assimilate to their surroundings. Then, as now, student bodies were comprised of young people, whose attention all too often turned to interests that had nothing to do with their studies. Cities had to respond to unique sets of demands and laws for these institutions, often laid down by kings and even popes. The presence of these external authoritative directives was a constant reminder of the "otherness" that universities embodied.[31] It grew to be a source of civic resentment in many cases. Royal protection saved the university from dissolution more than once in its early decades.[32]

A central concern of the masters at the University of Paris had been to gain some independence from their overseer. As a cathedral school, Notre Dame was presided over by a chancellor, also known as *scholasticus*, or *magister scholarium*.[33] As a member of the cathedral chapter, he was outside of the school's authority, and answerable only to the bishop. He was not a teacher himself, yet the masters were subject to him. This could naturally lead to the abuse of his power, and the inevitable conflict that such abuse brought.

Throughout the 12th century, the secular masters had struggled to gain their independence and assert their rights. The decretal, *Quanto Gallicana ecclesia*, issued by Pope Alexander III in 1170–72, recognized the masters' rights, though some abuses certainly continued. The temptation incurred by the authority to wield power over a group who could do nothing about it must have been great indeed.[34]

The transformation from a Paris cathedral school to a proper "university" began in the later 12th century, when the large number of students arriving demanded expansion, and the chancellor's position became unmanageable. The masters had grown to such numbers that they had effectively formed their own *universiti*, or guilds. However, this transition was not without difficulties. Essentially, the process involved a break from the cathedral school, with the secular masters taking over the authority formerly held by the chancellor and the chapter. A new *universitas* emerged, one that was still somewhat subject to ecclesiastical authority, but which had many new independent privileges and its own laws, agreed on by the masters without Church input. Perhaps inevitably, this brought about some conflict with the cathedral and the town.[35] These new positions of power were acknowledged by Pope Innocent III in the early 13th century, though he made attempts to define and set limits on their spheres of control. The idea of an independent center of learning, at least partially free of church control would certainly have left some with a feeling of unease. In the year 1215, official statutes were set forth defining the powers of the masters. Though limitations were placed on their activities, this was nevertheless a major advancement. The masters' hard-won victory was to be a central issue in their feud with the friars, which was shortly to ensue.

It was into this environment of newly-attained independence that the friars arrived a few years later to establish their schools. No one questioned the piety of Francis or Dominic. Indeed, both were canonized, in 1228 and 1234, respectively. Thus, the arrival of the Franciscans and Dominicans was no cause for alarm among the secular masters, even when Dominic sought admittance for his institution into the university; Pope Honorius III offered his congratulations to the university when it accepted the Dominicans into the fold in 1220. The orders, with their vows of poverty and strong emphasis on education (particularly the Dominicans) and missionary work (both), seemed welcome additions to the city.[36] Certainly, the city authorities must have thought with relief that such students would not be of the more rowdy disposition that the university could attract. The friars' school became increasingly popular, because they were not bound by the same practices as those of the seculars. A clerk might have no "job security" at all after receiving his degree, whereas a friar need not worry about advancement, debts, or other such burdens. A friar could devote his whole life to academic study and teaching at one of his own order's schools. This explains why the friars produced so many intellectual giants in the 13th and 14th centuries, as they were free of the secular burdens, and devoted to learning.[37]

The first real signs of trouble were revealed during the Great Dispersion of 1229–30, which arose as the result of riots that had broken out from a tavern brawl during the carnival of 1228–29. Young notes that the dispersion was also "the most notable instance of any strain on the relationship between the university and the crown."[38] It was sparked off by a group of students in the suburb of Bourg of Saint Marcel, who, according to Matthew Paris, happened on a delightful discovery: they found in a particular tavern a case of the best wine.[39] Undoubtedly they consumed too much of it.

It was from this point that trouble came. In a scene that almost seems a cliché, an argument about the bill arose. The inebriated students moved fairly quickly from heated words to blows, and a fist-fight broke out. However, the keeper of the tavern was not to be beaten by young trouble makers, and called for help. His reinforcements managed to soundly defeat the drunken rabble, sending them fleeing with many bruises and pains for their troubles.[40]

Medieval city taverns were odd places. They were settings for socialization, which could be friendly or otherwise. Popular imagination, then as now, views them as dens of iniquity, filled with gamblers, prostitutes, ruffians, and criminals spoiling for a fight, the "devil's monastery."[41] Without a doubt, these elements were present in a good many of them. Taverns sold wine in pots (a generous amount for the price), usually surplus from domestic producers. Its quality varied, but if the purpose were merely to get drunk, it would more than suffice. Taverns also served as meeting places for the public, and could be considerably more reputable, but the clergy (and perhaps general public opinion) tended to condemn them all without making any distinction between them.[42] Indeed, it was their very reputation for licentiousness that attracted so many young students, eager to blow off steam, drink, and indulge in illicit sexual encounters.

Returning to the Saint Marcel incident, after being dispersed, the chastised clerks were not about to accept humiliation in such a manner, and they returned in larger numbers the following day to enact revenge. In the course of the mayhem, they broke into the tavern, and proceeded to beat the inn-keeper and his friends, helping themselves to more wine, before emerging out into the streets for a grand bout of drunken loutishness, causing much upset and some damage, "at the expense of peaceable citizens."[43]

At this point, the city guard arrived and further violence erupted. The clerks, in various states of alcoholic incapacity, had no chance against even a small group of armed fighters. Though the number of guards in the city was limited, they relied on nearby neighbors of the offended and any witnesses (who were bound by law to intervene) to help them put down violence and criminal behavior.[44] Such assistance required no training or procedures for how it was to be enforced. Indeed, in suppressing the uprising, the soldiers and their helpers killed several students. The masters at the university were incensed, but their complaints to the papal legate were in vain. He was under the influence of the canons of Paris, who by now did not look kindly on the university.

At the heart of this conflict were the students' privileges. As masters, they were entitled to two specific legal protections, which as we have seen, were given royal backing by the king. The first was the *privilegium canonis*, which assigned clerics (and by extension, students) a sacred status. It was not only forbidden to use violence against them, it was actually considered a sacrilege that should lead to immediate excommunication. This was an excommunication of such severity that it could only be lifted by a penitential journey and audience with the pope. There were exceptions, especially in regards to students who had not attained puberty (which often occurred later in age than now); unruly schoolboys could be beaten for bad behavior, for example. Nevertheless, the masters would not sit idly by and watch their students be assaulted by town ruffians, regardless of what they had done.

The second protection was the *privilegium fori*, which stated that all clerics were under the sole jurisdiction of the Church courts. No royal or town court could try them for any crime, much less pass any sentence or carry out punishment. Effectively, they were immune from any prosecution, and punishments generally were no more than demands for penance, or at worst, excommunication and the loss of clerical status.[45] It is easy to see how a town could become resentful, and how a gathering of rowdy young students could lead to disaster. Students often gained a sense of cockiness because of their status, including a lack of a sense of self-preservation. As Baldwin notes, "the tonsure, the outward sign of clerical status, was more of a protection than the helmet."[46]

In response to the violence, the university, which insisted that its students were innocent of any crime, called a strike wherein the masters resolved to leave the city in protest for six years if no redress was made, a powerful threat, given the economic damage that such a drastic action would inflict. However, the city refused to comply and as a result, the masters did disperse.[47] Some of them never returned; they journeyed to England to take up positions at Oxford and later, Cambridge at the invitation of Henry III.[48] Others went to smaller *studia generalia* such as Toulouse or Rhiems. The *studia* of Angers may, in fact, date its very existence and origin to this act of protest. There was a feeling among many masters who left that they would be better off in other locations who would appreciate their services more than Paris had done, and that they would be free of ecclesiastical interference and civil hostility.[49]

However, there were those in authority who were rightly fearful of the economic damage to the city as a result of the loss of its student population, a logical result of so many masters leaving the city. Ultimately, Pope Gregory IX, a strong supporter of the university, intervened and ordered the king of France and the queen mother, Blanche of Castile (who had initially ordered the soldiers to quell the riots)[50] to punish the offenders within the guard. Redress was made, tempers calmed down, and by 1231, the masters who still remained were again teaching.[51]

This might have been the end of the whole affair. However, one major problem existed throughout it all: the actions of the friars during the dispersion. During the strike, the *studiae* of the Franciscans and Dominicans had refused to cease instruction in their own schools. Their position was that, as the students involved in the initial disturbance had not been from their orders, they were under no obligation to comply with a general university strike. Further, during the strike, the friars had rather audaciously opened their schools to secular students to compensate for the lack of secular university instruction, and continued to teach these students thereafter. This greatly displeased the remaining masters. These actions crossed territorial lines that the masters had drawn long before and that had not previously been questioned.

The controversy concerned one man in particular, a Dominican theologian named Roland of Cremona, who had been sent from his own school to the university to pursue further theological studies. By the year 1228, he was nearing the completion of his work and was about to take the title of "master." During the dispersion, a master named John of St. Giles, who opposed the strike, remained at the university, allowing Roland to finish his studies. As a result, in 1229, the Bishop of Paris granted Roland the license of theology. This was given without the approval of the theological faculty, who were absent because of the strike. This unusual and somewhat devious action meant that the Dominicans now had their first master on the university's faculty of theology, without the majority of the masters' consent.[52]

Things were to become worse for the secular masters. Soon after the strike had ended, John of St. Giles (also a member of the theological faculty) joined the Dominicans, apparently in the middle of a sermon![53] Shortly after this, Alexander of Hales, one the most renowned secular theologians of the day, assumed the Franciscan habit, but importantly, without giving up his position on the theological faculty. Thus, only fifteen years after their arrival in Paris, the friars now held three of the twelve theology faculty positions. Three regent masters, along with their students and importantly, the money that those students brought, had now gone over to the fraternal orders.[54] This abrupt change marked the beginning of the masters' resentment of the friars, a tension which would deepen and finally explode into open hostility two decades later.

In the years immediately following their return, the masters saw their positions and power further encroached upon and diminished, and their rights as independent teachers curtailed. Other religious orders, perhaps encouraged by the gains of the mendicants, began to occupy chairs on the faculty of theology, as some masters joined these orders. Among these at various times were the Cistercians, the Premonstratensians, and the other two main orders of friars: the Augustinians and the Carmelites. By the year 1254, only three chairs remained in secular hands, three others belonging to the friars, a further three being held by cathedral canons, and the remainder being dispersed among the additional orders.[55]

The secular theologians, quite rightly, saw their hard-won power and prestige falling away from them. It seemed that nothing could prevent the wholesale loss of their positions, or the independence that they enjoyed. Worse still, the mendicants had succeeded in gaining papal support, previously given to the secular masters; indeed, a good part of the reason for their tremendous success was this support. Papal action could bestow new benefits without being answerable to anyone, though this also meant that privileges could be revoked. As such, the friars were determined to keep in the good graces of the pope and ensure that they always had a strong lobby at the Papal Curia.[56]

Another consequence was that this support allowed the friars to establish succession in teaching positions, meaning that the theology chairs could never revert back to secular control, but would remain in the possession of their particular orders, in perpetuity. The angered masters believed this to be an unfair distribution of power which was not representative of the total secular student population. With nine faculty of theology chairs under the control of the mendicant and religious orders, there was an obvious lack of representation for the secular theology students.[57] In addition, there was certainly a professional and intellectual jealousy present, as the friars clearly had the superior thinkers in their ranks.[58] Among the mendicant holders of the coveted faculty positions would be Hugh of St. Cher, the Franciscan Bonaventure, and the great Dominican Thomas Aquinas.[59]

The Franciscans had also succeeded in gaining favor in very powerful circles, especially with Pope Innocent IV (1243–54), and King Louis IX (r. 1226–70), who chose his confessors from among them.[60] Louis, of course, had a reputation for considerable piety, and it is worth devoting time here to studying his relationship with the friars. They were established in France when he was a child. By coincidence, he ascended to the French throne in 1226, the same year that Francis died. The new order was immediately devoted to the twelve-year-old king, and apparently sent him as a coronation gift the pillow that Francis had used up until his death.[61] From a young age, Louis was intertwined with the orders and their affairs.

He helped them to acquire properties in Paris, and ensured that churches were built for them. He requested that his own children be educated by friars.[62] He oversaw the construction of the beautiful Sainte-Chapelle, his private chapel on the Île de la Cité. This building was designated to house a fragment of the true cross, and the crown of thorns, relics he had purchased from Emperor Baldwin II of the Latin Empire of Constantinople between 1239 and 1241. The emissaries that Louis sent to the great ancient city to acquire these precious relics were Dominicans.[63] Clearly, he trusted them completely. One of his chief preachers and associates was Bonaventure, the great Franciscan philosopher and teacher, noted for his large number of sermons.

Louis' two crusades (1248 and 1270) were supported in earnest by the Franciscans; both were disastrous failures (he died during the second one), but the wealth, time, and effort that he spent on them showed his level of devotion to a Christian cause he believed in deeply, and he kept friars as his confessors after returning from his first crusading effort.[64] He is the only French monarch to be canonized, by Pope Boniface VIII in 1297. His support for the friars thus lent them considerable power and influence.

Indeed, it was said of him (often angrily rather than reverently) that he would rather have been a friar than a king, and there is some truth to this. Louis was famous for his outward shows of piety, from his humble, non-kingly dress to his insistence on celebrating the monastic hours. He would, for example, rise at night to celebrate matins, just as monks did, no doubt to the consternation of his family and servants.[65] Louis loved sermons and the friars' emphasis on preaching thus made a positive impression on him.[66] He may have been something of a preacher himself, particularly to the friars.[67] He was known to attend Dominican lessons, insisting on sitting on the floor and refusing to take a seat when one was offered to him by the students.[68]

These public displays of piety actually brought considerable criticism, often directly to his face. Indeed, a case can be made that the university quarrels were in part influenced by a growing opposition to the king's religiosity, especially as far as it concerned his crusades.[69] Louis' failure ignited a popular uprising, the Shepherds' Crusade, a peasant movement following an elderly monk named Jacob, who initially sought to rescue the imprisoned king following the first of his crusades (he was held captive in Egypt), even obtaining some favor from Louis' mother. However, it descended into anarchy (with particular violence directed against the friars in various towns and cities), and was suppressed.[70]

Louis seems to have preferred a more informal approach to royal conduct in general, which put him at odds with a strict society that had very clear ideas about what a king should be and how he should act. His religious humility was such that he was genuinely open to criticism, even inviting it, but he could also feel stung by it,[71] viewing it as a reminder from God to remain humble. His responses to critiques and insults were generally remarkably measured, when many other monarchs would simply have had the offending person imprisoned and executed.

Louis would have been delighted to have been a younger son in the royal family, and thus able to enter one of the mendicant orders. He even considered abdicating more than once to fulfill that desire, though he confessed that he could not have chosen between them.[72] Though the mantle of kingship fell to him, he tried to behave like a friar whenever he could. For this, he was openly criticized and mocked. His servants were said to have called him "Friar Louis," a woman once (with great hostility) accused him of behaving more like a friar than a king, and even his own wife detested the simple mendicant habits that he was prone to wearing, viewing them as utterly unworthy of the King of France.[73] Given his enamored relationship to the mendicants, it becomes clear that this support would cause trouble for the secular masters as the conflict escalated.

A period of uneasy and increasingly cool relations now began between the factions of secular and friar. Unfortunately, there is little surviving detail of the exact course of the disintegrating relationship between them, but it is not difficult to imagine the attitude of the masters. They almost certainly saw their livelihoods at risk, and their whole existence as an independent entity seemed in danger of being eliminated. The friars, on the other hand, probably viewed themselves as the superior educators and the rightful holders of positions of instruction in theology. Even among the supposedly humble, it would not have taken much for egos on both sides to be inflated and alternately damaged.

In the year 1250, matters took a turn for the worse. Until that time, members of the mendicant orders had not formally applied for the license of theology from the university. It is possible that the friars believed that to ask for such a conferral in order to obtain a faculty position was an act of pride which violated the rules of their respective orders. There was no prohibition against such a petition in their rules, however, so the actual reason is unclear.[74] Given that various orders held so many positions on the faculty already, there may have simply been no need.

On May 30, 1250, Innocent IV issued a bull to the university chancellor granting him permission to bestow the license "according to his conscience," whether it was formally applied for or not. Though no specific references were made to the friars regarding this decision, it was clear that they would be the most favored in such a situation. This move effectively eliminated any remaining secular control over the choice of faculty. It allowed new members to be chosen without election by the seculars, and undermined what remaining power the masters retained in this area.[75]

In response, the masters decided to take action. In 1252, they passed the *statutum de promovendis* – the first statute that is recorded by any faculty at the university— against the friars, with the intent of controlling their admission. According to the new rules, in the future, all applicants would have to have studied at a recognized school at the university where they had been examined, and also to have lectured at one of these schools. Furthermore, no religious order was to have more than one college and one position on the theological faculty. This last move was a direct attempt to limit mendicant power. The failure to comply with these ordinances would result in the expulsion of the offender from the society of masters.[76]

For a brief time, this move was successful; given that the decision had been made in a proper assembly, the university was within its rights to enact such legislation.[77] Further, while Innocent IV was a supporter of the friars, he was also sympathetic to the concerns of the masters. Therefore, he tried to maintain a balance in his support for both parties.[78] It seems that his bull concerning the university selection process had not specifically been intended to favor the mendicants after all.

The Dominicans, who held two theology faculty positions, suddenly found themselves in the unfortunate situation of being forced to relinquish one of their chairs, which they had no intention of doing. As a result of their defiance, they were summarily expelled from the university in the same month as the issuance of the statute. This tense situation continued for just over one year, until March 1253. At that point, a series of events occurred that was to lead to a bitter war of words, an outright power struggle between the factions, and ultimately, the invocation with renewed force of the ever-present medieval fear of the impending apocalypse.

During Lent in 1253, another student-city conflict broke out, once again as the result of a tavern brawl, wherein one student was killed by the constabulary and their assistants, and several others were imprisoned. While the students were being interrogated, they were severely abused and suffered broken bones, among other injuries.[79] The university's response was swift and took the same form as in 1229: a strike. The resulting economic pressures eventually forced the city to make reparations. Indeed, in this case it seems that the actions of the guards were wholly unjustified; in a dense and crowded city, it was not just the criminally-minded who were spoiling for a fight. Two of those responsible for the beatings were hanged, and the others were banished from Paris.[80] The university made its peace with the city, but the friar/master conflict exploded into the open, and was to have far-reaching consequences.

Once again, the friars refused to participate in the strike, unless their second chair was returned. By doing this, they eliminated the university's leverage to stop all classes.[81] This had as much to do with their hostility toward the secular faculty because of the harsh new statutes, as it did with their feelings of being unconnected to the events which led to the strike. Indeed, none of their students seemed to be involved, so there was doubtless some sense of moral superiority in contrast to the masters' inability to control the behavior of their raucous students. However, the masters' response to their provocative decision was quick and merciless: the mendicant holders of faculty positions were officially expelled and also excommunicated. Henceforth, all magisterial candidates would be required to swear an oath of loyalty and observance to the university's statutes, with the defiance of a strike being grounds for permanent dismissal.[82] The Franciscans eventually agreed to this provision, but the Dominicans did not. Their response to the judgement was equally defiant; they appealed to their allies, the king and the pope.[83]

Pope Innocent IV, still seeking reconciliation between the opposing factions, sought first to reestablish the friars' positions. On July 1, 1253, he wrote a letter nullifying the excommunications, and urged the masters to readmit them to the faculty. The masters solidly refused despite his pleas, and as a result were themselves suspended from their offices.[84] The masters responded by setting down their position, recounting the gradual erosion of their rights and privileges, and the need to maintain their control. They aimed their attack particularly at the Dominicans, who they accused of making their support for the university conditional on the retention of both faculty chairs (which was true). Further, the masters also stated that the Dominicans sought perpetual possession of the chairs (also true), and that they had falsely obtained papal letters of support through their deceptions (this was an invention, but no doubt it was believed by many). In addition, the masters held that the friars created, by their very presence, an unwelcome competitive spirit and a disloyalty to the university. They took to enticing students into their classes and orders, inspiring many to become friars themselves, they lived off of alms instead of fees, and clearly did not feel bound to adhere to university demands and regulations.[85] In the autumn of 1253, the masters once again issued their statute. When they made an attempt to post the edict on the door of the Dominican *studia*, it resulted in heated words, and a violent clash that drew blood.[86] For the first time, friars had been drawn into physical conflict.

Relations between the masters and the mendicants continued to deteriorate. In another effort to resolve the conflict, Innocent IV asked both parties in August 1253 to send delegations to Rome, so that he might mediate the dispute and come to some solution.[87] Both agreed, and in the spring of the following year, the masters' delegation set off, led by Guillaume de Saint-Amour, the most vociferous opponent of the mendicants and the recognized leader of the masters. His education was considerable and his background was most impressive. Born in Saint-Amour in Burgundy (the modern-day Franche-Comté region) around 1200, he achieved a high status at the university in a relatively short time. He had received a Master of Arts by the year 1228. He studied Canon Law and received his doctorate in late 1238. He was also canon of Beauvais and rector of the church of Guerville. In addition, he was granted the care of souls in Granville in 1247, though he remained only a sub-deacon in Paris.[88]

Guillaume is a central figure in this episode, for he was to introduce a radical new element into the debate. Through his arguments, the conflict was moved from a mundane power struggle into an all-out war between the forces of good and evil, set against the backdrop of the coming apocalypse. This elevation to a spiritual level says as much about Guillaume's personality and temperament as it does about any reality, or even any existing aspect of the conflict. Up until this time, the conflict had remained mostly in the realm of the physical world, and concerned rights and privileges. The "man from Saint-Amour" (as his partisan, Jean de Meun would later enshrine him), in playing up existing fears, was about to take things to a different level entirely.

When he formulated these ideas, and how they exactly took shape are unclear, but we do know that along with the professional resentment of the friars, there arose in some the fear that they were actually deceitful agents of evil. This seems not to have been merely another secular tactic to stir up anger at and mistrust of the mendicants, as some have suggested,[89] but rather a genuine (if initially minor) fear born out of what was eventually seen as incontrovertible evidence of the approaching doom. In this, Guillaume differed from some of his contemporary and later fellow critics of the friars. He declared that these new orders were irredeemable agents of evil, heralds of Antichrist, and worthy only of elimination. His writings would continually stress this and he would be committed to it. Other critics of the friars were more cautious, seeing the orders as once worthy, but now fallen, and in need of renewal and reform.[90] Humbert of Romans and the Dominicans did not take kindly to Guillaume's accusations and shot back he and his supporters were the true devils, Leviathan and Belial.[91]

At this time of increasing hostilities, accusations, and counter-accusations, there appeared in Paris "an outrageously heretical work,"[92] now lost, by a Franciscan friar named Gerard of Borgo San Donnino, a lector in theology at the Franciscan convent in Paris.[93] Titled *Introductorius ad Evangelium Aeternum* ("Introduction to the Eternal Gospel"), it intended to offer one side in an ongoing debate about how the Rule of the Franciscans was to be interpreted.[94] However, its introduction also presented a radical vision of medieval cosmology that effectively denounced orthodox teaching. In it, Gerard saw a new world coming shortly, wherein the current Gospel and Church would be overthrown by a Third Testament, the *Eternal Gospel of the Holy Spirit*, just as the New Testament had replaced the Old. This new Church would be administered by the friars, the only ones pure and worthy enough to do so, because the hierarchical Church had become evil and corrupt.

Gerard was clearly a fanatic and had only a small following among Parisian Franciscans. The main cause for concern was that he had based his writings very loosely on the predictions of Joachim of Fiore (*ca.* 1130–1201/2), a Calabrian abbot who claimed the gift of prophecy.[95] There was considerable interest in Joachim's works among the Franciscans, despite some of his ideas having been condemned at the Fourth Lateran Council in 1215 (though he was not). Many other friars commented on his works in a more balanced fashion than had Gerard, though whole "schools" of followers developed, and sayings were often attributed to Joachim that were either distortions of his words, or simply things that he had not said at all (Gerard was guilty of both offenses).[96]

One of the central concerns of Joachim's writings was the appearance of Antichrist, which he believed would happen in the mid–13th century. This prediction was taken seriously by many in the Church, for there seemed to be much evidence to bear it out, despite a tendency to deny the validity of apocalyptic prophecy, at least in any official capacity. Joachim's later followers fixed the year precisely at 1260, based on his complex calculations that there were three ages (symbolizing the Trinity), and that each age lasted for 42 generations. Given that a generation was approximately thirty years, the length of each age was about 1260 years. He had seen the first age as being from the time of Moses until Christ, and that the second age was thus soon to come to an end. One of the pseudo–Joachimite writings states this explicitly: "When 1,260 years have passed after a blessed virgin has given birth, then Antichrist, filled with the devil, will be born."[97]

Joachim never proclaimed the downfall of the Church, merely that the monastic, contemplative life would take precedence in the Third Age, as wealth, power, and corruption fell away. However, this age would be born with terrible birth pangs, including the coming of Antichrist. His more revolutionary followers read much into his words that he had not intended.

Despite the biblical warning that no one could know the exact hour of the return of Christ and the Day of Judgement (Matthew 24:36),[98] medieval minds were seemingly obsessed with searching for clues. Predictions such as Joachim's haunted the minds of the educated, those who saw many signs of the last days in the deterioration of social structures and continuing war and strife.

Indeed, despite the recent annihilation of the Cathars, Christendom had been unable to fully regain the Holy Land from the Muslims in more than a century-and-a-half of military campaigns, and King Louis' own crusades, the largest and most expensive ever undertaken, ended as miserable failures. Louis being held for ransom was a sure sign of God's displeasure. The pious Louis was deeply troubled for the last 20 years of his life, and died rather pathetically of dysentery in Tunisia during his second crusading attempt.

Around Europe, conflict and animosity raged. A civil war brewed in England between Henry III and his barons, a hold-over from the days when his father, King John, had been forced to sign the Magna Carta. In the south of Italy, the Holy Roman Emperor, Frederick II had for decades been hostile to the papacy, having been denounced by the pope as the Antichrist (though also praised as a hero by many). Further, he crowned himself as the King of Jerusalem in 1229, an indication to his enemies that the last days were at hand. His death in 1250 did not settle the matter, for his sons continued the war of words (and arms). While Frederick consorted with Muslims, rumors circulated among the educated of the mysterious and terrifying Mongols ravaging as far west as Poland and Hungary in 1241.

The Flagellants also began to appear for the first time, "with their eerie, candlelit, and banner-laden processions of itinerant penitents, flogging themselves bloody with whips, spikes, and flails."[99] They would become a fixture of the medieval landscape in the next century, and a symbol of anguished and pitiful repentance, when the Black Death ravaged the continent and left at least a third of Europe's population dead. It is not clear whether they were directly influenced by Joachimite eschatology, or if they were merely another byproduct of the general heightened fears of the age.

The combination of these various factors aroused feelings of unease, anger, and fear among many. The appearance of Gerard's heretical work, which purported to be based on Joachim's predictions but was in fact a grand distortion, if not an outright fabrication, was proof to some masters at the university that they were no longer combating mere human opponents. Antichrist was about to enter their midst, if he had not done so already.

Guillaume and his party entered Rome with 32 excerpts from Gerard's work which he and the other masters felt to be heinous errors. Among these were: that the *Eternal Gospel* would be superior to the teaching of Christ and all of the New and Old Testaments, that it would follow in succession to the gospel of Christ, and that the New Testament would not endure.[100] His efforts were successful in establishing a commission of cardinals to review the work. It was indeed judged to be heretical, and Pope Alexander IV condemned it on November 4, 1255.[101]

The masters had issued a letter to the Church prelates in February 1254, outlining their many grievances with the friars, specifically the Dominicans.[102] They also accused them of vanity, by wanting to raise themselves up with the title of "master" against the very teachings of Christ to the contrary.[103] Guillaume would also reiterate this serious charge. They made various practical accusations related to the structure of the university: that the friars had refused to obey a strike as a means of gaining another chair, that Roland of Cremona's chair was gained through deceit, that the second Dominican chair was not obtained properly, and that these additional mendicants were causing a decrease in the number of chairs available to the masters.[104]

The masters appealed to the authorities to save the university. Perhaps somewhat surprisingly, they succeeded spectacularly in defending many of their positions and in receiving papal favor. Pope Innocent IV became convinced of their plight and on July 4, 1254, he issued a declaration which upheld the masters' statute. Later, on November 21, he issued what was almost a total condemnation of the friars' actions, *Etsi animarum*.[105] In it, he imposed severe restrictions on fraternal actions, particularly concerning the administration of confession and the celebration of Mass.[106] He justified this by saying that their competition with the masters was causing a negative image of the friars to develop, and that this in turn was bad for the Church. Their rights to preach, hear confessions, and instruct remained intact, but limits were placed on where and how they could do so.[107] It was a fabulous victory for Guillaume and his partisans; they were granted virtually everything they had set out to achieve. The friars were furious, maintaining that their loss of privilege had come about by the masters' lies. However, papal support for the masters was very short-lived. Sixteen days after issuing *Etsi animarum*, Innocent IV died.[108] Some enemies of the friars would later comment that the Dominicans had earnestly prayed for his death.[109]

This ill-timed misfortune proved to be a disaster for the secular faculty, and marked a turning point in the master/friar conflict. One of the great issues in electing the new pope was the conflict and the future of the mendicant orders. As fate would have it, Innocent IV was succeeded by Raynald of Segni, who adopted the name Alexander IV; he was no less than the Cardinal Protector of the Franciscans,[110] and his papacy would spell disaster for the secular faction. In December 1254, with the bull *Nec insolitum*, he annulled *Etsi animarum*, removing Innocent's restrictions on the friars concerning preaching, confessions, and the administration of the sacraments. In April 1255, he issued the *Quasi Lignum Vitae* ("The Cross of Life"), which attempted to rewrite the masters' statute by giving certain powers over to the chancellor, effectively eliminating secular control and strongly favoring the friars. In addition, it ordered that all the expelled friars be readmitted with full privileges at once.[111] Looking at these new decrees, it is obvious that the masters were given very harsh and unfair treatment by the new pope. Indeed, he seemed to be intent on punishing them for their actions against his beloved friars. He also had little understanding of the issues, and was effectively stripping the secular masters of rights they had held for nearly 50 years, rights obtained from the papacy itself.[112]

The masters refused to abide by these new strictures, boldly calling the papal issue the *Quasi Lignum Mortis* ("The Cross of Death"), and their response was to threaten to dissolve the university. They reached the point of making a drastic decision: rather than be forced to associate with the friars under these outrageous new regulations, they would relinquish their privileges, dissolve the *consortium magistrorum*, (in effect, the university), and walk away. The university had degenerated into something far different than a *universitas* for them, and they would not be compelled to keep it together if they could not do so with the rights they had held for so long.[113] The institution to which they were being ordered to readmit their expelled enemies would simply no longer exist.

By October, the masters more formally dissolved their organization. The situation in the city grew even tenser. The Dominican Humbert of Romans noted that by the end of 1255, the masters had effectively blacklisted the Dominicans and incited hostility against them. The friars were subjected to verbal abuse in the streets, and had things thrown at them (garbage, small rocks, etc.). The point was clearly to make their lives as miserable as possible and to treat them as traitors to the university, so that they would be afraid to walk the streets.[114] Indeed, King Louis had to assign a unit of armed guards to escort them about the city.[115] The papal response in December was to order the bishops of Auxerre and Orleans to excommunicate the masters and to enforce *Quasi Lignum Vitae*. Interestingly, the bishops were less than enthusiastic about carrying out his request, having their own political issues with the pope and the friars.[116]

In the grander scheme of things, the papacy's actions only increased the fears among some masters of something more sinister at work. Indeed, if some had been skeptical before, these new regulations may well have brought them over to the very unsettling idea that they were dealing with more than just privileges, economics, and details of bureaucracy. In the winter of 1255–56, Guillaume de Saint-Amour wrote a polemical work entitled *Tractatus Brevis de Periculis Novissimorum Temporum ex Scripturis Sumptus* ("The Brief Tract Concerning the Perils of the Last Times from the Citation of Scripture"). The work, which shall be considered in more detail in the next chapter, was anything but brief, being instead a detailed treatise that purported to show the clear signs of the coming dangers, through biblical exegesis. It cleverly drew parallels between the current events in Paris and New Testament eschatology, yet carefully refrained from outright associations with or condemnations of any particular group. Guillaume understood that obvious attacks on the friars would get him nowhere with the new pope.

Interestingly, Louis IX intervened at this point, trying to negotiate a settlement that would be acceptable to both sides. He convinced the opponents to submit their complaints to arbitration. A synod was held in Paris, with the archbishops of Rheims, Sens, Rouen, and Bourges. In March 1256, the arbiters produced a settlement that surprisingly, was agreeable to both sides. That should have settled the matter once and for all, but Pope Alexander was decidedly against any such peaceful solutions, given his intense dislike of the masters. He declared the settlement void, and instead urged the friars not to give away anything to the masters, since God was on their side.[117] He seems to have believed that the masters were being led astray by a small number of malcontents, and he wanted them sidelined so that the university could return to normal.[118] He was not well-informed about the severity of the situation, possibly as a result of being misled by some of the mendicant lobbyists. Indeed, this ridiculous and poor decision only made things worse. Then, Guillaume made a dreadful error, and set up his own fall.

In June 1256, he preached a Pentecost sermon on the topic of those who would follow Christ, drawing from John 14:23.[119] Guillaume began his sermon decrying the sin of hypocrisy (a charge so often leveled at the friars over the centuries), saying that it is found everywhere, even among many in the Church, the nobility and kings. He goes on to lament that certain kings waste their time getting out of bed in the middle of the night to celebrate monastic hours, when they should devote their time to masses (as Henry III did). Certain kings are so in love with the poor that they do not even dress in a kingly fashion, and instead pretend to be poor themselves. They waste their money on foolish wars wherein good Christians are killed. Guillaume argues that these behaviors are against scripture; a king is supposed to look kingly, rich, and impressive and administer justice; this is what God wants. And a true king surrounds himself with proper courtiers, not vagabonds and egotistical, self-righteous preachers who beg for their food. A king should not be a beggar.[120]

The target of this attack is clear. No one who heard or read the work would have any doubt as to that. Guillaume was essentially calling the king a would-be pauper, and insulting his ability to rule. Louis' response was quick, but measured. While a more hot-tempered king might well have imprisoned him, Louis simply dispatched clerks to Rome with copies of Guillaume's writings, including the scandalous sermon.[121] He probably wanted any judgement to come from the pope, rather than himself. Indeed, if he had taken action, it might well have proven Guillaume's point, that he was hopelessly in league with the friars, and incapable of independent thought or proper rule. Guillaume was ordered to appear in Rome to defend himself, where he faced not only Bonaventure, but also Thomas Aquinas, to argue for his opposition.

As one would expect, *De periculis* was not well-received by the papacy, and only added to the masters' troubles when it was condemned in October 1256. Though it was not branded as heretical, Alexander IV deemed it "perverse and reprehensible against the power of the pope and the Curia."[122] Every copy was ordered to be burned; possessors of it thereafter would be excommunicated.[123] In an age when books were hand-copied and only existed in preciously small numbers, this was a serious and damning response. Clearly, his attempt to stamp out Guillaume's work failed, as multiple copies eventually surfaced and had considerable influence on later writers.

In that same month, an even greater misfortune befell the masters: both Aquinas and Bonaventura were accepted as members of the faculty of theology. Two of the greatest minds of the 13th century were now in positions of authority at the University of Paris. This twist of events was to be one the most significant events in Guillaume's downfall. Brilliant theologian though he was, he was no match in a debate for their intellectual capacity and rhetorical skills; no one could have been. However, his efforts were not a total failure. In going up against an intellectual titan in Aquinas, Guillaume forced him into taking a defensive position about the role of the Dominicans at the university. While there was never a chance that such a man, backed by a sympathetic pope, would lose, Guillaume managed to fare far better than he has perhaps been given credit.[124]

He had already been expelled from the university and excommunicated in June of that year, and after his unsuccessful defense of *De Periculis*, he knew he was beaten.[125] In August 1257, the pope prohibited him from returning to Paris, effectively banishing him from the city. He also deprived Guillaume of his offices and the ability to preach or lecture, not only in Paris, but in other universities. Bologna, for example, had just enough free-thinkers, including anti-papal factions; for the pope, Guillaume's ideas might well have been dangerous there. In the same month, Louis IX sent him into exile from France. It seems that Louis was also instrumental in the punishment handed down by the pope.[126] He had quietly but forcefully made it known whose side he favored, and that he would not tolerate such defiance from the masters again. However, as we will see, the criticisms of Louis were not silenced by his actions, and in fact, his response brought them more into the open, especially from literary circles in Paris. While some were already proclaiming him a saint, as Little notes, "a few others, though, unfortunate enough to face him in a deadly political battle, felt they had been beaten down by an accomplice of anti–Christ."[127]

This bitter turn of events must have hit Guillaume especially hard. He had expended a great amount of energy and effort in formulating and defending his ideas, which, as far as we can determine, were sincere and born of genuine fear. His commitment to warning of the impending end continued throughout his time away. During his exile, he wrote another treatise, *Collectiones catholicae et canonical scriptural*, essentially a restatement of *De Periculis*, completed in 1266, further invoking apocalyptic themes, including certain writings attributed to the German mystic Hildegard of Bingen (1098–1179). These prophecies contained denunciations of clerical corruptions and heresy in view of signs and prophecies. They were popular at the time, and were being adopted and fitted into an eschatological model which focused on the friars.[128] Pope Clement IV received the *Collectiones* on October 18, 1266, and while noting its similarity to his previous tract, allowed Guillaume to return to France; he chose to return to his native Saint-Amour.[129] He lived until 1272, still the object of ecclesiastical enmity.[130]

The masters were ultimately forced to readmit the friars to the university. Nevertheless, support for Guillaume remained strong for a time. Indeed, a series of correspondences written by him in exile in defiance of papal prohibition briefly resurrected the debate. For the most part, the masters remained loyal to him, and repeatedly appealed to the pope to reinstate him, a plea which was always rejected.[131] This negative response was not received well in Paris, and riots occurred on more than one occasion in protest. Alexander would not budge, however, believing that this rather localized conflict was tied to a much larger issue, that of papal authority. Some of Guillaume's supporters eventually gave in and recanted, and were thus allowed to return to the university, effectively reestablishing it.[132] Alexander's heavy-handed approach generally worked, and by 1259, he boasted of a university at peace once again.[133]

By 1260, when the Antichrist notably failed to appear (yet again), the university had mostly returned to its normal operations,[134] though conflicts would arise again over the next several decades. It was little consolation to the masters at the time, but Alexander had been the exception to the tradition of papal support, with his flagrant and obnoxious backing of the friars in total defiance of university tradition. Having viewed this as a local dispute, he failed to grasp the seriousness of the master's complaints, and just how hard-won their rights had been. Alexander died in 1261, and was succeeded by Urban IV. From this time, the masters were able to regain some of their lost power, and restrict some of that of their opponents. The university would not again face such hostility from the papacy, even though it was forced to co-exist with the friars. Regardless of this improvement in fortunes, some still feared that more evil forces were at work, and saw treachery in the actions of the mendicant orders. Further, as we will see, there were those in the literary and poetic spheres who were not about to let the matter rest.

Guillaume's own supporters spoke up again at the end of the decade, attempting to win for him a return from exile, and to reignite the polemics against the friars. Gerard of Abbeville (*d.* 1272), a university secular theologian, wrote his *Contra adversarium perfectionis Christianae* in about 1269, once more questioning the legitimacy of religious mendicancy.[135] The work stopped short of calling for the abolition of the orders, as Guillaume had done, but prompted replies from both Aquinas and Bonaventure.[136] Gerard's contemporary, Nicolas of Lisieux expressed similar sentiments in his *Liber de Antichristo*.[137] However, the skillfulness with which both friars wrote their defenses was enough to effectively bring an end to these kinds of written theological debates over mendicancy for a long time, up until the mid–14th century.[138] Some masters themselves came under scrutiny at this time for their adherence to various Aristotelian philosophies, the so-called Latin Averroists (from the commentaries on Aristotle of the Spanish Muslim Averroes). They were condemned in 1270 by the bishop of Paris.[139]

Issues came to a boil again at the Council of Lyon in 1274, where there were calls to abolish the friars altogether. This did not happen, of course, but it was set out in the decree *Religionem diversitatem* that the regulations of the Fourth Lateran Council from 1215—that no new orders were to be created with new rules—should be enforced. This led to the abolition of various orders of friars, sparing only the Franciscans, Dominicans, Carmelites, and Augustinians. While these orders had certainly proven themselves to be useful in many ways, some argue that the Franciscans, already the subject of so much controversy over their ideals and actual practices, were spared at least in part due to the eloquence and persuasive abilities of Bonaventure.[140]

The friars' fortunes improved during the papacy of Martin IV, another strong supporter. In his *Ad fructus uberes* of 1281, he authorized them to preach in any diocese without first having to seek the approval of the local bishop.[141] This naturally did not please those bishops, who saw it as a threat to their abilities to oversee their parishes, as well as a loss of income for local churches. In France, they mounted a concerted effort to have the bull annulled, with the full support of the secular masters. At an assembly in Paris in November 1290, however, their hopes were crushed, when Cardinal Benedict Gaetani (later the controversial Pope Boniface VIII) told them quite clearly that the bull would not be annulled. Instead, he blocked their efforts to further hinder the bull with their own acts, and told the masters that the Curia would destroy the university before removing the friar's privileges.[142] Ultimately Gaetani, as Boniface, would reverse his strong position and issue *Super cathedram* in 1300, which would indeed restrict some of the friars' actions (including reviving the requirement for a bishop's approval to preach) in an attempt at compromise[143] (we will examine Boniface more in chapter 6). Later university partisans, such as Jean de Pouilly and Jean d'Anneux, would continue the antifraternal diatribes well into the first few decades of the 14th century.[144] Jean d'Anneux, a secular theologian like Guillaume de Saint-Amour, made use of similar apocalyptic attacks, and referenced the language of his predecessor.[145]

However, the university did not again see the same levels of conflict, and the secular masters were able to regain some of their prestige. Bert Roest notes, "With the relative decline of papal power in the closing decades of the thirteenth century, and with royal backing of university autonomy, the university as a body gradually strengthened its position. By 1318, the university was strong enough to ask from all its members an oath of full obedience to its statutes. The friars conceded without much demur."[146]

We turn our attention now to looking more closely at the works of Guillaume de Saint-Amour, and examining how they were so contentious and offensive. His fearless denunciation of the friars and the king was remarkable, given the intolerance of dissent in the wake of the Albigensian Crusade and other events of his time.

The Perils of the Last Times: The Writings of Guillaume de Saint-Amour

De Periculis Novissimorum Temporum is a detailed and at times tedious work that sets out Guillaume's principal arguments in great detail. The focal point is indicated in the title, the "Perils of the Last Times." It is an exegetical exercise which draws primarily from the New Testament and its glosses to present an understanding of the dangers that Guillaume and his supporters (such as Gerard of Abbeville and Nicolas of Lisieux) clearly felt were present.[1] The biblical passage from which Guillaume drew his title is II Timothy 3:1. Relevant sections of verses 1 through 6 include: in the last days, there will approach dangerous times; there will be men who love themselves, but have no love and no peace; they will have the outward appearance of devotion, but will refuse its power, and so they should be avoided; they are those who penetrate houses, deceiving weak women (burdened with sin and led by their desires).[2]

The phrase "penetrate houses" (*penetrant domos*) became a major focus of his concern, for Guillaume held that the friars were "penetrating" not just houses, but everywhere. They had used their wiles to endear themselves to the university, and were employing the same tactics to deceive many others and lead them astray, especially those with wealth and power, most importantly Louis IX and the papacy. Throughout his works, he identified three groups of guilty parties that pointed to the friars: the Pharisees, the pseudo-apostles, and the "antichrists," groups which would often be found in later antifraternal writings.[3]

De Periculis was as popular as it was controversial, and he revised it four times in 1256. Today, it survives in more than 60 manuscript copies, proof that papal condemnation was not nearly as effective as hoped.[4] It is composed of a prologue and 14 chapters, wherein he offers his arguments against the friars, heavily supported by biblical citations to prove his points. In the prologue, he announces that the "unworthy" professors of the faith who study in Paris (of which he is one) have taken it upon themselves as frequent inspectors of scripture (even though their work is inadequate to the task), to warn of the dangers of these last times, which are threatening the whole of the Church.⁵ Traver has suggested that this could indicate that Guillaume collaborated on this work with other secular masters at the university.⁶ For those who do not believe his words, he calls for a Church council instead of scholastic disputation and debate on the subject.⁷ He stresses that this work is not intended to attack any person or status which the Church has approved (a carefully-worded disclaimer), but rather is intended to instruct the Church in the reality of these dangers, and to speak against sin and evil.⁸ He cleverly and repeatedly stresses (including in his defense to the papacy) that since he attacks no one in particular, those who take offense at his words must have something to hide.⁹

There follows an extended commentary on II Timothy, and on scriptural descriptions of the coming of Antichrist,¹⁰ and questions about lawful preaching and authority to perform pastoral duties. The office of preaching cannot just be assigned at will. Mortals may not change that which has been ordained by God; even bishops cannot lawfully preach outside of their diocese. Thus, if those who freely penetrate houses claim they are divinely sent, they are false.¹¹ Guillaume held that there were two orders or classes in the Church, the upper (bishops, deacons, and priests) and the lower (the laity and regulars).¹² There can be no "third order," which is what the friars presumed to be.¹³ In chapters 3 and 4, he writes that these men will deceive others and be very persuasive. Their audiences will welcome them, believing them to be holy, and with this acceptance, they will bring many dangers to the Church.¹⁴ In chapter 5, he complains that these false prophets are able to hear confessions, even though they may not lawfully do so, which makes them penetrators of houses, as well as thieves and masters of seduction, of both men and women. Those who do not take care to resist or do not see the evil they bring will perish with them.¹⁵

From chapter 7, he begins to give more detailed lists of the signs and dangers: they are thieves, they are false prophets, they are wolves in sheep's clothing, and they are corrupt and will reject Christ.¹⁶ In chapter 8, he stresses that it is probable that the end of the world is immanent, since this age has lasted longer than those that came before it, and Christ will return soon.¹⁷ He lists eight signs of the coming end. The first is the appearance of the *Eternal Gospel*; the second is that this work was submitted for examination in Paris, indicating that it was being preached; the third concerns exegetical work on the book of Daniel and the writing on the wall at Belshazzar's banquet, as relating to the *Eternal Gospel*; the fourth sign is that in this time, some men will appear to be holier, but will actually displease Christ; the fifth is that these falsely pious will be challenged and will react angrily; the sixth is that certain preachers will seek to glorify themselves as they achieve positions of power in the Church; the seventh is that certain men, seeming holy, will in fact reject Christ and follow the *Eternal Gospel*; the eighth sign is that some will notice these dangers and make them public. He clearly was including himself and his followers in this scenario; their work is proof of the other signs.¹⁸

Chapters 9 to 11, discuss how the Church should combat this danger, investigating and removing such false preachers, making use of secular force, if necessary,¹⁹ advice that ironically sounds very much like a request for the Inquisition's duties. Chapter 12 is largely devoted to his previous arguments from his questions and sermons (some of which we will examine below), much of it having to do with issues of begging by the able-bodied; such individuals should be expelled from the Church, since they violate the actions of Christ and his apostles, actions which they claim to follow.[20] Chapter 13 is devoted to where such false prophets will be found, for they are not among the Jews, the Muslims, or even the obvious heretics. They will be hidden, and will seem to be pious Christians, particularly those who are very studious. They are learned but do not know the truth.[21] This was an obvious insult to the friars at the university, especially the likes of Bonaventure and Aquinas.

Based on all of this, he concludes the work by identifying 41 "signs"[22] that the friars are indeed false apostles, including: pride, deceit, consorting with women, deviations from Gospel teachings, greed, lying, living in idleness, and a host of similar offenses. Each sign is accompanied by a supporting biblical verse (or verses) and a gloss on its meaning. The list is long, but worth noting, as many of these accusations would surface repeatedly in attacks against the friars in the future.

True apostles, he writes, do not engage in these activities: 1. They do not enter into houses and lead women astray. 2. They do not deceive the simple, or seduce them away from God. 3. If they refuse to be corrected when they are wrong and cannot endure it, they are not true. 4. They do not act in a boastful manner, or give themselves praise for show. 5. They do not ask for letters of commendation to make themselves appealing to others though introduction. 6. They do not seek to be commended; they delay glory, and give it to God. 7. They do not try to preach without being sent to do so. 8. False apostles will claim that they are authorized by God, though they are not; even miracles can be worked with diabolical powers. 9. The false call their practices true religion when they are not; they feign knowledge and commit sacrilege. 10. These false apostles live by begging and preaching from the gospel without the authority to do so, rather than by their own labor. 11. The 11th sign repeats the 6th verbatim. 12. True apostles do not preach for temporal gain (including money), praise, or honor. 13. False apostles claim to have a greater zeal for saving souls (and thus greater authority) than parish priests. 14. True apostles do not engage in wordplay and eloquence. 15. True apostles do not offer up flattery, especially for profit. Those who linger in courts and insinuate themselves to the nobility, therefore, are false. 16. False apostles engage in deceiving and extorting goods under the pretense of friendship. 17. False apostles angrily argue against the truth, if it is inconvenient to them. 18. True apostles do not bring trouble to or wish harm on those who reject them, since this desire to be accepted is a worldly vanity. 19. Further, true apostles do not try to coerce rulers (who favor them) to act against those who have rejected them. 20. True apostles have an understanding of history, but also of what is to come, and do not dismiss these dangerous times. 21. True apostles do not desire the material wealth of those who hear them; they are not ravenous wolves, certainly not by begging, unless it comes from true authority. 22. True apostles endure their sufferings with patience and forbearance, turning the other cheek and not resorting in anger to an eye for an eye. 23. Likewise, these true apostles should suffer and be hated initially, prevailing only later. If they are loved immediately, they are false. 24. Apostles who seek glory by preaching to foreign peoples (who already have their own apostles), and do so uninvited in these courts and synods are false. 25. True apostles do not seek praise, even when their efforts benefit the Church. 26. Likewise, true apostles do not try to please men, or seek their favor. 27. True apostles gratefully accept the food and drink given to them, and do not try to obtain more lavish meals. 28. True apostles praise the law of Christ above all, and if they do not condemn works such as the *Eternal Gospel*, they are false. 29. As with food, true apostles do not seek out lavish accommodations, but are content with what they are offered, and only from the worthy, not those who offer anything other than from piety. Those who seek out evil men to obtain gifts in exchange for hiding their sins are false. 30. Likewise, true apostles do not meddle in others' affairs just to receive nourishment. 31. True apostles do not brag about their miracles, or indeed, those that God has worked through them, so that they can increase their standing. 32. True apostles always seek the glory of Christ, not their own. 33. True apostles do not seek to be a part of the feasts, celebrations, or ceremonies of the wealthy and worldly, but rather flee from them. 34. True apostles do not seek out the tables of others in order to give them flattery and recline in idleness. 35. True apostles hate no one, following the command of Matthew 5:44. They love their enemies, including those who despise them. 36. Those apostles who are false will respond in anger when questioned as to whether they are true or false. They will also seek revenge by aligning themselves with worldly powers that assault truth. 37. True apostles do not try to preach to those already converted, but rather go to those in need of conversion. 38. Likewise, true apostles go on their own missions, not another's. 39. True apostles do not brag or claim for themselves anything but what God gives to them. 40. True apostles do not rely on logic and reasoning. 41. True apostles neither love carnality nor anything that hinders their service to God; those that engage in simony are also false. 42. Finally, true apostles do not try to make friends in the world.[23]

Throughout this exhaustive account, however, Guillaume is careful not to link these agents of Antichrist directly with the friars, or to accuse them of devilry, though this was clearly the implication. *De Periculis* contains no references to the friars themselves. However, his treatise was clearly not coincidental to the events occurring in Paris, especially given that he was the head of the delegation seeking their disempowerment. What Guillaume attempted in writing his work in such a thinly-veiled manner was a legal maneuver. Knowing that he would have to appear before a synod of bishops to defend his potentially heretical work, and further, against charges that he had defamed the friars (who were, after all, given sanction by the pope), he could quite honestly and truthfully answer that he had never spoken against any order that was sanctioned by the church.[24] As noted above, his prologue stated as much. He would argue that he was merely pointing out the many "perils" which existed everywhere, and that readers could make up their own minds. This was a clever move, but one that ultimately failed to save him from the pope's wrath.

Guillaume leveled the charge of men "loving themselves" (*seipsos amantes*) against the friars, because he saw that they were surrounding themselves with wealthy and powerful individuals instead of the poor, ignoring university statutes (to him, a sign of arrogance), and living luxuriously rather than humbly, as their founders had intended. Both orders seemed to be infected with pride, a sin as deadly as lust, gluttony, and sloth, all of which he also saw in their behaviors. We can see here the beginning of the stereotype of the friar that would last for so long: the lazy, often obese friar living off of others' work, stuffing himself with food and wine, drunk, lustful, and indulging in all manner of sins and hypocrisy. It was a potent image that would take hold, capture the imagination of the literate and the humble, and reemerge in ridicule, satire, anger, and resentment for centuries.

One of Guillaume's specific tactics was to draw parallels between the Pharisees of the New Testament and this new group of hypocrites and deceivers, which he asserted were everywhere. Indeed, he delivered a public sermon, *De Pharisaeo et publicano*, in August 1256. He opened it with a rather pompous statement, drawn from Luke 18:11, saying that he gives thanks to God that he is unlike certain men: a robber, unjust, or a tax collector.[25] Though again, he does not refer to the friars specifically, there can be no doubt that they are the subject of the attack. He states that it should be noted that the Pharisees were a religious order among the Jews, just as there are now regular orders "among us."[26]

After labeling the Pharisees as hypocrites, he draws parallels between them and the hypocrites of his own time. To indicate further the subject of his attack without actually naming them, he draws on the entirety of Matthew 23, a long sermon wherein Jesus admonishes the Pharisees for their hypocrisy and outward show of piety, while inwardly they have become sinful and rotten. Guillaume made particular use of Matthew 23:6–10, to draw attention to a current controversial subject at the university: the mendicant desire to be known and treated as *magisteri* (masters). Guillaume could not have asked for a better scriptural support for his hostility to the idea. Concerning the Pharisees, the gospel records that Jesus said that they love to be called "master" by all. However, one should not desire to be called "master," for there is only one Master, but all will be brothers. Further, true apostles will not be called "teachers" (or again, "masters"): because their true teacher is one, Christ.[27]

"Rabbi," which he translated as "master," gave Guillaume all the scriptural evidence he needed for his attack. The reference to *fratres* ("brothers") provided an extra link. The fact that Guillaume and his associates had long held and fiercely defended the title of "master" for themselves was of little importance to his argument, for in his view it was the present-day "Pharisees" that wrongly coveted this designation, not the seculars, who had been rightfully granted their privileges from the pope himself. Guillaume proceeded to draw many other parallels between the Pharisees and the always-unnamed friars, moving beyond the criticisms of Matthew 23 to include a variety of other references.[28] Constant repetition was a method of reinforcing the idea of mendicant duplicity.

The second of Guillaume's tactics was to link the friars with vague references to the *pseudoapostoli*, false prophets and deceivers mysteriously alluded to in the New Testament. The reason for this connection stemmed largely from the Franciscans' claim to be both the inheritors of, and those who had revived, the true apostolic tradition, the *vita apostolica*, when they embraced poverty and renunciation, and went into the world to do good works and preach. As we have seen, Guillaume and his supporters believed that the Franciscans had strayed far from their original intentions, playing right into the devil's hand with their obvious corruption, accumulation of wealth, and preoccupation with other worldly cares.

Guillaume even questioned Francis's sanctity in his response to Bonaventure's *De mendicitate*, demanding proof for an alleged miracle, and noting that even with such proof, an evil man can work miracles.[29] Francis was a popular saint, so this was a bold statement. It was probably unwise for him to make it, but in the heat of dispute and debate, he recorded his controversial thoughts, just as he did in numerous other writings. Geltner has further noted that Guillaume offered a "jarring dismissal of St. Francis's and St. Dominic's lives as exemplary,"[30] making no distinction between the odious act of mendicancy and those who practiced it. In any case, Guillaume took up and exploited the fears of those who believed that the order was undermining the duties and authority of the Church, which, according to tradition, operated by the concept of apostolic succession. One of the central arguments of medieval antifraternal tracts is that despite their claims, these new orders did not imitate the lives of the original apostles, and certainly were not the inheritors of their traditions in any legitimate way.[31] He was essentially accusing them of being frauds.

Guillaume went further and questioned the validity of the friars to perform any Church functions at all, citing Romans 10:15, which asked how anyone would be able to preach unless they are sent.[32] Guillaume interpreted this to mean "sent" by apostolic succession, which was the privilege of the hierarchical Church alone. Thus, the friars became to him *non missi* ("not sent"). This left him open to charges that he was challenging papal authority, as both orders had been approved by the pope, Christ's representative on earth. Guillaume saved himself by upholding the concept of Church hierarchy, and stressing that neither the pope nor Francis and Dominic had intended to undermine its structure. The friars, however, were now doing just that, in defiance of their founders. He argued that they were performing the traditional functions of the clergy without being a part of the hierarchy, and that this represented a great danger to the multitude of Christians. Too many "apostles" would destroy the unity of the Church.[33]

Guillaume's next strategy was to see the coming apocalypse in the presence and actions of the friars. It is on this point that *De Periculis* takes its strongest position. In addition to the verses in II Timothy, the work contains numerous other references to the *pseudoapostoli*, such as Matthew 24:11, which states that many pseudo-prophets will rise up, and will deceive those around them.[34] Likewise there is a warning in I John 2:18, which notes that many Antichrists have arisen.[35]

He saw in the warning of II Timothy 3:6 (penetrating houses to lead weak-willed women astray) an alarming similarity to the association between the friars and the Beguines.[36] As we have seen, these communities of women arose at approximately the same time as the friars, during the wave of revived spirituality that swept through Europe. He was very suspicious of their interactions, even intimacy. He insisted that the Beguines were not generally old widows and such, but rather were young and beautiful, and thus would have been prime recruiting material for a popular religious movement, especially one with ulterior motives. He observed that the friars visited their houses, and stayed to "talk" with them, offering "consolation" and the hearing of confessions. Even worse, the friars were known to beg on behalf of the Beguines, and tried to keep these women sequestered from the world at large. To Guillaume, this implied many things, chief among them an undue influence on impressionable young minds, and very likely consorting with them in sexual ways which were forbidden by their vows.[37] The Beguines and their suspected licentious behavior would also come under attack from Jean de Meun in his continuation of the *Roman de la Rose*.[38]

Guillaume also saw the *penetrant domos* phrase in a more figurative sense, meaning that the friars had additionally seduced the hearts of weak men (which, in his view, made them more like women, who by their nature, so the medieval mind believed, were easily deceived) as well as the "Mother Church" itself. This was the greatest danger, for it seemed that the devil had succeeded in "penetrating" the very house of God, beginning the third and final persecution of the Church. The first had been the early martyrs, the second, the Church Fathers' battles with heresy; this new conflict was a sign of the beginning of the end.

Regardless of his motives or intentions to protect university privileges, it seems that Guillaume was genuinely afraid of the apocalypse, and saw himself as a champion of truth and the true Church. He has been accused in modern times of merely employing apocalyptic imagery to further his arguments against the friars for the benefit of the secular masters' standing and privileges, and this may be true in part. However, considering that he produced such a large volume of writing involving complex and carefully-researched biblical exegesis to prove his arguments, it is difficult to believe that he was merely jealously guarding his university position.[39] *De Periculis* and his other writings were a call to restore the established Church order, which had been badly damaged by these dangerous innovations.[40] Whatever his faults, Guillaume was a competent scriptural exegete, and his knowledge of biblical passages and the *Glossa Ordinaria* shows through in his writings, whatever conclusions one can draw about his interpretations. He made the arduous journey to Rome, risked being branded a heretic, suffered excommunication and banishment, and yet still held to his beliefs, including writing in exile and living in peril of harsher punishment.

In the end, he may have seen his life and work as a failure, for nothing that he set out to accomplish came to pass. However, history has a way of making the proclamations of the powerful seem foolish and impotent. Despite the early papal bans on his work, and the order by Pope Alexander IV for all copies of *De Periculis* to be burned, Guillaume's antifraternal tracts were ironically destined to become the most widely-read texts of their type well into the Reformation. His influence was great, and extended into several areas beyond theological speculation or scholastic debate. Evidence of his ideas can be found in such diverse areas as the works of Boccaccio, Gower, and Chaucer. During the Renaissance, some of his themes were taken up by Rabelais (*Pantagruel*) and Machiavelli (*Clizia*), as well as by Marlowe (*Doctor Faustus*).[41] The English religious reformer, John Wycliff, and his followers the Lollards (who were branded as heretics and persecuted in the 14th and 15th centuries) certainly employed the antifraternal polemics of Guillaume, calling for the abolition of the friars, and some taking the argument further to demand the abolition of the Church itself.[42]

Guillaume's writings were not the only source of antifraternal material, but they showed an astonishing persistence over the centuries. Geltner, as we have seen, argues that the notion of an unbroken European tradition of antifraternal sentiment originating with Guillaume is misplaced, and that even some of his own followers differed in their approach to dealing with the problem. Guillaume called for the outright abolition of all mendicant orders, for example, whereas other critics merely wanted to limit their power and return them to the state in which they were believed to have originated. Nevertheless, Guillaume's work had a tendency to reappear over the next several hundred years whenever it was useful.[43]

Perhaps the most audacious aspect of his efforts is not just the attack on the friars, but that they held up a whole society to criticism. The papacy, monarchies, prelates, and others were, in his view, equally responsible for the sorry state of affairs that allowed the friars to flourish. Their actions (or inactions) had created a climate of hypocrisy that was ripe for the emergence of Antichrist. It was when he stressed these faults by connecting them to Louis IX that his real downfall came.[44]

De Periculis was Guillaume's greatest work, but he contributed other important writings to the conflict which merit some further study: his two disputed questions, *De quantitate eleemonsynae* and *De valido mendicante* (both written in response to assertions made by the Franciscan Bonaventure); his three extant Paris sermons (*Qui amant periculum*, *Si quis diligit me*, and *De pharisaeo et publicano*); and his *Responsiones* to the charges brought against him.[45]

The questions date from the autumn of 1255,[46] and are Guillaume's response to defenses made of mendicancy by Bonaventure, by then the *de facto* chief apologist for the Franciscans.[47] At the time, he could not be recognized as a master due to the ongoing conflict, and so confined himself to duties within the order.[48] In his *De paupertate quoad abrenuntiationem*, Bonaventure argues that renouncing worldly possessions (both personal and communal) was relevant to attaining perfection as a Christian.[49] He immediately proceeds with an extensive list of biblical citations in support of this, beginning with Matthew 19:21, which advises that perfection is achieved by selling all of one's goods and following Christ.[50] Bonaventure interprets this to mean that Christ did not call his followers to attain wealth, nor indeed to work in manual labor, but rather to live lives of contemplation.[51] Christ was completely poor, unable to pay for anything, and so those who do likewise truly imitate him.[52] After these biblical references, he then goes on to cite numerous writings by saints and Church fathers, who reinforce the argument, including Ambrose, Jerome, and Augustine.[53] Not only do these authorities provide weight to the argument, but reason itself supports it. Renunciation removes the lure to cupidity and avarice.[54] He concludes his first argument by stating that this kind of deep renunciation is not only sufficient to Christian perfection, "but even of super-abundant Christian perfection."[55] There follows a lengthy listing of possible objections to his position, which he answers in detail.[56]

Guillaume issued his *De quantitate eleemosynae* in response. He begins with the question, is it permissible to give away everything, keeping nothing for oneself? Making use of a standard format, he first presents 14 arguments in favor of a "yes" answer, citing passages from the gospel and psalms.[57] Quickly, however, he moves on, to show that this is not the path of the true Christian. Giving away everything one has is in fact a kind of prodigal behavior, a form of lavishness and wastefulness that is not permitted.[58] He proceeds with a series of scriptural references and glosses to support his position, including Romans 12:1, concerning reasonable service.[59] Since the gloss adds a warning about anything added to this being too much, Guillaume makes the argument that this kind of excessive poverty, which involves renouncing even food, is sinful, for it will cause one's death. To give away everything in favor of begging (in the hopes of obtaining food) is therefore not permitted.[60] He proceeds with an extended section of scriptural citations to make the argument that those who are able-bodied should not beg. Poverty is an evil that makes one forget the eternal, and it should not be glorified.[61] He asserts, quoting Augustine, that possessions can be held in common, namely the resources of the Church, which thus leads to the perfection of the Christian life.⁶² Holding on to certain possessions will in fact, prevent the need for begging, since begging can lead to all manner of sins: flattery, theft, lying, even suicide and murder.⁶³ By giving up all possessions and work to be self-supporting, for example, one could eventually kill oneself, if the source of charitable food donations ever ends. Thus, such an individual is deliberately risking death, which is a sin.

He takes things further in his *De valido mendicante*. Probably issued in November of 1255, the work "represents an attempt on his part to gain the initiative in the Parisian friar/secular debates."⁶⁴ There are different types of beggars, he argues. Those who are legitimate—the poor, pilgrims, students, and the sick—beg from necessity. The sick and the poor are often unable to work. Students and pilgrims may be able to work, but will not always be in their current impoverished state (studying or going on pilgrimage), so it is acceptable to give to them. Those beggars who are not legitimate are those who have made a "profession" of it; they are capable of manual labor, but for various reasons, they choose not to engage in it, and therefore, they must be denied any alms. Further, they should be excommunicated.⁶⁵ Christ did not beg for his bread, Guillaume asserts, and any who try to link their begging with apostolic traditions are lying. It is too easy for one to become corrupted by this practice, and seek profit and gain from it, while pretending to be pious.⁶⁶ This charge against the friars will be repeated again and again over the centuries, and we will examine many examples of it in succeeding chapters.

Bonaventure's next work, the *De paupertate quoad mendicitatem* (also known as *De mendicitate*), takes the defense of mendicancy further in a lengthy discourse of propositions and objections. Guillaume probably had access to a late version (*reportatio*), but not the final copy (*redacto*) of the question from which to base his responses. This copy does not seem to be in a form which Bonaventure had approved, and was probably released before he had a chance to properly review it. As such, the version of Bonaventure's arguments that is found in editions of his works is not exactly the same as the one that Guillaume attempted to refute. They are at times very similar, but do have differences, and the final edition is expanded in portions. The essential question is the same: whether begging is a way to achieve Christian perfection.⁶⁷ For Bonaventure, he spent a considerable amount of effort formulating support for an answer in the affirmative. For Guillaume, the answer was a resounding "no."

Bonaventure begins his work with the format of objections to mendicancy, the ultimate aim, of course, being to refute them, indeed, making use of Guillaume's own objections.⁶⁸ In the next section, he delves into defending the mendicant way of life, beginning by offering that Christ told his apostles to undertake their journeys with no money, as recorded in Matthew 10:9.⁶⁹ He continues with a complex argument about Christ receiving a child, with reference to Luke 9:48; Christ notes that whoever shall receive the child in his name, also receives him.⁷⁰ Since a gloss on the text equates the child with the poor,⁷¹ Bonaventure seizes this opportunity to make a strong claim, as Traver notes, "as no one is poorer than a beggar, Christ's request must especially hold true for the poor beggar. And as Christ would not have intended that the faithful receive beggars if mendicancy were evil, begging must therefore be an act of Christian perfection."⁷²

Such arguments may seem convoluted, far-fetched, and even amusing to modern readers, but were taken very seriously at the time. Theologians and philosophers expended a great amount of intellectual energy in formulating these very precise points to reinforce and defend an overall position. Bonaventure clearly believed earnestly that his order was doing the right thing, and that receiving alms for leading holy lives was in no way sinful or contrary to the apostolic tradition and *imitatio Christi*. Further, the order was approved by the pope, so any criticisms were a direct questioning of papal authority.[73] This was a common fallback argument that the friars would resort to over the centuries.

Guillaume believed just as fervently in the opposite. His response to *De mendicitate* repeatedly stresses that to live from begging when not required to do so is sinful and worthy of excommunication. It encourages avarice and other sins, is degrading in a non-holy way, and an order based on this idea is a novel development that is tantamount to heresy. It has nothing to do with the actions of the first Christians, who in any case, were not bound by the same rules, and who did indeed own possessions in common.[74] In addition, though Francis himself may have begged, this cannot be used as an example, since in those early times, Guillaume asserts, the Franciscan brethren also worked.[75]

And so it went on, with no clear winner or sign of any end to the debate. Bonaventure wrote yet another response to Guillaume's response, titled the *Replicatio adversus objectiones postea factas*. The tit-for-tat nature of their arguments and counterarguments begins to look futile and shows that neither man was going to back down. However, Guillaume was not content to let the issue be decided only by such endless intellectual sparring. He wanted to take his arguments to his congregation, which is exactly what he did in a series of sermons about the conflict. These sermons (of which three are extant) date from either 1255 or 1256,[76] and as we saw in chapter 2, Guillaume conveys his feelings vividly and without self-censorship.

Of the three surviving, the earliest is *Qui amant periculum*, "He who loves danger (will perish from it)."[77] He says that he knows of many dangers afflicting the Church, and so he cannot remain silent, but must speak up about them. However, since this news does not please everyone who hears it, some have come forth to slander him, but the truth is with him.[78] He is greatly concerned with hypocrisy, which has infected the whole of the Church.[79] Therefore this sermon is necessary, he stresses, and he offers five extensive sections on the dangers of hypocrisy: First, the fact that such dangers must appear before Antichrist. Second, what exactly the dangers will be, which he will show. Third, from whom these dangers will arise. It will not be from the kings or soldiers, but rather those who profess sanctity and hide their evil and deceit behind it. Fourth, he reveals the manner in which these individuals will introduce such dangers into the world. Fifth, how one can read the signs to identify these individuals. Much of this reiterates *De Periculis*, often in a summarized form, but the intent is the same. He attacks the *Eternal Gospel* again, and stresses that the end is coming soon. As Traver notes, "The friars' stated purpose ... is to appropriate the office of preaching to themselves, to deceive the laity, and to set the stage for the Antichrist's arrival."[80]

His sermon *Si quis diligit me* ("If a man loves me, he will heed my words") changes the form of attack, and goes after the friars' patrons, including Louis IX, which in hindsight was a terrible mistake. As we have seen, Louis initially tried to work out a compromise between the seculars and the friars, and he might have remained sympathetic, if not for Guillaume's acidic words.[81] This sermon ruined his chances of gaining any further favor with the king, who dispatched envoys and a copy of *De Periculis* to Rome for examination, thus leading to Guillaume's downfall.

While seemingly a sermon on love, it is about how one should truly love God, binding himself to his creator. One cannot pretend true religion merely by wearing a humble garment. Those that do so are Pharisees.[82] One can see immediately that this was a poor choice of words, given Louis' preference for humble clothing, including dressing like a Franciscan. Unfortunately, Guillaume made things far worse when he criticized hypocrisy in the royal courts. As we have seen, he refers to kings who perpetually hear masses and imitate the poor in their clothing, surrounding themselves with deceivers.[83] This sermon was to be perhaps the "final nail in the coffin," as he effectively eliminated any hope of keeping royal favor, and was already at odds with the Church establishment. In his zeal to expose hypocrisy, he badly misread his influence and popularity at the court. Geltner has suggested that Guillaume probably preached such words out of despair, having realized that even if Louis continued with his arbitration, he was still too firmly on the side of the friars ever to treat the seculars fairly.[84]

In his next sermon *De pharisaeo et publicano*, he expands on the Pharisee links to the friars and once again, the theme of hypocrisy. He draws parallels between the ancient Jewish hypocrites and the new hypocrites that behave in the same manner,[85] desiring, for example, to be seated with the highest-ranking nobles, rulers, and prelates at their banquets, stuffing themselves with good things to eat; indeed, food is their true God.[86]

Guillaume's powerful arguments were ultimately unsuccessful, but his exile prompted others to take up the cause. In his own time, he had a profound influence on two of his presumed followers in Paris, destined to become the greatest French vernacular poets of the later 13th century: the trouvère Rutebeuf and the poet Jean de Meun.[87] Therefore, we now turn first to the writing of Jean de Meun, for his extensive continuation of Guillaume de Lorris' *Roman de la Rose* ensured that the work became the most popular French-language poem for nearly two centuries after its completion. It was therefore instrumental in the dissemination of Guillaume de Saint-Amour's views, through the character and discourse of one of the strangest figures in medieval French literature, *Faus Semblant*, or "False Seeming."

4

Antichrist's Boy: False Seeming, the Apocalypse and the Roman de la Rose

The *Roman de la Rose* is the most imposing French literary work of the Middle Ages, a lengthy allegorical poem that enjoyed tremendous popularity in its own time (and for centuries afterward), and sparked considerable controversy. Surviving in as many as 250 manuscript copies, its complexities and multiple layers of meaning have attracted countless readers and scholars over the centuries. It is comparable to the *Divine Comedy* and the *Canterbury Tales* in the scale of its achievement, though it is less well-known than these, outside of the field of medieval studies and to literary specialists.[1]

Unlike other major medieval works, the *Roman* is the product of two different authors who lived at different time periods and took differing approaches to telling this complex allegory of love. The first of these, and the creator of the work, was Guillaume de Lorris, about whom virtually nothing is known. Lorris is a town east of Orleans, and it seems that he lived until 1230–40, though the exact date of his death is unknown. He probably worked on the poem between about 1225 and 1230. This is an educated guess, based in part on the assertion of the poem's continuator, Jean Chopinel (or Clopinel), commonly known as Jean de Meun (or Meung). He states in the work that he is continuing the poem more than 40 years after Guillaume's death.[2] Guillaume's portion of the poem stops at slightly more than 4,000 lines, while Jean's continues the work to a massive 21,700, more than four times the length of the original. It is generally assumed that Guillaume's is an unfinished work, and that Jean took it upon himself to complete the story, though in a style quite different than that of his predecessor.

Jean's biography is only slightly more revealing. Presumably born at Meung-sur-Loire around the time that Guillaume died, he is thought to have attended the University of Paris, been a contemporary of poets such as Rutebeuf (see chapter 5), and to have been well acquainted with the secular/friar conflict, including the fall and banishment of Guillaume de Saint-Amour. Scholars believe that Jean undertook his work on the continuation of the poem between 1269 and 1278, though Lecoy has suggested that 1275 was the probable date for completion, owing to Jean's reference to a particular order, the Sack Friars, which was suppressed in 1274.[3] Jean died in 1305, or perhaps slightly earlier, and the Paris home that he lived in seems to have been donated later as a gift to the Dominican order, ironic given the antifraternal tone of several key parts of his work.[4]

Guillaume's major innovation was to provide a vivid dream allegorical narrative about love, a genre that he may well have invented.[5] His work has been described as courtly, unreal, refined, and concerned with the "art of love." Jean's continuation, by contrast, is more grounded in reality (despite its continuing use of allegory), and offers greatly expanded, almost encyclopedic, monologues from various characters, as well as a general satirical theme in its often caustic commentary. His figures speak far more than they act. These speeches by various characters are lengthy expositions that modern readers can find tedious, but that are rich sources of reference to classical literary influence and commentary on issues of the time, as we will see below. Themes of deceit are common in the continuation, and differing figures address them in differing ways.[6] Themes of sexuality run through the entirety of both sections of the poem, of course, and the narrative on one level is a kind of strange erotic dream.[7]

Allegory is a complex subject and there is still debate about its exact meaning. A simple definition might be the use of some type of imagery to represent deeper meanings, though a full discussion is not possible here.[8] Arden offers a useful definition: "Medieval allegory is like modern fantasy or science fiction literature, in which the reader is taken to a strange, wonderful land where things are not what they seem at first, where anything can happen, and where the experience unfolds slowly to reveal its meaning only at the end (if at all)."[9]

The story, told in first-person, seems simple enough at first. It concerns a young man, *Amant*, or the Lover, who at the age of 20 (an age when Love exacts a tribute from the young), lies down, and in sleep has a vivid dream. On a May morning, he wanders along a river, which takes him to a walled garden. The Lover is charmed by birdsong, and searches for an entrance. On the walls outside are paintings of vices that are uncourtly and unwelcome within, including Hate, Villainy, Covetousness, Felony, Avarice, Sadness, Envy, Old Age, Hypocrisy, and Poverty. He meets Idleness, and she lets him in, telling him that the garden belongs to *Deduit*, or "Merriment," and that his friends there enjoy all of life's pleasures. He views Gaiety singing as the others dance: Idleness, Beauty, Courtesy, Wealth, Youth, and others. Also there is the God of Love (the lover of Beauty), adorned in a robe of flowers.

The Lover tours the garden, accompanied by the God of Love, and peers into the fountain of Narcissus, where he sees rosebushes, and among them, the most beautiful bud of all, which is, as Luria notes, "a pudendal emblem representing the young girl whom the Lover comes to love—and especially that part of her which he chiefly craves."[10] The God of Love lets loose his arrows and the young Lover is smitten; he will never recover. He promises to serve the God of Love, who takes him as his vassal, and gives him love's ten commandments, and companions to accompany him, including Hope.

The Lover goes to where his beloved rose dwells, and is greeted by Fair Welcome, who is the only one who can give the Lover his desire. The Lover approaches his rose, but cannot touch her, for Resistance, Foul Mouth, Fear, and Shame intervene and send Fair Welcome fleeing. The Lover despairs. He is counselled by Reason, who advises him to abandon his quest, but he angrily refuses to do so, and she leaves. More to the Lover's liking, *Amis*, or "Friend," now appears to give his own advice. He must win the trust of Resistance, by offering the assurance that what the Lover wants is the right to love, not the physical gratification it brings. This is done, and Fair Welcome once again leads the Lover to the rose, a beautiful, but unopened bud. The Lover is able to obtain a kiss after some further pleading, but he is immediately blocked when Foul Mouth informs Jealousy of what has happened. Jealousy orders the construction of a tower in the garden's center to imprison Fair Welcome, with guards posted at each of its four corners, and stationed within, *La Vieille*, the Old Woman tasked with watching Fair Welcome personally. The Lover despairs, and here ends Guillaume's portion of the *Roman*.

The vivid, and even bizarre imagery of the poem is striking, and yet it did not have the impact that Jean's continuation would. Guillaume presumably intended to finish the work, but died before being able to do so.[11] The task was eventually taken up by Jean de Meun, who created one of the most enduring and influential literary works of the Middle Ages. Jean's continuation of the original poem is an encyclopedic work that contains a much larger collection of commentary on all types of love than is found in Guillaume's portion. It introduces several characters who are not in the earlier poem, one of the most important of them being *Faus Semblant* ("False Seeming"), who we will examine in detail below.

His narrative begins immediately where Guillaume's ends, with the Lover despairing in his quest to win the rose. He once more encounters Reason, and she again counsels him to abandon his foolish desire, and cultivate more elevated forms of love. Her speech is given 3,000 lines (about one-seventh of the entire poem's length), and yet she still makes no impact, for the Lover is determined, and she departs.

The Lover next revisits Friend, who gives him advice that is essentially the opposite of Reason's, assuring him that he will again see Fair Welcome and have his rose, but that he must use deceit and manipulation to do so. As we will see, this idea also features strongly in the words of False Seeming, who carries it to extremes in his discourses; most importantly, he evokes the apocalyptic and antifraternal sentiments of the university masters. Jean uses the deception employed by the Lover as a representation for a greater threat. Friend's discourse is nearly as long as Reason's (2,700 lines), and covers all manners of methods as to how the quest might be completed. He speaks of how to keep a woman's love, as well as various diversions, such as his account of a Golden Age before the vices, whose arrival brought about the world of unhappiness, conflict, and even private property.[12]

The Lover then meets Wealth, who also chases him away from the castle, telling him that lovers do not keep the gifts that she bestows on them, and therefore she hates them. The God of Love appears to chastise him for giving his ear to Reason. The Lover swears that he is devoted to love's cause, and the God of Love resolves that there will be an attack on the Castle of Jealousy. He summons his barons, including False Seeming, to draw up a plan. It is decided that False Seeming and his companion, Constrained Abstinence, will attack Foul Mouth; others will attack Fear, Resistance, and the Old Woman. The God of Love asks False Seeming where he may be found if he is needed. False Seeming launches into his remarkable monologue (1,000 lines), which is unsettling and revealing; we will return to this below. He urges the God of Love to take a chance on him and his unpleasant methods to help the Lover win the rose.

And so, the attack begins. False Seeming and Constrained Abstinence, disguising themselves as pilgrims, go to Foul Mouth, who suspects nothing and greets them. Constrained Abstinence delivers a sermon to him, accusing him of slandering others, which he denies. When False Seeming produces evidence of it, Foul Mouth kneels down to confess his sins. Taking advantage of his unprotected state, False Seeming takes hold of his throat, strangles him, and cuts out his tongue. They then throw the body in the castle moat, opening a way into the tower.

Finding the Old Woman, the false pilgrims, accompanied by Courtesy and Generosity, persuade her to take a wreath of flowers to Fair Welcome, and to let him speak to the Lover. Before she will let Fair Welcome see the Lover, however, she offers him her own advice (in 2,000 lines) on all matters pertaining to love. She is old and bitter and wants Fair Welcome to take revenge on suitors by fleecing them of their wealth. Sell your love, she says, and promise the rose to all, manipulating men.

Fair Welcome receives her advice, but not without doubts. Again, the Lover is admitted and they converse, but the Lover oversteps, and tries to touch the rose. Resistance once again appears, joined by Fear and Shame, and they lock up Fair Welcome. The Lover begs to be locked up with him, but they set to attacking and beating him. He cries for help and the God of Love's forces arrive to rescue him.

Interestingly, Jean pauses at this moment to insert another aside. He defends himself against charges that he has used obscene language, that he has criticized feminine manners and ways, and that he has attacked the religious via False Seeming. He then returns to the battle, describing a series of hand-to-hand combat scenes. However, the attack goes poorly for the God of Love's forces, and he is forced to call a truce, sending for his mother, Venus. She and her son vow to destroy Chastity.

Jean at this point enters into another seeming digression, as we are introduced to Nature, whose "confession" is over 3,000 lines long, as significant as the discourses of Reason and Friend. She laments how all things must die, but notes that species continue because death cannot trap all of them at once. She is heartened by the oath of Venus and the God of Love, but still must confess to her priest, Genius, who first gives a 400-line sermon on the dangers of women, before he will hear her.

Nature confesses that all of creation does the bidding of the Creator except for Man, the only component of the cosmic order that choose to rebel against her. He indulges in sin and vice, and will be condemned to hell for it, which will vindicate her position. She entreats Genius to go to the army and explain the need for natural acts of love, and to excommunicate those who do not follow these guidelines. Genius does her bidding, and is welcomed by the forces of Love. He delivers a 1,000-line sermon on the virtues of procreative sex and the heavenly garden that awaits those who adhere to this practice, as well as the evils of homosexual love. He offers a description of this paradise and then departs.

The final attack begins, as Venus takes a leading role, leading the assault on the castle. She demands that the guards in the tower surrender, but they refuse. In response, she threatens to scatter the roses of Chastity everywhere, among the religious and the laity. She sees an arrow slit between two pillars, atop of which is a beautiful statue of a woman, recalling the story of Pygmalion. Now the Lover, disguised as a pilgrim (like False Seeming and Constrained Abstinence before him), approaches the structure. Venus shoots a flaming arrow into the castle tower, and its defenders flee, clearing the way. Fair Welcome is saved from the fire, and he at last offers the rose to the Lover.

In this last moment, the Lover brandishes his large staff and pouch with two hammers. He inserts is staff into the arrow slit, finding resistance, but at last succeeding. He believes he is the first (but may not be the last) to pass into this shrine. He approaches the bush and plucks the rose, noting that he broke a bit off the bark and spilled some of the seed. He offers his thanks to those who have aided him and his curses to those who have opposed him. Then it is day, he awakes, and the poem ends.

The modern reader can be forgiven for being amused or even bewildered by the heavy-handed innuendo in this last scene, which leaves little to the imagination, but is also immediately problematic and disturbing. Many, both in medieval times and modern, have seen this scene as describing a rape. Such offensive imagery was not unknown in other medieval literature; even in song, a number of trouvère pastourelles tell of knights riding out in May and having their way with young country maidens, whether such ladies consented or not. There is an added layer to this representation, however, that may offer further clues as to Jean's intention. The key to this is the character of False Seeming, his personification of hypocrisy, and his lengthy diatribe against the mendicants, which we will now examine.

From the point that the poem introduces False Seeming, and he begins his speech, the reader is aware that there is something wrong with him. His name is likely derived from a reference in a poem by the trouvère Rutebeuf entitled *La Complainte de Maistre Guillaume de Saint Amor*. In it, Rutebeuf lists many of the vices that have been unleashed upon the university:

Ypocrisie
Et Vaine Gloire, et Tricherie,
Et Faus Samblant, et Dame Envie.[13]

Rutebeuf probably created the name from a passage in *De Periculis*, chapter 3:

Pseudo simulant charitatem, ut decipiant.[14]
"They pretend charity, in order to deceive."

Jean borrowed this name for his infamous allegorical figure, and Rutebeuf was probably a chief source for the verses that follow.[15] Like Rutebeuf, he seems to have been a partisan of the secular masters and a supporter of Guillaume de Saint-Amour, whose writings he references in False Seeming's monologue.[16] False Seeming's discourse is different from the others; he does not speak about love in the same manner, and his words are filled with antifraternal sentiment throughout. He attacks the friars and their hypocrisy, at times boldly, at times subtly, while simultaneously representing a certain kind of religious hypocrite, not religion as a whole. Jean creates False Seeming as a character that is the very thing he attacks, who boasts of doing what he condemns.[17] His nature and the attacks on religious hypocrisy had precedents in other literature; Jean Batany posits a relation between False Seeming and Reynard the Fox[18] (who we will examine in detail in chapter 6). However, the specific attention False

Seeming gives to various groups and events over such a long speech is remarkable. We will examine here some of the most critical and obvious references in the poem.

The scene begins with the presentation of False Seeming to the God of Love, after which he delivers a long monologue about both his own deceitful nature, and the equally dishonest nature of the hypocrites in Paris. Jean employs a particularly useful literary tool, as it allows False Seeming to be at one with the friars, while at the same time condemning them, a perfect illustration of the falseness of his character. The tone is set at the beginning, when he announces to the barons that those who wish to know him should look for him in the world or in the cloister, for he lives only in these areas, but in one more than the other (the religious). Those who are religious are more covert, those who are in the world are more open. False Seeming stresses that he does not attack the true religious life of humility and service, even if he does not love it, but rather the false religious, who are little more than criminals wearing a habit that conceals the evil in their hearts.[19] Indeed, Stakel has noted that clothing itself can be a form of deceit.[20] Further, if there are such wolves among the "new apostles," then the Church is in danger.[21]

The anticlerical and antifraternal sentiment is clear. Jean, via his allegorical figure, informs the reader that falsehood is everywhere, and he strongly implies that it is more often among the religious and mendicant orders. He also takes care not to condemn the genuinely religious, just as Guillaume de Saint-Amour did not.

False Seeming then embarks on a long and sustained attack on the friars, taking up many of the themes used in the masters' tracts and complaints during the conflict. A particularly notable passage concerns the mendicants' supposed state of poverty and living on alms. He swears that it is not written anywhere that Christ or his apostles, when they walked the earth, were ever seen begging for their bread, for they did not wish to do so. The university masters had already stressed this point.[22]

False Seeming's, and thus Jean's, central statement echoes that of Guillaume and the masters—that one's livelihood should be earned through work if at all possible, and not through begging. This was the practice of St. Paul and the apostles, they argued; if one does not work, one does not eat. The friars, by obtaining their needs through charity when they are perfectly capable of doing work, are committing a grave sin, ignoring the very actions of the apostles they claim to emulate. There are only special circumstances when one is permitted to beg, he says, and he outlines them clearly. These conditions are taken directly from Guillaume de Saint-Amour's writings.[23]

Interestingly, False Seeming upholds the religious life as exemplified by the Templars and the Hospitallers (the knightly monastic orders founded during the crusades to guard the way to Jerusalem for pilgrims and tend to the sick, respectively), as well as the examples of the Cistercians and Cluniacs, because they do not beg.[24] Within a generation of Jean's completion of the *Roman de la Rose*, the Templars would be dissolved by Philip the Fair, being accused of heresy, owing mainly to jealousy surrounding their vast wealth, power, and perceived influence.[25] Like the friars, both orders existed outside of the formal Church hierarchy, and were answerable only to the pope. They were thus able to secure several privileges for themselves, including immunity from excommunication, a benefit that no other orders had. In addition, the rituals and practices of the Templars in particular were shrouded in secrecy, arousing suspicions that they were obscene and even blasphemous. It is possible that since anti–

Templar sentiments already existed at the time of Jean's writing, this is an ironic attack on any orders believed to have grown wealthy with little or no work. Indeed, by the mid–13th century, the income of the Templars was believed to be four times that of the king of France. Remembering that False Seeming paradoxically embodies the very characteristics that he condemns, his emulation of the Templars may be a subtle means of showing his own amity toward his deceitful kindred spirits. However, the Templars and Hospitallers (who were often embroiled in their own bitter feuds with one another) operated in a manner entirely different than the Franciscans and Dominicans, effectively being "crusading monks" who were not concerned with the laity.

In referring to Guillaume directly, False Seeming asserts that the university and the general public gave their support to him. After listing the acceptable cases when one may beg, he notes that the "man from Saint-Amour" lectured and preached on this very topic, along with other theologians in Paris. Indeed, False Seeming exclaims, may the bread and wine of communion not help him if Guillaume did not have the full support of those who heard him preach.[26]

False Seeming deplores the banishment of Guillaume by Pope Alexander IV, and accuses Hypocrisy, False Seeming's own mother, of being the chief cause.[27] This is a bold statement, for it asserts that not only the friars, but also the pope and those responsible for the banishment (including by association, King Louis IX) were hypocrites. In a time when political and religious dissent was increasingly not tolerated, these were brave words, indeed. As we will see in chapter 5, Rutebeuf made similar accusations in some of his poems. Related to this, there is a reference to Guillaume's courage in writing *De Periculis*. False Seeming notes that Guillaume committed a terrible fault against False Seeming's mother, Hypocrisy, in writing this book, which exposed her life for all to see.[28] In other words, Guillaume's work detailed the friars' hypocrisy, laying bare all of their faults.

False Seeming then scorns the request that he take up honest work, for he is the very embodiment of the hypocrisy and laziness of the friars. Rather, he prefers to pray in front of others, concealing his foxlike qualities under a cloak of falsehood and hypocrisy.[29] He elaborates on his avaricious qualities by stating that he wishes to amass all that he can in both wealth and power. Thus, he will only hear the confessions of the rich, for the poor have nothing to offer him. His whole attention is focused on what he can acquire.[30] He also states that he prefers the company of women, be they, "empresses ... queens ... high-ranking palace ladies ... beguines ... [or] nuns and young girls ... provided that they are rich and beautiful."[31] These words reiterate the widespread suspicion that the mendicants' associations with women were anything but pious, a charge that will arise again later in his discourse, and through the actions of Constrained Abstinence.

Up to this point, False Seeming's invective reinforces the seculars' accusations that the friars spent all of their time among the wealthy, obtaining positions, favors, and material wealth while espousing poverty and humility. He exhibits a casual and cruel disregard for the poor, when he states that even if he sees all of them naked and cold, in their "stinking dunghills," afflicted with hunger, he has no time to be involved in their business. If he were forced to go to a hospital (for the poor and sick), he would give them no comfort, for they simply have nothing to offer to him in return, not even a bite to eat.[32]

This is a harsh condemnation of the perceived sins and callous attitudes of the friars, but False Seeming is not finished. He then revives the comparison of the friars to the Pharisees, recalling the prohibition on seeking to be called "master," as the seculars had pointed out. Indeed, these hypocrites wear fancy clothes, he says, and like to be greeted on the street. They especially love being called "master," despite the biblical warning against it,[33] a charge drawn directly from Guillaume de Saint-Amour's sermon, *De Pharisaeo*. Rutebeuf used this accusation as well in his poetry.[34]

Then he follows with a reference to the masters' accusation that the friars falsely obtained papal documents of approval for their actions. He states that so that they might earn praise, they lie about their nature to the rich to obtain letters of recommendation about their supposed holiness. With these, they can convince the whole world of their goodness and virtues.[35]

This leads to the first reference to Antichrist and an indication of a deeper, apocalyptic meaning. False Seeming proudly proclaims that he is one of "Antichrist's boys," a thief of whom it is written that he will wear a cloak of holiness and pretend to be religious. These are the ones who seem like sheep, but underneath are hungry wolves.[36] Rather than merely being an antifraternal diatribe, such references show a concern for the apocalyptic fears of the 1250s and 1260s, and allow for a means to link this sequence with the work as a whole.

From this first reference, the discourse takes a decidedly apocalyptic turn, giving attention to the great heresy of the *Eternal Gospel* of Gerard, and the righteous role of the masters in resisting it. False Seeming says of the friars that they cannot be recognized by their clothing alone, for they are full of tricks and falsehood; one must inspect their deeds to be truly protected.[37] Further, if the university (which has the "key" of Christianity) had not offered its protection, everything would have been lost in 1255. In that year, with evil intentions, the *Eternal Gospel* was unleashed on the world. It was from the devil while claiming to bring the Holy Spirit, and deserved only to be burned.[38] The university, though "asleep" (dispersed), was able to rouse itself and take up the defense of true religion. Arming itself with that faith, it stood against this monstrosity and handed it over to the cardinals for examination.[39] The *Eternal Gospel* was actually released earlier than 1255, a discrepancy in Jean's reckoning.

Given this event, apocalyptic fears were roused. He talks of the fate of those who have protested against it as opposed to the friars, who presumably are for it. All are awaiting Antichrist; those who will not follow him will die, whereas the friars and hypocrites will incite hatred of the true defenders of faith by their lies and deceit.[40] False Seeming proudly proclaims the deplorable state of the world, brought about by the actions of his family, his mother Hypocrisy and his father *Baraz* ("Fraud"). He boasts that Fraud is the emperor of the world, and that Hypocrisy is its Empress. Regardless of those who adhere to true religion, his royal line still reigns strongly. They rule in every kingdom, and quite rightly so, for they understand how to deceive and seduce, such that no one even realizes that they have been deceived.[41] These are truly the "last times." This is the age which was warned of in the New Testament, and which Guillaume de Saint-Amour rightly recognized. The stage is clearly set for the beginning of the end.

False Seeming directs his next attack to the Beguines, continuing the apocalyptic theme by invoking the spirit of the warning in II Timothy. The friars were indeed "penetrating" the houses of women by their association with these Beguines, and arousing suspicion as to their relationships behind closed doors. He accuses them of deceit, saying that if they are indeed other than what they seem (communities of devoted religious women) and seek to gain favor by trickery, then it is good for the hypocrites to seek them out, using their communities as a base to do their deceptive work.[42]

Here is where False Seeming pauses to stress that his repeated attacks are not directed at the truly religious, those who are humble and do good works. Indeed one should not show scorn to those whose habit is filled with humility, only to those who hide their pride underneath it. Even God will not value one who claims to be humble while secretly enjoying all worldly delights.[43]

Returning to the Beguines, and indeed, all deceivers, he asks, who can excuse them? When any who claim to have left the world in a false show of piety while secretly enjoying earthly pleasures and growing fat on them, such a one indeed is the dog who greedily returns to its vomit.[44] His attack has become increasingly slanderous, and it is with these malicious words that he brings his discourse to a close.

He is thereafter sworn into the service of the God of Love, and into the army which will lay siege to the Castle of Jealousy. However, as we have seen, he and Constrained Abstinence are to undertake a special mission, one which makes full use of their deceitful qualities, and provides yet another opportunity for an attack on the friars. The immoral actions of this pair, who are dressed to represent mendicants, are reprehensible, and provide a final condemnation of the friars before this sequence draws to a close.

The two prepare to make their way to the castle, guarded by Foul Mouth. In doing so, they disguise themselves as mendicant pilgrims, showing deceit by their outer appearance, when evil lies underneath. Constrained Abstinence arrays herself as a Beguine, and the narrative takes full opportunity to mock and condemn them. She has a rosary that was given to her by her friar confessor, who visited her often, more than any others, and delivered to her many fine "sermons." Indeed, her "confessions" were of such a great level of devotion, that it often seemed that they had two heads together under a single headpiece.[45] This bit of sarcastic humor, suggesting that the Beguines indulged in sexual affairs with the friars, has much in common with fabliaux stories about lecherous priests and monks, as we will see in chapter 6. So shameless are their actions that they never omit "confession," even on account of others. His description of her strays into apocalyptic territory. He remarks that she appeared like the "dirty bitch," the pale horse of the Apocalypse, soiled with hypocrisy.[46]

False Seeming assumes the role of a friar, Brother Seier, whose identity is not known, but was perhaps a representative of the friars during the conflicts with the secular masters.[47] In any event, False Seeming is also identified as resembling a Jacobin, transformed from "handsome Robin in the Dance." Robin was a common name for a young village man who indulged in foppish behavior.[48] Indeed, the story of *Robin and Marion* was popular in France at this time, and found its finest expression in the plays and music of the trouvère Adam de la Halle,[49] a contemporary of Jean de Meun, but its significance here may relate to how clothing represents different identities.[50] It may also refer to the springtime setting and theme of love in the larger work. Though it is expressed that the "Jacobins are all worthy men," one feels that this is an ironic statement, as it is immediately followed by yet another warning not to be deceived by appearances.[51]

Before murdering Foul Mouth, False Seeming delivers one last, subtle attack on the Parisian friars. In playing the role of a confessor, he espouses a belief attributed to them: that they saw themselves as being outside and above the Church hierarchy because they were morally superior and would be the only true servants of God in the forthcoming third age. He states that, being from an order, he is the highest rank of confessors that exist, for as long as the world will be. He is also the wisest and most learned; no prelates can match him. Indeed, he has the license of Divinity, and has lectured for a long time.[52] This recounts the controversy surrounding the granting of the license in theology; the mendicants offered their own qualifications and often did not seek the university's, feeling that theirs were sufficient. Following the papal decree that the chancellor bestow it on whomever he wished, the friars were no longer forced to have to ask for it, arousing deep resentment among the masters.

Then Foul Mouth kneels to confess; False Seeming seizes him, strangles him, and cuts out his tongue. This barbaric betrayal is a final and powerful statement against the friars and religious hypocrites, for it asserts that their intentions can be murderous, and that they will do anything to achieve their aims.[53] The sequence comes to a close as the two also murder the sleeping Norman guards, which further stresses this point. From here, False Seeming and Constrained Abstinence make their exit from the poem, to appear briefly again and be referred to in a handful of instances, discussed below.

As if to give strength to the argument that the attack is not directed at religion, but rather at falseness and hypocrisy in the garb of holiness, the narrative once again takes the opportunity during a side address to women to state the nature of the indictment. Jean writes that if people complain and are angry at him about False Seeming's words and actions, he answers that it was never his intention to speak against those who genuinely follow the religious life and do good works, regardless of the robe they wear (presumably that of a friar or any other). Rather, he lets fly his critical arrows where they will, and in their random wounding (one can avoid being wounded by avoiding hypocrisy), he hopes that the world will recognize that there are those in the world and in the cloister who are hypocrites. They are unlawful and were cursed by Jesus.[54]

Thus the polemic and violence of the False Seeming episode ends. This singularly curious account has caused much speculation and debate concerning the reason for its inclusion, and what it might mean. There have been commentaries that have insisted that it is not related to the plot, but rather, is a digression allowing Jean de Meun to vent his anger about his master's treatment, just as Rutebeuf had also done. However, this argument seems a superficial reading of the discourse that ignores its possible link with the rest of the poem. The relation between this sequence and the story as a whole is perhaps not readily apparent, but we will now examine some of those connections, by considering themes of apocalyptic anticlericalism and antifraternalism, as they relate to the larger work.

The sequence throughout is supportive of the efforts of Guillaume de Saint-Amour and is devoted to a discussion of Antichrist and the last times. For this reason, Richard Emmerson and Ronald Herzman have argued that the scene must be considered in terms of medieval apocalyptic, which is significant and present in the work as a whole.⁵⁵ There is much to be gained through an analysis of the poem in this context, for it is rich in such imagery and symbolism, and draws on the prevailing apocalyptic themes of the time. In order to gain some understanding of these themes, we will briefly examine the nature of medieval apocalyptic. This will shed light upon False Seeming's discourse as well as other references to apocalypticism in the work. A full treatment of medieval eschatology is a study in itself, and is not possible here. However, an outline of apocalyptic beliefs and scriptural exegesis is appropriate, given that these ideas occupied a significant place in medieval thought.

The word "apocalypse" derives from the Greek *apocalypsis*, meaning "the uncovering of hidden things," especially divine mysteries. Apocalyptic literature and narratives exist from several centuries before the Christian era, most often in Jewish writings. Their intent was to give encouragement in times of suffering, to advise their audience to be strong in faith, for the suffering will pass and better things will come. Jewish theology intended this in a temporal sense, i.e., that goodness would be restored at an actual future date rather than in the afterlife. This is the focus of the Old Testament books of Isaiah, Ezekiel, and Daniel, written during periods of dispersion and suffering at the hands of foreign invaders.

Several writings in the New Testament contain apocalyptic imagery. Revelation is, of course, the most well-known, but there are such themes in the gospel of Mark (written after the destruction of the Second Temple in 70 CE), and in the Pauline and Pseudo-Pauline corpus, such as the previously discussed II Timothy, attributed to St. Paul by a later writer. These writings borrowed imagery from the Old Testament to obtain authority and reinforce their impact.

The book of Revelation, ascribed to John of Patmos, is a bizarre mixture of images and coded language. It borrows heavily from the book of Daniel, which gives a clue to its original audience and the purpose for which it was written. In all likelihood, Revelation was written for a group of Jewish Christians who were suffering persecution under the Roman Emperor Domitian, who demanded worship, which both Jews and Christians refused to give. Much of the imagery cryptically addresses their suffering, for to have said anything openly would have meant certain death. It alludes to Rome as the new Babylon and the Greater Beast, and Domitian as the lesser Beast (a re-born Nero) identified by the infamous number 666 (616 in earlier versions). Its intention is not to predict the future (the suffering described within was very much a current event), but to stand as both a warning and a comfort to contemporary and future generations to be strong in their faith, the main theme of any apocalyptic literature.

As the centuries progressed, however, perceptions of this book and other New Testament apocalyptic writings began to evolve into a belief that they were a prediction of the dangers yet to come, a warning of the signs of the coming judgement. Early interpretations in this fashion still tended to see these works as symbolic. St. Augustine felt that Revelation encompassed the entire history of the world since the coming of Christ, seeing the 1,000 year binding of the devil as signifying the advent of the Church.⁵⁶ He warned against overly-literal interpretations of apocalyptic writings. It was true, he said, that the images dealt with events to come, "but until these events occur, the prophetic symbols must be interpreted with care and not applied naively to contemporary events."⁵⁷ As for predicting the time when these events would occur, a common practice among worried Christians, Augustine advised that it is not for humanity to know, and God "relaxes" the fingers of those attempting to calculate the date.[58]

As the centuries progressed, however, this advice was ignored, and the trend became to interpret apocalyptic signs and symbols in terms of historical events, a kind of theological 20/20 hindsight. This practice is noticeable in the writings of the Venerable Bede (7th and 8th centuries), and is continued in the first compilations of the *Glossa Ordinaria*, incorrectly ascribed to Walafrid Strabo in the 9th century, but now believed to have been overseen by Anselm of Laon in the early 12th century.[59] By the 12th and 13th centuries, elaborate interpretations had developed, linking specific symbols with specific people or events. This is best typified in the writings of Joachim and his over-zealous followers. Such action was not considered heretical if it did not contradict Church doctrine, but it did open the door to conflict and controversies. Thus, the various heads of the seven-headed dragon (Revelation 12) came to symbolize Herod, Nero, Muhammad, and Saladin, among others.

Saladin was the most recent of these, and he quickly assumed the status of the "sixth head." This worthy Muslim opponent of Richard the Lionheart was famed for his chivalry, and had won many Christian admirers. He was the subject of praise by both chronicler and poet. This situation certainly must have worried orthodox theologians, who saw danger in the emulation of an infidel. If good Christians could be led astray into reverence for such a "sinner," then surely he must be one of the deceivers and persecutors of the Church. All that then remained then was for the seventh deceiver to be revealed. Amid growing apocalyptic fears in the 13th century, the all-important seventh head could be identified with anyone or any group, exactly what happened in the polemics of Guillaume de Saint-Amour and the other masters.

As we have seen, Guillaume was a capable scriptural exegete, who understood and quite probably believed in the prevailing fears, especially the Joachimite writings. He knew these works, and was happy to use Joachim when it suited him.[60] Throughout his writings, Guillaume listed examples of events that could be linked to biblical prophecy. He made full use of the current exegetical methods and theological reasoning in stating his case against the friars.

This apocalyptic tradition is prominent in the discourse of False Seeming and in other references in the *Roman de la Rose*. False Seeming is one of "Antichrist's boys." He represents the greatest of hypocrites, who is the forerunner of the arrival of Antichrist. There had been several, the "heads" previously identified, and False Seeming's deceptive evil stands for the hypocrites who now signal that accursed figure.[61]

By presenting False Seeming as both a false friar and as the progenitor of Antichrist, the narrative reinforces Guillaume de Saint-Amour's assertion that the friars are the servants of evil and a sign of the end. This is developed later in the poem after the Old Woman's speech, when the Lover observes the scene at the beginning of the attack on the Castle of Jealousy. He describes False Seeming as the son of Hypocrisy, herself angry at the virtues. Significantly, he notes that Constrained Abstinence is now pregnant by False Seeming, and will soon give birth to Antichrist, as is written in a book (Revelation? *De Periculis*?). False Seeming is thus the false religious hypocrite, preaching the holy life, while indulging in carnality with his Beguine companion.[62] They undoubtedly defeated the guards at the gate, and the Lover offers his prayers for them. Anyone who wishes to be a traitor should make False Seeming his master, for then he may practice his deceit while pretending to be simple and innocent.[63] Remarkably, it is clearly stated that False Seeming (the false friar) and Constrained Abstinence (the Beguine) will beget Antichrist. The final age has dawned, to be ushered in by the sins and deceits of the religious hypocrites and false deceivers. Jean conveys strong feelings of support for Guillaume's position, and the fear of doom that the friars bring.

This antifraternal discourse is fascinating, though one must question the reason for its inclusion in what is presented as an allegorical treatise about love. Is it merely Jean's version of the poems of Rutebeuf, but written on a much larger scale? Scholars such as William Ryding, Charles Muscatine, and C.S. Lewis argued that it is such a distraction, an unjustifiable inclusion of irrelevant meanderings and digressions that are a fatal fault of Jeans' poem.[64] However, such readings do a disservice to the complexity of the sequence, and ignore the impact of a pivotal event in the story, one which helps to define the nature of the Lover's quest. False Seeming's "digression" is actually quite important, and its placement is deliberate.

False Seeming is introduced after the long aside wherein the narrator explains the situation which has led him to continue the poem. The reader is given historical background which is helpful in allowing Jean's writing to be dated with some accuracy. In mentioning Guillaume de Lorris, Jean is acknowledging his predecessor, perhaps ironically, as a servant of Love. One can hardly miss the word-play between "Guillaume the Lover" and Jean's admiration for Guillaume "of Holy Love," who is mentioned in the subsequent section.[65] The reader is temporarily brought back into the real world, though the allegorical imagery is retained through the continued presence of Guillaume de Lorris' characters, and the commentary concerning his service to them. Thus, history and reality are blended with the dream and fantasy of the poem.

This is the same technique used for False Seeming's monologue. It is at once solidly concerned with the real world of university conflicts and apocalyptic expectations, and at the same time does not ignore the Lover's quest, because False Seeming is testifying as to why he must assist in the capture of the rose. This skillful blend of fantasy and reality helps to introduce more fully a theme that has been hinted at throughout the poem, and foreshadowed in the previous section with Friend, that trickery and hypocrisy are necessary tools to complete the quest. The presumed deceit and lewd conduct of the friars provides the perfect vehicle with which to illustrate this argument. Brownlee argues that the entire continuation of the *Roman* is in one sense a parallel of Gerard's *Eternal Gospel*, which was to succeed the New Testament just as Jean's portion of the poem was to succeed Guillaume's. This also accounts for the placement of the False Seeming discourse at this point in the story and gives a reason for mingling fantasy with history.[66] The friars, in being cast in the role of false prophets who "penetrate the houses of women" to lead them astray, find their parallel in both False Seeming, who "penetrates" the Castle through deceit in the initial assault, and in the ultimate winning of the rose by the Lover, when, aided by the forces of Hypocrisy, he "penetrates" the "inner sanctuary."

Indeed, False Seeming and the Lover can be seen as two of a kind in that their prime love is for themselves, just like the friars. The Narcissus fountain of the earlier portion of the poem suggests the idea of foolish self-love, as pointed out by Emmerson and Herzman. This is further illustrated by the Pygmalion *exempla* of obsession, self-love, and idolatry.⁶⁷

It is significant that it is the gazing into the fountain of Narcissus that causes the Lover to fall in love with the rose, thus beginning the story, and that the Pygmalion account occurs just before he finally obtains his desire. Thus idolatry and self-love both begin and end the quest for the rose. The two examples reflect one another, just as the Lover gazes into the reflection in the fountain, and Jean calls his continuation "The Mirror for Lovers." There is much complex word-play and double meaning in the imagery here, which is not immediately apparent.

Further, the concept continues to be linked to the actions of the friars. Fleming notes that the phrase *seipsos amantes* ("loving themselves"), which derives from II Timothy to describe false prophets (one that the antifraternal writers used often) has an obvious relation to False Seeming who boasts of his self-gratifying behavior. The Lover's stubborn desire to have his rose bears an obvious similarity, as well; both are primarily lovers of themselves.⁶⁸ Indeed, he observes: "If Amis represented the worldly attitude toward innocence, in all its cynicism and sentimentality, Faussemblant pre-eminently represents the conscious worldly perversion of the channels of supernatural grace which alone offered remedy, in medieval theology, for man's fall from innocence."⁶⁹ They are alike in that both live by the idea that the ends justify the means.⁷⁰ False Seeming is thus crucial to the whole poem. Stakel argues that he "serves additionally as the magnetic center of a conceptual field of deceit spanning the 17,000 lines of Jean de Meun's continuation ... it would be surprising if Faux Semblant, the actor, were intended to be only of incidental interest."⁷¹

Is the poem a condemnation of amorous love? Some have seen it as such and have argued that Jean's continuation refutes the romantic and courtly images evoked in Guillaume de Lorris' portion.⁷² In an effort to show continuity, Alan Gunn has quoted the discourse of the God of Love, which states that Jean will serve him "his whole life," to show that Jean had a full understanding of Guillaume's intent—to teach the commandments of love. This, Gunn argues, is the purpose of his continuation, "whatever digressive material may be found in the poem." He assumes from a letter written to Philip IV prefacing Jean's translation of Boethius, that Jean is "a teacher of the methods by which one might win success in love." Therefore, the continuation "is in full accord with Guillaume's conception of the allegory of the Rose."⁷³ However, to teach something is not necessarily to endorse it. Gunn does not discuss the potential irony in this sequence and that Guillaume's work may be just as ironic and potentially satirical.⁷⁴ Further, his argument essentially dismissed the False Seeming episode as unnecessary, which is clearly not the case.

How then can the two portions of the *Roman de la Rose* be viewed as being unified? The answer, of course, lies in the interpretation of Guillaume's section. What is important here is not only modern critical observation, but also the manner in which Jean may have read the text. It is not possible to say for certain how Jean viewed Guillaume's original poem. However, it is possible that the traditional interpretation of Guillaume's work as a joyous celebration of spring and courtly love is overstated and incorrectly assumed. There are many images in the first poem that hint at the irony of the Lover's quest. Concerning the unpleasant figures outside the garden, for example, there are some which are not necessarily worthy of condemnation, such as Old

Age and Poverty. While such concepts have no place in the world of courtly love, to read their exclusion from the garden as being only for negative reasons requires accepting Guillaume's portion solely as a celebration of courtly love, which is by no means certain. There may be some irony in this sequence, and an implication that the Lover's pursuit is artificial, removed from the real world where problems exist, hence the use of the dream format. Other figures seem to hint at hidden themes, especially *Papelardie* (a kind of clerical hypocrisy in the 13th century),[75] described as the image of a hypocrite, who is not afraid to do evil in secret, when she cannot be seen.[76] Given that Guillaume de Lorris wrote his initial poem from 1225 to 1230, it is interesting to speculate on the meaning of this passage, since the first real controversy with the Parisian friars was occurring then, with the elevation of the Dominican Roland of Cremona to the faculty of theology under suspicious circumstances.

In any event, Jean may have seized on these images and brought them into the garden and the quest, but their existence in the original poem shows that Guillaume was aware of them. The presence of both Hypocrisy and Poverty, two of the central themes of the attack on the friars, could be more than a coincidence. The unhappy figures banished from the garden may show that the world outside is not as pleasant as that of the Lover's fantasy, and that courtly love is an illusion, a dream. Fleming has posited that *Papelardie* represents "the trivial hypocrisy of lovers who change their minds."[77] This fickleness is not permitted to enter the garden. However, False Seeming, the far greater evil, is able to live there and move about quite freely.[78] Thus, Jean has elaborated a simpler theme into one that is central to his continuation.

The ending of Guillaume's poem leaves the Lover unfulfilled. Though Jean records that he died, there is little evidence to prove that this interrupted the poem. It may simply be a poetic device, or perhaps an excuse to continue the work, as Jean felt that there was much more to be said. If Guillaume's text is also ironic in presenting the Lover's actions as a quest of folly, then it is entirely fitting that he should have remained unsatisfied at the poem's conclusion, for his desires were foolish and irrational. Indeed, this would illustrate the lack of true happiness that characterizes amorous pursuits, just as Reason warned. Guillaume's true intentions may never be fully known.[79] However, if Jean read his poem as an ironic work, his own addition would be appropriate, showing as it does the consequences of romantic love, and the extremes necessary to derive satisfaction from it. The fact that Jean's continuation begins with a much longer discourse from Reason, who again discourages romantic love, might indeed support this.

After Reason's exit, the Lover meets Friend again, who takes up the theme of deceit to win the rose. He says that to win Fair Welcome's favor (and thus the rose's), the Lover must do whatever he thinks will please Fair Welcome. If he does this, the Lover will not face rejection, and will attain his desire.[80] Initially, the Lover reacts with shock at such tactics, insisting that no man who is not a hypocrite would resort to such devilish actions.[81] Friend replies simply that those who are at war must seek out such solutions to their problems.[82]

The stage has been set; after being told by Reason that amorous love is inferior, this sequence begins to illustrate why, for the seed of deception planted by Friend bears fruit in the murderous actions of False Seeming and Constrained Abstinence. In his own way, Friend is also false, and what he offers is a false friendship. His "war" to win the rose, exemplified by the army of Love and the assault on the castle, may also have parallels in the war against God, conducted by the deceitful servants of Antichrist. Penn Szittya puts forth an interesting theory concerning this similarity, which will be examined below.

Even Nature's long confession to Genius, wherein the procreative urge is recognized as natural, does not automatically give approval to the Lover's desires. Nature giving her assent is perhaps nothing more than an allegorical expression of the natural forces behind his urges. It is fitting, then, that she approves of his quest; indeed, she cannot do otherwise. This sequence may be an acknowledgement of the forces of nature driving the Lover's lusts without being an attempt to justify them. She hardly speaks of his quest at all, except at the end of her discourse. Much of her speech is concerned with theological speculation, and the divine order of creation.

She makes her confession to Genius, a mock priest, and thus anticlerical themes are also present. She refers to False Seeming and Constrained Abstinence, calling up the apocalyptic imagery associated with them. She sends greetings to the forces of Love, except for False Seeming, because he consorts with criminals and the hypocrites warned of by scripture, those that are called pseudo-prophets. One should fear such people. They are only a part of the God of Love's army because he knows that it would have been impossible to achieve the Lover's goal without them, otherwise they would have been expelled from his presence. Given that they are essential, Nature is prepared to pardon them, if there are those who will advocate for them in the cause of true love.[83] This suggests that the Lover himself is a hypocrite. Nature plainly states that it is impossible to pursue this romantic quest without the tricks of deceivers and pseudo-prophets who lead women astray.

Further, when Genius addresses the God of Love and his forces to give them Nature's approval for their objective, Love adorns him with a chasuble (an outer garment worn when celebrating the Eucharist), and gives him a ring, a crosier, and a mitre.[84] These are the symbols of bishop and pope, of ecclesiastical authority, which Genius has no right to wear, for if the forces of the Lover require deceit and hypocrisy to succeed, then it is these same qualities which vest Genius with his position. Here the poem seems to imply that the authority of the papacy and bishoprics may be falsely given. Genius, in ecclesiastical garb, unwittingly gives sanction to an undertaking of hypocrisy and trickery, even though he preaches the opposite, just as Pope Alexander IV gave his unconditional support to the "deceitful" friars.

Genius devotes the majority of his speech to imploring his audience to seek not the garden wherein the delights of love are to be found, but rather that garden which is the eternal paradise, i.e., heaven. He contrasts the features of both gardens and finds the fountain of life preferable to the fountain of Narcissus. The situation is complicated by the fact that the forces of Love do not understand Genius' speech, for no sooner does he complete this sermon, than they proceed forth to attack the castle, in total opposition to what he has just advised. Genius himself does not seem to be completely aware of what he says, being a false priest, implying an element of foolishness in both parties. All of this is revealing commentary on the Paris debates.

Thus, apocalypticism again appears, and is carried through to the conclusion, when the forces of Love are victorious. The Lover assumes the role of a pilgrim (just as False Seeming had), and in a series of puerile sexual metaphors, describes his "penetration" of the last defenses and his "plucking" of the rose. As we have seen, the action described is essentially a rape. Indeed, the sequence bears a strong resemblance to the False Seeming episode. Both the Lover and False Seeming must disguise themselves in pious and honorable outer garments to conceal their actual motives, again evoking the warning of II Timothy, and fears of the friars being deceivers in holy garb. In reference to the union between False Seeming and Constrained Abstinence, for example, Szittya observes: "The liaison between Astenance Contrainte and False Seeming has resulted in precisely what the Lover himself has been desiring so long—physical union. False Seeming's abstinence, like the Lover's, was a sham, hiding secret desires."[85]

Further, concerning the parallels in their respective pilgrimages and the Lover's quest, Szittya observes that the final 10,000 lines of the poem are concerned with the allegorical battle to attain the rose in the castle: "This amorous assault is reminiscent of the traditional psychomachia and other allegorical battles in which figures of evil besiege the Castle of the Soul or the church ... Jean de Meun parodies just such a battle in having the band of Amour attack the Castle of Jealousy led by a friar and a Beguine who are the parents of Antichrist. The deflowering of the Rose is a romance parody of the rape of the church."[86] Indeed, Stakel comments, "It is love allied with Faux Semblant that forms the context for the interpretation of the allegory. The lover's final act reveals that he has retained the teachings of Faux Semblant: clad in pilgrim garb he plucks the rose after having promised Bel Accueil to commit no 'outrage.' Venus takes the castle, but Faux Semblant takes the rose."[87]

At the point of plucking the Rose, the poem ends. There is no epilogue, no denouement; the dreamer simply awakens "straightaway." No further elaboration or explication is given (or necessary); the deed has been done, the deception is complete. Having heard the testimony of all concerned, the reader is left alone to muse on the morality of the Lover's actions, and the implications of the danger to the church that such deceptions pose. These are powerful symbols and warnings. The use of this imagery for such an extended literary work requires an investigation into the intentions of its author, and a consideration of the sincerity of his polemic.

Considering the complexity of this entire apocalyptic theme, and the controversial nature of the subject matter, the problem arises as to whose voice is heard in the overall story. Is it Jean de Meun who is cautioning about the deceits of amorous love, or is this merely a poetic device? From the evidence given in this discussion, it seems that the voice of caution is indeed Jean's, and that False Seeming is the key to arriving at that conclusion. We have seen that False Seeming's speech is not just a digression, but rather is related to the overall theme of the poem because the deception he celebrates is a crucial element in the effort to win the rose.

Are the antifraternal feelings expressed in False Seeming's hypocritical words and deeds reflective of Jean's own? It would seem so. Even those critics who argue that this section is unrelated to the work as a whole generally agree Jean's sentiments were with the masters. If Jean had no connection with or interest in the university debate, it is doubtful that he would have expended so much energy expressing distaste for the friars, religious hypocrites, and the outcome of the controversy. Further, if the discourse of False Seeming were not related to the rest of the poem, there would have been absolutely no point in including it at all. If, on the other hand, the speech is integrated into the poem, as several scholars have argued, then it would, if insincere, be a terribly lengthy diatribe (even for Jean) just to make a point about deception. Indeed, the charge of lack of sincerity on Jean's part would be similar to such charges against Guillaume de Saint-Amour; there is little evidence that both men were not sincere in their writings.

Given, then, that Jean is a supporter of Guillaume, and shares his apocalyptic fears, it may be that Jean's personal view of romantic love is in accord with that of Reason and cautions against the deceitful and impetuous actions of False Seeming and the Lover. Though it is stated in the aside that Jean will be a "faithful servant" of Love and scorn Reason (the basis of Gunn's argument), it is the God of Love who speaks here, the same god who is about to align himself with the vices of hypocrisy and deceit. His word can hardly be trustworthy, just as he must accept False Seeming on faith, without any guarantee of loyalty.[88]

Great care is taken to link False Seeming with the remainder of the story, for as Nature says, his help is invaluable to the quest and he must be pardoned, albeit unwillingly. Since this deceit is necessary to win the rose,[89] the quest can hardly be noble or holy, but rather it is hypocritical and perhaps runs the risk of damnation. The object of an "apocalyptic" quest should (to medieval minds) be one's salvation, but here, the hypocritical quest leads to just the opposite, as the Lover has not gained a spiritual reward, but rather the gratification of his earthly desires. In addition to the romance parody that Szittya suggests, the poem takes on the quality of a parody of an apocalypse, for the conclusion inverts standard apocalyptic themes. The dark period of suffering which the Lover experiences is his own agony at being unable to have the rose, hardly suffering worthy of the apocalyptic tradition. His emergence from this period of despair (the kind that apocalyptic literature invariably describes) results in his plucking of the rose, which is exactly what he set out to do. He has learned nothing and has certainly not achieved salvation. The threat of the coming of Antichrist remains; indeed, that part of the story is never resolved. The Lover has acted in the manner of False Seeming and the friars, becoming in effect a "pseudo-apostle" himself, serving his own selfish desires even in the face of doom.

This is not to say that Jean's continuation is completely anti-love in its content. There are many themes and strands woven into the tale, not all of which condemn love. However, one of these themes is a cautionary tale of the potential dangers and vices involved in an overly-zealous romantic pursuit. The Lover is obsessed and will allow nothing to deter him from the object of his desire. It is this obsession, even avarice, which causes him to align himself with the deceivers to gain his ends, and which Jean seems to condemn so strongly, for it leads to foolish and even desperate measures. The poem is less an indictment of love, than a condemnation of deceitful acts. The Lover, in his desire for the rose, allows himself to be led astray by deception, and even to take part in it, just as Guillaume de Saint-Amour felt that those of his day were being led astray by the deceptions of the friars.

Jean was never specifically condemned in any capacity by the Church, and the *Roman* was, perhaps surprisingly, largely received favorably until the beginning of the 15th century.[90] The work would influence generations of poets, particularly in France. In the 1280s/90s, Gui de Mori (possibly a pseudonym) produced his own adaptation, *Le Remaniement du Roman de la Rose*, with hundreds of new interpolated lines,[91] including additional dialogue from False Seeming that at times tones down the harshness, recounts recent conflicts, and perhaps seeks to put an end to them.[92] At some point after the 1280s, a sizeable interpolation in False Seeming's speech also appeared, with stronger antifraternal themes, which we will discuss in more detail below. In the mid–14th century, Guillaume de Deguilleville, a poet and Cistercian monk wrote his *Pèlerinage de la vie humaine*, a kind of "response" to the *Roman de la Rose*, calling into question its moral tone and conclusions.[93] The great 14th-century poet and composer Guillaume de Machaut certainly made use of the poem's allegorical imagery in his own work, including the God of Love, Reason, and False Seeming.[94] In England, Chaucer knew the work well and may have translated part of it into English.[95] The dream narrative format also influenced the style of Langland's *Piers Plowman* and Gower's *Confessio Amantis*.[96] As Luria notes, "by the latter half of the fourteenth century, the Roman de la Rose had provided western European poetry with an allegorical locus, a set of allegorical personifications, and an archetypal fable"[97] for the many types of love.

Recently, Geltner has made the case that False Seeming represents less of a direct attack on mendicancy and the friars, and more a kind of "Cretan liar" figure,[98] whose purpose is to condemn religious hypocrisy in general.[99] He notes that False Seeming "does not *depict* anyone; he *typifies* hypocrisy. The character is a personification and an allegory, created by Jean de Meun to represent the nature of all liars, not all friars."[100] There is a considerable amount of ambiguity in his speech, as befits one who is deceptive and unclear about his intentions. For example, his costumes and roles are not only those of a friar, but of all classes of society, and so he should not only be affiliated with the mendicant orders.[101] Indeed, though referred to as a friar in the poem, he is more often depicted as a Benedictine monk in the illuminations that adorned manuscript copies of the poem,[102] suggesting that hypocrisy is universal: it thrives among the friars, in the hierarchical Church, and at the court. As we have seen, he both condemns evil, trickery, and deceit, and embodies the very things he condemns. Can we be certain that he is only a friar when he pretends to be so many things?

Approximately 30 percent of the surviving *Rose* manuscripts contain a later interpolation of about 150 lines added to False Seeming's speech, that directly attack the friars' right to preach. This seems to be a response to Pope Martin IV's bull of 1281 affirming that privilege and removing the parish priests' exclusive right to hear confessions.[103] The unashamedly partisan tone of the lines suggests a renewal in the fight against the friars, and perhaps a feeling that False Seeming's discourse did not go far enough in singling them out as targets of hypocrisy and evil. The language is even more harsh, condemning the "friar wolf, who devours all"[104] and lurks everywhere. It is unclear as to why these lines were added. Geltner offers that perhaps it was thought that the original speech did not go far enough and was viewed as too ambiguous in tone to be an adequate antifraternal attack.[105] However, it might have been added for emphasis, in response to what were seen as new and continuing abuses of power. It may have been a commentary on the events of the 1280s, written to bring the poem "up to date."

Jean blended antifraternalism, apocalyptic fears, courtly love, and caution to resist hypocrisy and deception in a most complex manner. The apocalyptic view is not the sole approach to interpreting the poem, but it is a particularly prominent theme that Jean obviously intended to impress on his readers. In this, he was quite successful, for the debate concerning these issues has produced much insightful commentary showing the multifaceted nature of the work. Careful reading of the text reveals that Jean was quite deliberate both in his placement of False Seeming's monologue and in relating it to the work as a whole. As such, it remains a most unusual and fascinating episode in medieval literature.

By the time that Jean completed his poem, French literature had flowered into an astonishing variety of works, and a rich musical culture of courtly songs was firmly established. We now turn our attention to these, for the Church and the friars did not escape the notice of either poet or musician.

5

Poetry and Song in 13th-Century France: Rutebeuf, the Trouvères and the Goliards

By the mid–13th century, French culture already possessed an astonishing literary heritage, including many works which are still read and loved today. Such masterpieces as the *Song of Roland*, the *Lais* of Marie de France, the stories of Tristan and Iseult, and various Arthurian Romances are standard works in university courses on medieval French literature. Others, such as Jean Renart's *Guillaume de Dole* and Gautier de Coincy's *Miracles de Nostre-Dame* deserve wider attention by modern audiences. The songs and poetry of the troubadours in the south and the trouvères in the north dominated monophonic secular music. They influenced musical styles in Germany and Italy, and to a certain extent, eclipsed efforts to create a similar tradition in English.[1] Paris was certainly one of the great hubs of creative activity, though Arras, as we will see below, offered its own unique output of jongleur[2] activity, as well as of poetry and early drama.

In the midst of this remarkable and flourishing literary world, we encounter the enigmatic figure of Rutebeuf (fl. 1248–85), who was a skilled poet living in Paris at the exact time that the university quarrels were occurring.[3] A versatile trouvère,[4] he created poetry in a large number of genres. Indeed, he wrote in more genres than any other medieval poet, though interestingly, none of his works are in the typical formats such as courtly love songs or lengthy romances, for which the trouvères were best known. Further, his pieces were not intended to be sung, as was the case with so much of the trouvère output,[5] but were read or recited. He made great use of the form known as the *dit*, which means "spoken," and is a first-person narrative employing allegory and other techniques to express its ideas. It is particularly well-suited to oral presentation, and we may presume that many of his works were intended to be read aloud, being the perfect choice for invective and polemic. His surviving corpus includes 56 works recorded in twelve manuscripts.

Little is known about his life, so no comprehensive biographical sketch can be drawn. Even his name is a pseudonym; he describes it as being play on words, saying he derived it from *rude boeuf* and *rude oeuvre*, "coarse ox" and "rustic work," respectively. Suppositions that he may have been a minstrel or a jongleur are nothing more than that. More likely, he seems to have had some clerical background, for he read and translated Latin to the extent that he was familiar with medieval and classical sources such as Ovid (the *Metamorphoses*), of which he translated portions and offered commentary. He was certainly familiar with the life of a university student. Regalado observes: "His *Dit de l'université* is a sympathetic account of a peasant boy come to study in Paris who soon squanders his hard-earned funds on pretty city girls."[6] This is almost a stereotype example of the kinds of young men who got into the trouble that led to the university strikes. Was he a student during the quarrels? Were his poems offering an eyewitness account of the conflicts? Is *l'université* something of an autobiography? He goes on to mention that students like nothing better than good drink, and references the fateful tavern brawl of Lent in 1253, that led to the strike and closure of the university.[7] It would be wonderfully tempting to hypothesize that he was one of those very students involved, or at least knew them, but we can only speculate.

He may give some tantalizing glimpses into his later life in certain poems, such as *Le Mariage Rutebeuf* ("The Marriage of Rutebeuf"), where he states that on the 2nd of January in 1261, he married an ugly fifty-year-old woman, who had no dowry, but at least she would not betray him.[8] This may be nothing more than a comic conceit; he exhibits this "making the best of things" attitude frequently, and to obvious satirical effect. However, it seems that he later did have to endure many hardships from being poor, possibly related to a gambling habit. He notes that gamers have taken all of his wealth from him, but he has also tricked other gamers, for wealth comes and goes. Still, the dice have robbed him of his clothes and are killing him, lying in wait to attack him.[9] Nevertheless, his work brought him into contact with many of the nobility and even royalty of his time, including King Louis' daughter Isabelle, and Alphonse of Poitiers, Louis' brother and one of Rutebeuf's benefactors. A number of his poems include appeals for noble and royal support, often rather brazen, especially in view of his satirical attacks on Louis IX.[10]

We know that he lived in Paris and spent much of his life there, though he may have come from the Champagne region. His *Dit des Cordeliers*, an early poem from 1249, is set in Troyes and in the poem, he gives his support to the Franciscans there,[11] an interesting position given his later stand against the friars; at some point over the next few years, he was to turn strongly against them. Concerning this, Geltner has noted that it is unclear if he objected to mendicancy in general, or only the actions of the Parisian friars.[12]

Rutebeuf was deeply immersed in the politics and day-to-day affairs of his city, and this is reflected in his poetry. Subjects in his work include the king, propaganda for the crusades (including the ill-fated venture in 1270 that cost Louis IX his life; these were probably commissions rather than expressions of his true feelings), the university and all of its attractions and troubles, various religious figures (especially the friars and the problems they bring), and daily life. His poetry is uniquely urban, and shows an intimate knowledge of Paris and indeed, a love for his adopted home. He had no interest in the fancies of some of his contemporaries, such as Arthurian myth, the pains of love, and debates on the nature of courtliness, though he did write ribald fabliaux and a poem related to the stories of Reynard the Fox (which contained much satirical commentary on the friars).[13] Rather, he was very concerned with writing about and criticizing, when appropriate, the political and religious issues of the day.

The events at the university and the controversy surrounding the friars were of particular interest to him, and are reflected in a series of poems, written at the height of the conflict and in its aftermath.[14] He makes use of an astonishing variety of literary techniques to put forth the case in favor of the secular masters against the friars, indeed, as Regalado notes, "Dream allegories, battles of vices and virtues, animal satires, complaints attributed to the church personified— all the resources of the Latin and French satirical tradition are brought to bear on partisan concerns."[15] His poems cover many of the issues we examined in chapter 2, namely the rise of the friars in power and numbers, and how they threaten the established order, the writings and unjust fate of Guillaume de Saint-Amour, and the various conflicts over university rights and privileges that the mendicants sought to appropriate for themselves.[16] These works were essentially part of a campaign, political propaganda to emphasize the plight of the masters.

As we have seen, the masters made a concentrated effort to tarnish the reputation of the friars, knowing that they survived by the goodwill of the general population. Quite simply, if people could be turned against them, the friars would have far greater difficulty in surviving by their means: begging and alms. Rutebeuf's poetic skills in the vernacular suited this need well. He did not contribute new ideas to the debate, and did not need to. He only had to express the issues in a way that would catch the attention of the audience; but who were his listeners? Certainly the masters and friars involved, but also the students and religious authorities.[17] It is possible that the general public may have heard his works, spoken in the streets or in taverns. Indeed, in 1255 (in the midst of the crisis), the king forbade drinking in taverns, other than by standing or quickly passing through, obviously in an attempt to prevent gatherings of crowds who might hear dangerous ideas. He also forbade blasphemies against God, Mary, and the Saints under penalty of severe punishment; it may be no coincidence that these two restrictions are listed together. In Louis' mind, there was certainly a link between antifraternal sentiment (especially when directed against his beloved Franciscans) and blasphemy.[18]

At the same time, Pope Alexander was also concerned about the circulation of any work showing support for the exiled Guillaume de Saint-Amour, given that, in a letter to the bishop of Paris in 1259, he ordered the destruction by burning of Guillaume's *De Periculis*. In addition, all other pamphlets, poems, and songs in written forms were to be burned,[19] with no appeal accepted or mercy given. Clearly, there were enough of these diatribes and satires in existence to motivate him to take such a drastic action; he obviously feared another widespread outbreak of antifraternal sentiment. One can easily imagine poems like Rutebeuf's (and probably others of lesser quality which have not survived) finding their way through the city streets, and jongleurs openly singing scandalous songs to their fiddles, with lyrics mocking the friars and various authorities.[20] The defiance was at times blatant; according to Alexander's letter, one lay official even tried to distribute antifraternal writings to a congregation in the middle of a Palm Sunday sermon by Thomas Aquinas![21]

Rutebeuf's poems belong to this category of blunt and straightforward criticism and satire. They have a directness that contrasts sharply with the verbosity, appeals to scripture, and endless theological speculations of the Latin works. One of the key figures in his antifraternal writings is *Ypocrisie*, or Hypocrisy, a new addition to the cast of characters in allegorical poetry, though warnings against hypocrisy had biblical antecedents. The wolf in sheep's clothing was the classic metaphor, appearing in many medieval writings.[22] Rutebeuf's Hypocrisy is the first appearance of a fully-fledged allegorical figure of that name, however, and would become very important in the morality literature of the next century. Hypocrisy is, of course, a major concept in Jean de Meun's continuation of the *Roman de la Rose*, being False Seeming's mother. For Rutebeuf, *Ypocrisie* represents the friars, who are undermining the Church. She makes her first appearance in *Du Pharisien*, where she is portrayed as a relative of Heresy.[23] Rutebeuf devotes a considerable amount of verse to describing her reach and influence, noting that she has many followers, especially those that claim humility and dress "simply."[24] The use of Hypocrisy, especially in *Du Pharisien*, ties in with Guillaume de Saint-Amour's own works linking the friars to that reviled biblical group. In employing a new allegorical figure, Rutebeuf makes his case strongly.[25]

He was also quite willing to inveigh against the mendicants directly, without recourse to allegory. In his *La Discorde de l'Université et des Jacobins*, he attacks the Dominicans for undermining the university that they should be supporting. They proclaim how they forbid anger, but then they stir it up to advance themselves. They should be friends with the university, which gave them books, money, and food when they first arrived in Paris, but now they repay that kindness with betrayal, trying to dismember the university, recalling the story of how St. Nicholas saw the pickling body parts of three boys or young clerks (killed by an evil butcher) and brought them back to life.[26] In *La Bataille des Vices contre les Vertus*, he stresses that originally, they were humble, begging for their bread, but that has given way to vanity and ambition. They are now lords over kings, prelates, and counts.[27] In *Des règles*, he resorts to the charge that would dog the mendicants for centuries; that they seek out only the wealthy through deceit, in search of gifts and donations.[28] They give out false hopes of heaven to these deluded rich men, tricking them into buying their way to salvation.[29]

Making things worse, there is an escalation in their devious goals, which he implies in successive works. Regalado observes: "The friars' ambition appears to reach higher with each poem: while in the *Discorde* they want to possess the University and in the *Bataille* to control the King, in *Des Jacobins* they aspire to be apostles seated with Christ himself, and think their greedy feasts to be the Holy Supper."[30] As we have seen, this escalation is also found in the masters' writings, which evolved from defenses of their privileges to notions of the Last Times and Antichrist.

He was also deeply concerned with the plight of the masters in light of what he saw as great injustices done against them by the pope. In 1257, Rutebeuf wrote his *Le Dit de Guillaume de Saint-Amour*, where from the very first lines, he boldly proclaims to prelate, prince, and king that Guillaume's banishment is unjust.[31] As a follow-up in 1259, his *Complainte de Guillaume* takes the outrage at this unjust act to a new level, as he gives voice to the Church herself, who laments Guillaume's ongoing banishment, and says that she will mourn for him if he dies. He has spoken the truth, she says, and this has cost him and others dearly, but God can end this strife, if he chooses.[32] Works such as this prompted the harsh papal response to burn all dissenting writings, an order which was destined to fail.

Indeed, when the new pope, Urban IV, was elected in 1261, Rutebeuf responded with a new poem, *Le Dit d'Hypocrisie*, which wasted no time in denouncing the corruption of the Papal Curia under Alexander IV, a bold move in light of the still-existing ban on these kinds of writings. Rutebeuf presents the work as a dream narrative, probably in homage to Guillaume de Lorris' portion of the *Roman de la Rose*. If so, this raises the question as to whether this homage to the original *Rose* inspired Jean de Meun to take up his own continuation, an interesting but unanswerable question. In the poem, Rutebeuf takes an active part, journeying to Rome and meeting the figure of *Cortois*, who becomes his guide. *Cortois* makes it clear that the friars have seized power in Rome through their influence, and that figures such as Hypocrisy, Vainglory, and Avarice are now in attendance.[33] Eventually, *Cortois* is elected pope (a reference to the recent papal election), which offers some chance for improvement.

If Guillaume spoke up for truth, others have not. In *Des règles*, Rutebeuf condemns the other masters and prelates, who he says have bowed to the friars in fear, by not protesting Guillaume's exile and by not defending their positions against unjust papal rulings. Their punishment will be hell for their cowardice.[34] In the *Dit de Sainte Eglise*, he excoriates the cowardly masters again. The friars teach false doctrines and have become powerful, and by not opposing them more strongly, the masters have become the torturers and executioners of God.[35] Again, God will punish this cravenness. In *Complainte de Guillaume*, the Lady Church once again speaks, bemoaning her sad situation and the weakness of the masters.[36]

All of this is very bold, indeed. What are we to make of this man, who repeatedly wrote such damning charges against the friars, in defiance of papal orders and royal decrees? We must remember that "Rutebeuf" is a pseudonym, and appears nowhere outside of his own writings. This was a wise choice in a time when such impertinence could lead to exile, imprisonment, or worse. He may have used this name to be able to criticize in anonymity and safety. It calls to mind the letters of the 18th-century anonymous satirist Junius, who openly criticized corruption and immorality in the British government between 1769 and 1772 in a series of missives to the *Public Advertiser* (a newspaper of the time), taking it to a personal level by naming names.[37] The effect was similar to Rutebeuf's invective, and led to much discussion and debate among the public. Rutebeuf does mention at the opening of *Des règles* that he writes despite the dangers, showing that he was aware of the seriousness of his charges.[38] Further, he states in *Les Ordres de Paris* that he might be in danger because of his work.[39] We do not know whether this is true, or again, poetic license. Perhaps he was only a poet-for-hire, reflecting in his words the ongoing public debates, paid to influence opinion without interjecting his own beliefs.[40]

The overall effectiveness of his works is not clear, however. Certainly they provided additional "ammunition" for the masters' cause. There was indeed a change in public sentiment, as we have seen, requiring guards to defend the friars against townspeople's attacks.[41] We must also recall that the Dominicans served as papal inquisitors, a very real and frightening task, so standing up to them took no small amount of courage. In any case, there is no record of him, or any other writers, being punished for their antifraternal work, other than the papal ban. Guillaume de Saint-Amour was the sole victim, perhaps serving as a scapegoat and an example.[42]

Rutebeuf's literary and musical contemporaries weighed in on the issues as well, though not nearly to the degree that he had. There are a number of songs and poems that survive that show the popularity of mendicant ridicule, exactly of the type that Alexander forbade. While we unfortunately do not have surviving examples of street songs,[43] various pieces discussed the issues within the courts.

Earlier trouvères had indulged in clerical satire, so it is not surprising that the friars would come under their attack eventually. Guiot de Provins from the Champagne region (*d.* after 1208), for example, wrote both songs and his lengthy *Bible*, a moral satire. His musical work had some influence on his German counterparts, the *Minnesingers.* Despite becoming a monk himself from 1195, he humorously noted in his *Bible* that the reason that the Black Monks (the Benedictines) change priors frequently is because the old ones might stink if left in one place for too long.[44]

Rutebeuf's near contemporary Adam de la Halle (*ca.* 1237–1288, or possibly as late as 1306) noted in his song *Glorieuse Vierge Marie*, how the Enemy, filled with pride, has attacked the clergy and the Jacobins (Dominicans) with poisoned arrows, because greed reigns over them, and of how with envy, he strikes at monks and abbots.[45] While this is a more general mention of Church corruption, he notes that the friars' avarice makes them the devil's target.

Adam ranks as one of the most important of the last generation of trouvères. Also known as *Adam le Bossu*, or "Adam the Hunchback" (a name which he insisted was a family name and not a description of his appearance),[46] he is notable to this study because he may have been a secular cleric who studied at the University of Paris, though this is not certain.[47] If so, he would not have been the first trouvère cleric.[48]

In his *Jeu de la feuillée* from *ca.* 1276, Adam crafts a first-person narrative that many scholars consider to be at least semi-autobiographical. In it, he expresses his desire to leave his wife in the city of Arras and return to Paris to continue his studies, but ultimately he never leaves. The play is also symbolic, with stock characters, and the figure of "Adam" may well have biblical connections, so it is uncertain how true this intention was.[49] The work uses a mixture of real people, fictional creations, and allegorical figures. It has frequently baffled later scholars, with its seemingly incoherent assemblage of scenes and characters, long-lost jokes, and references to things forgotten, but it is clearly intended to satirize events and social classes in Arras, particularly clerics and monks.[50] It is thematic, rather than chronological. Events take place in the real world, but the play includes a significant scene in the middle, wherein fairies intrude and engage in a lengthy dialogue, which will remind modern readers of similar fantastical scenes in Shakespeare's *A Midsummer Night's Dream*. Adam represents the prince of the fairies as Hellequin, who will be seen again in the *Roman de Fauvel* as the Erlking (see chapter 6), and later as the comical Arlecchino (Harlequin) in the *Commedia dell'arte*.[51]

The play uses Adam's predicament about returning to Paris to study as the setup for its farce. His father is not willing to fund his adventure, and Adam wants to leave behind his wife before he gets her pregnant. There is a back-and-forth exchange between several characters about the issue of clerical bigamy, which addresses an infraction newly regulated by the Council of Lyons in 1274 (which, as we have seen, also suppressed various minor mendicant orders). Pope Gregory X stripped various secular clerics of their offices for engaging in prohibited marriages, which included second marriages by either spouse, or marrying a woman of "loose morals." These clerics lost their privileges (including tax exemption), and it seems that a good number in Arras were affected (indicating that abuses of the system were common there).[52]

Such clerical bigamists are ripe for satire, but one character, Master Henri, makes a forceful argument against the ruling, wondering why other Church officials such as prelates can have all the women they want, while clerics cannot even remarry. Such prelates are consumed by lust and sin, but still to get to keep all of their powers. Rome has reduced a third of its clerics to a kind of slavery.[53] Gillot responds that the pope who decreed this is lucky to be dead, for a cleric named Plumus would most certainly have deposed him and told him to go to hell, where he may actually be now.[54] It is implied that Plumus is mad,[55] and most certainly not a cleric who attends to his duties, but this is still a shocking statement to make about a pope in a medieval document. Conversely, the play's fool, the *dervés*, identifies himself with pope and king, and delivers condemnations of the corruption in Arras.[56] He is the "holy fool," who delivers wisdom to those with the sense to hear it.

The monk who appears throughout the play brings with him many of the abuses we have already seen, especially those of a financial nature. He is a charlatan, and first appears offering to help cure madness (a frequent theme in the play) by telling the others to offer prayers to St. Acaire; he has seen much success from this in the past, but of course, one also needs to offer money.[57] Later, when the monk falls asleep in a tavern (during the final scene of the play), the inn keeper resolves to stick him with the bar bill, a way of making him pay back some of the money he has effectively stolen by soliciting funds for St. Acaire. He has clearly been interested in his own gain, not the well-being of others.[58] The monk has fallen asleep before, during the scene with the fairies, and the implication is that he is also guilty of the Deadly Sin of sloth.[59] The inn keeper threatens physical violence against the monk if he is not paid.[60] The monk leaves his saint's relics as surety, promising to return (which also shows how little they actually matter). Eventually he does come back, and pays up.

The play ends with no resolution to Adam's story, serving rather as a social commentary and satire on current events in his city. The monk is the final character on stage, and he resolves to leave, because there is no one left to cheat out of their money.[61] While the Adam of the play may never achieve his ambition to return to Paris, it is the monk who ultimately loses the most, that is, salvation.[62] Scholars are still debating how much any of this reflects Adam's real life.[63] McGregor notes that when the host invites Adam to join in mocking the monk, it may represent "an antipathy for *clergie* as a whole, and for Adam's vision of it in particular,"[64] though the character's response to this invitation is not revealed.

Whatever his background, Adam's peers seemed to regard him as well-educated, so there may be truth in the wishes of the story's main character. A play written after his death, the *Jeu de la pèlerin*, assigns him the title of "master," that designation which we have seen to be so contentious. Further, the miniature portrait of him in the *Chansonnier d'Arras* (a manuscript from *ca.* 1278 featuring the works of various trouvères over several generations) depicts him with a clerical tonsure and seated at a desk with writing tools.[65] This does not prove he was a secular master, of course, but it may be another clue to his professed desire to resume studies in Paris.[66] If he was a cleric and had connections with Paris, he surely would have been familiar with the conflicts of recent decades. His comment about the greed of the Dominicans in *Glorieuse Vierge* may reveal some of his personal thoughts on the issues.

Interestingly, the jongleurs and players of Arras had established a brotherhood around 1175, the *Confrérie des jongleurs et bourgeois d'Arras*, based on a miracle story about the Virgin Mary offering a cure to an outbreak of ergotism (grain contaminated by the ergot fungus) in their city in the early 12th century. She appeared to two jongleurs and offered them the wax from her holy candle, which when mixed with water, would cure those afflicted. The brotherhood was effectively a lay religious order, receiving the support of the clergy (ultimately taking the Bishop of Arras as their patron) and the Benedictine abbey of Saint-Vaast, as well as the Franciscans and Dominicans in a charter from 1241; the jongleurs reenacted the miracle story in a liturgical drama for Assumption Eve.[67] It was a rare example of jongleurs aligning themselves with the Church, instead of being condemned by it.

Returning to the trouvères, the repertoire contains various anonymous religious songs (written down in the later 13th century) that make passing references to hypocrisy and quite possibly the friars.[68] All of these examples survive with music, and were presumably performed for various noble audiences, who would almost certainly have been aware of the conflicts occurring in Paris.

Et cler et lai begins with an exhortation to both clergy and laity to listen to a new song in praise of Mary.[69] After prayers for mercy and intercession, it stresses that every mendicant (beggar) should hold her dear in his words and deeds.[70] While not a specific reference to the friars ("mendicant" could refer to beggars in general), the opening lines addressing clerics and laity point to this possibility. If so, it doesn't condemn them, but rather reminds them of their duty, perhaps with the implication that they do not always remember it.

A stranger piece, *Quant froidure trait a fin*, speaks of a heaven of delights (including those of the flesh), where wine flows, where no pain, no poor, and no brothers exist.[71] The description resembles those of medieval Islamic visions of paradise more than Christian.[72] What is striking here is the use of the word *frerin*. While this might mean "brothers" in a literal sense, it could easily be a reference to the friars, and is probably a play on words, especially since it is linked with the word *povre* or "poor" in the same line. Certainly some of those who heard this work could have made that association. The poem may well be saying that there are no friars in this paradise, a paradise that includes the same kinds of pleasures that the friars were often accused of indulging in. The work ends by saying that Christ delivered the world from the snare of Isengrin, the wolf from the Reynard branches, who we will discuss in the next chapter.[73] Isengrin is one of the many "wolf in sheep's clothing" figures, a literal representation of the hypocrisy metaphor.

The song *Au douz commencement d'esté* offers a broader anticlerical theme, noting that truth is nowhere to be found, not among the bishops or the "white abbots" (most likely the Cistercians). The narrator is disappointed by this, for they now endorse falsehood and condemn the poor, and both clerics and laity have been seduced by flattery.[74]

Likewise, *Por ce que verité die* offers a general condemnation of hypocrisy, saying that those whose bodies are filled with hatred and greed cannot be free of it no matter how often they attend church.[75] Indeed, God entreats us to leave hypocrisy behind.[76]

Its forceful message is both direct and ambiguous enough that it could have been interpreted in the minds of some listeners as referring to the friars.

The trouvères, of course, held many different viewpoints and political opinions, and among their number are those who actively allied with the friars. A notable example of such a supporter is Thibaut IV, King of Navarre and Count of Champagne. Probably because of his royal status, more of his songs survive with music than from any other trouvère, and they are of high quality. Thibaut was gifted in artistic abilities, but less so in other areas. He was notably at odds with King Louis VIII, oddly enough, over issues of Jewish rights; Thibaut wanted to protect them and the extra tax income they generated. He was widely rumored to have had an affair with Blanche of Castile, Louis VIII's widow and mother of Louis IX. His attempt at a crusade in 1239–41 was a mix of miserable failure and unintended victory,[77] though he wrote four songs about his preparations for it.[78]

And while he found himself at odds with French royalty and even officials in the Church, he was a firm enemy of heretics, and gave his backing to the Dominican Inquisition, particularly one odious and arrogant individual, Friar Robert le Bougre, said to be an ex–Cathar, and who was exceptionally devoted to his new profession. Through Robert's efforts, Thibaut oversaw the public burnings of more than 180 accused heretics in Mont-Aimé in Champagne, shortly before embarking on his crusade.[79] This action may well be offensive to modern sensibilities, but shows the conviction of believers in a time wracked by dissent and heretical charges. Thibaut gave his full support to the Dominicans' work in the region of Champagne.[80] It must be noted that as lord of the region, he had a claim to the property of those executed, a fine financial incentive when he was seeking to raise money for his crusade.[81] It may be difficult to believe that he would have sanctioned the murder of at least 180 people just for financial gain, though far more heinous crimes had occurred during the Albigensian Crusade. More likely, he wanted to show his genuine penitence ahead of his crusade and also repair some of the damage he had caused in past relations with the papacy and French royalty.[82]

Inspired by his beliefs, he also wrote a mysterious song, a religious *serventois* entitled *Dieus est ensi conme est li pelicans* ("God is like the Pelican").[83] In it, he specifically condemns those who have turned from God. The language is surprisingly reminiscent of the invectives of the antifraternal writers. Indeed, he laments that pride, deception, felony, and treason are found everywhere, but instead of casting his anger toward the friars, he instead notes that it is only because some churchmen have abandoned sermons and taken up arms against heretics that anyone believes in God at all,[84] a reference either to the Albigensian Crusade, or to the crusade for which he was preparing. He goes on to condemn the *papelards*, the hypocrites who are killing God and his children. They are foul, evil, stinking, and vile, and with their false words they murder simple folk and make the world rock on its foundations. They take away joy and peace and will carry that burden to hell.[85] All of this would seem quite at home in the *dits* of Rutebeuf, who also uses the term *papelard* in his depictions of worldly hypocrisy. Here, however, Thibaut invokes these images to condemn heretics and the enemies of the Church, most likely the Cathars, though possibly also the Muslims he is going to face.[86] Thibaut was unapologetic in defending the Church, and believed that the friars did important work in rooting out heresy. The horror of Mont-Aimé is proof enough of that.

Elsewhere, the courtly audiences of France repeatedly showed that they had a taste for the unconventional, the obscene, and the dangerous, and perhaps most of all, the novel. We will examine the scandalous fabliaux and Reynard branches in the next chapter, but another artistic musical form captured the courts' attention at the time, one that appeared in the first decades of the 13th century, and enjoyed tremendous popularity well into the 14th: the polyphonic, and often polytextual motet. The motet is a type of polyphonic musical composition, which arose from the styles of religious music created at Notre Dame Cathedral in Paris. It could be in two, three, or four parts, where the bottom line was most often a fragment of chant that had been assigned a new rhythmic pattern. These pieces often appear with separate texts, rhythmic styles, and even different languages in each vocal line (French and Latin). The texts might also mix secular and religious ideas into one piece, i.e., a vernacular text about spring, and a Latin text about Easter, for example, playing off of one another. The effect was quite striking, and motets became very popular.

Some examples of these anonymous polyphonic vocal pieces reveal sentiments by now very familiar. In *L'estat du monde, et la vie / Beata viscera*, a two-part motet from the Montpellier Codex,[87] the main vocal text laments how life gets worse each day, for those that outwardly look holy in fact are not. They are filled with hypocrisy and lies, and seek power and its reputation. The text explicitly names the Jacobins (Dominicans) as among the worst offenders, as well as others from minor orders.[88] Another piece, *A Cambrai avint l'autrier*, offers quite a change in tone, telling a ribald and comic story about Sohiers, a cooper who gets entangled with the Beguines, out of his own schemes and trickery. The song relates how they often receive him, but not because he has a good name; rather it is because of his large "walking stick."[89] As we have seen, many had made similar charges about their lechery.

Another piece, *Fole acoustumance*, resembles the dark tone of *L'estat*, and finds the narrative voice in the top line filled with a heavy heart. Making use of allegory, the text relates that Envy and Villainy grow in power day by day while Courtesy and her friend Generosity flee. Hypocrisy is advancing, may God curse her! Anyone who stands up to her will inevitably receive blame from others for doing so. The richest and most powerful are the ones at fault; France has died because of their deceptions and *false seeming*. The world mocks the nation of France for its fallen state, while Hypocrisy makes all abandon friendship and generosity, and the greedy do not refuse power.[90] The condemnation of Hypocrisy and the mention of "false seeming" would appear to be direct references to the works of Rutebeuf and Jean de Meun. While the friars are not specifically named, the similarity of this motet to one condemning the Dominicans, and another mocking the Beguines suggests a fraternal target. A fourth motet in this collection, *O natio*, is in Latin; it prays for deliverance from the sin of pride.[91] It is not clear if these pieces were by the same composer, or were grouped together because of their common theme.

The trouvères and other composers who wrote all of this music tended to be settled in various regions, affiliated with various courts. They were not the stereotypical "wandering minstrels," more properly known as jongleurs. However, there was another group of poets who reveled in their vagabond lifestyle, and many did indeed travel far and wide. They have been grouped together (often erroneously) under the name of the "goliards."

The origin of the word "goliard" is uncertain. It may derive from the Latin *gula*, or "gluttony," though some poets themselves liked to link it with Golias, the biblical Goliath. There may also be a connection to a reference by the Cistercian abbot Bernard of Clairvaux, who called his Parisian scholastic enemy Pierre Abelard "Goliath," an insult in the ongoing war of words between them in the first half of the 12th century.[92] Some of Abelard's poems may have ended up in later goliardic collections, such as the original *Carmina Burana*, thus strengthening this connection.

The goliards represent a unique group of poets and satirists in medieval European literature, with (among other subjects) songs that mock and condemn Church corruption dating back considerably earlier than the 13th century; the first goliards (or rather, those who wrote in Latin on similar topics) appeared in the later 10th century, but reached their full flowering in the 12th. Thus, their tradition was already well established by the time that fraternal criticism appeared. Interestingly, those associated with this group were almost exclusively clerical students, particularly from the universities in France, Italy, Germany, and England by the 13th century. They wrote primarily in Latin on a wide variety of themes. Topics for their songs included celebrations of drink and music, gambling and feasting, women and love, debates, religious and institutional corruption, the welcoming of spring, and songs of genuine piety... in short, they exhibit a panorama of subjects as varied as the students who composed them.[93] Further, some had a tendency to wander from town to town and school to school, bringing the charge of vagrancy against them not unlike one of the chief criticisms of the friars.[94] Or, they might be clerics, more properly thought of as "wandering scholars" than true goliards, who had failed to secure a permanent Church position after their studies, and so took to the road, a controversial decision. The Church itself had criticized the *gyrovagi*, a pejorative label for those who roamed freely,[95] dating back to the Benedictine Rule, which condemned wandering monks. Indeed, some antifraternal writers identified the friars with these wanderers, and used the Rule as proof of their concerns.

Yet it would be a mistake to compare the goliards to modern students indulging in the party atmosphere of a university, or the "frat boy" mentality. They were not merely lazy vagabonds. Their works were often extremely well written and offered insight into many issues of the time. Indeed, they likely played up their loutish behavior as part of the satirical picture that they painted, exaggerating aspects of their lives for comic and satiric effect. They mocked both other topics and themselves.[96]

As an example, the famed Archpoet (*ca.* 1130 – *ca.* 1165) made such sentiments clear (whether truly or for dramatic effect) in his *Estuans intrinsecus*, or "The Confession of Golias." In this classic "manifesto" of goliardic philosophy, he delights in celebrating his drunkenness and love of a wanton life. He freely admits that he is on the way to perdition, shunning a virtuous life and doing things that he should not. He has little hope for heaven, since his soul is probably already lost.[97] Later, he expresses his desire to die drinking in a tavern, wine at hand. He hopes that a choir of angels will sing to God, asking him to spare this drunkard.[98] A number of modern scholars do not link the Archpoet with the goliards, believing his lowbrow poetry to be merely a conceit for courtly audiences.[99]

In any case, their conduct did not sit well with the Church, and on several occasions, it took actions to limit and censure them. A large number of examples survive from numerous Church councils that issued edicts trying to control them, often prohibiting clerics and students from going to taverns, gambling with dice, and playing musical instruments (especially in a church). Such regulations were also sometimes directed at clerics in holy orders to prevent them from being tempted into the vagabonds' way of life. The fact that these edicts had to be continually reissued shows the extent of the undesirable behavior, and that the goliards routinely ignored the rulings.[100]

Goliardic verse contains a wealth of content about factional Church disputes. Before the friars, there were poems and verses written by clerics and goliards attacking monks, sometimes with great emphasis and vitriol.[101] The writings once attributed to Walter Map illustrate this clearly. Map was of Welsh origin, born between 1137 and 1140, and after studying in Paris, was attached to the court of King Henry II of England. Later he assumed ecclesiastical duties, including archdeacon of Oxford and more than once was a candidate for a bishopric. His attributed work contains many examples of condemnation of Church corruption, especially of the Cistercians, the Templars, and the Hospitallers. The long poem, *Metamorphosis Goliae Episcopi* ("The Metamorphosis of Bishop Golias") includes a defense of clerical scholars against the intrusion of monastic interference in their work; the reference to Bernard's attacks on Abelard is clear. The author makes a strong point at the poem's conclusion that such hooded meddlers (the monks) are in fact evil and impious, the heirs to Pharaoh, appearing outwardly to be holy, but harboring superstitions within. This "cowled flock" should be scorned and driven from the schools of philosophy, where they have no place.[102] Such language is strikingly similar to that of Guillaume de Saint-Amour, Rutebeuf, and Jean de Meun, yet appearing about a century earlier in a similar context. As Regalado notes, "The University quarrel is, then, part of a continuing history of rivalry between different ecclesiastical branches."[103] Interestingly, in the early years of the Dominicans' existence, there was a prohibition on excessive study of Classical writing; it was essentially the same kind of interference with learning that the *Metamorphosis* poem rails against,[104] though it was directed inwardly.

The *Carmina Burana* is the most well-known and extensive collection of goliardic and related verse from the Middle Ages. A selection of these works was made famous by the 20th-century composer Carl Orff, whose orchestral setting focused mainly on the springtime and love poems. The original manuscript, compiled in the first half of the 13th century, and containing considerably older poetry, as well as some later additions, features a good number of poems that condemn Church practices such as simony (the act of paying for sacraments or positions of power within the Church) and other vices. The first 55 texts are devoted to morality and satire.

Licet eger cum ergotis (CB 8) by Gualterius de Castillione (*ca*. 1135—*ca*. 1179) from about 1170, boldly claims in its opening verse that Church leaders now practice their imitation of Christ from a distance.[105] Further, lay persons no longer have respect for the clergy, since the Church is bought and sold, debased. Altars and the Eucharist are auctioned to the highest bidder, though this kind of purchased salvation has no value.[106] The poem continues with lurid descriptions of how the Church is drenched with money, and how wealthy old men can give in to their every whim.

The undated *O curas hominum* offer similar sentiments, noting that as soon as a holy position is bought, the concern for the flock fades away. Their words betray their hidden sentiments.[107] Curiously, the poem ends with a comment about how the

Simonists reign, which is hardly surprising, when dogs are given the faith.[108] It is worth noting that though the poem likely predates the founding of the mendicant orders, Dominic sometimes referred to himself as a "dog of the Lord," or *Domini canis*, a pun on *Dominicanus*, the name for the order. A later antifraternal polemicist could certainly have seen this as a useful poem for engaging in wordplay.

The famous and humorous drinking song, *In taberna quando sumus*, is also undated, but in its colorful roster of those to whom the jolly poem offers its toasts are the errant brethren or friars, and the dispersed monks.[109] One should not assume that this is a blanket assertion about all religious orders; it may be only a toast to those who have fallen, but the fact that it exists here shows that the idea of the fallen monk or friar was well embedded in popular culture and thus easy to mock.

Another work, *Deduc, Sion*, by Philip the Chancellor (*ca.* 1160/70–1236), offers a harsh condemnation of Church corruption, saying that a sickness in its head now infects the entire body,[110] and that the Church has become a den of thieves.[111] Philip was chancellor of Notre Dame, a gifted poet, and possibly a composer. He may have opposed the friars at one point, but this is unclear. Such was the popularity of his output, that some of his works were used over a century later in the *Roman de Fauvel*, which we will examine in chapter 6.

That the goliards wrote their satires in Latin made them something of an anachronism by the mid–13th century, when vernacular languages were fast overtaking the old language as the means of communicating in the courtly realm.[112] Yet the vernacular polemicists of the 13th and 14th centuries were actually drawing on the rich tradition of Latin satire and critique which had come before them.[113]

There is a surviving goliardic critique of the friars from the second half of the 13th century, *O spina noxia latet in lillio*, from an English manuscript possibly dating between 1261 and 1265. This document contains a miscellany of important works, including the famed English round, *Sumer is icumen in* (in its only surviving source, which includes the music), the fables of Marie de France, and a number of goliardic poems, among many other selections.[114] The anonymous author was possibly English, but shows knowledge of the French polemics regarding the friars, making use of proverbs and animal imagery as Rutebeuf had done to condemn them.[115] The poem opens with striking metaphors for the friars' trickery, including the hidden spines in the lily, treacherous tongues, and poison hidden in a jar of honey. The basilisk, the scorpion's tale, the snake's tooth, and the sword all are used as damning imagery. The author wishes for protection from the web of fraud and false brethren.[116] Clearly, it was a simple matter to take the existing goliardic tradition of attacking corrupt monks and clergy, and fit the friars into it.

While trouvères, jongleurs, and goliards entertained audiences with their songs, developments in vernacular poetry offered new and rich sources of inspiration for writers, some of which were quite shocking. Ribald animal tales, obscene fabliaux, and a devilish horse featured in some of the most remarkable literature of the French Middle Ages, and as always, the Church and friars were not spared, whether it was a figurative tweak on the nose, or a full theological body blow.

Scandalous Fables and Vulgar Animals: Reynard, the Fabliaux and Fauvel

The Roman de Renart

"No one gets around Reynard. Reynard leads everyone by the nose. Reynard wheedles and coaxes: he is well versed in villainy. No one, however much his intimate, profits from associating with him."[1]

This description of the famous trickster fox appears in the opening to Branch IV of the *Roman de Renart*, and sums up his duplicitous nature perfectly. Trusting Reynard is a mistake, for he will always betray those who do so, while appearing to be their true friend. It is not difficult to see how this model for a character could easily be used in anti–Church criticism.

By the Middle Ages, the fox already had a long history of being viewed as duplicitous and dangerous in Christian tradition, going back to biblical references.[2] In the Book of Judges, Samson uses 300 foxes, attaching torches to their tails, to destroy the grain supplies of the Philistines, along with their olive groves and vineyards.[3] Foxes ruin the vineyards in the Song of Songs.[4] Later commentators, such as Pope Gregory the Great (6th century), stated that foxes are cunning creatures, hiding in holes and always running crookedly; they might even be demons in disguise.[5] St. Ambrose (4th century) comments at length on how heretics are like foxes.[6] Isidore of Seville (7th century) wrote that foxes pretend to be dead, to lure in prey, tricking them.[7] In the 13th century, the English Franciscan Bartholomaeus Anglicus echoed these ideas, adding considerably more detail about the fox in his encyclopedia, *De proprietatibus rerum*.[8] Medieval bestiaries did the same.[9] Thus, in his deceitful behavior, the fox is like the devil, but the truly holy will not be lured in by his tricks.

So ingrained was this idea that in Adam de la Halle's *Jeu de la feuillée*, when Douce (a woman of suspected "loose morals") responds to accusations by one Rainelet that she is a prostitute, she tells him, "Damn your red head!" His red hair, real or symbolic, associates him with the fox's red fur, and identifies him to her as a liar and a devil.[10]

In the real world of farmers and country folk, the fox was a scourge, a taker of chickens and lambs, and a competitor for game birds and other small animals. Thus, the character of Reynard came with quite a negative history and reputation, one that was already well known to his medieval audiences. Indeed, one version announces that Reynard is a creation of Eve, who, after expulsion from Eden, made only wild creatures, while Adam made useful animals. Reynard is a product of vanity and wildness, and is not directly a creature of God.[11]

Reynard and his animal cronies are part of a colorful French "romance" which is not a unified work at all, but rather a collection of 26 short tales (referred to as "branches"), to which various (mostly anonymous) writers contributed over a period of several decades, beginning in the later 12th century. A good number of these stories had been completed by about 1200, and so were set down before the rise of the mendicant orders, but the corpus of work continued to inspire new poems, including a contribution by Rutebeuf, and translations into other languages, such as English and Dutch. So popular were the Reynard stories over the centuries that the very word *renard* has come to mean "fox" in French, replacing the older *goupil* (from the Latin *vulpecula*).[12] The poems are beast tales, wherein anthropomorphic animals take the lead roles, and their comic, satirical, and even violent adventures show the failings and foibles of the human race.[13] Richard Kaeuper notes that these works are essentially parodies of the hugely popular *chanson de geste* poems that circulated so widely, and are a product of the unique political atmosphere under the Capetian kings of the time, noting their frequent combination of hope for justice in the courts, which is often dashed by unfairness and the harsh reality of how human systems operate.[14]

Though the characters are representative of more than just animals, these works differ from dream allegories in that they present a largely realistic world, one that their audiences would easily recognize. Indeed, Owen notes that "the setting for Reynard's adventures is no fantasy realm, but takes us down the highways and more often byways of rural France, offering glimpses of real townships and villages sometimes identified by name.... This is the real world, and the sight of the costumed beasts galloping through it on horseback is the illusion."[15] The characters frequently morph back and forth from courtiers to animals, from upholding chivalric ideals to scavenging for food.[16] The rural setting contrasts with Rutebeuf's urban locations, and as we will see, his own contribution to Reynardian lore is more in his own writing style than that of the other Reynard branches, since his focus is again on the troubles of Church and State in his city.

The cast of characters is well known to students of French literature: Reynard, the anti-hero, the trickster fox whose schemes cause so much havoc, yet who always seems to come out on top (earning him amused admiration from his audience); Ysengrin (or Isengrim), the wolf, his sworn enemy, dull-witted and often the victim of his tricks, but who always returns for more; their wives, Hermeline and Hersent, respectively, who despite their own faults, may have more sense than their husbands; Noble the king lion, well-meaning, but sometimes easily deceived; Chantecler the rooster (who will find his way into Chaucer's *Nun's Priest's Tale*), and Bernard the donkey who is a priest, perhaps a telling commentary: the ass is a holy man, and shares a name with the most famous theologian of the 12th century.[17] There are many others: Bruin the Bear, Tibert (Tybalt) the Cat,[18] Baldwin the Ass, Sir Tardy the Snail... all representatives of various aspects of medieval French literary society.

Court and Church were ripe for mockery, and the stories do so with glee. These are not high-brow writings, but rather revel in their sauciness, prominently featuring violence, sex, and cynical humor at the expense of others. Nevertheless, they often contain simple morals or proverbs as a means of cloaking the tales in respectability.[19] As such, they resemble the fabliaux, which we will examine later in this chapter. Still, many scholars believe that the poems are not about moralizing, but rather are a kind of literary game that makes fun of other forms.[20]

The earliest French poem is now numbered as Branch II, and dates from the 1170s. It is attributed to the cleric, Pierre de Saint-Cloud (who also produced what is referred to as Branch Va). He may have compiled stories and story lines from earlier sources for some of the other poems, and he certainly drew on them for inspiration in his own work. One of these sources was the Latin poem *Ysengrimus*, attributed to one Nivard of Ghent, about whom almost nothing is known. This work, drawing on the Latin tradition of beast fables going back to Aesop, has some affinities with goliardic repertoire, though it is not a song, but rather an epic poem of more than 6,500 lines divided into seven lengthy books. Dating from about 1148–50, it introduces the wolf, Ysengrimus and his enemy, the fox Reinardus. Throughout a series of comic adventures, Reinardus gets the best of the wolf by trickery, just as his French incarnation would do decades later. One of the work's key themes is the mockery of the corruption of various monastic figures, particularly those that engage in simony, just as the goliardic works do. Ysengrimus himself is the representation of the greedy monks, led astray by his desire for more wealth and gain. At the end of the poem, he is flayed and thrown to the pigs, a horrible if fitting end to a sinful life.[21] Many medieval Christians believed that this death-by-devouring by pigs was also the fate of Muhammad, the Prophet of Islam, further emphasizing what was to them the wolf's evil nature. The poem holds up monastic circles to ridicule, possibly as a result of the disastrous failure of the Second Crusade, preached with such fervor by the Cistercian Bernard of Clairvaux, who was left dejected and humiliated in its aftermath, and was sharply criticized by some.[22]

An earlier Latin poem, the *Ecbasis captivi*, was written in the Vosges region (modern-day north-eastern France, though the story is German in content) in the mid–11th century, and has the distinction of being the earliest surviving medieval work to feature anthropomorphic animals, with characters similar to those in the Reynard material. These include a fox, a wolf, and a lion, and a rivalry between the wolf and the fox. In the story, a runaway calf is captured by a wolf, but manages to escape. The wolf relates an "inner fable" about how the fox and wolf became enemies. There are strong monastic allusions (probably to real individuals) showing that even at this early stage, the failings and hypocrisy of monks were subjects of discussion in courtly literature.[23]

Returning to the later 12th century, in the decades after Pierre's work, more writers added their own interpretations of the Reynard story, expanding his world and offering other viewpoints. We do not know the identities of most of these poets and trouvères, though there are some speculations. Only two others are named, the Priest of La Croix-en-Brie (Branch IX), and Richard de Lison (Branch XII, itself an anticlerical parody). Interestingly, Owen notes that Branch VII, written around 1200 and given the rather grim title of "Reynard Eats his Confessor," is an anticlerical satire set in a specific region north of Paris that seems to be pointing to actual individuals. The author of this diatribe is suspected of being a cleric with strong opinions or perhaps even a defrocked priest.[24] We will examine this work in more detail below.

Other branches, such as XII, hold up both court and Church to ridicule, but do so with less vehemence and vitriol. Reynard and Ysengrin actually take on the roles of religious in some stories, but their reasons for doing so are hardly pure. Ysengrin once pretends to aspire to be a monk to gain access to Reynard's home, and to join the monks that he thinks are there eating all of the delicious food. There are no monks eating in Reynard's home, of course; it is merely Reynard's lie for another of his cruel jokes. The wolf is a liar, as well; he makes his offer merely to satisfy his voracious appetite.[25] The underlying message is that many who go into the clergy do so less from pure and godly motivations, and more from a desire for wealth, gratification, and advancement.

Despite such anticlerical themes, Kathryn Gravdal has argued that these tales are in general more parody than satire. She notes: "parody and satire are quite distinct systems of text production. Parody is a textual play on literary traditions and conventions, while satire is a literary commentary on the real world."[26] The animals in the Reynard stories tend to represent types of humans (rather than individuals), even stereotypes.[27] Stereotyped figures in medieval literature refer to literary genres, as well as social norms, and "discursive practices, such as rhetoric."[28] Parody, then, seeks to deflate, to mock, and breaks the rules of literary conventions. It is an "authorized transgression" of society's hierarchies and codes as they are expressed in literary form.[29] The clergy (and later the friars), as subjects of such ridicule, were as good a group as any for this, particularly as so many seemed so filled with their own self-importance, but they were not the only objects of farcical scorn. Gravdal maintains that the Reynard stories of the 12th and 13th centuries are essentially parodies, and have often been misread as satirical.[30] However, Branch VII certainly has no small amount of a bitter satirical air about it, and Rutebeuf would introduce satirical jabs at the friars in his own contribution, as would later writers, as we will see below.[31]

Satire, in this definition, offers specific critiques about specific groups or individuals, and often has much more to do with political content and real-world themes, actively condemning its intended targets,[32] the friars being the obvious example. As Laura Kendrick notes, medieval satire is "episodic and appears within works such as romances, fables, sermons, visions, songs, or other medieval genres."[33] Furthermore, such satire was often deliberately partisan in content, aimed at the enemies of the writer or those of his patron, with a view not only to pointing out their faults, but even insulting them.[34] The writings of Jean de Meun and Rutebeuf can clearly be seen as examples of the latter, whereas the fables and animal stories tended toward the parodic. We also find inter–Church satire, rivalry, and sarcasm, such as in the fables of the English preacher Odo of Cheriton (*d.* 1246/47). In one of his tales, a cat becomes a monk, and is able to lure a suspicious mouse too close. The mouse asks what will become of the cat's monastic vows if he eats him. The cat replies that when he wants to be a monk, he is, but when he wants to be otherwise, he is a canon.[35]

Whether parody or satire, the Reynard branches are filled with mockeries of human failings, especially those of the Church, and of monks in particular. Monks are often represented in human form, rather than as animals, and their behaviors are anything but holy.³⁶ As Gravdal notes, villainy is held up as something comical. Injustice rules the world, and the trickster Reynard, who is portrayed as a noble, inverts the whole concept of what such an individual is supposed to do.³⁷ Indeed, the audience laughs at both the winners and the losers.³⁸

In Branch IV, Reynard tricks Ysengrin into falling down a well on the grounds of a Cistercian monastery, where, he notes, the monks are especially malicious.³⁹ The wolf has stumbled into the monastery in the midst of a wilderness, and at first thinks it to be the abode of demons, where no food will be found.⁴⁰ When the duped wolf is eventually hauled up from the well, the monks attack him: the abbot with a large mace, the prior with a candlestick, and the monks with clubs, with which they set upon Ysengrin and beat him nearly to death.⁴¹ Clearly, these monks are violent when they need to be, just as monks (in the form of the military orders) and the Church itself had become more violent in the aftermath of the crusades.

When facing possible torture and execution for his misdeeds in Branch I, Reynard moans that he wishes he were in the monastic communities of either Cîteaux (the Cistercians) or Cluny (the Benedictines), only he would probably soon have to leave, since there are so many bad monks among them.⁴² The comedy here is that the reprobate Reynard sees the monks as worse than he is, and that he could not stand to be around them for long.

In Branch VII, the animals again assume religious roles. This particularly vitriolic branch seems to have more venom than is usual, and as mentioned, may be the work of a cleric deprived of a position or otherwise wronged. Reynard finds an abbey near Compiègne (just north-east of Paris) with the choicest and tastiest chickens. A servant catches him in the act, and locks him in the coop. The angry monks arrive, again armed with clubs, ready to strike him down. Reynard shakes with fear, saying to himself that monks are so unmannered and ferocious that they would not be moved by his prayers for deliverance. He wishes he had a priest to confess to, and so be absolved.⁴³ As for the monks, he decides that just because they wear black and are called holy means nothing. They are insane and would be better off known as devils, who are also colored black.⁴⁴

He escapes, but not before suffering 14 injuries at their hands. Finding a safe haven, he lets out seven farts,⁴⁵ one each for his father, mother, all other ruffians and gluttons, the chicken he has eaten, the peasant who stacks hay, his love Hersent (Ysengrin's wife, but in this poem portrayed as Reynard's true love), and for Ysengrin, who he hopes will come to a bad end.⁴⁶ He then settles down, and prays to God to save all criminals, traitors, and gluttons, and those who love good food more than their clothes, and live by trickery. As for monks and abbots, priests and hermits, he prays that God may inflict them with great torments.⁴⁷

After sleeping, he awakens to find he is trapped by a rising river. A kite, Sir Hubert, happens to fly over and settles down next to him. He is a confessor, and is ready to hear Reynard's confession. Reynard confesses to hating all who are good and honest, and says he would gladly join the Cistercians and wear a hair shirt, except that he has a recurring body pain preventing it. As for the Benedictines, they do not care for anyone who is not in good health. Further, he cannot speak Latin, and enjoys a good morning meal.⁴⁸ In any case, the rule of the Benedictines is too harsh, he announces. They need a rule that permits them to have sex once a week, which would make them a better order. However, the woman who they have sex with would have to leave once they were finished, and not return until the next week, because these monks are so lecherous they would wear her out, and would end up fighting over who gets to go first.[49] The Cistercians, by contrast, are so severe that one could die from their fasting and keeping vigils, their singing and laboring.[50]

A lengthy section then follows where the confessor rebukes Reynard for his wickedness, and drones on at length about the sexual appetites and wantonness of Hersent, which angers Reynard and he threatens to eat Hubert. Yet Reynard confesses further about his bad deeds, comparing them to a list of real people, and saying that he is worse than all of them.[51] This provide us with clues about the author's opinions and intent. Finally after more heated exchange and threats (including calling the confessor a hypocrite), and a false promise of peace, Reynard eats the kite, and so ends the tale.[52] This violent and insult-filled poem is interesting for its specifics: names, places, actions, etc. In targeting the Cistercians and Benedictines, as well as individuals, it is closer to the antifraternal writings of a half-century later, where the friars were often accused of many of the same crimes: lechery, violence, and outward shows of piety. As we can see from these few examples, the anticlerical themes of the Reynard branches are numerous.[53]

New stories continued to be written and circulated throughout the 13th century, though the original French "roman" reaches its conclusion with the twenty-sixth poem. By the time of the university conflicts, they were well known stock characters, and they would provide a useful vehicle for secular partisans to attack the friars. Indeed, Rutebeuf made use of them in his *Renart le Bestourné*. Though classified as one of his "misfortune" poems, the work seems to criticize Louis IX through use of the thinly-disguised Noble the lion representing him, and by stating that he is being led astray by deceivers. This was not his only reference to the trickster fox; Reynard had appeared in other poems, where his trickery was compared to that of the friars.[54]

Renart le Bestourné opens in a manner similar to the earlier Reynard stories, as exemplified in Owen's rhyming translation:

> Reynard is dead, yet lives in style;
> Reynard is base, Reynard is vile
> But Reynard reigns.
> Lording it over the king's domains.[55]

Soon after this, however, the poem abandons any sense of narrative, discarding the usual tales of trickery and slapstick humor in favor of invective against the foolishness of a king who would allow himself to be so deceived. Interestingly, this type of opening was a technique sometimes used by the friars themselves: they would begin a sermon with a more popular set of references and *exempla* (such as with chivalric themes or other *chanson de geste* material, or even an event drawn from local life), and then segue from there into the more important matters of the sermon's content.[56] Preachers used these *exempla* to spice up their sermons, with a view to imparting some important moral lesson. Short and to the point, they offer insight into the minds of both the preacher and his lay audience, as well as their world.[57] So, perhaps in his Reynard poem, Rutebeuf is deliberately turning their style back on them, using a popular character to attract the listeners' attention before launching into his dire warnings about the gullible monarch and the doom that threatens the world.

The exact objects of his criticism are difficult to identify, but a good argument can be made that Reynard represents the friars.[58] The fox of his poem is darker than in previous incarnations, being linked to great evil.[59] Rutebeuf notes that Reynard's kin are numerous, and a large number of them are about in the land.[60] Noble the lion trusts Reynard completely, but this is a mistake, and if the king does not return again to God, the fox will bring terrible misfortunes.[61] The king is so in thrall to the fox that he doesn't hear the gossip that is spoken about him and his gullibility, or the jokes made at his expense.[62] All of this sounds very familiar and exactly describes the masters' criticisms of Louis and his devotion to the Franciscans.

The poem continues by naming other beasts in the king's court, those found in earlier Reynard tales: Ysengrin, Roenal the dog, and Bernard the donkey priest. These would lead his armies into war, but there would be no honor or victory.[63] This could be a reference to Louis' preparations for his second crusade of 1270, a political satire on the various factions of his court with Reynard representing the friars, and Bernard as the other clergy. Together, they have turned Noble away from being a good ruler, and now his court is more like a hermit's abode.[64] The land is in danger because of them, and the Beast (of Revelation) may appear at any moment.[65] The irony of a beast poem warning of the coming of the Great Beast would probably not have been lost on medieval audiences.

Reynard flourished in other adventures, such as the Middle English *þe vox and þe wolf*, preserved in only one manuscript, and dating from between 1275 and 1300. It is the earliest surviving beast fable in English, and retells the story of Reynard tricking Ysengrin into a well. Then at Matins, the wolf is discovered, set upon, and beaten, in this version by friars.[66] The story is rich with anticlerical allegory, including images of the deceptive fox-priest and the angry,stupid, and violent mendicants.[67]

Various French works continued to keep the wily fox alive, and they targeted friars along with other religious hypocrites. Jacquemart Giélée wrote *Renart le Nouvel* between 1288 and 1292. Containing social commentary on the events of the time, it notes that Reynard will assume the grey habit (a reference to the Franciscans) and use hypocrisy to deceive the mendicants and military orders.[68] The Dominicans, seeing that he is wealthy, ask him to join them, that he may bring his wealth to their order. Reynard declines but offers his son Renardiel to them, and his younger son, Rousiel, to the Franciscans. At the end of the work, father and son sit atop the Wheel of Fortune, which no longer turns.[69] The poem has interpolated musical works, like the exquisite *Roman de Fauvel* that would follow it (see below).[70] The last major iteration of the Reynard stories is *Renart le Contrefait* ("Reynard the Hypocrite"), surviving in two versions, the first written between 1319 and 1322, and the second between 1328 and 1342, by Evesque de Troyes, probably a defrocked cleric who had become a spice merchant. It is a massive poem (more than 40,000 lines), with prose additions, containing many diverse, and at times, unrelated elements, though it also draws from the earlier branches, putting a greater emphasis on satire.[71] Like *Fauvel*, it owes a debt to the *Roman de la Rose* and False Seeming, and contains references to both, showing its literary influences.[72]

Geoffrey Chaucer made use of Reynardian themes in the Canterbury Tales. In his *Nun's Priest's Tale*, there is a fox, "Rossel," (likely derived from Reynard's Franciscan son Rousiel),[73] as well as an ass, "Brunel," which recalls an earlier satirical donkey, Burnellus (see below). The cock-priest and the friar-fox in this tale are vivid examples of anticlerical and antifraternal characterization.[74] Reynard also featured in English literature of the 15th century; in 1481, William Caxton brought out *The Historie of Reynart the Foxe*,[75] which popularized the character in England. There is also a translation into Middle Dutch, the *Van den vos Reynaerde*, by Willem die Madocke maecte (*ca.* 1200 – *ca.* 1250).[76] Reynard even tricked his way into Scotland. In the 1480s, the Scottish poet (known as a "makar") Robert Henryson (*fl.* 1460–1500) offered Reynardian material as part of his *Morall Fabillis of Esope the Phrygian*, where the fox appears in five of the fables, and is called "Lowrence."[77]

The persistence of this wily trickster in literature down the centuries is a testament to his enduring appeal, an antihero always ready for mischief, and to tweak the nose (and sometimes much worse) of authority, whether courtly or religious; the friars were only one of many groups on whom Reynard unleashed his cruel humor. Stories of the trickster fox have survived into the modern era, and been adapted in a multitude of ways,[78] for as his medieval audience knew well, "Reynard lives on!"

The Fabliaux

Scandalous, obscene, scatological, ribald, irreverent, anticlerical, antifeminist… all of these adjectives and many others have been used to describe the fabliaux, that unique body of French literature that circulated widely from the 12th to the 14th centuries,[79] though most were composed between about 1200 and 1340. Some 160 tales in octosyllabic couplet form survive, spread over 43 or so manuscripts (mostly from the 13th century).[80] They are a uniquely northern French phenomenon, though they would influence comic works over a much larger area in later times; writers who drew from fabliaux plots and themes include Chaucer, Boccaccio, Rabelais, and Molière.

The poems were circulated both in oral and written forms, and while most of the authors are anonymous, there does seem to be a bias toward clerical sources of authorship, i.e., the literate clerks who were church-educated, essentially those same secular clergy who opposed the friars in Paris, and also wrote goliardic poetry.[81] Indeed, many of these clerics were probably of that wandering status, educated but unemployed, and thus resorting to writing (and perhaps reciting) ribald literature for money, just as did the jongleurs.[82] Charles Muscatine notes that "clerks are, interestingly, the only class of people uniformly admired in the fabliaux,"[83] which further points to their identity as the authors. One may as well praise one's own when writing parody and satire. They drew from a long-standing tradition: an early Goliardic song collection from the mid–11th century, the *Cambridge Songs*, contains several fabliaux-like themes.[84]

The audience seems to have been the entire panoply of French culture and life (though probably not the devout King Louis IX). Scandalized 19th-century scholars could not fathom such works being anything but low-brow entertainment; the great French literary scholar, Joseph Bédier,[85] held to this theory. In contrast, the Danish Per Nykrog argued in the 1950s that they were enjoyed by a more courtly audience,[86] and were less about real social institutions than playing with courtly literature.[87] Muscatine and others have since made a strong case for the works being popular across all social classes.[88] Performed from memory by jongleurs and minstrels, many were written down for posterity, and for the amusement of the literate.[89] They were as likely to have been heard in courtly halls as in taverns and at market fairs, and their appeal seems to have been universal, their controversial themes notwithstanding. The origins of some of the tales have been identified, but many remain obscure, and theories have ranged from ancient Rome to India and Persia, while many may have been spontaneous creations from medieval France.[90] Part of their popularity was due to their compact form. Bloch notes that unlike epics and cycles, "the fabliaux offer a quick fix.... They are short and dirty; but they clean up their own mess, and they never leave any loose ends."[91]

Remarkably, given their obscene and frequent anticlerical content, fabliaux and related stories and anecdotes appear in a number of preaching collections. Brian J. Levy notes, "some of the most direct evidence that we possess of the fabliaux's performance potential comes from the *artes prædicandi* [arts of preaching]. Throughout the various collections of *exempla*, which bear full witness to the practical eclecticism of the medieval sermon, are to be found a number of recognisable fabliaux or fabliaux analogues."[92] These include examples in the writings of Jacques de Vitry (1160/70–1240, Bishop of Acre and later a cardinal) and various Dominican and Franciscan collections in both England and France.[93] Offering up the same stories to an audience that had heard them from jongleurs was an effective means of gaining and holding an audience's attention.

Several themes abound in the various fabliaux. They are not generally concerned with courtly life. Indeed, commoners mainly populate the tales, and many stereotypes repeatedly emerge: peasants are generally stupid and crude, women are deceitful, and not to be trusted, husbands are suspicious and jealous, clergy and monks are lustful and greedy, and use their positions of power to gain their desires. Those low-born who attempt to climb the social ladder (whether by bribes or other means) and put on noble airs only end up looking foolish. Unlike dream allegories or some animal fables, there is a surprising realism to the stories, often including small details about everyday life. The question of how accurate these portrayals are is of course, open to debate. Muscatine has argued for a fairly faithful representation: "Fabliaux characters act according to an ethos, explicit or implicit, that is rooted in the everyday life of the culture."[94] Conversely, Bloch observes, in discussing the scatological poem, *De la Crote*: "As a presentation of 'the way things really were' in the thirteenth century, as a 'window' upon the medieval world, does this tale mean that peasant couples in northern France exposed their genitals and tasted each other's excrement to chase away the boredom of long winter nights? Probably not."[95]

However, there is certainly attention given to the details of daily life, and the celebration of simple pleasures, what Muscatine refers to as "hedonistic materialism."[96] He further observes an affinity between these poems and the Reynard branches, for their use of everyday settings and themes.[97] Indeed, "a certain malicious intelligence is several times referred to as *renart* in the fabliaux,"[98] though of course, the Reynard stories, as we have seen, parody courtly literature far more, even as they also deliver anticlerical content.[99] Bloch further notes that "unlike other literary forms of the period—the elevated epic, the courtly romance, and lyric verse, which are meant to inspire noble deeds or lament unhappy love—these often scandalous works are filled with the celebration of bodily appetites: sexual, economic, gastronomic, and yes, even the human need for laughter."[100] The stories repeatedly praise good food, good sex, money and wealth, and coming out on top by using one's wits.[101] The constant recurrence of these hedonistic themes seems to point to the fabliaux not being so much a reaction against established mores and institutions, but rather a system of values existing alongside of them.[102] The stories are "archeological evidence: fragmentary remains, preserved in written form, of an important stratum of the culture that has otherwise left few traces."[103]

The language is earthy and uncensored; the equivalent word for "fuck" appears in some 25 of the poems,[104] while "cunt" is another favorite. Such words themselves were probably not particularly shocking to their audiences, merely being vehicles for telling a story whose humor was found in other elements.[105] Over time, they seem to have been viewed as increasingly offensive, particularly in more high-brow courtly literature, so their use diminished.[106] Depictions of sexual activity are frequent and explicit, often with word-play, euphemism, and humor,[107] though in some ways, they are also conservative. The scenes are brief, the missionary position is by far the most often presented; depictions of oral sex are rare, and homosexuality generally shows up for accidental comic effect.[108]

Perhaps disturbingly for modern audiences, castration and other mutilations are often employed for humorous effect,[109] as in *Le Prestre crucifé*, or "The Crucified Priest," which also displays a good example of the anticlerical themes so common in these works. Roger, a carver of crucifixes and statues, returns home to find his wife, as he had suspected, with her lover the priest, Father Coustanz, though they are dining rather than having sex; this is a frequent prelude to sexual activity in the fabliaux. Hearing that he is returning, she hastily advises the priest to hide in the carver's workshop, remove his clothes, and pretend to be a crucifix statue.

The husband sits down, dines with his wife, and then goes to work in his shop. Knowing full well what the priest's plan is, he asks his wife to bring a candle to light the way. She has no choice but to agree, or else she would give away their deception. The carver goes straight to the naked priest, and announces that he must have been drunk when carving the work, for he has made a terrible mistake in carving genitalia on the image, and will rectify his sinful error. He proceeds to take his knife and remove the poor fellow's testicles and penis, leaving him with nothing. Coustanz runs away, the carver shouting that his crucifix is escaping. A townsman overhears the chase, and strikes the escaping priest, causing him to fall down into the muck. The carver drags him back to his home, and forces him to pay a large sum to be released. The moral of the story is that no clergyman should ever be having an affair with a married woman, or he will sacrifice his balls in payment, just as Coustanz left his "three hanging ornaments."[110] The tale ends, and we presume, much laughter followed.

This is a typical example of several fabliaux themes: the deceptive woman, illicit sex, violence as humor, the cuckolded husband, and the lustful clergyman. How and why were such tales so widely popular with various social classes, defying Church teachings, and even holding up the institution's representatives to such mockery? Indeed, to give only one example, the fabliaux and other writings of Gautier le Leu (early to mid–13th century) at times bordered on blasphemous and obscene, not only mocking Christ, but also extolling the glories of female genitalia with an "almost hysterical enthusiasm."[111]

There are many answers of course, an obvious one in this instance being that the priest was the sinner, the one who had betrayed his office and indulged in fleshly pleasures that were not permitted to him, a common fabliaux theme. The Church seemed to be engaged in a constant battle to keep its errant clergy in line,[112] and tales such as this reflect well-known issues about clerical corruption. The moral clearly states that a priest has no business doing such things, and if he does, he should be punished. There is a larger theme, then, summarized in the moral; the ribald and violent tale is simply a way of expressing it. Indeed, some morals may have been attached to ends of these tales to give them a greater air of respectability.[113] The fact that the lustful priest is such a stock character in these stories shows the extent to which it was probably a joke among the laity, and seeing a corrupt priest getting what was coming to him must have been very satisfying. The anticlerical themes could be justified then as being in defense of true religion against these charlatans and scoundrels.[114]

Various scholars have argued about the nature and even the existence of anticlerical themes in the fabliaux. Earlier studies tended to accept that such negative depictions reflected the reality of the times, while later scholars countered that they were more a kind of literary device. Indeed, Burrows notes that "a man sworn to charity and chastity, members of whose social group would be unlikely to be members of the audience, was an ideal candidate when the tale called for a party who merited defeat."[115] He argues convincingly that the tales do contain anticlerical and satirical elements, that the term "anticlerical" does not necessarily imply outright hostility toward the clergy, and that satire merely "denotes the process whereby a text presents an image of an extratextual referent which through content or context negatively deforms the target."[116] In that sense, these works are most certainly anticlerical to at least some degree. The fact that such stereotypical representation exists to such an extent implies something about the audiences' attitudes.[117] There is certainly a theme of lay superiority: "through their negative stereotyping, the texts deny the greater virtue in sexual and financial affairs which was so essential to the Church's attempts to assert the priesthood's difference from, and superiority to, the laity."[118]

As such, these tales were also fitting for antifraternal satire, and we will examine two of them here, *Les Braies au Cordelier* and Rutebeuf's *Freire Denise le Cordelier*. "Cordelier" refers to the belts of cord or rope worn by the Franciscans, and in these stories, the friars are guilty of the same misdeeds that their priestly counterparts are.[119]

Les Braies au Cordelier ("The Cordelier's Britches") dates from the middle of the 13th century, and features many of the familiar fabliaux tropes, including the cheating wife, the foolish cuckolded husband, and her lover the clerk, who naturally is portrayed in a positive light.[120] The Franciscan in the story is mentioned as such five times in the poem, both as a *cordelier* and a friar minor. The Franciscan convent at Orleans, where the tale takes place, is also named.[121] These are unusually specific references for a fabliau, and O'Gorman believes that "this insistence betrays a clear intent to denigrate a religious order whose original aspirations had already been subverted."[122]

In the story, the friar is, rather surprisingly, not the butt of a joke or even of slander and derision. Rather, he is merely a small part of the main plot. The unfaithful wife has her clerk as a lover, and schemes of how to see him. On one occasion, her husband must make a long journey to Meung-sur-Loire (curiously, Jean de Meun's home town) to attend a market, and he must leave at dawn. She tells the clerk to stay awake all night and await his departure. The husband wakes up, it is dark, and he leaves. Her lover sneaks in and they embrace.

However, it happens that the husband has awoken far too early, for his traveling companion informs him (after being roused from sleep) that it is not yet midnight. Learning of his mistake, he returns home, knocking loudly at the door. Realizing that they are about to be caught, the clerk hides, but forgets to take his britches. Forcing his way in, the cuckolded husband goes to his wife, who first pretends to be asleep, and then to awaken, crying out that she is being attacked. He husband calms her and explains what happened, and they then sleep until dawn. He rises, puts on the clerk's britches without seeing that they are not his, and leaves again. The clerk emerges safely from his hiding place, and he and the wife engage in their love-making.

The clerk then wants to leave without being seen, but realizes his britches are gone. This causes them both much anguish, but the lady devises a plan, for she is cunning like Reynard the Fox.[123] The clerk sneaks away and she goes to a Franciscan brother, to whom she confesses everything and asks for his help. Should the husband become suspicious when he discovers he is wearing someone else's clothing, she will say that the friar lent her a pair of his britches, so that she could stow them under her pillow, as an aid for her to conceive a child. She asks for him to back her up in this lie, and he gladly agrees to do so.

At the market, the husband discovers his purse is missing due to not wearing his own britches, and he immediately suspects trickery. Returning home, he angrily accuses his wife of infidelity, but she gives him the false explanation, and invites him to take the britches to the friar to confirm it. He goes to the friar, who laughs and whispers in his ear the very same story. The husband is relieved, leaves the britches with the friar, and returns home, where he apologizes to his wife. Her deception is so well done that she can now have her clerical lover with impunity at any time, for the husband will never again suspect her of wrongdoing. And so ends the story.

It is a classic fabliau, where cunning and wit win out over foolishness. This amoral resolution contributed to the comic effect of the story, and was common in the genre, as it was in the Reynard branches.[124] Gravdal notes about Reynard and his ilk something that could just as well be said of the cast of fabliaux characters: "The failure to trick is punished; the ability to trick is rewarded."[125] As with Reynard, the trickster is applauded, just as a modern audience might secretly admire the skill inherent in the perfect crime.[126] While the friar is not mocked or condemned in the story, his behavior is deceptive and he is complicit in her adultery. He happily helps the wife to cheat on her foolish husband, and does so without guilt. His actions permit their affair to continue. Implicit in the story, then, is the notion that one can rely on a friar to be deceptive, to take the side of Reynard in trickery.

A more direct attack on the friars comes from, naturally, Rutebeuf in his contribution to the genre. It is not surprising that he would use the fabliaux format to "take a shot" at the friars, as it is a style into which he could easily adapt a story for his invective. *Freire Denise* is the tale of a Franciscan, Simon, who conspires to smuggle Denise, a young woman whom he desires, into his house by disguising her as a young friar herself. At the beginning, Rutebeuf offers a criticism of mendicant hypocrisy very similar to those in his *dits*.[127] A monk is not a monk merely by wearing a habit, and even if his clothing looks poor, his behavior must match his garment or else it is false. Many like to show off their presumed virtue, but they are like trees that present beautiful flowers but bear no fruit.[128] Indeed, those that do this deserve a shameful death.[129]

He continues by noting that the young lady was very desirable, with at least 20 suitors, but she wanted to live a holy life. By chance, a certain friar caught her attention while visiting the family home. She begs him to obtain her mother's blessing so that she can enter a convent, and the friar is most happy to help, but of course, he desires for her something much different than a religious life. He offers to sneak her into his house posing as a young friar minor. Rutebeuf again condemns his deception, saying that she wants to serve God, but he serves another, and will get his just reward from that one.[130] The friar is wicked, because their goals are completely opposite; she wishes to withdraw from the world, while he, burning with lust, already has plans for them to bathe together.[131]

Denise sneaks away at the appointed time, causing great sorrow for her mother. She cuts her hair, receives the tonsure, and puts on men's clothes. The friar welcomes her, and Rutebeuf again condemns him, saying he is in league with the Enemy.[132] Though she is exemplary in her duties, he "converts" her to his ways, and she learns an "unfamiliar leisure activity" that the others do not know about; she gladly learns "his Lord's prayer."[133] The euphemisms are obvious and as explicit as the poem ever gets.

It happens that the two visit the home of a knight and his lady. She correctly guesses that "brother Denise" is not a young man. She asks for the men to leave while Denise hears her confession. This alarms Simon, who is wary of being found out, as are all friars. Simon offers to hear her confession instead, saying that Denise is incompetent, but the lady is insistent. They retire to her private chamber, where she confronts the young "friar," asking her whatever possessed her to take on such an absurd vocation. Denise tries to defend her position, but fails, and crying, she begs not to be exposed, confessing how the friar lured her from her home.

The furious lady calls in the friar and in her husband's presence, yells at him, calling him a hypocrite and saying he leads a false life. It would be good, she declares, to take that cord he wears around his waist and hang him with it.[134] She accuses him of being virtuous on the outside but rotten inside, and says that his whole community is neither good nor noble, trying to deny others music and dance, and instruments such as citoles, vielles and tabors,[135] and indeed "all of the delights of minstrelsy."[136]

For his lies, she says, he will pay. She wants to lock him in a box, but he begs for mercy, face down, arms stretched out to form the cross. Her husband takes pity on him, and lifting him up, tells him that he can save himself by obtaining 400 livres, to pay for Denise to be wed. Simon happily agrees and since the friars are so wealthy, it will not be a problem to produce that much money. He then hastily exits their home and the story.

The lady keeps Denise in her company, and promises to keep her secrets, saying she may marry any man she desires. The lady sends for Denise's mother, and the two are reunited, the mother being told that Denise has been at a convent. Finally, it is noted that Simon has paid her dowry and she is then married to a knight, with whom she has far more honor and happiness than she ever had with the friar.[137]

Considering the invective that Rutebeuf addresses to Simon and the Franciscans in the poem, as well as the lady's condemnation and threat of death, the friar's fate is rather unusual. Muscatine calls the poem's ending "weak."[138] One could say that the friar got off very lucky, in view of the fate of the crucified priest, and many others of the religious class who come to such bad ends in fabliaux poems. Indeed, Regalado notes that the work "has more in common with fabliaux about lustful priests such as Rutebeuf's own *Sacristain* than with the University polemic."[139] One reason for this, she notes, may be that the Dominicans wielded more real power at the time than did the Franciscans, and thus were a bigger target for political satire and condemnation. The Franciscans' "pretension of extreme austerity" makes them ripe for mockery; when they fail to live up to this impossible ideal, it is all the more comic. Fabliaux-type stories are thus perfect for portraying them as hypocritical, lustful buffoons, who burn all the hotter because of their self-enforced celibacy.[140] In any case, Friar Simon does not need additional punishment in the story, since Rutebeuf has already stated that he will receive the ultimate punishment in the afterlife.

Punishment for wrongdoing would figure strongly in the last work we will survey here. The remarkable story in poetry and music of a vice-ridden horse that brings ruin to a kingdom perfectly captured the tumultuous events of the early 14th-century French court.

The Roman de Fauvel

"I would rather be a swineherd than curry Fauvel."[141]

The *Roman de Fauvel* is a singularly curious and highly important work of poetry, art, and music from early 14th-century France. Written in two versions between 1310 and 1314 by the royal clerks Gervais de Bus and Chaillou de Pesstain, a more elaborate and interpolated edition was created before 1320 (probably about 1317), with extended poetry and 169 musical pieces (monophonic and polyphonic) that spanned more than a century of French styles, dating back as far as 1200. The lavish presentation of this work, preserved in the Bibliothèque nationale de France manuscript Paris, BN fr. 146 is one of the glories of medieval art.[142] Its intricate blend of poetry, notated music, and illuminations is unparalleled, with all three masterfully woven together to tell a single story. It is the most important window we have into the music-making of the time. Given its controversial subject matter, its survival in such an edition is all the more remarkable.[143]

Making use of allegory (though not using a dream narrative as in the *Roman de la Rose*), this story is a true satire, a controversial commentary on the sorry state of affairs for both Church and Crown in a turbulent period. Among the events that occurred at about the same time as its creation were the end of the troubled reign of Philip IV, called "the Fair" (1285–1314), the suppression of the Knights Templar from 1307 to 1312, the beginning of the Avignon Papacy (from 1309), and the Great Famine beginning in 1315.[144] Additionally, Philip the Fair's feud with Pope Boniface VIII, which began in the 1290s, was still remembered by many, and we will examine this in more detail below.

The story of Fauvel also certainly drew a good amount of its inspiration from the life and death of Enguerran de Marigny, the chamberlain to King Philip. He came from a minor noble family and was in service to the king by the mid–1290s. By 1305, he had been appointed the king's chamberlain, and continued to rise in power, with the blessing of both king and nobility. Around 1313, however, things began to go wrong for him. As often happens to those who acquire too much power and wealth too soon, Marigny overstretched his reach and was filled with more ambition than many at the court could tolerate, especially Philip's son Louis of Navarre (who would become King Louis X), though the king continued to favor him. In particular, Marigny offended both Louis and Charles de Valois, Philip IV's brother. Charles was a man of limited abilities and great ambition who nevertheless thought highly of himself, enough so that Marigny's encroachment on duties he presumed were his led to a feud between the two. Charles wanted revenge, and after Philip IV died in 1314, he sought it. The king's death removed the royal protection afforded to Marigny, and Charles moved ahead with his plan, having him accused of mismanaging finances and taking bribes. Initially cleared of these charges in January 1315 (since the accusations were false and Marigny could prove it), Louis X nevertheless proposed to banish him, but Charles was not satisfied. Using his influence, he was able to bring charges of sorcery and necromancy against Marigny. These were absurd charges, but this time, it worked. Marigny was found guilty in March 1315 and hanged in April.[145]

The *Roman de Fauvel* takes the side of Marigny's enemies, employing in its satire a warning about trying to climb too high above one's station, thus displaying pride, vanity, and avarice. Indeed, the whole of the second book of the *Roman* seems to be a commentary on this, and on his downfall in particular.[146] Specific musical pieces in the work relate directly to his execution and the dangers to the political order of things that schemers and usurpers bring.[147] Drawing on well-established animal imagery, the motet *Garrit gallus* presents a deceitful fox who has tricked the old Noble the lion. Margaret Bent notes, "the fox is not only Marigny but also the antecedent of Fauvel and the Renard of earlier romans, in which the lion-king Noble is deceived by Renard the wily fox, a clear model for King Philip as the blind lion and Marigny as the fox."[148] Fauvel's palace has paintings of the story of Reynard, further strengthening the connection.[149] The author of the Chronique métrique (an account of the kingdom of France from 1300 to 1316 that is found in the *Fauvel* BN fr. 146 manuscript) states that a crowd denounced Marigny "as a thieving 'Renart' who had despoiled the kingdom, as he went to Judgement at Vincennes in 1315."[150]

The story references many other current events, including the suppression of the Templars (on accusations of heresy, sodomy, black magic, and other trumped-up charges, believed by many at the time to be true), and the death of the Holy Roman Emperor Henry VII, probably of malaria. Interestingly, some believed him to have been poisoned by his Dominican confessor,[151] further proof, if any was needed, of the extent to which vice and corruption had infiltrated the halls of power. The poem recalls this incident, and supports the poisoning theory.

Philip IV's biography is filled with stories of his conflicts and power struggles, especially with religious institutions, and most notably with Pope Boniface VIII.[152] Born Benedetto Caetani, this future pope was under the care of Franciscans from an early age, eventually rising through the hierarchy of the Church to become a cardinal and part of the Roman Curia. He was elected pope in December 1294, succeeding Celestine V, who resigned, having reigned only since July of that year. Celestine was clearly not up to the task, being a humble Benedictine monk who had no interest in politics and power. An unsubstantiated rumor suggested that Caetani had convinced or intimidated him to resign, and there were further whisperings that he had bought the papacy with bribes. As pope, the ambitious Boniface set about consolidating papal power to an even greater extent than had been seen before. He annulled the majority of his predecessor's acts, and fearful that supporters of Celestine (including Philip IV) would try to re-install him as an antipope in opposition to Boniface, he had him imprisoned. Celestine died ten months later, prompting his supporters to declare that Boniface had him murdered. The evidence is unclear, though it certainly would have been in Boniface's best interests for Celestine to be dead. The former pope was very elderly (more than 80), however, so he may well have died of natural causes, or the stresses of his incarceration.

Boniface's attitude toward the friars was mixed. As a cardinal and papal legate in Paris, he had strongly supported their position in yet another conflict with the university in 1290, over the issue of pastoral privileges. As we have seen, he quite clearly declared that the university did not have the right to deprive the friars of any such privileges, and that the Curia would destroy the university before it would let that happen.[153] These were harsh and threatening words, yet as pope in 1300, he issued the bull *Super cathedram*, which attempted to regulate the friars' activities, by affirming their right to preach, but requiring them to have a license to hear confessions, and giving bishops control over their local flocks. Further, they were not to preach while a bishop was doing so, and had to pay their parish church one-quarter of all gifts and legacies. This seemed a huge victory for the seculars, but in some ways was a compromise that tried to allow the friars to continue their activities without additional conflict.[154] The bull failed to resolve the problems, however, and a series of popes had to re-issue it throughout the 14th century, usually at the request of bishops and priests who accused the friars of repeatedly violating its orders.[155]

As pope, Boniface insisted on absolute power over the world's affairs. His bull of 1302, *Unum sanctam*, stated that it was necessary for every human being to be subject to the pope in order to attain salvation.[156] This applied to monarchs, as well as to the poorest. As this came after several years of conflict with Philip IV over issues concerning power and taxation of the clergy (for wars and other expenses), the king was understandably furious. He had long held that the king bowed to no one, the pope included, and so had a refutation of the bull written by the Dominican theologian John of Paris. Boniface responded by excommunicating the king. Philip and his advisors shot back with a barrage of accusations against the pope, including: heresy, simony, sodomy, idolatry, practicing sorcery and black magic, denial of the souls' existence, murdering Celestine V, and usurping the papal position.[157] More than twenty bishops and archbishops took the king's side. One of Philip's councilors, Guillaume de Nogaret (also excommunicated), devised a scheme to seize Boniface in Italy and bring him to France, where he could be deposed. The plan succeeded initially, and Boniface was taken prisoner in early September 1303, but an uprising of papal supporters allowed him to escape three days later. He was not to live long, however, dying on October 11, 1303. Again, lurid rumors circulated that it was not a normal death, but that he had committed suicide, possibly by gnawing through his own arm or bashing his head against a wall.[158] A popular prophecy had stated that Boniface would "enter like a fox, reign like a lion, and die like a dog."[159]

After his death, the French Crown pressed for a posthumous trial that would convict him of the crimes of which he had been accused.[160] The charge of heresy was central, and was clearly a politically motivated attack, by a monarchy that prided itself on having a long family history of defending religion against heretics. Indeed, in a show of defiance, Philip also pressed for the canonization of Boniface's predecessor, Celestine V, as a way of underscoring just how evil Boniface had really been.[161] Nothing was ultimately to come of it, and Boniface was declared orthodox by the Council of Vienne in 1311–12. Philip dropped his accusations against the pope in exchange for being absolved of any responsibility for his actions against Boniface.

These conflicts clearly reveal the problems of authority in the highest positions of power, and the corruption that inevitably came with them. Philip's actions against the Knights Templar were yet another in a line of battles he fought with ecclesiastical institutions. His trumped-up charges (again including heresy and sodomy) were successful in having the order suppressed by Pope Clement V. All of this would certainly have been in the minds of the creators of the *Roman de Fauvel*, and other satirical writers of the time. The seemingly endless series of wars, both actual and ideological, along with the greed and self-interest displayed by so many who held authority, created a situation ripe for satire and condemnation.

The *Roman de Fauvel* was a response to just such troubling times. Implying that neither Crown nor Church serves justice any more, it tells the tale of a horse (sometimes thought of as a donkey), *Fauvel*, whose name is an acronym for the vices: **F**laterie (Flattery), **A**varice (Greed), **V**ilanie (Guile), **V**arieté (Inconstancy), **E**nvie (Envy), and **L**acheté (Cowardice). In a further play on words, the word *fauvel* also means "veiled lie" or "veil of falsity."[162] The connection with *Faus Semblant* is already clear. The color *fauve* (Old French *falve*), or "tawny" had its own associations with evil, and also came to mean a wild animal. Fauvel, like False Seeming, is one of "Antichrist's boys," a forerunner of his appearance and the end of the world. In the second half of the poem, for example, Lady Fortune accuses Fauvel of serving Antichrist, and therefore of deserving death.[163] Drawing on some of the familiar motifs of the beast fables, the Reynard branches, and the *Roman de la Rose*, the story became something else, a unique work in medieval literature.

The character also recalls a donkey, Burnellus, from a monastic satire, the *Speculum Stultorum*. Written by the monk Nigel de Longchamps in 1179, it tells the story of a vain ass, Burnellus, who desires to have a longer tail. He tries to do this by medicine and fails. Next, he goes to the University of Paris to study, but also fails at that. He then resolves to create a new monastic order, a combination of all the others, but without their hard work and deprivation. Eventually, he is recaptured by his master.[164] There are various criticisms of the clergy and ruling classes (and a later version from the 14th century was expanded to include the friars).[165] His series of failures serves as a caution to those (especially clergy) who by their vanity seek to rise above their station in the world.

The *Roman de Fauvel* takes a similar position. As the tale begins, Fauvel is brought out of his stable and into the royal palace where he is given undeserved power. Lady Fortune defies Reason, and allows him to become the master of the house. He is soon attended, served, and flattered by both king and pope, and a host of clergy, friars, nobility, and others, implying that all earthly authority ultimately gives in to corruption and sin. The English phrase "to curry favor" derives from the original "to curry Fauvel," which describes how the powerful bow low to attend to the animal. The pope even grooms him, proclaiming (with the agreement of the cardinals) what a beautiful beast he is![166]

Just prior to this, the motet *Jure quod in opera* references the rumor that Emperor Henry VII was murdered by his Dominican confessor, via poison in his communion wine. There is a stern warning to beware of false prophets, and wolves dressed in sheep's clothing, the reference from Matthew 7:15 that had by then become a standard antifraternal statement.[167]

Examples such as this, the poem states, prove that the natural order is reversed and humanity is now ruled and deceived by an animal and by bestial qualities.[168] Fauvel, of course, desires ever more power, and to hold on to the good luck that he has attained. The Church has given over its power (derived from God) to him, a horrible state of affairs. The conductus[169] *Floret fex favellea* proclaims that Fauvel's dregs flourish, and the world changes. The Papal Curia has become like iron, and now Fauvel is exalted. The poor are held in contempt, and the masses now adore an animal. Crime abounds, faith has been buried, and truth has fled.[170]

The friars are given special attention, and a conductus, *Vehemens indignacio*, is devoted to their deceptions. Stating that a "savage indignation" disturbs the narrator, the text condemns the friars with all of the vehemence of the writings of Guillaume de Saint-Amour and Rutebeuf. The friars do not practice what they preach; they come like lambs, but are wolves in disguise. Because of their failings, the laws of the Church are dying. They want the attention of the wealthy, and seek out large tables so that many will celebrate them. They want to secure favor from the courts and the pope, and when a Church official is dying, they try to make one of their own his successor. Finally, they wear simple clothing to appear humble, which disguises their true ambitions.[171]

Returning to the poem, it then notes that Francis and Dominic founded worthy and humble orders, but now they are infested by the evil of Fauvel. The friars bring back young women who they consort with[172]; they are not truly religious, being instead devoted to this world. To leave the world for the religious life, and then return to the world is like a dog returning to its vomit, another reference to the actions of fools in Proverbs.[173] The friars appear to be poor, but have wealth. They renounce everything, but then want everything. They are a "disorderly" order, whom Fauvel has granted the right to have possessions.[174]

Other orders, such as the Templars, are heretics and have also been consumed by sin,[175] but at least they have been punished for it.[176] The courts are no better, or for that matter are any of the other non-religious classes. All have fallen and the world must surely be near its end. False Seeming and Disloyalty rule over the world.[177] Book one ends here.

Fauvel is drunk with power now. In his splendid if false court, he is attended by his various courtiers, vices including Vanity, Deceit, Perjury, Envy, Sloth, and dozens more.[178] He seeks to wed Lady Fortune, so that he will always control his fate; she has granted him much, but he worries that she may take it away at any time, as is her way.[179] The courtiers approve of this impossible idea, and so they journey to Macrocosm, where she resides, so that Fauvel can make his case and ask for her hand in marriage.[180]

A lengthy section follows wherein Fortune talks of herself and her purpose. She is accompanied by Lady Vainglory, who draws the attention of those who have achieved great heights, in order that they do not notice they are about to fall.[181] Fauvel expresses his love for Fortune in a series of songs, but she rejects him; the two spar back and forth for some time. No one can control fate for long, however, and she finally rebuffs him, foretelling his own downfall. However, she does offer instead to let him marry Vainglory, as a kind of consolation.[182]

He happily agrees, and a conductus, *Gaudet Falvellus nimium*, proclaims that he celebrates too much, believing he has Fortune's favor. Now, foul and corrupt, he will be married to Vainglory.[183] He and his entourage return to Paris, where he prepares a lavish wedding, attended by all of the vices and their disreputable followers.[184] Fauvel throws a grand banquet with much food and music, to be followed by a tournament the next day, a contest between the vices and the virtues. That night, the activities of their unholy marriage bed are accompanied by loud celebrations from noisy and obnoxious street musicians below their chamber, singing obscene little songs.[185] This street music, or *charivari*, has a long tradition in France and other countries, often associated with loud noises (such as the banging of pots) at the homes of newlyweds. One of the *sotte chanson* refrains is a nonsensical lyric mentioning Hellequin, whom we encountered in Adam de la Halle's *Jeu de la feuillée*.[186]

The next day, the tournament begins.[187] All of the combatants are splendidly arrayed, but the virtues are welcomed at their pavilion by the archangel Gabriel, a sure sign of divine support; he offers them heavenly bread and wine, which fills them completely.[188] The tournament progresses, and one by one, the virtues overcome the vices.[189] Fauvel is dejected, and he and Vainglory leave the field to retreat to the palace.[190] Amid the celebrations, Lady Fortune again predicts his fall, saying that he is damned, but not for some time, and not until he has done much harm to the land.[191]

Fauvel and Vainglory go on to sire many little Fauvels, who will run rampant through "the garden of sweet France."[192] To make matters worse, Heresy offers to bathe Fauvel and his progeny in the fountain of youth.[193] Ultimately, Fauvel's immediate fate is to bring more evil and spread sin throughout the land, though his reign will end eventually. The work concludes with the hope that corruption may yet be overcome, addressing Lady Fortune, then the Virgin Mary, and finally praying to God for deliverance. Until then, however, the author announces that it is time for a drink of wine![194]

This remarkable work is very complex, and its astonishing weaving of verse, music, and artwork is unique. The structure of the fr. 146 manuscript, and the layout of the pages seems to be in parody of a standard medieval format of a central text with glosses and annotations on the sides, by reversing this and frequently having the main text to the sides, reinforcing the idea of the world turned on its head and the natural order reversed.[195] Given the strong anti–Marigny nature of the text, some have concluded that the manuscript may have been produced with the approval and perhaps the sponsorship of Charles de Valois.[196] Some of his enemies may well have been targets for the *Roman's* satire.[197] Certainly there are also themes of both instruction and warning to the young King Philip V (who ascended to the throne in January 1317, after his older brother, Louis X died, as did Louis' newborn son) to beware of the many dangers that plagued his father's reign, including ambitious advisers and treacherous clergy,[198] as well as his brother's weaknesses and ineptness in his short reign.[199] The ascension of Philip V may have been the catalyst for the whole work.

The *Roman de Fauvel* draws on existing literary works, referencing its great predecessor, the *Roman de la Rose*.[200] An important passage describes how Hypocrisy is at Fauvel's court. She appears humble on the outside, but inwardly is very clever, hiding great pride. She may appear religious, or as a woman of the world. She may be a Franciscan or a Dominican, a master or a servant. She prays in front of people but has a "little fox" in her heart (with its obvious Reynardian reference).[201] Seated with her is, significantly, False Seeming. However, the author does not wish to discuss them further, for nothing good is in them. He recommends instead that those who wish to know more go and read the *Roman de la Rose*.[202] It is notable that the story of Fauvel shares this key character, even if only briefly, and invites the reader to learn more from the earlier work.[203] The fact that Hypocrisy is also present and that she may show herself so falsely to the world, especially in the habit of a Franciscan or Dominican would seem to be significant as well, evoking the imagery in the monologues of False Seeming. Keven Brownlee has noted how Fauvel and False Seeming are portrayed in similar ways (using very similar language), both as deceivers and robbers.[204]

Criticisms are both overt and subtle. For example, Roesner has shown that the motet *Favellandi vicium*, a work which decries "fauvelling" and greed, has as its musical basis an earlier work in which the Franciscans are praised. Given the close association between the Friars Minor and the Capetian kings, this may be a subtle swipe at that relationship. Indeed, he notes that, "One might draw an ironic comparison between the renunciation of wealth (along with other ties to the material life) pursued by the friars, and the 'fex avaricie' of *Favellandi vicium*."[205] In a later motet, *In nova fert*, a Reynard-like fox (representing Marigny) deceives and blinds the lion (the king), ravaging the kingdom.[206]

The artwork in the manuscript is also remarkable; there are 77 illuminations of great detail and originality.[207] They may have been created by a Parisian artist named Geoffroy de Saint-Léger, and represent both original motifs and borrowed ones from existing iconography.[208] Depictions of Fauvel himself are of interest, for they put at the center of the story the technique of human/animal hybridization more commonly found in the margins of medieval manuscripts.[209] Fauvel is portrayed in a variety of forms: all animal, animal headed and human bodied, and human headed with an animal body. He is only portrayed as entirely an animal in the first illustration of him; thereafter, he assumes one of his hybrid forms. The metamorphosis into something other than his original state is, of course, a commentary on the upended order of things, of how it is wrong to aspire to be something that one is not (Marigny, for example). Further, as Michael Camile notes, "if human beings and animals can change shapes, then the definition of man as 'made in God's image' is thrown into confusion, and with it the whole hierarchy of creation."[210] Seeking to be something other than what was ordained by God is sinful and is the cause of the great upheaval and distress of the times. When men, particularly the clergy, behave like animals, they become monsters and undermine the whole of creation.[211]

Fauvel's changing appearance can be said to represent his two-faced nature, bestial when lording it over others, falsely human when trying to woo or flatter. The depictions are not only mandated by the text, however, as Camille shows.[212] Nevertheless, the human-headed but animal-bodied Fauvel frequently appears in his courtship of Fortune. Such human-faced images were most commonly associated with sexual themes, the handsome young man's face concealing bestial urges behind it, a topic most often found in marginal imagery, but here made central to stress Fauvel's dark intentions.[213] Fauvel is not unlike medieval representations of the serpent tempting Eve, who is shown with a woman's head but a snake body, hiding its deception behind its human face.[214] However, Fauvel is a beast pretending to be a man.

Such human-animal hybrids were, of course, commonly used in satirical writings, and there are a number of images of friars presented as foxes or wolves in medieval marginalia. Camille notes a good example in a missal from Amiens of 1323, which shows in the margins of one folio a Franciscan fox and a Dominican wolf (Reynard and Ysengrin, respectively) worshipping a kingly lion, who represents Pride. Such images "are denunciations of the self-importance of the new orders but more specifically are attacks on the wealth and prestige they had attained by the end of the thirteenth century."[215]

Reception of the poem was mixed, and there were attempts to ban it for its unflattering portrayal of the corrupting nature of power. However, the text version survives in several copies.[216] The illuminated manuscript presents an interesting question: despite being a superb collection of poetry and music, it is not certain if the work was even intended for performance, certainly not beyond a small audience of king and courtiers. If it were performed, it would take several evenings to play out as a complete whole. It is doubtful that this exquisite masterpiece was ever seen or heard beyond such a group of the powerful, though it enjoys frequent revivals in modern early music performances and recordings.[217]

As the 14th century progressed, with all of the ills it would bring, France found itself frequently rivaled in the literary sphere by its northern neighbor, England. The two countries were inextricably linked, of course, but though French had been the language of the English courts since 1066, the English language was beginning to flower and come into its own. The next chapter surveys the works of Chaucer, Langland, and Gower, and we find that the friars were very much a topic of interest to them, just like their French counterparts. What they had to say about the fraternal orders was not at all flattering.

7

England: The Turbulent 14th-Century, and the Writings of Chaucer, Langland and Gower

England was to present its own unique forms of mendicant criticism, though as we will see in this chapter and the next, they also revived many of the same themes and accusations that had arisen at the University of Paris. Was there a continuous tradition of antifraternal polemic that could be traced back in an unbroken line from 14th-century England to 13th-century France, as Szittya proposes?[1] Or, as Geltner has argued, were these episodes less related, with the later writings more often being examples of independent, even spontaneous attacks?[2] Both positions have merit.

Certainly, the antifraternal sections of English poetic works of the later 14th century had their roots in the religious writings of FitzRalph and Wycliff (who we will examine in detail in chapter 8). Poorly written polemical poetry often accompanied various conflicts with friars, but out of these events, as we saw in France, some masterpieces also arose. And so it was in England, where the second half of the century was quite different than the first (nearly all such surviving poetry in English dates from after 1360),[3] and the age-old fears of the end of the world assumed a frightening new reality after a series of unimaginable disasters.

History might have taken a very different path if not for the major calamity of the 14th century: the Black Death, which ravaged Europe. The appalling loss of life (at least one third of the population, and possibly more) turned society upside down, encouraged extreme penitential movements such as the Flagellants to become even more prominent, resulted in new persecutions of Jews (who were accused of poisoning waters to cause the pestilence) and other minorities, and called into question the very offices that held the world together, namely Church and State. England was no exception to this upheaval. Interestingly, the religious orders of all kinds were more susceptible to the appalling fate of the plague's victims, given their communal lifestyles. The friars, who some even tried to blame for the pestilence,[4] saw larger losses than monastic communities, with as much as 60 percent of their number felled. This was perhaps due to their urban dwellings, as well as their wanderings, which brought them into contact with the lay world in a way that cloistered monks did not experience. Other writers, such as the Benedictine John of Reading, blamed the friars for trying to appropriate (i.e., "steal") the goods of plague victims, since their wealth seemed to mysteriously increase in the aftermath of the calamity.[5] Indeed, a group of Augustinian friars in Winchester simply moved, without permission, into another dwelling in the city center (presumably deserted and better), abandoning their older convent and its graves.[6]

Curiously, one of the lingering charges that would be brought against English friars by religious and secular writers was that they were proliferating at an alarming rate. This had been a common complaint in France in the 13th century, but it is not borne out by statistics about the friars' expansion in the following century. After the plague, the losses sustained by the orders could not possibly have contributed to this accusation, yet it is prominent in the works of such writers as Langland and Gower. Szittya proposes that the charge refers less to an actual growth of numbers (though all orders did recover somewhat in the decades following the calamity), and more to a symbolic growth in false prophets as the world neared its end, a theme that could be traced back to Guillaume de Saint-Amour. This multiplicity is also opposed to unity, one of the chief principles of God,[7] thus "proving" the opposition of the friars to the divine order.

The great writers in English: Chaucer, Gower, and Langland, would not seem to have had the same devotion to antifraternal sentiment as Rutebeuf might have, or even Jean de Meun, though we will examine one controversial theory about Langland below, that he was himself a friar, which, if true, would give him a deeply vested interest in the mendicant problem. The reason that these poets expressed such strong antifraternal sentiments in some of their writings may relate less to personal feelings about the issues, and more to that ever-present sense of decay and the ending of the world, particularly after the plague.[8] This chapter will examine specific writings of all three, as well as a few other relevant poems.

This brings us to the concept of "estates satire," widely employed when discussing these writings, but perhaps not always understood or used accurately. With antecedents in the 12th and 13th centuries, it found a greater flowering in England in the 14th, where concern about the order of all things was great, especially in the aftermath of the plague. Broadly defined, there were seen to be three estates which made up the whole of medieval society in a traditional feudal system: The First Estate was the Church, the representative of God on earth, headed by the pope and administered by the various ranks of cardinals, priest, monks, and other clergy. They were those who prayed. The Second Estate was the nobility, those to whom was entrusted temporal power. Inclusive of the knights, they were those who fought. The Third Estate was essentially all others (peasants and laborers), whose duty it was to provide food and support for those who prayed and fought.

This concept had been given articulation in England by the Anglo-Saxon monk Ælfric of Eynsham (*ca.* 955–1010/20), a prolific writer in Old English. He notes in his *Qui sunt Oratores, Laboratores, Bellatores*, that "there are three orders set in unity— these are labourers, beadsmen, soldiers. *Labourers* are they who obtain with soil our subsistence; *Beadsmen* are they who intercede with God for us; *Soldiers* are they who protect our towns, and defend our soil against an invading army."[9] The idea goes back even earlier, to King Alfred, who noted in his translation of Boethius' *Consolation of Philosophy* that in order for a king to reign properly, he must have "prayer-men," "army-men," and "workmen."[10] That such an order relies on certain stereotypical views of each class is obvious, and this helps reinforce the satirical content of many writings that refer to it.

The satire then, was a critical examination of these estates and their failure to live up to their duties, as ordained by God. Gower's work in particular offers very strong indictments of all classes and professions in the estates, religious and earthly. *Piers Plowman's* "field of folk" shows all of the members of the estates, between heaven and hell, wandering about. Chaucer's "General Prologue" to the *Canterbury Tales* has been seen as an example of such satire, but his portraits of the Canterbury pilgrims are much more ambiguous and subtle than Gower's clear-cut condemnations. Indeed, his details of these pilgrims can be seen as a description of a tradition breaking down, and an illustration of the conflict between old and new.[11] We will examine his vague portrait of his Friar below.

Obviously, after the plague, traditional societal structures and functions began to shift and change. The decimation of the peasant population contributed to these changes, as those who survived found themselves and their labor in a much more valuable position. Fewer farmers meant that those who were left could begin to charge more for their services, and demand better treatment. This fracturing of the traditional social structure was one of the causes of the Peasants' Revolt in 1381 (we will examine Gower's response to this later in the chapter), which was predicated on a demand for the end to serfdom. New classes, such as merchants and non-religious clerks (Chaucer could be said to belong to both), also appeared in greater numbers, no longer conforming to the typical estate model.

Such changes also saw the beginning of a true middle class, with its possibility of upward mobility, and so threatened to upend the entire feudal system. Indeed, Chaucer's own granddaughter Alice was eventually made Duchess of Suffolk, and became deeply involved in the complex royal politics of England in the 15th century. This came about through her marriage to William de la Pole, Earl of Suffolk (which was actually her third marriage after the deaths of her previous noble husbands), a testimony to the ability of those of lower standing to achieve higher status, which would have been unthinkable in previous centuries.[12]

Chaucer, Langland, and Gower, among others, were writing at exactly the time that all of these momentous events were happening: the Black Death and recurrence of plague in subsequent decades (less forceful than the initial outbreak, but still terrifying and devastating), the Hundred Years' War between England and France, the Western Schism, and the Peasants' Revolt. There can be little wonder, then, that many believed the world to be in decline and soon to end. Yet at the same time, a great flowering in English arts and literature was taking place, not to be equaled again until the Elizabethan era.[13] Their writings are deeply complex and cannot be seen as simply advocating one position or another. Criticisms of the friars are found in all three, but are only one aspect of a much wider literary picture. Writings against the friars certainly carried on (or perhaps revived) the older literary traditions of critique, satire, and condemnation.

Mockery of various classes of religious figures was already known in vernacular

English writings. The poem "The Simonie," from Edward III's reign, is a condemnation of that practice and of the comfortable lives of Church representatives. Indeed, it boldly states that there is no easier profession than that of the monks, canons, and friars, who live lives of luxury and gluttony.[14] The work then turns its attention specifically to the four orders of friars. It charges that they would preach more for a bushel of wheat than to save a soul from hell, and that greed reigns. They will prefer to grant penance to the rich who offer them gifts, rather than to the poor who have none to give. If a powerful man dies, they will fight for his body, to bury it in their grounds.[15] The work deals with the estates and seems to have been popular; Chaucer may have known of it.[16] Two other English poems from after 1382 (and possibly Lollard in origin)[17] offer similar hostile attitudes, one concluding that for a mere six pennies, a friar will absolve a sinner of slaying his father and mocking his mother.[18]

Geoffrey Chaucer

Well known and widely loved, the writings of Chaucer stand as a crucial landmark in the development of the English language. Many would consider him the father of English literature, and countless generations have been entertained, amused, and captivated by his works, most notably *The Canterbury Tales*. By writing in English, rather than the preferred languages of Latin or French, he elevated the English language to a new status, and gave it a courtly and artistic legitimacy that it had not previously possessed.[19] Though he was acclaimed in his own lifetime, we know less about his early and late life than perhaps we should. However, given his prominence as a writer and government bureaucrat and diplomat, there are hundreds of documents that mention him.

The dates of his birth and death are uncertain, though they were possibly 1343 to October 25, 1400. The location of his birth is not known, though it was likely in London. His name most likely derives from the French *chausseur*, or "shoemaker,"[20] but his family included vintners (both his father and grandfather) who had roots in Ipswich in the mercantile profession. Through his family connections, he was brought into service to the Countess of Ulster (wife of the Duke of Clarence), and from there became a part of the courtly circle where he would remain for the rest of his life. During the 1360s and 70s while in service to King Edward III, he seems to have traveled widely, to Flanders, France, Spain, and Italy. He may have met the great French chronicler Jean Froissart, who was almost an exact contemporary, as well as other esteemed poets of his time, such as Petrarch, Boccaccio, and the French composer Guillaume de Machaut. In 1374, he received the job of Comptroller of the Customs for the port of London. By the early 1380s, he seems to have relocated to Kent, and there, perhaps naturally, began work on the *Canterbury Tales*. Among his many positions over the next two decades were serving as a member of Parliament for Kent from 1386, the clerk of the king's works in 1389 (an overseer of royal building projects), and the Deputy Forester in the royal forest of North Petherton in Somerset. Remarkably, he still found time to write, though the *Canterbury Tales* are incomplete, and scholars believe that the collection represents only a portion of the number he originally intended. By 1399, Richard II had been overthrown by Henry Bolingbroke (who crowned himself Henry IV).[21] After this event, Chaucer disappeared quickly from the records. He may have died suddenly on October 25, 1400. The engraving on his tomb states this, though it was placed there more than 100 years after his death, so it is far from certain. We do not know the cause of his death, if it did occur then.[22] Recent speculation that he was murdered by Henry IV's loyalists is intriguing, but unproven.[23]

These, then are some very basic biographical details of what seems to have been a remarkable life. Given Chaucer's literacy, highly important positions, courtly connections, and obvious education, it is interesting that he used antifraternal themes in his poetry, most notably in the "Summoner's Tale" from the *Canterbury Tales*, a ribald fabliau-like piece which makes a complete mockery of the friar in it.[24] What can be the reasons for this? In his treatment of other clergy in the tales (the Parson, for example), he is more inclined to depict at least some of them favorably.[25] This being the case, as Williams notes, "why is he apparently so hard on the way of life founded by Francis and Dominic, which gave the world Thomas Aquinas, Bonaventure, and Roger Bacon?... Surely, at the least, Chaucer could have given us a friar no farther from Francis or Dominic than the Monk is from Benedict or Bernard."[26]

This was influenced by a number of factors, including the courtly milieu in which he was immersed, which was attended much more by the secular clergy than the mendicant variety. There was also a greater sense of antifraternal feeling "in the air" in England at that time, owing to the polemic of the clergyman Richard FitzRalph (who we will examine in detail in chapter 8), who had resurrected some of Guillaume de Saint-Amour's attacks.[27] So, Chaucer may have been going with the fashion of the era, or he may genuinely have viewed the friars as degraded and corrupt orders, which had fallen far away from their founders' intentions. Ackroyd notes an apocryphal tale from a 16th-century English biographer, Thomas Speght (who published an edition of Chaucer's works in 1598) that as a young man, Chaucer was once "fined two shillings for beating a Franciscane Fryer."[28] This account was included as part of an assertion that Chaucer studied law, a debated, even doubtful, theory. However, such student lapses were common, as we have seen from the Paris examples, and the fine would have been appropriate for such a crime.[29] Was this incident true, and does it give some insight into Chaucer's later criticism and mockery of friars in the *Canterbury Tales*? Or is this merely wishful thinking on the part of an Elizabethan scholar, who wished to show that "our ancient and learned English poet" was not only a trained lawyer (thus "explaining" his literary genius), but also a kind of proto–Protestant reformer? We can only speculate.

Geltner argues that Chaucer's antifraternalism is overstated, as it has been for False Seeming's confession. There is ambiguity in his presentation of the friars, and his attack is on hypocrisy in general, not the friars as a singled-out group. Only those friars who have fallen are the targets of his satire.[30] Given the loathsome nature of the Summoner, his tale against his rival, the friar, can hardly be seen to have much validity, as their stories simply attack one another; they are two sides of the same, corrupt, hypocritical coin.

The *Canterbury Tales* is justifiably considered one of the great masterpieces of English literature, illuminating a cross-section of English society that gives us fascinating glimpses into the culture of the time. As noted, the work itself is unfortunately incomplete, at only 24 tales; Chaucer likely intended for there to be more in the collection, perhaps in imitation of the 100 stories in Boccaccio's *Decameron*. The scholarship devoted to the *Canterbury Tales* is vast and overwhelming to anyone approaching the work for the first time. Here, we will look only at the character of the Friar in the Prologue, and the depiction of friars in the "Summoner's Tale."[31]

The Prologue introduces the setup for the whole work, of how each pilgrim will tell stories to help pass the time on a pilgrimage to Canterbury from Southwark Cathedral in London in the springtime; the stories are presented as a contest for who can tell the best tale, and the winner will be awarded a free meal at the Tabard Inn in Southwark when they return. Using this simple plan, Chaucer launches into descriptions of the travelers who are making the pilgrimage, a hodge-podge of the high and low of society, the virtuous and the repulsive, the comic and the serious.

The Friar in the Prologue is named Hubert, and Chaucer devotes 63 lines to his description, a detailed account of his qualities. Perhaps surprisingly, the depiction is not overtly negative, but rather seems deliberately vague. It certainly alludes to the usual stock of charges leveled against the friars, but mostly stops short of outright condemnation. One explanation for this is that in view of the large-scale corruption and decay that was seen to be tearing at society, how could the friars be expected to behave any differently than others who were corrupted? They did indeed indulge in many sins, but so did the other inhabitants of the three estates.[32]

Mann further points out that satire is a complex subject that "practices both selection and distortion, and that its relationship with 'historical reality' is therefore impossible to define with exactness."[33] Further, satire essentially creates its own life and ways of looking at things, which are independent of reality and exist in their own framework. So, we must consider Chaucer's description of the Friar in light of this observation.[34]

Chaucer gives a decent amount of attention to his Friar, describing him variously as both wanton and merry, and that none in the four orders (of friars) is equal to either his gossip or his fair language.[35] He is gifted in all of the usual mendicant offerings, including sweet speech, which of course, was a common fraternal stereotype, going back to Jean de Meun: the ability to speak with charm and thus influence others, for good or ill. This Friar associates with the best in society, but he also has fine musical skills[36] (recalling Francis' assertion that the Franciscans were "minstrels of God"; we will examine this later in the chapter). And yet, he is also deeply acquainted with the taverns and barmaids, more so than the needy or lepers, because there is no real advantage in being associated with such outcasts.[37] Here, we see a more typical antifraternal comment.

If a situation is beneficial or profitable to him, he is filled with courtesy and goodwill, indeed he is the finest of beggars.[38] Certainly his Friar has the qualities of greed and arrogance.[39] And yet, while Chaucer would seem to be condemning, or at the very least sarcastic, he ends by noting his genuine charm, saying that his eyes sparkle like stars on a frosty night when he has sung and harped, this most worthy Friar.[40]

In the "Summoner's Tale," the friar is a kind of "everyman" friar, not affiliated with any one order (various attempts in the past to link him to one particular order or another have been erroneous, or unconvincing at best), but showing the worst in all of them, not unlike False Seeming.[41] He is "a kind of 'stage friar' who sums up everything that is wrong with the mendicant orders from a fourteenth-century English peculiar point of view."[42]

This friar's vices are many—greed, hypocrisy, anger, gluttony, lying—all sins which had been leveled against the mendicants since the time of the university quarrels. The "Summoner's Tale" itself is a witty one, with its scandalous and scatological prologue, and its reliance on farting as the main source of humor.[43] It fits perfectly into the canon of the tales, and has a refreshing earthiness about it reminiscent of the French fabliaux, with which Chaucer was certainly familiar.[44] It is told by the Summoner as a direct retaliation to the "Friar's Tale" which comes before it, a story that ends with a wicked summoner being dragged down to hell by a demon, getting what he deserves for an unrepentant life. These two are placed in opposition to each other, illustrating, as Janette Richardson notes, "each other's moral degeneracy while simultaneously revealing their own defects."[45]

In medieval England, summoners were, as their name implies, those who were employed by the Church to summon people to ecclesiastical courts to hear charges against them, specifically religious crimes. It was an office easily prone to corruption, since summoners could take bribes to make a summons "disappear," or use the threat of a summons to extort money. It was a loathsome occupation, and such shady characters were probably widely feared and resented. Chaucer describes his Summoner as being physically repulsive, covered with sores, and prone to excess drinking. As such, the "Friar's Tale" which precedes this story is an attack on the very practice of summoning; the summoner answers this insult with his own tale.

In the prologue, the Summoner accuses the Friar of lies, and offers his own story in retaliation.[46] A friar is taken to hell by an angel and shown the torments and the damned, but he does not see a single one of his brethren anywhere. He is mystified by this and asks the angel if this is because the friars are possessed of such grace that none of them are in hell? The angel assures him that there are indeed many friars in hell, millions of them. He then takes the friar down to Satan, whom he commands to lift up his very wide tail (broader than a boat sail), and show his ass, to display where the friars are.[47] Satan does so, and in less than a minute, 20,000 friars emerge from his anus, swarming like bees all over hell. Soon, they return to their place, and Satan lowers his tail. The friar emerges from his dream shaking with fright, remembering the devil's ass, which is the heritage of the mendicants.[48]

With this, the tale proper begins. It concerns a certain friar who has come to the region of Holderness in Yorkshire to beg. He arrives at the house of one Thomas, who has in the past donated to him, but is now ill. Thomas' wife tells the friar that her child has recently died, and the friar assures her that he has had a vision of the child entering into heaven. He received this, he says, because friars are poor and humble, and thus closer to God. The friar then tells Thomas that he remains sick because he has not donated enough. When Thomas protests that he has given to many friars, but has not gained anything from it, the friar responds that this is because Thomas should have given all his money to him.

He then launches into a lengthy sermon on anger and its consequences, using several examples, and closing it by asking Thomas for money to help build the friars' new cloister.[49] The whole thing is a mixed jumble, of course, with out-of-context examples, and scriptural misinterpretation. Thomas has had enough, and offers a special gift to the friar, one that he is sitting on, but only on the condition that the friar shares it with his brothers. The friar agrees and proceeds to put his hand down

Thomas' back, greedily groping for his gift. At that point, Thomas lets out a loud fart, the likes of which even a horse pulling a cart could not have made.[50]

The friar becomes angry (of course, having just preached against it), and threatens revenge, but Thomas' servants chase him out. The friar is furious at the deception, and goes to the local lord to complain, asking how he could possibly divide a fart among twelve brethren. The lord's squire, Jankyn, has a clever suggestion: take a 12-spoked cartwheel, and have each of the other friars put his nose at the end of one spoke, around the wheel. Then the friar would sit in the middle and fart, and the spokes of the wheel would carry the smell to each of them.[51] The lord and lady deem this an excellent solution; Jankyn wins new clothing, and there ends the tale.

What are we to make of this ridiculous and seemingly juvenile story? On the surface, it seems little more than vulgar entertainment, a story with a fart-joke punch line in retaliation for another ribald story, two characters (the Friar and the Summoner) simply insulting each other's professions. Some early scholars suggested that the poem draws from an earlier fabliau for some of its themes, the 13th-century *Li Dis de le vescie à prestre* ("The Tale of the Priest's Bladder") by Jacques de Baisieux.[52] In this story, a sick priest informs two friars that he has already bequeathed all of his possessions to others, and has nothing to give to them. After much pestering from the increasingly annoyed friars, he agrees to give them something special after all. Delighted, they return with the whole chapter the following day to learn that he will leave them his bladder, which makes them extremely angry. Chaucer may have drawn on this story, though a number of scholars more recently have argued against it, seeing the "Summoner's Tale" as representative of general satiric and parodic themes, which Chaucer employed to craft a similar story.[53] Other tales and biblical motifs are possible influences.[54]

Regardless, the poem is rich with symbolic meaning, and reveals some surprising political and religious commentary. The vulgar yet bizarrely funny prologue has at least one identifiable precedent: a well-known story about how a monk has a vision of heaven, and learns that the Virgin Mary offers a home under her cloak to fellow monks of various orders. This account was first recorded by the Cistercian prior Caesar of Heisterbach, whose works circulated widely in Germany from the 13th century.[55] The prologue has an obvious similarity to this story, and is a satirical inversion of it. The truly holy find eternal bliss under the Virgin's cloak, while the friars instead suffer an eternity of torment in the devil's anus. Caesar's account seems to have found favor with the mendicant Carmelites, whose adoration of the Virgin was well known. Indeed, Carmelite iconography was known for depicting Mary spreading her cloak over a group of worshipping friars, so this prologue scene may well be a wry and perverse reference to that.[56]

The main tale is replete with complex imagery.[57] The friar is clearly hypocritical to an extreme degree, extolling the virtues of his order whole not embodying them in any way. There are many references to biblical scripture, and the friar is held up to ridicule for his foolish exegesis, and glosses.[58] Indeed, the use of glossing could be quite creative, and may relate to one of the great comic scenes. Francis was said to have detested money, likening it to snakes, rocks, dirt, and excrement. For a Franciscan to even touch money was to commit great offense.[59] Less than scrupulous friars devised a way around this prohibition by glossing the Franciscan Rule to indicate that they could handle money with sticks, thus not actually touching it.[60] Such obviously deceptive practices were condemned not only by antifraternal clerics, but also by the Spiritual Franciscans.[61] Chaucer's friar happily indulges in the sin of collecting money, however, going from house to house, "penetrating" them, and greedily seeking what he can get. After suffering the friar's inane sermon, Thomas offers him his special "gift," one that he must divide among his brethren. This gift is, of course, his fart. The friar even asks him at one point, "what is a ferthyng worth parted in twelve?"[62] with the obvious pun on "farthing" and "farting" and a hint of Jankyn's suggestion on how to divide the fart.

When the greedy mendicant places his hands into Thomas' bedclothes, he receives his nasty surprise. Indeed, since Francis himself compared money to excrement, does the friar not receive exactly what he should?[63] Further, since the friar himself is full of hot air (as evidenced by his long-winded sermon), it is only appropriate that he should receive the same. In contradiction to his own sermon about resisting anger, he flies into a rage, also ignoring Francis' own counsel about forbearance and enduring insults and humiliation, and immediately goes to the nobleman in a sulk. As much as anything, he cannot conceive of how to divide his "gift," proof again that he is more concerned with the letter than the spirit of his order's Rule.

Jankyn offers an amusing solution to his dilemma, but one with deeper meanings. The fart on the wheel is a comic reverse representation of Pentecost, a theory which was first proposed in the 1960s and has been the subject of much research and supporting evidence since.[64] Essentially, the act of a fart being spread equally among the brethren around a wheel is a satire on the image of the descent of the Holy Spirit to the disciples at Pentecost. This seemingly ridiculous comparison is supported by several facts. Looking at Acts 2:2, we see that the sound from heaven comes to the house of the disciples like a great wind blowing.[65] Further, Szittya notes that St. Augustine made use of an Old Latin version, which describes the sound "as if a violent flatus[66] was being produced." Even if Chaucer did not know the Augustinian usage directly (and it is certainly possible that he could have), the goliards definitely did, and their work, as we have seen, circulated widely.[67] The notion that the Holy Spirit appeared with a sound like a giant fart would have been too good to ignore for any comic writer. Thus the friars, who claimed to be upholding the true apostolic tradition, deserve to receive not the Holy Spirit, but only a loud and smelly fart. Various other aspects of the poem foreshadow the Pentecostal joke: references to the Old Testament, images of fire (both in Thomas' home and in the "fire" of anger), and the confounding of the friar's speech (as a reversal of the speaking in tongues), among many others.[68]

The Pentecostal theme may have derived from the Franciscan practice of holding their general chapter approximately every third year during the Feast of Pentecost.[69] While the friar of the tale is not Franciscan, this is one of several references, including the declaration that his brother friars own books that they will be forced to sell[70] (devotion to books was a quality most often associated with the Dominicans), plus the Carmelite satirical inversion in the prologue, that help to reinforce the notion that the friar symbolizes mendicants as a whole. The cartwheel itself may also evoke the Arthurian round table in parody, since the knights, according to a 13th-century account, met at Pentecost.[71] Curiously, Francis referred to his own friars as "knights of the round table,"[72] and this may be a further connection. Finlayson argues the tale is outright blasphemous, and the use of Pentecostal satire may call into question ecclesiastical authority, safely behind the mask of a foolish friar.[73]

The notion of Antichrist bringing down a false Pentecost existed in medieval thought, and was certainly used by the Oxford theologian John Wyclif[74] (who we will discuss in detail in the next chapter), well-known for his condemnation of the friars late in his life. Chaucer was likely familiar with his work, and would have known to him by sight, if not in person. Further, he was friends with certain knights at court who were Lollards, followers of Wyclif.[75] All of these factors show that the "Summoner's Tale" is far more than a simple ribald poem, but rather, one that raises some of the very same issues as the *Roman de la Rose* and other works before it.[76]

Chaucer was deeply influenced by the *Roman de la Rose*, as we have seen, translating at least a portion of it into Middle English.[77] Some have argued that other than the works of Ovid, the *Roman* was his greatest influence.[78] His *Legend of Good Women* begins with a dream vision in its prologue, complete with a meeting between a Lover and the God of Love, and dream visions are similarly found in various forms in his other works.[79] Scholars have noted the many similarities between False Seeming's boastful words and the "Pardoner's Prologue" from the *Canterbury Tales*,[80] in which the Pardoner lauds himself and admits to engaging in deceitful behaviors, showing letters of commendation, and adding Latin words in to make his sermons sound holy.[81] He is also a peddler of fake relics and false cures.[82] He only preaches for the money, and does not care about saving souls, which often happens.[83] He gets his revenge by spitting out venom under the guise of being holy.[84] The Pardoner is clearly a loathsome and hypocritical individual who delights in his corruption, as well as in good drink. The similarities to False Seeming are remarkable; Fansler notes that Chaucer puts translations of False Seeming's words into the mouths of both the Pardoner and the Friar.[85] The behaviors of both of these unpleasant characters point to what were obviously some widely-held views about Church corruption at the time. Corruption and sin feature prominently in *Piers Plowman*, and we now turn our attention to this enigmatic work.

William Langland

Unlike Chaucer, Langland presents us with a great mystery. Very little is actually known about his life, and much of what is speculated about him is drawn from his great work, *Piers Plowman*.[86] Indeed, while scholars have long assumed that Langland is the author of this Middle English masterpiece, that assumption is based on manuscripts identifying one Willielmi de Langlond, or Wilhelmus W. There is a reference in one version of the work that seems a pun on his name: "'I have lyved in londe,' quod I, 'my name is Longe Wille.'"[87] Thus "Wille Longelonde," could refer to the writer. Not all scholars are convinced of his identity, however, if indeed, there was a man by that name.[88] The question of authorship is difficult, because the work is a dream poem, and as such, how much is the narrator's voice and how much is allegorical is debatable. Hussey suggests that we take at least some of the limited autobiographical information at face value, since the idea of a fully fictional narrator is not one generally found in the literature of the time.[89] Scase doubts this, arguing that the supposed biographical revelations are in fact more typical of a "false confession" tradition.[90] In any case, the poem specifically states at its end that the author wakes, and begins to write about what he has just been dreaming.[91]

If we assume some truth to the autobiographical snippets, Langland was probably born about 1332, somewhere in the West Midlands, near Malvern, or perhaps closer to Wales,[92] for the dialect of the work seems to be from North-West Gloucestershire.[93] He may have died around 1386.[94] Little is known for certain of his life in between. At some point he seems to have gone to London, and settled in Cornhill, not the best of areas. He may have taken minor orders and been married to a woman named Kitte; they had a daughter named Calote.[95] His duties there included being a clerk who said masses for the dead.[96] If any of this is true, then we have some outline for his life, but only the barest of biographical sketches. None of it can be definitively proven, however.[97]

Piers Plowman itself is a strange work, difficult, dense, and even confusing for the modern reader. It does not have the ready accessibility of the *Canterbury Tales*, and is not easy to excerpt from, unlike those Tales which, though part of a larger narrative, stand on their own. This is perhaps one reason for its lack of familiarity, except among students and scholars of medieval English. It is a lengthy dream vision, like the *Roman de la Rose*, which puts it into that otherworldly, allegorical state, where fantastical imagery resides, and many truths can be learned. Unlike the *Roman*, the narrator wakes more than once, ponders the meanings of what he has witnessed, has waking visions, and then falls asleep again to continue his dream. It is written in alliterative verse, rather than rhyming couplets.[98]

The poem is further complicated by existing in four versions, labeled as A, B, C, and Z, respectively. Each version is different from the other, and the uncertainty surrounding the authorship of the poems is even more pronounced because of this. A is the shortest and earliest (prologue and 12 *passus*, or divisions), probably dating from after 1362. It is incomplete and breaks off at an inconclusive point in the story. Version B is considerably longer (and is the most often used and studied today, with a prologue and 20 *passus*), dated to before 1380. It is a revision of A, with much new material. Version C appears to be a revision of B (prologue and 22 *passus*),[99] dating from about 1388. The so-called "Z version" is controversial, and scholars are divided about whether it constitutes a unique version at all, containing a prologue, but only 8 *passus*. It may represent an early draft, but this is not certain.[100]

A blend of allegory and social commentary, as well as satire and a strong antifraternal theme, the story concerns the dream narrator's quest for a true and perfect Christian life. It is strongly critical of the fallen world, and this includes quite a few critiques of the friars and religious corruption. Throughout the work, as in the *Roman de la Rose*, there are many asides and discourses with allegorical figures.[101] It offers a kind of history of Christianity, frequently referencing the Old and New Testaments, and laments the sorry state of the world, which has failed to live up to the standards of a godly society. The corruption of religious institutions is much to blame for this, as are the wealthy among the laity, to whom the Church has failed to teach proper charity; thus they ignore the plight of the poor and suffering.

What follows is a brief summary of the B version: it begins in the Malvern Hills (near Herefordshire and Worcestershire). The narrator, named Will, falls asleep on a May morning near a brook, and has a dream. In it, he sees both a tower of Truth on a hill, and a dungeon of Wrong in a deep valley, representations of heaven and hell. In between these is a "fair field of folk," comprised of all manner of people: rich and poor, working and not, beggars and tramps, pilgrims on journeys, religious and laity, friars of all the orders, minstrels and fools... representing humankind, and how they are poised between the two great destinations. The poem offers many satirical descriptions of various inhabitants of the field.

Will ponders how one can live in the world, with all of its inherent corruption and sinfulness, and make a living, while still attaining salvation. Aided and guided by various allegorical figures, he desires to know the answers. He encounters the figure of Conscience, who convinces others to turn away from the Seven Deadly Sins and seek Saint Truth. Soon they meet a humble plowman named Piers (Peter), who offers himself as a guide on the narrator's quest. He says that he knows the way because of his clean life and common sense, and if they will help him plow his half-acre of land, he will assist them. His humility leads the narrator to suspect that he is in fact Christ (and this theme is explored near the end of the work, in the 19th *passus*). Piers is said to represent the notion of men working for their own relief in a world filled with sin. Eventually, Will awakens.

When Will sleeps again and re-enters his dream, Piers is gone. He continues his quest, looking for the figures of Dowel (Do-Well), Dobet (Do-Better), and Dobest (Do-Best),[102] but eventually he wakes again, and this time wanders the world for many years, pondering what he has seen, before being able to re-enter the dream world. At one point near the end of the poem, and during another time when he is awake, he has a vision of Christ arriving at Jerusalem on an ass, likening him to a knight whose destiny is to joust with Death in Piers' helmet and armor (representing human nature). Thereafter, he sees the passion, descent to hell, and resurrection before once again sleeping and dreaming. He finally beholds Piers, bloody and carrying a cross, who is identified with Christ. The poem ends on a dark theme, the coming of Antichrist, identified as happening in the poet's own time. The religious (especially the friars and other hypocrites) now follow Antichrist, and even in this age, line their pockets with gold. Holy Church is assaulted by Pride, aided by the friars' neglect and greed. The figure of Conscience goes to seek Piers, who might at last destroy Pride, and change the way that the mendicants behave. There is no guarantee of success, and the Church may fall. Reminiscent of the *Roman de Fauvel*, the poem ends on that uncertain note, with sin ravaging the world.

There is a great sympathy throughout the work for the commoner and laborer, who are frequently the victims of the interests of money and power. With that theme in mind, the poem is filled with antifraternal satire and commentary, employing all of the familiar charges against them: greed, hypocrisy, deceit, jealousy of other clergy, desire for power, the abuse of begging, etc. They appear more frequently than any other type of ecclesiastical characters, including both in the dreams and when the narrator is awake, and appear at key points in the poem, including the dramatic ending. With the exception of Francis and Dominic, there are no good friars to be found in the work.[103] Indeed the friar *Penetrans Domos* is clearly derived from the depictions of Guillaume de Saint-Amour and his partisans, and fits the apocalyptic themes of the poem.[104] These friars are ultimately symbolic, being set among the medieval ideas of eschatology and the fulfillment of history. Chaucer's friar is not a servant of

Antichrist, Langland's friars are. They are not the comically satirical representations of Chaucer, but have a place in salvation history, recalling the apocalypticism of earlier antifraternal works.

From the prologue, we read that the friars in the field are from all four orders, preaching for their own profit and to gain lavish clothing. They peddle charity for themselves and claim miracles, and mischief increases.[105] The poem links the friars with other suspect groups, such as beggars, wanderers (both worldly and spiritual), and importantly, minstrels. Beggars seek to avoid honest work, and minstrels seek to twist words and pervert the God-given gift of speech.[106] Minstrels occupied a curious place in medieval history, at once revered by the nobility and retained for their many entertainment skills, but also reviled by the Church, whose clergy denounced them in sermons. Edward III, still king when the first version of *Piers Plowman* was presumably written (he died in 1377), was very fond of minstrels, and kept a large retinue in his employ.[107]

Minstrels and friars are similar in many ways, the poem warns. Both they (along with the spicers) have met with and entertained the figure of Liar.[108] Indeed, both invent fictions in the hope of enticing the rich to invite them to feasts and give them gifts. Men should not, the poem warns, act as fiddlers and friars do, and attempt to enter other people's houses for these purposes, while neglecting their own homes.[109] Minstrels are opposed to the true speech of God, their speech instead being associated with vagabonds in taverns, and a fiddle that is out of tune.[110] "True" minstrels, or "Goddes glemen," are those that use their gift for the glory of God, not their own profit. Indeed, the poem frequently refers to minstrels in unflattering terms.[111] They bring only sorrow and enticement to sin ultimately, and lords would be better to have real beggars before them, the genuinely needy who are the true minstrels of God.[112] These will make a man truly laugh, and give him comfort when he is dying, whereas professional minstrels will lead him to Lucifer's feast, with foul speech, a lay of sorrow, and Lucifer's fiddle.[113]

So why is this connection so important to the narrator? One explanation of the association goes back to the tradition that Francis called his friars the *ioculatores Domini*, the "jongleurs" or the "minstrels of the Lord." The friars of the poem, however, are not these minstrels of God, but rather the low and corrupt *ioculatores*, nothing but tellers of tawdry tales, looking for a good meal and personal gain.[114] The poem contains the usual list of charges against the friars and their sinful behaviors.

However, Lawrence Clopper convincingly argues in his detailed study, *Songes of Rechelesnesse: Langland and the Franciscans*, that the position of the poem is not antifraternal at all, at least not in the sense of Wycliff or FitzRalph. Clopper asks a valid question: "Why did William Langland make his Wanderer an itinerant beggar at the same time that he singled out the mendicant orders as the most immoral of the clergy?"[115] Indeed, in the amended C text, there is a beginning scene in *Passus* V where Will is confronted by Conscience and Reason, who demand to know if he contributes any productive labor, given his admitted love of drinking and sleeping. He protests that he is too weak to work with farm tools, and too tall to bend down. Reason notes that he seems idle, and asks if he has lands to live off of, or if he begs at doorways or tries to freeload at churches on feast days, again things of which the friars were accused.[116]

The answer Clopper proposes is that Langland was a Franciscan himself and the work is a form of self-criticism of the order to encourage reform; the work has been mistakenly labeled as antifraternal. It is not a version of a lover's dream narrative, but rather the voice of the author, a deeply concerned friar, whose conscience compels him to plead for change.[117] He acknowledges some external criticisms as being entirely valid, while rejecting others.[118] For example, in assessing three main fraternal privileges: the right to preach, the right to bury, and the right to hear confessions, all of these were attacked by external critics, whereas internal criticisms never questioned the right of preaching. Similarly, Langland does not question the friars' right to preach, and in fact even defends the right at certain times without a bishop's authorization. These are not the words of someone seeking to abolish the mendicant orders.[119] Langland makes use of the term "perfect poverty," a phrase used only in Franciscan writings on poverty, particularly in those which predate the rulings of John XXII. From this, it can be inferred that Langland was appealing to an earlier period, perhaps even to the founding or an ideal age such as that of Bonaventure.[120]

There had long been issues of concern about renegades within the fraternal orders making public their writings of criticism about their fellow brothers, with punishments prescribed for doing so.[121] While critical, the poem also presents Franciscan ideas in a positive light,[122] actually illustrating the internal debate among Franciscans, Clopper argues, and the growing desire to see it return to its original intention.[123] Indeed, Will even takes on some mendicant characteristics, which could be suggestive of an association.[124] The poem suggests various connections between Will and the friars, which, if Clopper is correct, may be indicative of the identity of the poet. Like the friars, Will is a wanderer; we are told as much in the opening lines of the poem.[125] Even after he has awakened from the dream world in one instance, he wanders like a mendicant (i.e., a beggar) for some years.[126] Indeed, Clopper notes, "The poem seems to ask: What are the circumstances under which a person can be itinerant without committing sin or an illegal act? Who may justly take the alms of others?"[127] Piers Plowman mostly criticizes "mode, function, and appropriateness"[128] in mendicancy, not the act itself, or the friars' preaching. Subsequent readers of the poem have confused this reforming criticism of the Franciscans' failures with an external attack.

Was it Langland the impoverished cleric, the proto–Lollard,[129] or rather the determined reforming Franciscan? Was Langland the defender of the poor, or rather the conservative at heart who was horrified by the Peasants' Revolt and still wanted to maintain social order? Was there more than one author? Did Langland exist at all? These questions have conflicting answers as of yet, and will continue to entice readers and scholars for the foreseeable future.

John Gower

Gower was born around the year 1330, probably in Kent, into a wealthy Yorkshire family who held properties there, as well as in Kent, Suffolk, and Norfolk. Little is known of his younger life, but he may have trained in law (though he may not have practiced),[130] and resided in Kent or Suffolk before moving to London. He was obviously wealthy, and his writing talent brought him into the courtly sphere, like Chaucer. He relates in the prologue of the first edition of his *Confessio Amantis* (mid–1380s) how King Richard II once saw him in a boat on the Thames, and proceeded to invite him to his own royal barge, commissioning him to write a new work that Richard himself would read and ponder. This was the origin of his *Confessio*.

He seems never to have taken holy orders (or perhaps only minor ones), and married more than once, though from about 1377, he lived at the priory of St. Mary Overy in Southwark. He gave generously to the priory, and continued to live there for decades; indeed, he is recorded as having married in 1397, at nearly 70 years of age, and to have continued to reside at the priory afterward.

His friendship with Chaucer was well known. Chaucer dedicated his *Troilus and Criseyde* to him, calling him "moral Gower." Gower, in turn included a speech praising Chaucer, given by Venus near the end of his *Confessio Amantis*. When Chaucer went abroad in 1378, Gower was one of the individuals to whom he gave a power of attorney for his affairs in his absence.

Gower is best known for three works: the *Mirour de l'Omme* ("Mirror of Mankind"), the *Vox Clamantis* ("Clamoring Voice"), and the *Confessio Amantis* ("Lover's Confession"), written in French, Latin, and English, respectively, indicative of the multilingual environment of the court. They are linked by common themes of criticism of the three estates and the idea of the world in decline, its end immanent.[131]

One of his earlier works (which survives in a single manuscript), the *Mirour de l'Omme* was later retitled as the *Speculum Meditantis*, probably more closely to match his other major works. Written in the late 1370s, it is a massive allegorical poem of more 28,000 lines (though some leaves of the manuscript are missing, and it may have been over 30,000). Written in French, it is a commentary on virtue, vice, and morality, divided into ten sections. All of the estates come under fire here, for none are free of sin, all are fallen, and all must learn how to return to God via Christ. Beginning with a description of the devil's marriage to the seven daughters of sin, it also views the marriage of reason to the seven virtues, before beginning its condemnation of all levels of society.

Around 1380, Gower began to write the *Vox Clamatis*, which like its predecessor, also deals with sin and corruption. Interestingly it includes commentary on the Peasants' Revolt, and essentially sides with the aristocracy, which brutally suppressed the uprising. This remarkable event occurred in 1381, born out of a protest against unfair taxation and the lingering oppression of serfdom, which had survived the Black Death, but was changing because of the reduced peasant population in the plague's wake. Led by Wat Tyler, the movement achieved some early success when the peasants attacked London, destroying the Savoy Palace (residence of John of Gaunt) and other buildings, and murdering those that they presumed to be associated with the royal government. Richard II initially agreed to the movement's demand for the abolition of serfdom, but later succeeded in killing Tyler, and rescinded all concessions. The revolt ended, but was a dramatic foreshadowing of later revolutionary movements.[132] Gower was no revolutionary, and clearly believed in the established order, even with all of its inherent sinfulness. Yet this work also urges the king not to impose heavy taxes, to rule wisely, and to use justice to eliminate crime. Interestingly, Chaucer makes virtually no mention of the revolt, even though he may well have been able to witness it in part.[133]

By 1386, Gower had begun writing what would be his most acclaimed work, the one that essentially made his reputation as an English writer. The *Confessio Amantis* was written in English, apparently at the request of King Richard II after the barge meeting, who was concerned that not enough was being written in the native language. A very lengthy work at more than 33,000 lines, it was revised at least twice during the 1390s, and draws inspiration from the *Roman de la Rose*, again using the dream vision motif. In it, a lover has a dialogue, first with Venus, and later with her confessor, Genius (a familiar *Roman* character) about all manner of issues surrounding courtly love. During the confession, the Seven Deadly Sins are discussed, and Gower uses many *exempla* from classical and medieval sources. Genius recalls various tales, in a similar manner to the *Canterbury Tales*, to illustrate his points. In the end, the poet lets go of earthly love. The work is a major contribution to the English language of the time, like Chaucer's and Langland's, and one of the stories in it would serve as a source for *Pericles* by Shakespeare, a testimony to its importance.

In looking to Gower for antifraternal sentiments, we find an abundance of attacks and criticisms. When the *Mirour de l'Omme* finally comes to discuss the friars, Gower has much to say, and it is unflattering in the extreme. He notes that in viewing the estate of the friars, he is merely repeating what others are saying; it is common knowledge, perhaps even gossip. The friars, more than any others, are decaying and going bad, despite their claims to be the true inheritors of the discipleship of Christ. Far from this, the author asserts, the friars are mainly concerned with the ways of the world. They do have one thing in common with the original disciples: the first disciples were not "poor"; though they had nothing, they had everything in terms of spiritual riches. The friars likewise have everything, but theirs is a material wealth. They do not share what they have with the poor, but rather hoard it for themselves.[134]

Further on in the poem, he notes that the friars preach their poverty, but always stretch out their hands to receive more wealth. They hide their greed, and thus their order is perverted; its purpose is to deceive and trick. They love their comfortable lives, and have no desire to work, never seeking it out. They are like vagrants and do not do what they are called to do. It is the author's opinion that they look for rewards without earning or deserving them.[135] They travel about in pairs, traversing the country, always seeking to attain more wealth, and combining their efforts to acquire it. They deliberately lie, so that they can flatter and encourage others to sin (and fleece them of money). One of the pair is Friar Hypocrisy, who is the confessor to the author's lady, while the other is Friar Flattery, who is to give her absolution.[136] Indeed, he may even encourage her to sin more, since he can so easily give such absolution.[137] These attacks and accusations continue for more than 500 additional lines in the poem, and are very typical of the types of accusations we have seen so often.[138]

In his *Vox Clamantis*, he devotes a considerable portion of the fourth book to attacking the friars, from chapters 16 to 24.[139] Many of the familiar charges are leveled against them: the friars have grown too great in number; they pretend humility and poverty; they preach against sin publically, but in private they encourage it; they help wives to commit adultery; they seek out only the wealthy; they take on rights that belong to others in the Church, though they are not necessary to the Church; they have deceived the pope; they are not necessary to society, and indeed they live off of it since they refuse to work; they ensnare children into their orders; they hide treachery in their hearts; they are dispersed over the earth like the Jews, but live in luxurious dwellings that even kings do not have; they neglect their own rules and the intentions of their founders... the list goes on to the point of tedium. Nothing here is new, but the amount of space devoted to it, even in such a long work, is striking. Despite these harsh sentiments, Gower was in no way advocating for the abolition of the established Church, and perhaps surprisingly, he does not call for the total suppression of the mendicant orders, only that they be tightly controlled and disciplined.[140]

He remained a faithful Catholic to the end of his life. Indeed, he had nothing but scorn for John Wycliff and the Lollards, just as he had for Wat Tyler and the rebellious peasants. He clearly states in the Prologue to the *Confessio Amantis*, for example, that it is a terrible thing for Christians to abandon unity and become torn apart by dissent (likely a reference to the ongoing papal schism of the time between Rome and Avignon).[141] Envy has caused Wycliff to utter his heresies, Gower charges, and the Lollards who came after him are schismatic. It is better for men to plow their fields (perhaps a reference to *Piers Plowman*) and have faith through revelation than to know the scriptures by heart like clerics, presumably a reference to the Lollard wish for the Bible to be translated into English and made available to all.[142]

Gower expressed strong opinions about the various religious controversies shaking society in his time, which not only saw lay arguments come to prominence, but also continuing inter–Church factional divides. England had long had its own issues of sectarian religious conflict. Criticism of the friars from monks or clergy, while drawing on French models, was to assume its own unique identity in the 14th century. The result was very nearly a proto–Protestant movement, a century and a half before the Reformation came to England.

English Religious Criticism: Matthew Paris, Oxford University, Richard FitzRalph and John Wyclif

Antifraternal attitudes among members of the Church hierarchy in England were varied and numerous. Quite often, they resulted from the same concerns that were present in France: suspicions of the friars as entities outside of the traditional Church structure, fears of their secret motives and possible connections to Antichrist, jealousy of their popularity and intellectual skills, and annoyance at their infringing on pastoral activities traditionally only accorded to priests and bishops. In this chapter, we will examine some of these issues through the writings of regular and secular clergy, noting how such concerns became more intense after the middle of the 14th century.[1] Antifraternal English writers generally levelled five charges against the friars: that their numbers were excessive, that they were hypocrites, that they violated and abused their vow of poverty, that they infringed on the rights of the secular clergy, and that they vigorously defended themselves but attacked other religious orders and groups.[2]

Matthew Paris

Matthew Paris was a unique figure in 13th-century English monastic circles. A Benedictine monk at the abbey of St. Alban's north of London, he was a chronicler and unusually, a gifted illuminator of his own works, as well as having great skills in cartography.[3] Born around 1200 and probably dead by 1259,[4] he was mostly likely English, despite his name. Speculations that he may have studied at the University of Paris are just that, and definitive biographical material is sparse, largely coming from his own writings. He produced a number of important works, including the *Chronica Majora*, the *Historia Anglorum*, and the *Flores Historiarum*, as well as lives of Edward the Confessor and St. Alban.[5] The *Chronica Majora* is a history of the world from the biblical creation to Matthew's own day, the *Historia Anglorum* is, as the name implies, an English history, while the *Flores Historiarum* is a shorter tome that draws on the writings of an older monk, Roger of Wendover (*d.* 1236). Matthew worked continually on these, amassing an enormous amount of historical and contemporary information, which at times seems random and inconsistent, with a number of dubious accounts.[6]

He was notoriously outspoken, particularly in the *Chronica Majora*, criticizing the pope and the Roman Curia, England's political failings, and the friars, among other subjects. Indeed, so terse were his words that he felt obliged to edit out some of the more offensive passages toward the end of his life; this may have been done out of fear of causing offense (especially to the king),[7] or perhaps it was regret from an older man who wanted to earn his salvation and felt that his judgmental pronouncements would not put him in good favor with his creator. Thankfully, his edit was not thorough, and we have many of the entertainingly harsh passages left intact in what is known as the C version of the manuscript. These give important insights into his personality.[8] We will examine some of his criticisms below.

Though he was primarily focused on writing and illustrating, he once made a remarkable journey to Norway.[9] For the most part, however, he seems to have been content with his monastic life at St. Alban's, though this was not always the secluded life that one might expect. The political and religious affairs of England and Europe interested him greatly, and he was always questioning the abbey's many visitors about events happening in the larger world.[10] St. Alban's was regularly in contact with greater England. Situated only a day's journey north of London on a major route to the North, it was frequently visited by those in power, including King Henry III on nine recorded occasions between 1220 and 1259.[11] The number of notable individuals with whom Matthew met and conversed is remarkable, and include Henry III and his wife Queen Eleanor, various earls (among them Richard, Earl of Cornwall, Henry III's brother), Bishop Robert Grosseteste of Lincoln, and those from much farther away, such as King Haakon IV of Norway, and Bishop Waleran of Beirut.[12] Indeed, Matthew viewed such prestigious individuals as the best sources when compiling his own writings. As Weiler notes, "his definition of what was reliable and trustworthy also tells us something about his concept of truth, about what he deemed newsworthy, and about the social dimension of truth. In very basic terms, the more high-ranking the informant, the more reliable was the information he had to offer. Wherever possible, Matthew thus sought to link his information to people of great status."[13]

Matthew's work on the events of his own time is of great interest to medievalists, and to this study. A conservative Benedictine monk with a great sense of English national pride, he developed very strong opinions about those institutions and individuals that he felt were failing the Church and the English government, including both a succession of popes and Henry III, as well as the friars. As a monk of St. Albans, he sided with other organizations similar to his own against unwanted intrusions. He was "against any attempt at interference with the privileged social existence of the monks of his own day."[14] His portion of the *Chronica Majora* (it extended after his death) is never short of colorful descriptions and criticisms. It covers a huge range of topics from events all over Europe, reflecting his wide-ranging interest in the affairs of the time, though the work was principally meant to be a chronicle of England. He was certainly not an objective reporter of news in any modern sense. Indeed, he had his own agendas, and often retold events in the way he believed that they should have occurred.

Matthew also tended to put his critiques into the mouths of others, a useful means of avoiding some controversy and conflict by passing the blame on to another and taking on the role of a mere reporter.[15] In a speech he records as given by Robert Grosseteste in 1253, for example, he has the bishop state that if the pope and friars do not do enough to combat heresy, they are equally guilty and would suffer "eternal death" unless they stopped condoning sin.[16] In the pursuit of heresy, however, the friars could be equally sinful. He denounces the Dominican Robert le Bougre (to whom the trouvère king, Thibaut IV had given his support, as we have seen) for his abuses as an inquisitor. Matthew notes that he condemned and executed many innocent and simple people and so was punished with perpetual imprisonment.[17]

The pope and Papal Curia came under considerable criticism.[18] He writes on several occasions that Pope Innocent IV was at least in purgatory for his sins[19]; a series of storms and floods in 1250, he asserts, were due to God's anger at the sinful Curia.[20] Matthew was especially critical of papal methods of raising money for crusading efforts and other such ventures. Indeed, when the king or pope taxed the poor, it greatly aroused his anger; he considered such actions to be extortion.[21] When both the Franciscans and Dominicans were employed in these efforts, he vented against them, noting how far their orders had fallen from the ideals of Dominic and Francis. Pope Gregory IX made use of the friars to preach, promote, and collect money for his proposed crusade of 1234–35, to which Matthew caustically commented that the friars were caught up in pomp and showy signs of piousness, and were received lavishly in towns and abbeys. They were supposed to be humble orders, but clearly these brethren enjoyed the celebrity and ceremony that came with their task. He charged that they would absolve those who took crusading vows if such would-be pilgrims paid them enough money.[22]

In another account from 1247, he decries two deceitful English Franciscans, Alexander and John, who are sent by the pope to wander England to extort money (his exact word) from the wealthy. Concealing their greed like wolves in sheep's clothing (once again that comparison appears), they sought out permission from the Henry III with not only papal bulls, but innocent looks and speech, in order to deceive him. Once he had granted his permission for their work, they took to the road dressed in lavish fashion, more like knights than monks, including boots with spurs and colored hose, to the disgrace of their order. They proceeded to go to various prelates, demanding money on pain of dreadful punishment. Both the Bishop of Lincoln and the abbot of St. Alban's refused their outlandish demands, and they went away with threatening language on their tongues.[23] Matthew records that the pope also attempted the same actions in France, but the French king refused and the friars went away "empty-handed amid universal sneers and derision,"[24] more a commentary on Matthew's personal feelings than an accurate retelling of events. Louis, as we have seen, was very devoted to the fraternal orders.

Matthew's dislike of the friars probably came from his strong sense of allegiance to the Benedictine order, which he felt was the true inheritor of monastic tradition, carrying it directly from St. Benedict. These new friars were upsetting the old established ways with their presumptuous innovations.[25] He even accused some of them of forcing their way into existing monasteries to set up their own altars,[26] and considering themselves superior to monks, looking down on them.[27] He notes in an entry dated to 1246 that the Dominicans began as humble preachers, but now, less than

30 years after their appearance, they seek power and veneration by the prelates of the Church. They want to be not only preachers, but also confessors, usurping what is not theirs to claim; even worse, they have the support of Pope Gregory IX.[28] They live in extravagant luxury, he says in a 1243 entry, in their costly and sumptuous buildings.[29] The Dominicans have been successful in having the pope grant them the privilege that their members not be allowed to transfer to other orders, even though they receive deserters themselves. This runs contrary to the Rule, he argues, as well as the golden rule of not doing unto others what one would not want done to oneself. As we have seen, Benedict himself had condemned the idea of a wandering monk. Matthew claims that this new privilege was obtained because many who had joined the Dominicans were having second thoughts. They had not found what they wanted spiritually, and regretting their choice, they desired to leave[30]; the Dominican order had to take action to prevent that, or they would have lost many members.

The Franciscans have also taken on actions which are offensive and inappropriate, he says. For example, they were appointed by the pope to sell the belongings of those that die intestate, and take that money for the Church. Matthew is happy to report that this odious papal decree has been revoked. That the Franciscans agreed to it at all was scandalous and shameful to their order.[31] He does allow that the greedy pope made many of the friars his tax collectors against their will, which nevertheless damaged their respective orders' reputations.[32]

He notes with some sarcasm that both orders have become the counsellors of kings, and have made those royal residences so much their homes that said houses are now clothed in the low attire of the friars.[33] In the case of Louis IX, this was quite true. Further, since the friars did not seek hierarchical advancement in the Church, they had achieved these royal positions because such rulers saw them, rightly or wrongly, as having no ambitions.[34]

He reiterates this in the closing to the year 1250, wherein he notes a half-century of important events. He describes how new orders have sprung up everywhere: Franciscans, Dominicans, Carmelites, Cruciferi, and Beguines, all of whom initially embraced poverty and holiness, devoting themselves to study and preaching. However, within a few years, pride had crept back in, and some now lived in lavish houses, collected taxes, and extorted money for the papacy (even if unwillingly).[35]

The *Chronica* did not circulate widely; indeed, outside of St. Alban's, it was mostly unknown[36] and thus cannot be said to have had an influence on later antifraternal writings. However, it does give us a fascinating insight into the mind of a prominent Benedictine writer, the most important chronicler of his time. The fact that he was willing to record such sentiments, even in the privacy of his abbey for the personal use of the other monks, shows that there was probably a discomfort in some monastic circles with the rapid rise of the mendicant orders and their newly-granted privileges.[37] Matthew did gain fame in the decades after his death by his contributions to the *Flores Historiarum*, which was updated and continued by others into the 14th century.[38]

In the decades after Matthew's life, there were other instances of monastic/mendicant conflict in England, but they were relatively rare, and it is possible, as Szittya notes, that the two institutions "maintained an uneasy peace."[39] There were also examples of cooperation and goodwill between them, particularly in study and learning.[40] Given that the Inquisition was not established in England, the friars there did not assume the villainous role as its enforcers and the inevitable negative reactions to it that certainly would have arisen. There were some striking examples of antifraternal rumor-mongering, however, such the chronicler Thomas Walsingham (like Matthew, a monk at St. Alban's, *d.* 1422) recording how King Edward III's mistress, Alice Perrers, was in league with a Dominican friar, who pretended to be a physician, but was secretly a sorcerer practicing black magic. Walsingham noted that this friar's magic had allowed Alice to become the king's mistress, and his potions, spells, and wax effigies allowed her to obtain whatever she wished from Edward. The friar was eventually arrested and handed over to his order for punishment.[41] Such accusations were fed in part by a feeling that the friars had endeared themselves too well to the royals, and were unduly influencing them.[42]

English resistance to the friars' presence more often flared up in less esoteric forms, notably at the University of Oxford, where, though not as dramatic, apocalyptic, and vitriolic as in Paris, by the 1320s there were certainly a handful of antifraternal tracts circulating among the secular masters and other clergy. The friars had come to Oxford early on in their existence, the Dominicans in 1221, and the Franciscans in 1224. The Dominicans were single-minded in establishing themselves in the city (having arrived from France), and had declined offers of houses from both Canterbury and London, opting instead for the university town.[43] They were eager at this early stage to recruit from the best minds in the country. The first Franciscans were, by contrast, native Englishmen, and initially they stayed with the Dominicans, though they quickly obtained their own house.[44]

Further expansion for both came in 1229 with two events. The first was the dispersal at Paris, which led to not only certain seculars leaving the city, but friars, as well. In both cases, some of the dispersed were English, and decided to return to their own country, rather than stay in a turbulent foreign city. A number of friars journeyed to Oxford and were incorporated into the houses there. The second event was the arrival of Jordan of Saxony, who came to preach and to ignite interest in the Dominican order, though his presence had the effect to drawing new recruits to both orders.[45]

The Franciscans attracted the interest and teaching skills of Robert Grosseteste (*ca.* 1175–1253), first chancellor of the university (though not named as such) and later Bishop of Lincoln, which greatly enhanced their status at the university. He was elected to his bishopric in 1235, and so was drawn away from Oxford, but he maintained an active support for the Franciscans, and friendships with prominent Dominicans, notwithstanding the occasional conflict as reported by Matthew Paris. Grosseteste (literally "big head," though how he acquired this amusing name is not known) is regarded as one of the great scholars and thinkers of the 13th century, a scholastic philosopher with a keen interest in the world. He was skeptical of the new Aristotelian ideas, but made use of scientific methods in their infancy and authored a number of treatises on such subjects as astronomy, light, mathematics, and tidal movements.[46] Roger Bacon noted his indebtedness to Grosseteste's work, and praised him for his efforts in promoting learning in mathematics, languages, and the sciences. Grosseteste was generally supportive of the Franciscans and their commitment to poverty, holding that such a state was similar to that before the fall of humanity,[47] though as we have seen in Matthew Paris' account, he was not above criticizing them for extravagance unsuited to their impoverished ideal.

Oxford seems an unlikely place for a university of international stature to have appeared, unlike Paris. Originally created as an Anglo-Saxon fortification against invading Danish forces, it was also a located at a suitable place on the Thames for crossing animals ("oxen-ford"). Evidence exists for Roman and Iron Age settlements in the area.[48] Unlike London, Oxford was geographically well-situated between many urban centers, including London, Bristol, Cambridge, Worcester, and Warwick, among others.[49] It was already a center of learning by 1200, but had been home to teachers and students for a long time before.[50]

By 1214, it had a charter, granted by Innocent III, outlining various rights and privileges for the masters.[51] The university chancellorship was inaugurated at about this time, and grew with the university, a situation quite different from that in Paris. There was less interference by the Bishop of Lincoln (under whose authority the university rested) for control over the university, in contrast to ecclesiastical meddling in Paris. As such, the secular masters from the start had greater autonomy; they chose their own chancellor, rather than having him imposed on them. As Leff notes, "Whereas after 1231 the chancellor of Paris had little of his original powers beyond conferring the license, at Oxford he combined these original powers with those of the Paris rector and chief magistrate of the city."[52] Inevitably, such power would lead to "town-gown" clashes as in Paris, though given the unique situation at Oxford, complaints were nearly always resolved in the university's favor, much to the chagrin and resentment of the townspeople and officials. Indeed, such tensions and conflicts would characterize the relations between the university and the town until the later 14th century. It was the king of England, not the pope, who judged conflicts, and the monarchy was well disposed toward the university and its scholars. Again, Leff notes, "Compared with Paris the influence of pope and church upon events in Oxford was nonexistent. Indeed, except for the initial charter of liberties of 1214 and their confirmation by Innocent IV in 1254, what official contact there was with the pope came mainly through the initiative of the kings."[53] Town officials were routinely humiliated and subjected to unfair decisions and favoritism that sparked violence.[54]

The friars were destined for their own conflicts with the university over similar issues to those in Paris, namely the controversy over whether a friar had to be a graduate of the arts before being accepted to study for the license in theology. They felt that they should be exempt from this requirement, given their own conditions on what subject matters they could study (the liberal arts contained "profane" subjects not suitable for a friar).[55] Further, they had their own *studia*, which they claimed were equal in educational value, and should be acceptable in lieu of the university requirements. The secular masters argued that no one should be exempt. In 1253, the Franciscan Thomas of York sought to be admitted as a master of theology, though he had not undertaken the study of the arts. Ultimately, he was allowed to do so (no doubt over some fierce objections) with the proviso that it not be permitted in the future. This was not strictly followed, however, and friars continued to be admitted without meeting the requirement, though it gave the university the power to decide just who would be accepted.[56] In 1256, Thomas wrote *Manus quae contra omnipotentem tenditur*, defending the Franciscans against charges by Guillaume de Saint-Amour and others.[57]

Conflicts also arose between the Oxford Franciscans and Dominicans in the

1260s. By this time, there was a rivalry, since both were trying to recruit and admit the best and brightest students to their orders. Apparently, there was so much attempted "poaching" going on (both trying to steal members away from each other), that Pope Clement IV intervened to put a stop to it, though not entirely successfully (interestingly, a short Latin poem by a Glastonbury monk written some decades later and with an Oxford setting, describes Francis and Dominic as the two thieves flanking Christ at the crucifixion).[58]

In response, the Dominicans at the university began to charge the Franciscans with many of the abuses that others were already doing, namely betraying the wishes of their founder and effectively lying to prospective recruits and students. With the poverty controversy still circulating, they stepped up their attack in 1269. Evans notes that the Dominicans accused the Franciscans of hypocrisy, claiming that "they were as disputatious and greedy as anyone else. Solomon of Ingham went so far as to say that the Franciscans were destined for hell because they broke their vows by owning property."[59]

Despite the controversy of such a statement, the head of the Dominican order in England, Robert Kilwardby (*ca.* 1215–79, and later Archbishop of Canterbury) refused to punish Solomon or move him away from the university. This entrenched attitude shows how much of a rift already existed between the two orders. After being elected to the Canterbury bishopric, he skillfully presided over the transition between kings. Henry III's long reign ended in 1272 with his death, and his son Edward I assumed the throne, but Kilwardby then turned his attention away from political matters and back to the theological. He was stubborn, to be sure. In 1271, he had been asked to review a series of undesirable questions that had been circulating in university circles, questions which raised uncomfortable issues in the opinion of the Church (the freedom to spread unconventional ideas was certainly not a right at the time). In 1277, he responded with a list of 30 propositions, known as the "Oxford Condemnations," which the Arts faculty was forbidden to teach (a similar action had recently occurred at the University of Paris).[60]

Unfortunately for him, some of his bans included certain teachings of Thomas Aquinas, related to the doctrine of unicity of form.[61] As can be imagined, this did not please his superiors, as Evans observes: "The Order had invested much reputational capital in getting him [Aquinas] to provide standard manuals of instruction such as the *Summa Theologiae*. Doubts about some of his arguments among the Oxford Dominicans were not welcome."[62] Thus, at a general chapter meeting in 1278, the Dominican Bishop of Corinth issued a stern rebuke to Kilwardby, and messengers were sent to Oxford with the authority to punish anyone who held to Kilwardby's restrictions.[63]

In the early 14th century, ongoing tensions became more pronounced, though not to the extent that they had in Paris a half century earlier, and friars contributed considerably to scholarship and learning throughout the century,[64] even in the face of new tensions. In 1303, the university began requiring the friars to give their exam sermons (by which they would be accepted into the study of theology) away from their own houses, prompting complaints.[65] This may have been a deliberate act on the part of masters wishing to limit the number of friars undertaking theology degrees, for in 1311, a new statute appeared requiring all who aspired to lecture on the Bible to possess a bachelor of theology degree. This new demand forced all friars to lecture and make commentary on the *Sentences* of Peter Lombard, a standard requirement for secular students.[66] The Dominicans were furious and protested the new ruling. One, Hugh of Sutton, refused to obey the new decree and was expelled. In response, the Dominicans appealed to the Papal Curia, and a kind of settlement was reached and confirmed by the king, though this did not satisfy them. They went further and appealed directly to Pope John XXII, who wrote a response telling the university not to hold to this requirement, and instructed the Curia to enforce his decision. Remarkably, the university ignored him, and got away with it. By 1320, another settlement was reached, but the university did not have to relinquish its statutes to achieve it.[67] The papacy simply did not have the same authoritarian influence in Oxford as it did in Paris.

The 1320s would unfold with more conflicts. As we have seen, Pope John XXII was not especially amenable to Franciscan complaints, and removed the fiction of papal ownership of Franciscan property.[68] Though he did condemn the antifraternal writings Jean de Pouilly (a master at the University of Paris) in 1321,[69] for his position on the friars' privilege of confession, John showed far less sympathy for the Franciscans and their breakaway sect of devotees to absolute poverty, declaring the Spirituals' beliefs to be heretical. These radicals, of course, felt that wealth was antithetical to the meaning and purpose of religious life, and that its holders could thus be deprived of it. John's ruling completely reversed the position of Pope Clement V (suppressor of the Templars), who in his bull of 1312, *Exivi de paradiso*, had attempted a compromise of sorts, commending the rigorousness of the Spirituals, and effectively allowing two forms of devotion to poverty in the order.[70]

Further, John's bull *Quorundum exigit* declared that obedience to the pope was more important than poverty.[71] The conflict came to a boil in 1328, when a group of Franciscans, angered by the pope's treatment, declared him a heretic[72] and fled to the protection of the excommunicated Louis IV of Bavaria (1282–1347), Holy Roman Emperor from that same year. Louis, like so many holy roman emperors, had been in conflict with the pope. In 1328, he made a brazen assault on the papacy, entering Rome and having himself crowned as emperor. Soon after, he declared John XXII deposed and installed a Franciscan Spiritual, Pietro Rainalducci, as an antipope, Nicholas V (his pontificate lasted from 1328 to 1330). Supporters of the revolt had included the scholar Marsilius of Padua, the great English Franciscan philosopher William of Ockham, and the Franciscan minister general Michael of Cesena, quite a distinguished group of thinkers to be so openly in revolt against the Avignon pope.[73] Ultimately, this rebellion failed. Rainalducci eventually submitted at Avignon, was absolved in 1330, and remained there at the papal palace under house arrest until his death in 1333. Ockham and Cesena fled to safety with Louis, and followed him to Munich, still at odds with the Church and excommunicated,[74] though Pope Innocent VI "rehabilitated" both of them in 1359, after their deaths.

English theologians would retain a confrontational attitude in some of their religious outlooks, not only toward the friars but toward the papacy. Though it might be erroneous to consider this an ongoing "antifraternal tradition" in English thought, there is no doubt that the writings of Guillaume de Saint-Amour and others did circulate among secular theologians at Oxford and elsewhere. The controversies of the previous decades, while not of the magnitude of those in Paris, certainly would have made some masters and other clergy predisposed to a disliking for the friars. Indeed, there is ample evidence of this in the form of manuscripts containing writings against the friars, most dating from 1350 onward, but often containing earlier writings, including *De Periculis* itself, or substantial quotations from it.[75] It is difficult to determine if Guillaume's work was unknown in England prior to this, whether there was insufficient interest in such writings, or if the subject matter was too controversial and thus was disseminated more quietly.[76] There also were undoubtedly manuscripts that do not survive. However, by the middle of the century, a keener interest in these older polemics was appearing. In the post–Black Death society, uncertainty reigned, apocalyptic fears were heightened, and scapegoating and blame were on the rise. Antifraternal sentiments may well have increased due to this combination of factors.[77]

In May 1356, secular clerics presented a bill of complaints to a London council. In it, they noted the abuses that the friars repeated regularly, including living lavishly in expensive houses, riding about on horses, ignoring laws, flattering the nobility for favors, and slandering the clergy. They interfered in politics to try to increase their influence and wealth, harming the English Church. The bill further charged that they had abused the powers of confession, absolving penitents too easily, in exchange for generous payments.[78]

Opposition to the friars was not only from clerics. Uthred (or Uhtred) of Boldon (*ca.* 1315/20–1396/7) was a Benedictine monk at Oxford University, who quarreled with the friars over issues of monastic ownership and wealth. In the 1360s, the Dominican William Jordan drew up a list of Uthred's propositions that he believed to be in error. Uthred responded, and a war of words ensued; he accused the friars of being like Cain, the first murderer, for destroying true brotherhood.[79] The association of the friars with Cain was revived by FitzRalph and Wyclif, as we will see below. The Archbishop of Canterbury ultimately intervened in 1368, and silenced both sides, forbidding discussion of certain of the propositions at all.[80]

Sometime after 1350, a certain Jacobus, began work on a massive encyclopedia, *Omne Bonum*, which was to contain "all good things." He may have been an English Cistercian monk, or more probably a clerk of the Exchequer, in service to Edward III.[81] This alphabetic work contained beautiful illuminations as well as marginal notes for the entries. What marks this work as unusual is that a number of its entries are decidedly hostile to the friars, a curious situation in a book about "all good things." In entries such as "Fratres," "Apostoli," and "Ffariseus," there are extended quotes from Guillaume de Saint-Amour, and the negative viewpoints seem to be taken as a given.[82] It contains all of the expected attacks, including: hypocrisy, unrealistic vows of poverty, condemnation of begging, their craving of wealth and position, unfair and undeserved papal privileges, and charges of being false apostles and deceivers.

There are sections by known writers, such as Jean d'Anneux, another French secular master who wrote against Franciscan privileges and the order's rule, and was equally hostile to both the orthodox brothers and the Spiritual heretics. He wanted the pope to withdraw such favors, since they had acted like ungrateful and disobedient children. His work dates from the later 1320s, but found its way into an English book nearly 30 years later, a testimony to its importance at least to some.[83] Likewise, there is a work by Thomas de Wilton, an English scholar who studied at Merton College in Oxford, and later took up a position as a master at the University of Paris, before returning to London in the 1320s. He devotes much of this work to condemning begging by the able-bodied, a clear attack on the friars.[84] Eschatological attacks continued in various ways, such as in the warnings of John Grandisson, Bishop of Exeter, who in 1358–59, wrote to his whole diocese to beware of certain hypocrites, who in this last age, were leading people astray. These individuals were the heralds of Antichrist, he stressed, and included friars who claimed to have a license to preach when they did not. His apocalyptic language was remarkably similar to that of Guillaume de Saint-Amour.[85]

Perhaps the most important writer included in *Omne Bonum*, certainly to the modern medievalist, is Richard FitzRalph, and it is to his writings that we now turn.

Richard FitzRalph

FitzRalph (*ca.* 1299/1300–60) was Archbishop of Armagh in Ireland, an Anglo-Norman from a wealthy family in Dundalk (near the modern border between Northern Ireland and the Republic).[86] Already active at Oxford in the 1320s, he was by the early 1330s the vice-chancellor, probably chosen not for any remarkable original thought, but for his sound beliefs and commitment to teaching, as well as a willingness to undertake bureaucratic responsibilities.[87] He weathered a crisis at the university, the Stamford Schism (a town-gown conflict, as well as disagreements between students from different regions),[88] and made his first journey to papal Avignon in late 1334 (a city which would later be very important in his conflict with the friars). Thereafter, he returned to England, having been appointed as Dean of Lichfield Cathedral in December 17, 1235.[89] He returned again to Avignon in 1337 and remained there until 1344. In 1346, he was appointed to the position of Bishop of Armagh in Ireland, being consecrated in July, 1347.

During this time, he was a prolific preacher, and he recorded his Latin sermons in his so-called "Diary," which gave dates and locations for the delivery of each. He may have intended for them to be gathered together in a collection, though this did not happen in his lifetime. His sermons, like many others, reveal his concerns about abuses of the clergy, but also for matters of law-breaking, violence, fraud and other crimes committed against the Irish (an interesting position to take, given the frequent racism of the Anglo-Norman colonists toward the Irish natives), illegal business transactions, and many other vices. Indeed, nothing seems to have been off-limits. As might be expected, his condemnations of clerical abuses were somewhat muted in his Avignon sermons, but when it came to the friars, he had less desire to self-censor.[90]

What is remarkable about FitzRalph is that until 1350, at least in public, he was a good friend to the fraternal orders, and had cordial relations with many friars, both at Avignon and in England and Ireland. As late as 1349 in Avignon, he was invited to preach at mendicant houses (where he praised St. Francis), and he also noted that he had relatives who had joined the Franciscan order in his home town of Dundalk.[91] However, by July 1350, he appealed in his *Unusquisque* sermon[92] to Pope Clement VI and the Curia to revoke the friars' privileges, thus beginning a decade of hostilities with the friars and polemical writings against them that grew increasingly vitriolic.[93] This particular attack seems to have been in response to a mendicant *propositio* to have the pope to rescind aspects of *Super cathedram*, Pope Boniface VIII's bull from 1300, which as we have seen, set certain restrictions on the friars in relation to other clergy. For various reasons, this seems to have aroused FitzRalph's anger, and prompted his response. He claimed that if anything, the bull was not specific enough in defining the friars' privileges and was too harsh on the other clergy. Importantly, it marks the beginning of what would come to define FitzRalph's position on the friars and mendicancy, namely that they had no place in the Church and were now causing great harm by their very presence.[94]

Historians have puzzled over this seeming sudden change of heart. Katherine Walsh notes that it is remarkable that someone who had what seemed to be genuine friendships with various friars "should suddenly become their most bitter opponent and should devote the last years of his life to a systematic attempt to undermine their privileges, their way of life, even their *raison d'être*."[95] However, a deeper study reveals that relations may not have been as warm as they seemed, and that as early as his time as Dean of Lichfield, he may have been aware of certain mendicant practices that bothered him.[96] In 1349, before his appeal to the pope, he had been asked to be a part of a commission to consider some of the long-standing Franciscan issues (poverty, possessions, and the imitation of Christ, among others).[97] Though they failed to reach definitive conclusions, FitzRalph continued to study the matter, and the result was, in 1356, his *De pauperie Salvatoris*, which considered at great length the issue of holy poverty, and whether mendicancy could truly lay claim to being an authentic *imitatio Christi*. We will examine this work in more detail below.

By the time of FitzRalph's appeal, Europe had just passed through the dreadful scourge of the Black Death. As we saw in chapter 7, the friars and monastic communities were not immune to this, and had suffered heavy losses, due in part to a genuine sense of duty, as many friars compassionately entered plague-stricken areas to minister to the sick and comfort the dying. As a result, there were considerable depletions of numbers in the mendicant houses, leaving important positions that needed to be filled. This inevitably led to a relaxation in the rigorous standards for admission into the orders, to replace the dead quickly. These positions were thus often taken up by those who were too young or unsuitable for such responsibilities, and this may have contributed to a kind of degradation in the quality of friars, whether in their education or personal behaviors.[98] Further, as Walsh points out, there are a conspicuous number of Anglo-Irish critics of the friars from the mid–14th to the mid–15th centuries, suggesting that there were specific ongoing issues about mendicant behavior in Ireland that provoked harsh responses.[99]

Indeed, his earlier reservations seem to become more crystalized after his assumption of the bishopric in Armagh, which was beset with troubles, including strife between natives and colonists, and the opportunities for exploitation that undoubtedly abounded. The friars there may well have been guilty of any number of offenses, taking advantage of their special status to get away with various questionable activities. The secular clergy objected (as they often did) to these privileges and it is possible that the friars resisted and hindered FitzRalph's attempts at reforming a system in need of it. When one group has a "good thing going," it is not usually receptive to changes that undermine that. That other Anglo-Irish clergy voiced similar criticism of the friars may well indicate just how deep the problem was in that Irish diocese.

These were not new objections; they were essentially the same as had been raised in the past, but FitzRalph focused on the Franciscans for their special emphasis on poverty and the presumed moral superiority that it gave them. Clopper further observes that in 1357, FitzRalph noted that he had heard a friar preach on poverty, expounding a Spiritual doctrine on poverty and dominion of the type that had been condemned by John XXII.[100] To summarize, FitzRalph was concerned with two particular aspects of the friars, which by now had been debated numerous times. The first was that of the poverty of Christ and its relation to his apostles and subsequent followers. The second was the various privileges granted to the friars, giving them leave to perform tasks normally reserved to priests and bishops, with the addition of immunity from any clerical jurisdiction except the papacy.

As with many antifraternal writers, FitzRalph felt that Francis's teachings regarding poverty and ownership had been misunderstood by his followers, and taken to extremes which the founder never intended. He argued that giving up private property did not include the renunciation of the right to own community property, for example. As for duties, he believed that there were problems with their privileges, including the ability to preach, to hear confessions, and even to bury the laity in their grounds, while being exempt from any oversight.[101] He took exception to the mendicant practice of burying the dead in their own cemeteries, rather than those of the deceased's parish churches, and in two vernacular sermons directed at the laity, stated that such an act led to the damnation of those interred.[102] The reasoning behind this, he argued, was that the friars, with their massive powers in the confessional, had convinced many of the laity to leave generous donations to the convents, and agree to burial in their churchyards, convinced that doing so would offer them a better chance at salvation. Naturally, they sought out the wealthiest among the laity, to increase their chances of receiving generous legacies.[103] The conflict over this was so strong that there are stories of rival churches digging up corpses and stealing and then reburying them, which would be almost comical if not so macabre.

He argued that the friars were simply not a part of the hierarchical structure of the traditional Church, and so had no real right to the privileges that they claimed and sometimes abused. In his *Unusquisque*, for example, he criticizes friars who arrogantly preach in the vicinity of a parish church while the priest is saying mass, a distraction that takes away from the purpose of the mass. The priest will only preach at that time, but friars can preach any time that they wish, an advantage they should not have and that should be abolished.[104] Further, if confession is to be allowed to any of the religious other than priests, it should have been given to the already-existing monastic orders.[105] The only time that friars should be able to hear confession is if it were so granted by a visiting bishop to fill a need, and only on condition that they were subject to that bishop's authority. This, to him, was an adequate compromise.[106] Their desire to be confessors was in direct opposition to the vows of humility and poverty that they took, making even nobility and kings subordinate to them. This was certainly a perversion of the original intentions of the order, though it also probably indicates the very real resentments that the clergy felt in having this right usurped.[107] With this kind of power and the influence that came with it, the friars had the ability to decide just how much penance a particular sinner would have to undertake, and FitzRalph accused them of deliberately offering easier penances to their wealthier flock, the ones more inclined and capable of making generous donations to Franciscan convents.[108] He was careful, however, not to criticize the popes who had granted them privileges, only to say that since the friars had abused these gifts, they should be deprived of them.[109] He was certainly making some sweeping generalizations, but it is obvious that he was passionate about rectifying these perceived abuses.

His *De pauperie Salvatoris* took these arguments and developed them in detail, questioning the entire concept of mendicancy having a basis in the actions of Christ and the apostles. Here, he introduced the notion of dominion founded on grace, a concept that was taken up by John Wyclif (as we will see below), and other reformers such as the Czech priest, Jan Hus. Essentially, this meant that the right to have authority over things, to exercise jurisdiction, and to own property came from God. Only a just Church and its faithful members therefore have a right to rule. Those who fall away from the Church such as heretics, or the unbaptized (which were never a part of it) have no such right, though he stops short of supporting the idea that their property and possessions can be confiscated, even if they have forfeited the right to retain them.[110] Just such a position was useful to the Church in dealing with groups such as the Cathars, or Jews and Muslims.[111]

Ironically, this theory had been expounded by Giles of Rome in his *De ecclesiastica potestate* at the beginning of the 14th century.[112] Giles was the doctor of the Augustinian friars, but his viewpoint was taken up by other theorists, and eventually found its way into FitzRalph's thinking.[113] However, it would be wrong to see his position as a forerunner to the later thoughts of the reformers, even if they adopted it. FitzRalph was essentially a conservative theologian intent on preserving the structure and sanctity of the established hierarchical Church, not a revolutionary bent on its destruction.[114]

De pauperie Salvatoris is divided into eight books that address various aspects of poverty and dominion, though the eighth book may have been written in response to mendicant criticisms of the previous books. The first five provide an extensive discourse on dominion, and the problems of ownership.[115] For example, would private property exist at all if not for the fall of Adam and Eve? Theologians wrestled with such questions, and FitzRalph could not provide definitive answers, though he did assert in Book V, "that before the fall all temporal possessions had been common to all men, and that private property was introduced to the world only as a result of sin."[116] Therefore, those who were Godly and in a state of grace, shared equally in the dominion over all things; the friars could not renounce everything and still claim to be in that state of grace. He wanted to distinguish between *proprietas*, or property ownership, and *dominium*, or lordship. The lordship that humanity has is only on loan from God; it is a right of usage under certain conditions that can be revoked. Having lordship over something does not guarantee the right to use it.[117]

Books VI and VII focus on poverty, and include the idea that no vow of poverty should ever be so extreme that it threatens one's life. Voluntary poverty is entered into according to the circumstances of the situation; indeed, Christ and his apostles most definitely held certain possessions which were more than what they absolutely needed, and did so with the intention of using them in the future. Therefore the renunciation of everything was not in keeping with apostolic practice. Only in certain cases would a vow of extreme poverty be acceptable, and only within the confines of Church approval. It simply would have been irresponsible for the Church to have "no concern for the morrow," when its duties required much careful planning, as well as the necessary wealth and property to enact them.[118] FitzRalph was not making a distinction between Conventual Franciscan practice and that of the Spirituals, though the latter would have been the more obvious target for his argument. Indeed, this treatise is directed at the friars as a whole, even if much of his argument does seem to be slanted toward Franciscan beliefs. The modern reader might well consider this nothing more than a justification for the ecclesiastical hoarding of wealth, while claiming it was for a higher good. James Doyne Dawson has suggested that *De pauperie* was not necessarily equivocating mendicancy with the friars, but rather was opposing the acts which they engaged in, i.e., confession and absolution. As such, he inadvertently sided with the Spirituals, many of whom wanted to be free of these priestly duties. He articulated his attack on mendicancy itself later in his *Defensio curatorum*.[119]

FitzRalph charged that the Franciscans had worn their supposed poverty as a badge of honor, acting as if they were superior to other orders of friars, all the while safe in the knowledge that their property came under the pope's protection, which offered such holdings a security that no one who was involuntarily poor had; the destitute layman could not look to the pope to safeguard his home.[120] Though this was no longer official, since John XXII's abolition of the practice of papal ownership, it was still a point of contention. As a result of so many violations of their privileges (and they were always trying to gain more, or improve the existing ones, he said), and their special exempt status from any kind of regulation outside of that of the pope, the friars (and by this he meant all of them) were a burden to the Church, one that it could no longer afford. He appealed again for the abolition of all mendicant privileges, as well as any for other monastic orders. His demands would have essentially resulted in the disbanding of the orders of friars altogether,[121] a remarkably controversial position that had not had such lengthy and forceful arguments since the writings of Guillaume de Saint-Amour, even if he did not adopt the same apocalyptic reasoning.

Essentially, since dominion required grace, the friars were not like the apostles, but rather like Adam and Eve. By their sinful actions, the friars' work was no longer valid, and they had lost their grace. Therefore, all of their activities were invalid and illegal, particularly the hearing of confession and preaching. They could not give absolution and their sermons meant nothing.[122] Preaching without a license could eventually lead to charges of heresy, though FitzRalph did not pursue this.

Of course, the friars took immediate exception to his positions, especially after he aired them publically in four sermons in London over the winter of 1356–57, while he was there on diocesan business. He delivered them in English, but the surviving versions were written down in Latin.[123] These sermons featured an even harder line than *De pauperie Salvatoris* had, possibly because he was still clarifying his position at the time of writing his treatise.[124] Sermon I talks of the poverty of Christ, but stresses that he never would have begged, for voluntary begging would have been contrary to his dominion. In Sermon II, he continues this theme, noting that no scripture records Christ ever begging voluntarily. If the Franciscans truly wish to emulate Christ, it cannot be by a vow of a lifetime of willful begging. Sermon III addresses issues concerning the friars directly, stressing that parish priests and bishops, by virtue of being a part of the hierarchical Church, have superiority over the friars for the same duties.[125]

At this point, the friars responded as a group. Representatives of each of the four orders met and drew up a list of twenty supposed errors in FitzRalph's sermons, in London and elsewhere, and the Augustinian Friar John of Arderne delivered it to the residence where FitzRalph was staying. He was either not at home, or in no mood to confront an angry Augustinian friar, so John left a copy, after publically reading out their response.[126]

FitzRalph shot back with a fourth sermon, accusing the friars of "seducing with empty words"[127] and responding to each of the charges. It is an angry sermon that touches on apocalyptic themes. As Szittya notes, "This is the most intemperate outburst of FitzRalph's career, and it shows that he could, if he would, come at the friars from the same point of the compass as William of St. Amor."[128]

The conflict was now escalating and the next battleground would be Avignon. In response to FitzRalph's sermons, the friars had appealed to the pope. FitzRalph shot back with his *Defensio curatorum* to respond officially to the friars' charges of errors. He delivered this to the pope in November, 1357, and it was destined to become his most widely-read theological work at the time.[129] He claimed that he had only been drawn into this particular conflict recently, and by accident, based on the events in London[130] (though, as we have seen, the events in Ireland had predisposed him toward an increasingly negative view of fraternal activities). He put forth a petition that the friars' charges against him be dropped, and that they be stripped of their position, asking a commission of cardinals to hear his complaint, rather than a Curial court. He produced a *Libellus* in 1357, in which he made 33 charges of his own against the mendicant orders; as if in an attempt to outdo this, the friar's own *Libellus* contained 64 charges against him.[131] He accused them of abusing their privileges, though was careful not to name names or give specific instances. One odd persistent charge from the *Defensio* was that friars were buying up all available books so that none were left for his students.[132] The friars countered that he was too vague in his accusations (implying perhaps that he could not prove them), but was slandering them and conducting a campaign of propaganda against them. FitzRalph's lawyer responded that he was talking about all of Christendom (implying that these abuses were that widespread), and that it would be tedious to catalog them all.[133] This was quite a slap in the face to the friars, but they did not back off, and the war of words continued. FitzRalph produced two more works in his ongoing campaign, *Objectiones et responsiones*, which reveal its contents in its title, and *De audientia confessionem*.[134]

It would be fascinating to know how this conflict would have resolved (though a victory for FitzRalph would have been less likely),[135] but fate intervened. FitzRalph died in November 1360, and less than a year later, so did Roger Conway, one of his chief Franciscan opponents, as well as two of the adjudicating cardinals. As a result, the whole thing dissipated, probably to the great relief of the pope. No decision was ever made one way or the other, and the Church was able to dodge the issue for a while longer.

FitzRalph's legacy was to be remembered as an opponent of the friars, one of the most vocal since the days of the Paris quarrels, and yet this issue only preoccupied him for the last decade of his life, particularly from 1356 to 1360. His unwavering position was that the friars endangered the Church, and were an illegal addition to it that needed to be corrected, possibly even abolished.[136] He and Wyclif are often grouped together because of their antifraternal sentiments. In fact, their approaches to the friars and the role of the Church were very different, as we will see. It is to the life and writings of John Wyclif that we now turn.

John Wyclif

Wyclif (*ca.* 1331–84) stands as the most important figure in the English religious controversies of the 14th century. Hailed by the 16th-century reformers in England as a proto–Protestant, his works were condemned, damned, praised, and ultimately had tremendous influence on the political and religious upheavals of the next three centuries. The exact year of his birth is not known; it may have been any time between 1320 and 1330, or perhaps slightly later.[137] Born in Yorkshire, his family was not especially notable, but seemed to be improving their status in the world, an increasingly common occurrence among the growing middle class. By the early 1350s, he was at Oxford, and would have witnessed one of the more dramatic town-gown disputes, the St. Scholastica's Day riot, in February 1355.

As we have seen, Oxford had a long and ugly history of these kinds of conflicts, but this one was particularly violent. It began with an argument between students and the innkeeper at the Swyndlestock tavern about the poor quality of wine,[138] which turned into a brawl and escalated into a town-wide conflict that lasted for three days. Though this sounds like something from a modern comedy sketch, it became very violent and bloody. Indeed, gangs of supporters for both sides met in the High Street and battled. Certain friars attempted to put a stop to the fighting, but were also viciously attacked. Some of the townspeople went further and sacked various academic halls, looting and burning them, and killing students and masters.

The furious university authorities appealed directly to the king and the Bishop of Lincoln. The king happened to be nearby and sent judges to hear the cases of both sides. Predictably, they ruled in favor of the university, and the mayor, among others, was imprisoned. To make things worse, the bishop placed the town under excommunication (but not, we presume, the university) for a year, and thereafter, the mayor and various townspeople were forced to pay for a yearly mass to be said for the souls of those who had died in the riot. All of this led to new rights being granted to the university, on top of the ones they already held, making the defeat and humiliation of the town that much more pronounced.[139] For the townspeople, their hatred of both the secular clerics and the friars only increased.

Thus, Wyclif had entered a dynamic academic world, one that was not as peaceful as we tend to think such institutions are today. Oxford's university was clearly important to the king and bishop in the larger scheme of things, so much so that they were prepared to do almost anything to keep it there, no matter what conflicts arose. Such a place would prove to be a fertile ground for Wyclif's volatile ideas. He was a fellow of Merton in 1356 (indicating that he had taken his bachelor's degree), and Master of Balliol College by 1361. He was soon serving as a parish priest in Fillingham in Lincolnshire, and then at Ludgershall in Buckinghamshire, eventually returning to Oxford.[140]

An incident occurred in 1367 that may be significant in the development of his views about religious orders and the Church. In 1361, Simon Islip, the Archbishop of

Canterbury, had attempted a new experiment in student living. He founded Canterbury Hall as a community where monks from Canterbury and secular students would live together, an idea that seems ill-advised based on all that we have seen so far, though was clearly intended as a way of trying to promote harmony between rival groups. Disagreement started soon after, and by 1365, the archbishop appointed John Wyclif as the new warden of the house. It is not absolutely certain if this was the same John Wyclif, but it seems probable. However, the monks resented the seculars having such a role and protested. By 1367, the new archbishop Simon Langham intervened and removed Wyclif, replacing him with a monk and ejecting Wyclif and his partisans. Eventually, the hall became fully monastic and the experiment failed.[141] If this was the same Wyclif, the episode may have shaped some of his ideas about Church abuses of power and the preferential treatment given to orders of all kinds.

Oxford had been characterized by friars of outstanding intellectual ability, from Roger Bacon to William of Ockham and Duns Scotus, all Franciscans. Wyclif, like FitzRalph, was of the secular clergy, and in his scholastic philosophy he took the side of realism, as opposed to the nominalism of Ockham and others.[142] Briefly, realism held that the fundamental structure of the world exists independently of the mind, in the form of universals, whereas nominalists asserted that only individual things exist, not essences or universals, which are merely abstractions from individual things which we then name as being of this universal sphere. Objects that seem to be familiar are not connected by anything other than the names that we assign to them. Realists would counter that there is indeed an essence which is common to such things, but exists apart from them. Wyclif defended the realist position in his *Summa de Ente*, written between 1365 and 1371. He firmly believed that devotion to nominalism led to heresy, ironic since in his later life, he was accused of heresy, yet remained a devoted realist.[143]

He received his doctorate in theology in 1372, and secured the patronage of John of Gaunt, Duke of Lancaster. John was the third son of Edward III and had tremendous wealth and power, at times acting as ruler of England in all but name. Wyclif's family lived on lands under his lordship, and it is possible that this is how John learned of him.[144] This alliance was to prove crucial during the 1370s, for such protection allowed Wyclif to formulate dangerous ideas in relative safety.

He became further involved in politics when asked to take part in a delegation to Bruges, over a long-standing dispute between the English crown and the papacy. The popes had for some time claimed the right to tax the English clergy for their own purposes, but also to appoint those of whom they approved to prominent positions. In order to attain these positions, the candidates had to pay the papacy a fee for the right, as much as a whole year's worth of income. The English kings, preferring to be able to tax the clergy for their own uses, were not happy with this practice. In 1371, Wyclif attended a meeting of Parliament, wherein two friars defended the position of the crown, stating that the king had the right to tax clergy and even confiscate Church property if needed. Doubtless, this was not well-received by papal officials. Wyclif's delegation in 1374 (though he was not its leader) failed to resolve this issue, but from it, he produced a work in three books on the concept of dominion by 1376, clearly influenced by FitzRalph, *De civili dominio*,[145] or "On Civil Dominion."

His propositions are fairly straightforward. In Book I, he states that the sinner has no right to dominion or ownership. He is by nature unjust, and therefore cannot possess things justly. Conversely, the one who is in the state of grace possesses everything, for he is "the adoptive son of God,"[146] and like Adam before the fall, a lord of all that can be seen. All Christians are in this state, and thus all are lords, holding everything in common.[147] He follows with various theoretical writings about the nature of monarchy and tyranny, how taxes should be rendered, and the morality or not of slavery (he tends to believe it is not, except in certain exceptional circumstances).[148]

The natural question, of course, is how is one to know who has God's grace and who does not? How is one to know if a sinner is wielding power unjustly? As Kenny notes, "Wyclif is exasperatingly reluctant to spell out this obvious difficulty and to offer an answer to it."[149] What he does do, however, is stress that some sinners are so obvious that it is a Christian's duty to reject them. Who are these sinners? His controversial answer is that they are often found among the clergy. As such, a lay ruler is justified in taking away the wealth and property of the Church, if it can be shown that individuals or a community are abusing their privileges.[150] Likewise, tithes can be withheld, if the clergy in question do not perform their duties properly, and the money rather can be given directly to the poor who need it more,[151] depriving the errant clergyman of his possessions. In *De ecclesia*, he further asserts that the pope need not be followed if he is not in the state of grace, for then he is not a member of the true Church, and he cannot demand to be followed to attain salvation.[152] In *De civili dominio*, he had written that a pope can lawfully be disobeyed by secular rulers, if he ceases to obey the gospel, for even popes can sin. If they become too filled with their own self-importance, they would be committing blasphemy, and paving the way for Antichrist.[153] Despite this, an evil and corrupt priest can still be a vehicle for grace, if God wishes it.[154]

Though *De ecclesia* was not life-changing, it clearly showed the direction in which his thought was taking him. Several key points, including the supremacy of scripture, the notion of those living in grace as predestined, and the uncertain nature of papal power, were all to figure prominently in his later works. As expected, John of Gaunt and the nobility of England were quite delighted by these arguments, and gave him their backing. William Courtenay, later Archbishop of Canterbury, was not so pleased. He summoned Wyclif to an ecclesiastical tribunal in St. Paul's Cathedral, held in London in February of 1377. Wyclif was accompanied by no less than John of Gaunt and Henry Percy (the latter of whom would be given the titles of 1st Earl of Northumberland and Marshal of England). With such powerful protectors, there was little that the incensed Courtenay could do, beyond a barrage of words, though another riot ensued.[155]

Meanwhile, Pope Gregory XI received news of Wyclif's writing and was equally unhappy. Identifying eighteen offending propositions in the work, he sent bulls to the king, bishops, and the University of Oxford, commanding them to investigate whether Wyclif was teaching these positions. If so, he was to be jailed. This could have ended Wyclif's career, but nothing came of it. The university agreed to some light confinement (a limited house arrest). The bishops were not able to take real actions against him, for they were warned off by the Queen Mother. Instead, they tried to silence him by forbidding him from spreading these ideas in his sermons and lectures. The king's council, in a deliberate act of defiance, decided to employ Wyclif as a consultant,[156] another shot in the ongoing row with the papacy and its ambitions.

Ultimately, Gregory did not live long after this, dying in March 1378. The new pope, Urban VI, seemed the type who might be receptive to reforms and criticisms, and Wyclif was not only relieved but hopeful. However, Urban ignited new controversies by his overbearing leadership style, insisting that cardinals should neither accept gifts, nor live lives of luxury (Wyclif would have agreed with this). The cardinals who elected him rebelled, saying they had done so only under pressure from locals to elect an Italian pope. A new conclave of French cardinals met in September 1378, and elected another pope, Robert of Geneva, who took the name Clement VII.[157] Gregory had returned the papacy to Rome, but now Clement fled back to Avignon, taking those loyal to him and leaving Urban without many of his advisers. He had to reform the college, and as Kenny notes, "even of these, six proved unfaithful, and the new Pope had them tortured by a Genoese pirate and thrown into the sea."[158] This kind of brutality would give credence to Wyclif's claims about the sinfulness of popes, and cause many to question their loyalties.

Thus began the Western Schism, which would last until 1417, and create a spiritual crisis in the Western Church. The Catholic Church today calls the Avignon popes of this period "antipopes," and their legitimacy is not recognized. At the time, however, different nations allied themselves with the competing papal sees, England supporting Urban and Rome, while France sided with Clement in Avignon. The laity were confused as to which side they should support, or if they should support either Urban or Clement at all. Indeed, at one point the absurdity led to the election of a third pope, Alexander V.[159] The friars were also divided. The Dominicans were initially split, some supporting Avignon, though in 1389, the newly-elected general Raymond of Capua settled the matter by giving support to Pope Urban VI and Rome.[160]

Back in England, these events put a temporary stop to further papal investigation into Wyclif's potentially dangerous writings. Urban had no time to worry about what his predecessor had done, and if he had, he still would not likely have risked antagonizing the English over the matter and losing their tentative support. For Wyclif, the whole debacle of the schism must have begun to undermine his faith that the Church was still the valid institution for the Christian religion. Two increasingly unworthy clergymen hurling insults at each other did not make for a unified Church; rather, it was embarrassing and outrageous. He referred to them in *De ecclesia* as "pseudomonks" that breed schism between them.[161]

From this time until his death in 1384, his conflicts with the Church became more pronounced and bitter. Until the later 1370s, Wyclif, like FitzRalph, had cordial relations with many friars, who often shared his increasingly critical views of the bloated Church hierarchy and its failures. The shift toward hostility may have begun after a group of friars joined with the Archbishop of Canterbury to oppose Wyclif's ideas on clerical poverty and the divesting of the Church's wealth.[162] It escalated during the conflicts over the Eucharist, as we will see below.

In 1378 and 1379, he produced three works (part if his theological *summa*) on the Church, the king, and the power of the pope, respectively.[163] He came to believe that the "true" Church was the "invisible" Church of those predestined for heaven. The "visible" Church, comprised as it was of humans and institutions, only had value if individual clergyman were also a part of the invisible Church. Thus, the sacraments had no guaranteed authority.[164] His increasing dissatisfaction with the papacy and its behavior led him to argue that while there is a need for a pope, individual popes have been "Antichrists." In *De ecclesia*, he condemned Gregory XI for his many abuses, including taking money from English tithes to secure a good marriage for his nephew, supporting other relatives in luxury, buying his brother out of a deserved imprisonment, and having thousands killed for his own gain. Such a man was a heretic and never a worthy leader of the Church, but rather a servant of the devil.[165] Further, in *De potestate papae*, he states that no one is obligated to obey any of the clergy unless they adhere to true Christian teachings, and this goes for the popes in both Rome and in Avignon. The faithful should wait for the true pope to be revealed.[166] However, he also pointed out that there was no specific biblical mandate for a pope to exist at all.[167] Indeed, Antichrist may have been "simply the Pope gone astray."[168]

Wyclif was treading into dangerous territory with these observations, yet still remained under the general protection of the English nobility. His downfall came with his writings on the Eucharist and transubstantiation, in which he condemned the nominalists and drew in the friars, who responded angrily. The debate is a complex one about the nature of the bread of the host, and pitted him against the friars' nominalist position. Essentially, it was agreed by all parties that the consecrated host was transformed into the body of Christ, even if it still resembled bread to all outward appearances. An explanation offered for this, by both Thomas Aquinas and William of Ockham, was that the substance of the bread changed, but the "accidents" of its physical nature, shape, color, taste, texture, etc., did not. Thus, it looked like bread, but was not bread in its substance, but something else.[169]

Wyclif could not accept this, and from 1379, he began to assert that such a belief was heresy. It violated his realist position, since all being reflected an ideal essence. Accidents could not happen without a substance. That the friars and nominalists held to this position showed that they were "worshippers of signs" and had reduced this sacrament to nothing more than a sign.[170] In effect, they had become idolaters, venerating the sign rather than God. As we have seen, Wyclif had a profound dislike for nominalism and increasingly identified the friars with the adoration of signs, i.e., outward show, and so was able to link them to the nominalists he detested. Signs should not be revered over those things which they signify, a practice that he believed was endangering the Church. As Szittya summarizes, "Wyclif connected the nominalist metaphysics of the friars with their (as he saw them) heresies, blasphemies, and apostasies of the Eucharist, of penance, of Scriptural interpretation, of the ordination of priests, of the nature of religion."[171]

Wyclif attributed the errors in the interpretation of the Eucharist to Innocent III, another pope he disliked, since it was he who first allowed the Franciscans and Dominicans to come into existence. Innocent's decretal *Cum Marthe* (1201) seemed to indicate that an accident could exist without a substance, though Wyclif conceded that this may not have been his intention.[172] Worse, in this time when Satan was unleashed and the friars arose, Innocent had instigated the idea of annual private confession in his canon *Omnis utriusque sexus* at the Fourth Lateran Council in 1215. Wyclif argued that this put too much emphasis on the "sign" of outward penance. Sinners would believe that simply uttering words absolved them, and confessors could abuse the practice by using it for monetary gain, exactly as he charged the friars were doing. It should be enough to be contrite and repentant in one's own heart and soul.[173]

He accused the friars of extolling their habits, which are only signs of religion, not religion itself. If clothing and its accoutrements truly represented religion, it would be possible to cloak an ass in a habit and he would be a friar.[174] This amusing image is rather strikingly reminiscent of Fauvel, Reynard, and other such beastly representations of false holiness.

Though the friars were not initially the main focus of his attacks (which at this point were devoted to a broader anticlericalism that happened to include them along with the Church), they reacted swiftly and angrily to his accusations. He lost friends among them almost overnight. Adam Stockton, an Augustinian friar in Cambridge, had supported Wyclif's writings on papal power, calling him a *venerabilis doctor* in 1379. However, with these new writings, Adam changed that praise in 1381 to read *execrabilis seductor*.[175] This reversal in opinion was followed by others, and soon enough, Wyclif found that many of his old allies had deserted him. In late 1380, the chancellor of Oxford University, William Barton (a rival of Wyclif's), established a commission of twelve doctors, charged with examining Wyclif's writings. Half of them were friars, and all were hostile to him, condemning two of his propositions: "that the substance of bread and wine remain after consecration, and that the body of Christ is not corporally but figuratively present in the sacrament."[176] He was threatened with the expected measures for a man of his position, including excommunication, removal from the university, and imprisonment. Wyclif tried appealing to the king, and John of Gaunt met with him, cautioning that he should hold his tongue, but whether because of sincere belief, a desire to answer the friars' charges, or stubbornness, he continued his antifraternal and anticlerical stance. His response to the committee was typical of his acidic and provocative words, showing a remarkable defiance, even arrogance. He wrote in his *De blasphemia* that the devil was "deficient in arguments... but in order to make it more colorful he has brought together six or seven who are jealous of the truth into a conclave and they make the truth which displeases them into a heresy."[177]

Further complications arose in the aftermath of the Peasants' Revolt of 1381. One leader of the revolt, John Ball, was reported to have confessed to being a loyal follower of Wyclif for two years; he was later executed and quartered. The story of his purported confession is most likely untrue, but in the circumstances of the time, it did not bode well for Wyclif.[178] Having written that the taking of ecclesiastical property was acceptable if those holders of it were unjust, it would have been easy to pin the murder of Archbishop Sudbury on Wyclif, by accusing him of inciting insurrection.[179] In February 1382, the four mendicant orders in Oxford wrote to John of Gaunt, complaining that the followers of Wyclif had blamed them for fomenting the revolt because they were lazy and taught others to be like them, and failed to carry out their confessional duties properly. They struck back, implying that Wyclif was the true cause of the uprising.[180] Wyclif ultimately responded "that the tumultuous 1381 uprising and the death of Archbishop Sudbury would never have occurred had temporal lords been appropriately vigilant in rooting out priestly corruption."[181]

Then in May 1382, the new archbishop, Courtenay (Wyclif's old enemy) called a council, later known as the "Earthquake Synod." The various bishops and clergy reviewed 24 of Wyclif's propositions, declaring ten of them heretical, and the other fourteen "erroneous." Sixteen of the seventeen doctors were friars, so the outcome was a foregone conclusion.[182] During this meeting, however, an earthquake struck London, damaging buildings, and sending the attendees running in fear. They thought that God was judging them, but Courtenay countered that the earthquake was a favorable sign, the earth letting loose unpleasant air. The writings of heretics were similar to these noxious fumes, he said, and also needed to be expelled.[183] Wyclif, naturally, took the opposite view and saw the earthquake as a judgement from God on those unjustly persecuting him.

A Carmelite friar delivered the decision to Oxford's chancellor, who was not so receptive. The university initially came to Wyclif's defense, once again agitated about outside interference in its affairs, making it quite clear that the friar would come to harm if he tried to publish the council's condemnation. For once, however, the university had to capitulate, when the Privy Council forced the chancellor to assent to the synod's judgement, and publish the condemnations at St. Mary's Church. However, he censured one of Wyclif's enemies who had called the supporters of Wyclif "Lollards," an insult deriving from the Middle Dutch *lollaert*, meaning "mumbler."[184] Strangely, this epithet stuck, and thereafter, Wyclif's supporters were named the Lollards, spreading to become a major heretical movement in England into the 15th century. We will briefly examine Lollardy as part of the heritage of Wyclif, with its own antifraternal writings, below.

Meanwhile, having seen his fortunes changing for the worse, Wyclif had withdrawn from Oxford by 1381 to the rectory in Lutterworth, where he lived for the rest of life.[185] He did not forgive the friars for their actions, however, and in these last few years, he devoted a considerable amount of ink to attacking them ferociously, in both writings and sermons. Others took up his cause as well, and English-language "Wyclif-fite sermons" began to circulate. Frequently attributed to him, their authorship is most often dubious, but they share his passion for accusing the friars of all manner of misdeeds. For example, the sermon "On the Leaven of Pharisees," dating from the 1380s, notes that friars (possibly with a nod to the notion of them being the "minstrels of God") spend holy days dabbling in witchcraft and songs, playing harp or gittern (a small lute-like instrument), or dancing and other such vain trifles, all to try to attract women and lure them into sin.[186] The passage calls to mind Chaucer's description of his friar's musical abilities and Langland's minstrel references.[187]

The friars responded with equal vitriol; one Carmelite called him a fox during a sermon, an obvious reference to the diabolic behavior of the trickster animal, and recalling scenes of Reynard in clerical robes.[188] Likewise, it is possible that depictions of carved foxes in robes preaching to geese on some English misericords (wooden shelves as part of folding seats in a church) are warnings against following the deceit of the Lollards.[189]

Wyclif managed to escape being brought to trial for heresy and imprisoned or executed (dying of a stroke in December 1384),[190] but his exile no doubt left him bitter and ready to step up his verbal attacks.[191] By 1381, he had already completed his treatise on blasphemy, which is filled with anticlerical and antifraternal polemic, levelling charge after charge against the Church.[192] After defining blasphemy, he asserts that its root is the Roman Curia, and that it has twelve branches, the "twelve daughters of the diabolic Leech" (i.e., Satan): the pope, the cardinals, the bishops, the archdeacons, the officials (chancellors), the rural deans, the rectors, the "inferior" priests, the monks, the friars, the clerks ("door keepers"), and the questers (tithe collectors).[193] Multiple chapters cover all of these in detail.

Such a comprehensive list for his vitriol shows that he objected to the institutional Church as a whole, though he seems to have reserved a special place for the friars that had turned against him, and the cardinals.[194] Delighting in word-play and acronym, he asserts that the very name "cardinal" indicates that they are dear to the devil ("**CAR**ior **DI**aboli **NA**tus, **LI**cium **S**eminator"),[195] and keepers of his apostates ("**C**ustos **A**postatarum **R**egni **D**iaboli, **I**uvans **N**equissimum **A**d **L**egem **I**udicis **S**opiendam").[196] The friars, as both Wyclif and FitzRalph had charged, were in effect, descendants from the time of Cain, the first murderer. Indeed, the four orders' names allowed Wyclif to create another acronym: CAIM, for the **C**armelites, **A**ugustinians, Jacobites, and *Minores*, or Franciscans.[197]

He devotes three chapters of *De blasphemia* to attacking the friars. They take children into their orders to corrupt them, they are traitors, they are answerable to no one, they blaspheme, and they obey no laws. The best solution is to abolish them. They live in communities for no good reason, communities which have grown excessively rich (while they pretend to be holy by not personally touching money), and they are burdened with traditions such that even their founders (good honest men) would not recognize them. He then quotes a list of attacks from FitzRalph, including that they beg while being fully able to work, they concoct clever ways to evade following their respective rules, they appoint others to touch money for them, and always interfere in secular affairs. He revives the issue of his Oxford condemnation (a grudge that he never let go), insisting that the ruling was due to Satan and the misinterpretation of scripture.[198] Indeed, in his brief *Descriptio fratris*, he describes the friars as being the Devil incarnate, who are spreading discord through the Church.[199] Szittya notes rather amusingly that his short treatise *De fratribus* has "no visible structure or purpose to the work beyond the aggregation of insult."[200]

He also invoked apocalyptic themes in his attacks on the clergy and friars. They never had the urgency of Guillaume de Saint-Amour's tracts, though he acknowledged Guillaume's efforts in attempting to stop the friars near the beginning.[201] For Wyclif, the friars were one part of an overall pattern of decline and sinfulness that would bring about the end of the world, whereas for Guillaume, they were the principle harbingers of it. Wyclif did not attempt to show that the end was immanent, asserting in the tradition of Augustine that we do not know, however, it certainly must be near.[202] He stated that the four "sects" of monks, friars, clergy, and canons were rife with heresy, and were persecuting the Church with their hypocrisy.[203] Indeed, Lahey has argued that opposition to such sects was at the heart of his antifraternal and anticlerical views.[204]

Studies of English antifraternal writings have often grouped Wyclif and FitzRalph together, understandably, because they were both major religious figures in England, and each had a particular disliking for the friars, though Wyclif is more remembered as an opponent of the Church as a whole, whereas FitzRalph wanted to reform it.[205] As Lahey has recently shown, however, their approaches to the friars were very different, bearing little resemblance to one another.[206] Wyclif in general was not interested in the writings of more recent scholars from his century, looking back instead to luminaries such as Anselm, Bernard, and especially Robert Grosseteste. However,

FitzRalph was one of the few for whom Wyclif made an exception, reviving his *De pauperie* as part of his attack on mendicant practices, and ultimately using it against the pope as well,[207] something that would no doubt have horrified FitzRalph, devoted as he was to the Church hierarchy and its preservation.

Interestingly, both claimed that the friars had been responsible for the decline in student numbers at Oxford. Secular students had been offended by their teaching and recruiting methods, and thus the university population declined by tens of thousands. This was a ridiculous exaggeration and had no basis in truth. At the time, the whole population of Oxford would not have been more than a few thousand at most, though the Black Death certainly had taken a toll and reduced overall numbers.[208]

Both made use of the Bible almost exclusively in their attacks, citing the authority of scripture to show how the friars had failed to live up to their ideals. It was their approach to the Bible that marked their differences. For Wyclif, it was "the final iteration of a universal the primary reality of which lies in God's understanding, while FitzRalph had the more mundane view that it is a divinely inspired book written by men,"[209] though both stressed its literal nature, as opposed to it being symbolic or allegorical. Further, Wyclif argued for the necessity of grace in understanding scripture to a far greater extent than FitzRalph.[210] This led FitzRalph to allow for the possibility of extra-scriptural authority in the governance of the Church. Thus, the friars were not invalid because they claimed to have been called by God, but because they had abused their privileges.[211]

Wyclif, by contrast, deferred to the Bible as the absolute authority, imbuing it, as Lahey notes, with almost a kind of personhood.[212] It was inerrant, and if someone found a supposed contradiction in its passages, the fault was with that exegete, not the text itself. The student had failed to grasp the deeper meaning. The Bible therefore was to be used to judge all other innovations and developments, and it needed to be made freely available to all, clergy and laity.[213] He also had no interest in the scribes who wrote the original scrolls; it was the texts themselves as a living Word of God that concerned him. As such, no human-created texts could come close to it in authority. With this position, he was to assert that the friars had no right to exist at all, because nothing in the scriptures offered any precedent for such an organization, regardless of what they might claim. Those orders (in fact, both mendicant and monastic)[214] who live by their complex rules were essentially saying that the law of God given by Christ was incomplete, and needed to be amended over 1,000 years later[215]; for Wyclif, this was an absurd proposition.

As noted, he evaded being tried for heresy, possibly due to some minor capitulations in some of his writings; he seemed willing to back off from some of his positions. As Margaret Aston observes, his "works are peppered with protestations of his readiness to be corrected, but they usually read rather in the nature of challenges to anyone who could prove him wrong by scripture."[216] This may have removed some pressure from him during his lifetime and he was buried in consecrated ground, but in 1415 at the Council of Constance (which also ended the Western Schism, reestablishing the papacy in Rome), he was declared a heretic. The reformer Jan Hus was also condemned, having traveled to the council under a guarantee of safe conduct. He was seized, convicted of heresy, and burned at the stake.[217] In 1428, Richard Flemming, Bishop of Lincoln, saw to it that Wyclif's bones were disinterred, burned, and the ashes scattered in the River Swift near Lutterworth, to prevent them from becoming religious relics. This was done at the order of Pope Martin V.[218]

Despite his condemnations, Wyclif in fact had some curious commonalities with the friars, including a desire to preach to the poor and the common people without hierarchical interference, as well as sharing with the Dominicans a distrust of certain Aristotelian philosophies when such ideas seemed to demand that traditional religious teachings accommodate them, rather than the other way around. One of his chief reasons for criticizing the friars so harshly was that that he saw most of them as failures, abandoning their ideals. He believed that there were still a few of the true faithful among them, and he hoped that they would rise up again and renew their commitment to that noble cause, as William of Ockham had attempted to do.[219]

More surprisingly, he may in his old age have approved of the idea of poor preachers, whose goal was to go and minister to the masses and bring new life and enthusiasm back to the faith, liberating them from sectarianism and returning them to true religion. However, not all scholars accept that he was directly involved in this.[220] Some have even considered the possibility that under differing circumstances, he might have become a friar himself,[221] however, from a young age, he chose a different path. Lahey has suggested that Wyclif desired to be better than either Francis or Dominic, and to inaugurate a true change in the practices of the Christian religion,[222] but it is unclear if he intended to start a movement of the kind that developed into the Lollards. Nevertheless, given how his ideas were taken, adapted, and spread despite persecution, in both England and Bohemia, it is easy to see why the 16th-century English reformers looked back to him and claimed him as one of their own.

In the years after his death, the Lollard movement gathered strength. This was not so much an organized sect with one leader; rather, they were scattered groups who held to Wyclif's ideas, but also developed their own, and who were no longer associated with Oxford University.[223] Indeed, Wyclif's first followers had been colleagues at the university, led by Nicholas of Hereford (*d. ca.* 1420), who later recanted and helped in persecuting those who held to his former beliefs.[224] From 1412, the University of Oxford was forced to swear that it would not teach Wyclif's works.[225] However, it is important not to conflate "Wyclifism" with Lollardy.[226] Lollards did not adhere to one centralized doctrine, but shared various views in common, focused on condemning the corruption of the Church and its hierarchy, as well as criticizing various practices and beliefs. They were also resolutely antifraternal.[227]

In 1395, a group of Lollards presented Parliament with the "Twelve Conclusions of the Lollards," which laid out in English a series of statements and grievances. The twelve issues were: that faith, hope, and charity have fled from the English Church, corrupted by Rome; that the priesthood of the Church is not that which Christ gave to his apostles, but rather is obsessed with rites and signs; that clerical celibacy leads to sodomy; that the sacrament of bread (the Eucharist) leads most into idolatry; that exorcisms and blessings of all kinds, incense, oils, and holy water are forms of necromancy; that clerics should have no worldly power, for this conflicts with their religious duties; that alms given to clergy for prayers for the dead are selective, false, and not far from simony; that undertaking pilgrimages and the veneration of relics are forms of idolatry; that confession gives priests the false power of absolution and increases their pride; that wars, both temporal and spiritual, fought without genuine revelation are contrary to the New Testament, which teaches love and mercy, not slaughter; that female vows of continence lead to unwanted pregnancy and abortion; and that excessive ornamentation and craft in Churches is wasteful and unnecessary.[228]

These accusations and condemnations struck at the very heart of the English Church, and obviously were not received kindly. In 1401, Parliament passed into law *De heretico comburendo*, overseen by King Henry IV, who despite being John of Gaunt's son, was not interested in protecting unorthodox ideas. It addressed the issue of the Lollard heretics, describing them as a wicked new "sect" that was spreading dangerous teachings. If any so accused refused to repent, they were to be arrested, tried, and burned at the stake.[229] This striking development effectively brought a kind of inquisition to England for the first time. It remained the law of the land until set aside by Henry VIII. His daughter Mary revived it during her brief reign (which re-imposed Catholicism on England), but Elizabeth I permanently repealed it.[230]

Oxford University was likewise forbidden to teach Wyclif or promote Lollardy in any way, though this was not as successful as hoped. Archbishop Arundel in 1407 drew up a list of thirteen guidelines for preventing the university from teaching any Lollard doctrines, going so far as to demand an oath of loyalty in 1411. The university, not used to being pushed, appealed to Henry IV, and threatened Arundel himself with excommunication, given that these demands were effectively breaking his own loyalty oath as a university member. He responded by placing the university under a local interdict. The dispute escalated, but the university appealed to the pope, who lifted the sentence, and order was restored. Once again, the University of Oxford simply did not have to back down.[231]

Perhaps the most famous of the Lollard "martyrs" was Sir John Oldcastle, a soldier and one-time friend of Prince Henry (the future King Henry V). Considered a model for Shakespeare's Falstaff,[232] he ran afoul of the establishment for his Lollard sympathies, and was tried and convicted of heresy in 1413. Henry V granted a temporary stay of execution, but during that time, he escaped from the Tower of London and hatched a plot with fellow Lollards in 1414 to kidnap the king. This was foiled, though he again escaped, only finally being captured and executed by burning in 1417.[233]

Opposition to Lollard beliefs was also intellectual. In 1426, a Carmelite friar, Thomas Netter of Walden, produced his *Doctrinale antiquitatum fidei eccleaisæ catholicæ*, a three-volume tome devoted to attacking the errors of Wyclif, and by extension, FitzRalph. He was a fervent persecutor of Wyclif's ideas and the Lollards, as well as those of Hus, and his apology for Catholic doctrine continued to be influential for centuries. He was devoted to the notion that it was not for the laity to understand the complexities of religion, but merely to believe.[234]

Regardless of these attacks, the Lollards were committed to spreading their message in English,[235] and produced unauthorized (and thus heretical) English translations of the Bible.[236] Indeed, Church authorities protested with the time-honored position that the Bible was only for those with the learning and qualifications to interpret it, not to be given freely to those incapable of understanding it properly.[237] While Wyclif seems to have supported the idea of vernacular readings of scripture, there is little evidence that he wrote in English or sought to have his Latin works translated.[238] After his death, some of his sermons were translated, and a large number in English were attributed to him.[239] The Lollards were also vigorous in their denunciation of the friars, and various major works in English illustrate this. The first is *Jack Upland*, written in the 1390s. Fashioning itself in some ways as a "sequel" to Piers Plowman by using some of its themes, it is filled with apocalyptic imagery and laments how the Church has been infiltrated by the disciples of Antichrist. It accuses the friars of being at the forefront of the Church's corruption and deceit, and of being latter-day Pharisees. It poses more than 60 questions to the friars, demanding to know just which side they are on. Around 1419, a friar took the time to respond to the work, producing *Friar Daw's Reply*, answering each of the questions posed in *Jack Upland*. A Lollard of the mid–15th century composed a reply to this response, *Upland's Rejoinder*, surviving in the margins of a copy of *Daw's Reply*.[240] This back-and-forth sparring over the course of more than 50 years shows just how divided the two sides were, and that the Lollards were not eradicated, despite the repression of *De heretico comburendo*.

A further important work is *Pierce the Plowman's Crede*, an obvious imitation of *Piers Plowman*. Written between 1393 and 1401, it tells of a poor man who wants to learn the Apostles' Creed, and so consults the four orders of friars. However, they are useless, spending their time either denouncing one another, or trying to get money out of him. He concludes that they are ignorant, and so finds a humble plowman, Piers, who is able to give him the knowledge he seeks. The friars are portrayed as burdened with many vices, including having mistresses, extorting money from housewives, and even murdering their own when they do not make enough money from begging. What is worse, they accuse each other of vices, further displaying their hypocrisy and evil nature. Evidence for Lollard authorship of the work can be found throughout, as James M. Dean notes: "The author of *PPC* develops stereotypes for each of the four orders; and these stereotypes owe much to Lollard views. The Franciscans are the most hypocritical because they try to appear the most humble; the Dominicans are the most arrogant as well as the richest, most avaricious order; the Austins are the most vicious in attacking the other orders; and the Carmelites are the most straightforward, and outrageous, in begging for money. Piers, however, speaks approvingly of the founders of the fraternal orders, Francis and Dominic, but he censures their followers as evil. At one point Piers invokes Wyclif as a truthteller who cautioned the friars against their iniquitous behavior."[241]

Finally, there is *The Plowman's Tale*, a Lollard text dating from about 1400 that only survives in later, adapted 16th-century versions, which attribute authorship to Chaucer, and make it one of the *Canterbury Tales*. This was an attempt to identify Chaucer as a proto-reformer with sympathies for Wyclif, exactly what the reforming Tudors would have liked to believe of him, though this was not likely the original author's intent.[242] Indeed, editions of the *Canterbury Tales* included the work until 1775.[243] The work is a general anticlerical poem, attacking friars as well as bishops, cardinals and the pope. In the story, a plowman leaves his work to join a pilgrimage to Canterbury. When asked to share a story, he relates the situation of conflict between the clergy and the "lollers" who are being oppressed. A griffin (representing the Church) and a pelican (a traditional symbol of Christ, naturally representing the Lollards) debate over who has the most virtue, and the pelican gets most of the dialogue, triumphing in the end.[244]

Lollardy persisted in various ways into the 16th century, and while it cannot be said to have had a major impact on genesis of the English Reformation, those that still quietly held such views were undoubtedly welcomed into the reformers' fold. Wyclif, FitzRalph, Chaucer, and Langland were all lauded as speakers of the truth, 150 years or more before their time. Their real or imagined criticisms of the friars, whether through mockery and satire, or outright denunciation, ensured that they would have an honored place in the remembrance of the English during the 16th century and beyond.

Conclusion

The presence of the "other" was always a reason for distrust and antipathy in medieval European society: Jews, Muslims, lepers, and heretics. Many critics saw the friars as a kind of "other," one erroneously and dangerously given rights and privileges that they should not have possessed. Indeed, the friars were from the beginning outsiders, not a part of the traditional Church hierarchy. Almost immediately, this made them suspicious in the eyes of some, whether traditionalists or reformers. They had certain privileges also held by both the clergy and the monastic houses, but answered only to the pope, and could engage in certain activities with virtual impunity, such as preaching where they wished. It is not surprising that such special rights granted to new organizations with no long-standing traditions would stir up antagonistic feelings. The irony is that over time, they were absorbed into that same Church hierarchy, becoming an integral part of the institution that many of them initially criticized, or from which they wanted to be separated.

A combination of clerical and ecclesiastical jealousy and protectionism led to increasing resentment about perceived mendicant encroachment on the traditional rights of the clergy. That the friars defended themselves vociferously, at times even angrily, often only encouraged more criticism. A major divide in these wars of words was over how the Church was to be structured, whether it was immutable or could accept change. Some of the fiercest critics of the fraternal orders, such as Guillaume de Saint-Amour, held that they had no place, were dangerous, and needed to be abolished. Others were less adamant in their attacks, seeing the friars as failed organizations in need of reform. In this, they shared many views in common with reform-minded friars themselves. Roger Bacon, Bonaventure, the Spirituals, and perhaps William Langland were among the Franciscans seeking to correct deficiencies in their order. The Dominicans, founded as preachers and scholars, and not hounded by the same problems of absolute poverty, fared better in this regard.

Some of these same issues were addressed by the laity. Antifraternal theologians found allies in vernacular poets, some of them adopting broader anticlerical traditions for use in their works. Whether substituting the friars for other clergy and monks in parodies like the Reynard branches, or offering up blistering satires such as in the works of Rutebeuf and Jean de Meun, vernacular poets and writers in both France and England found much in the fraternal orders to examine, question, criticize, mock, and even condemn. However, they did not limit their verbal assaults to the friars alone. Religious figures of all kinds that took vows and acted holy, but sometimes did not live up to those vows, were ripe for the picking in comic and satirical literature; the friars were in this sense no different than the monks and priests who had come before them, but their special positions and their exceptional vows of poverty made them easy targets. The four mendicant orders weathered these challenges and survived into the Renaissance and beyond. However, greater trials awaited them.

Antifraternal writings gathered strength again during the Reformation, in the seemingly endless Protestant and Catholic conflicts of the 16th and 17th centuries, and during the time of the French Revolution. While *De Periculis* may not have inaugurated an unbroken tradition of antifraternal writing from the mid–13th century, it did feature prominently in the works of some later religious reformers who wanted to mine its contents for use in their own situations. John Foxe (1516/17–87) wrote approvingly of Guillaume de Saint-Amour in his *Acts and Monuments* (popularly known as *Foxe's Book of Martyrs*), for example, listing Guillaume's proofs (here numbered at 39) that the friars were false apostles.[1] Guillaume's complete works were eventually published in 1632 in France, and again in 1690 in England[2]; the earlier of these was done in an attempt to link Guillaume with current Protestant sentiments,[3] as was also done with Wyclif's works. The English reformers, such as Foxe, were particularly receptive to Guillaume's inflammatory words, and the friars, like monks, became targets because of their wealth and supposed corruption in England, gradually becoming extinct in the wake of the actions of Henry VIII and the Protestants who came after him.[4]

In France, the friars survived the Reformation, but endured their own series of crises, culminating in the suppression of the orders by the Assembly in 1790, during the French Revolution that some of them had initially supported. As a result, hundreds, if not thousands, were persecuted, imprisoned, and even executed, while untold numbers fled the country. What Guillaume de Saint-Amour had so fervently wished for but failed to achieve was finally accomplished by Republican revolutionaries more than five centuries later.[5] The Dominican order in particular was nearly wiped out in France, and this was not the end of their troubles; by the mid–19th century, their numbers overall had been drastically reduced.[6]

The wide range of antifraternalism, from comic mockery to bloody violence, could not have had a single origin. Rather, various aspects of and actions by the orders brought out numerous responses in different times and regions. While the people of Languedoc cowed before the Inquisition and many undoubtedly secretly burned with hatred for the Dominicans who presided over it, Rutebeuf at the same time openly mocked and condemned the Parisian Jacobins as hypocrites and deceivers. While FitzRalph called for the curtailing of Franciscan privileges to the point of effectively ending the order, artists depicted friar-foxes deceiving their congregations, and Chaucer wrote a ribald tale about thousands of false friars living in Satan's anus. This is a remarkable diversity of attacks for a common target.

Ultimately, the friars succeeded because of the wide-ranging popularity of their ideas and ideals. Despite frequent and pointed attacks in all of the forms we have surveyed, the orders were attractive to a large portion of the populace, whether as potential recruits or as benefactors and seekers of spiritual counsel. The complex arguments of scholastics and theologians were of little concern to the medieval everyman, and the parodies and satires penned by vernacular writers, while finding a wide audience who undoubtedly laughed at their often cruel jests, did not dissuade the many supporters of all social classes who sought out the friars for confession or the rites of sepulture.

The friars failed and were dispersed during the Protestant and revolutionary movements which came long after their founding, but during the Middle Ages, they remained one of the most important and influential groups of the reformed Church, despite turmoil within them and assaults from without. Their successes defied efforts to suppress or substantially alter them, and yet, they have never quite removed the tarnish of those times, which labeled Franciscans as gluttons and drunks, and Dominicans as insidious agents of a police state. If these stereotypes are untrue and slanderous, they nevertheless are a legacy of a time when opponents of the orders for various reasons felt emboldened to speak their minds, and commit to permanent record their thoughts and concerns. As Geltner notes, "the threat of change rather than routine, action rather than stillness, drives societies to protest, to fight, and to record."[7]

The changes in Europe from the 12th to the 14th centuries were dramatic and had long-lasting consequences, including the rise of popular piety and heresy, the burgeoning market economy and beginning of the middle class, the flourishing of non-monastic education and the importance of the new universities, the devastation of the Black Death, the demands for greater rights for commoners (from Magna Carta to the Peasants' Revolt), and outright criticisms of the Church and papacy when they failed (as they frequently did). That the friars would be seen as both allies and enemies through such upheavals is not surprising. That they survived and thrived is a testimony to their appeal and resilience. That these criticisms came from so many different sources shows that the tapestry of medieval life and society was as rich, colorful, and vibrant as in any age.

Appendix A

Art Bibliography and Resources

For a number of the writings discussed in this book, there are remarkable, beautiful, and varied examples of artwork in many medieval manuscripts. Often such illuminations and miniatures relate closely to the texts, highlighting certain points in the story, or playing off of them with visual puns. This appendix lists art resources for further study. Generally, these are not included in the main bibliography, unless there is significant overlap with other aspects of the given subject.

Avril, François. *Manuscript Painting at the Court of France: The Fourteenth Century*, translated by Ursule Molinaro. New York: George Braziller, 1978. A general overview.

Benton, Janetta Rebold. *Holy Terrors: Gargoyles on Medieval Buildings*. New York: Abbeville Press, 1997. A splendid collection of color photographs.

Camille, Michael. *The Gothic Idol: Ideology and Image-Making in Medieval Art*. Cambridge: Cambridge University Press, 1989, reprinted 1992.

_____. "Hybridity, Monstrosity, and Bestiality in the *Roman de Fauvel*." In *Fauvel Studies: Allegory, Chronicle, Music, and Image in Paris, Bibliotèque Nationale de France, MS Français 146*, edited by Margaret Bent and Andrew Wathey, 161–74. Oxford: Oxford University Press, 1998.

_____. *Image on the Edge: The Margins of Medieval Art*. London: Reaktion Books, 1992, reprinted 2012. This is a delightful study of the grotesque, vulgar, and funny imagery that finds its way so often into the margins of medieval manuscripts.

Fleming, John V. *The Roman de la Rose: A Study in Allegory and Iconography*. Princeton: Printceton University Press, 1969. Contains 42 images, for which he give analysis. See figure 4 with its fox image (discussed at 24–26), and at 169, for the Lover and False Seeming in MS Garret 126, fol. 77v, which has an image of both bowing to the god Love as brothers, thus stressing the connection between them.

Flores, Nona C. "'Effigies Amicitiae... Veritas Inimicitiae': Antifeminism in the Iconography of the Woman-Headed Serpent in Medieval and Renaissance Art and Literature." In *Animals in the Middle Ages: A Book of Essays*, edited by Flores, 167–95. New York: Routledge, 1966. Reprinted as part of Routledge Medieval Casebooks, 2000.

Hardwick, Paul. *English Medieval Misericords: The Margins of Meaning.* Woodbridge: Boydell, 2011.

Kauffmann, Martin. "Satire, Pictorial genre, and the Illustrations in BN fr. 146." In *Fauvel Studies: Allegory, Chronicle, Music, and Image in Paris, Bibliotèque Nationale de France, MS Français 146*, edited by Margaret Bent and Andrew Wathey, 285–305. Oxford: Oxford University Press, 1998.

Lewis, Suzanne. *The Art of Matthew Paris in the Chronica Majora.* Berkeley: University of California Press, 1987. A remarkably detailed study of his illustrations, with numerous reproductions.

MARGOT. "Reading the *Roman de la Rose* in Text and Image," accessed March 3, 2014: http://margot.uwaterloo.ca/ROMAN/miniatures.php, a good collection of color reproductions of various *Rose* illuminations, with bibliographic information for each.

Matthew Paris. *Historia Anglorum, Chronica majora*, Part III, covering 1250–1259. Royal MS 14 C VII, British Library Digitised Manuscripts, accessed February 18, 2014: http://www.bl.uk/manuscripts/FullDisplay.aspx?ref=Royal_MS_14_c_vii. This is a digitized version of this manuscript. The page also has an extensive bibliography.

"Misericords of the World," accessed January 15, 2014: http://www.misericords.co.uk. Contains numerous color photographs of these remarkable church carvings.

Mühlethaler, Jean-Claude. *Fauvel au pouvoir; lire la satire médiévale.* Nouvelle Bibliothèque du Moyen Age 26. Paris: Champion, 1994. See 413–35 for a complete listing of the *Fauvel* miniatures.

Randall, Lilian M.C. "Exempla as a Source of Gothic Marginal Illumination." *The Art Bulletin* 39, 2 (1957): 97–107. Discusses the use of *exempla* in mendicant sermons, and the use of marginal art to illustrate text, which served a similar purpose. The article contains a variety of images of friars, monks, and animal fables, as well as imagery from Reynard branches and other anticlerical themes. She notes at 107: "There can remain little doubt concerning the iconographic analogies between exempla and Gothic marginal illustrations. The prolific use of exempla, particularly by the preaching friars, after the first quarter of the thirteenth century, served to disseminate far and wide facts and legends which had heretofore been known to only a select few who had access to books. Since these themes began to appear in increasing numbers in the margins of manuscripts after the middle of the thirteenth century, the exempla must certainly be considered as one of the primary motivating factors for the emergence of Gothic marginal illumination."

Roman de Fauvel, Bibliothèque Nationale's website, accessed November 12, 2013: http://gallica.bnf.fr/ark:/12148/btv1b8454675g. This is a full reproduction of the illuminated manuscript, beautifully digitized.

Le Roman de Fauvel in the Edition of Messire Chaillou de Pestain: A Reproduction of the Complete Manuscript Paris, Bibliothèque Nationale, fonds francais 146. Introduction by Edward H. Roesner, Francois Avril, and Nancy Freeman Regalado. New York: Broude Brothers, 1990. A facsimile edition.

"*Roman de la Rose* Digital Library," accessed January 21, 2014: http://romandelarose.org. Contains digitized versions of many manuscripts.

The Romance of the Rose, translated by Charles Dahlberg. Hanover, NH: University Press of New England, reprinted 1983. The book contains 64 reproductions of manuscript illuminations, see the list of illustrations beginning at 453.

Stinson, Timothy L. "Illumination and Interpretation: The Depiction and Reception of Faus Semblant in *Roman de la Rose* Manuscripts." *Speculum* 87. 2 (2012): 469–498.

Varty, Kenneth. *Reynard, Renart, Reinaert: And Other Foxes in Medieval England : The Iconographic Evidence.* Amsterdam: Amsterdam University Press, 1999. This book contains over 250 illustrations of representations of Reynard and his cronies, and other foxes in English sources.

Vaughan, Richard. *The Illustrated Chronicles of Matthew Paris.* Stroud, Gloucestershire, UK: Alan Sutton, 1993. This book contains English translations with a selection of Matthew's drawings from manuscript sources.

Appendix B

Music Bibliography and Resources

As with art, there are a good number of music manuscripts surviving from the Middle Ages, containing secular or sacred music, or a mixture of both. This appendix lists several collections of music, most often transcribed into modern notation, for those interested in exploring these pieces further, as well as additional studies, and links to performing ensembles.

Bibliography

Brownlee, Kevin. "Machaut's Motet 15 and the 'Roman de la rose': The Literary Context of 'Amours qui a le pouoir/Faus Samblant m'a deceu/Vidi Dominum.'" *Early Music History* 10 (1991): 1–14.

Butterfield, Ardis. *Poetry and Music in Medieval France: From Jean Renart to Guillaume de Machaut*, Cambridge Studies in Medieval Literature. Cambridge: Cambridge University Press, 2002.

Clemencic, René. Ulrich Müller, Michael Korth. *Carmina Burana*. München: Heimeran Verlag, 1979. This book was produced to accompany a series of recordings made by the Clemencic Consort in the late 1970s.

Dillon, Emma. *Medieval Music-Making and the Roman de Fauvel*. Cambridge: Cambridge University Press, 2002. This looks at the role of music in the *Fauvel* manuscript, also taking into account the greater world of manuscript production at the time.

Epstein, Marcia Jenneth, ed. and trans. *Prions en chantant: Devotional Songs of the Trouvères*. Toronto: University of Toronto Press, 1977. An excellent collection of transcribed melodies from France. Religious poems were sometime set to existing secular melodies and vice versa; some of these songs certainly had non-religious origins.

Helmer, Paul, ed. *Le premier et le secont livre de Fauvel: In the version preserved in B.N. f. fr. 146*, Wissenschaftliche Abhandlungen, 70,1. Ottawa: Institute of Medieval Music, 1997. Contains the *Fauvel* music in transcription.

Hoppin, Richard. *Medieval Music*. New York: W.W. Norton, 1978. A classic general history of medieval music.

Leach, Elizabeth Eva. *Guillaume de Machaut: Secretary, Poet, Musician*. Ithaca: Cornell University Press, 2011. An excellent study of the greatest French composer of the 14th century.

McKinnon, James, ed. *Antiquity and the Middle Ages: From Ancient Greece to the 15th Century*. Music and Society. Englewood Cliffs, NJ: Prentice Hall, 1990. This work contains a number of useful studies, covering such topics as music in Paris, in England, and at the royal courts.

Roesner, Edward H. "Labouring in the Midst of Wolves: Reading a Group of 'Fauvel' Motets." *Early Music History* 22 (2002): 169–245.

Rosenberg, Samuel N., and Hans Tischler, eds. T*he Monophonic Songs in the Roman de Fauvel*. Lincoln: University of Nebraska Press, 1991. As the title indicates, this is a complete collection of the single-line melodies from the *Fauvel* manuscript, with complete texts and translations; an indispensable resource.

Saltzstein, Jennifer. "Cleric-Trouvères and the Jeux-Partis of Medieval Arras." *Viator* 43 (2012): 1–17.

_____. *The Refrain and the Rise of the Vernacular in Medieval French Music and Poetry*, Gallica 30. Woodbridge: D.S. Brewer, 2013. Surveys the use of French refrains as sources of knowledge in music, with attention given to Adam de la Halle and Guillaume de Macaut.

Schrade, Leo, ed. *The Roman de Fauvel, The Works of Philippe de Vitry, French Cycles of the Ordinarium missae*, Polyphonic Music of the Fourteenth Century I, commentary volume published separately. Monaco: Éditions de l'Oiseau-Lyre, 1956. The first volume in a large, ongoing series, this book contains all of the multi-part pieces from the *Fauvel* manuscript, and complements the Rosenberg and Tischler.

Tischler, Hans, ed. *The Montpellier Codex: Fascicles 3, 4, and 5*, vol. 2. Madison: A-R Editions, Inc., 1978. This is an edition of the polyphonic motets popular in 13th-century France, including multi-texted pieces on any number of subjects. Fascinating music, well worth exploring.

Van der Werf, Hendrik. *The Extant Troubadour Melodies: Transcriptions and Essays for Performers and Scholars*, texts edited by Gerald A. Bond. Rochester: the author, 1984. This is a collection of the surviving troubadour melodies and their variants, though not the complete texts (which would have made the book a multi-volume work).

Wilkins, Nigel, ed. and trans. *The Lyric Works of Adam de la Halle*, Corpus Mensurabilis Musicæ. Hänssler-Verlag: Amcrican Institute of Musicology, 1967. All of Adam's melodies, a surprisingly large output.

Yudkin, Jeremy. *Music in Medieval Europe*. Englewood Cliffs, NJ: Prentice Hall, 1989. See especially "The New Music of Paris," 357–431, for a study of the music that would have been heard during the secular/friar conflict and beyond.

Performing Ensembles

Including discographies in a book is always a rather questionable practice, since they inevitably will become out-of-date quite soon. While there are "classic" recordings in any genre, it seems better to include links to ensembles performing these medieval repertoires, and who have made recordings of the music and related repertoires discussed in this book.

Alla Francesca: performing a variety of medieval repertoires, this splendid French group produced a recording based around the *Roman de la Rose*: http://allafrancesca.fr.

The Boston Camerata: over its long history, this excellent group has produced numerous recordings, including songs from the *Carmina Burana*, and a *Fauvel* program, which it continues to perform live: http://www.bostoncamerata.com.

Clemencic Consort: produced a series of goliardic and *Carmina Burana* recordings in the late 1970s. The group is still active under its director, René Clemencic: http://www.clemencic.at/en/index_en.html.

Dufay Collective: a British favorite, the Dufay Collective is known for its clever imagery and quirky sense of humor (not to mention its unusual website!). The group has produced recordings of medieval French and English repertoire, among many others: http://www.dufay.com.

Ensemble Gilles Binchois: this French group has released an astonishing number of recordings, ranging from early medieval to Renaissance, including a beautiful CD of French poly-textual motets: http://gillesbinchois.com.

Fortune's Wheel: an American ensemble that has produced two very fine recordings, one of French repertoire (including Adam de la Halle's pieces), and another of medieval English music: http://www.fortuneswheel.org.

Gothic Voices: founded by medieval musicologist Christopher Page. In the 1980s and early 90s, the group released a series of CDs devoted to French vernacular music, including poly-textual motets, and pieces by Philip de Vitry and Guillaume de Machaut, among many others. They have also produced a number of recordings of English sacred music from the 14th century: http://www.gothicvoices.co.uk.

Hilliard Ensemble: a British institution, the Hilliards announced their retirement in 2014, after 40 years of performances and recordings. Among their dozens of recordings are two of medieval English music (from the 12th to the 15th centuries), and a classic recording of the work of Perotin, the great polyphonic composer at Notre Dame in Paris at the beginning of the 13th century, whose style was still being sung in the cathedral during the master/friar conflict: http://www.hilliardensemble.demon.co.uk/.

Lionheart: a New York-based vocal ensemble that performs both medieval and Renaissance music, they have an exquisite CD of music of Notre Dame in Paris from *ca.* 1200: http://www.chantboy.com/lionheart.

Micrologus: an Italian ensemble more often devoted to medieval Mediterranean repertoire, they did produce a spirited recording of Adam de la Halle's "Le Jeu de Robin et Marion": http://micrologus.it.

Sequentia: one of the finest of medieval ensembles, and active since the 1970s, the group has recorded a remarkable number of programs over the years, including a two-disc set devoted to the trouvères, and a recording of motets by Philippe de Vitry, an important contributor to the *Roman de Fauvel*: http://www.sequentia.org.

Sinfonye: directed by composer Stevie Wishart, Sinfonye has a number of vibrant and beautiful recordings covering a variety of repertoire, including a striking CD devoted to the motets of the *Montpellier Codex*: http://www.loganartsmanagement.com/sinfonye.html.

Tim Rayborn: it may be presumptuous for the author to include his own work among such esteemed groups, but he has produced a recording of medieval English music from the 13th and early 14th centuries, with several noted guest artists: http://www.timrayborn.com.

Chapter Notes

Introduction

1. Trinity College Cambridge MS 1144 fol. 58v: "Freers, freers, wo ye be | *ministri malorum*! | For many a mannes soule brynge ye | *ad penas inffernorum*." This bilingual poem is in a modern edition, *Medieval English Political Writings*, James M. Dean, ed. (Kalamazoo: Medieval Institute Publications, 1996), available online at the University of Rochester: http://d.lib.rochester.edu/teams/publication/dean-medieval-english-political-writings, accessed February 15, 2014.

2. This was not always the case. The earliest Robin Hood stories date from later than the reigns of Richard and John. Robin came to inhabit a mythical time that made use of the crises of the English crown in the 1190s and into the first decade of the 13th century, but he stood as a folk hero for all times.

3. Penn Szittya, *The Antifraternal Tradition in Medieval Literature* (Princeton: Princeton University Press, 1986). This is an excellent introduction to writings against the friars from a variety of outside critics, with a focus on English sources. Extensively researched and detailed, it remains one of the best books on the subject, though some of its conclusions have been questioned in recent years. See also Szittya, "The Antifraternal Tradition in Middle English Literature," *Speculum* 52, 2 (1977): 287–313.

4. Szittya, *Antifraternal Tradition*, ix.

5. See G. Geltner, *The Making of Medieval Antifraternalism: Polemic, Violence, Deviance, & Remembrance* (Oxford: Oxford University Press, 2012), a recent excellent overview; Geltner, "William of Saint Amour's *De periculis novissimorum temporum*: a False Start to Medieval Antifraternalism?" *Defenders and Critics of Franciscan Life*, Michael F. Cusato & G. Geltner, eds. (Leiden: Brill, 2009), 105–18; and Geltner, "*Faux Semblants*: Antifraternalism Reconsidered in Jean de Meun and Chaucer," *Studies in Philology* 101 (2004): 357–80. Geltner is a leading scholar in the field, whose work is offering a fresh examination of the antifraternal subject.

6. Geltner, *Making of Medieval Antifraternalism*, 16, and 24–25.

7. Ibid., 134–36. For a study of anticlerical attitudes, see José Sánchez, *Anticlericalism: A Brief History* (Notre Dame: University of Notre Dame Press, 1972).

8. Geltner, *Making of Medieval Antifraternalism*, 41. See also chapter 7.

9. Ibid., 136.

10. Ibid., 94.

11. Ibid., 99. See Donald F. Logan, *Runaway Religious in Medieval England, c.1240–1540*, Cambridge Studies in Medieval Life and Thought, 4th ser., 32 (Cambridge: Cambridge University Press, 1996), 241–50. For the Dominicans in a larger context, see Geltner, *Making of Medieval Antifraternalism*, 90–93. He notes, for example at 92, *n*35, that prisons for disobedient and fallen brothers were required at all Dominican convents or provinces from 1238.

12. Geltner, *Making of Medieval Antifraternalism*, 93. His focus is on the Dominicans, but could be applied equally to other friars as well.

13. Carolly Erickson, "Fourteenth-Century Franciscans and their Critics," *Franciscan Studies* 35 (1975), 118. However, see *n*43; some have suggested this was merely an excuse for a lack of religious devotion. See also 119–20.

14. Frances Andrews, *The Other Friars: The Carmelite, Augustinian, Sack and Pied Friars in the Middle Ages* (Woodbridge: Boydell, 2006).

15. Pertaining to preaching, as one example; the Franciscans and Dominicans had more freedom to preach in a given diocese, whereas Carmelites and Augustinians needed a license to do so. This issue was addressed by the papal bull *Super cathedram* in 1303, which we will discuss in chapters 2, 6, and 8.

Chapter 1

1. Dominique Iogna-Pratt, *Order and Exclusion: Cluny and Christendom Face Heresy, Judaism, and Islam (1000–1150)*, trans. Graham Robert Edwards (Ithaca: Cornell University Press, 2002), 110. For a brief biographical sketch of Peter, see Heinrich Fichtenau, *Heretics and Scholars in the High Middle Ages, 1000–1200*, trans. Denise A. Kaiser (University Park: Pennsylvania State University Press, 1998), 57–58.

2. The Reform is a vast topic, with numerous studies. Pope Gregory VII was its most enthusiastic supporter, but it continued into the 12th century. For summaries see Karl F. Morrison, "The Gregorian Reform," *Christian Spirituality—Origins to the Twelfth Century*, Bernard McGinn, John Myendorf, and Jean Leclercq, eds., (London:

SCM, 1989), 177–93, and I.S. Robinson, *The Papacy 1073–1198: Continuity and Innovation* (Cambridge: Cambridge University Press, 1990). See also Tim Rayborn, *The Violent Pilgrimage: Christians, Muslims and Holy Conflicts, 850–1150* (Jefferson, NC: McFarland, 2013), 16–18. For the life of Gregory VII, see H.E.J. Cowdrey, *Pope Gregory VII, 1073–1085* (Oxford: Oxford University Press, 1998). The killing of Peter of Bruys may have had political motives as well as religious ones, involving trade and a struggle for control of the region between the Counts of Toulouse and Barcelona, see Iogna-Pratt, *Order and Exclusion*, 110.

3. C. H. Lawrence, *The Friars: The Impact of the Early Mendicant Movement on Western Society* (London and New York: Longman, 1994, reprinted as *The Friars: The Impact of the Mendicant Orders on Medieval Society*, 2013), 15. This is an excellent brief introduction to the friars and their times.

4. For a summary of the founding of the Cistercians, see Rayborn, *The Violent Pilgrimage*, 76–79.

5. Iogna-Pratt, *Order and Exclusion*, 109.

6. Peter the Venerable, *Contra Petrobrusianos hereticos*, James Fearns, ed., Corpus Christianorum Continuatio Mediaevalis 10 (Turnhout: Brepols, 1968). Iogna-Pratt offers a comprehensive study of Peter the Venerable's refutation in part II of *Order and Exclusion*, 99–261, so we will not offer excerpts from the work here.

7. See Rayborn, *The Violent Pilgrimage*, 97–111, for a summary of Peter's monumental Islamic studies project. This was not an undertaking of interfaith dialogue, but a deliberate effort to aid in evangelizing and refuting the supposed Islamic heresies.

8. The Church had long charged that heretics did not venerate the cross; Peter and his followers demonstrated this perfectly. The accusation was also applied to Jews, who did indeed view it as a form of idolatry. See Iogna-Pratt, *Order and Exclusion*, 188. See also 183; the act of burning the cross was a way of "punishing" the instrument of Christ's death.

9. See chapter 8 for a study of Wyclif.

10. Iogna-Pratt gives a summary in *Order and Exclusion*, 2–3, and a more detailed examination of these five points at 109–110. These were taken from Peter the Venerable's *Contra Petrobrusianos*, since those of Peter of Bruys do not survive, see also 144.

11. Ibid., 114 and 253–54.

12. A quick internet search will reveal any number of websites of contemporary Protestant churches and thinkers who view Peter of Bruys in a favorable light, and see him as a proto-reformer long before Luther. This is, of course, a matter of opinion, but some of these arguments fail to examine the larger issues of the time.

13. Fichtenau, *Heretics and Scholars*, 59. He believes the designation "of Lausanne" to be in error, calling him Henry the Monk, though he also shows at 59 that Henry was not likely actually from a monastery. A summary of Henry's life and activities is at 59–61.

14. Ibid., 59 and 61.

15. Ibid., 58. See also Iogna-Pratt, *Order and Exclusion*, 256.

16. Fichtenau notes in *Heretics and Scholars* at 67 that evidence for this name only dates from the 14th century. He provides a summary of Waldes's life at 67–69. For a longer summary, see C. H. Lawrence, *The Friars*, 19–22. For more detailed works, see Gabriel Audisio, *The Waldensian Dissent: Persecution and Survival, c.1170–c.1570*, Cambridge Medieval Textbooks (Cambridge: Cambridge University Press, 1999), and Jean Gounet and Amédée Molnar, *Les Vaudois au moyen-âge* (Turin: Claudiana, 1974). See also Michael Frassetto, *Heretic Lives: Medieval Heresy from Bogomil and the Cathars to Wyclif and Hus* (London: Profile, 2007), 56–74.

17. Lawrence, *The Friars*, 20.

18. Fichtenau, *Heretics and Scholars*, 67.

19. Lawrence, *The Friars*, 23. See also Fichtenau, *Heretics and Scholars*, 66–67. For more detailed studies of the Humiliati, see Frances Andrews, *The Early Humiliati*, (Cambridge: Cambridge University Press, 1999); Sally Mayall Brasher, *Women of the Humiliati: Lay Religious Order in Medieval Civic Life* (New York: Routledge, 2003); and John B. Wickstrom, "The Humiliati: Liturgy and Identity," *Archivum Fratrum Praedicatorum* 4 (1992): 1–32.

20. Lawrence, *The Friars*, 24. See also Fichtenau, *Heretics and Scholars*, 67 and 260.

21. καθαροί, *katharoi*, "the pure," or "the pure ones," though this is not certain.

22. Private email correspondence with Stephen O'Shea. The association of cats with evil was widespread in medieval Europe. The German for heresy, *die Ketzerei*, is from the same root.

23. As with many of these topics, the literature on the Cathars and Catharism is vast. Standard books include Malcolm Barber, *The Cathars: Dualist Heretics in Languedoc in the High Middle Ages* (Harlow, UK: Longman, 2000); Malcolm Lambert, *The Cathars* (Oxford: Blackwell, 1998); Anne Brenon, *Le Vrai Visage du catharsime* (reprinted Cahors: La Louve éditions, 2008); and Jean Duvernoy, *Le Catharisme*, Vol. 1: *La Religion des cathares*, and Vol. 2: *L'Histoire des cathares* (Toulouse: Privat, 1976 and 1979). See also his more recent *Cathares, Vaudois et Beguins, dissidents du pays d'Oc, Domaine Cathare* (Toulouse: Privat, 1994), which includes study of the Waldensisans and Beguines in the south. A good study of the whole of the Cathar movement, the Albigensian Crusade that resulted, and the Inquisition that followed it, is Walter L. Wakefield, *Heresy, Crusade, and Inquisition in Southern France, 1100–1250* (New York: Allen and Unwin, 1974). A very readable and compelling popular account of the Cathars and the Albigensian Crusade is Stephen O'Shea, *The Perfect Heresy: The Revolutionary Life and Death of the Medieval Cathars* (New York: Walker, 2000). One of the best introductions to the Albigensian Crusade is Joseph R. Strayer, *The Albigensian Crusades* (Ann Arbor: University of Michigan Press, rep. 1992); see also the recent work by Mark Gregory Pegg, *A Most Holy War: The Albigensian Crusade and the Battle for Christendom* (Oxford: Oxford University Press, 2008) as well as his "On Cathars, Albigenses, and Good Men of Languedoc," *Journal of Medieval History* 27 (2001): 181–190. A broader view of dualism in the Middle Ages is Steven Runciman, *The Medieval Manichee* (Cambridge: Cambridge University Press, 1991). For general histories of heresy in the Middle Ages see Michael Frassetto, *Heretic Lives*, Heinrich Fichtenau, *Heretics and Scholars*, Yuri Stoyanov, *The Other God: Dualist Religions from Antiquity to the Cathar Heresy* (New Haven, CT: Yale Nota Bene, 2000); Leonard George, *The Encyclopedia of Heresies and Heretics* (London: Robson, 1995); Malcolm Lambert, *Medieval Heresy: Popular Movements from the Gregorian Reform to the Reformation* (Oxford: Blackwell, 1992); Walter L. Wakefield and Austin P. Evans, eds., *Heresies of the High Middle Ages* (New York: Columbia University Press, 1969, reprinted 1991); R.I. Moore, *The Formation of a Persecuting Society* (New York:

Blackwell, 1987); and Moore, ed. *The Birth of Popular Heresy*, Medieval Academy of America Reprints (Toronto: University of Toronto Press, 1975, reprinted 1995).

24. For studies of this complex and fascinating belief, see Geo Widengren, *Mani and Manichaeism* (London: Weidenfeld and Nicholson, 1965); Jason David BeDuhn, *The Manichaean Body: In Discipline and Ritual* (Baltimore: Johns Hopkins University Press, 2000, republished 2002); and Iain Gardner and Samuel N. C. Lieu, *Manichaean Texts from the Roman Empire* (Cambridge: Cambridge University Press, 2004). See also the above-mentioned Runciman, *The Medieval Manichee*.

25. Fichtenau, *Heretics and Scholars*, 66–67.

26. The term "troubadour" originally referred to these poet-musicians in the south, who wrote in the language of Occitan, a distinct tongue having more in common with Catalan than northern French. The name has at times been mistakenly used as a more generic term, or a synonym for minstrel. The first known troubadour was Guillaume IX, Duke of Aquitaine, grandfather of Eleanor of Aquitaine, who was herself a great patron of troubadours in the later 12th century. Their culture thrived until many were dispersed by the Albigensian crusade, when they were forced to flee to Spain and Italy. Some went to Northern France and adopted the French language of the trouvères. For an excellent introduction to the history and culture of the time, see Linda M. Paterson, *The World of the Troubadours: Medieval Occitan Society, c. 1100–1300* (Cambridge: Cambridge University Press, 1993). For a comprehensive look at all aspects of the troubadours, including texts, music, culture, and dissemination, see F.R.P. Akehurst and Judith M. Davis, eds., *A Handbook of the Troubadours* (Berkeley: University of California Press, 1995). A good analysis of the extant melodies is Elizabeth Aubrey, *The Music of the Troubadours* (Bloomington: Indiana University Press, 1996). For a collection of the surviving melodies, see Hendrik van der Werf, *The Extant Troubadour Melodies: Transcriptions and Essays for Performers and Scholars*, Gerald A. Bond, ed. texts (Rochester, NY: the author, 1984). For a collection of the poems of the trobairitz (the female troubadours), see Meg Bogin, *The Women Troubadours* (New York: Norton, 1980); a number of notable noble women contributed poems to the genre, with one extant musical work by the Contessa de Dia.

27. It was so named because of the belief that a good number of adherents to Catharism resided in the city of Albi, northeast of Toulouse.

28. "Caedite eos. Novit enim Dominus qui sunt eis," recorded by Caesarius of Heisterbach (*ca.* 1180–*ca.* 1240), a fellow Cistercian. Caesarius Heiserbacencis monachi ordinis Cisterciensis, *Dialogus miraculorum* 2, Joseph Strange, ed. (Cologne: J.M. Heberle, 1851), 296–8. For a study of Cistercian activities during this period, see Beverly Mayne Kienzle, *Cistercians, Heresy, and Crusade in Occitania, 1145–1229* (Woodbridge: Boydell and York Medieval Press, 2001).

29. For a history of the final decades of the religion, see René Weis, *The Yellow Cross: The Story of the Last Cathars, 1290–1329* (New York: Random House, 2001), and Stephen O'Shea, *The Friar of Carcassonne: Revolt against the Inquisition in the Last Days of the Cathars* (New York: Walker, 2011).

30. See *n*167 below.

31. See Szittya, *Antifraternal Tradition*, 7, *n*5, for some referenced examples.

32. For an additional summary of the social conditions of the time, see Lawrence, *The Friars*, 1–4, and 218.

33. Ibid., 165, and 219–220. See also 87.

34. See ibid., 225–28.

35. Guillaume de Saint-Amour, as we will see in the next two chapters, was not overflowing with praise for Francis or Dominic.

36. From the earliest days of the Franciscan order, they had a confrontational attitude toward Islam, seeing it as a perfect ideology against which to set their preaching. The story of Francis meeting with the Egyptian Sultan Malik al–Kamil to convert him to Christianity is one instance, see *n*37 below. There is also the claim that Francis was pleased when he heard that a group of his friars had gone to their deaths for insulting the Prophet Muhammad and condemning Islam in the presence of Muslims in Seville in 1219. Led by one Berard of Carbio, who was fluent in Arabic, they were taken to Marrakech, and then sent home, but they returned. They were subsequently tortured and beheaded, making them the order's first martyrs. Francis is said to have proclaimed them to be true Friars Minor for their sacrifice. See *Passio Sanctorum Martyrum, Frairum Beraldi*, Analecta Franciscana 3 (Florence: Frati Editori di Quaracchi, 1897), 579–596. Instances of Franciscans actively seeking death through denouncing Islam in Spain and North Africa became more common as the 13th century progressed, and bear a striking similarity to an earlier episode, the Spanish Martyr's Movement in mid–9th-century Córdoba in southern Spain. Groups of determined Mozarabic Christians actively sought out martyrdom as a protest against Muslim rule by verbally attacking Islam and Muhammad. For an account, see Rayborn, *The Violent Pilgrimage*: 130–39. The Dominicans were also devoted to evangelizing the Muslims in Spain, establishing a school in Barcelona to study Arabic in 1259. See Lawrence, *The Friars*, 202–03. For the early Dominicans and Islam, see Thomas F. O'Meara, O.P., "The Theology and Times of William of Tripoli, O.P.: A Different View of Islam," *Theological Studies* 69 (2008): 80–98. For Dominican crusade preaching, see Lawrence, *The Friars*, 185–88.

37. For a full account, see John Tolan, *St. Francis and the Sultan: The Curious History of a Christian-Muslim Encounter* (Oxford: Oxford University Press, 2009).

38. Lawrence, *The Friars*, 27. For an edition of Thomas of Celano's writings, see *St. Francis of Assisi According to Brother Thomas of Celano: His Descriptions of the Seraphic Father. A.D. 1229–1257*, H.G. Rosedale, ed. (London: J.M. Dent, 1904). For a modern edition of Thomas' *Life*, and a detailed study of Francis's early life see Regis J. Armstrong, J. A. Wayne Hellmann, William J. Short, eds., *Francis of Assisi: The Saint*, 3 vols., vol. 1: Early Documents (New York: New City Press, 1999). For an edition of *The Mirror of Perfection* (the biography of Francis from the 1240s), see Rosalind B. Brooke, ed., *Scripta Leonis, Rufini et Angeli, Sociorum S. Francisci* (Oxford: Clarendon Press, 1970, rep. 1990).

39. We will examine some of his writings in defense of mendicancy during his feud with Guillaume de Saint-Amour in chapter 3.

40. This was not successful, as Thomas' works survive in modern editions, see *n*38. For a summary of some of the other issues with these lives, dating, and sources, see Lawrence, *The Friars*, 28–30.

41. Biographies and studies of Francis are numerous to the point of confusion for anyone looking for an introduction. A comprehensive recent study is Augustine Thomp-

son, O.P., *Francis of Assisi: A New Biography* (Ithaca: Cornell University Press, 2012). An excellent collection of general essays of the early years of the order is Michael J. P. Robson, ed., *The Cambridge Companion to Francis of Assisi* (Cambridge: Cambridge University Press, 2012). For a study of Francis's conception of poverty, which would be so essential to the Franciscans, see Kenneth Baxter Wolf, *The Poverty of Riches: St. Francis of Assisi Reconsidered* (Oxford: Oxford University Press, 2003). A study placing Francis in the context of the time is Adrian House, *Francis of Assisi: A Revolutionary Life* (Mahwah, NJ: Hidden Spring, Paulist Press, 2001). This work has received some criticism for its inconsistent approach to the works of Francis's first biographers, however. A classic study is Father Cuthbert (O.S.F.C.), *Life of St. Francis of Assisi* (London: Longmans, Green and Co. 1914). For good general studies of the order, see Michael Robson, *The Franciscans in the Middle Ages* (Woodbridge: Boydell, 2006), and John Moorman, *A History of the Franciscan Order, from its Origins to Year 1517* (Oxford: Clarendon Press, 1968).

42. Lawrence, *The Friars*, 30–31.

43. Detailed in ibid., 32. See also K. Esser, O.F.M., *Die opuskula des hl. Franziskus von Assisi*, Editiones Collegii S. Bonaventurae ad Claras aquas (Rome: Grottaferrata, 1976), 439.

44. Lawrence, *The Friars*, 32.

45. For a discussion of the debate on Franciscan poverty, as well as disorder and lapses in obedience at this early stage, see David Burr, *The Spiritual Franciscans: From Protest to Persecution in the Century after Saint Francis* (University Park: Pennsylvania State University Press, 2001), 15–30.

46. Lawrence, *The Friars*, 35–36.

47. For an edition, see Herbert Grundmann, "Die Bulle Quo elongati Papst Gregors IX," *Archivum Fratrum Historicum* 54 (1961): 1–25. An edition and translation is also at the website "Francis and Clare of Assisi, Early Documents": http://franciscantradition.org:8080/FAED/index.jsp?workNum=043&p=570, accessed December 27, 2013: "Super quo duximus respondendum, quod si rem sibi necessariam velint fratres emere vel solutionem facere pro iam empta, possunt vel nuntium eius, a quo res emitur, vel aliquem alium volentibus sibi elymosinam facere, nisi iidem per se vel per proprios nuntios sol-

vere maluerint, presentare; qui taliter presentatus a fratribus non est eorum nuntius, licet presentetur ab ipsis, sed illius potius, cuius mandato solutionem tacit, seu recipientis eandem."

48. Jonathan Robinson, at the University of Toronto, provides an edition in Latin and English at his website: http://individual.utoronto.ca/jwrobinson/translations/innocent4_lat-eng_ordinem-vestrum.pdf, accessed December 27, 2013. See 3: "cui domus, & loca praedicta cum Ecclesiis, ceterisque suis pertinentiis (quae omnia in jus, & proprietatem Beati Petri suscipimus) omnino tam in spiritualibus, quam temporalibus immediate subesse noscuntur." Text drawn from J. H. Sbaralea and C. Eubel, eds., *Bullarium franciscanum*, 7 vols. (Rome: Vatican, 1759–68, and 1898–1904), 1:400a–02b, 114.

49. Lawrence, *The Friars*, 40.

50. For an excellent summary of the Franciscan rift in the early years as a result of these papal rulings, see Gordon Leff, *Heresy in the Later Middle Ages: The Relation of Heterodoxy to Dissent, c. 1250-c. 1450* (Manchester: Manchester University Press, 1967, reprinted 1999), 51–166.

51. Geltner, *The Making of Medieval Antifraternalism*, 56, referencing the *Chronica Fratris Jordani* 5, H. Boehmer, ed. (Paris: Libraries Fischbacher, 1908), 5–6: "Unde accidit, ut interrogati, si essent heretici et si ad hoc venissent ut Teutoniam inficerent sicut et Lombardiam prevertissent, et respondissent 'ia,' quidam ex ipsis plegati, quidam incarcerati et quidam denudati nudi ad choream sunt ducti et spectaculum ludecre hominibus sunt effecti."

52. However, see Geltner, *The Making of Medieval Antifraternalism*, 56–57 for additional thoughts.

53. Salimbene is a major source for 13th-century Franciscan history. See *Cronica Fratris Salimbene de Adam*, Oswald Holder-Egger, ed., Monumenta Germaniae Historica Scriptores 32 (Hannover: Verlag, 1905–13). For a more recent edition, see Salimbene de Adam, *Cronica*, Giuseppe Scalia ed., 2 vols. Corpus Christianorum Continuatio Mediaevalis, 125 and 125A (Turnhout: Brepols, 1998–99). For an English translation, see the *Chronicle of Salimbene De Adam*, Joseph L. Baird, B. Guiseppe, and J. R. Kane, eds., (Binghamton, NY: Medieval & Renaissance Texts & Studies, 1986).

54. Geltner, *The Making of Medieval Antifraternalism*, 57, referencing the Scalia edition of the

Cronica, 56: "Dixit igitur michi pater meus: 'Fili dilecte, non credas istis pissintunicis'"; and "'Comendi te mille demonibus, maledicte fili, et fratrem tuum qui hic tecum est, qui etiam de decepit. Mea maledictio vobiscum sit perpetuo, que vos infernalibus commendet spiritibus.'" See also Geltner, "Mendicants as Victims: Scale, Scope, and the Idiom of Violence," *Journal of Medieval History* 36 (2010): 131–32.

55. Lawrence, *The Friars*, 107.

56. ibid., 46.

57. See Raphael M. Huber, "Elias of Cortona (c. 1180–1253): Minister General of the Friars Minor," *The Catholic Historical Review* 22, 4 (1937): 395–408. See also Lawrence, *The Friars*, 48–50.

58. Burr, *The Spiritual Franciscans*, 9. See 9–10 for a discussion of why there were so many supporters of expanding the Franciscan's duties.

59. Ibid., 10.

60. Lawrence, *The Friars*, 52.

61. There are a number of histories of the order and of Dominic, though surprisingly, not as many good scholarly works in English as one might expect. A standard biography is M.H. Vicaire, *Histoire de Saint Dominique*, 2 vols. (Paris: Les Éditions de Cerf, 1957), translated by Kathleen Pond as *Saint Dominic and His Times* (Green Bay, WI: Alt Publishing, 1964). For a comprehensive study of the order, see William A. Hinnebusch, *The History of the Dominican Order: Origins and Growth to 1500*, 2 vols. (New York: Alba House, 1966 and 1972). For a study of the Dominicans in England, see Hinnebusch, *The Early English Friars Preachers* (Rome: Ad S. Sabinae, 1951). For an excellent selection of writings in English from the first decades of the order, see Simon Tugwell, ed., *Early Dominicans: Selected Writings*, The Classics of Western Spirituality (Mahwah, NJ: Paulist Press, rep. 1999). A collection of works relating to the life of Dominic can be found in Francis C. Lehner, ed., *St. Dominic: Biographical Documents* (Washington, D.C.: Thomist Press, 1964), available online at: http://domcentral.org/blog/st-dominic-biographical-documents, accessed December 28, 2013. Latin sources include Vladimir Koudelka and Raymondo Loenertz (eds.), *Monumenta diplomatica S. Dominici*, Monumenta ordinis fratrum praedicatorum historica 25 (Rome: Institutum historicum fratrum praedicatorum, 1966). A history of the order's masters is Antonin Mortier, *Histoire des maîtres généraux de l'Ordre des Frères Prêcheurs* (Paris: A. Picara,

1903–20). See also the Latin language history of Angelus Maria Walz, *Compendium historiae Ordinis Praedicatorum* (Rome: Herder, 2nd ed. 1948), and Vicaire's French-language translation of sources, *Saint Dominique de Caleruega: D'après les documents du XIIIe siècle* (Paris: Éditions du Cerf, 1955).

62. Lawrence, *The Friars*, 67. He notes the story that Dominic happened to stay at an inn at that time, where the innkeeper was a Cathar. Dominic was shocked and apparently stayed up all night, arguing with the man about the error of his ways. Cathars were generally not impressed by what the Church had to say, however, so Dominic's words likely had little effect.

63. A full account can be found in the writings of Jordan of Saxony. See H.C. Sheeban, ed., *Libellus Iordani de Saxonia*, Monumenta Ordinis Fratrum Praedicatorum Historica 16 (Rome: Institutum Historicum Fratrum Praedicatorum, 1935), 36. The Cistercians had been well aware of the Cathars for some time. Correspondence between Bernard of Clairvaux and Eberwin of Steinfeld in the 1140s and Bernard's 65th sermon on the Song of Songs (1144) show great concern for their beliefs and practices. See Walter Wakefield, Austin Patterson Evans, *Heresies of the High Middle Ages*, 126–38. For the full text of Bernard's sermon in Latin, see Jean Leclercq, C.H. Talbot, and H.M. Rochais, eds., *Sancti Bernardi Sermones super Canitca canticorum*, Sancti Bernardi Opera, I-II (Rome: Edizioni Cisterciensi, 1957–58), II, 172–77. Iogna-Pratt suggests in *Order and Exclusion* at 126 that this sermon may instead have been written in response to the activities of followers of Henry of Lausanne in Toulouse.

64. Lawrence discusses issues of dating the meeting, including the claims of Thomas of Celano, in *The Friars*, 68, and *n*6.

65. See Marie-Humbert Vicaire, "L'ordre de Saint Dominique en 1215," *Archivum Fratrum Praedicatorum* 54 (1984): 5–38, for a discussion of this early stage in the order's development.

66. For a study of this early approval, see Patrick Zutshi, "Letters of Pope Honorius III Concerning the Order of Preachers," *Pope, Church and City: Essays in Honour of Brenda M. Bolton*, Frances Andrews, Christoph Egger, and Constance M. Rousseau, eds. (Leiden: Brill, 2004), 269–86.

67. For a study of this fascinating figure and the culture of Languedoc at the time, see N. M. Schulman, *Where Troubadours were Bishops: The Occitania of Folc of Marseille (1150–1231)* (New York: Routledge, 2001).

68. For a collection of essays on the Dominican presence in Toulouse and the south, see *Saint Dominique en Languedoc*, Cahiers de Fanjeaux 1 (Toulouse: Éditions Privat, 1966), and *Les Mendiants en Pays D'oc au XIIIe siècle*, Cahiers de Fanjeaux 8 (Toulouse: Éditions Privat, 1973).

69. For an account of Raymond's life leading up to his conflict with the Church and the relative tolerant nature of Toulouse, see O'Shea, *The Perfect Heresy*, 44–54. See 161–68 for the siege of the city and the death of Simon de Montfort. On Raymond's humiliation by the pope, see Fichtenau, *Heretics and Scholars*, 150–51.

70. Lawrence, *The Friars*, 73–74.

71. Ibid., 75.

72. Lawrence discusses Dominic's wishes and the urban environment in ibid., 79–80.

73. For studies of the Inquisition, a good, brief general introduction is Bernard Hamilton, *The Medieval Inquisition* (Teaneck, NJ: Holmes & Meier, 1981). An overview is found in Lawrence, *The Friars*, 188–94. See also Edward Peters, *Inquisition* (Berkeley: University of California Press, 1989). A thorough study, including many translations of key texts relating to the southern heretics is Walter L. Wakefield, *Heresy, Crusade and Inquisition in Southern France, 1100–1250*. See also the detailed account of a specific instance in Mark Gregory Pegg, *The Corruption of Angels: The Great Inquisition of 1245 –1246* (Princeton: Princeton University Press, 2006). A recent excellent anthology of writings about both the Cathars and the Inquisition is Catherine Léglu, Rebecca Rist, and Claire Taylor, eds., *The Cathars and the Albigensian Crusade: A Sourcebook* (Abingdon: Routledge, 2014); an important work featured in this book (207–36) is the *Chronicle of William Pelhisson*. The original text is printed in Célestin Douais, ed., *Les sources de l'histoire de l'inquisition dans le midi de la France, aus XIIIe et XIVe siècles* (Paris: Victor Palmé, 1881), 81–118. Another important account available in translation is W. A. Sibly and M. D. Sibly, eds., *The Chronicle of William of Puylaurens: The Albigensian Crusade and Its Aftermath* (Woodbridge: Boydell, 2003). The original, also with French translation, is Jean Duvernoy, ed., *Guillaume de Puylaurens, Chronique 1145–1275: Chronica magistri Guillelmi de Podio Laurentii* (Paris: CNRS, 1976). On the issues of Catharsim in Toulouse, see John H. Mundy, *The Repression of Catharism at Toulouse*, Studies and Texts 74 (Toronto: Pontifical Institute of Medieval Studies, 1985). For a study of the testimonies of those accused, and the problems with translation (they gave their answers in Occitan, which was translated into Latin by the inquisitors), see John H. Arnold, *Inquisition and Power: Catharism and the Confessing Subject in Medieval Languedoc* (Philadelphia: University of Pennsylvania Press, 2001). For the techniques used by the inquisitors, see James Buchanan Given, *Inquisition and Medieval Society: Power, Discipline, and Resistance in Languedoc* (Ithaca, NY: Cornell University Press, 1997). A classic work is Arthur Stanley Turberville, *Medieval Heresy & the Inquisition* (London: Lockwood, 1920). A study of the impact of the Inquisition in Aragon (an ally to Count Raymond in his resistance to the Church's taking of his lands), see Damian J. Smith, *Crusade, Heresy and Inquisition in the Lands of the Crown of Aragon: (c. 1167–1276)* (Leiden: Brill, 2010).

74. We will discuss Robert and his relation to the trouvère king, Thibaut IV, in chapter 5.

75. See Nancy Freeman Regalado, *Poetic Patterns in Rutebeuf: A Study in Noncourtly Poetic Modes of the Thirteenth Century* (New Haven: Yale University Press, 1970), 172, *n*65, referencing Ralph Francis Bennett, *The Early Dominicans: Studies in Thirteenth-century Dominican History* (Cambridge: Cambridge University Press, 1937), 129. For a study of Humbert, see Edward Tracy Brett, *Humbert of Romans: His Life and Views of Thirteenth-century Society* (Toronto: Pontifical Institute of Mediaeval Studies, 1984).

76. For further study, see Marie-Humbert Vicaire, "La prédication nouvelle de prêcheurs méridionaux au XIIIe siècle," *Cahiers de Fanjeaux* 6 (1971): 21–64, especially 38–40.

77. O'Shea, *The Perfect Heresy*, 199–200.

78. *Les sources de l'histoire de l'inquisition*, 88: "Eodem tempore, est mortuus in dicto Burgo quidam hereticus, Galvanus nomine, archimandrita magnus Valdensium. Quod magistrum Rotlandum nun latuit, et publice hoc retulit in sermone, et convocatis fratribus et clero et aliquibus de populo, iverunt confidenter ad domum ubi dictus

hereticus obierat, et eam funditus destruxerunt, et fecerunt eam locum sterquilinii, et dictum Galvannum extumulaverunt, et de cimiterio Villenove, ubi sepultus fuerat, extraxerunt. Corpus vero illius per villam cum ingenti processione traxerunt, et in loco communi extra villam combusserunt. Hoc ad laudem Domini nostri Jhesu Christi et beati Dominici actum est, et ad honorem Romane et Catholice ecclesie, matris nostre, anno Domini M.CC.XXXI." For an English translation, see Wakefield, *Heresy, Crusade and Inquisition*, 210.

79. The Premonstratensians are an order of Canons Regular founded in 1120, by St. Norbert at Prémontré, near Laon, France, drawing influence from Bernard of Clairvaux's Cistercians. Still active today, their website contains historical information: http://www.premontre.org, accessed December 30, 2013.

80. Paul B. Pixton, "Conrad of Marburg," *Medieval Germany: An Encyclopedia*, John M. Jeep, ed. (New York: Garland, 2001), 230–31.

81. Lawrence, *The Friars*, 191.

82. See Holly J. Greico, "Franciscan Inquisition and Mendicant Rivalry in Mid-Thirteenth-Century Marseille," *Journal of Medieval History* 34 (2008): 275–90.

83. Larissa Tracy, *Torture and Brutality in Medieval Literature: Negotiations of National Identity* (Woodbridge: Boydell, 2012), 22.

84. Christine Caldwell Ames, *Righteous Persecution: Inquisition, Dominicans, and Christianity in the Middle Ages* (Philadelphia: University of Pennsylvania Press, 2009), 199.

85. See *n*73 above for editions of William's writings. See also Lawrence, *The Friars*, 192–93.

86. A more lengthy account is in Stephen O'Shea, *The Perfect Heresy*, 191–93.

87. *Les sources de l'histoire de l'inquisition*, 93–94: "Tunc commota est villa valde contre Fratres, et mine et verba multa fuerunt contra eos supra modum, et multi hereticales incitabant populum ut lapidarent Fratres, et domus eorum omnino diruerentur, quia probos homines, ut dicebant, et conjugatos accusabant injuste de heresi. Et sic faciebant multa consilia contra fratres."

88. Ibid., 90: "Quosdam alios mortuos condempnavit, et trahi fecit et comburi. Unde moti Aibienses voluerunt eum submergere in fluvio Tarni, et percussum, laniata veste, facie sanguinolenta, ad instanciam quorumdam, dimiserunt eum."

89. Ibid., 91–92: "Deprimebantur autem illis temporibus in terra illa catholici, et persequtores hereticorum in multis locis occidebantur, licet dominus Raymundus comes promisisset in forma pacis, quod per quinquennium daret, pro unoquoque heretico vel heretica, illi qui eos caperet duas marchas argenti, et post quinquennium unam tantum. Quod et factum fuit multoties. Sed majores de terra et potenciores milites et burgenses et alii defendebant dictos hereticos et celabant, et persequtores eorum percuciebant, vulnerabant et occidebant, quia consilium principis erat corruptum in fide notabiliter, et ideo multa mala fiebant in terra contra Ecclesiam et fideles."

90. The account of the storming of the town and the killing of the two friars is retold in a rather thrilling and cinematic manner by O'Shea in *The Perfect Heresy*, 208–10.

91. Susan Taylor Snyder, "Orthodox Fears: Anti-Inquisitorial Violence and Defining Heresy," *Fear and Its Representations in the Middle Ages and Renaissance*, Anne Scott and Cynthia Kosso, eds. (Turnhout: Brepols, 2002), 92–104, see especially 101.

92. Ibid., 94.

93. Geltner, *The Making of Medieval Antifraternalism*, 58–59.

94. Two recent works are Donald Prudlo, *The Martyred Inquisitor: The Life and Cult of Peter of Verona (+1252)* (Aldershot: Ashgate, 2008), and "The Assassin-Saint: The Life and Cult of Carino of Balsamo," *The Catholic Historical Review* 94 (2008): 1–21. Carino later repented of his action and became a Dominican lay brother.

95. O'Shea, *The Friar of Carcassonne*: 53.

96. Geltner, *The Making of Medieval Antifraternalism*, 123. See also 104 (where he asserts that the friars' approach to their own suffering unintentionally fueled further antifraternal sentiments) and 129.

97. Ibid., 124.

98. Ibid., 66.

99. Ibid., 114, and 125–26.

100. See ibid., Appendix I: "Aggression against Mendicant Friars and Convents until 1400," 140–153, and Geltner, "Mendicants as Victims," 126–41. This is an excellent introduction.

101. Burr, *The Spiritual Franciscans*, 263. This would be the cause of much hostility when the Dominicans stepped up persecution of the Spirituals in the early 14th century. In one of the more ridiculous examples, during a raid on Scotland in 1335, some English sailors attacked a Franciscan convent, stole its bell, and sold it to some English Dominicans in their home town of Newcastle! See Geltner, "Mendicants as Victims," 135.

102. On violence within the Franciscan order in the 14th century, see Erickson, "Fourteenth-Century Franciscans," *Franciscan Studies* 35, 132–35.

103. Geltner, "Brethren Behaving Badly: A Deviant Approach to Medieval Antifraternalism," *Speculum* 85 (2010): 51. See the entire article, 47–64, for a more detailed discussion of deviance and disobedience in the Dominican order. See also Michael Vargas, *Taming a Brood of Vipers: Conflict and Change in Fourteenth-Century Dominican Convents* (Leiden: Brill, 2011), which, while focusing primarily on Spanish Dominican houses, provides useful insights into how the order dealt with disobedience, crime, and the punishment of its members. See also Vargas, "Weak Obedience, Undisciplined Friars, and Failed Reforms in the Medieval Order of Preachers," *Viator* 42, 1 (2011): 283–308. See also the Introduction to this book, *n*11.

104. See Geltner, *The Making of Medieval Antifraternalism*, 51–54 for a more detailed analysis. See also 71, which notes that the simple fact that the friars lived in urban environments meant that they would be more susceptible to all kinds of violence (theft, murder, military) that had nothing to do with their vocation.

105. Geltner, "Mendicants as Victims," 129–30.

106. Ibid., 131.

107. For examples, see René Nelli, "Le Catharisme vu à travers les troubadours," *Cathares en Languedoc*, Cahiers de Fanjeaux 3 (Toulouse: Privat, 1968), 177–97.

108. Elizabeth Aubrey, *Music of the Troubadours*, 23. For some examples of his rhetorical method in his antifraternal poems, see Nathaniel B. Smith, "Rhetoric," *A Handbook of the Troubadours*, F.R.P. Akehurst and Judith M. Davis, eds. (Berkeley: University of California Press, 1995), 413, 415, and 449.

109. For selections of Peire's poetry, see Rialto online: http://www.rialto.unina.it/BdT.htm, accessed February 2, 2014; an alphabetical listing of troubadours' works is here, including Ab votz; v. II: "mas Jacopi apres maniar n'an queza, | ans desputon del vi cals meillers es | et an de plaitz cort establia | et es

Vaudes qui·ls ne desvia | e los sicretz d'ome volon saber | per tal que mieills si puoscon far temer." http://www.rialto.unina.it/PCard/335.1%28Vatteroni%29.htm, accessed February 2, 2014.

110. Ibid., III: "Esperitals non es la lur paubreza: | gardan lo lor prendon so que mieus es; | per mols gonels tescutz de lan'englesza | laisson selis car trop aspres lur es,"

111. Ibid., VII: "S'ieu fos maritz molt agra gran fereza | c'om desbraiatz lonc ma moiller segues | qu'ellas ez els an fauda d'un'amplesza | e fuec ab grais fort leumen s'es enpres; | de beguinas re no·us diria | tals es turgua que fructifia: | tals miracles fan, so sai hieu per ver | de sains paires saint podon esser l'er."

112. We will discuss Ysengrin in detail in chapter 6; he was an important character in the branches of Reynard the Fox.

113. http://www.rialto.unina.it/PCard/335.31%28Vatteroni%29.htm, accessed February 2, 2014, I: "Li clerc si fan pastor | e son aussizedor | e semblan de santor; | can los vei revestir | e prent m'a souvenir | de n'Alengri, c'un dia | volc ad un parc venir | mas pels canx que temia | pel de mouton vestic | ab que los escarnic | pois manget e trazic | la cal que l'abelic."

114. Ibid., II: "Rei et emperador | duc, comte e comtor | e cavallier ab lor | solon lo mon regir; | eras vei possezir | ha clercs la seingnoria | ab tolre et ab trair | et ab ypocrizia | ab forssa et ab prezic,"

115. Ibid., VI: "Clergues, qui vos chauzic | ses fellon cor enic | en son comde faillic | c'anc peior gent non vic."

116. An edition of the complete poem is available on the Institut d'Estudis Catalans website. Its *Corpus des Troubadours* is a digitization of Vicenzo Crescini, *Manuale per l'avviamento agli studi provenzali* (Milano: Hoepli, 1926). For the poem, see: http://trobadors.iec.cat/veure_d_fra.asp?id_obra=416, accessed February 2, 2014.

117. See O'Shea, *The Friar of Carcassonne*, 56–60, for a detailed summary, including the text of the letter. See also Jean-Marie Vidal, *Un inquisiteur jugé par ses victimes: Jean Galand et les Carcassonnaise (1285–1286)* (Paris: Picard, 1903), 40–41, for the full text of the appeal.

118. O'Shea, *The Friar of Carcassonne*, 60.

119. For two recent studies of Bernard's life, see Alan Friedlander, *The Hammer of the Inquisitors: Brother Bernard Délicieux and the Struggle against the Inquisition in Fourteenth-Century France*, Cultures, Beliefs, and Traditions 9 (Leiden: Brill, 2000), and Stephen O'Shea, *The Friar of Carcassonne*. O'Shea's book is a riveting account of the dramatic events of the time, comparable to his previous work, *The Perfect Heresy*, with an excellent sense of narrative and description.

120. See O'Shea, *The Friar of Carcassonne*, 65–69.

121. Ibid., 78–82. See also Friedlander, *Hammer of the Inquisitors*, 55–56.

122. See Friedlander, *Hammer of the Inquisitors*, 93.

123. O'Shea, *The Friar of Carcassonne*, 97. See 85–98 for the full remarkable account. See also Friedlander, *Hammer of the Inquisitors*, 96.

124. Ibid., 129–34. See also 47 and 49 for some discussion of the conditions. Oddly, inmates were expected to pay for their housing and food, an additional humiliation to being incarcerated.

125. Ibid., 146–152.

126. See Jean Duvernoy, *Le Procès de Bernard Délicieux 1319* (Toulouse: Pérégrinateur, 2001), 155–57. O'Shea summarizes in *The Friar of Carcassonne*, 156–161.

127. O'Shea, *The Friar of Carcassonne*, 168–73. Part of this unusual lenience may have been due to the influence of Queen Joan, who died in childbirth in April 1305, and had long been sympathetic to Bernard's cause. See Friedlander, *Hammer of the Inquisitors*, 223–24.

128. On Bernard's relationship to the Spirituals, see Burr, *The Spiritual Franciscans*, 191–94

129. O'Shea, *The Friar of Carcassonne*, 178.

130. See ibid., 184–87, and Friedlander, *Hammer of the Inquisitors*, 256.

131. Michel de Dmitrewski, "Fr. Bernard Délicieux, O.F.M. Sa lutte contre l'inquisition de Carcassonne et d'Albi, son procès, 1297–1319," *Archivum Franciscanum Historicum* 17 (1924): 486. Gui was made famous as the principal villain in Umberto Eco's *Name of the Rose*.

132. See Duvernoy, *Le Procès de Bernard Délicieux*, 147.

133. Ibid., 151.

134. For a full summary of the trial, see O'Shea, *The Friar of Carcassonne*, 187–207.

135. For recent studies of Clare, her spirituality, and her relationship to Francis, see Maria Pia Alberzoni, *Clare of Assisi and the Poor Sisters in the Thirteenth Century*, William Short and Nancy Celaschi, trans. (St. Bonaventure, NY: Franciscan Institute Publications, 2004); Lezlie Knox, "Clare of Assisi: Foundress of An Order?" *Spirit and Life* 11 (2004): 11–29; Margaret Carney, *The First Franciscan Woman: Clare of Assisi and her Form of Life* (Quincy: Franciscan Press, 1993); Margaret Carney, "Francis and Clare: A Critical Examination of the Sources," *Laurentianum* 30 (1987): 25–60. For Clare's writings see Regis J. Armstrong, ed. and trans., *Clare of Assisi—The Lady: Early Documents* (New York: New City Press, 2006).

136. For a survey of the early relations between male and female Dominicans, and Dominic's own attempts to establish women's communities, see Maiju Lehmijoki-Gardner, "Dominican Order," *Women and Gender in Medieval Europe*, Margaret Schaus, ed. (New York: Routledge, 2006), 223–24.

137. For a summary of women's issues and the monastic houses that cast off some of the nunneries, see Lawrence, *The Friars*, 76–78. See also Walter Simons, *Cities of Ladies: Beguine Communities in the Medieval Low Countries, 1200–1565* (Philadelphia: University of Pennsylvania Press, 2001), 22: "All the religious orders that came to the fore in the twelfth century—the Premonstratensians, Arrouaisians, Cistercians, and so on—eventually abandoned the experiment and segregated male and female religious, or simply stopped admitting women."

138. In addition to Simons' *Cities of Ladies* (which gives good information about the movement's origin), a good short summary of the movement is Simons, "Beguines," *Women and Gender in Medieval Europe*, 66–69. A study of the movement's early years is Carol Neel, "The Origins of the Beguines," *Signs* 14, 2 (1989): 321–41. On the development of beguinages in Northern France, see Penelope Galloway, "'Discreet and Devout Maidens': Women's Involvement in Beguine Communities in Northern France, 1200–1500," *Medieval Women in Their Communities*, Diane Watt, ed. (Toronto: University of Toronto Press, 1997), 92–115. See also Dennis Devlin, "Feminine Lay Piety in the High Middle Ages: The Beguines," *Medieval Religious Women, Vol. 1: Distant Echoes*, John A. Nichols and Lillian Thomas Shank, eds. (Kalamazoo: Cistercian Publications, 1984), 183–97. For online resources, see Abby Stoner, "Sisters Between: Gender and the Medieval Beguines," *Ex Post Facto* IV, 2 (Spring 1995), at: http://userwww.sfsu.edu/epf/journal_archive/volume_IV,_no._2_-_sp._1995/, accessed December 29, 2013.

See also Jennifer Deane, "'Beguines' Reconsidered: Historiographical Problems and New Directions," *Monastic Matrix*, 2008 (*Commentaria* 3461), online at: http://monasticmatrix.org/commentaria/beguines-reconsidered-historiographical-problems-and-new-directions, accessed December 29, 2013.

139. On Lambert, see Simons, *Cities of Ladies*, 24–34. Though not the Beguines' actual founder, he was certainly a part of the ever-growing movement of new religious ideas that was challenging the status quo.

140. Mechthild was a German Beguine, later affiliated with both the Dominicans and Cistercians, whose most famous work is *Das fließende Licht der Gottheit* (The Flowing Light of the Godhead). For a modern edition, see Frank Tobin, ed. and trans., *The Flowing Light of the Godhead*, Classics of Western Spirituality Series (New York and Mahwah, NJ: Paulist Press, 1998). For biographical information, see Bernard McGinn, *The Flowering of Mysticism: Men and Women in the New Mysticism (1200–1350)* (New York: Crossroad Herder, 1998), 222–244. Saskia Murk-Jansen surveys Mechthild, as well as other Beguine mystics in *Brides in the Desert: The Spirituality of the Beguines* (Maryknoll, NY: Orbis Books, 1998).

141. Walter Simons, "Beguines," 68. Burr, in *The Spiritual Franciscans*, 91, considers the use of the term in a more general sense, as it was applied to other members of the laity who acted as if in religious orders. It could also simply mean a very pious individual, who could be very orthodox or completely heretical in belief. The word "mumbler" may also point to the origin of the term "Lollard," see chapter 8.

142. Stoner, "Sisters Between," 11–12.

143. A useful study of the male and female movements is Ernest W. McDonnell, *The Beguines and Beghards in Medieval Culture* (New Brunswick, NJ: Rutgers University Press, 1969).

144. A full treatment of the Spirituals is not possible here, but a number of good studies can be recommended. A standard history of the Spirituals is David Burr, *The Spiritual Franciscans*, and Duncan Nimmo, *Reform and Division in the Medieval Franciscan Order* (Rome: Capuchin Historical Institute, 1987). See also Malcolm D. Lambert, *Franciscan Poverty: The Doctrine of the Absolute Poverty of Christ and the Apostles in the Franciscan Order, 1210–1323* (London: S.P.C.K., 1961).

A classic study is Decima L. Douie, *The Nature and the Effect of the Heresy of the Fraticelli* (Manchester: Manchester University Press, 1932). Perhaps the most well-known representation of the Spirituals in modern times is their portrayal in the novel *The Name of the Rose*, by Umberto Eco, William Weaver, trans. (New York: Harcourt Brace Jovanovich, 1983, reprinted several times).

145. The best study of Olivi's life and thought is David Burr, *Olivi and Franciscan Poverty: The Origins of the Usus Pauper Controversy*, Middle Ages Series (Philadelphia: University of Pennsylvania Press, 1989). See also Lawrence's summary in *The Friars*, 60–62. See David Burr, for an edition of Olivi's commentary on the *usus pauper*, *De usus pauper, the quaestio and the Tractatus* (Firenze-Perth: Leo S. Olschki, University of Western Australia Press, 1992). See also Burr and David Flood "Peter Olivi: On Poverty and Revenue," *Franciscan Studies* 40 (1980): 18–58, and Burr, *The Spiritual Franciscans*, 51–54, 56–65, and 269, for a brief overview of Peter's fairly reasonable position on *usus pauper*, which the commission set up to review it nevertheless rejected. For a detailed study of Vatican manuscripts and their annotations about Olivi's censure, see Sylvain Piron, "Censures et condamnation de Pierre de Jean Olivi: enquête dans les marges du Vatican, Mélanges de l'Ecole française de Rome," *Moyen Age*, 118, 2 (2006): 313–73. He argues that these show that the reviewers had an existing list of doctrinal errors before identifying those passages in Olivi's writing which they later deemed to be incorrect. For a short summary of the *usus pauper* controversy, see Lawrence, *The Friars*, 60–62.

146. Burr, *The Spiritual Franciscans*, 52.

147. Lawrence, *The Friars*, 61–62. See also chapter 8.

148. See ibid., 171–77 for charges levelled against the Spirituals in France, and 199–200 for comparisons to other heretical groups, by Pope John XXII. Burr also offers at 110 that it was not in the best interests of Spirituals to associate with heretical groups in their earlier days, but by the middle of the 14th century when they had been pushed to the margins and condemned, they may have been more influenced from other outlawed groups.

149. For recent thorough studies of the poverty controversy, see Patrick Nold, *Pope John XXII and his Franciscan Cardinal: Bertrand de la Tour and the Apostolic Poverty Controversy* (Oxford: Oxford University Press, 2003); Virpi Mäkinen, *Property Rights in the Late Medieval Discussion on Franciscan Poverty* (Leuven, Belgium: Peeters, 2001); and Melanie Brunner, "Papal Interventions in Mendicant Organisation: Pope John XXII and the Franciscans," *Franciscan Organisation in the Mendicant Context: Formal and Informal Structures of the Friars' Lives and Ministry in the Middle Ages*, Michael Robson, Jens Röhrkasten, eds. (Berlin: LIT Verlag, 2010), 353–75. See also Lawrence's summary in *The Friars*, 62–64. For a Latin and English edition of the chronicle of Nicolaus Minorita, see *Nicolaus Minorita: Chronica, Documentation on Pope John XXII, Michael of Cesena and the Poverty of Christ with Summaries in English*, Gedeon Gal and David Flood, eds. (St. Bonaventure, NY: Franciscan Institute Publications, 1996). For an online English translation of *Ad conditorem canonum*, John Kilcullen and John Scott, trans., see Macquarie University: http://www.mq.edu.au/about_us/faculties_and_departments/faculty_of_arts/mhpir/politics_and_international_relations/staff/john_kilcullen/john_xxii_ad_conditorem_canonum, accessed January 3, 2014.

150. A short introduction is in James Hannam, *God's Philosophers: How the Medieval World Laid the Foundations of Modern Science* (London: Icon, 2010), 135–51. A good collection of studies on Bacon is *Roger Bacon and the Sciences: Commemorative Essays*, Jeremiah Hackett, ed., Studien und Texte zur Geistesgeschichte des Mittelalters 57 (Leiden: Brill, 1997). For his works, see the extensive page at the Stanford Encyclopedia of Philosophy: http://plato.stanford.edu/entries/roger-bacon, accessed March 2, 2014. See also Brian Clegg, *The First Scientist: A Life of Roger Bacon* (New York: Carroll & Graf, 2003), though this work tends to accept some older, disputed views of Bacon as factual.

151. See, for example, David C. Lindberg, *Roger Bacon and the Origins of Perspectiva in the Middle Ages: A Critical Edition and English Translation of Bacon's Perspectiva with Introduction and Notes* (Oxford: Oxford University Press, 1996).

152. Bacon may have written a treatise called the *Epistola de Secretis Operibus Artis et Naturae, et de Nullitate Magiae* (the "Letter on the Secret Workings of Art and Nature, and on the Vanity of Magic"), which actually dismisses

magic, but does contain information about alchemical processes, a possible formula for gunpowder, as well as ideas for flying and underwater machines. A translation of this work (said to have been in the possession of Dr. John Dee, astrologer to Queen Elizabeth I) appeared in England in 1659, titled *Friar Bacon, His Discovery of the Miracles of Art, Nature, and Magick*. For an online version, see http://www.sacred-texts.com/aor/bacon/miracle.htm, accessed December 30, 2013. A modern translation by Michael S. Mahoney is online at: http://www.princeton.edu/~hos/h392/bacon.html, accessed December 30, 2013. Elizabethan plays and literature supported the idea of Bacon as a sorcerer of some power (giving him a Faustian biography), see Clegg, *The First Scientist*, 165–66, but the legend had existed for centuries. In the 1380s, a physician from Dalmatia named Peter of Trou claimed that Bacon had many magical powers, including the ability to make a bridge appear out of thin air to cross a river, as well as possessing a magical mirror that allowed the viewer to see anywhere in the world, see Clegg, ibid., 165.

153. Ibid., 76.

154. Ibid. Rufus taught at both Oxford and Paris between the years 1231 and 1255. Bacon seems to have disliked him intensely.

155. See Jeremiah Hackett, "Roger Bacon: His Life, Career, and Works," *Roger Bacon and the Sciences*, 13–17.

156. John S. Brewer, ed,. *Fr. Rogeri Bacon Opera quædum hactenus inedita* (London: Longman, Green, Longman, and Roberts, 1859), 399: "Consideremus religiosos; nullum ordinem excludo. Videamus quantum ceciderunt singuli a statu debito, et novi ordines jam horribiliter labefacti sunt a pristina dignitate. Totus clerus vacat superbiæ, luxuriæ, et avaritiæ. Et ubicunque congregantur clerici, sicut Parisius et Oxoniæ, bellis, et turbationibus, et cæteris vitiis scandalizant totum populum laïcorum."

157. Ibid., 401: "Certe si fidem istius sacramenti, et reverentiam, et devotionem haberent homines sicut deberent et tenentur, non corrumperent se tot erroribus, et vitiis, et malitiis; sed scirent omnem sapientiam et omnem veritatem salutiferam in hac vita."

158. Lawrence, *The Friars*, 203.

159. For an edition of the *Opus majus*, see *Roger Bacon, Opus majus*, 3 vols., John Henry Bridges, ed. (London: Williams and Norgate, 1897–1990). For a study of Bacon's concerns, see Timothy J. Johnson, "Preaching Precedes Theology: Roger Bacon on the Failure of Mendicant Education," *Franciscan Studies* 68 (2010): 83–95.

160. Ibid., 86–88.

161. Ibid., 92.

162. The account is recorded in the *Chronicle of the Twenty-Four Generals* written *ca.* 1374 by Arnald of Sarrant. *Chronica XXIV Generalium Ordinis Fratrum Minorum (1209–1374)*, Analecta franciscana 3 (Florence: Frati Editori di Quaracchi, 1897), 360: "Continens aliquas novitates suspectas, propter quas fuit idem Rogerius carceri condemnatus." For an English translation, see Noel Muscat, *The Chronicle of the Twenty-Four Generals of the Order of Friars Minor* (Malta: TAU Franciscan Communications, 2010), 488. Michael H. Shank discounts the idea that Bacon was imprisoned in "Myth 2: That the Medieval Christian Church Suppressed the Growth of Science," *Galileo Goes to Jail, and Other Myths about Science and Religion*, Ronald L. Numbers, ed. (Cambridge: Harvard University Press, 2009), 21. See also D.C. Lindberg, "Medieval Science and Its Religious Context," *Osiris* 10, Constructing Knowledge in the History of Science (1995): 60–79. He notes at 70: "his imprisonment, if it occurred at all (which I doubt) probably resulted from his sympathies for the radical 'poverty' wing of the Franciscans (a wholly theological matter) rather than from any scientific novelties which he may have proposed." Hannam discounts the incarceration story, as well, *God's Philosophers*, 144–45, where he notes at 144: "if Bacon had been a supporter of these spiritual Franciscans … he could have got into a great deal of trouble. However, the allegation that Bacon's science led to his imprisonment finds no support in the historical record." Clegg believes that the incarceration took place, *The First Scientist*, 143, on the grounds that Bacon produced no writings at all during the 1280s, though this could have been due as much to the general prohibition. He admits, however, at 143 that "there is never likely to be absolute proof that Bacon was imprisoned by d'Ascoli."

163. Recorded by Bartholomew Cotton, a Benedictine monk of Norwich. See the *Historia Anglicana (449–1298)*, Henry Richards Luard, ed., Rolls Series 16 (London: Longman, Green, Longman, and Roberts, 1859), 431: "Tempore sub eodem generalis minister ordinis Sancti Francisci per mundum universum visitando, in Hirlandiam causo visitandi accessit, et in capitulo suo generali xvi, fratres cum confratribus suis interfecti sunt, nonnulli vulnerati sunt, et quidam eorum per regem Angliæ incarcerati sunt." See also Ignatius Fennessy, "The Chapter at Cork 1291: A Gory Franciscan Story," *Irish Theological Quarterly* 70 (2005): 283–285, and Geltner, *The Making of Medieval Antifraternalism*, 70, where he lists a series of other violent clashes between various branches of friars in Germany and England. See also 131, regarding factional disputes.

164. As we will see in chapter 8, the Benedictine monk Matthew Paris had some very harsh opinions about the Franciscans.

165. See Geltner, *The Making of Medieval Antifraternalism*, 70, n118.

166. See Laura Kendrick, "Medieval Satire," A Companion to Satire: Ancient and Modern, Ruben Quintero, ed. (Oxford: Wiley, 2007), 61–62.

167. George Gordon Coulton, in *Five Centuries of Religion*, Vol. 2 (Cambridge: Cambridge University Press Archive, 1927), presents a practically dizzying array of examples of medieval inter–Church criticisms, polemic, and insults in his two appendices, "Contemporary Generalizations," 504–50, and 553–647, translated into English and featured in small portions for easy reading. It includes criticisms of monks, friars, priests, and all other religious vocations, made by their fellow clergy. Well worth taking the time to peruse, this is a goldmine of quotes that show just how fractured the Church was from the 12th century onward.

168. Lawrence, *The Friars*, 152–53.

169. Geltner discusses this further in *The Making of Medieval Antifraternalism*, 4–5, and 13.

Chapter 2

1. See Andrew G. Traver, "Secular and Mendicant Masters of the Faculty of Theology at the University of Paris, 1505–1523," *The Sixteenth Century Journal* 26, 1 (1995): 137–155, for a discussion on how the conflicts continued in various forms well into the Renaissance, especially 137–38, n1 and n2, for bibliographic citations. He observes at 137–38: "While the secular masters struggled to require the religious masters to recognize university statutes and to adhere to the corporative privileges, the mendi-

cants flaunted papal exemptions and slighted episcopal and papal restrictions placed upon their magisterial activities. Opposition between these two groups continued well into the sixteenth century." For a good general overview of secular-mendicant conflicts in the universities at Paris, Oxford, and Cambridge, see Bert Roest, *A History of Franciscan Education (c. 1210–1517)* (Leiden, Brill, 2000), 51–64.

2. Penn R. Szittya, *Antifraternal Tradition*, 11. See also Lawrence, *The Friars*, 130, for some discussion the location of their first school. For other good general discussions on the conflict, see James Doyne Dawson, "William of St. Amour and the Apostolic Tradition," *Mediaeval Studies* 40 (1978): 223–38; Decima L. Douie, *The Conflict between the Seculars and the Mendicants at the University of Paris in the Thirteenth Century*, Aquinas Paper no. 23. London: Blackfriars, 1954; M.M. Dufeil, *Saint Thomas et l'histoire* (Aix-en-Provence: C.U.E.R.M.A., 1991), a collection of essays, many of which relate to the secular-mendicant conflict; and Peter R. McKeon, "The Status of the University of Paris as Parens scientiarum: An Episode in the Development of its Autonomy." *Speculum* 39 (1964): 651–75 (which presents in detail a discussion of the problems of dating certain letters and sermons related to the conflict in the 1250s). Also related to this is Alan E. Bernstein, "Magisterium and License: Corporate Autonomy against Papal Authority in the Medieval University of Paris," *Viator* 9 (1978): 291–307, and Andrew G. Traver, "Rewriting History? The Parisian Secular Masters' Apologia of 1254." *History of Universities*, Volume XV: 1997–1999, Peter Denley, ed. (Oxford: Oxford University Press, 2000): 9–45. The *Chartularium Universitatis Parisiensis*, ed. Henricus Denifle, O.P., and Aemilio Chatelain (Paris: Ex Typis Fratrum Delalain via Sorbone Dicta, 1889), vol. I (hereafter referred to as Chart. I) is an edition of many of the correspondences from popes, university officials, and royals, containing the extant records of the occurrences at the University of Paris in the Middle Ages, as recorded by Matthew Paris and other writers. A major collection of Matthew's work is found in Matthew Paris, *Chronica Majora*, ed. Henry Richards Luard, 7 vols. (Rolls Series, LVII, London: Longman, 1872–82). We will survey Matthew in more detail in chapter 8. Additional key works are listed below.

3. See G. Geltner, "William of St. Amour's *De periculis novissimorum temporum*: A False Start to Medieval Antifraternalism?" in *Defenders and Critics of Franciscan Life, Essays in Honor of John V. Fleming* (Leiden: Brill, 2009), 107. See also Lawrence, *The Friars*, 39 and 46–47; see also 48 for some of the conflicts between the Franciscans and Dominicans over how educated their brethren should be. Geltner's translation of *De periculis* will be considered in more detail in chapter 3.

4. Lawrence, *The Friars* 84.

5. Szittya, *Antifraternal Tradition*, 11.

6. John W. Baldwin, *The Scholastic Culture of the Middle Ages, 1000–1300* (Prospect Heights, IL: Waveland Press, 1971, reissued 1997), 44. This is a good short introduction to medieval education. For the general structure of the university, its curriculum, information on student life, and how it was organized, see J.E. Healey, "The Medieval University," *CCHA Report* 17 (1950): 65–77. He notes at 65 that the archetypal universities were Paris and Bologna, and that "every other university was a conscious and deliberate imitation." The importance of the University of Paris helps to explain why the king and popes were so interested in the outcome of the secular-mendicant conflict. For studies of the early university environment in Paris, see Stephen C. Ferruolo, *The Origins of the University: The Schools of Paris and their Critics, 1100–1215* (Stanford: Stanford University Press, 1998); Olaf Pedersen, *The First Universities: Studium Generale and the Origins of University Education in Europe* (Cambridge: Cambridge University Press, 1997); and Hilde de Ridder-Symoens, ed., *A History of the University in Europe. Vol. I: Universities in the Middle Ages* (Cambridge: Cambridge University Press, 1992).

7. Baldwin, *Scholastic Culture*, 42.

8. Gordon Leff, *Paris and Oxford Universities in the Thirteenth and Fourteenth Centuries*, (New York: John Wiley & Sons, Inc., 1968), 15–16. This is an important source in English for understanding the Paris conflict. See also Pearl Kibre, *Scholarly Privileges in the Middle Ages*, Mediaeval Academy of America (London: William Clowes and Sons, 1961); and Palémon Glorieux, "Le conflit de 1252–1257 à la lumière du Mémoire de Guillaume de Saint-Amour" in *Recherches de théologie ancienne et medieval*, 24 (1957), 364–72, a short chronology of the major events of the first debate. Glorieux has written numerous other articles and books on the history of the University of Paris, and the mendicant debate in particular; he is regarded as one of the leading scholars on the subject in the French language.

9. Simone Roux, *Paris in the Middle Ages*, Jo Ann McNamara, trans. (Philadelphia: University of Pennsylvania Press, 2009), 98.

10. Leff, *Paris and Oxford Universities*, 16.

11. Lawrence, *The Friars*, 12. The universities did not completely displace cathedral and monastic schools, however, see Leff, *Paris and Oxford Universities*, 116.

12. For an excellent overview of the topic in the 13th and 14th centuries, see William J. Courtenay, "Inquiry and Inquisition: Academic Freedom in Medieval Universities," *Church History* 58, 2 (1989): 168–181.

13. Roux, *Paris in the Middle Ages*, 9–10.

14. Joseph and Frances Gies, *Life in a Medieval City* (New York: Harper Perennial, 1981), 164. Leff, however, is less sure that the number can be determined, *Paris and Oxford Universities*, 9. See also G. Geltner, ed. and trans., *William of Saint-Amour: De periculis novissimorum temporum*, Dallas Medieval Texts and Translations 8 (Paris and Louvain: Peeters, 2008), 5.

15. Leff, *Paris and Oxford Universities*, 9.

16. Ibid., 16.

17. McKeon, "The Status of the University of Paris," 652. Importantly, see Spencer Young, "'Consilio hominum nostrorum': A Comparative Study of Royal Responses to Crisis at the University of Paris, 1200–1231," *History of Universities* 22, vol. 1, ed. Mordechai Feingold (Oxford: Oxford University Press, 2007), 1–20.

18. Young, "A Comparative Study of Royal Responses," 2–3.

19. Ibid., 3. See the *Chronica Magistri Rogeri de Hoveden*, ed. William Stubbs, 4 vols., Rolls Series 51 (London: Longman & Co., 1871), IV, 121.

20. Young, "A Comparative Study of Royal Responses," 4.

21. Ibid., 5–6. Some of the political issues included the conflict between Henry II and Thomas Beckett (many masters sided with Beckett), as well as problems concerning the king's own complex marriage troubles.

22. Ibid., 11.

23. Leff, *Paris and Oxford Universities*, 16–17.

24. Ibid., 18. The *studium*

came to be seen as effectively the third of a three-part structure, the Church, imperial authority, and the universities, that governed Christendom. The *studium generale* was seen as an authorized school, given its privileges by the pope. See Lawrence, *The Friars*, 14, and Leff, 21–22.

25. Baldwin, *Scholastic Culture*, 43.

26. Lawrence, *The Friars*, 138. See also Leff, *Paris and Oxford Universities*, 6–8.

27. Joseph and Frances Gies, *Life in a Medieval City*, 164. See also Healey, "The Medieval University," 76.

28. Baldwin, *Scholastic Culture*, 51.

29. Geltner, *Making of Medieval Antifraternalism*, 99–100. See Ruth Mazo Karras, *Common Women: Prostitution and Sexuality in Medieval England* (New York: Oxford University Press, 1996), 30 and 45.

30. Ibid., 46–7.

31. Leff, *Paris and Oxford Universities*, 19–20. See also, Baldwin, *Scholastic Culture*, 43.

32. Leff, *Paris and Oxford Universities*, 2.

33. Ibid., 20.

34. Leff discusses the early years of the university and its struggles for legitimacy in great detail at 20–29. For the text of Alexander's decretal, see Chart. I, *Introductoria*, 4.

35. Leff, *Paris and Oxford Universities*, 22.

36. Szittya, *Antifraternal Tradition*, 11.

37. Lawrence, *The Friars*, 136. See also 127, which notes that the friars actively sought out recruits in university cities for this very reason.

38. Young, "A Comparative Study of Royal Responses," 7. He covers the event and its relation to royalty in some detail at 7–12.

39. "Invenerunt ibi casu vinum optimum in taberna quadam et ad bibendum suave." Hastings Rashdall, *The Universities of Europe in the Middle Ages*, ed. A.B. Emden, and Sir Frederick Maurice Powicke, 3 vols. (London: Oxford University Press, 1936), I, 334, *f.*, drawn from Chart. I, 214.

40. Rashdall, *Universities of Europe*, 334–5.

41. Roux, *Paris in the Middle Ages*, 188.

42. Ibid.

43. Rashdall, *Universities of Europe*, 335.

44. Roux, *Paris in the Middle Ages*, 41. For an account of the soldiers and their response, see Matthew Paris, *Chronica Majora* III, 166–67.

45. Baldwin, *Scholastic Culture*, 47–8. Baldwin also notes that this was complicated by the legal precedent set by the conflicts between Henry II and Thomas Beckett, 48–9, see *n*21 above. See also Young, "A Comparative Study of Royal Responses," 4. The text of the students' immunity from civil prosecution is in Chart. I, 1: "Ad hec in capitale Parisiensium scolarium pro nullo forifacto justicia nostra manum mittet; sed si visum fuerit illud esse arrestandum, per justiciam ecclesiasticam arrestabitur et arrestatum custodietur, ut de illo capitali fiat quod per ecclesiam fuerit legitime judicatum. Quod si tali hora fuerint scolares arrestati a preposito nostro, quod non possit ecclesiastica justicia inveniri vel statim haberi, faciet prepositus noster in aliqua scolaris domo eosdem sine omni injuria sicut supra dictum est custodiri, donec justicie ecclesiastice tradantur." The citizens of Paris were even obliged to defend a student being attacked. See, for example, Chart. I, 1: "Si alicui scolari ab aliquo laico injuriam fi erialiquis viderit, quod super eo testimonium perhibebit veritati; nec se subtrahet aliquis ne videat. Et si contigerit quod aliquis scolarem percusserit, nisi super se defendendo, si scolaris maxime armis percutiatur, aut fuste, aut lapide, omnes laici qui viderint bona fide comprehendent illum malefactorum vel malefactores et tradent justicie nostre, nec se subtra[h]ent ne videant vel comprehendant vel testimonium veritati perhibeant. Sive autem malefactor captus sit super ipsum forifactum, sive non, nos legitimam inquisitionem faciemus et fi delem, sive per clericos sive per laicos seu per quascumque personas; et prepositus noster et justicie nostre idem facient."

46. Baldwin, *Scholastic Culture*, 49–50.

47. Szittya, *Antifraternal Tradition*, 12, Leff, *Paris and Oxford Universities*, 31, Young, "A Comparative Study of Royal Responses," 8. Matthew Paris records that the masters were furious, see *Chronica Majora*, III, 168: "Indignum enim sibi videbatur, quod tam levi nacta occasione, quorundam contemptibilium clericulorum trangressio in praejudicium totius redundaret universitatis; sed poenam daret in ultione, qui culpam perpetravit in transgressione. Sed cum tandem omnimoda eis justitia tam a rege et legato, quam ab episcopo civitatis, denegata fuisset, facta est universalis discessio magistrorum et scolarum dispersio, cessante doctorum doctrina et discipulorum disciplina, ita quod nec unus famosus ex omnibus in civitate remanserit."

48. Chart. I, 64: "Unde vestre duximus universitati significandum, quid si vobis placeat ad regnum nostrum Anglie vos transferre et in eo causa studii moram facere."

49. Rashdall, *Universities of Europe*, 336–7.

50. An act to which some of the masters "even accused the queen of having engaged in an infamous sexual liason [sic] (*infamem concordiam*) with the papal legate, Romano Frangipani," Young, "A Comparative Study of Royal Responses," 8. Blanche seems to have been somewhat rash; Matthew Paris records that she did not take any counsel in making her decision, and acting with violent inclination, she ordered the retaliation, see *Chronica Majora* III, 167: "At illa muliebri procacitate simul et impetu mentis agitata, prepositis civitatis et quibusdam ruptariis suis dedit ilico in mandatis, ut sub omni celeritate armati ab urbe exeuntes, hujus violentiae auctores, nulli parcentes, punirent." There is no doubt Blanche was a formidable woman. Married to Louis VIII, son of Philip Augustus, she assumed regency at his death in 1226, and she ruled capably until Louis IX reached his majority in 1234, more than once securing the kingdom through conflict and treaties. Louis IX was certainly under her influence for the remainder of his life. She died in 1252, just as the university conflict was intensifying.

51. Rashdall, *Universities of Europe*, 337. See also the accounts in Chart. I, 66, 67, 69, 70, and 71. There was a whole series of correspondences aimed at reinforcing the university's privileges after this affair, which included some compromises about scholars not being permitted to carry weapons and the right of the Bishop of Paris to punish students' bad behavior. See Leff, *Paris and Oxford Universities*, 31–32. The papal bull *Parens scientiarum* was another victory for the masters at this time, guaranteeing their rights over the chancellor, Chart. I, 79.

52. Szittya, *Antifraternal Tradition*, 13.

53. Lawrence, *The Friars*, 129.

54. Szittya, *Antifraternal Tradition*, 13.

55. Leff, *Paris and Oxford Universities*, 38–39. See Chart. I, 230 for a detailed description.

56. Lester K. Little, "Saint Louis' Involvement with the Friars," *Church History* 33 (1964): 136

57. Leff, *Paris and Oxford Universities*, 39.

58. See Geltner, *Making of Medieval Antifraternalism*, 108–09. See Szittya, *Antifraternal Tradition*, 4, which notes that by the 14th century, these great thinkers "had taken over the intellectual leadership of the church."

59. Aquinas' writings were adopted as the official teachings of the Dominicans in 1309, though not without some controversy, including opposition to some Thomist philosophies among the Franciscans. See Lawrence, *The Friars*, 148–50, for a summary. See also Leff, *Paris and Oxford Universities*, 214–15, for a survey of how Aristotelian thought became accepted in the Dominican order.

60. Lester K. Little, "Saint Louis' Involvement with the Friars," 127. Of the three known names of the confessors, all were friars. Two were Dominicans, Geoffrey of Beaulieu and William of Chartres, both biographers of the king. One was a Franciscan, John of Mons. Geoffrey oversaw the distribution of alms at the court, but accompanied Louis on his failed first crusade, being imprisoned with him in Egypt, while the king awaited ransom for his freedom. Geoffrey also administered last rites to the king on his second failed crusade in 1270. Much less is known about William and John, but they also accompanied the king to Tunis, and undoubtedly assisted in returning the king's bones to France after his death. See Little, 128–27.

61. Little, "Saint Louis' Involvement," 127. See also Lucas Wadding, *Annales Minorum*, 3rd. ed., 25 vols. (Frati Editori di Quaracchi, 1931–34), II, 184. The Irishman Wadding (1588–1687) was a Franciscan friar who produced the *Annales* in the years 1625–1654. Republished several times over the centuries, it is one of the great histories of the Franciscan order.

62. Lawrence, *The Friars*, 166 67.

63. Little, "Saint Louis' Involvement," 128.

64. See Lawrence, *The Friars*, 170–73, for a discussion of the role of mendicant confessors at the courts of France and England.

65. Little, "Saint Louis' Involvement," 128. See also Geltner, *De periculis*, 9–10.

66. Little notes at 129 an amusing contrast between Louis and Henry III of England, also a deeply religious king. It seems that Henry was obsessed with celebrating mass, often several times a day. It was said that while in Paris to negotiate with Louis in 1259, Henry would stop at every church along the way to see Louis to hear its mass, causing ridiculous delays. This prompted the church curates to take action and not celebrate until after the king had passed them by. If necessary, they were permitted to close the church doors in his face! This contrast does show how Louis' emphasis on preaching and personal piety rather than the grandeur of the mass made him feel naturally drawn to the supposed simplicity of the friars.

67. See William Chester Jordan. "Louis IX: Preaching to Franciscan and Dominican Brothers and Nuns," *Defenders and Critics of Franciscan Life*, 219–35.

68. Little, "Saint Louis' Involvement," 131.

69. See Jean Richard, *Saint Louis: Crusader King of France* (Cambridge: Cambridge University Press, 1992), 405–16. See also Geltner, *De periculis*, 12–13.

70. See Lawrence, *The Friars*, 177–78, and *n*30 and *n*31.

71. A good discussion of Louis' responses to criticism is William Chester Jordan, "The Case of Saint Louis," *Viator* 19 (1988): 209–17.

72. Ibid, 215. See also William Chester Jordan, *Louis IX and the Challenge of the Crusade: A Study in Rulership* (Princeton: Princeton University Press, 1979), 188–90.

73. Jordan, "The Case of Saint Louis," 214. See, for example Guillaume de Saint-Pathus, "Vie de saint Louis," in *Recueil des historiens des Gaules et de la France* 20, Martin Bourquet, ed. (Paris: V. Palmé, 1840), 106: "Fi! fi! deusses tu estre roi de France? mont mieux fust que un autre fust rois que tu; car tu es tant seulement des frères Meneurs, des frères Preescheurs et des prestres et des clers; grant damage est que tu es roi de France, et cest grant merveille que tu nes bouté hors du royaume." See also Geltner, *De periculis*, 10.

74. Rashdall, *Universities of Europe*, 336, *n*.

75. Szittya, *Antifraternal Tradition*, 13, and Leff, *Paris and Oxford Universities*, 39.

76. Szittya, *Antifraternal Tradition*, 13, Leff, *Paris and Oxford Universities*,39. Chart. I, 200, see also 219.

77. Peter R. McKeon, "The Status of the University of Paris," 655.

78. Leff, *Paris and Oxford Universities*, 40.

79. Rashdall, *Universities of Europe*, 377.

80. Szittya, *Antifraternal Tradition*, 11. See also, Baldwin, *Scholastic Culture*, 43.

81. McKeon, "The Status of the University of Paris," 655.

82. Szittya, *Antifraternal Tradition*, 14.

83. For the full account see Chart. I, 252–58.

84. Leff, *Paris and Oxford Universities*, 40.

85. Jacques Le Goff. *Intellectuals in the Middle Ages*, trans. Teresa Lavender Fagan (Oxford: Blackwell, 1993), 98. See also Leff, *Paris and Oxford Universities*, 40–41.

86. Szittya, *Antifraternal Tradition*, 14.

87. Ibid., 15.

88. A. J. Heiman, "William of St. Amour," *New Catholic Encyclopedia*, XIV, 936.

89. For example, see McKeon, "The Status of the University of Paris," 670. He argues that Guillaume's attack "appears to be only a rhetorical device ... the *De Periculis* is a parody on Joachim and the Joachites ... its commentary is intended as a jest," yet he offers no further evidence for this assertion.

90. Geltner, "William of St. Amour's *De periculis*," 114. See also Geltner, *De periculis*, 6–7.

91. Geltner, "William of St. Amour's *De periculis*," 118.

92. Szittya, *Antifraternal Tradition*, 15.

93. Rashdall, *Universities of Europe*, 385.

94. Geltner, "William of St. Amour's *De periculis*," 108.

95. Szittya, *Antifraternal Tradition*, 25.

96. For a study of manuscripts and the differences between those who followed Joachim and those who adapted and altered his ideas to other apocalyptic themes, see Fabio Troncarelli, "Early Joachimism and Early Franciscanism: Manuscript Evidence of a Common Destiny," *Franciscan Studies* 69 (2011): 141–151.

97. Szittya, *Antifraternal Tradition*, 27, and *n*46: "Cum fuerint anni completi mille ducenti et decies seni post partum virginis alme, tunc Antichristus nascetur demone plenus," see also 25–7. Matthew Paris would record these same words, with a change of date to 1,250 years, see Szittya, 104.

98. "De die autem illa et hora nemo scit, neque angeli caelorum nisi solus Pater." *Biblia Sacra Juxta Vulgatam Clementinam*, 7th ed. (Madrid: La Editorial Catolica, 1985).

99. Szittya, *Antifraternal Tradition*, 27. For an account of a violent confrontation between flagellants and Dominicans in Germany (resulting in the death of one friar), see Geltner, *Making of Medieval Antifraternalism*, 122, and *n*77.

100. "Quod Evangelium eternum, quod idem est quod doctrina Joachim, excellit doctrinam Christi et omne novum et vetus Testamentum ... quod evangelio Christi aliud evangelium succedet ... quod novum Testamentum non durabit in virtute sua...," see Chart. I, 225, and M.M. Dufeil's *Guillaume de Saint-Amour et la polémique universitaire parisienne, 1250–1259* (Paris: Picard, 1972), 101. See also McKeon, "The Status of the University of Paris," 659–60.

101. He did so more quietly, however, not wanting to draw attention to its relationship with the Franciscans.

102. Traver discusses this document at length in "Rewriting History," 9–45. He looks at the various accusations and presents evidence that while the masters had legitimate grievances, they were also guilty of stretching the truth on several issues, especially regarding how long some rights had been held, how the Dominicans had cheated to gain another chair, and how many of those chairs were now lost to the masters, when they were entitled to them.

103. Matthew 23:8–10. The passage in question concerns how the friars were welcomed by the university and at first served Christ, but then became desirous of titles and power, leading to the strife now rampant: "Novissime autem diebus nostris quidam viri regulares, qui fratres Predicatores dicuntur, Parisius in parvo numero viventes sub quadam pietatis ac publice utilitatis specie subingressi una nobiscum theologie studium ferventer et humiliter sunt aggressi, propter quod a majoribus nostris et nobis benigue recepti, sincere caritatis brachiis amplexati, in domo nostra propria, in qua usque hodie commorantur, quam eis ad inhabitandum concessimus, hospitati, alimento tam doctrine quam corporali diligentius educati, plurimisque beneficiis nostris et antecessorum nostrorum potiti, per ingressum scolasticorum nostrorum in scientia simul et in numero adeo sunt dilatati, quod jam ubique terrarum per multa collegia sunt dispersi. Ceterum cum ab initio sue institutionis elegisseut in humilitate perfecta Christo Domino famulari, consequenter nescimus quo ducti spiritu contra evangelicam perfecto humilitatis quam fuerant professi regulam (qua dicit Dominus ad perfectos: 'Nolite vocari Rabbi,' et paulo post: 'Ne vocemini magistri,' in primo magisterii prohibens appetitum, in secundo magistri etiam interdicens vocabulum) honorem sollempnis magisterii et magistrorum cathedras ambientes, tamen propter quandam atrocem injuriam et famosam nobis illatam translata majori parte studii Parisiensis Andegavis, in illa paucitate scolarium, que remansit Parisius, desiderio suo politi, conniventibus episcopo et cancellario Parisiensibus, qui tunc erant, in absentia magistrorum sollempne magisterium et unam magistralem cathedram sunt adepti." The letter is quite lengthy and addresses a number of other issues. See Chart. I, 230, for the full text.

104. Traver, "Rewriting History," 9–10.

105. Chart. I, 240.

106. Szittya, *Antifraternal Tradition*, 15–16.

107. Little, "Saint Louis' Involvement with the Friars," 138, and Chart. I, 240.

108. Szittya, *Antifraternal Tradition*, 16.

109. Little, "Saint Louis' Involvement with the Friars," 139.

110. The role of the Protector had existed since the 1220s, and its purpose was to give the Franciscans ongoing representation to the Papal Curia, see Lawrence, *The Friars*, 182.

111. Leff, *Paris and Oxford Universities*, 42–43, and Szittya, *Antifraternal Tradition*, 16–17. See also McKeon, "The Status of the University of Paris," 658.

112. Leff, *Paris and Oxford Universities*, 42. See also, Geltner, *De periculis*, 10–11.

113. Leff, *Paris and Oxford Universities*, 43.

114. Ibid., see also Chart. I, 273.

115. Little, "Saint Louis' Involvement with the Friars," 140.

116. McKeon, "The Status of the University of Paris," 667: "But Alexander had underestimated, or chose to ignore, the nature and extent of the protests. These bishops, as bishops, had no desire to further papal aims or to aid the mendicants, and Alexander's orders received, in all cases, either no attention at all, or very cursory and tardy action. The letter depriving William [i.e., Guillaume] of his benefices was not made public; in fact William was later able to say that he had never known of it."

117. Ibid., 140–41. Chart. I, 268–70.

118. McKeon, "The Status of the University of Paris," 667. Alexander also wrote a condescending letter to the masters, urging them not to be led astray by Guillaume, but to return to obedience. Chart. I, 271: "Et certe nisi motum mentis nostre, quem transgressionis vestre stimulus concitavit, a pena vindicte vobis merito infligendo hoc potissime temperasset, quod simplicitatem vestre multitudinis ab astuta malitia paucorum et precipue magistri G. de Sancto Amore credimus fuisse seductam, oculus vester, quem caligo superbie nimium obumbravit, virga correctionis debite illustratus patenter agnosceret, quam stultum sit et detestabile apostolice sedis equissimis ordinationibus et litteris contumaciter obviare. Sane quia filiorum errantium disciplinam magis cupimus quam vindictam, universitatem vestram affectione paterna rogamus per apostolica vobis scripta districte precipiando mandantes, quatinus noxia seductorum vestrorum consilia et erronea vestigia penitus declinantes juramento seu statuto vel quacumque obligatione, per que precepti nostri executio impediri valeat vel differri, nequaquam obstantibus, prefatas ordinationem et sententias reverenter et humiliter omni occasione postposita post susceptionem presentium observetis."

119. "Any who love me will obey my teaching. My Father will love them, and we will come to them and make our home with them." *Vulgata*, 1058: "Respondit Iesus et dixit ei: Si quis diligit me sermonem meum servabit et Pater meus diliget eum et ad eum veniemus et mansiones apud eum faciemus."

120. Little, "Saint Louis' Involvement with the Friars," 141–142. The relevant text of the sermon is found in Palémon Glorieux, *Répertoire des maîtres en théologie à Paris au XIIIe siécle*, 2 vols. (Paris: J. Vrin, 1933–34), I, 345: "Peccatum ypocrisis in paucis ese solobit modo in tantum crevit quod devenit usque ad episcopos, parochiales sacerdotes, milites, burgenses, reges et principes et similiter de multibus. Unde similiter dolendum est unde in media nocte modo reges surgunt ad matutinas dicendas et in die audiunt sex paria missarum ad votum et dimittunt causas pauperum sequentium curiam suam indiscussas et non portarent unum pulchram robam (interlin.: vestem) tamen bene permitterent unum bellum oriri vel fieri in quo mille christiani interficerentur, bene de suis extorsionibus redderent X solidos vel V sed nullo modo redderent unam comitivam nec unam villam vel castellum, et tamen a scripturis non habemus quod reges debent surgere ad matutinas de nocte et cetera et quod debere induere vestes de villi pano, sed bene invenio quod debent induere vestes preciossisimas non in

talibus consistit officium regis sed in faciendo judicum et justitiam et.judicando abbacias et ecclesias et de sedondo et procurando pacem sua terre. Ieronimus—utere deliciis non pro te sed pro regno ut timorem .i. curias ad justicias exercendas, ipse loquitur cuidam regi qui forte benignus erat et ideo ordinavit ecclesia quod papa equitat cum freno de strig. aurato bene et rubea que potest invenire et ferunt milites seilicet quando equitat unum pannum de serico super caput eius, non deberent regibus consulere homines boni quod essent begini sed quod facerent elemosinas et vacarent semper iusticie et judicia facienda. Unde decretum dicit XXIII q V Regum est facere justitia et indicium non invenitur quod rex debeat esse beginus, de nobis clericis notandum."

121. Little, "Saint Louis' Involvement with the Friars," 142.

122. Leff, *Paris and Oxford Universities*, 45. Chart. 288, 291.

123. Chart. I, 288: "*Tractatus brevis de periculis uovissimorum temporum*, nuncupalur, tanqnam iniquiin, scelestum et execrabilem, et institutiones ac documenta in eo tradita utpote prava, falsa et nefaria de fratrum nostrorum consilio auctoritate apostolica reprobanius et in perpetuum condempnamus, districte precipientes, ut quicumque labellum ipsuin habuerit, eum infra octo dies, ex quo hujusmodi nostram reprobationem et condempnationem sciverit, prorsus in toto et in qualibet sui parle comburere et abolere procuret." See also Geltner, *De periculis*, 18, *n*72.

124. John Fleming, *The Roman de la Rose: A Study in Allegory and Iconography* (Princeton: Princeton University Press, 1969), 164. See also, Fleming, "The Collationes of William of Saint-Amour against S. Thomas," *Recherches de théologie ancienne et médiévale* 32 (1965 b): 132–38.

125. See Leff, *Paris and Oxford Universities*, 45–46.

126. Little, "Saint Louis' Involvement with the Friars," 143. See also Geltner, *De periculis*, 18–19.

127. Ibid., 146.

128. For a study of her writings in the antifraternal context, see Kathryn Kerby-Fulton, "Hildegard of Bingen and Anti-Mendicant Propaganda," *Traditio* 43 (1987): 386–99. There were authentic comments, and a pseudo–Hildegard prophecy (probably deliberately misattributed to give it more credibility), *Insurgent gentes*, circulating in the 1250s, both of which were known to Guillaume, see 393–98.

These prophecies continued to be popular with antifraternal polemicists (especially in England) well into the 14th century. See also Geltner, *Making of Medieval Antifraternalism*, 42, and *n*78.

129. Geltner, *Making of Medieval Antifraternalism*, 23.

130. Heiman, "William of St. Amour," 937.

131. Leff, *Paris and Oxford Universities*, 45–46. See Chart. I, 309, 332, and 343. Louis IX made one attempt on the masters' behalf, and failed. See Chart. I, 353, 355–57, and chapter 3.

132. Some had done so as early as the end of 1256, realizing that they could not win against such a stubborn pope, McKeon, "The Status of the University of Paris," 674. Their letter contained five points, wherein they agreed to obey the pope, receive back the friars, not swear to any oaths in contradiction to these things, not remove the *studium* from Paris again, and to denounce *De Periculis*. Chart. I, 293. This must have been humiliating and demoralizing for them.

133. McKeon, "The Status of the University of Paris," 675. Chart. I, 331, 340.

134. Leff notes, for example, that even in 1261, after several years of struggle with the friars, the masters were able to enforce quite a bit of power and retain many rights and privileges, among them, "exemption from summons outside Paris; their own seal; the right to tax members for university purposes; ... and freedom, periodically renewed, from the ban of excommunication without papal consent." *Paris and Oxford Universities*, 33. For source references, see Chart. I, 142, 165, 352, 376, and 161, 383, 405, and 406 (the ban on excommunication, reiterated several times).

135. For an edition, see S. Clasen, "Tractatus Geraldi de Abbatisvilla 'Contra adversarium perfectionis Christianae,'" *Archivum Franciscanum Historicum* 31 (1938): 284–329, and 32 (1939): 89–200.

136. Geltner, *Making of Medieval Antifraternalism*, 23–24, and see 21 for some differences between Guillaume and later French and English writers. See also Marianne Schlosser, "Bonaventure: Life and Works," *A Companion to Bonaventure*, Jay M. Hammond, Wayne Hellmann, and Jared Goff, eds. (Leiden: Brill, 2013), 48–49. The works were Bonaventure's *Apologia pauperum*, and Aquinas' *De Perfectione Vitae Spiritualis contra Doctrinam Retrahentium a Religione*.

137. Geltner, *Making of Medieval Antifraternalism*, 23. Nicolas was in contact with Guillaume, who was very glad for his support, see Traver, *Opuscula*, 80 and *n*184. For an edition, see "Liber de Antichristi," *Veterum scriptorium et monumentorum historicum* IX, Edmond Martène and Ursin Durand, eds. (Paris: Montalant, 1733), cols. 1271–1446, reprinted in *Burt Franklin: Research & Source Works Series* 276 (New York: Burt Franklin, 1968). See also Palémon Glorieux, "Une offensive de Nicolas de Lisieux contre sainte Thomas d'Aquin," *Bulletin de Littérature Ecclésiastique* 39 (1938): 121–29, and Andrew Traver, "The Liber de Antichristo and the Failure of Joachite Expectations," *Florensia* 14 (2001): 1–12.

138. Geltner, *Making of Medieval Antifraternalism*, 24.

139. Lawrence, *The Friars*, 146–47. See 144–45 for some discussion of the controversies about the introduction of these Greek and Arabic philosophical works into Christian thought. See Leff, *Paris and Oxford Universities*, 221–40 for a detailed summary. See also Chart. I, 486–87. For Aristotle in the curriculum, see Leff, *Paris and Oxford Universities*, 131–32.

140. Schlosser, "Bonaventure: Life and Works," 49. See also Lawrence, *The Friars*, 158–59, and A.G. Rigg, "The Lament of the Friars of the Sack," *Speculum* 55, 1 (1980): 84–90. The Sack friars were unpopular with the other mendicant orders, see 85.

141. Lawrence, *The Friars*, 159. For a useful summary of the events between 1269 and 1281, see Leff, *Paris and Oxford Universities*, 263–70.

142. Ibid., 160. See Le Goff, *Intellectuals of the Middle Ages*, 103, for a translation of key points of his harsh address.

143. For an edition, see *Corpus juris canonici* 2, A.L. Richteri, ed. (Leipzig: Tauchnitz, 1879), cols. 1161–64.

144. For Jean de Pouilly, and Jean d'Anneux, see chapter 8, and the extended survey of d'Anneux's work in Szittya, *The Antifraternal Tradition*, 81–93.

145. Szittya, *Antifraternal Tradition*, 85–93. One of his works, "Filios enutrivi," is quoted at length in a mid-14th-century treatise called *Omne bonum*, which we will examine in chapter 8.

146. Bert Roest, *A History of Franciscan Education*, 58. For a good overview of life in the city and university in the decades after the Quarrels, see William J. Courtenay, *Parisian Scholars in the Early Four-

teenth Century: A Social Portrait (Cambridge: Cambridge University Press, 2004).

Chapter 3

1. See Szittya, *Antifraternal tradition*, 24, for more on the relationship between this biblical exegesis and antifraternal sentiment.
2. *Vulgata*, 1153–4: "1. Hoc autem scito, quod in novissimis diebus instabunt tempora periculosa: | 2. erunt homines seipsos amantes ... | 3. sine affectione, sine pace, criminatores ... | 5. habentes speciem quidem pietatis, virtutem autem eius abnegantes. Et hos devita: | 6. ex his enim sunt qui penetrant domos et captivitatis ducunt mulierculas oneratas peccatis, quae ducuntur variis desideriis." English translation by Tim Rayborn.
3. Szittya, *Antifraternal tradition*, 32.
4. Andrew Traver, *The Opuscula of William of Saint-Amour: The Minor Works of 1255–1256*, Beitrage zur Geschichte der Philosophie und Theologie des Mittelalters 63 (Münster: Aschendorff Verlag, 2003), 31. See also 34–38 for questions about the dating, which place the work in later 1255 through to a completed version in 1256.
5. Guillaume de Saint-Amour, *De periculis novissimorum temporum*, G. Geltner, ed. and trans., 38: "Nos igitur christiane fidei professores—licet indigni—Parisius studentes, qui ex assumpto gignasio sanctas scripturas, quamvis exiliter secundum tenuitatem ingenii, tamen frequentius intuemur, attendentes in illis literis pericula novissimorum temporum vel eis similia toti ecclesie inminere quasi iam de prope." See also 15–18 for a brief overview of the contents. This book contains the full Latin text with parallel English translation. This relatively new translation is invaluable for the study of Guillaume and his work, and is used as the reference in the notes below. Though not a full critical edition, it is the first proper English translation, and also has an illuminating introduction. For earlier editions, see the Conclusion, *n*2. A new English translation by Jonathan Robinson of the 1690 version, which differs somewhat from Geltner's, can be found online in pdf format: http://individual.utoronto.ca/jwrobinson/translations/wsa_de-periculis.pdf, accessed February 5, 2014. The quality of *De periculis* as a polemical tract is much debated, with some seeing it as little more than a mediocre attempt. See Geltner, *De Periculis*, 1, and *nn*3–4.
6. Traver, *Opuscula*, 39 and *n*49.
7. *De periculis*, 42: "Quoniam parati sumus ad omnem obiectionem circa istam materiam faciendam, opitulante domino, respondere, non per disputationem et altercationem philosophicam ac sophisticam, que ad nichil utilis est nisi ad subversionem audientium, sed potius per collationem katholicam, que sola debet esse inter servos Christi."
8. Ibid., 44: "Protestamur autem ab initio, quod omnia que hic ad cautelam et instructionem ecclesie universe, non contra personam aliquam, nec contra statum aliquem ab ecclesia approbatum; sed contra peccata malorum et pericula ecclesie generalis dicturi sumus."
9. See Traver, *Opuscula*, 78–79, for a specific example in his *Responsiones* to the papal examination. See also Szittya, *Antifraternal Tradition*, 18.
10. *De periculis*, 46–53. The Timothy passages were essential to Guillaume's argument. See Traver, *Opuscula*, 40, and *n*53, where he observes: "In fact, William relies so heavily upon II Tim. 3, that Thouzellier has called *De Periculis* merely a commentary on it. 'La Place du *De periculis*, 75.'"
11. *De periculis*, 52–59. See also Traver, *Opuscula*, 40–43.
12. Leff, *Paris and Oxford Universities*, 261.
13. *De periculis*, 16. See also Geltner, *Making of Medieval Antifraternalism*, 21–22.
14. *De periculis*, 58–65.
15. Ibid., 66–71.
16. Ibid., 72–77.
17. Guillaume saw that the world was a series of ages, *De periculis*, 76: "Post vero sextam etatem, que est pugnantium, cum qua currit VII etas, que est quiescentium, non est ventura etas alia nisi octava, que est resurgentium. Ergo nos sumus in ultima etate huius mundi, et ista iam duravit per mille ducentos LV annos. Verisimile est ergo quod nos sumus prope finem mundi."
18. Ibid., 76–85. See also Traver's analysis in *Opuscula*, 45–47, and Szittya's in *Antifraternal Tradition*, 28–31.
19. *De periculis*, 85–91.
20. Ibid., 91–105. See also Traver, *Opuscula*, 47–50.
21. *De periculis*, 107–111.
22. There are 42 listed, but sign 11 repeats sign 6 exactly.
23. See *De periculis*, 112–139, for the full list.
24. Szittya, *The Antifraternal Tradition*, 18.
25. "Deus gratias tibi ago, quod non sum sicut ceteri hominum: raptores, iniusti, velut etiam hic Publicanus."
Andrew Traver, *Opuscula*, 191. The whole of the sermon is at 191–205.
26. Ibid., 191: "Circa primum, notandum est quod Pharisaei erant quidam religiosi apud Iudaeos, sicut sunt apud nos regulares."
27. *Vulgata*, Matt 23: 6–10, 984: "6. Amant autem ... 7. ... vocari ab hominibus Rabbi. 8. Vos autem nolite vocari Rabbi: unus enim Magister vester, omnes autem vos fratres estis. ... 10. Nec vocemini magistri: quia Magister vester unus est, Christus."
28. See, for example, Szittya, *Antifraternal Tradition*, 36–7.
29. Traver, *Opuscula*, 134–35. See also Geltner, *De periculis*, 8.
30. *De periculis*, 20.
31. Szittya, *Antifraternal Tradition*, 45
32. *Vulgata*, 1102: "Quomodo vero praedicabunt nisi mittantur?"
33. Szittya, *Antifraternal Tradition*, 45–6.
34. *Vulgata*, 985: "Et multi pseudoprophetae surgent, et seducent multos."
35. Ibid., "Et nunc antichristi multi facti sunt." 1176.
36. Szittya, *Antifraternal Tradition*, 59. See also chapter 1 for more information on their associations with the friars, and the controversies surrounding them.
37. Ibid., 59–60.
38. See chapter 4.
39. Szittya wryly remarks that Guillaume's work is "an effort of crabbed polemic that staggers the imagination," *Antifraternal Tradition*, at 45. It is highly unlikely that so much work would have been put into his attacks had they been insincere.
40. *De periculis*, 14.
41. Ibid.,19. See also Geltner, *Making of Medieval Antifraternalism*, 28.
42. See chapter 8 for a detailed look at Wyclif's writings against the Church and the friars.
43. See *De periculis*, 18–22, for a more detailed analysis of the work's influence, or lack thereof. See also Geltner's later article, "William of St. Amour's *De periculis*," in *Defenders and Critics of Franciscan Life*, 105–118.
44. See *De periculis*, 2–3, and 9–10, for more discussion of the shifts in society (following Louis' failed crusade) that brought about this situation, and 17 for its references to Louis IX.
45. Andrew Traver provides an

excellent study of the sermons, and the debate with Bonaventure in *Opuscula*. He also provides a very good summary of *De Periculis* at 31–52. For Traver's critical edition of his responses to Bonaventure of 1255, see also his "William of Saint-Amour's Two Disputed Questions *De quantitate eleemosynae* and *De valido mendicante*," *Archives d'histoire doctrinale et littéraire du moyen âge* 62 (1995): 295–342. Jonathan Robinson asserts that it was Guillaume's sermons which brought him the condemnation, and resulting excommunication and exile, rather than *De periculis*, in "Qui praedicat periculum in illo peribit: William of St-Amour's Anti-Mendicant Sermons," *Weapons of Mass Instruction: Secular and Religious Institutions Teaching the World, Proceedings of a St. Michael's College Symposium* (25–26 November 2005), ed. Joseph Goering, Francesco Guardiani, and Giulio Silano (Ottawa: Legas, 2008), 51–63. Robinson has provided an extensive list of useful translations on his website, available in pdf format. These are not critical editions, but are nevertheless very helpful: http://individual.utoronto.ca/jwrobinson/#Translations, accessed November 11, 2013. See especially his edition of *De periculis* (in which he points out differences to Geltner's edition): http://individual.utoronto.ca/jwrobinson/translations/wsa_de-periculis.pdf; his translation of Guillaume's *Qui amant*: http://individual.utoronto.ca/jwrobinson/translations/William-QAP.pdf; and his translations of Bonaventure's writings on renunciation and mendicancy, *De paupertate quoad abrenuntiationem*: http://individual.utoronto.ca/jwrobinson/translations/bonaventure_2.1-abrenuntiationem.pdf; and *De paupertate quoad mendicitatem*: http://individual.utoronto.ca/jwrobinson/translations/bonaventure_2.2-mendicitate.pdf.

46. For questions about the uncertainty of the dates, see Traver, "Two Disputed Questions," 296–97.

47. See Lawrence, *The Friars*, 57–60, for a summary of his defenses of the Franciscan order. He argued, for example, that the shift in the order's focus from absolute poverty to a training ground for qualified preachers and academics was a logical growth, and need not be shunned or seen to be in opposition to the order's original intentions.

48. Traver summarizes the situation and the questions in *Opuscula*, 7–29.

49. Bonaventure, *Opera Omnia*, 10 vols. (Quaracchi: Colegium S. Bonaventurae, 1882–1902), V, 124–28, 125: "Circa primum sic proceditur et quaeritur, utrum christianae perfectionis sit abrenuntiare omnibus, tam in communi quam in privato. Et quod sic, videtur." There follows a long list of biblical verses in support of his argument.

50. *Vulgata*, 980: "Ait illi Iesus: Si vis perfectus esse vade vende quae habes et da pauperibus et habebis thesaurum in caelo et veni sequere me."

51. Bonaventure, *Opera Omnia*, V, 125, 1: "Constat, quod Dominus istum ad divinitas non vocabit, et tamen renuntiare omnibus consulebat; nec ad opera manualia, immo ad contemplativam."

52. Ibid., 125, 8: "Si ergo Christus tantae paupertatis fuit, quod non potuit solvere denarium; manifestum est, quod fuit in summa paupertate." And 126, 12: "Sed qui abrenuntiat omnibus eius paupertatem imitatur."

53. Ibid. The full listing is at 126–27, paragraphs 15–25.

54. Ibid., 127–28, paragraphs 26–32.

55. Robinson, trans., *De paupertate quoad abrenuntiationem*, 9. Bonaventure, *Opera Omnia*, V, 129: "Abrenuntiare omnibus tam in privato quam in communi est christianae perfectionis, non solum sufficientis, sed etiam superabundantis."

56. Bonaventure, *Opera Omnia*, V, 129–34.

57. Traver, "Two Disputed Questions," 323–324.

58. Ibid., 324: "Dare omnia et nichil retinere ad sustentacionem vite prodigalitas est. Ergo non licet."

59. *Vulgata*, Rom 12:1, 1104: "Obsecro itaque vos fratres per misericordiam Dei ut exhibeatis corpora vestra hostiam viventem sanctam Deo placentem rationabile obsequium vestrum."

60. Traver, "Two Disputed Questions," 324. "Sed non retinere victum est nimis quia hoc est sibi mortem ingerere. Ergo non licet omnia dare sub spe mendicandi."

61. Ibid., 324–28. See especially # 9 at 327: "Ergo inopia facit oblivisci eterna. Ergo malum," and # 10 at 328: "Ergo potenti operari non licet mendicare."

62. Ibid., 330: "Expedit facultates ecclesie possideri, et proprias perfectionis amore contempni. Non enim proprie sunt, sed communes ecclesie facultates."

63. Ibid., 328: "Si dat omnia sic ... quia exponit se periculis multorum peccatorum, scilicet adulationis, detractionis, furandi, periurandi, declinandi a iustitia, ut ostensum est supra; vel periculo mortis corporalis quam evitare posset sine peccato, si necessaria vite retineret." See also Traver, *Opuscula*, 8–9.

64. Traver, *Opuscula*, 8.

65. Ibid., 10. See Traver, "Two Disputed Questions," 341: "Sed qui mendicant, cum possit vivere de labore corporis iustitiam negligit quia facit contra doctrinam Apostoli, et excommunicari debet, ut dictum est supra. Ergo tali non est dandum."

66. Traver, *Opuscula*, 10–11. Traver, "Two Disputed Questions," 342: "Quod queritur de predicatoribus, utrum possint petere, credo quod non, ne videatur esse occasio avaritie.... Vel ne videantur committere symoniam, si obtentu predicationis recipient; precipue illi, qui non sunt apostoli nec vices eorum gerant."

67. For a discussion of some of the differences and the relationship between the two versions, see Traver, *Opuscula*, 12–14, and 22–28.

68. Ibid., 15, which offers a summary of the methods used.

69. *Vulgata*, Matt. 10:9, 971: "Nolite possidere aurum neque argentum neque pecuniam in zonis vestris."

70. *Vulgata*, Luke 9:48, 1023: "et ait illis: Quicumque susceperit puerum istum in nomine meo me recipit et quicumque me recipit recipit eum qui me misit nam qui minor est inter omnes vos hic maior est." Traver erroneously cites it as Luke 9:42 at 16, *n*45.

71. Traver, *Opuscula*, 16, and *n*46.

72. Ibid., 16.

73. Bonaventure, *Opera Omnia*, V, 138: "Nam si quis impugnare et improbare velit omnem mendicandi modum in servis Christi, impugnare videbitur non tantum ordinem pauperum, verum ipsum summum pontificem, qui approbavit hunc vivendi modem." See also Traver, *Opuscula*, 25–26, and Lawrence, *The Friars*, 157.

74. The full text in a critical edition of the response is in Traver, *Opuscula*, 123–54, and the back-and-forth arguments are excellently summarized at 15–29.

75. Ibid., 18, and *n*65.

76. For questions about the uncertainty of the dating, see ibid., 53–57. The issue is surprisingly complex, and various scholars have weighed in with different opinions. For a study of his sermons, see Jonathan Robinson, "Qui praedicat periculum," 51–63.

77. For analysis, see Traver, *Opuscula*, 58–63. For an edition, see 155–78.

78. Ibid., 155: "Ego scio ecclesiae quaedam pericula imminere, et non potest esse quin secundum quod possum tacere, sed oportet ut ea manifestem secundum quod possum elicere ex scripturis. Sed quia non placet omnibus audire huiusmodi pericula, ideo quidam audientes me de his loqui derident, et detrahunt mihi; sed ego habeo veritatem mecum."

79. Ibid., 156: "Et ideo periculum aliorum peccatorum non est commune omnibus sicut peccatum hypocrisis, quo fere tota ecclesia vel pro maiori parte infecta est."

80. Ibid., 63.

81. See chapter 2, and Traver, *Opuscula*, 64–65.

82. Ibid., 181: "Et talis religio potest esse ita bene sub scarleto, sicut sub sacco, sive sub burello. Unde religio non est in dividendo se ab aliis per habitum, sed in uniendo se Deo per amorem. Qui autem habet habitum religionis, si non sit intus religio."

83. Ibid., 181–83.

84. Geltner, *De periculis*, 10–11.

85. For the text of the sermon see Traver, *Opuscula*, 191–205. The poet Rutebeuf would take up these themes in two of his works, *Du Pharisien* and *Des règles*. We will survey Rutebeuf's inflammatory poems in detail in chapter 5.

86. Traver, *Opuscula*, 194–95.

87. Traver notes some of this influence in ibid., 80–81.

Chapter 4

1. The number of works on the *Roman de la Rose* always growing. There are two standard editions of the poem: Ernest Langlois, ed., 5 vols. (Paris: Librairie Ancienne Honoré Champion, 1914–24), and Félix Lecoy, ed., 3 vols. (Paris: Champion, 1965–70). More recently, there is the easily available edition in original text and modern French for the Livre de Poche series, Armand Strubel, ed., and based on two separate manuscripts (Paris: La Librairie générale française, 1992). Verse numbering varies slightly between these editions; we will use the Lecoy version (a standard scholarly edition) for all subsequent quotes, and verse numbers. The standard English translation is Charles Dahlberg, *The Romance of the Rose* (Princeton: Princeton University Press, 1971, 3rd ed.,1995), based on the Langlois edition. A dated, but still excellent study guide is Maxwell Luria, *A Reader's Guide to the Romance of the Rose* (Hamden, CT: Archon Books, 1982). See also Heather M. Arden's good short guide, *The Romance of the Rose* (Boston: Twayne Publishers, 1987, and more recently, see her *The Roman de la Rose: An Annotated Bibliography*, Garland Medieval Bibliographies 8 (New York: Garland, 1993). Key general studies include Alan M. Gunn, *The Mirror of Love: A Reinterpretation of the "Romance of the Rose"* (Lubbock: Texas Tech University Press, 1952); D.W. Robertson, Jr., *A Preface to Chaucer: Studies in Medieval Perspectives* (Princeton: Princeton University Press, 1962), which, despite its title, has much important information on the *Roman*; John V. Fleming *The Roman de la Rose: A Study in Allegory and Iconography* (Princeton: Princeton University Press, 1969); and C.S. Lewis, *The Allegory of Love* (Oxford: Clarendon Press, 1936), though his theories about the differences between Guillaume and Jean, and Jean's lack of skill were later disputed and disproven. Other important studies include Kevin Brownlee and Sylvia Huot, eds., *Rethinking the Romance of the Rose: Text, Image, Reception* (Philadelphia: University of Pennsylvania Press, 1992), and Douglas Kelly, *Internal Difference and Meanings in the Roman de la Rose* (Madison: University of Wisconsin Press, 1995). On comparison with Dante and Chaucer, see John Fyler, *Language and the Declining World in Chaucer, Dante, and Jean de Meun* (Cambridge: Cambridge University Press, 2007). The "Les Archives de littérature du Moyen Âge" (ARLIMA) web page for Jean de Meun has an extensive bibliography: http://www.arlima.net/il/jean_de_meun.html, accessed January 22, 2014. For an online resource of manuscripts, see the "*Roman de la Rose* Digital Library": http://romandelarose.org. This work should not be confused with the *Roman de la Rose* by Jean Renart, a different poem with musical interpolations written around 1200, also known as *Guillaume de Dole*.

2. [10587–90], III, 166–67: "Car, quant Guillaumes cessera │ Johans le continuera │ Emprès sa mort, que je ne mente,│ Anz trespassez plus de quarante." The verse numberings of Langlois differ slightly from those of Lecoy. See also Luria, *A Reader's Guide*, 6.

3. Félix Lecoy, "Sur la date du *Roman de la Rose*," *Romania* 89 (1968): 554–55. Jean mentions the Friars of the Sack at line 12,137, who were suppressed at the Council of Lyons in 1274.

4. Jules Quicherat, "Jean de Meung et sa maison à Paris," *Bibliotèque de l'Ecole des chartes* 41 (1880): 46–52.

5. Maxwell Luria, *A Reader's Guide*, 7–9, and 36, which also references in translation Lecoy's work.

6. Susan Stakel, in *False Roses: Structures of Duality and Deceit in Jean de Meun's "Roman de la Rose,"* (Stanford: ANMA Libri, 1991), offers a useful listing of how the various characters make use of deceit as a topic at 43–45. See also 33–35, for a discussion of wordplay. See also Maxwell Luria, *Reader's Guide*, 41 and 46, the latter noting the differences between the central character's speeches in Jean's continuation.

7. Maxwell Luria, *Reader's Guide*, 48–49.

8. Arden devotes a useful chapter to allegory in the poem in *Roman de la Rose*, 43–66, as does Luria in *Reader's Guide*, 36–47.

9. Arden, *Roman de la Rose*, 45.

10. Luria in *A Reader's Guide*, 42.

11. On this, see ibid., 10.

12. Interestingly, Wyclif and FitzRalph would also discuss aspects of the Golden Age before the Fall of Man in their own writings against the friars in the 14th century. The idea of dominion and questions of private property were invoked. See chapter 8.

13. Rutebeuf, *Poèmes concernant l'Université de Paris*, H.H. Lucas, ed. (Paris: Libraire Nizet, 1952), 41. We will discuss his works in more detail in chapter 5.

14. Geltner, *De periculis*, 60.

15. Fleming, *Allegory and Iconography*, 25.

16. Ibid., 162, where he notes: "Some knowledge of the antifraternal hermeneutics of William of Saint-Amour greatly aids one's reading of Jeans' poem." For a more detailed study, see Daniel Poirion, "Jean de Meun et la querelle de l'Université de Paris: Du libelle au livre," *Traditions polémiques* 2, Nicole Gazauran and Jean Mesnard, eds. (Paris: Ecole Normale Supérior des Jeunes Filles, 1985), 9–19.

17. See John Fleming, *Allegory and Iconography*, 165–66 for more study and debate. Stakel, in *False Roses*, gives several examples at 51, and see also 100–101 for more on False Seeming's dual nature. See also Gabriella I. Baika, "'Double-Talk' (*Bilinguium*) in *Faus Semblant's* Discourse in the Roman de la Rose," *Medievalia et Humanistica* 35 (2009): 15–32, for more on False Seeming's duality, and his relation

to Guillaume de Saint-Amour's concern for signs of the last times, as well as to the concept of "double-talking," expounded in detail by the 13th-century Dominican William Perault.

18. Jean Batany, *Approches du Roman de la Rose* (Paris: Bordas, 1972), 104–05.

19. [10976–996], II, 84–85: "Baron, entendez ma sentence | Qui Faus Semblant vodra connoistre | si le quiere au siecle ou en cloistre; | nul leu fors en ces .II. ne mains | mes en l'un plus, en l'autre mains. | ... Religieus sunt mout couvert | seculer sunt plus aouvert. | Si ne veill je mie blamer | religion ne defamer: | en quel que habit que l'en la truisse | ja religion, que je puisse | humble et leal ne blamerai. | Ne porquant ja ne l'amerai. | G'entent des faus religious | des felons, des malicieus | qui l'abit en veulent vestir | et ne veulent leur queur mestir."

20. See Stakel, *False Roses*, 52–54, where she gives numerous examples of the different names and uses for clothing. See 55 for a discussion of Jean's insistence that not all who wear habits are deceivers. See also R. Howard Bloch, *The Scandal of the Fabliaux* (Chicago: University of Chicago Press, 1986), 33–34.

21. [11103–108], II, 88: "S'il a guieres de tex loveaus | entre tes apostres noveaus | Iglise, tu iés maubaille; | se ta citez est assaille | par les chevaliers de ta table | ta seigneurie est mout endable."

22. [11263–272], II, 93: "Si puis bien jurer sanz delai | qu'il n'est escrit en nule lai | au mains n'est il pas en la nostre | que Jhesucrit ne si apostre | tant con il alerent par terre | fussent onques veü pain querre | car mendier pas ne voloient | (ainsinc preechier le soloient | jadis par Paris la cite | li mestre de divinité)";

23. [11345–452], II, 95–99. See also chapter 3.

24. [11384–394], II, 97.

25. See chapter 6 for more on Philip the Fair and his conflicts with the pope and Templars. The satirical *Roman de Fauvel* was created out of this turbulent time.

26. [11458–468], II, 99: "Se cil de Saint Amor ne ment | qui desputer solait et lire | et preeschier ceste matire | a Paris avec devins. | Ja ne m'eïst ne pains ne vins | s'il n'avoit en sa verité | l'acort de l'Université | et du peuple communement | qui oait son preeschement. | Nus preudon de ce refuser | ver Dieu ne se peut escuser":

27. [11475–478], II, 99: "ou estre baniz du rïaume | a tort, con fu mestre Guillaume | de Saint Amor, qu'Ypocrisie | fist essillier par grant envie."

28. [11482–484], II, 100: "Vers ma mere trop mesprenoit | por ce qu'il fist un noveau livre | ou sa vie fist toute escrivre,"

29. [11492–494], II, 100: "J'aim mieux devant les genz orer | et affubler ma renardie | du mantel de papelardie."

30. [11535–536], II, 101: "En aquerre est toute m'entente | mieuz vaut mes porchaz que ma rente."

31. Dahlberg, *Romance*, 203. [11547–556], II, 102.

32. [11215–223], II, 92: "Quant je voi touz nuz ces truanz | trembler sus ces fumiers puanz | de froit, de fain crier et brere | ne m'entremet de leur affere. | S'il sunt a l'Ostel Dieu porté | ja n'ierent par moi conforté | car d'une aumosne toute seule | ne me pestroient il la gueule | qu'il n'ont pas vaillant une seiche."

33. [11595–606], II, 103: "Leur philateres eslargissent | et leur finbries agrantissent | ... et aiment que l'en les salue | quant il trespassent par la rue | et veulent estre apelé mestre | ce qu'il ne devroient pas estre | car l'esvangile vet encontre | qui leur desleauté, demontre."

34. Nancy Freeman Regalado, in *Poetic Patterns in Rutebeuf*, 140–45, gives a discussion of the relationship between Jean and Rutebeuf, and their use of common themes in their antifraternal attacks, among which is the Pharisee allusion. This will be discussed further in chapter 5.

35. [11639–644], II, 104–05: "Et pour avoir des genz loanges | des riches homes par losanges | empetrons que letres nous doignent | qui la bonté, de nos tesmoignent | si que l'en croie par le monde | que vertu toute en nous habonde."

36. [11683–688], II, 106: "Je sui des vallez Antecrit | des larrons don il est escrit | qu'il ont habit de sainteé | et vivent en tel sainteé | Dehors semblons aigneus pitables | dedanz somes lous ravisables";

37. [11757–759], II, 108: "Ja ne les connoistrez aus robes | li faus treïstres pleins de lobes; | leur fez vos esteut regarder | se vos volez bien d'eus garder."

38. [11761–776], II, 108–09: "Et se ne fust la bon garde | de l'Université, qui garde | la clef de la crestienté | tout eüst esté, tourmenté | quant par mauvese entencion | en l'an de l'incanacion | .M. et .II.C. .V. et .L. | n'est hom vivanz qui m'en desmante | fu baillez, c'est bien chose voire | por prendre conmun examplaire | un livre de par le deable | c'est l'*Esvangile Pardurable* | que li Sainz Esperiz ministre | si con il apparoit ou tistre | ainsinc est il entitulez; | bien est digne d'estre brulez."

39. [11795–802], II, 109: "L'Université, qui lors iere | endormie, leva la chiere; | du bruit du livre s'esveilla | n'onc puis guieres ne someilla | ainz s'arma por aler encontre | quant il vit cel horrible montre | toute preste de batailler | et du livre aus juges bailler."

40. [11815–820], II, 110: "Ainsant Antecrist atendrons | tuit ensemble a lui nos tendrons. | Cil qui ne s'i vorront aherdre | la vie leur convedra perdre. | Les genz encontre eus esmovrons | par les baraz que nous covrons,"

41. [11867–876], II, 111–112: "De tout le monde est empereres | Baraz, mes sires et mes peres; | ma mere en est empereriz. | Maugré, qu'an ait Sainz Esperiz | nostre puissant lignage reigne. | Nous reignons or en chascun reigne | et bien est droiz que nous resnons | qui tretout le monde fesnons | et savons si les genz deçoivre | que nus ne s'en set aperçoivre";

42. [11919–922], II, 113: "Et s'il sunt autres qu'il ne semblent | qu'ainsint la grace du monde emblent | la me veill enbatre et fichier | por decevoir et por trichier," See also Stakel, *False Roses*, 81–82.

43. [11923–931], II, 113: "Si ne veill je pas por ce dire | que l'en doie hunble habit despire | por quoi desouz orgueill n'abit: | nul ne doit haïr por l'abit | le povre qui s'en est vestuz; | mes Dex nou prise .II. festuz | s'il dit qu'il a lessié, le monde | et de gloire mondaine habonde | et de delices veust user."

44. [11932–938], II, 113: "Qui peut tel beguin escuser? | Tex papelarz, quant il se rant | puis va mondains deliz querant | et dit que touz les lessiez | s'il en veust puis estre angressiez | c'est li mastins qui glotement | retorne a son vomissement." Referencing Prov. 26:11, *Vulgata*, 601: "Sicut canis qui revertitur ad vomitum suum, sic imprudens qui iterat stultitiam suam."

45. [12020–034], II 116: "unes paternostres i a | a un blanc laz de fil pendues | qui ne li furent pas vendues; | donees les li ot uns freres | qu'el disoit qu'il estoit ses peres | et le visitoit mout sovent | plus que nul autre du covent; | et il sovent la visitoit | maint biau sarmon li recitoit. | Ja por Faus Semblant nou lessast | que sovent ne la confessast | et par si grant devocion | fesoient leur confession | que .II. testes avoit ensemble | en un chaperon, ce me semble."

46. [12037–040], II, 116–17: "El resembloit, la puste lisse | le cheval de l'Apochalipse | qui senefie

la gent male | d'ypocrisie tainte et pale"; See Susan Stakel, *False Roses*, 48–49, where she suggests that this pale coloring, mentioned earlier in the poem, is a result of hunger. See also Szittya, *Antifraternal Tradition*, 33, for an examination of Guillaume de Saint-Amour's use of the horses of the apocalypse in his *Collectiones*, which may have had some influence on Jean.

47. [12052–54], II, 117: "Faus Semblant, qui bien se ratorne | ot, ausinc con por essaier | vestuz les dras frere Saier." Concerning the identity of this figure, Lecoy remarks in the notes at 290: "Si le nom du frère Saier ... renvoie à un personnage réel, il ne nous est plus possible, aujourd'hui, de l'identifier."

48. Stakel, *False Roses*, 54.

49. We will examine Adam's work in more detail in chapter 5. This Robin was not initially related to Robin Hood.

50. Stakel, *False Roses*, 54–55.

51. [12097–116], II, 118–19.

52. [12309–323], II, 125: "car je sui d'ordre et si sui prestres | de confessier li plus hauz mestres | qui soit, tant con li mondes dure ... | Si rai un mout grant avantage: | prelat ne sunt mie si sage | ne si letré, de trop con gié. | J'ai de divinité, congié | voire, par Dieu, pieça leü."

53. See Fleming, *Allegory and Iconography*, 170–71 for some further discussion on how this relates to the Lover's quest. See also Stakel, *False Roses*, 56–57.

54. [15213–234], II, 213: "Et se gent encontre moi groucent | qui se troublent et se corroucent | qu'il santent que je les remorde | par ce chapistre ou je recorde | les paroles de Faus Semblant ... | je faz bien protestation | qu'onques ne fu m'antanacion | de parler contre home vivant | sainte religion sivant | ne qui sa vie use en bone euvre | de quel que robe qu'il se queuvre | ainz pris mon arc et l'antesoie | quex que pechierres que je soie | si fis ma saiete voler | generaument por affoler. | Por affoler? Mes por connoistre | fussent seculier ou de cloister | les desloiaus genz, les maudites | que Jhesus apele ypocrites,"

55. Richard Kenneth Emmerson and Ronald B. Herzman, "The Apocalyptic Age of Hypocrisy: Faus Semblant and Amant in the Roman de la Rose," *Speculum* 62 (1987): 612: "The net cast by apocalyptic imagery and allusions in the Roman is wide enough to deserve careful analysis, because it provides insight into the fundamental questions that arise in any interpretation of the poem and that are still very much in debate."

56. Saint Augustine, *The City of God Against the Pagans*, William Chase Green, trans., 7 vols. (London: William Heineman, 1960), VI, 294–5: "Non itaque per totum hoc tempus quod liber iste complecitur, a primo scilicet adventu Christi usque in saeculi finem, qui erit secundus eius adventus, ita diabolus alligatur ut eius haec ipsa sit alligata, per hos intervallum quod mille annorum numero, appellat non seducere ecclesiam, quando quidem illam nec solutus utique seducturus est."

57. Emmerson and Herzman, "Apocalyptic Age of Hypocrisy," 615.

58. Augustine, *City of God*, 80–1: "Omnium vero de hac re calculantum digitos resolvit et quiescere iubet ille qui dicit: Non est vestrum scire tempore, quae Pater posuit in sua potestate."

59. For a recent study, see Lesley Smith, *The Glossa Ordinaria: The Making of a Medieval Bible Commentary* (Leiden: Brill, 2009). For an edition (erroneously ascribed to Strabo), see *Patrologia Latina*, Jacques Paul Migne, ed., vols. 113 and 114 (Paris: Imprimerie Catholique, 1852). See also online the French site: http://www.glossae.net.

60. Marjorie Reeves, *The Influence of Prophecy in the Later Middle Ages* (Oxford: Clarendon Press, 1969), 62–63.

61. Emmerson and Herzman, "Apocalyptic Age of Hypocrisy," 620–1.

62. See Fleming, *Allegory and Iconography*, 163–64, for some debate on the issue of chastity. See also Stakel, *False Roses*, 49–50. She notes, however, that Constrained Abstinence is actually refraining from food, not sex, see 48–49.

63. [14709–722], II, 197–98: "Ce fu Faus Samblant, li traïstress | le filz Barat, li faus ministres | dame Ypocrisie sa mere | qui tant est au vertuz amere | et dame Attenance Contrainte | qui de Faus Samblant est enceinte | preste d'anfanter Antecrit | si con je truis an livre ecrit. | Cil la desconfirent sanz faille | si pri por eus, vaille que vaille. | Seigneurs, qui veust traïstres estre | face de Faus Samblant son mestre | et Contrainte Attenance preingne: | double soit et simple se faigne."

64. William Ryding, "Faus Semblant: Hero or Hypocrite?" *Romanic Review* 60 (1969): 163; Charles Muscatine, *Chaucer and the French Tradition: A Study in Style and Meaning* (Berkeley: University of California Press, 1957), 73; and C.S. Lewis, *The Allegory of Love* (London: Oxford University Press, 1938), 142.

65. Kevin Brownlee, in "The Problem of Faux Semblant: Language, History, and Truth in the Roman de la Rose," *The New Medievalism*, Marina S. Brownlee, Kevin Brownlee, and Stephen G. Nichols, eds. (Baltimore: Johns Hopkins University Press, 1991), 271, *n*17, remarks: "Manuscript evidence offers an interesting commentary on Jean's substitution of Guillaume de Saint-Amour for Guillaume de Lorris as primary subtext for the Faux Semblant episode. Several thirteenth, fourteenth, and fifteenth century rubricators confuse the two Guillaumes, going so far as to attribute to Saint-Amour the authorship of the first part of the Rose."

66. Ibid., 253–71. He notes at 268–9: "On a variety of levels, then, the *Evangile Pardurable* is presented as an inscribed, negative version in miniature of Jean de Meun's book. As such, it functions in tandem with Faux Semblant's presentation of *De Periculis* simultaneously to expand the scope of the Rose as literary-poetic enterprise and to problematize the very terms of this enterprise, both structural and linguistic.... Love's structural model of the continuation of the Rose appears as potentially dangerous, when seen from Faux Semblant's new 'historical' perspective."

67. Emmerson and Herzman, "The Apocalyptic Age of Hypocrisy," 629–30.

68. Fleming, *Allegory and Iconography*, 166–7.

69. Ibid., 167.

70. Ibid., 170.

71. Stakel, *False Roses*, 46. See also 58.

72. Lewis, *Allegory of Love*, and Norman Cohn, *The World-View of a Thirteenth-Century Intellectual* (Newcastle upon Tyne: University of Durham Press, 1961), for example. This was also a common perception throughout the 19th century; see Dahlberg, *Romance of the Rose*, 2–3 for a brief discussion.

73. Gunn, *The Mirror of Love*, 26

74. See Luria, *A Reader's Guide*, 34–35, for thoughts on the idea that Guillaume's portion was also intended to be satirical.

75. Deriving from *paper*, "to eat" and *lard*, indicating one who eats meat on religious days when meat should not be eaten. See Arden, *Roman de la Rose*, 113, *n*5.

76. [406–410], I, 13: "Une autre en ot aprés escrite | qui sembla bien estre ypocrite. | Papelardie ert apelee. | C'est cele qui en recelee, | quant nus ne s'en puet penre garde | de nul mal fere n'est coarde";

77. Fleming, *Roman de la Rose*, 170.

78. Ibid.

79. David Hult, in *Self-Fulfilling Prophecies: Readership and Authority in the First Roman de la Rose* (Cambridge: Cambridge University Press, 1986), argues in his chapters "The Allegory of Incompletion" and "The Allegory of Love," at 160–185, that Guillaume de Lorris' poem is indeed complete in and of itself. For example, he states at 175: "To assert that the *Roman de la Rose* is an unfinished poem is at best a naive judgement that takes little account of the intricacies latent in a tale whose self-conscious manipulation of a sequence of narrative voices risks threatening, if not eradicating, a single authoritative voice." Thus, the poem is too complex to be dismissed so easily, and should not be read merely as incomplete.

80. [7759–764], I, 238: "Briefement fetes en quelque place | quan que vos pensez qu'il la place. | S'ainsinc le fetes, n'ene doutez | ja n'i seroiz arriers boutez | ainz vendrez a vostre propos | tout ainsinc con je le propos."

81. [7765–767], I, 238: "Douz amis, qu'est ce que vos dites? | Nus hom, s'i n'iert faus ypocrites | ne feroit ceste deablie."

82. [7789–790], I, 239: "Conpainz, conpainz, ce doivent querre | cil qui sunt en aperte guerre."

83. [19315–320 and 19329–338], III, 80–81: "fors seulemant a Faus Semblant | por qu'il s'aut james assemblant | avec les felons orguilleus | les ypocrites perilleus | des quex l'Escriture recete | que ce sunt li pseudo prophete. | ... Trop font tel gent a redouter | bien les deüt Amours bouter | hors de son ost, s'il li pleüst | se certeinement ne seüst | qu'il li fussent si necessaire | qu'il ne peüst sanz eus riens faire. | Mes s'il sunt advocat por eus | en la cause au fins amoureus | don leur mal saient alegié | c'est barat leur pardone gié."

84. [19447–450], III, 84: "Tantost li diex d'Amours affable | a Genius une chasuble; | anel li baille et croce et mitre | plus clere que cristal ne vitre."

85. Szittya, *Antifraternal Tradition*, 188.

86. Ibid., 189.

87. Stakel, *False Roses*, 82.

88. See ibid., 60–61, for thoughts on False Seeming's important relation to the God of Love and the poem as a whole.

89. Ibid., 58–59, explores this important idea further.

90. See John Fleming, "The Moral Reputation of the Roman de la Rose before 1400," *Romance Philology* 18, 4 (1965): 430–35, especially 431 and 434.

91. For a recent edition, see Andrea Valentini, *Le remaniement du "Roman de la Rose" par Gui de Mori. Étude et édition des interpolations d'après le manuscrit Tournai, Bibliothèque de la Ville 101*, Collection des Anciens auteurs belges, Collection in–8°, nouvelle série 14 (Brussels: Académie royale de Belgique, 2007).

92. See Lori Walters, "Gui de Mori's Rewriting of Faux Semblant in the Tournai Roman de la Rose," *The Medieval Opus: Imitation, Rewriting and Transmission in the French Tradition*, Proceedings of the Colloquium held at the Institute for Research in the Humanities, October 5–7, 1995, Douglas Kelly, ed. (Amsterdam: Rodopi, 1996), 261–76, especially 267–68.

93. For an edition, see *Le Pèlerinage de la Vie Humaine*, J.J. Stürzinger, ed. (London: Nichols & Sons, 1893). See also Stephanie A. Viereck Gibbs Kamath, "Naming the Pilgrim: Authorship and Allegory in Guillaume de Deguileville's *Pèlerinage de la vie humaine*," *Studies in the Age of Chaucer* 32 (2010): 179–21.

94. For a further discussion of Machaut and the *Roman's* influence on later generations of poets, see Luria, *Reader's Guide*, 60–62. See also Kevin Brownlee, "Machaut's Motet 15 and the 'Roman de la rose': The Literary Context of 'Amours qui a le pouoir/Faus Samblant m'a deceu/Vidi Dominum,'" *Early Music History* 10 (1991): 1–14, especially 12–14. This particular work features the Lover and False Seeming in different vocal lines with different text (a common motet technique in the 13th and 14th centuries).

95. See Luria, *Reader's Guide*, 75–76, for some discussion on just what portions of the surviving Middle English version may be attributed to Chaucer.

96. See chapter 7.

97. Luria, *Reader's Guide*, 62–63.

98. This was an ancient paradox, formulated at least as early as the 6th century BCE, and known as Epimenides' Paradox. Essentially, if all Cretans are liars, and a Cretan says this is so, then he must be lying. If this is the case, not all Cretans are liars, so he may be telling the truth. But how can all Cretans be liars if he is telling the truth? See Geltner, *Making of Medieval Antifraternalism*, 29 and 32–33. On this, see also Daniel Heller-Roazen, *Fortune's Faces: The Roman de la Rose and the Poetics of Contingency* (Baltimore: Johns Hopkins University Press, 2003), 132–35.

99. Jill Mann has suggested a similar view, though she feels that the connections between False Seeming and the friars are clear. See *Chaucer and Medieval Estates Satire* (Cambridge: Cambridge University Press Archive, 1973), 226, n70, and 38, an important work that we will return to in chapter 7.

100. Geltner, "Faux Semblants: Antifraternalism Reconsidered," 365.

101. Ibid. 361–62.

102. Geltner, *Making of Medieval Antifraternalism*, 33. For further study of False Seeming in manuscript art, see Timothy L. Stinson, "Illumination and Interpretation: The Depiction and Reception of Faus Semblant in *Roman de la Rose* Manuscripts," *Speculum* 87, 2 (2012): 469–498.

103. See chapter 2, and Geltner, *Making of Medieval Antifraternalism*, 33–35. For further analysis, see Geltner, "Faux Semblants: Antifraternalism Reconsidered," 365–69 and 376–80, and Sylvia Huot, *The Romance of the Rose and its Medieval Readers: Interpretation, Reception, Manuscript Transmission* (Cambridge: Cambridge University Press, 1993), 236–39.

104. Geltner, *Making of Medieval Antifraternalism*, 35: "frère Leus, qui tout deveure."

105. Ibid., 36–37.

Chapter 5

1. An excellent study on French poetry and music from the beginning of the 13th century through the 14th is Ardis Butterfield, *Poetry and Music in Medieval France: From Jean Renart to Guillaume de Machaut*, Cambridge Studies in Medieval Literature (Cambridge: Cambridge University Press, 2002).

2. Jongleurs were professional itinerant musicians and story-tellers in medieval France. The word derives from the Old French *jogleour*, and from the Latin *joculator* a "joker." The word "juggler" is also related. They were frequently condemned by the Church and were considered to be very low on the social scale.

3. In this opening section, I am indebted to the work of Nancy Freeman Regalado, for her excellent summary of Rutebeuf's life, "Rutebeuf," in *Key Figures in Medieval Europe: An Encyclopedia*, Richard Kenneth Emmerson and Sandra Clayton-Emmerson, eds., Routledge Encyclopedias of the Middle Ages (New York: Routledge, 2006), 581–83. Likewise, her *Poetic Patterns in*

Rutebeuf is still the principal study in English of Rutebeuf's works, and has been very helpful in creating this chapter. Scholarship on Rutebeuf is relatively rare in English, and as expected, considerably more is available in French. To date, no complete edition of his poems has been translated into English, which is surprising given his importance. A classic edition of his poems is Achille Jubinal, ed., *Œuvres complètes de Rutebeuf, trouvère du XIII*^{e} *siècle* (Paris: Paul Daffis, 1874). A more recent edition of the Old French texts (and considered the scholarly standard), see *Œuvres completes de Rutebeuf*, ed. Edmond Faral and Julia Bastin. 2 vols. (Paris: Picard, 1959 and 1960), which is used in all excerpts in the notes that follow. For an edition with modern French translation, see *Rutebeuf, Œuvres completes*, ed. and trans. Michel Zink. 2 vols. (Paris: La Librairie générale française, 1989–90). A short article on Rutebeuf's use of wit and self-deprecation is Charles H. Post, "The Paradox of Humor and Satire in the Poems of Rutebeuf," *The French Review* 25, 5 (1952): 364–68. For a study of Rutebeuf's seemingly contentious relationship with King Louis IX (including the king's role in the University Quarrels), see Edward Billings Ham, *Rutebeuf and Louis IX*, Vol. 42 of Studies in the Romance languages and literatures (Chapel Hill: University of North Carolina Press, 1962), a short monograph; later scholars have questioned some of Ham's conclusions. French studies are more numerous and varied, and include: Ari Serper, "L'Influence de Guillaume de Saint-Amour sur Rutebeuf," *Romance Philology* 17 (1963): 391–402; Omer Jodogne, "L'anticléricalisme de Rutebeuf," *Lettres Romanes* 23 (1969): 219–44; Jean Dufournet, "Sur trois poèmes de Rutebeuf: La Complainte Rutebeuf, Renart le Bestourné, et La Pauvreté Rutebeuf," *Hommage à Gérard Moignet*, Travaux de Linguistique et de Littérature 18, 1 (1980): 413–28; and Jean Subrenat, "Fabliau et satire cléricale: la specificité de Frere Denise par Rutebeuf," *Risus Mediaevalis: Laughter in Medieval Literature and Art*, Mediaevalia Lovaniensia, series I, studia 30, Herman Braet, Guido Latré and Werner Verbeke, eds. (Leuven: Leuven University Press, 2003), 143–153.

4. The trouvères were the northern French counterpart to the troubadours, writing in the *langue d'oïl*, or Old French, as opposed to the Occitan or *langue d'oc* of the troubadours. Chrétien de Troyes (fl. 1160s-80s) is generally seen as being the first trouvère, particularly known for his Arthurian romances. These poet-musicians came from all social classes, including the very poorest up to royalty, such as Thibaut IV, who we will discuss later in the chapter. Unlike the troubadours, whose culture was damaged and scattered by the Albigensian Crusade, the trouvères continued to flourish until at least 1300, though some consider Guillaume de Machaut (*ca.* 1300–77) as the last trouvère, at least in part due to his fondness for continuing to write monophonic songs (i.e., those with only a single line of melody), when all of his courtly contemporaries by then focused exclusively on polyphonic music. Machaut also wrote exceptional polyphonic compositions (including the landmark *Messe de Notre Dame*), but retained a fondness for the lai, an older monophonic musical form known for its length.

5. Of the more than 2,100 trouvère poems that survive, fully two-thirds of them have melodies, a remarkable situation in view of the paucity of survivals in the troubadour tradition, where only about 250 melodies survive. The Albigensian Crusade and general hostilities toward the south by the north no doubt contributed to the tragic loss of so much of the secular music of medieval Occitania.

6. Regalado, "Rutebeuf," 581. See *Le Dit de l'Université de Paris* [27–28], I, 375: "Par chacune rue regarde | Ou voie la bele musarde."

7. *Li Dit de l'Université de Paris* [32–39], I, 375: "Ne fait or boen ci semancier | En Quaresme, que hon doit faire | Choze qui a Dieu doit plaire. | En leu de haires, haubers vestent | Et boivent tant que il s'entestent; | Si font bien li troi on li quatre | Quatre cens escoliers combatre | Et cesseir l'Universitei."

8. *Le mariage Rutebeuf* [35–38], I, 548: "Et si n'est pas gente ne bele; | Cinquante anz a en s'escuele | S'est maigre et seche: | N'ai pas paor qu'ele me treche."

9. *De la Griesche d'Yver* [43–49], I, 523: "Li enviaul que je savoie | M'ont avoié quanques j'avoie | Et forvoié | Et fors de voie desvoié. | Fols enviaus ai envoie | Or m'en souvient | Or voi je bien tout va, tout vient." Further, at [85–86], 524: "Griesche li a coru seure | Desnué l'a en petit d'eure." For the dice reference, see [52–57], 523: "Li dé que li decier ont fet | M'ont de ma robe tout desfet | Li dé m'ocient | Li dé m'aguetent et espient | Li dé m'assaillent et desfient | Ce poise moi." The word *griesche* seems to refer to a type of dicing came that came from Greece, known as "griesche," see Jubinal, *Œuvres completes*, I, 24–25, n1.

10. See, for example, *La Povreté Rutebuef* [1–18], I, 570–571: "Je ne sai par ou je coumance | Tant ai de matyere abondance | Por parleir de ma povretei. | Por Dieu vos pri, frans Rois de France | Que me doneiz queilque chevance | Si fereiz trop grant charitei. | J'ai vescu de l'autrui chatei | Que hon m'a creü et prestei | Or me faut chacuns de créance | C'om me seit povre et endetei | Vos raveiz hors dou reigne estei | Ou toute avoie m'atendance. | Entre chier tens et ma mainie | Qui n'est malade ni fainie | Ne m'ont laissié deniers ne gages. | Gent truis d'escondire arainie | Et de doneir mal enseignie."

11. *Cordeliers* refers to the lengths of rope that the Franciscans wore as belts about their robes.

12. Geltner, *De periculis*, 19–20.

13. *Renart le Bestorné* is his addition to the Reynardian corpus. Recent English editions of four of his fabliaux can be found in Nathaniel E. Dubin, trans., *The Fabliaux*, introduction by R. Howard Bloch (New York: Liveright/Norton, 2013). We will discuss both of these important genres, and examine Rutebeuf's contribution to them in chapter 6.

14. Regalado, in *Poetic Patterns in Rutebeuf*, makes an interesting comparison between Rutebeuf and Jean de Meun, in how they depict the university conflict, at 146: "If Jean de Meun is the historian of the quarrel, Rutebeuf is the war correspondent under fire at the front lines."

15. Regalado, "Rutebeuf," 582. See also her *Poetic Patterns in Rutebeuf*, 113–14,

16. Regalado lists the poems addressing the mendicant issues in "Rutebeuf," 582, and their themes: "The proliferation of mendicant orders in Paris (Ordres de Paris, Chanson des ordres, Des béguines); the struggle between mendicants and secular clergy for parish privileges and university chairs (Discorde de l'université et des Jacobins, Des règles, Dit de sainte Église, Bataille des vices et des vertus, Des Jacobins); the writings of William of Saint-Amour, banished leader of the university masters (Dit and Complainte de Guillaume)." Other relevant poems were Du Pharisien and Le Dit d'Hypocisie. For an excellent short summary of the poem's contents online, see Juliet O'Brien's pdf, "The Paradoxical Heroism of Rute-

beuf's Antimendicant Poems, Jean de Meun's *Roman de la Rose* and Chaucer's *Summoner's Tale*. Three Approaches to the Problem of Truth." (2002), 5–8: http://blogs.ubc.ca/mdvl302/files/2012/01/comm-sample-rose2.pdf, accessed February 16, 2014. The whole work is worth reading for its insightful observations on Rutebeuf's work and False Seeming.

17. Regalado, *Poetic Patterns in Rutebeuf*, 106 and 108–09.

18. René de Lespinasse, ed., *Vie et vertus de Saint Louis*, Petits Mémoires sur l'histoire de France I (Paris: Société bibliographique, 1877, reprinted in facsimile by Elibron Classics, 2001), 164: "L'année où les troubles de l'université eurent lieu (1255), le Roi défendit de boire dans les tavernes, autrement que debout et en passant; il interdit aussi les blasphèmes contre Dieu, la sainte Vierge et les saints; tout individu convaincu d'avoir blasphémé, était sévèrement puni d'une amende et d'une peine matérielle."

19. *Chart.* I, 391, 342: "Necnon et quosdam alios libellos famosos in infamiam et detractionem eorundem fratrum ab eorum emulis in litterali et vulgari sermone necnon rismis et cantilenis indecentibus de novo ut dicitur editos, quos tibi exhiberi facias, detentores ad exhibitionem ipsorum per censuram ecclesiaticam appellatione postposita compellendo, convocatis magistris et scolaribus parisius existentibus facias publice coram omnibus igne cremari."

20. For some observations on the role of the poet and jongleur in social satire, and the hostility toward them, see Regalado, *Poetic Patterns in Rutebeuf*, 88–91.

21. *Chart.* I, 391, 342: "Pretercea Guillotum bedellum scolarium nationis Picardorum pro eo, quod sue salutis immemor ia dominica de Ramis Palmarum proximo preterita predicante dilecto fllio fratre Thoma de Aquino ejusdam Ordinis Predicatorum quendam libellum famosum, quem utpote contra cosdem fratres editum publice reprobaveras, contempta excommunicationis sententia, quam in omnes auctores, detentores et publicatores ipsius libelli auctoritate ordinaria promulgasse diceris in conspectu cleri et populi tunc ibidem existentium in tui et ipsorum fratrum injuriam publicaro presumpsit, excommunicatum presentibus magistris et scolaribus supradictis studeas nuntiare, privando ipsum nichilominus perpetuo bedellionatus officio, ila quod illud nec por se neque per alium decetero exercere presumat, nec etiam salarium aliquod sibi, quem de civitate Parisiensi sublato appellationis obstaculo perpetuo procures expellere."

22. See Regalado, *Poetic Patterns in Rutebeuf*, 137–40 for a discussion of earlier examples.

23. *Du Pharisien* [6–9], I, 251: "A vous toz faz je ma clamor | D'Ypocrisie | Cousine germaine Heresie | Qui bien a la terre saisie." See also Nancy Regalado, *Poetic Patterns in Rutebeuf*, 140–41.

24. *Du Pharisien* [50–57], I, 252–53: "Ainz est certaine: | Granz robes ont de simple laine | Et si sont de simple couvaine | Simplement chascuns se demaine | Color ont simple et pale et vaine | Simple viaire | Et sont cruel et deputaire | Vers cels a cui il ont afaire."

25. See Regalado, *Poetic Patterns in Rutebeuf*, 114, and 142–43 for some additional analysis, and a comparison with Jean de Meun's similar creation. However, she notes at 121–23 that Jean more directly translated Guillaume's writings about mendicancy than did Rutebeuf, arguing that Jean was more versed in scholastic argument and approached the subject from a more academic than propagandistic point of view.

26. *La discorde de l'université et des jacobins*, [9–16], I, 239: "Sor Jacobins est la parole | Que je vous vueil conter et dire | Quar chascuns de Dieu nous parole | Et si desfent corouz et ire | Que c'est la riens qui l'ame afole | Qui la destruit et qui l'empire: | Or guerroient por une escole | Ou il vuelent a force lire," [25–32], 239–40: "Chascuns d'els deüst estre amis | L'Université voirement | Quar l'Université a mis | En els tout le bon fondement: | Livres, deniers, pains et demis; |Més or lor rendent malement | Quar cels destruit li anemis | Qui plus l'ont servi longuement," and [35–36], 240: "Chascuns a son pooir desmembre | La mesnie saint Nicholas";

27. *La bataille des vices contre les vertus* [58–69], I, 307: "Si vindrent assez humblement: | Du pain quistrent, tel fu la riegle | Por oster les pechiez du siecle. | S'il vindrent chiés povre provoire | Tel bien comme il ot, c'est la voire | Pristrent en bone paciance | El non de sainte penitance. | Humilitez estoit petite | Qu'il avoient por aus eslite: | Or est Humilitez greignor | Que li Frere sont or seignor | Des rois, des prelas et des contes." See also Nancy Regalado, *Poetic Patterns in Rutebeuf*, 117–18. See also 120 for some discussion of how in this poem, jongleurs were also accused of being freeloaders.

28. *Des règles* [106–14], I, 273: "Encor est ceste gent si chiene | Quant un riche homme vont entor | Seignor de chastel ou de tor | Ou userier ou clerc trop riche | (Qu'il aiment miex grant pain que miche) | Si sont tuit seignor de leenz: | Ja n'enterront clerc ne lai enz | Qu'il nes truisent en la meson. | A ci granz seignors sanz reson!"

29. *Des règles* [37–39], I, 271: "Qui porroit paradis avoir | Aprés la mort por son avoir | Bon feroit embler et tolir."

30. Regalado, *Poetic Patterns in Rutebeuf*, 119.

31. *Le dit de Guillaume de Saint-Amour* [1–5], I, 243–44: "Oiez, prelat et prince et roi | La desreson et le desroi | C'on a fet a mestre Guillaume: | L'en l'a bani de cest royaume! | A tel tort ne morut més hom."

32. *Complainte de Guillaume* [156–61], I, 264: "S'il muert por moi, s'ert de moi plains. | Voir dires a cousté a mains | Et coustera | Més Diex, qui est et qui sera | S'il veut, en pou d'eure fera | Cest bruit remainder."

33. See Regalado, *Poetic Patterns in Rutebeuf*, 146–50 for a detailed summary. The full poem with further analysis is in *Rutebeuf* I, 286–98. See also Nancy Regalado, *Poetic Patterns in Rutebeuf*, 163–64.

34. *Des règles* [68–76], I, 272: "Nostre prelat sont enragié | Si sont decretistre et devin. | Je di por voir, non pas devin: | Qui por paor a mal se ploie | Et a malfetor se souploie | Et por amor verité lesse | Qui a ces deux choses se plesse | Si maint bone vie en test monde | Qu'il a failli a la seconde!"

35. *La Dit de Sainte Eglise* [37–48], I, 280: "Vous devin, et vous discretistre | Je vous jete fors de mon titre | De mon titre devez fors estre | Quant le cinqueime esvengelitre | Vost on fere mestre et ministre | De parler dou roi celestre. | Encor vous teront en champ [p]estre | [Si] com autre berbiz chanpestre | Cil qui font la novelle espitre. | Vous estes mitres, non pas mestre: | Vous copez Dieu l'oreille destre | Diex vous giete de son regitre." See also Regalado, *Poetic Patterns in Rutebeuf*, 125, *n*16, for how this passage may reference the *Eternal Gospel*.

36. *Complainte de Guillaume* [44–54], I, 260: "Comment souffrez en tel lien | Mestre Guilliaume | Qui por moi fist de teste hiaume? | Or est fors mis de test roiaume | Li bons preudon | Qui mist cors et vie a bandon. | Fet l'avez de Chastel Landon | La moquerie: | Me vendez, par sainte Marie! | J'en doi plorer, qui que s'en rie: | Je n'en puis mais."

37. A recent study of this fascinating individual is Linde Katritzky, *Johnson and the Letters of Junius; New Perspectives on an Old Enigma* (New York: Peter Lang Publishing, 1996). He has never been definitively identified, though the favorite candidate is Sir Philip Francis, a politician and writer of pamphlets, noted for his good education.

38. *Des règles* [1–7], I, 269: "Puis qu'il covient verité tere | De parler n'ai je més que fere. | Verité ai dite en mains leus: | Or est li dires pereilleus | A cels qui n'aiment verité | Qui ont mis en auctorité | Tels choses que metre n'i doivent."

39. *Les Ordres de Paris* [57–60], I, 325: "Nus n'en dit voir c'on ne l'assomme: | Lor haïne n'est pas frivole; | Je qui redout ma teste fole | Ne vous di plus, més qu'il sont homme."

40. Regalado holds to this view, which she summarizes in *Poetic Patterns in Rutebeuf*, 255.

41. See chapter 2. An account from 1256, recorded by Matthew Paris, gives a good example of public hostility. *Chronica Majora* V, 599: "Subsannavit populus, elemosinas consuetas subtrahendo, vocans eos hypocritas, et Antichristi successores, pseudoprædicatores, regum et principum adulatores et consiliatores, ordinariorum contemptores, et eorundem supplantatores, thalamorum regalium subintratores, confessionum prævaricatores, qui peragrantes ignotas provincias peccandi audaciam subministrant." See also Regalado, *Poetic Patterns in Rutebeuf*, 168–171, for some of the Dominican reactions to the anger against them.

42. Regalado, *Poetic Patterns in Rutebeuf*, 173–74.

43. Popular songs tended not to have been written down, a costly and time-consuming exercise that was still largely used for religious music. The secular music that does survive (and we are fortunate that there are still large amounts of it from France in this period) tends to be found in manuscripts created due to wealthy patrons employing literate clerks and music notationists to preserve art songs for posterity. Large numbers of trouvère songs survive this way.

44. *Les oeuvres de Guiot de Provins, poète lyrique et satirique*, John Orr, ed. (Manchester: Manchester University Press, 1915), 43, 1080–88: "'por coi remuent les priours | si sovent ? se n'est pas raisons, | destrutes en sont les maisons' – | de ceu me travaillent il molt. | Mais, tant i ait, je lor respond | que por ceu sovent les remuent | que paor ont que il ne puent, | et por ce les vont remuant | que il ne deviegnent puant –" For an introduction to the work, see xx-xxxii.

45. Nigel Wilkins, trans., *The Lyric Works of Adam de la Halle*, Corpus Mensurabilis Musicæ (Hänssler-Verlag: American Institute of Musicology, 1967), 24 (includes music): "D'orgueil a ja traitié clergie | Et Jacobins de bons morsiaus | Car en aus regne gloutrenie | Mais ceus espargne de Chitiaus! | Moines, abbés a trait d'envie | Et chevaliers de reuberie | Prendre nous cuide par monchiaus | Encore a fair pis li mauvais oisiaus | Car de luxure a toute gent plaïe." The complete works in text form with parallel modern French translations (and melodies included at the end) is Pierre-Yves Badel, ed. and trans., *Adam de la Halle: Œuvres complètes*, Lettres gothiques (Paris: Librairie générale française, 1995); see 104–06 for the poem.

46. See the poem *C'est du roi de Sezile*, Badel, *Adam de la Halle*, [70], 378: "On m'apele Bochu, mais je ne le sui mie."

47. For the issues surrounding the debate, see Jennifer Saltzstein, *The Refrain and the Rise of the Vernacular in Medieval French Music and Poetry*, Vol. 30 of Gallica (Woodbridge: D.S. Brewer, 2013), 114–123.

48. For a study of the flourishing of clerical trouvères in the second half of the 13th century in Arras, see Jennifer Saltzstein, "Cleric-Trouvères and the Jeux-Partis of Medieval Arras," *Viator* 43 (2012): 1–17.

49. Helen Solterer, "Theater and Theatricality," *The Cambridge Companion to Medieval French Literature*, Simon Gaunt and Sarah Kay, eds. (Cambridge: Cambridge University Press, 2008), 184–85.

50. Two translations of the play are worth investigating: *The Play of Madness*, Guy Mermier, trans., Studies in the Humanities 22 (New York: Peter Lang, 1997), offers a side-by-side edition with the original text and an English translation. A detailed study and analysis is Gordon Douglas McGregor *The Broken Pot Restored* (Nicholasville, KY: The French Forum, 1991). For some early ideas on the live presentation of the play, see Thomas Walton, "Staging 'Le Jeu de la Feuillée,'" *The Modern Language Review* 36, 3 (1941): 344–350. For an illuminating study of the social background and the environment in which Adam wrote the play, see Frederick W. Langley, "Community drama and community politics in thirteenth-century Arras: Adam de la Halle's *Jeu de la feuillée*," *Drama and Community: People and Plays in Medieval Europe*, Alan Hindley, ed. (Turnhout: Brepols, 1999), 57–77.

51. Memier, *The Play of Madness*, notes at 117, *n*123 that the character was believed in earlier times to be the descendant of the Saxon king, Herla, who was doomed to wander without ever setting foot on mortal ground. Christian lore made Hellequin into a devil. Indeed, the bump on the forehead of Arlecchino's *Commedia* mask is sometimes seen as a reminder of the horns from the devil masks of medieval mummer's plays. As in the *Commedia*, Adam has downplayed the darker origins of the character, making him more reminiscent of Shakespeare's Oberon, stern but not diabolical.

52. McGregor, *The Broken Pot*, 34 *n*4. For a complete summary of the decrees of the council, see *Papal Encyclicals Online*: http://www.papalencyclicals.net/Councils/ecum14.htm, accessed November 13, 2013.

53. Memier, *The Play of Madness*, [434–36], 36: "Certes li meffais fu trop grans | Et chascuns le pape en cosa | Quant tant de bons clers desposa." [446–56], 36: "Comment ont prelas l'avantage | D'avoir femes a remuier | Sans leur previlege cangier, | Et uns clers si pert se franquise | Par espouser en sainte eglise | Feme qui ot autre baron? | Et li fi a putain, laron | Ou nous devons prendre peuture | Mainent en pechié de luxure | Et si goent de leur clergie! | Romme a bien le lierche partie | Des clers fais sers et amatis."

54. Ibid., [462–69], 38: "Li papes qui en chou ot coupes | Est eüreus quant il est mors: | Ja ne fust si poissans ne fors | C'ore ne l'eüst deposé. | Mal li eüst onques osé | Tolir previlege de clerc | Car il li eüst dit esprec | Et si eüst fait l'escarbote."

55. Madness plays a key role in the play, both with the fool, and in other characters' behaviors. For a brief summary, see Memier, *The Play of Madness*, xxi.

56. McGregor, *The Broken Pot*, 112–13. The idea of the fool as the speaker of truth when no one else can is ancient, perhaps best known in Shakespeare's *King Lear*. For a good study of the fool as a worldwide phenomenon throughout the centuries, see Beatrice K. Otto, *Fools Are Everywhere: The Court Jester around the World* (Chicago: University of Chicago Press, 2001). On scandal and satire in Arras, see also Nancy Regalado, *Poetic Patterns in Rutebeuf*, 80, and *n*21.

57. Memier, *The Play of Madness*, [332–37], 26: "Souvent voi des

plus ediotes | A Haspre no moustier venir | Qui sont haitié au departir | Car li sains est de grant merite | Et d'une abenguete petite | Vous poés bien faire du saint." See also Carol Symes, *A Common Stage: Theater and Public Life in Medieval Arras* (Ithaca: Cornell University Press, 2007), 188, and McGregor, *The Broken Pot*, 91.

58. McGregor, *The Broken Pot*, 111.

59. Ibid., 116.

60. Memier, *The Play of Madness*, [964–66], 88: "Et or me faites tout escout: | Metons li ja sus qu'il doit tout | Et que Hane a pour lui jué." [995–96], 92: "Li moines—Ostes, me ferés vous dont forche? | Li ostes—Oïl, se vous ne me paiés." See also McGregor, *The Broken Pot*, 120–21.

61. Memier, *The Play of Madness*, [1094–97], 102: "Je ne fai point de men preu chi | Puis que les gens en vont ensi | N'il n'i a mais fors baisseletes | Enfans et garchonaille."

62. McGregor, *The Broken Pot*, 129.

63. McGregor offers some thoughts on the subject, ibid., 65–66.

64. Ibid., 121.

65. Saltzstein, *Refrain and the Rise of the Vernacular*, 117.

66. Ibid.

67. For a summary of this miracle and the formation of the brotherhood, see Symes, *A Common Stage*, 84–93.

68. An excellent modern collection of these is Marcia Jenneth Epstein, ed. and trans., *Prions en chantant: Devotional Songs of the Trouveres* (Toronto: University of Toronto Press, 1977).

69. Ibid., 190, I: "Et cler et lai | tout sanz delai | or ecoutés m'etante: | chançon ferai | si chanterai de la roïne genet."

70. Ibid., V: "chascun mendis | en fais, en dis | vos doit avoir mout chiere."

71. Ibid., 242, II: "Tuit lu deduit enterin | sont en cel riche regné: | autant prise on le vin | comme l'eue dou fossé. | Tuit sont riche et assizé | n'i a povre ne frein." Epstein translates the word as "mendicants."

72. Ibid., 242–43. Indeed, Epstein notes at 243 that for the fifth stanza (which opens by comparing the earth and sky to ink and parchment) the "earliest source [for this imagery] would appear to be the Koran (Ch. 31, 27)."

73. Ibid., 242, V: "conçut le douz enfantin | qui le monde a deliver | dou laz au mal Ysengrin."

74. Ibid., 206–07, III: "Je ne sai querre verité | que chascuns l'acoile endroit soi: | en evesque n'en blanc abé | n'en truis je point, ce poise moi | car gieus a si touz sousplanté | qu'en justifie fausseté | et qu'on dampne povre home versai." IV: "Par flaterie sont guilé | toutes les gens, et cler et lai."

75. Ibid., 202–03, II: "Ensit est d'ypocresie: | qui le cors a plain d'envie | ne par dehors ne pert mie | ainz sont tel fois au mostier | que leur cuers est en folie."

76. Ibid., III: "et nos prie d'esloigner | doubleise d'ypocresie."

77. For a detailed account, see Sidney Painter, "The Crusade of Theobald of Champagne and Richard of Cornwall," *A History of the Crusades*, Kenneth Setton, ed., 3 vols. (Philadelphia: University of Pennsylvania Press, 1962), 2, 463–85. He notes with humor at 464: "if one wished to write a burlesque of the crusades, one could do no better than to give an accurate account of the events of this expedition." Yet the crusade accomplished much, in spite of its participants' actions, setting the stage for Louis IX's far more ambitious venture a decade later.

78. These are surveyed by the author in Tim Rayborn, "The Crusade Songs of Thibaut IV," *Series Intendere, In Celebration of the Twenty-Fifth Anniversary of the Centre for Medieval Studies at Leeds University*, Sharon Hanen, ed. (Leeds: Centre for Medieval Studies, 1994), 45–51. For an edition of Thibaut's poems, see Axel Wallensköld, ed., *Les Chansons de Thibaut de Champagne* (Paris: Édouard Champion, 1925).

79. Michael Lower argues that Thibaut was an enthusiastic supporter of this mass execution as a part of his readying himself for the crusade. See "The Burning at Mont-Aimé: Thibaut of Champagne's Preparations for the Barons' Crusade of 1239," *Journal of Medieval History* 29 (2003): 95–108. He notes at 106 that Mont-Almé had a history of heretical activity, so the executions were probably held here to make a point that such beliefs would not be tolerated. Robert was a particularly odious individual, who was relieved more than once of his duties by the papacy, presumably because of his excessive zeal and cruelty. Matthew Paris noted that he was punished by being imprisoned for life, see chapter 8. An early but useful study of Robert and the French Inquisition is Charles H. Haskins, "Robert Le Bougre and the Beginnings of the Inquisition in Northern France," *The American Historical Review* 7:4 (1902): 631–652.

80. Michael Lower, "The Burning at Mont-Aimé," 103.

81. Ibid., 104–05.

82. Ibid., 106–07.

83. God as a pelican was a common medieval religious allegory; it was believed that the pelican would wound itself to feed its young, sacrificing itself in the way that Jesus had done for all humankind.

84. Wallensköld, *Les Chansons de Thibaut*, 195: "Mult par est or nostre estaz perilleus; | Et se ne fust li essamples de ceus | Qui tant aiment et noises et tençons | – Ce est des clers qui ont lessié sarmons | – Por guerroier et por tuër les genz – | Jamès en Dieu ne fust nus hons creanz."

85. Ibid., 196–97: "Savoz qui sont li vil oisel punais | Qui tuënt Dieu et ses enfançonèz? | Li papelart, dont li nons n'est pas nèz. | Cil sont bien ort et puant et mauves; | Il ocïent toute la simple gent | Par leur faus moz, qui sont li Dieu enfant. | Papelart font le siecle chanceler; | Per saint Pere, mal les fet encontrer: | Il ont tolu joie et solaz et pès. | Cil porteront en Enfer le grant fès." I am indebted to Dr. Rosalind Brown-Grant, University of Leeds, who some years ago provided me with translations of the four crusade songs and this *serventois*.

86. Rayborn, "Crusade Songs," 50.

87. The *Montpellier Codex* is a large collection of these pieces and others, mostly dating from 1250 to 1300, and probably compiled around 1300. Despite its name, it probably originated in Paris, where these pieces were in such fashion during that time period.

88. Hans Tischler, ed., *The Montpellier Codex: Fascicles 3, 4, and 5, vol. 2* (Madison: A-R Editions, Inc., 1978), no. 46, 18–19: "L'estat du monde et la vie | va empirant cahscun jour | car plein d'orgueil et d'envie | sunt cil qui samblent meillor. | Par dehors ont religious atour | et par dedans sunt plein d'ypocrisie | de fausseté, de dolour | penant se vont d'avoir non de mestrie | pour tost monter en henor. | Ja ne lairai que ne die: | Li Jacobin et li frère menor | sunt tout itel li pluisor." The "minor orders" here may refer to smaller groups of mendicants such as the Friars of the Sack and the Pied Friars, who were forced to disband in 1274 by the Council of Lyons. For an account of these groups, see Frances Andrews, *The Other Friars*.

89. *Montpellier Codex*, no. 48, 19: "A Cambrai avint l'autrier | que Sohiers li cuveliers | par son angin et son art | se mella de grant barat.

| A Camptiré s'en ala | as beguines s'acointa. | Mes sachiés tot vraiement | qu'antr'eles communaument | le revidoie[n]t souvent: | et ne mie por son non | ains ert por son grant bordon."

90. *Montpellier Codex*, no. 50, 20, v. 6–47: "Mes en remembrance | ai fet un nouvel deschant | que duel et pesance | doivent avoir moult grant | li vaillant | quant envie | et vilenie | vont de jour en jour montant | cortoisie | av[e]ques s'amie | largesce s'en vet fuiant. | Papelardie | que Dieus la maudie! | Que que nus en die | vet mes avant | n'est nus en vie | por qu'il en mesdie | que l'on ne l'en voist blasmant. | Chascun le va redoutant | n'il nest mie | grant folie | car li plus riche et li plus puissant | vont mes tel vie menant | valor ne sens ne clergie | ne vont mes nule rien prisant | tout ont mes truant. | Morte est France | par tel decevance | par tel *faus semblant* [emphasis mine] | Tant est mes pleine de tel viltance | que trestout li monz s'en vet gabant | c'est grant duel et grant mescheance | que tel guile dure mes tant | qu'ypocrisie | seur toute rien vivant | vet compaignie | et grant despense eschivant | trop sont chiche, angoisseus et tenant | seignorie | nebaillie | ne vont refusant | mes de lors biens ne se sent *nus*."

91. *Montpellier Codex*, no. 47, 19.

92. Peter's scholasticism was in conflict with Bernard's more conservative theology, resulting in a heated war of words that Bernard eventually won. For a survey of the conflict, see Jonathan Robin St. John, *The Conflict of Authority Between Peter Abelard and Bernard of Clairvaux: Theological and Historical Issues Reconsidered* (Portland: Reed College, 1996). For a survey of the end result, see Constant J. Mews, "The Council of Sens (1141): Abelard, Bernard, and the Fear of Social Upheaval," *Speculum* 77 (2002): 342–82. Bernard calls Abelard a "Goliath" in reference to his intellectual magnitude, but he confidently asserts that he is the David who will bring him down. See Bernard, *Epistola* 189 to Pope Innocent II, in *Sancti Bernardi Opera*, Jean Leclercq ed., 8 vols. (Rome: Editiones Cistercienses, 1957–77), 8, 13–14: "Stans ergo Golias una cum armigero suo inter utrasque acies, clamat adversus Phalangas Israel exprobatque agminibus sanctorum, eo nimirum audacias quo sentit David non adesse."

93. Classic studies and collections of goliard poetry include John Addington Symonds, *Wine, Women, and Song* (London: Chatto and Windus, 1907, reprinted from 1884); Karl Breul, *The Cambridge Songs: A Goliard's Songbook of the Eleventh Century* (Cambridge: Cambridge University Press, 1915, reissued by Cambridge University Press, 2009); and Helen Waddell, *The Wandering Scholars* (London: Constable & Robinson, 1927, reprinted by Dover, 2000), a dense study of the poets' history (and Classical roots) and translation of various poems that is still a valuable resource. A collection of English translations is George F. Whicher, *The Goliard Poets: Medieval Latin Songs and Satires* (New York: New Directions, 1949, reprinted by Greenwood Press, 1979). More recently, see René Clemencic, Ulrich Müller, Michael Korth, *Carmina Burana* (München: Heimeran Verlag, 1979), a collection of sheet music, original texts, and translations into modern German to accompany the Clemencic Consort's recordings of goliardic repertoire. See also Le Goff, *Intellectuals in the Middle Ages*, 24–35.

94. Waddell discusses the long-standing Church controversies over wanderers in "The Ordo Vagorum," chapter 8 of *Wandering Scholars*, 177–213.

95. Ibid., 179. See also Nancy Regalado, *Poetic Patterns in Rutebeuf*, 119, and n8, 119–120, referencing Waddell.

96. Jill Mann investigates this duality in "Satiric Subject and Satiric Object in Goliardic Literature," *Mittellateinisches Jahrbruch*, Band 15 (1980): 63–86. See also Kendrick, "Medieval Satire," 567, and chapter 6 for more on satire vs. parody.

97. Whicher, *The Goliard Poets*, 106–08: "Mihi cordis gravitas | res videtur gravis | iocus est amabilis | dulciorque favis. | Quicquid Venus imperat | labor est suavis | que nunquam in cordibus | habitat ignavis. | Via lata gradior | more iuventutis | inplico me viciis | immemor virtutis | voluptatis avidus | magis quam salutis | mortuus in anima | curam gero cutis."

98. Ibid., 110: "Meum est propositum | in taberna mori: vinim sit appositum | morientis ori | ut decant cum venerint | angelorum chori: | 'Deus sit propitius | huic potatori!'"

99. See, for example, Peter Dronke, *The Medieval Lyric* (Woodbridge: D.S. Brewer, 1968, reprinted 1996), 21–22: "The Archpoet's picture of the vagabond-poet (whatever element of literal truth it may have contained) has been drawn for the sophisticated entertainment of that international set of diplomats and legislators, high-born scholars and prelates who surrounded the Emperor, whose lingua franca was Latin, and among whom the Archpoet probably, by his birth and position, moved as an equal." See also Richard Hoppin, *Medieval Music* (New York: W.W. Norton, 1978), 262: "By the thirteenth century, *goliardus* was a term of reproach and contempt, but it did not apply to men such as Philip the Chancellor or to the three great poets of the twelfth century: Hugh Primas of Orléans, Walter of Châtillon, and the Archpoet." Jan Ziolkowski argues the same in "Archpoet," *Medieval Germany: An Encyclopedia*, Routledge Encyclopedias of the Middle Ages, John M. Jeep, ed. (New York: Routledge, 2001), 21–22, saying that the Archpoet's praise of the drunken, Bohemian lifestyle, "may be little more than a stance struck by the poet to entertain his audience."

100. Waddell devotes an entire lengthy appendix (E) to a list of Church Councils in *Wandering Scholars*, with quotes concerning their attempts to curtail unsavory clerical behavior, 267–94 (Dover edition). The sheer number is remarkable and borders on comical in its seeming futility, something with which the goliards would no doubt have been amused.

101. See Le Goff, *Intellectuals of the Middle Ages*, 32, where he refers to goliardic criticism of monasticism as "a rejection of an entire part of Christianity."

102. Thomas Wright, ed., *The Latin Poems Commonly Attributed to Walter Mapes* (London: Camden Society, 1841, reprinted New York: AMS Press, 1968), 21–30, v. 56: "Grex est hic nequitiæ, grex perditionis | impius et pessimus hæres Pharaonis | speciem exterius dans religionis, sed subest scintillula superstitionis." v. 59: "Quicquid tantæ curiæ sanctione datur | non cedat in irritum, ratum habeatur | cucullatus igitur grex vilipendatur | et a philosophicis scolis expellatur. – Amen." For a modern English translation, see C. Stephen Jaeger, *Ennobling Love: In Search of a Lost Sensibility The Middle Ages* (Philadelphia: University of Pennsylvania Press, 2011), 229–240.

103. Regalado, *Poetic Patterns in Rutebeuf*, 97.

104. "Die Constitutionen des Prediger-Ordens vom J. 1228," in *Archiv für Litteratur- und Kirchengeschichte des Mittelalters*, Heinrich Denifle and Franz Ehrle, eds. (Berlin: Weidmannschen Buchhandlung, 1885), 222, no. 28 (*De magistro studentium*): "In libris gentilium et philosophorum non student, etsi ad

horam inspiciant. Seculares sicencias non addiscant, nec etiam artes quas liberales vocant, nisi aliquando circa aliquos magister ordinis vel capitulum generale voluerit aliter dispensare; sed tantum libros theologicos tam juvenes quam alii legant." Also partially quoted in Waddell, *Wandering Scholars*, 143.

105. Available online at the *Bibliotheca Augustana* website: http://www.hs-augsburg.de/~harsch/Chronologia/Lspost13/CarminaBurana/bur_car0.html. See: http://www.hs-augsburg.de/~harsch/Chronologia/Lspost13/CarminaBurana/bur_cmo1.html#008, I: "presides ecclesie | imitantur hodie | Christum a remotis," accessed February 2, 2014.

106. Ibid., III: "Iacet ordo clericalis | in respectu laicalis | sponsa Christi fit mercalis | generosa generalis | veneunt altaria | venit eucharistia | cum sit nugatoria | gratia venalis."

107. http://www.hs-augsburg.de/~harsch/Chronologia/Lspost13/CarminaBurana/bur_cpo1.html, IV: "Honorum titulis | carens ambitio | cum ficto gaudio | pretendit singulis | osculum amoris | sed eminet | cum obtinet | baculum pastoris. | quos mens intus clauserat | mores ostentat libere | quod occultum fuerat | verbo prodit et opera," accessed February 2, 2014.

108. ibid, V: "donum Sancti Spiritus | sic venit iam Simonibus. | conformatur penitus | si danda fides canibus," accessed February 2, 2014.

109. http://www.hs-augsburg.de/~harsch/Chronologia/Lspost13/CarminaBurana/bur_cpo1.html #196, IV: "Octies pro fratribus perversis | novies pro monachis disperses," accessed February 2, 2014.

110. http://www.hs-augsburg.de/~harsch/Chronologia/Lspost13/CarminaBurana/bur_cmo4.html# 034, II: "Ad corpus infirmitas | capitis descendit | singulosque gravitas | artus apprehendit," accessed February 2, 2014.

111. Ibid., III. "Vide, Deus ultionum | vide, videns omnia | quod spelunca vispillonum | facta est Ecclesia," accessed February 2, 2014.

112. Regalado, *Poetic Patterns in Rutebeuf*, 82.

113. For a survey of possible goliardic influence in the works of Chaucer, see James A. S. McPeek, "Chaucer and the Goliards," *Speculum* 26, 2 (1951): 332–336. For Langland's use of goliardic verse, see John Chamberlin, *Medieval Arts Doctrines on Ambiguity and Their Places in Langland's Poetics* (Montreal: McGill-Queen's University Press, 2000), 82–83.

114. For the manuscript, additional information, and a summary of its contents, see the British Library website, Manuscript Display, *Harley MS 978, f.* 98v, col. I: http://www.bl.uk/manuscripts/FullDisplay.aspx?ref=Harley_MS_978, accessed November 3, 2013. The poem is also found in transcription in Wright, *Latin Poems*, 236–37.

115. Regalado notes some similarities in *Poetic Patterns in Rutebeuf*, 135–36, n16.

116. Wright, *Latin Poems*, 236–37. The text, worth quoting in full, reads: "O spina noxia latet in lillio: | o lingua perfida pacis in filio | venenum conditur in mellis dolio | frumentum læditur a tristi lolio | regnat iniquitas in æqui solio | fidem perfidia pellit exilio | vix potes credere patri, nutricio | matri vel filiæ, fratri vel socio. | Minatur syrius mortem in radio in visu regulus, in cauda scorpio | in dente coluber, princeps in gladio | fuca simplicitas in falso labio | dentem vipereum ubique timeo | venenum adhibent unguentes oleo | qui tecum loquitur, te capit laqueo | mel ore preeferens, pungit aculeo. | Nullus nocivior hoste domestic| in magno decipit, sicut in modico | de non ambiguis aperte judico de fratris laqueis vix pedem explico | occulte lacerat bonum quod egero | malum exaggerat si quid offendero. | Longum est dicere fraudes quas perfero | jam nulli credere possum de cætero | jam cantum flebilem quem mæstus concino | preces accumulans hie fine termino | a falsis fratribus et fraudis glutino | ut me protegere cura sit Domino."

Chapter 6

1. *The Romance of Reynard the Fox*, The World's Classics, D.D.R. Owen, trans. (Oxford: Oxford University Press, 1994), 81. *Le roman de Renart*, Ernest Martin, ed. (Strasbourg: Trübner, 1882), IV [23–28], 146–47: "De Renart ne va nus a destre: | Renars fet tot le monde destre | Renars atret, Renars acole | Renars est molt de male escole. | De lui ne va coroies ointes, | Ja tant ne sera ses acointes."

2. For a short account of medieval views on the fox, as well as some naturalistic history, see Joan V. Chadwick, "The Fox: A Medieval View, and Its Legacy in Modern Children's Literature," *Between the Species* (Winter/Spring 1994), 71–75.

3. *Vulgata*, Iudices 15: 4–5, 208: "Perrexitque et cepit trecentas vulpes caudasque earum iunxit ad caudas et faces ligavit in medio: quas igne succendens dimisit ut huc illucque discurrerent quae statim perrexerunt in segetes Philisthinorum quibus succensis et conportatae iam fruges et adhuc stantes in stipula concrematae sunt in tantum ut vineas quoque et oliveta flamma consumeret."

4. *Vulgata*, Canticum Canticorum 2:15, 615: "Capite nobis vulpes vulpes parvulas | Quae demoliuntur vineas | Nam vinea nostra floruit."

5. Gregory the Great, *Patrologia Latina* 76, J.-P. Migne, ed. (Paris: Garnier, 1857), *Liber* 19, 96: "Vulpes valde fraudulenta sunt animalia, quae in fossis vel specubus se abscondunt; cumque apparuerint, nunquam rectis itineribus, sed tortuosis anfractibus currunt. Volucres vero, ut novimus, alto volatu se in aera sublevant. Nomine ergo vulpiam dolosa atque fraudulenta, nomine autem voluerum, haec eadem superba daemonia designantur."

6. Ambrose, *Patrologia Latina* 15, J.-P. Migne, ed. (Paris: Garnier, 1845), *Exposit. evang. Luc*, VII, 1707, 31: "Hæreticis autem vulpes comparat. Denique cum gentes vocet, hæreticos excludit. Vulpis enim plenum fraudis est animal, foveam parans, et in fovea semper latere desiderans: ita sunt hæretici, qui domum sibi parare non norunt, sed circumscriptionibus suis alios decipere conantur." His diatribe continues for some time, with scriptural references.

7. *Isidori Hispalensis episcopi Etymologiarum sive Originvm libri XX*, 2 vols. ed. W. M. Lindsay (Oxford: Oxford University Press, 1911), 2. *De bestiis*, XII, ii, 29: "Vulpes dicta, quasi volupes. Est enim volubilis pedibus, et numquam rectis itineribus, sed tortuosis anfractibus currit, fraudulentum animal insidiisque decipiens. Nam dum non habuerit escam, fingit mortem, sicque descendentes quasi ad cadaver aves rapit et devorat."

8. Robert Steele produced a translation of the work, *Medieval Lore* (London: King's Classics, 1907); a scan of the 1483 Anton Koberger edition (from the collection of the University of Madrid) is available at the Internet Archive, https://archive.org/details/deproprietatibu00anglgoog, accessed November 10, 2013.

9. A beautiful modern edition and translation of a 13th-century English bestiary, Oxford M.S. Bodley 764 (Bodleian Library) is *Bestiary*, Richard Barber, trans. (London: Folio Society, 1992). The fox is featured at 65–66, where his diabolical nature is reiterated. A study of bestiaries (including a cat-

alog of surviving manuscripts) is Ann Payne, *Medieval Beasts* (New York: New Amsterdam Books, 1990); the fox is discussed at 45.

10. Memier, *The Play of Madness*, [271], 20: "Tien! Honnis soit te rouse teste!" See also 111, *n*55.

11. See Luke Sunderland, "*Le Cycle de Renart*: from the *Enfances* to the *Jugement* in a Cyclical *Roman de Ren*art Manuscript," *French Studies*, 62, 1 (2008): 6–7.

12. The name was probably Germanic in origin, Reginhard, or Reinhard.

13. The bibliography of Reynard studies is vast. Many editions of the original poems exist, including detailed studies of individual branches. A classic edition is *Le roman de Renart*, Ernest Martin, ed, from which these notes will use text examples (for copyright reasons). However, these excerpts should be compared to more modern editions, bearing in mind that different manuscripts have different branch numberings. See, for example, *Le roman de Renart*, Tome 1 (Branches I-XI), Jean Dufournet, Laurence Harf-Lancner, et al, ed. and trans. (Paris: Campion, 2013), and *Le roman de Renart*, 2 vols., Jean Dufournet and Andrée Méline, eds. (Paris: Flammarion, 1985). Another more complete collection is *Le roman de Renart*, Armand Strubel, with Roger Bellon, Dominique Boutet, and Sylvie Lefèvre, eds. Bibliothèque de la Pléiade 445 (Paris: Gallimard, 1998). A classic history of the poems, and study of their place in the literature of medieval France is John Flinn, *Le Roman de Renart dans la littérature française et dans les littératures étrangères du Moyen Âge* (Toronto: University of Toronto Press, 1963). *Reinardus: Yearbook of the International Reynard Society* is a yearly journal of Reynard, beast fables, and fabliaux studies which is an excellent resource for those interested in all aspects of these genres. A general study of the Reynard branches is J.R. Simpson, *Animal Body, Literary Corpus: The Old French Roman de Renart* (Amsterdam: Rodopi, 1996). A study of the use of beast fable in social commentary is Arnold Clayton Henderson, "Animal Fables as Vehicles of Social Protest and Satire: Twelfth Century to Henryson," *Third International Beast Epic, Fable and Fabliau Colloquium*, Jan Goossens and Timothy Sodmann, eds. (Münster: Böhlau Verlag Köln Wien, 1979), 160–173. See also Danielle Buschinger and André Crépin, eds. *Comique, satire et parodie dans la tradition renardienne et les fabliaux*, (Göppingen, Kümmerle: Göppinger Arbeiten zur Germanistik 391, 1983). For the representation of monks, see Arnold Clayton Henderson, "Foolish foxes and comic Cistercians: the Roman de Renart, branch IV," *Épopée animale, fable et fabliau*, Mediaevalia 78, Marche romane, 28: 3–4 (1978): 49–57. A discussion of blasphemy, or the lack thereof, in the Reynard branches is found in Evelyn Birge Vitz, "La liturgie, Le Roman de Renart, et le problème du blasphème dans la vie littéraire au Moyen Age, ou Les bêtes peuvent-elles blasphémer?" *Reinardus* 12 (1999), 205–225. A consideration of Rutebeuf's relation to the Reynard corpus is Jean Dufournet, "Rutebeuf et le Roman de Renart," *L'information littéraire* 1 (1978): 7–15, reprinted in *L'univers de Rutebeuf*, Medievalia 56 (Orléans: Paradigme, 2005), 41–60; and more recently, Jean Dufournet, *Du "Roman de Renart" à Rutebeuf* (Caen: Paradigme, 1993). For representations of deceit, see Gaston Zink, "Le vocabulaire de la ruse et de la tromperie dans les branches x et XI du *Roman de Renart*," *L'information grammaticale* 43 (1989): 15–19. On the origins of medieval beast fables, see Roger Bellon, "Du temps que les bestes parloient. À propos de la création des animaux dans *Le roman de Renart*," *Recherches et travaux* 3 (Grenoble: Université Stendhal–Grenoble, 1989): 21–33. A useful study of the differences between beast tales and fables is Lilian Schutter, *Misconceptions about Beast Fables and Beast Tales, and the Role of the Fox in All of It*, M.A. dissertation, Rijksuniversiteit Groningen, 2008. For a study of the first branches of Reynard, see Anthony R. Lodge, and Kenneth Varty, *The Earliest Branches of the Roman de Renart*, Synthema 1 (Louvain, Belgium: Peeters, 2001). A history of beast fables from the 8th century to the 12th is Jan M. Ziolkowski, *Talking Animals: Medieval Latin Beast Poetry, 750–1150* (Philadelphia: University of Pennsylvania Press, 1993). A comprehensive (if overwhelming) bibliography of Reynard studies can be found at the Reynard page on the website of "Les Archives de littérature du Moyen Âge" (ARLIMA), accessed November 4, 2013, http://www.arlima.net/qt/renart_roman.html, last updated in May 2011. See also Kenneth Varty, *The Roman de Renart: A Guide to Scholarly Work* (Lanham, MD: Scarecrow Press, 1998) for a more dated, but still useful bibliography in print form.

14. Richard W. Kaeuper, "The King and the Fox: Reactions to the Role of Kingship in the Tales of Reynard the Fox," *Expectations of the Law in the Middle Ages*, Anthony Musson, ed. (Woodbridge: Boydell, 2001), 9–21, especially at 20–21. The Capetians were an ancient dynasty of French monarchs dating back to 987 that ruled France for over 800 years.

15. Owen, *Reynard the Fox*, xiii-xiv. See also Kathryn Gravdal, *Vilain and Courtois: Transgressive Parody in French Literature of the 12th and 13th Centuries* (Lincoln: University of Nebraska Press, 1989), 93, where she notes that "It is this literary construct of the rural space that constitutes the interpretant of the *Roman de Renart*." This book is devoted to a study of literary parody in medieval French texts.

16. Gravdal, *Vilain and Courtois*, 93 and 97.

17. Over a century later, Fauvel the horse (or donkey) would epitomize clerical and courtly corruption, as we will see. Bernard also features in Branch VIII, where Reynard, dressed as a pilgrim, meets the donkey as he eats thistles in a ditch. Certainly there are anticlerical undertones to this imagery.

18. In *Romeo and Juliet*, Mercutio addresses Tybalt as the "king of cats," (Act III, Scene I) showing that even in Shakespeare's time, the name was still associated with the feline of the Reynard stories.

19. Owen, *Reynard the Fox*, xi.

20. Kaeuper, "The King and the Fox," 11.

21. A classic edition of the poem is Ernst Voigt, *Ysengrimus* (Halle: Verlag der Buchhandlung des Waisenhauses, 1884). For an English translation with comprehensive commentary, see Jill Mann, *Ysengrimus: Text with Translation, Commentary, and Introduction* (Leiden: Brill, 1987). Mann has revised this work with a new edition and different materials in *Ysengrimus* (Cambridge: Harvard University Press, Dumbarton Oaks Medieval Library, 2013). Mann discusses the history of beast fables in "Beast epic and fable," *Medieval Latin, an Introduction and Bibliographical Guide*, Frank A. C. Mantello and Arthur G. Rigg, eds. (Washington, D.C.: Catholic University of America, 1996), 556–61. See also her discussion of the satiric elements of the poem (including the wolf-as-monk motif) in "The Satiric Fiction of the Ysengrimus," *Reynard the Fox: Cultural Metamorphoses and Social Engagement in the Beast Epic from the Middle Ages to the Present*, Kenneth Varty ed., Berghahn Series, vol. 1 of Polygons:

Cultural Diversities and Intersections Series (New York: Berghahn Books, 2003), 1–16. Not all scholars have assumed a direct connection between this work and the later Reynard tales. However, L.G. Donovan has argued strongly for a relationship with the Reynard branches and for direct influence on them; see Donovan, "Ysengrimus and the Early Roman de Renard," *Canadian Journal of Netherlandic Studies* IV, 1 (1983): 33–38. See also Gravdal, *Vilain and Courtois*, 89.

22. Mann, "The Satiric Fiction of the Ysengrimus," 13–14. For a summary of the preaching of the Second Crusade and various reactions to its failure, see Rayborn, *The Violent Pilgrimage*," 84–90.

23. For an analysis of this work, see A.K. Bate, "Narrative Techniques in the Ecbasis Captivi," *Canadian Journal of Netherlandic Studies* IV, 1 (1983): 3–8. For an edition with commentary, see Edwin H. Zeydel, ed. and trans., *Ecbasis Cuiusdam Captive Per Tropologiam: An Eleventh-Century Latin Beast Epic*, University of North Carolina Studies in the Germanic Languages and Literatures (Chapel Hill: University of North Carolina Press, 1964).

24. Owen, *Reynard the Fox*, xviii.

25. See Martin, *Renart*, III [215–361], 137–41, where Reynard tells Ysengrin that he is a member of the Tironesian Order, a Benedictine monastic order founded by Bernard of Thiron in the early 12th century, west of Chartres. Their specific naming has a comical purpose in that they were very ascetic, and would not have been feasting on lavish food, as Reynard proclaims. Ysengrin wants to join to partake of all of the good food he smells. See also Owen, *Reynard the Fox*, 76–78.

26. Gravdal, *Vilain and Courtois*, 6. See also 95 for a discussion of parody of battles and clichés in the epic literature of the time.

27. Owen, *Reynard the Fox*, xii-xiii.

28. Gravdal, *Vilain and Courtois*, 4.

29. Ibid., 9 and 83.

30. She devotes her third chapter to a discussion of the Reynard branches as parody, ibid., 81–112.

31. Gravdal considers his contribution to be "obscurantist satire," a type that refers to the alluding to obscure and cryptic topics, often unrecognizable. See ibid., 163, n23.

32. Ibid., 85. For a more detailed discussion of medieval satire, see Karen Klein, *The Partisan Voice: A Study of the Political Lyric in France and Germany, 1180–1230* (The Hague: Mouton, 1971), 31–54.

33. Laura Kendrick, "Medieval Satire," 52.

34. Ibid., 62.

35. See Arnold Clayton Henderson, "Of Heigh or Lough Estat": Medieval Fabulists as Social Critics," *Viator* 9 (1978): 279. For an edition of the fables, see *The Fables of Odo of Cheriton*, John C. Jacobs, ed. and trans. (Syracuse: Syracuse University Press, 1985).

36. For a discussion of the roles of the various human characters in the Reynard stories (in the French, and also the German and Dutch versions), see Sharon Short Robertson, "Those Beastly People: a Study of Human Beings in Animal Epics," *Canadian Journal of Netherlandic Studies* IV, 1 (1983): 63–68.

37. Gravdal, *Vilain and Courtois*, 103 and 111.

38. Ibid., 109.

39. Martin, *Renart*, IV, [103–06], 149: "Li moine retendront son gage | O lui meismes on ostage: | Car felon sont a desmesure. | Qui chaut? toat est en avanture."

40. Ibid., [194–96], 151: "'Ci conversent' dit il 'malfe | Qant l'en n'i puet trouver viande | Ne rien de ce que on demande.'"

41. Ibid., [405–12], 157–58: "Li frere apellent les serjanz | Par temps iert Ysengrins dolenz. | Li abbes prent une macue | Qui moult estoit grant et cornue | Et li priours un chandelier. | Il n'i remest moine ou moustier | Qui ne portast baston ou pel: | Tuit sont issu de leur hostel."

42. Martin, *Renart*, Ia [1010–16], 29: "Molt he l'ore que je tant vif | Quant je serai demein peudus. | Qar fusse je moignez rendus | A Clugni ou a Cleresvax! | Mes je conois tant moines fax | Que je croi q'issir m'en conviegne. | Por ce est meus que je m'en tiegne."

43. Martin, *Renart*, VII [150–56], 245: "'Ha' fet il, 'moignes sont si fier | Et gens de molt male manere | Rien ne feroient por proiere. | Ha, que ferai? se prestre oüsse | Corpus domini recoüsse | Et a lui confes me feïsse."

44. Ibid., VII [161–68], 245–46: "'Por ce qu'il vestent capes noires | Si les apele l'en provoires: | Mes il sont tuit con forsenez. | Meuls les puis apeler maufez: | Maufe sont noir et cist ausi. | Bien les puis apeler einsi. | Ce me convient en esprover | Bien les puis einsi apeler.'"

45. Seven farts can mock many things, as seven was an important medieval symbolic number: seven deadly sins, seven virtues, seven liberal arts, seven days of the week, seven sacraments, seven trumpets and seals of the apocalypse, etc. The number was used in *chansons de geste*, which the Reynard branches parody, see Catherine Hanley, *War and Combat, 1150–1270: The Evidence from Old French Literature* (Woodbridge: DS Brewer, 2003), 147.

46. Martin, *Renart*, VII [221–35], 247: "Il a mis la coe en arcon | Si fist set pes en un randon. | 'Icist premiers soit por mon pere | Et l'autre por l'arme ma mere | Et li tiers por mes bienfetors | Et por toz aprealeceors | Et li quars soit por les jelinez | Dont j'oi rongies les escines | Et li quins soit por le vilein | Qui ici aüna cest fein. | Li sistes soit par druerie | Dame Hersenz ma douce amie | Et li semes soit Ysengrin | Qui dex doinst demein mal matin | Et male encontre a son lever. | Male mort le puisse acorer!'"

47. Ibid., VII [247–60], 248: "Que dex garisse toz larons | Toz traïtors et toz felons | Toz felons et toz traïtors | Et toz aprimes lecheors | Qui meus eiment les cras morsaux | Qu'il ne font cotes ne mantax | Et toz cous qui de barat vivent | Et qui prenent quanqu'il consivent. | 'Mes as moignes et as abez | Et as provoires coronez | Et as hermits des boscagez | Dunt il ne seroit nuz damagez | Pri deu qu'il doigne grant torment | Si qu'en le voie apertement.'"

48. Ibid., VII [353–66], 251: "Je hax hom frans et debonaire. | Volentiers preïsse la haire | Et devenisse moignes blans: | Mes j'ai un mal parmi les flans | Qui chascun jor par droite rente | Me reprent bien vint fois ou trente. | Et je sai bien que moignes noir | Trestos sont faillis et por voir | N'ont cure d'ome s'il n'est seins | Ou s'il n'est clers ou chapeleins. | Sire, je ai molt grant essoigne | Que je ne puis devenir moigne: | Car je ne sai parler latin. | Si monguz volentiers matin."

49. Ibid., VII [383–403], 252: "De ce esploistent il molt mal | Q'entr'eus ne font un jeneral | De toutre une fois la semeine | S'en seroit l'ordre molt plus seine. | Et quant il oüssent fotu | Et ele eüst le cul batu | Si la meïssent hors de cloistre | Tant que il fust saisons de croistre. | Car se remanoit au covent | Il la foutroient trop sovent. | Si n'en porroit soffrir la peine | Car trop sont lecheor li moine. | Il la conbriseroient tote | Si que ja mes ne tendroit gote. | Et il porroit bien avenir | Que grant mal en porroit venir | Que il entr'eus se conbatroient | Si que il s'escerveleroient. | Car chascun volroit fotre avant | Ausi li viel con li enfant | Et li serjant conme li mestre."

50. Ibid., VII [409–13], 252: "Li

blans ordres par est si fors | Nus n'i entre qui n'i soit mors | De jeüner et de veiller | De chanter et de versellier | Et d'ovrer et de laborer."

51. Ibid., VII, the complete list is at lines [684–706], 260–61.

52. Ibid., VII [840–44], 264: "Et Renart bet a lui decoivre: | Si l'ot encois tot devore | Que en oüst son pie torne. | Ha las! ci a mal pecheor | Qui a mangie son confessor."

53. See Muscatine, *Old French Fabliaux*, 162–63, for some analysis of branch XIV, "Reynard's Confession."

54. In *La Discorde de l'Université et des Jacobins* and *Des règles*, for example. Regalado discusses these in *Poetic Patterns in Rutebeuf*, 132–34. See also 135–36 for his uses of animals in general.

55. Owen, *Reynard the Fox*, 256. For *Renart le Bestourné*, see Faral and Bastin, eds., *Rutebeuf*, [1–4], I, 537–38: "Renars est mors: Renars est vis! | Renars est ors, Renars est vils: | Et Renars regne ! | Renars a moult regné el regne"; This edition is used for all excerpts from the poem below.

56. Regalado, *Poetic Patterns in Rutebeuf*, 152, *n*39. See also 151–52, for the drama of the opening lines of his Reynard poem. The use of *exempla* in friars' sermons was well known, and not always liked. See David Jones, *Friar's Tales: Thirteenth-Century Exempla from the British Isles* (Manchester: Manchester University Press, 2011), which contains sermons translated into English from the Franciscan *Liber Exemplorum*, from *ca.* 1275. See 9–11 for a brief history. For an edition of the manuscript, see A.G. Little, ed., *Liber exemplorum ad usum praedicantium* (Aberdoniae: Typis academicis, 1908). See also D. L. d'Avray, *The Preaching of the Friars: Sermons diffused from Paris before 1300* (Oxford: Clarendon Press, 1985).

57. David Jones, *Friar's Tales*, xi.

58. For some disputes over the identities of the objects of the poem's attacks, see ibid., 133–34, especially *n*12.

59. Aurélie Barre, "Le renard de Rutebeuf," *Cahiers de recherches médiévales et humanists* 14 (2007): 259: "Avec Rutebeuf, le renard est devenu une figure politique et religieuse. L'image de l'animal est plus noire que dans les récits antérieurs, elle est fortement liée à la vision biblique: le renard y est une incarnation du diable ou de Judas, dont il a la couleur rousse, et plus généralement le symbole des hérétiques.... Le goupil rusé devient pour les récits épigones une image du diable."

60. Faral and Bastin, *Rutebeuf* [25–27], I, 538–39: "Renars a moult grant norreture: | Moult en avons de sa nature | En ceste terre."

61. Ibid., [31–36], I, 539: "Me sires Nobles li lyons | Cuide que sa sauvations | De Renart viegne. | Non fet, voir (de Dieu li soviegne!) | Ainçois dout qu'il ne l'en aviegne | Domage et honte."

62. Ibid., [37–45], I, 539–40: "Se Nobles savoit que ce monte | Et les paroles que l'en conte | Parmi la vile,—| Dame Raimborc, dame Poufile | Qui de lui tienent lor concile | Ça dis, ça vint | Et dient c'onques més n'avint | N'onques a franc cuer ne sovint | De tel geu faire!"

63. Ibid., [86–103], I, 541–42: "Et se son ost estoit mandez | Par bois, par terre | Ou porroit il trover ne querre | En qui il se fiast de guerre | Se mestier iere? | Renars porteroit la baniere | Roneaus, qu'a toz fet laide chiere | Feroit la bataille premiere | O soi nului: | Bien vos puis dire de celui | Ja nus n'avra honor de lui | De par servise | Quant la chose seroit emprise | Ysengrins, que chascuns desprise | L'ost conduiroit | Ou, se devient, il s'en fuiroit | Bernars l'asne les desduiroit | O sa grant croiz."

64. Ibid., [141–43], I, 543: "Mon seignor Noble ont tuit getié | De bons usages: | Ses ostex samble uns recluxages."

65. Ibid., [155–57], 544: "La chose gist sor tel endroit | Que chascune beste vodroit | Que venist l'Once."

66. For editions, see *Middle English Humorous Tales in Verse*, George H. McKnight, ed. (Boston: D.C. Heath, 1913), 25–37. The text of this is available online at the "Corpus of Middle English Prose and Verse": http://quod.lib.umich.edu/c/cme/AGD2855.0001.001/1:4?rgn=div1;view=fulltext, accessed January 20, 2014. For a more recent edition, see also *Middle English Literature*, Charles W. Dunn and Edward T. Byrnes, eds. (New York: Routledge, 1990), 166–73. For an online modern translation, see the "Medieval Forum" at San Francisco State: http://www.sfsu.edu/~medieval/complaintlit/fox_wolf.html, accessed January 20, 2014. For an early study, see G. H. McKnight, "The Middle English Vox and Wolf," *PMLA* 23, 3 (1908): 497–509.

67. For a good study of anticlerical elements in the poem, see Sacvan Bercovitch, "Clerical Satire in 'þe Vox and þe Wolf,'" *The Journal of English and Germanic Philology* 65, 2 (1966): 287–294.

68. Nancy Regalado, *Poetic Patterns in Rutebeuf*, 185. For an edition, see Jacquemart Gielee, *Renart le Nouvel*, Henri Roussel, ed. (Paris: SATF, 1961), and his study, *Renart le Nouvel de Jacquemart Gielée* (Lille: Étude littéraire, 1984). For dating and diverging versions, see John G. Roberts, "Renart Le Nouvel—Date and Successive Editions," *Speculum* 11, 4 (1936): 472–477.

69. See Charles Dahlberg, "Chaucer's Cock and Fox," *The Journal of English and Germanic Philology*, 53, 3 (1954): 278, for further discussion.

70. See John Haines, *Satire in the Songs of Renart le Nouvel*, Publications Romanes et Franaises 247 (Geneva: Droz, 2010). See also Elizabeth Eva Leach, "Renart le Nouvel: Beast satire with songs": http://eeleach.wordpress.com/2013/05/06/renart-le-nouvel/, accessed January 20, 2014.

71. For an edition of the later version, see *Renart le contrefait*, ed. Gaston Reynaud and H. Lemaitre (Paris: Champion, 1914, rep. Genève: Slatkine, 1975). For an early study, see Gaston Raynaud, "Renart le Contrefait et ses deux rédactions," *Romania* 37 (1908): 245–283. See also Chantal de Saulnier, "Le clerc auteur et personnage dans Renart le contrefait," *Le clerc au Moyen Âge*, Senefiance 37 (Aix: CUERMA, 1995), 515–528; and Nancy Regalado, *Poetic Patterns in Rutebeuf*, 185–86. For textual relationships between *Renart le contrefait* and Chaucer's *Nun's Priest's Tale*, see Edward Wheatley, "The Nun's Priest's Tale," *Sources and Analogues of the Canterbury Tales*, Robert M. Correale and Mary Hamel, eds., Vol. 1 (Woodbridge: Boydell, 2002), 449–52 and 474–86.

72. See G. Ward Fenley, "Faussemblant, Fauvel, and Renart le Contrefait: a Study in Kinship," *The Romanic Review* 23, 4 (1932): 323–331. This short study examines the similarities between the three, and looks at cross-references to each in the respective works. See also Nancy Regalado, *Poetic Patterns in Rutebeuf*, 134, where she notes that the poets who wrote such works "could speak not only more clearly but more safely through the mouth of an animal." Fenley concurs with this at 330.

73. Dahlberg, "Chaucer's Cock," 279.

74. Ibid., 283–90.

75. An edition of Caxton's print is *The History of Reynard the Fox: William Caxton's English Translation of 1481*, Early Prose Romances, Henry Morley, ed. (London: Routledge, 1889). For Reynardian literature in England, see

Kenneth Varty, "Reynard in England: from Caxton to Present," *Reynard the Fox: Social Engagement and Cultural Metamorphoses in the Beast Epic from the Middle Ages to the Present*, Kenneth Varty, ed. (New York: Berghahn Books, 2000), 163–74. See also N.F. Blake, "William Caxton's Reynard the Fox and His Dutch Original," in his *William Caxton and English Literary Culture* (London: Hambledon Press, 1991), 231–58.

76. For a recent edition, see *Of Reynaert the Fox*, Thea Summerfield, trans., André Bouwman and Bart Besamusca, eds. (Amsterdam: Amsterdam University Press, 2009). See also Paul Wackers, "Medieval French and Dutch Renardian Epics: Between Literature and Society," *Reynard the Fox: Social Engagement and Cultural Metamorphoses*, 55–72.

77. For an online edition of the complete fables, see the University of Rochester site, "The Morall Fabillis": http://www.lib.rochester.edu/camelot/teams/morfram.htm, accessed January 20, 2014. See also at the same site, Robert L. Kindrick, "The Morall Fabillis: Introduction": http://d.lib.rochester.edu/teams/text/kindrick-poems-of-robert-henryson-morall-fabillis-introduction, accessed January 20, 2014. For translations of two of the fox fables, see Seamus Heaney, trans., *Robert Henryson: The Testament of Cresseid & Seven Fables* (New York: Farrar, Straus and Giroux, 2009).

78. One of the more unpleasant examples was as a Dutch anti-Semitic diatribe masquerading as a children's story, *Van den vos Reynaerde*. It appeared in 1937 in a Dutch national socialist journal, and was made into a cartoon in 1943, though never aired at the time. It featured a rhinoceros with a large nose (representing a stereotyped Jew) that is killed by Reynard, along with many others of his kind. Disney had plans for making its own Reynard cartoon, but after concerns that the subject matter would be unsuitable for a children's film (and rightly so!), the character morphed into an animated version of Robin Hood, keeping the fox as Robin, and the wolf as the Sheriff of Nottingham that he defeats. The author saw this film as a young child on its initial release in 1973, and has been a devoted medievalist ever since.

79. The number of fabliaux studies has grown rapidly in the past several decades. An excellent new edition in English, containing 69 of the tales (one wonders if that number is a deliberate humorous choice?) is Nathaniel E. Dubin, trans. *The Fabliaux*, with a fine introduction by noted scholar R. Howard Bloch. The book contains the original Old French texts with parallel modern English rhyming translations. Older collections in English include *The French Fabliau B. N. MS. 837*, Raymond Eichmann and John DuVal, eds. and trans., Garland Library of Medieval Literature, Series A, 16–17, 2 vols. (New York: Garland, 1984–1985); Robert L. Harrison, *Gallic Salt: Eighteen Fabliaux Translated from the Old French* (Berkeley: University of California Press, 1974); *Bawdy Tales from the Courts of Medieval France*, Paul Brians, ed. and trans., (New York: Harper and Row, 1972); and *Fabliaux: Ribald Tales from the Old French*, Robert Hellman and Richard O'Gorman, eds. and trans. (New York: Crowell, 1965). For modern French translations alongside the original texts, see Jean Dufournet, *Fabliaux de Moyen Âge* (Paris: Flammarion, 1998). For a complete modern edition in Old French, see Willem Noomen and Nico van den Boogaard, *Nouveau recueil complet des fabliaux* (NRCF), 10 vols. (Assen and Maastricht: Van Gorcum, 1983–98). A good introduction to the works is Charles Muscatine, *The Old French Fabliaux* (New Haven: Yale University Press, 1968). For a thorough analysis of various sexual and violent themes (more for scholars than general readers), see R. Howard Bloch, *The Scandal of the Fabliaux*. One of the earliest major studies is Joseph Bédier, *Les fabliaux: Études de littérature populaire et d'histoire littéraire du moyen âge* (Paris: E. Bouillon, 1895). Another classic study, though with some now-disputed conclusions is Per Nykrog, *Les fabliaux*, Étude d'histoire littéraire et de stylistique médiévale (Copenhagen: Munksgaard, 1957). Anne Cobby discusses anticlerical themes (or lack thereof, in her opinion) in "L'anticléricalisme des fabliaux," *Reinardus* 7 (1994): 17–29; see also the important study by Daron Burrows, *The Stereotype of the Priest in the Old French Fabliaux: Anticlerical Satire and Lay Identity* (Bern: Peter Lang, 2005). A study of the comedy of the fabliaux is the collection of essays edited by Kristin L. Burr, John F. Moran, and Norris J. Lacy, *The Old French Fabliaux: Essays on Comedy and Context* (Jefferson, NC: McFarland, 2007). For a recent bibliography of studies, see Anne Cobby, *The Old French Fabliaux*, Research Bibliographies and Checklists, New Series, 9 (Woodbridge, Tamesis, 2009). A comprehensive listing of works (editions, books and articles) is at the "Fabliaux" page of Les Archives de littérature du Moyen Âge (ARLIMA), accessed November 26, 2013: http://www.arlima.net/eh/fabliau.html#biblio.

80. Muscatine suggests that the variety of collections, which have no obvious order, and are often bound with any number of other subject matter, were copies made for private collectors, who gathered them one story at a time, *Old French Fabliaux*, 11. For an additional consideration of the number of poems, see Daron Burrows, *The Stereotype of the Priest*, 31–33. He also notes at 39 that "the standard collections of *fabliaux* are utterly artificial," and attempts to codify them will always be problematic, depending on definition, content, etc.

81. See Stephen L. Wailes, "Vagantes and the Fabliaux," *The Humor of the Fabliaux: A Collection of Critical Essays*, Thomas D. Cooke and Benjamin L. Honeycutt, eds. (Columbia: University of Missouri Press, 1974), 43–58. See at 58: "The shared literary traditions of Latin and French texts suggest a shared sociological basis, one that was more likely in authorship than in audience."

82. Muscatine, *Old French Fabliaux*, 9–10.

83. Ibid., 10.

84. See Peter Dronke, "The Rise of the Medieval Fabliau: Latin and Vernacular Evidence," *Romanische Forschungen* 85, Bd., H. 3 (1973): 278–89.

85. Bédier, *Les fabliaux*.

86. In his *Les fabliaux* of 1957.

87. See Gravdal, *Vilain and Courtois*, 84.

88. Muscatine, in *Old French Fabliaux*, discusses this debate at length in the chapter "The Social Background," 24–46.

89. See Brian J. Levy, "Performing Fabliaux," *Performing Medieval Narrative*, Evelyn Birge Vitz, Nancy Freeman Regalado, and Marilyn Lawrence, eds. (Woodbridge: Boydell, 2005), 123–49, for a discussion of how the fabliaux may have been performed by these jongleurs.

90. Bloch offers an introduction to fabliaux origin theories in *Scandal of the Fabliaux*, 1–3, and in his introduction to *Fabliaux*, xiv-xvii. See also Peter Dronke, "The Rise of the Medieval Fabliau," 275–297. See also Burrows, *The Stereotype of the Priest*, 41–41, for some 11th and 12th-century Latin works that may have had influence.

91. Bloch, *Scandal of the Fabliaux*, 127.

92. Brian J. Levy, "Performing Fabliaux," 123.
93. Ibid., 124–26. See also n56 above. On the topic of music, see Epstein, *Prions en chantant*, 9: "Recent scholarship has linked the nascent Franciscan order with the rise of vernacular devotional lyric in Italy and England."
94. Muscatine, *Old French Fabliaux*, 72. See also 55, 59, 68–69, 71–72, and 152.
95. Bloch, *Scandal of the Fabliaux*, 53. See also 56–58.
96. Muscatine, *Old French Fabliaux*, 73. He further notes: "The attitude is manifest at once in the remarkable interest the fabliaux have in food and eating."
97. Ibid., 16.
98. Ibid., 17.
99. Ibid.
100. Bloch, *Scandal of the Fabliaux*, xxi.
101. Muscatine, *Old French Fabliaux*, 92, and 95–98. See also 124, and 183, n10.
102. Ibid., 153–56, and 167.
103. Ibid., 165.
104. Ibid., 110. However, see also Bloch, *Scandal of the Fabliaux*, 89.
105. Muscatine, *Old French Fabliaux*, 109.
106. Ibid., 133–38, where he notes that Guillaume de Lorris advises to guard against such language, as does Jean Renart. He writes at 138: "Whatever the state of verbal taboos may have been in the pre-courtly period, it would seem inevitable that in proscribing certain words and expressions, in banishing them from its newly exclusive social sphere, the courtly tradition made those words and expressions more obscene, and newly vulgar."
107. See ibid., 110–15 for a fuller analysis of terms and comic euphemisms.
108. Ibid., 125.
109. Bloch offers analysis of the castration themes, *Scandal of the Fabliaux*, 61–66. See also 83, and 110–11, where he discusses the tradition of deformity as a source of humor going back to Aristotle. Muscatine's analysis in *Old French Fabliaux* is at 125–28. For a deeper analysis of violent fabliaux themes, see Larissa Tracy, "The Uses of Torture and Violence in the Fabliaux: When Comedy Crosses the Line," *Florilegium* 23, 2 (2006): 143–68.
110. Dubin, *Fabliaux*, "Le Prestre crucifé" [99–11], 54: "si comme fist prestres Coustanz | qui I laissa les .iii. pendanz." The complete text runs from 48–55.
111. Muscatine, *Old French Fabliaux*, 160. For a study, see Charles Harold Livingston, *Le Jongleur Gautier Le Leu: Étude Sur Les Fabliaux*, Harvard Studies in Romance Languages (Cambridge: Harvard University Press, 1951; New York: Kraus Reprint, 1969).
112. Muscatine, in *Old French Fabliaux*, 193, n55, lists various records kept by the Church of clerical misdeeds and sins, and actions taken to correct them.
113. Ibid., 102.
114. Muscatine, ibid., discusses this further at 93–94, and also at 131–32. See also 161–62 for the sadistic anticlericalism of the poem *Richeut*. See also Bloch, *Scandal of the Fabliaux*, 36–37. For a valuable in-depth study of the representations of clerical characters in the poems, see Daron Burrows, *Stereotype of the Priest*.
115. Burrows, in *Stereotype of the Priest*, summarizes the debate at 15–18. One early theory suggested that the stories were in part a reaction to the burning of heretics in northern France, though this is not now strongly supported, see 17.
116. Ibid., 20. See 19–21 for a more detailed explanation of the terms, which helps clarify what the author intends in discussing their application to these works. He notes at 29–30, for example that just because not every priest is portrayed badly in the tales does not mean that they contain no anticlerical content as a whole.
117. Ibid., 30. See also Gravdal, *Vilain and Courtois*, 144, where she notes that our image of medieval people quaking in fear at an all-powerful Church is a misrepresentation.
118. Burrows, *Stereotype of the Priest*, 121.
119. For some general observations about friars and the fabliaux, see Regalado, *Poetic Patterns in Rutebeuf*, 179–80.
120. A comprehensive modern critical edition that compares the poem to other similar works is Richard O'Gorman, ed., *Les Braise au Cordelier* (Birmingham, AL: Summa, 1983). For questions of the date, see 3–5. O'Gorman places it between 1240 and 1260, and thinks it is contemporary with Rutebeuf, with whom the anonymous author of *Les braise* "shared a real contempt for the Minorites." For a modern English translation, see Raymond Eichmann and John DuVal, *The French Fabliau B. N. MS. 837*, I, 202–17.
121. O'Gorman, *Les Braise au Cordelier*, 4 and 7.
122. Ibid.
123. *Les Braise au Cordelier*, Eichmann and DuVal, *The French Fabliau*, [238–39], 210: "La dame sot molt de renart: | engingneuse fu de toz cors." Reynard's reputation for trickery was so well established that he could easily be referenced in other stories involving deception.
124. See Gravdal, *Vilain and Courtois*, 101. See also 165, n33.
125. Ibid., 102.
126. Muscatine, *Old French Fabliaux*, 159.
127. Burrows notes in *Stereotype of the Priest*, 167, n10, that "Frere Denise includes more than fifty lines of virulent diatribe against the mendicants, which constitutes the longest of any such polemical outbursts in the texts commonly recognized as fabliaux." See also Bloch, *Scandal of the Fabliaux*, 44, and Regalado, *Poetic Patterns in Rutebeuf*, 181–82. See also Mary E. Leech, "Dressing the Undressed: Clothing and Social Structure in Old French Fabliaux," *Comic Provocations: Exposing The Corpus of Old French Fabliaux*, Holly A. Crocker, ed. (New York: Palgrave Macmillan, 2006), 90–93.
128. Dubin, *Fabliaux*, "Freire Denise," [1–11], 78.
129. Ibid., [12–13]: "Bien dovroient teil gent morir | vilainnement & a grant honte."
130. Ibid., [92–95], 84: "Cele a son cuer a Dieu donei | cil ra fait dou sien ateil don | qui bien l'en rendra guerredon."
131. Ibid., [95–108].
132. Ibid., [142–44], 86: " Li freres, cui li anemis | contraint & sermon & argue | out grant joie de sa venue"
133. Ibid., [161–79], 88.
134. Ibid., [244–48], 92: "Fauz papelars, fauz ypocrite | fause vie meneiz & orde! | Qui vos pendroit a vostre corde | qui est en tant de leuz nöee | il avroit fait bone jornee!"
135. The citole is a kind of early guitar, whose heyday was in the 13th and 14th centuries in France and England. The vielle is an early fiddle. The tabor is a large drum. All were probably used in dance music.
136. Dubin, *Fabliaux*, "Freire Denise," [261], 92: "& toz deduiz de menestreiz."
137. Ibid., [299–336], 96–98.
138. Muscatine, *Old French Fabliaux*, 30–31.
139. Regalado, *Poetic Patterns in Rutebeuf*, 181.
140. Ibid., 180.
141. Rondeau: "Porchier mieus estre ameroie," *The Monophonic Songs in the Roman de Fauvel*, Samuel N. Rosenberg and Hans Tischler, eds. (Lincoln: University of Nebraska Press, 1991), 44.

142. The manuscript is available for viewing online in beautiful full color scans at the Bibliothèque nationale's website, accessed November 12, 2013: http://gallica.bnf.fr/ark:/12148/btv1b8454675g. A facsimile of the work is *Le Roman de Fauvel in the Edition of Messire Chaillou de Pestain: A Reproduction of the Complete Manuscript Paris, Bibliothèque Nationale, fonds francais 146*, introduction by Edward H. Roesner, Francois Avril, and Nancy Freeman Regalado (New York: Broude Brothers, 1990).

143. The work has been edited and prepared in modern editions a number of times over the past century, though no published English translation has yet appeared. A recent edition in parallel medieval and modern French verses is *Le Roman de Fauvel*, Armand Strubel, ed. and trans., Lettres Gothiques (Paris: Librarie Général Française, 2012); this is the edition used for all text quotes in the notes below. The earlier classic edition is *Le Roman de Fauvel par Gervais de Bus, publié d'après tous les manuscrits connus*, Arthur Långfors, ed., (Paris: Société des anciens textes français, 1914–19). The music of the manuscript is available in various modern editions: the polyphonic pieces in *The Roman de Fauvel, The Works of Philippe de Vitry, French Cycles of the Ordinarium missae*, Leo Schrade, ed., Polyphonic Music of the Fourteenth Century I, commentary volume published separately (Monaco: Éditions de l'Oiseau-Lyre, 1956). The monophonic pieces appear, with translations and commentary in *The Monophonic Songs in the Roman de Fauvel*. Another collection of musical scores is *Le premier et le secont livre de Fauvel : In the version preserved in B.N. f. fr. 146*, Paul Helmer, ed., Wissenschaftliche Abhandlungen, 70:1 (Ottawa: Institute of Medieval Music, 1997). An essential collection of essays on various aspects of the work and the manuscript is *Fauvel Studies: Allegory, Chronicle, Music and Image in Paris, Bibliotheque Nationale MS Francais 146*, Margaret Bent and Andrew Wathey, eds., (Oxford: Clarendon Press, 1998); several entries from this collection are used in this chapter. For a study of the music itself and how it is intertwined with the culture of medieval French manuscript preparation, see Emma Dillon, *Medieval Music-Making and the Roman de Fauvel* (Cambridge: Cambridge University Press, 2002). An early look at the interpolations is Emilie Dahnk, *L'Hérésie de Fauvel*, Leipzig romanistische Studien, Literaturwissenschaftliche Reihe 4. (Leipzig-Paris: C. & E. Vogel, 1935). A useful study of satirical aspects is Jean-Claude Muhlethaler, *Fauvel au pouvoir: Lire la Satire médiévale*, Nouvelle bibliothèque du Moyen Âge, 26 (Paris: H. Champion; Genève: Slatkine, 1994), and also his "Le dévoilement satirique. Texte et image dans le Roman de Fauvel," *Poétique* 146 (2006): 165–179. A discussion of the use of the allegorical virtues and vices is Nancy Freeman Regalado, "Allegories of Power; the Tournament of Vices and Virtues in the *Roman de Fauvel* (BN MS Fr. 146)," *Gesta* 32, 2 (1993): 135–146. A look at how the music reflected issues in the troubled court of the time is Edward H. Roesner, "Labouring in the Midst of Wolves: Reading a Group of Fauvel Motets," *Early Music History* 22 (2003): 169–245. For a good online summary of the work and its time, see Andrew Wathey, *Roman de Fauvel*: http://musicologicus.blogspot.com/2007/05/roman-de-fauvel.html, accessed February 16, 2014.

144. Each of these topics merits study on its own. A standard biography of Philip the Fair is Joseph Strayer, *The Reign of Philip the Fair* (Princeton: Princeton University Press, 1980). For his early life and difficult nature, see E.A.R. Brown, "The Prince is Father of the King: The Character and Childhood of Philip the Fair of France," *Medieval Studies* 49 (1987): 282–334. For the suppression of the Templars, see Malcolm Barber, *The Trial of the Templars* (Cambridge: Cambridge University Press, Second Edition, 2006). A history of the Avignon papacy and the events of the larger world around it is Edwin Mullins, *The Popes of Avignon: A Century in Exile* (Katonah, NY: BlueBridge, 2008). An introduction to the Great Famine can be found in John Aberth, *From the Brink of the Apocalypse: Confronting Famine, Plague, War and Death in the Later Middle Ages* (London: Routledge, 2000), chapter 1.

145. Bent and Wathey, "Introduction," *Fauvel Studies*, 9–10. For additional studies on the relation of Fauvel to the political scene of the time, see Malcolm Vale, "The World of the Courts: Content and Context of the *Fauvel* Manuscript," *Fauvel Studies*, 591–98, and Andrew Wathey, "Gervès du Bus, the *Roman de Fauvel*, and the Politics of the Later Capetian Court," *Fauvel Studies*, 599–613. See also Edward Roesner, *et al.*, *Le Roman de Fauvel*, 48–53, and Jean Favier, *Un conseiller de Philippe le Bel: Enguerran de Marigny*, Mémoires et documents publiés par la Société de l'école des Chartes 16 (Paris: Presses Universitaires de France, 1963), 198–99.

146. Jean Favier, *Un conseiller*, 67, 173, and 198–99. However, see also Bent and Wathey, "Introduction," *Fauvel Studies*, 18, which discusses some of the problems of dating regarding Marigny as the sole, or even the main target. There may have been other enemies of the king also being addressed.

147. In the polyphonic motet *Aman novi / Heu Fortuna / Heu me*, Bent and Wathey, "Introduction," *Fauvel Studies*, 10. The other two motets are *Tribum que non abhorruit* and *Garrit gallus*. For specific questions of dating the so-called "Marigny motets," see Margaret Bent, "Fauvel and Marigny: Which Came First?" *Fauvel Studies*, 35–52. *Tribum que* and *Garrit* both make use of animal imagery. See also Roesner, et al., *Le Roman de Fauvel*, 50–53.

148. Bent, "Fauvel and Marigny," 44.

149. Strubel, *Le Roman de Fauvel* [1393–94], 278: "Et de Renart toute l'histoire | Y estoit painte a grant memoire."

150. Nancy Freeman Regalado, "The *Chronique métrique* and Moral Design of BN fr. 146: Feasts of Good and Evil," *Fauvel Studies*, 472–73. See also n23: "Et disorient: 'Avant Renart, | Honte te dointe saint Lienart! | Ton barat et ta tricherie | A touz nous a tolu la vie. | L'avoir du rëaume as emblé.'"

151. Bent and Wathey, "Introduction," *Fauvel Studies*, 10. A motet at the beginning of the *Roman* references this supposition, see below.

152. For details of Boniface's controversial life and papacy, see Agostino Paravicini Bagliani, *Boniface VIII: Un pape hérétique?* (Paris: Payot, 2003). For his conflict with Philip IV, see Charles T. Wood, *Phillip the Fair and Boniface VIII: State vs Papacy* (New York: Holt, Rhinehart, and Winston, 1967).

153. See chapter 2. See also Katherine Walsh, *A Fourteenth-Century Scholar and Primate: Richard FitzRalph in Oxford, Avignon, and Armagh* (Oxford: Clarendon Press, 1981), 354. We will return to this work in chapter 8.

154. Ibid., 355.

155. Ibid., 407.

156. *Unum sanctam*, registers of Boniface VIII in the Vatican archives, "Reg. Vatic.," L, fol. 387: "Porro subesse Romano Pontifici omni humanae creaturae declara-

mus, dicimus, definimus, et pronuntiamus omnino esse de necessitate salutis."

157. For a summary of the charges, see Jeffrey Denton, "The attempted trial of Boniface VIII for heresy," *Judicial Tribunals in England and Europe, 1200–1700: The Trial in History*, Maureen Mulholland and Brian Pullan, eds., with Anne Pullan (Manchester: Manchester University Press, 2003), I, 117–19. An edition of the charges is found in Jean Coste, ed., *Boniface VIII en procès: Articles d'accusation et dépositions des témoins* (Pubblicazioni della Fondazione Camillo Caetani, Studi e Documenti d'Archivio 5 (Rome: L'Erma di Bretschneider, 1995). See also Leff, *Paris and Oxford Universities*, 48–49, for how the feud between king and pope affected the University of Paris. See also O'Shea, *Friar of Carcassonne*, 30–32.

158. For a summary, see E. R. Chamberlin, *The Bad Popes* (New York: Dorset Press, 1986), 102–04.

159. Referenced in the *Chronique métrique*. See Nancy Freeman Regalado, "The *Chronique métrique*," *Fauvel Studies*, 472, and *n*22.

160. See Denton, "The attempted trial of Boniface," 117–28 for a study of the whole affair.

161. Ibid., 122–23.

162. Bent and Wathey, "Introduction," *Fauvel Studies*, 1.

163. Strubel, *Le Roman de Fauvel* [4015–20], 502: "Fauvel, que fusses tu tuez | Quant a si mal seigneur tu es! | Antecrist si est ton droit sire: | Tu es mauves, et il est pire! | Son garcon es et son message."

164. For short survey, see A.G. Rigg, *A History of Anglo-Latin Literature, 1066–1422* (Cambridge: Cambridge University Press, 1992), 102–04. For an edition, see *Speculum Stultorum*, John H. Mozley and Robert R. Raymo, eds. (Berkeley: University of California Press, 1960).

165. See for example, Mann, *Chaucer and Medieval Estates Satire*, 43, where she notes that Burnellus is delighted that as a Dominican, he will appear like a king, and everyone will honor him. See also Mann, "The 'Speculum Stultorum' and the 'Nun's Priest's Tale,'" *The Chaucer Review* 9, 3 (1975): 262–282. For the complete text of the antifraternal interpolation, see *Speculum Stultorum*, 183–88. See also Kendrick, "Medieval Satire," 58–60.

166. Strubel, *Le Roman de Fauvel* [105–116], 144: "Le pape se siet en son siege | Jadis de pierre, or est de liege | Fauvel regarde en sa presence | A cui l'en fet grant reverence | Que l'en torche au soir et au main. | Le pape si li tent la main | Par le frain doucement le prent | De torcher nului ne reprent | Et puis frote a Fauvel la teste | En disant: 'Ci a bele beste!' | Li cardinal dient pour plere: | 'Vous dites voir, sire saint Pere!'"

167. Ibid., *Jure quod in opera*, Duplum [22–34], 142: "Jure quod in opera | Davitico prestolatur | Cesareo funere | Jacobitis applicator: | 'Etenim homo pacis mee, in quo speravi | Qui edebat panes meos, magnificavit | Super me supplantacionem!' | Sacramento protinus clam toxicato potatur | Henricus; per facinus auro dato violator. | Sie quod dixit Dominus | De hisdem verificatur: 'Veniunt falsi prophete in vestimentis ovium | Lupi autem interius rapaces!'"

168. Ibid., [259–62]: "Fauvel est beste non resonnable. | Chose apparant et non estable | Plain de fallace, vuit de voir, Figure pour gent dechevoir."

169. The conductus was a type of religious lyric (but not liturgical), most often in Latin, composed for one or more parts. They were extremely popular from the later 12th century through the early 14th. Some may have been adoptions of melodies of popular secular songs in vernacular languages, in order to Christianize them and make them acceptable in the view of the Church.

170. Rosenberg and Tischler, *Monophonic Songs*, 20: "Floret fex favellea | Mundus innovator | Curia fit ferrea | Fauvel exaltatur. | Quisque pauper hodie | In contemptum datur | Formatus in specie | Christi vir dampnatur | Incensate bestie | Plebs congratulatur. | Nunc est locus sceleri | Fides datur funeri | Veritas fugatur."

171. Ibid., see 42–43 for the complete Latin text.

172. Mann notes several other examples of accusations of fraternal lechery in *Chaucer and Medieval Estates Satire*, 228, *n*91.

173. Prov. 26:11, *Vulgata*, 601: "Sicut canis qui revertitur ad vomitum suum, sic imprudens qui iterat stultitiam suam." See also chapter 4, *n*44, where the passage is referenced in the *Roman de la Rose*.

174. Strubel, *Le Roman de Fauvel* [843–910], 224–230.

175. Ibid., [277–80], 160: "A Templier herese equipole | Cil qui de Fauvel fait ydole | Beste est Fauvel, et cil est beste | Qui li fait ne honeur ne feste."

176. For further discussion of the Templars and their perceived sinfulness, see ibid., [935–1035], 234–42.

177. Ibid., [1044–45], 244: "Faus Semblant et Deslouaité | One du monde la royauté."

178. The full list is in a Latin poem interpolated into the text, see ibid., *Carnalitas, Luxuria in Favelli palacio*, 280–84.

179. Ibid., [1772–75], 316: "Vous savez que n'ai point de fame | Mestier seroit qu'aucune dame | Qui bien me plairoit espousasse | Si que je me montepliasse." After a motet, *La mesnie fauveline*, Fauvel continues his monologue, resolving to ask Lady Fortune to marry him, though he concedes that she does not love him, [1776–1819].

180. Ibid., [1820–1905], 322–26.

181. Ibid., [1988–97], 335.

182. Ibid., [4108–35], 528–30.

183. Rosenberg and Tischler, *Monophonic Songs*, 123: "Gaudet Falvellus nimium | Quia per infortunium | Credit habere graciam | Fortune per licenciam | Quam habuit redeundi | Omnis spiritus immundi | Repletus immundicia | Ducantur Vana Gloria." See also the section of the main poem that follows, Strubel, *Le Roman de Fauvel* [4140–4151], 533.

184. Strubel, *Le Roman de Fauvel* [4149–4151], 533: "Touz ses amis sans demourer | Ha mandé aus noces venir | Car trop grant feste veilt tenir."

185. The texts and music for all of these short refrains can be found in Rosenberg and Tischler, *Monophonic Songs*, 127–31.

186. For the music, see ibid., 128. See also Strubel, *Le Roman de Fauvel*, 587, *n*2, for some discussion of Hellequin's identity.

187. The tournament seems to be modeled on a real-life event in 1313, wherein Philip IV knighted his sons and son-in-law, Edward II of England. See Bent and Wathey, "Introduction," *Fauvel Studies*, 11, and *n*41, with reference to a detailed study by Elizabeth Brown and Nancy Regalado.

188. Strubel, *Le Roman de Fauvel* [5121–5136], 614.

189. Ibid., a lengthy sequence detailed in lines [5285–5562], 626–644.

190. Ibid., [5575–78], 644: "S'en va Fauvel quant il eschape | Et Vainne Gloire o sa grant chape | Courrouciee o sa corte honte | Par un pou qu'elle ne s'afronte."

191. Ibid., [5615–26], 648.

192. Ibid., [5750–54], 656: "C'est le jardin de douce France. | Hé! las! com c'est grant mescheance | De ce quen si tres beau vergier | S'est venu Fauvel herbergier."

193. Ibid., [5763–82], 658.

194. Rosenberg and Tischler,

Monophonic Songs, 150: "Ci me faut un tour de vin. | Deus! Quar le me donnez!"

195. Bent and Wathey, "Introduction," *Fauvel Studies*, 8.

196. Ibid., 14.

197. Ibid., 19.

198. Ibid., 17–18. For more in-depth analysis, see Elizabeth A. R. Brown, "*Rex ioians, ionnes, iolis*: Louis X, Philip V, and the *Livres de Fauvel*," *Fauvel Studies*, 54–72. For a study of the motet *Servant regem / O Philippe / Rex regum*, which addresses Philip V directly, see Emma Dillon, "The Profile of Philip V in the Music of Fauvel," *Fauvel Studies*, 215–31.

199. Brown, "*Rex ioians*," 65. Louis X reigned only from 1314 to 1316.

200. For a further discussion of some literary similarities, especially in regards to the expanded Fauvel resembling the continuation of the *Roman de la Rose* and how the authors of both represent themselves, see Kevin Brownlee, "Authorial Self-Representation and Literary Models in the Roman de Fauvel," *Fauvel Studies*, 73–103.

201. Strubel, *Le Roman de Fauvel* [1611–28], 306. See also Regalado, *Poetic Patterns in Rutebeuf*, 175.

202. Ibid., [1629–34], 306: "Faus Semblant se sist pres de li | Mais de ceste ne de celi | Ne vous veil faire greigneur prose | Car en eus nul bien ne repose. | Et qui en veult savoir la glose | Si voist au romans de la rose."

203. For additional analysis, see Brownlee, "Authorial Self-Representation," 75–77, and 76, n5 and n6.

204. Ibid., 97–98, for a textual comparison.

205. Edward H. Roesner, "Labouring in the Midst of Wolves: Reading a Group of 'Fauvel' Motets," *Early Music History* 22 (2002): 187. See 186–91 for a full discussion.

206. Ibid., 225–28, though the fox is overthrown, see 233.

207. While a detailed study of the *Fauvel* manuscript art is worthwhile, it is not feasible to do so here. See Jean-Claude Mühlethaler, *Fauvel au pouvoir; lire la satire médiévale*, Nouvelle Bibliothèque du Moyen Age 26 (Paris: Champion, 1994), 413–35, for a listing of miniatures. For a good general survey of the art of the time, see François Avril, *Manuscript Painting at the Court of France: The Fourteenth Century*, Ursule Molinaro, trans. (New York: George Braziller, 1978). For additional references to the art of *Fauvel*, see Appendix A.

208. For a more detailed study, see Martin Kauffmann, "Satire, Pictorial genre, and the Illustrations in BN fr. 146," *Fauvel Studies*, 285–305. He also considers the relation of royal imagery in the manuscript to royal seals.

209. For an excellent study of hybrids, grotesques, and obscene images in medieval illuminated manuscripts, see Michael Camille, *Image on the Edge: The Margins of Medieval Art* (London: Reaktion Books, 1992, rep. 2012).

210. Michael Camille, "Hybridity, Monstrosity, and Bestiality in the *Roman de Fauvel*," *Fauvel Studies*, 162.

211. Ibid., 164.

212. Ibid., 166.

213. Ibid., 168–70.

214. Ibid., 170. See also Nona C. Flores, "'Effigies Amicitiae... Veritas Inimicitiae': Antifeminism in the Iconography of the Woman-Headed Serpent in Medieval and Renaissance Art and Literature," *Animals in the Middle Ages: A Book of Essays*, Nona C. Flores, ed. (New York: Routledge , 1966, reprinted as part of Routledge Medieval Casebooks, 2000), 167–95.

215. Michael Camille, *The Gothic Idol: Ideology and Image-Making in Medieval Art* (Cambridge: Cambridge University Press, 1989, reprinted 1992), 267, which also includes the image in question, drawn from the Hague, Koninklijke Bibliotheek, MS 78.D.40. See also Camille "Hybridity, Monstrosity, and Bestiality," 166, for some similarities to the representations of Fauvel.

216. For a discussion of manuscript copies and circulation, see Roesner, "Labouring in the Midst of Wolves," 171–72, and 171, n4.

217. See appendix B.

Chapter 7

1. Szittya, *Antifraternal Tradition*. He devotes a chapter to the dissemination of Guillaume de Saint-Amour's work in England in ecclesiastical circles, 62–122. We will examine some of this source material in greater detail in chapter 8.

2. Geltner, "Faux Semblants," 357–80, and "A False Start to Medieval Antifraternalism?" 105–18.

3. Szittya, *Antifraternal Tradition*, 191.

4. See Geltner, *Making of Medieval Antifraternalism*, 121, and n74, for an account of such accusations in France. See 119–123 for a broader survey.

5. Ibid., 121–22. For the text of the accusation, see *Chronica Johannis de Reading et Anonymi Cantuariensis 1346-1367*, James Tait, ed. (Manchester: Manchester University Press, 1914), 109–110.

6. Aubrey Gwynn, *The English Austin Friars in the Time of Wyclif* (Oxford: Oxford University Press, 1940), 77–78.

7. Szittya, *Antifraternal Tradition*, 227: "Here the friars' multiplicity is directly related to the eschatological multiplicity of the false prophets whose advent Christ prophesied and of similar multitudes in the epistle of John: 'nunc Antichristi multi facti sunt, (1 John 2:18); 'multi pseudoprophetae exierunt in mundum' (1 John 4:1)." See 223–27 for a more detailed analysis of the numbers of religious houses in the wake of the plague's devastation.

8. Ibid., 184, where he posits these three "must have taken it [antifraternal polemic] up because it accorded with their own imaginative and symbolic perspective on English society and the decline of the world."

9. Walter William Skeat, ed., *Aelfric's Lives of Saints*, Early English Text Society (London: N. Trübner & Co., 1900), [812–818], 120–23: "Is swa-ðeah to witenne þæt on þysre worulde synd þreo endebyrdnysse on annysse gesette. Þæt synd *laboratores. oratores. bellatores*. *laboratores* synd þa þe urne bigleafan beswincað. *oratores* synd þa ðe us to gode geðingiað. *bellatores* synd þa ðe ure burga healdað. and urne eard be-weriað wið onwinnendne here."

10. Giles Constable, *Three Studies in Medieval Religious and Social Thought: The Interpretation of Mary and Martha, the Ideal of the Imitation of Christ, the Orders of Society* (Cambridge: Cambridge University Press, reprinted 1998), 279: "These then are the king's materials and his tools to reign with: that he have his land well-peopled; he must have prayer-men and army-men and workmen (gebedmen, fyrdmen, weorcmen). You know that without these tools no king can exhibit his craft." Walter J. Sedgefield, ed., *King Alfred's Old English version of Boethius De consolatione philosophiae* (Oxford: Clarendon Press, 1899), 40: "bið þonne cyninges his tol mid to riscianne, þ^t he hæbbe his lond fullmonnad; he sceal habban gebedmen , fyrdmen , weorcmen. Hwæt, þu wast þætte butan þissan tolan nan cyning his cræft ne mæg cyðan." Constable discusses these early descriptions of the three orders in England at 279–81.

11. See Mann, *Chaucer and Medieval Estates Satire*. She dis-

cusses how such satire is defined at 3–4. See also 7, for how Chaucer seems to have held that such specialized places were detrimental to society. See also Kendrick, "Medieval Satire," 64–68.

12. Alice lived a remarkable life, one that her grandfather could not have envisioned, witnessing various events during the Wars of the Roses. She lost all three of her husbands, and was deeply unpopular at times. A survey of her life can be found in Marjorie Anderson, "Alice Chaucer and Her Husbands," *PMLA* 60, 1 (1945): 24–47. A comprehensive online biography of Alice is Susan Higginbotham, "The Indomitable Duchess: Alice Chaucer, Duchess of Suffolk": http://www.susanhigginbotham.com/blog/posts/the-indomitable-duchess-alice-chaucer-duchess-of-suffolk/, accessed October 27, 2013.

13. Peter Ackroyd, *Chaucer: Ackroyd's Brief Lives* (New York: Doubleday / Nan A. Talese, 2005), 105–08.

14. Thomas Wright, *The Political Songs of England: From the Reign of John to that of Edward II* (London: Camden Society, 1839), 330: "Religioun was first founded duresce for to drie; | And nu is the moste del i-went to eise and glotonie. | Where shal men nu finde fattere or raddere of leres? | Or betre farende folk than monekes, chanons, and freres? | In uch toun | I wot non eysiere lyf than is religioun."

15. Ibid., 330–31.

16. Mann, *Chaucer and Medieval Estates Satire*, 310.

17. See chapter 8 for more on the Lollards.

18. Thomas Wright, ed. *Political Poems and Songs Relating to English History, Composed During the Period from the Accession of Edward III to that of Richard III*, 2 vols. (London: Longman, Green, Longman, and Roberts, 1859), I, 270: "Wyde are thair wonnynges, and wonderftdly wroght; | Murdre and horedome ful dere has it boght. | With an O and an I, for six pens er thai fayle, | Sle thi fadre, and jape thi modre, and thai wyl the assoile." The full texts of both works, *Song against the Friars*, and *On the Minorite Friars*, are available at 263–70. The work is available as print-on-demand from Cambridge University Press: http://www.cambridge.org/us/academic/subjects/history/british-history-1066–1450/thomas-wrights-political-songs-england-reign-john-edward-ii.

19. It has been said that English survived rather than developed in the immediate centuries after 1066, but this an overstatement. The Anglo-Saxon language had achieved great heights in its poetry through the 11th century (Beowulf, of course, and many other fine examples), until the Normans brought their own customs and French language into the new court, replacing the Anglo-Saxon nobility and the need for Old English. Indeed, all of the medieval kings of England spoke French as a first language, and in the earlier age following the conquest, many never bothered to learn English. Henry IV (reigned 1399–1413) was the first monarch for whom English was his native language, over 300 years after the Norman Conquest, though Richard II, as we will see in this chapter, greatly encouraged its use. Nevertheless, the common people continued to speak English despite their new Norman yolk, and a decent amount of English poetry from the intervening centuries survives, though much more perished, accidentally or otherwise, over the centuries. It is frequently of high quality, and shows that the language was vibrant and evolving, absorbing French influences and slowly changing into the language we know today. A good introductory anthology of works from the 13th to the early 16th centuries is Maxwell S. Luria and Richard Hoffman, eds., *Middle English Lyrics* (New York: Norton, 1974). Chaucer, and to a lesser extent, Langland, and Gower, raised English up to a literary standard from which it has never been displaced. For an excellent short history of English, see "The History of English": http://www.thehistoryofenglish.com/index.html, accessed February 25, 2014.

20. Peter Ackroyd, in *Chaucer*, notes that the name may also derive from *chauffecire*, "to seal with hot wax in the manner of a clerk," at 1, though this is less likely.

21. Not all friars were pleased with this action, and some spoke out against it in sermons. See Geltner, *Making of Medieval Antifraternalism*, 64–65, for some striking accounts of torture used against friars during the political upheavals of England in the later 14th and early 15th centuries. See also 65, *n*91.

22. There are many biographies of Chaucer, and as with Shakespeare, many summaries of his life added into prefaces to his writings. Notable comprehensive works include Martin M. Crow and Clair C. Olson, eds., *Chaucer Life-Records* (Oxford: Oxford University Press, and Austin: University of Texas Press, 1966), an enormous collection of all of the records mentioning him. At over 650 pages, it is very important and is the standard reference. See Derek Brewer, *Chaucer and His World* (New York: Dodd, Mead, 1977); Donald R. Howard, *Chaucer: His Life, His World, His Works* (New York: Dutton, 1987); and Derek Pearsall, *The Life of Geoffrey Chaucer*, Blackwell Critical Biographies 1 (Oxford and Cambridge, MA: Blackwell, 1992), one of the best studies. Three more recent works are Peter Ackroyd, *Chaucer: Ackroyd's Brief Lives*; Peter Brown, *Geoffrey Chaucer*, Authors in Context (Oxford: Oxford University Press, 2011); and Ardis Butterfield, *Chaucer: A London Life* (London: I.B.Tauris, 2013). The standard complete edition of Chaucer's works is Larry D. Benson, general ed., *The Riverside Chaucer*, third edition (Oxford: Oxford University Press, 2008).

23. Terry Jones, *Who Murdered Chaucer? A Medieval Mystery* (New York: Thomas Dunne, 2004). Jones (of Monty Python fame, and an avid medievalist) enlisted the aid of a number of scholars of English literature in preparing this intriguing work, so it has scholarly merit, but the central thesis is unproven, and probably unprovable. There are simply not enough records surviving to fill in the picture, tantalizing though its speculations may be.

24. There are also antifraternal themes in other works. See, for example, N R. Havely, "White Words, False World: Chaucer's Pandarus and the Antifraternal Tradition in *Troilus*, Books I-III," *Medium Aevum* 61, 2 (1992): 250–60.

25. Arnold Williams, "Chaucer and the Friars," *Speculum* 28 (1953): 499. This is one of the most important early studies about Chaucer's relationship to the friars and how he portrayed them.

26. Ibid.

27. Ibid, 513.

28. Related in Ackroyd, *Chaucer*, 24. The edition, *The workes of our Antient and learned English Poet, Geffrey Chaucer* (London: George Bishop, 1598), was reprinted in 1602 with corrections and again over the next few decades. For a discussion of the process involved in editing and presenting the text (Chaucer's English was quite different than Shakespeare's), see H.G. Wright, "Thomas Speght as a Lexicographer and Annotator of Chaucer's Works," *English Studies* 40 (1959): 194–208.

29. Ackroyd, *Chaucer*, 24–25.

30. Geltner, "Faux Semblants," 369–76.

31. For a good introduction that also provides an excellent summary of the friars' history up to Chaucer's time, see Karl T. Hagen, "A Frere Ther Was, A Wantowne and a Meryee," *Chaucer's Pilgrims: An Historical Guide to the Pilgrims in The Canterbury Tales*, Laura C. Lambdin and Robert T. Lambdin, eds. (Westport, CT: Prager, 1996, rep. 1999), 80–92.

32. Mann offers a comprehensive and excellent analysis of the vagaries of the Friar's depiction in *Chaucer and Medieval Estates Satire*, 37–54. She notes, for example, at 54: "It is the consistent use of ambivalent words which make it hard to subject the Friar to moral analysis ... the narrator still does not dictate a moral attitude to us.... What emerges from the portrait is not just that the Friar does not live up to his ideals; it is that were he to do so, he would come into conflict with the audience's equally 'ideal' notions of social hierarchy. Looking back to the Monk's portrait, we can see the same tension between the spiritual and the social. An orthodox moralist might well blame the Monk for his 'lordly' aspect—but when monasteries are supported by manors, how can monks avoid acting like lords of them?" Thus, the friars have indeed sinned, but are they any guiltier in their transgressions than all the others?

33. Ibid., 8. See also 8–9 for consideration of how satirical writers employed the stereotypes of the estates to create their own versions, and 9, where she observes: "each satirist re-creates the estates stereotype afresh, 'seeing' for himself the vanity of women or the corruption of the clergy. But while his vision is conditioned by what is traditional, it will also reflect something of the immediate situation which he is analyzing in terms of the old formulae."

34. Ibid., 39.

35. General Prologue, [208–11] 26: "A frere ther was, a wantowne and a merye | A lymytour, a ful solempne man. | In alle the ordres foure is noon that kan | So muchel of daliaunce and fair langage."

36. Ibid., [236–39], 27: "Wel koude he synge, and pleyen on a rote | Of yeddynges he baar outrely the pris. | His nekke whit was as the flour-de-lys | Therto he strong was as a champioun."

37. Ibid., [240–48]: "He knew the tavernes wel in every toun | And everich hostiler and tappestere | Bet than a lazar or a beggestere | For unto swich a worthy man as he | Acorded nat, as by his facultee | To have with sike lazars aqueyntaunce. | It is nat honeste, it may nat avaunce | For to deelen with no swich poraille | But al with riche and selleres of vitaille."

38. Ibid., [249–52]: "And over al, ther as profit sholde aris | Curteis he was, and lowely of servyse. | Ther nas no man nowher so vertuous. | He was the beste beggere in his hous";

39. Mann offers some good concluding remarks on the friar's portrait in *Chaucer and Medieval Estates Satire*, 53–54, and at 54: "We may suspect that the Friar's portrait is so long and complex because his estate reveals more clearly than any other the gulf between the standards of an ordered society and of Christianity."

40. General Prologue, [269–71], 27: "Hise eyen twynkled in his heed aright | As doon the sterres in the frosty nyght. | This worthy lymytour was cleped Huberd."

41. John V. Fleming, "The Antifraternalism of the 'Summoner's Tale,'" *Journal of English and Germanic Philology* 65, 4 (1966): 688–89.

42. Ibid., 700.

43. For as thorough a study of medieval fart humor as one could want, see Valerie Allen, *On Farting: Language and Laughter in the Middle Ages* (New York: Palgrave Macmillan, 2010).

44. For an overview of Chaucer's French literary influences, see Helen Phillips, "The French Background," *Chaucer: An Oxford Guide*, Steve Ellis, ed. (Oxford: Oxford University Press, 2005), 292–312.

45. Janette Richardson, "Friar and Summoner, the Art of Balance," *The Chaucer Review* 9, 3 (1975): 235.

46. Summoner's Prologue, [1669–71], 128: "I yow biseke that, of youre curteisye | Syn ye han herd this false Frere lye | As suffreth me I may my tale telle."

47. Ibid., [1689–91], 128: "'Hold up thy tayl, thou Sathanas!' quod he; | 'Shewe forth thyn ers, and lat the frere se | Where is the nest of freres in this place!'"

48. Ibid., [1704–06]: "But natheles, for fere yet he quook | So was the develes ers ay in his mynde | That is his heritage of verray kynde,"

49. Though the sermon is intended to show the comic long-windedness of the friar, it makes use of dark *exempla*. One of the accounts is the friar's version of a story related by Seneca in his *De Ira* ("Concerning Anger"), 1.18: 3–6. The judge Gnaeus Piso orders the unjust executions of three innocent and virtuous soldiers, following the letter of the law, rather than admitting his own mistake. Aubrey Stewart, trans. *L. Annaeus Seneca, Minor Dialogs Together with the Dialog "On Clemency,"* Bohn's Classical Library Edition (London: George Bell and Sons, 1900). R.A. Pratt suggests that Chaucer most likely drew from a redaction of Seneca's work by the Franciscan John of Wales (d. ca. 1285) in his *Communiloquium sive Summa collationum*, rather than from a copy of the original work, see Pratt, "Chaucer and the Hand That Fed Him," *Speculum* 41 (1966): 621–642. For a summary of analyses of how this *exempla* relates to the larger tale, see John F. Plummer, ed., *A Variorum Edition of the Works of Geoffrey Chaucer, 2: The Canterbury Tales, 7: The Summoner's Tale* (Norman: University of Oklahoma Press, 1995), 170.

50. Summoner's Tale, [2144–51], 134: "And doun his hand he launcheth to the clifte | In hope for to fynde there a yifte. | And whan this sike man felte this frère | Aboute his tuwel grope there and here | Amydde his hand he leet the frere a fart | Ther nys no capul, drawynge in a cart | That myghte have lete a fart of swich a soun."

51. Ibid., [2263–74], 136: "And to every spokes ende, in this manere | Ful sadly leye his nose shal a frère | Youre noble confessour—there God hym save! | Shal holde his nose upright under the nave | Thanne shal this cherl, with bely stif and toght | As any tabour, hyder been ybroght | And sette hym on the wheel right of this cart | Upon the nave, and make hym lete a fart | And ye shul seen, up peril of my lyf | By preeve which that is demonstratif | That equally the soun of it wol wende | And eke the stynk, unto the spokes ende."

52. For a modern translation of the work, see Larry D. Benson and Theodore M. Andersson, *The Literary Context of Chaucer's Fabliaux* (Indianapolis and New York: Bobbs-Merrill, 1971), 354–59.

53. For a good discussion of this uncertainty, see Plummer, *The Summoner's Tale*, 9–16. Skeat was an advocate of the direct influence, as were other early scholars, though the consensus now is against a direct borrowing. For a study of a possible English fabliaux tradition pre-dating Chaucer, see Robert E. Lewis, "The English Fabliau Tradition and Chaucer's 'Miller's Tale,'" *Modern Philology*, 79, 3 (1982): 241–55. He seeks to answer the question (at 241): "Was there an English fabliau

tradition before Chaucer, and, if so, was Chaucer indebted to it?" There was such a tradition (with a pitifully small number of English survivals, only three before his time), and Lewis is inclined to believe that Chaucer did draw on it for some inspiration for his Miller's Tale, and did not essentially invent the English fabliau tradition himself.

54. Ibid., especially at 11–13.

55. Fleming, "Antifraternalism," 689. Caesar of Heisterbach, *Dialogus magnus visionum atque miraculorum*, ed. Joseph Strange (Köln, Bonn, and Brussels: J.M. Heberle, 1851) 12 vols., VII, 59.

56. Fleming, "Antifraternalism," 689, *n*.4. See also Fleming, "The Summoner's Prologue: An Iconographic Adjustment," *The Chaucer Review* 2, 2 (1967): 95–107, for a discussion of the Marian story in relation to lay confraternities, suggestive of how Chaucer may have learned of it. For information on source material, see Christine Richardson-Hay, "The Summoner's Prologue and Tale," *Sources and Analogues of the Canterbury Tales*, Robert M. Correale and Mary Hamel, eds., Vol. 2 (Woodbridge: Boydell, 2005), 449–77.

57. Extensive discussions and analyses of the tale and its influences can be found in the articles by Williams and Fleming (*n*25 and *n*41 above), as well as Fleming, "The Summoner's Prologue," 95–97; see also Penn R. Szittya, "The Friar as False Apostle: Antifraternal Exegesis and the 'Summoner's Tale,'" *Studies in Philology*, 71, 1 (1974): 19–46. Szittya updated this as chapter 6 of his book *The Antifraternal Tradition in Medieval Literature*: "Chaucer and Antifraternal Exegesis: The False Apostle of the *Summoner's Tale*," 231–46. A good recent study is Marie Borroff, *Traditions and Renewals: Chaucer, the Gawain Poet, and Beyond* (New Haven: Yale University Press, 2003), specifically the chapter "Dimensions of Judgment in the Canterbury Tales," 3–49.

58. Glossing was a form of explanatory notes to a scriptural or other religious text. It was used frequently and everywhere during the Middle Ages.

59. Fleming, "Antifraternalism," 695, noting an example from the *Speculum perfectionis*.

60. Williams, "Chaucer and the Friars," 507, referencing Decima Douie, *The Nature and the Effect of the Heresy of the Fraticelli* (Manchester: Manchester University Press, 1932), 102.

61. See chapter 1 for the Spirituals.

62. Summoner's Tale, [1967], 132.

63. Fleming, "Antifraternalism," 698–99.

64. The body of literary analysis of Chaucer's work is, of course, extensive. This note lists only some of the more important works regarding the layers of religious meaning in this tale. For detailed discussions of Pentecostal associations, see the classic thesis by Alan Levitan, "The Parody of Pentecost in Chaucer's Summoner's Tale," *University of Toronto Quarterly* 40 (1970–1): 236–46; and Bernard S. Levy, "Biblical Parody in the Summoner's Tale," *Tennessee Studies in Literature* 11 (1966): 45–60. Roy Peter Clark offers further biblical analysis in two articles: "Wit and Whitsunday in Chaucer's *Summoner's Tale*," *Annuale Mediaevale* 17 (1976): 48–57; and "Doubting Thomas in Chaucer's 'Summoner's Tale,'" *The Chaucer Review* 11, No. 2 (1976): 164–178. See also John Fleming, "Anticlerical Satire as Theological Essay: Chaucer's *Summoner's Tale*," *Thalia* 6 (1983): 5–21. More recently, see V.A. Kolve, "Chaucer's Wheel of False Religion: Theology and Obscenity in The Summoner's Tale," in *The Center and Its Compass: Studies in Medieval Literature in Honor of Professor John Leyerle*, Robert A. Taylor, et al., eds., Studies in Medieval Culture 33 (Kalamazoo: Western Michigan University Press, 1993), 265–96; Phillip Pulsiano, "The Twelve-Spoked Wheel of the Summoner's Tale," *Chaucer Review* 29 (1995): 382–89; Glending Olson, "The End of the *Summoner's Tale* and the Uses of Pentecost," *Studies in the Age of Chaucer* 21 (1999): 209–45. John Finlayson, in "Chaucer's *Summoner's Tale*: Flatulence, Blasphemy, and the Emperor's Clothes," *Studies in Philology* 104, 4 (2007): 455–470, discusses the various means of interpreting this tale, from parody to religious, from a Middle English fabliau to Chaucer as a kind of Lollard. See Derrick G. Pitard, Greed and Anti-Fraternalism in Chaucer's "Summoner's Tale," *The Seven Deadly Sins: From Communities to Individuals*, Richard Newhauser, ed. (Leiden: Brill, 2007): 207–27, who discusses how the friar's false and "empty words signify the impoverishment of clerical authority," at 227, something that Chaucer likely found tragic, but chose to communicate with humor. Olson, in "Measuring the Immeasurable: Farting, Geometry, and Theology in the 'Summoner's Tale,'" *The Chaucer Review* 43, 4 (2009): 414–

27, discusses the influence of geometry and measurement in the imagery of the 12-spoked fart wheel, especially as fostered by the so-called "Oxford calculators," scholars and logicians at Oxford University (1320s to 40s), who were almost obsessed with measurement, proportion, and mathematical relations for everything, even philosophical and theological issues. For a discussion of the relationship between the ending of the tale and the Peasants' Revolt of 1381, see Lee Patterson, *Chaucer and the Subject of History* (Madison: University of Wisconsin Press, 1991), 321. For a study of the fart as noise and how it relates to religion and politics in Chaucer's world, see Peter W. Travis "Thirteen Ways of Listening to a Fart: Noise in Chaucer's *Summoner's Tale*," *Exemplaria* 16, 2 (2004): 323–48, though the work is hindered somewhat by its excessive wordiness and overuse of academic terms.

65. *Vulgata*,1066: "Et factus est repente de caelo sonus tamquam advenientis spiritus vehementis et replevit totam domum ubi erant sedentes."

66. Szittya, *Antifraternal Tradition*, 233.

67. Ibid., 233, and *n*. 5. For possible connections, see James A.S. McPeek, "Chaucer and the Goliards," *Speculum* 26, 2 (1951): 332–36.

68. Szittya explores all of these in some detail, ibid., 233–36.

69. Ibid., 237, noting the Rule of both 1221 and 1223: "Omnes autem ministri, qui sunt in ultramarinis et ultramontanis partibus, semel in tribus annis, et alii ministri semel in anno veniant ad capitulum in festo Pentecostes apid ecclesiam sanctae Mariae de Portiuncula." *Regula* I, chap. 18, *Opuscula sancti patris Francisci assisiensis*, 3rd ed. (Quaracchi: Collegium S. Bonaventure, 1949), 48–49.

70. Summoner's Tale, [2107–08], 134: "'Now help Thomas, for hym that harwed helle! For ells moste we oure bookes selle.'"

71. Szittya, *Antifraternal Tradition*, 238, referring to a lost work of the goliard Walter Map (1140-ca.1210). This theme was later taken up in the 15th century by Thomas Malory. Kolve, in "Chaucer's Wheel of False Religion," suggests that the model for the wheel may have derived from a treatise by an Augustinian canon Hugh of Fouilloy (*d. ca*. 1172), but admits this is speculative.

72. "Isti sunt fratres mei milites tabulæ rotundæ." *Speculum perfectionis seu: S. Francisci Assisiensis*, Paul Sabatier, ed. (Paris: Fischbacher, 1898), IV, 72, 143.

73. See John Finlayson, "Flatulence, Blasphemy, and the Emperor's Clothes," 455–70.
74. Olson, "The End of the *Summoner's Tale*," 217–18.
75. Borrof, in *Traditions and Renewals*, at 30–31, discusses the connections between Chaucer and Wyclif. See also Andrew Cole, *Literature and Heresy in the Age of Chaucer* (Cambridge: Cambridge University Press, 2008), 75–99, for a thorough examination of possible Wycliffite references in Chaucer's texts. See 79, where he says of Chaucer: "By looking outside of the Tales, we will find that the poet's relationship to Wycliffism is greater than and different from what we have taken it to be—bound up ... with Wycliffism's most lasting contribution to English letters: the Wycliffite vernacular bible."
76. For a study of other possible connections to Wyclif, see Katherine Little, "Chaucer's Parson and the Specter of Wycliffism," *Studies in the Age of Chaucer* 23 (2001): 223–51.
77. For an edition, see *Riverside Chaucer*, 685–767.
78. Luria, *Reader's Guide to the Roman de la Rose*, 75.
79. See ibid., 78–82, for a summary of some of the chief influences and relations between Chaucer's works and the *Roman*.
80. See, for example, Luria, *Reader's Guide*, 82–83. See also Felicity Currie, "Chaucer's Pardoner Again," *Leeds Studies in English*, n.s. 4, (1970): 11–22, especially 14–15, 17, and 21.
81. *Pardoner's Prologue* [341–46], 194: "And after that thanne telle I forth my tales | Bulles of popes and of cardynales | Of patriarkes, and bishopes I shewe; | And in Latyn I speke a wordes fewe | To saffron with my predicacioun | And for to stire hem to devocioun."
82. Ibid., [347–76].
83. Ibid., [400–08], 195: "Of avarice and of swich cursednesse | Is al my prechyng, for to make hem free | To yeven hir pens, and namely unto me. | For myn entente is nat but for to wynne | And nothyng for correccioun of synne. | I rekke nevere, whan that they ben beryed | Though that hir soules goon a-blakeberyed! | For certes, many a predicacioun | Comth ofte tyme of yvel entencioun";
84. Ibid., [420–22]: "Thus quyte I folk that doon us displesances; | Thus spitte I out my venym under hewe | Of hoolynesse, to semen holy and trewe."
85. Dean Spruill Fansler, *Chaucer and the Roman de la Rose* (New York: Columbia University Press, 1914), 164. See 162–65 for a more detailed analysis. The work is now available free online at: http://books.google.com/books/about/Chaucer_and_the_Roman_de_La_Rose.html?id=rrYLAAAAYAAJ, accessed January 7, 2014.
86. The academic and critical literature on *Piers Plowman* is vast. Multiple editions of the work, conferences, and societies are devoted to the work. Recent scholarly editions of the various versions of the poem include: *Piers Plowman: The A Version*, George Kane, ed. (London: Athlone, 1988); *Piers Plowman: The B Version*, G. Kane and E. Talbot Donaldson, eds. (London: Athlone, 1988); *Piers Plowman: The C Version*, George Russell and George Kane, eds. (London: Athlone, 1997); *William Langland, Piers Plowman: A New Annotated Edition of the C-Text*, Exeter Medieval Texts and Studies, Derek Pearsall, ed. (Exeter, UK: University of Exeter Press, 2008); *Piers Plowman: A Parallel-Text Edition of the A, B, C, and Z Versions*, A. V. C. Schmidt ed., 2 vols. (Kalamazoo: Medieval Institute, 2011); and *Piers Plowman: The A Version*, Míceál F.Vaughan, ed. (Baltimore: Johns Hopkins University Press, 2011). Wendy Scase, in *Piers Plowman and the New Anticlericalism*, Cambridge Studies in Medieval Literature 4 (Cambridge: Cambridge University Press, 1989), argues that the poem was part of a new anticlerical sentiment that gripped England in the 14th century, one that of necessity bred a new form of literature; Anna Baldwin, in *A Guidebook to Piers Plowman* (Basingstoke: Palgrave Macmillan, 2007) presents a good introduction to the text and its sources. Kathryn Kerby-Fulton argues for the importance of *Piers Plowman* as an apocalyptic text in *Reformist Apocalypticism and Piers Plowman* (Cambridge: Cambridge University Press, 1990). John Bowers, in *Chaucer and Langland: The Antagonistic Tradition* (Notre Dame: University of Notre Dame Press, 2007), makes a case for Langland's work being more important than Chaucer's at the time, being far more widely disseminated and influential. Chaucer read Langland, but not the other way around. For a discussion of the use of English in theological considerations and the place of *Piers Plowman* (drawing different conclusions from Lawrence Clopper), see Paul Hardwick, *Raising Unruly Voices: The Laity, the Vernacular and the Church in Late Medieval England*, DPhil dissertation, University of York, 1997. For an online version of the B text, see the *Piers Plowman* page at the Corpus of Middle English Prose and Verse, University of Michigan / Oxford Text Archive, accessed January 3, 2014: http://quod.lib.umich.edu/c/cme/ppllan. The excerpts in these notes are drawn from this version, with references to more recent editions.
87. *Piers Plowman* B text, XV [152], See also Kane and Donaldson, *B Version*, 543.
88. See, for example, C. David Benson, "The Langland Myth," *William Langland's Piers Plowman: A Book of Essays*, ed. Kathleen M. Hewett-Smith (New York: Routledge, 2001), 83–99.
89. S. S. Hussey, in "Langland the Outsider," *Middle English Poetry: Texts and Traditions: Essays in Honour of Derek Pearsall*, Alastair J. Minnis, ed. (Woodbridge: Boydell and York Medieval Press, 2001): 129–37, at 130: "I have never been able to see the point of any other explanation of the relationship between author and persona, especially as fourteenth-century literature provides few or no examples of a wholly fictitious first person singular." This short article attempts to put together a more satisfying biographical picture of the elusive author by looking at the texts of *Piers Plowman* for clues. He notes at 129: "I hope that the first, and shortest section of this paper will be relatively non-controversial. The second is a little more tenuous, and the third can do no more than offer a few pointers towards one way in which we might look at Langland."
90. Scase, *New Anticlericalism*, 139–40.
91. *Piers Plowman* B, XIX [1]: "Thus I awaked and wroot what I hadde ydremed." See also Kane and Donaldson, *B Version*, 632.
92. Hussey, in "Langland the Outsider," 129–30, discusses some of the possible origins for Langland, including the Malvern Hills, where the poem also begins.
93. Michael Samuels, "Dialect and Grammar," *A Companion to Piers Plowman*, ed. John Alford (Berkeley: University of California Press, 1988), 201–22.
94. MS Rawlinson poet. 137, in the Bodleian Library, Oxford, writes of Langland that death struck him down unaware, and now he is buried beneath the earth. The author of this note, one John But, is thought to have died in 1387, indicating that Langland would have died some time before, but this is still conjectural. Hussey, in "Langland the Outsider," 131, observes: "But has been

identified either with a king's messenger who died in 1387, or with a Norfolk family whose members are associated in late fourteenth-century records with people of the surname *Rokele*. If he is but the messenger ..., then 1387 is the *terminus ad quem* for all three versions of the poem."

95. Ibid.

96. Russell and Kane, *C Version*, V [48], 289: "Thus y synge for here soules of suche as me helpeth."

97. This general short biography was pieced together by Walter William Skeat (1835–1912), whose version for the Early English Text Society from 1866 is still one of the standard editions. Skeat was a remarkable scholar of early English, working not only on *Piers Plowman*, but an edition of Chaucer, and Anglo-Saxon texts, among many others. Recently, C. David Benson, in *Public Piers Plowman: Modern Scholarship and Late Medieval English* (University Park: Pennsylvania State University Press, 2005) has re-examined the "Langland myth" constructed by Skeat, moving away from thinking of it as autobiography. He examines the effects of Skeat's constructed life of Langland, 3–42, noting at 4: "The Langland myth is a plausible explanation of the available evidence and may well be true, in whole or in part, but almost none of it can be verified ... Skeat's construction of a Langland biography ... was a major achievement that satisfied a real need." See especially 34–42 for a discussion of various modern interpretations of the historical validity (or not) of Langland and various theories about his life.

98. This is the technique of repeating a particular sound in a verse of poetry, rather than relying on rhyme. See, for example, the B version Prologue [17–19]: "A fair feeld ful of folk fond I ther bitwene | Of alle manere of men, the meene and the riche | Werchynge and wandrynge as the world asketh." See also Kane and Donaldson, *B Version*, 227–28. The tradition of alliterative poetry dated back to the Anglo-Saxon age, when it was a primary literary form (e.g., *Beowulf*). It is also found in the Old Norse *Poetic Edda*. The practice survived into Middle English, and can be found in other works, such as *Sir Gawain and the Green Knight*, where alliterative and rhyming verses both feature.

99. See Emily Steiner, *Reading Piers Plowman* (Cambridge: Cambridge University Press, 2013), 2–3 for more on the general history and number of extant manuscripts. Lawrence Warner has questioned the categorization of these texts as A, B, and C in that order, arguing that C may pre-date B. See *The Lost History of "Piers Plowman": The Earliest Transmission of Langland's Work* (Philadelphia: University of Pennsylvania Press, 2011).

100. Skeat first assigned the designation of "Z" to this version, though it tended to be ignored. In 1983, A.G. Rigg and Charlotte Brewer edited the text and proposed the notion that it was an earlier draft of A, which caused considerable controversy. George Kane, the poem's principal editor of the 20th century, denied any such identification. See George Kane, "The 'Z Version' of Piers Plowman," *Speculum* 60, 4 (1985): 910–930. Rigg and Brewer defended their position in *Piers Plowman: A Facsimile of the Z-Text in Bodleian Library, Oxford, MS Bodley 85* (Woodbridge: Boydell, 1994); see 1–22.

101. Roberta D. Cornelius posited an intriguing link between *Piers Plowman* and the *Roman de Fauvel*, noting both the name of deceit, or "Favel," who seeks to aid Fals, and the similarity in the courtships of both poems, Fauvel wishing to marry Fortune, and Fals wishing to marry Lady Meed. See "Piers Plowman and the Roman de Fauvel," *PMLA* 47, 2 (1932): 363–367. She notes at 367: "In both cases an unworthy person wishes to marry a wife who, judged by one side of her nature, is not his superior, but who, if other aspects of her character be considered, is much above him. In both cases a long journey is made by the hero and his followers for the sake of the prospective wedding. In neither instance does the intended wedding take place." She concludes that Langland knew the earlier work. For a detailed study of Lady Meed, see John A. Yunck, *The Lineage of Lady Meed: The Development of Mediaeval Venality Satire* (Notre Dame: Notre Dame UP, 1963). See also "Meed and Greed," San Francisco State Medieval Forum: https://www.sfsu.edu/~medieval/complaintlit/meed_intro.html, accessed February 25, 2014.

102. For more on these allegorical figures, see Rosanne Gasse, "Dowel, Dobet, and Dobest in Middle English Literature," *Florilegium* 14 (1995–96): 171–95.

103. Szittya devotes a lengthy chapter to studying the antifraternal references in the B poem, "The Friars and the End of Piers Plowman," in *Antifraternal Tradition*, 247–87.

104. Ibid., 3.

105. B *Prologue* [58–67]: "I fond there freres, alle the foure orders | Prechynge the peple for profit of [the wombe]:

Glosed the gospel as hem good liked | For coveitise of copes construwed it as thei wolde. | Manye of thise maistres mowe clothen hem at liking | For hire moneie and hire marchaundise marchen togideres. | Sith charite hath ben chapman and chief to shryve lords | Manye ferlies han fallen in a fewe yeres. | But Holy Chirche and hii holde bettre togidres | The mooste meschief on molde is mountynge up faste." See also Kane and Donaldson, *B Version*, 230–31.

106. See Szittya, *Antifraternal Tradition*, 251, for more on this.

107. The history of medieval minstrelsy in England is far more detailed and complex than it might seem to be. Still the best survey is Richard Rastall, *Secular Musicians in Late Medieval England*, Ph.D. diss. for Victoria University of Manchester, 1968. Rastall has noted that the work is being completely revised and will be published in 2014–15 by Boydell. A less useful, if well intended work is John Southworth, *The English Medieval Minstrel* (Woodbridge: Boydell, 1989), a book Rastall has excoriated in a review, and dismisses as little more than historical fiction, due to its lack of attention to key sources.

108. B, II [228–33]: "Ac mynstrales and messangers mette with hym ones | And [with]helden hym an half yeer and ellevene dayes. | Freres with fair speche fetten hymthen | And for knowynge of comeres coped hym as a frere; | Ac he hath leve to lepen out as ofte as hym liketh | And is welcome whan he wile, and woneth with hem ofte." See also Kane and Donaldson, *B Version*, 269.

109. B, x [92–95]: "Swiche lessons lordes sholde lovye to here| And how he myghte moost meynee manliche fynde—- | Noght to fare as a fithelere or a frere for to seke festes | Homliche at othere mennes houses, and hatien hir owene." See also Kane and Donaldson, *B Version*, 412.

110. B, IX [101–04]: "And siththe to spille speche, that spire is of grace | And Goddes gleman and a game of hevene. | Wolde nevere the feithful fader his fithele were untempred | Ne his gleman a gedelyng, a goere to tavernes." See also Kane and Donaldson, *B Version*, 398, and Szittya, *Antifraternal Tradition*, 253–54.

111. B, x [48–50]: "Ac murthe and mynstralcie amonges men is nouthe | Lecherie, losengerye and losels tales— | Glotonye and grete othes, this [game] they lovyeth." See

also Kane and Donaldson, *B Version*, 409.

112. B, XIII [422–39]: "That fedeth fooles sages, flatereris and lieris | And han likynge to lithen hem [in hope] to do yow laughe— | *Ve vobis qui ridetis* &c— | And yyveth hem mete and mede, and povere men refuse | In youre deeth deyinge, I drede me soore | Lest tho thre maner men to muche sorwe yow brynge: | *Consencientes et agentes pari pena punientur.* | Patriarkes and prophetes, prechours of Goddes words | Saven thorugh hir sermon mannes soule fro helle | Right so flatereris and fooles arn the fendes disciples | To entice men thorugh hir tales to synne and harlotrie. | Ac clerkes, that knowen Holy Writ, sholde kenne lords | What David seith of swiche men, as the Sauter telleth: | *Non habitabit in medio domus mee quifacit superbiam; qui loquitur iniqua...* | Sholde noon harlot have audience in halle ne in chamber | Ther wise men were— witnesseth Goddes wordes— | Ne no mysproud min amonges lordes ben allowed. | Clerkes and knyghtes welcometh kynges minstrales | And for love of hir lord litheth hem at festes | Muche moore, me thynketh, riche men sholde | Have beggeres bifore hem, the whiche ben Goddes minstrales." See also Kane and Donaldson, *B Version*, 509–11.

113. B, XIII : [449–56]: "Thise thre maner minstrales maketh a man to laughe | And in his deeth deyinge thei don hym gret confort | That bi his lyve lithed hem and loved hem to here. | Thise solaceth the soule til hymself be falle | In a welhope, [for he wroghte so], amonges worthi seyntes | There flatereres and fooles thorugh hir foule words | Leden tho that loved hem to Luciferis feste | With *turpiloquio*, a lay of sorwe, and Luciferis fithele." See also Kane and Donaldson, *B Version*, 511.

114. Szittya, *Antifraternal Tradition*, 252–255. See also *Speculum perfectionis*, 197–98: "'Nos sumus joculatores Domini et pro his volumus remunerari a vobis, videlicet ut stetis in vera paenitentia.' Et ait: 'Quid enim sunt servi Dei nisi quidam joculatores ejus qui corda hominum erigere debent et movere ad laetitiam spiritualem.'" Interestingly, Caesarius of Heisterbach, in his *Dialogus miraculorum*, Distinctio sexta 8, calls the simple minded ("simplices") the *ioculatores Dei*. Given that Francis, as noted in chapter 2, described himself as a *simplex et idiota*, could there be a connection to this earlier designation? The *Dialogus* was extremely popular, and given that Caesarius and Francis were close contemporaries, it is not improbable that Francis, or the scribe who wrote this story, knew of it. Are the simple and ignorant thus the true "minstrels of God?"

115. Clopper, *Songes of Rechelesnesse: Langland and the Franciscans* (Ann Arbor: University of Michigan Press, 1997), 69–70. He argues this thesis with clarity and elegance. It casts doubt on many of the long-held assumptions about the work, and if true, would overturn many beliefs that have been thought to be beyond debate. Suspicions about Langland's potential Franciscan connection are not new, however, as Szittya notes in *Antifraternal Tradition*, 248, n1. Clopper gives a comprehensive history of this unconventional theory at 15–19, which first appeared in the latter 19th century, but was initially dismissed, as much as anything due to a long association of the poem with Wycliff, Lollardy, and later, Protestantism. See his related articles "Langland's Persona: An Anatomy of the Mendicant Orders," *Written Work: Langland, Labor, and Authorship*, Steven Justice and Kathryn Kerby-Fulton, eds. (Philadelphia: University of Pennsylvania Press, 1997), 144–84, and "Langland's Franciscanism," *The Chaucer Review* 25, 1 (1990): 54–75. See also Szittya, *Antifraternal Tradition*, 265.

116. C, V [27–31]: "þenne hast þow londes to lyue by quod resoun or linage riche | þat fynt þe þin fode · for an ydel man þou semest | a spendour þat spende mot · or a spille-tyme | Or beggest þi byleue aboute at mennes hacches | Or fattest vpon fridaies · or feste daies in churche | þe whiche is lollarne lif þat litel ys preysed." See also Russell and Kane, *C Version*, 287–88.

117. Clopper, *Songes of Rechelesnesse*, 332. See also 69, n2, for his response to Wendy Scase, who posits in her *New Anticlericalism* that Langland was an external critic utilizing Franciscan ideas.

118. Clopper, *Songes of Rechelesnesse*, 70: "A number of more recent scholars ... now believe that the critique of the friars in Piers Plowman is closer to that of the rigorists and moderates within the Franciscan order than it is to that of the external critics.... In general, we might conclude that Langland adjudicates between those external critiques he believes to be accurate, because they reflect internal concerns about laxity, and those he rejects, because they are in opposition to the mendicant ideal." See also 10 and 325–333.

119. Ibid., 10–11. See also 42–43. For the issue of sermons and their content, see 84–85.

120. Ibid., 12, 19–20, and 35. For some thoughts on the relation between the poem's them and Bonaventure's Trinitarian doctrine, see 112–21.

121. See ibid., 44–47.

122. Ibid., 4.

123. Ibid., 11–12.

124. Szittya, *Antifraternal Tradition*, 247. See Clopper, *Songes of Rechelesnesse*, 23–24, for a discussion of the title of his work, of "Rechelesnesse" as a concept, and its relation to the Franciscan "minstrels."

125. B Prologue [1–8]: "In a somer seson, whan softe was the sonne | I shoop me into shroudes as I a sheep were | In habite as an heremite unholy of werkes | Wente wide in this world wondres to here. | Ac on a May morwenynge on Malverne hilles | Me bifel a ferly, of Fairye me thoghte. | I was wery forwandred and wente me to reste | Under a brood bank by a bourne syde." See also Kane and Donaldson, *B Version*, 227.

126. B, XIII [1–3]: "And I awaked therwith, witlees nerhande | And as a freke that fey were, forth gan I walke | In manere of a mendynaunt many yer after." See also Kane and Donaldson, *B Version*, 484.

127. Clopper, *Songes of Rechelesnesse*, 2.

128. Ibid., 75. See also 78 and 82–83.

129. Most scholars now reject any notion that Langland was a Wyclifite, see ibid., 63.

130. A recent study of Gower's extensive use of legal terminology in his writings and interest in the law of the time is Conrad van Dijk, *John Gower and the Limits of the Law*, Publications of the John Gower Society (Woodbridge: D.S. Brewer, 2013). The book examines the potential conflict between his devotion to the rule of law, and his use of *exempla* that frequently advocate for other forms of vengeance. Van Dijk reaffirms that it is not clear that Gower was a practicing lawyer, at 5. For more general studies, a standard book on Gower and his works is John H. Fisher, *John Gower, Moral Philosopher and Friend of Chaucer* (New York: New York University Press, 1964). For a good recent collection of general Gower studies, see Elizabeth Dutton, John Hines, and R. F. Yeager, eds. *John Gower, Trilingual Poet: Language, Translation, Tradition* (Cambridge: D. S. Brewer, 2010). There are many studies on Gower's work, especially the *Con-*

fessio Amantis. For a comprehensive recent online bibliography, see Georgiana Donavin and Meghan Hekker Nestel, "Bibliography of Gower Studies, 2005 to 2011," The Gower Project, accessed October 26, 2013: http://www.gowerproject.org/bibliography.htm. For translations of the major French and Latin works, see William Burton Wilson and rev. Nancy Wilson Van Baak, trans., *Miroir de l'omme—The Mirror of Mankind, by John Gower* (East Lansing: Colleagues Press, 1992); and Sian Echard and Claire Fanger, trans., *The Latin Verses in the Confessio Amantis: An Annotated Translation* (East Lansing: Colleagues Press, 1991). Additional Gower materials can be found at the website of the *International John Gower Society*: http://www.wcu.edu/johngower/index.html, accessed October 26, 2013.

131. Szittya, in *Antifraternal Tradition*, 214–222, offers analysis of some of the antifraternal passages in these works, with some text examples.

132. The revolt has been widely studied. Good introductions include R. B. Dobson, *The Peasants' Revolt of 1381*, 2nd ed. (London: Macmillan, 1983); Rodney Hilton, Bondmen Made Free: Medieval Peasant Movements and the English Rising of 1381 (London: Routledge, 1995); Alastair Dunn, The Great Rising of 1381: the Peasants' Revolt and England's Failed Revolution (Stroud: Tempus, 2002); and Dan Jones, Summer of Blood: the Peasants' Revolt of 1381 (London: Harper Press, 2010). For a survey of the thoughts and motivations of the common people of the time, and how this was reflected (or not) in the literature, see David Aers, "Vox Populi and the Literature of 1381," The Cambridge History of Medieval English Literature, David Wallace, ed. (Cambridge: Cambridge University Press, 1999), 432–53.

133. Ackroyd, *Chaucer*, 99–102.

134. George Campbell Macaulay, ed., *The Complete Works of John Gower*, The French Works (Oxford: Clarendon Press, 1899), [21181–92], 239: "Si nous agardons plus avant | L'estat du frère mendicant | N'ert pas de moy ce que je dis | Mais a ce que l'en vait parlant | Ensur trestout le remenant | Cist ordre vait du mal en pis: | Et nepourqant a leur avis | Ils diont q'ils a dieu le fils | Sont droit disciple en lour vivant | Mais j'ay del ordre tant enquis | Qe frères ont le siècle quis | Et sont a luy tout entendant."

135. Ibid., [21217–28]: "Ils nous prechont de la poverte | Et ont toutdis la main overte | Pour la richesce recevoir; | La covoitise ils ont coverte | Deinz soy, dont l'ordre se perverte | Pour enginer et decevoir | Les eases vuillont bien avoir | Mais les labours pour nul avoir | Ainz vont oiceus comme gent deserte | De nulle part font leur devoir: | Dont m'est avis pour dire voir | Q'ils quieront loer sanz decerte."

136. Ibid., [21241–52], 239–40: "Deux freres sont de la partie | Qui vont ensemble sanz partie | Les paiis pour environner; | Et l'un et l'autre ades se plie | Au fin que bien leur multeplie | Du siècle; dont sont mençonger | Pour blandir et pour losenger | Et pour les pecchés avancer: | L'un ad nown frere Ypocresie | Qui doit ma dame confesser | Mais l'autre la doit relesser | Si ad noun frere Flaterie."

137. Ibid., [21268–71], 240: "Dont il sovent plus entalente | Le pecché faire que laisser | Qant pour si poy voet relaisser."

138. For additional examples, see Mann, *Chaucer and Medieval Estates Satire*, 40 and 47–48.

139. George Campbell Macaulay, ed., *The Complete Works of John Gower*, The Latin Works (Oxford: Clarendon Press, 1902), 186–200. The section is too lengthy to include notable quotations here.

140. Ibid., chapter 17, 188: "Non peto quod periant, set fracti consolidentur, et subeant primum quern dedit ordo statum."

141. The Western Schism of 1378 to 1417 was largely the result of political feuding, leading to two separate popes (and at one time, three), residing in Rome and Avignon (in southern France), respectively. Useful general studies include Walter Ullmann, *The Origins of the Great Schism: A Study in Fourteenth-Century Ecclesiastical History*, (Hamden, CT: Archon Books, 1967); and Joëlle Rollo-Koster, Thomas M. Izbicki, eds., *A Companion to the Great Western Schism (1378–1417)*, Brill's Companions to the Christian Tradition, 17 (Leiden: Brill, 2009). See also chapter 8, *n*159, for additional resources.

142. George Campbell Macaulay, ed., *The Complete Works of John Gower*, The English Works (Oxford: Clarendon Press, 1901), [338–55], 14: "In holy cherche of such a slitte | Is for to rewe un to ous alle; | God grante it mote wel befalle | Towardes him which hath the trowthe. | Bot ofte is sen that mochel slowthe | Whan men ben drunken of the cuppe | Doth mochel harm, whan fyr is uppe | Bot if somwho the flamme stanche | And so to speke upon this branche | Which proud Envie hath mad to springe | Of Scisme, causeth forto bringe | This newe Secte of Lollardie | And also many an heresie | Among the clerkes in hemselve | It were betre dike and delve | And stonde upon the ryhte faith | Than knowe al that the bible seith | And erre as somme clerkes do." See also chapter 8.

Chapter 8

1. For an excellent lengthy summary of conflicts as well as cooperation and goodwill during this time period, see Arnold Williams, "Relations between the Mendicant Friars and the Regular Clergy in England in the Later Fourteenth Century," *Annuale Mediaevale* 1 (1960): 22–95. See also the important overview by Carolly Erickson, "Fourteenth-Century Franciscans and their Critics," *Franciscan Studies* 35 (1975), 107–135, and 36 (1976), 108–147.

2. Erickson discusses these in detail in her two articles.

3. The standard work in English on Matthew's life is Richard Vaughan, *Matthew Paris* (Cambridge: Cambridge University Press, 1958, reissued 1979). Vaughan also served as editor and translator of *The Illustrated Chronicles of Matthew Paris* (Corpus Christi College, Cambridge: Alan Sutton, 1993, reissued from an earlier edition in 1984 without manuscript images), a portion of the *Chronicle* dating from 1247 to 1250, translated into English, and accompanied by a selection of Matthew's drawings.

4. For questions about the dating of his death, see Vaughan, *Matthew Paris*, 7–11.

5. The complete Latin edition of the *Chronica* is *Matthæi Parisiensis: Monachi Santi Albani, Chronica Majora*, Henry Richards Luard, ed., Rolls Series, 7 vols. (London: Longman, 1872–82). An edition of the history of England is *Matthaei Parisiensis, Monachi Sancti Albani, Historia Anglorum, sive, ut Vulgo Dictur, Historia Minor. Item Ejusdem Abbreviatio Chronicorum Angliae*, Frederic Madden, ed., Rolls Series, No. 44, 3 vols. (London: Longmans, Green, Reader, and Dyer, 1866–69), now available as a print-on-demand book from Cambridge University Press: http://www.cambridge.org/co/academic/subjects/history/british-history-1066-1450/historia-anglorum-sive-ut-vulgo-dicitur-historia-minor-item-ejusdem-abbreviatio-chronicorum-angliae, accessed

December 1, 2013. An early translation of the English history into English (though problematic due to issues with the original manuscripts) is John Allen Giles, *Matthew Paris's English History. From the Year 1235 to 1273*, 3 vols. (London: Henry G. Bohn, 1852–53).

6. See Vaughan, *Matthew Paris*, 130–34. He notes, at 134, that concerning Matthew's stretching of the truth: "Matthew, then, has something of the forger in him. He is neither systematic nor thorough in his fraudulence, but his sporadic tampering with documentary sources, and misuse of historical material, as well as his many errors, make him basically unreliable as a historical source." However, see BjörnWeiler, "Matthew Paris on the Writing of History," *Journal of Medieval History* 35 (2009): 254–78, for some responses to this argument.

7. Matthew tended to support the barons in their quarrels with Henry III, see *Illustrated Chronicles*, xii.

8. See Vaughan, *Matthew Paris*, 117–24 for a detailed examination of the removal of controversial passages.

9. A recent study of this journey is Björn Weiler, "Matthew Paris in Norway," *Revue Bénédictine* 122 (2012): 153–81.

10. For a more detailed study of Matthew's relationship with the world beyond the cloisters, see Björn Weiler, "Matthew Paris and Europe," *Matthew Paris: Monk, Historian, Artist*, ed. J.G. Clark (forthcoming 2014), currently accessible from http://aber.academia.edu/BjörnWeiler, accessed December 1, 2013.

11. Vaughan, *Matthew Paris*, 11.

12. For a list of recorded visitors to St. Alban's, and those known to have conversed with Matthew, see ibid., 12–17. See also Vaughan, *Illustrated Chronicles*, x.

13. BjörnWeiler, "Matthew Paris on the Writing of History," 262.

14. Vaughan, *Matthew Paris*, 138.

15. Ibid., 135.

16. *Chronica Majora*, V, 402: "Potest ergo concludi, quod tam Papa, nisi ab hoc vitio cesset, quam dicti fratres, nisi curiosos se exhibeant ad arcendum talem, digni sunt morte, scilicet perpetua. Item dicit Decretalis, quod super tali vitio, videlicet hæresi, potest et debet Papa accusari." See also Björn Weiler, "Matthew Paris and Europe," 19.

17. *Chronica Majora*, III, 520: "Tandem abutens potestate sibi concessa et fines modestiæ transgrediens et justitiæ, elatus, potens, et formidabilis, bonos cum malis confundens involvit, et insontes et simplices punivit. Auctoritate igitur Papali jussus est præcise, ne amplius in illo officio fulminando desæviret. Qui postea, manifestius clarescentibus culpis suis, quas melius æstimo reticere quam explicare, adjudicatus est perpetuo carceri mancipari."

18. Vaughan, *Matthew Paris*, 140–42 discusses some of his chief grievances with the papacy and with corruption in the English government.

19. See for example, *Chronica Majora*, V, 471–72, an entry for 1254, where he describes at length a certain cardinal (whose name is withheld for precautionary reasons) as having a terrifying vision of Innocent's judgement. In the end God speaks, "Ait autem Dominus 'Vade, et pro meritis tuis mercedem apprehende.' Et sic ablatus est." His fate is thus unknown. See also at 491–92, where it is described that his successor, Alexander IV (the great enemy of the masters in Paris) has a vision of Innocent's fate, with similar vague revelations, but which greatly unsettles him.

20. *Chronica Majora*, V, 176–77: "Ut manifeste ira Dei tam in mari quam in terra mortalibus appareret, secundum illud Abacuc vaticinium, vindicta videretur peccatorum imminere; *Nunquid in fluminibus iratus es, Domine, vel in mari indignatio tua*? Et quid mirum? a Romana enim curia, quæ fons esse totius justitiæ teneretur, enormitates irrecitabiles emanarunt; quarum unam indignam scribi huic paginæ duximus inserendam."

21. Vaughan, *Matthew Paris*, 139, where he notes that again, Matthew uses the word "extortion" for essentially any royal tax. See *Chronica Majora*, III, 170–72, for two different entries where he condemns the actions of French papal extortionists. They wring money out of the poor (sometimes by force), both clerics and laity, for yet more violence and slaughter.

22. *Chronica Majora*, III, 287: "Sed cito in tantam nobilitatem, ne dicam arrogantiam, elevabantur Prædicatores et Minores, qui spontaneam paupertatem cum humilitate elegerunt, ut recipi curarent in cœnobiis et civitatibus in processione sollempni, in vexillis, cereis accensis, et in dispositione vestimentis festivis indutorum; et concessa est eis veniam multorum dierum suis conferre auditoribus, signatosque hodie eras data pecunia a crucis voto absolverunt."

23. *Chronica Majora*, IV, 599–600. His language is quite caustic in the opening section, 599: "Duo fratres de ordine Minorum, Johannes et Alexander, natione Anglici, potestatem a domino Papa optinentes extorquendi pecuniam ad opus domini Papæ, in Angliam ab ipso Papa destinantur. Qui multis bullatis litteris Papalibus armati et sub ovino vellere lupinam rapacitatem palliantes, post ad regem simplici intuitu, vultu demisso, sermone blando pervenientes, licentiam per regnum vagandi postulabant, auxilium ad opus domini Papæ caritatem petituri, nullam se cohertionem facturos asserentes. Ex licentia igitur domini regis, nihil sinistri super his meditantis, dicti fratres a cura regis, jam legati sophistici donis clericorum regalium superbientes, nobiles mannos obsidentes, sellis deauratis falerati, pretiosissimis vestibus adornati calceamentisque militaribus, quæ vulgariter *heuses* dicuntur, sæculariter, immo potius prodigialiter, calciati et calcarati, in læsionem et obprobrium ordinis et professionis suæ, profecti sunt, officio et tirannide fungentes legatorum, et procurationes exigentes et extorquentes xx. solidos pro procuratione parvum reputarunt." See also Vaughan, *Illustrated Chronicles*, 8–9 for an English translation.

24. Vaughan, *Illustrated Chronicles*, 9. *Chronica Majora*, IV, 600: "Eisdemque diebus, dominus Papa apices suos autenticos per sollempnes nuntios Prædicatores et Minores misit ad omnes Franciæ prælatos singillatim, supplicans ut unusquisque juxta suam possibilitatem sibi unam quantitatem pecuniæ accommodaret; et ipse proculdubio cum respiraret, quod cuilibet competeret, redderet indubitanter. Quod cum regi Francorum innotuisset, suspectam habens Romanæ curiæ avaritiam, prohibuit ne quis prælatus regni sui sub poena amissionis omnium bonorum suorum taliter terram suam depauperaret. Et sic cum sibilo et derisione omnium Papales legati sophistici, quorum humeris hoc officium incumbebat, inanes et vacui a regno recesserunt memorato."

25. Vaughan, *Illustrated Chronicles*, ix. For a further study of how the friars are portrayed in Matthew's work, see Williel R. Thomson, "The Image of the Mendicants in the Chronicles of Matthew Paris," *Archivum Franciscanum Historicum* 70 (1977): 3–34. On the importance of the Benedictines as guardians of tradition in Matthew's thinking, see Björn Weiler, "Matthew Paris and Europe," 23–24. See also Damien

Bocquet, "Un idéal de théocratie monastique au XIIIe siècle: Mathieu Paris, *Chronica Majora*, 1235–1259," *Revue Mabillon* NS 6 (1995): 83–100.

26. See Thomson, "The Image of the Mendicants," 18 and *n*1. See also 28.

27. Ibid., 24.

28. *Chronica Majora*, IV, 511–12: "Eodemque tempore, Fratres Prædicatores, limites paupertatis, quam professi sunt et nuper, [transcendentes], [jam ad superos gradus ascendere, venerari, et timeri a prælatis ecclesiasticis affectabant, et non jam tantum Prædicatores sed etiam esse confessores contendebant, usurpantes sibi officium ordinariorum, et haberi eosdem contemptui procurantes, quasi scientia et potestate insufficientes populum Dei regere et ecclesiae lora moderari. Unde multis discretis videbantur ordinem universalis ecclesiae, per sanctos Apostolos et sacros doctores nostros antecessores, de quorum sanctitate toti mundo constat, sancitum, nimis enormiter perturbare. Testificatum est etiam, quod ordo Sancti Benedicti vel ordo beati Augustini per multorum spatium sæculorum tantum non deliravit, quantum eorum, qui nondum in Anglia per triginta annorum spatium radicum propagines transplantavit]. Impetrato igitur a Papa Gregorio, qui specialiter eorum fautor erat, paucis evolutis annis inaudito privilegio, hoc etiam his temporibus novum, ad primum roborandum, [non sine ordinariorum jactura et præjudicio, a domino Papa sunt adepti.]" The sections in brackets were expunged in one of the copies of the *Chronica* as part of Matthew's purge of his harsh criticisms, but reserved in another.

29. *Chronica Majora*, IV, 279–80: "Et quod terribile est et in triste præsagium, per trecentos annos vel quadringentos, vel amplius, ordo monasticus tam festinanter non cepit præcipitium, sicut eorum ordo, quorum fratres, jam vix transactis viginti quatuor annis, primas in Anglia construxere mansiones, quarum ædificia jam in regales surgunt altitudines. Hi jam sunt, qui in sumptuosis et diatim ampliatis aedificiis et celsis muralibus thesauros exponunt impreciabiles, paupertatis limites et basim suae professionis, juxta prophetiam Hyldegardis Alemanniæ, impudenter transgredientes." See also Lawrence, *The Friars*, 108–11, for a discussion of the regulations about humble dwellings in the rules of both orders, and also of the building of large preaching churches for the friars, due to generous donations from the nobility and laity.

30. *Chronica Majora*, IV, 625: "Eodem anno fratres Prædicatores impetrarunt privilegium a domino Papa, ne liceat alicui fratrum ab eorum ordine ad alium transmigrare, nee alicui abbati vel priori aliquem talem suscipere, cum tamen ipsi transfugas suscipiant monachorum. Quod videtur dissonum rationi, et regulæ sancti Benedicti contrarium, necnon et huic præcepto naturali, 'Quod tibi non vis fieri, ne feceris alii.' Cum autem multi moribus, scientia, et genere pollentes ad eorum ordinem a sæculo convolarent, neque postea talem formam religionis, qualem se invenisse sperabant, reperiebant, sed pro claustro totius mundi latitudinem, præsertim cum in principio regulæ suæ reprobat sanctus Benedictus illud genus monachorum quod girivagum est, coeperunt dolere et poenitere, quod ad talem ordinem intrassent, et subterfugia quaerere contraria. Propter quod in eorum ordine majores censebantur, qui medium procurarunt moderatum." English translation, Vaughan, *Illustrated Chronicles*, 26.

31. *Chronica Majora*, IV, 604: "Per idem quoque tempus, propter scandalum indecenter per diversa climata ventilatum, cogentibus cardinalibus, revocatum est, quod paulo ante a domino Papa, [instigante manifesta avaritia,] fuerat constitutum, et ad quod fratres Minores, [in dampnum et scandalum ipsorum et sui ordinis læsionem,]" English translation, Vaughan, *Illustrated Chronicles*, 12. These words were also erased by Matthew in his attempt to purge his chronicle of its harshness.

32. *Chronica Majora*, IV, 612: "Utpote fratres Minores et Prædicatores, quos, ut credimus, invitos jam suos fecit dominus Papa, non sine ordinis eorum læsione et scandalo, [thelonearios et bedellos.]" English translation, Vaughan, *Illustrated Chronicles*, 18. See also *Chronica Majora*, IV, 635: "Verum non cessavit dominus Papa pecuniam aggregare tam in sua curia quam in remotis regionibus, faciens de fratribus Prædicatoribus et Minori[bu]s, etiam invitis, non jam piscatores hominum sed nummorum." For the English translation, see Vaughan, *Illustrated Chronicles*, 33–34.

33. *Chronica Majora* III, 627: "Et facti sunt eo tempore Praedicatores et Minores regum consiliarii et nuntii speciales, ut sicut quondam *mollibus* induti *in domibus regum* erant, ita tunc qui vilibus vestiebantur, in domibus, cameris, et palatiis essent principum."

34. Lawrence, *The Friars*, 221.

35. *Chronica Majora* V, 194–95: "Plurium ordinum fratres scatent, nunc Prædicatores, nunc Minores, nunc Cruciferi, nunc Carmelani. In Alemannia autem mulierum continentium, quæ se Beguinas volunt appellari, multitudo surrexit innumerabilis, adeo ut solam Coloniam mille vel plures inhabitarent. Prædicatores vero et Minores, primo vitam pauperem et sanctissimam deducentes, prædicationibus, confessionibus, divinis in ecclesia obsequiis, lectionibus, et studiis penitus intendebant, paupertatem voluntariam pro Deo, relictis multis reddituibus, amplectentes, nihil in victualibus usque in crastinum sibi reservantes; sed infra paucos annos sese sollicite instaurabant, ædificia sumptuosa nimis construentes; Papa insuper de ipsis licet invitis suos fecit thelonearios, et multiformes pecuniarum exactores, ..." English translation in Vaughan, *Illustrated Chronicles*, 201.

36. Vaughan, *Matthew Paris*, 153–54. He notes at 154 that "it is indeed extraordinary that the *Chronica Majora*, the fullest and most detailed of all medieval English chronicles, was virtually unknown outside St Albans during the latter part of the Middle Ages."

37. See William Chester Jordan, "The Anger of the Abbots in the Thirteenth Century," *The Catholic Historical Review* 96, 2 (2010): 219–233, for a good overview of how abbots fought back against lay rulers, bishops, and friars who encroached on their privileges, often with limited success.

38. Vaughan, *Matthew Paris*, 152–54.

39. Szittya, *Antifraternal Tradition*, 101. He notes several incidences of outbreaks of conflict in England, in areas such as Bristol, Scarborough, St. Alban's, and Bury St. Edmunds, among others. See 102–03, *n*85, for a listing of monastic chronicles detailing monk-friar hostilities. See also David Knowles, *The Religious Orders in England*, vol. 2 (Cambridge: Cambridge University Press, 1955, rep. 1979), 61–73.

40. See Joan Greatrex, "Monks and Mendicants in English Cathedral Cities: Signs of a Mutual Benefit Society?" *The Friars in Medieval Britain: Proceedings of the 2007 Harlaxton Symposium*, Harlaxton Medieval Studies 19, Nicholas Rogers, ed. (Donington, UK: Shaun Tyas, 2010), 97–106.

41. Ralph Hanna and Sarah

Wood, "Mendicants and the Economies of Piers Plowman," *The Friars in Medieval Britain*, 231–32; they also show how Alice may have served as a model for Lady Meed in *Piers Plowman*. For the account, see *The St Albans Chronicle, Volume I 1376–1394: The Chronica Maiora of Thomas Walsingham*, John Taylor, Wendy R. Childs, and Leslie Watkiss, eds. and trans. (Oxford: Clarendon Press, 2003), 47–49.

42. See Hannah and Wood, "Mendicants and the Economies," 228–29, for a listing of the English kings and nobles who made use of the friars' counsel in the 14th century.

43. Lawrence, *The Friars*, 131.

44. For a classic study, see A. G. Little, "The Franciscan School at Oxford in the Thirteenth Century," *Archivum Franciscanum Historicum* 19 (1926): 803–74.

45. Lawrence, *The Friars*, 131.

46. Works on Grosseteste are numerous. Some introductory studies include James McEvoy, *Robert Grosseteste* (Oxford: Oxford University Press, 2000), especially 51–61 for his relations with the friars. See also McEvoy, *The Philosophy of Robert Grosseteste* (Oxford: Clarendon Press, 1992), and R. W. Southern, *Robert Grosseteste: The Growth of an English Mind in Medieval Europe* (Oxford: Clarendon Press, 1986). See also the collection *Robert Grosseteste: Scholar and Bishop, Essays in Commemoration of the Seventh Centenary of his Death*, D. A. Callus, ed. (Oxford: Clarendon Press, 1955). For an excellent English translation of his letters, see *The Letters of Robert Grosseteste, Bishop of Lincoln*, Frank Anthony, Carl Mantello and Joseph Goering, eds. and trans. (Toronto: University of Toronto Press, 2010). For Grosseteste's relationship to the friars, see Gordon Plumb, "Robert Grosseteste and the Early English Franciscans," available online at: http://www.tssf.org.uk/study-and-prayer-papers/study-week-papers/302-robert-grosseteste-and-the-early-english-franciscans, accessed January 4, 2014. For a study of some of Grosseteste's scientific works (which also includes an excellent biography in chapter 2), see Matthew F. Dowd, *Astronomy and Compotus at Oxford University in the Early Thirteenth Century: The Works of Robert Grosseteste*, unpublished Ph.D., University of Notre Dame, 2003, available at: http://www3.nd.edu/~mdowd1/dowddissertation.html, accessed January 4, 2014.

47. James McEvoy summarizes in *Robert Grosseteste*, 53–54. He gives various anecdotes about their warm relations at 59–61.

48. G.R. Evans, *The University of Oxford, A New History* (London: I.B. Taurus, 2010), 79.

49. Leff, *Paris and Oxford Universities*, 76–77.

50. See ibid., 76–78, for a short summary. For a more detailed study, see R.W. Southern, "From Schools to University," *The History of the University of Oxford: Vol. 1, The Early Oxford Schools*, J.I. Catto, ed., (Oxford: Oxford University Press, 1984), 1–36. Evans also summarizes in *The University of Oxford*, 79–84.

51. Leff, *Paris and Oxford Universities*, 78–79. For much more detail, see M.B. Hackett, "The University as a Corporate Body," *The History of the University of Oxford: Vol. 1*, 37–95. See also Evans, *The University of Oxford*, 84–88.

52. Leff, *Paris and Oxford Universities*, 81. See also 75–76.

53. Ibid., 93.

54. See ibid., 82–97 for a comprehensive study. One does get the sense that the citizens of Oxford were treated very unfairly, as nearly every resolution to a conflict went against them. See 85–85, for a discussion of the unbreakable hold that the university had over the city. See also Evans, *The University of Oxford*, 111–12. Clerks were almost immune from prosecution, and could not even be held under arrest by bailiffs, but had to be returned to the university, which would decide its own punishment, if any. Burgesses fought back by attempting to cheat the university on goods, pricing, etc., but this had limited success.

55. See Lawrence, *The Friars*, 85 and 133, for notes about how the Dominicans grudgingly accepted the study of Aristotle and pagan philosophy as necessary to engage in scholastic debate, but did not wish to dwell on them.

56. Leff, *Paris and Oxford University*, 104. See also Lawrence, *The Friars* 134–35. This action may have been undertaken in imitation of the hard line that the secular masters of Paris had enacted at the same time.

57. For a study of Thomas' relation to the Parisian conflict, see Andrew G. Traver, "Thomas of York's Role in the Conflict between Mendicants and Seculars at Paris," *Franciscan Studies* 59 (1999): 179–202. For Thomas' letters with Franciscan master Adam Marsh (which reveal much biographical material), see *Epistolae in Monumenta Franciscana in Rerum Brittanicarum medii aevi scriptores*, ed. J. S. Brewer (London: Rolls Series, 1858) 4, 1: 75–489.

58. Szittya, *Antifraternal Tradition*, 194. An edition of the poem and another with a university setting is in A.G. Rigg, "Two Latin Poems Against the Friars," *Mediaeval Studies* 30 (1968): 106–18.

59. Evans, *The University of Oxford*, 94. See also William Page, ed., *The Victoria History of the County of Oxford*, vol. 2 (London: Archibald Constable, 1907), 110, for a listing of the other friars embroiled in the conflict. For a full account in Latin, see Andrew G. Little, Appendix C: "Controversy Between the Friars Preachers and Friars Minors at Oxford, A.D. 1269," *The Grey Friars in Oxford: Part I: A History of Convent*, and *Part II: Biographical Notices of the Friars*, (Oxford: Clarendon Press, 1892), 320–35. Solomon's charge is at 321: "Ex verbis tuis sic arguo: vos de non recipiendo peccuniam votum fecistis hec est major; assumo—et recepistis; ac concludo; ergo vos estis in statu dampnacionis."

60. See Leff, *Paris and Oxford Universities*, 208–09, and 300–01, for brief summaries.

61. On this doctrine, see Christopher Brown, *Aquinas and the Ship of Theseus: Solving Puzzles about Material Objects* (London: Continuum, 2005), 83–87.

62. G.R. Evans, *The University of Oxford*, 96.

63. An excellent summary of Kilwardby's life is online at Simon Tugwell, "Robert Kilwardby," *Oxford Dictionary of National Biography*, http://www.oxforddnb.com/view/printable/15546, accessed January 5, 2014. For more detailed surveys of the Condemnations, see L.E. Wilshire, "Where the Oxford Condemnations of 1277 directed against Aquinas?" *The New Scholasticism* 48 (1964): 125–32, and Wilshire, "The Condemnations of 1277 and the Intellectual Climate of the Medieval University," *The Intellectual Climate of the Early University: Essays in Honor of Otto Gründler*, N. van Deusen, ed., (Kalamazoo: Western Michigan University, 1997), 151–93, as well as J.F. Wippel, "The Condemnations of 1270 and 1277 at Paris," The Journal of Medieval and Renaissance Studies 7, 2 (1977): 169–201. See also Leff, *Paris and Oxford Universities*, 290–93.

64. Fort a brief survey, see William Abel Pantin, *The English Church in the Fourteenth Century, Based on the Birkbeck Lectures, 1948* (Cambridge: Cambridge University Press, 1955, reprinted 2010), 140–50.

65. Leff, *Paris and Oxford University*, 105. See 103–06 for a full

summary. See also Hastings Rashdall, "The Friars Preachers and the University," *Collectanea* II, M. Burrows, ed. (Oxford: Oxford Historical Society, 1890), 217–273, though as Leff notes, Rashdall perhaps overstates the importance of this conflict, trying to put it on par with those Paris. A conflict arose at Cambridge University in the same year, involving changes to the statutes, see A. G. Little, "The Friars v. The University of Cambridge," *The English Historical Review* 50, 200 (1935): 686–96.

66. Leff, *Paris and Oxford University*, 105. See also Evans, *The University of Oxford*, 113, and Evans, *John Wyclif, Myth and Reality* (Downers Grove, IL: IVP Academic, 2005), 106–113. The *Libri Quattuor Sententiarum* ("The Four Books of Sentences") was a theological compendium by Peter Lombard, written around 1150. It was a systematic organization of the glosses and commentary on biblical passages, which became a standard reference for 13th-century theology students. For a recent study, see Philipp W. Rosemann, *The Story of a Great Medieval Book: Peter Lombard's "Sentences"* (Toronto: University of Toronto Press, 2007). A good summary can also be found in Thomas M. Finn, "The Sacramental World in the Sentences of Peter Lombard," *Theological Studies* 68 (2008): 557–82. For a modern translation, see Peter Lombard, *The Sentences*, 4 vols., Giulio Silano, trans., Mediaeval Sources in Translation 42–43, 45, and 48 (Toronto: Pontifical Institute of Medieval Studies, 2007–2010). For the original text, see Magistri Petri Lombardi, *Sententiae in IV libris distinctae*, Ignatius Brady, O.F.M., ed., 2 vols., Spicilegium Bonaventurianum 4 and 5 (Grottaferrata [Rome]: Editiones Collegii S. Bonaventurae ad Claras Aquas, 1971–1981).

67. Leff, *Paris and Oxford University*, 105–06, and see also 175.

68. For a good summary, see M. D. Lambert, *Franciscan Poverty: The Doctrine of the Absolute Poverty of Christ and the Apostles in the Franciscan Order, 1210–1323*, revised edition (St. Bonaventure, NY: Franciscan Institute Publications, 1998), 208–46. For several studies of John XXII and the friars, see chapter 1, *n*147.

69. Szittya, *Antifraternal Tradition*, 80–81. For more on Jean, see J.G. Sikes, "Jean de Pouilly and Peter de la Palu," *English Historical Review* 49 (1934): 219–40. See also Katherine Walsh, *Fourteenth-Century Scholar and Primate*, 356–57. For a general background, see Michael J. Haren, "Friars as Confessors: The Canonist Background to the Fourteenth-Century Controversy," *Peritia* 3 (1984): 503–16.

70. See Clopper, *Songes of Rechelesnesse*, 29, 32, and 52–53. For the Latin text of the bull online, see *Papal Encyclicals Online*: http://www.papalencyclicals.net/Clem05/exivi-l.htm. For an English translation, see the Franciscan Archive: http://www.franciscan-archive.org/bullarium/exivi-e.html, accessed February 2, 2014.

71. See Clopper, *Songes of Rechelesnesse*, 54–55.

72. Two later Spirituals were burned at the stake in Avignon in 1354 for declaring the same thing, see ibid., 54–55. See also Patrick Nold, "Two Views of John XXII as a Heretical Pope," *Defenders and Critics of Franciscan Life*, 139–58.

73. Space prohibits a detailed examination of this event, but see Gordon Leff, *Heresy in the Later Middle Ages*, 238–55. See also Decima L. Douie, *The Nature and Effect of the Heresy of the Fratricelli* (Manchester: Manchester University Press, 1932), 153–208. Ockham came to believe that John was a heretic, see *William of Ockham: A Letter to the Friars Minor and Other Writings*, Arthur Stephen McGrade, ed., and John Kilcullen, trans. (Cambridge: Cambridge University Press, 1995), 3–15. On Cesena's troubles, see G. Knysh, "Biographical Rectifications in Ockham's Avignon Period," *Franciscan Studies* 46 (1986): 61–91. William of Ockham is a fascinating and complex figure, best known for his philosophy of Nominalism. Biographies and studies of his philosophy are practically countless. A good recent introduction is Rondo Keele, *Ockham Explained: From Razor to Rebellion* (Chicago and La Salle: Open Court Publishing, 2010). See also *The Cambridge Companion to Ockham*, Paul Spade, ed. (Cambridge: Cambridge University Press, 1999). For a comprehensive bibliography of 20th-century studies, see Jan Beckmann, *Ockham-Bibliographie, 1900–1990* (Hamburg: Verlag, 1992). For a recent study on his decision to throw in his lot with the rebels, see A.S. McGrade, "William of Ockham and Augustinus de Ancona on the Righteousness of Dissent," *Franciscan Studies* 54 (1994): 143–65. Another excellent resource, with a biography and summary of his major writings, as well as a large bibliography, is the William of Ockham page at the Stanford Encyclopedia of Philosophy: www.plato.stanford.edu/entries/ockham, accessed January 5, 2014.

74. See Gedeon Gál, "William of Ockham Died Impenitent in April 1347," *Franciscan Studies* 42 (1982): 90–95.

75. Szittya includes a study of the manuscripts in *Antifraternal Tradition*, 63–67, with a full listing of the English manuscripts at 64, *n*4. He offers an exhaustive study of the contents of these at 62–122, an excellent resource for further study. Oxford University had a series of conflicts with the friars in the 1350s, see Andrew Larsen, "The Oxford 'School of Heretics': the Unexamined Case of Friar John," *Vivarium* 37, 2 (1999): 168–77.

76. Szittya is of the opinion in *Antifraternal Tradition*, 66, that such works were more widely circulated than it might seem from the manuscript evidence, owing to the lack of documentation of the contents of manuscripts that were compendiums of multiple works. Given that *De Periculis* was also still under papal condemnation, it might have been read more quietly, the way that any banned book would be, which simply enhanced its appeal.

77. See Szittya, *Antifraternal Tradition*, 9.

78. Walsh, *Fourteenth-Century Scholar*, 407–08. See 407, *n*4, for the manuscript source of the bill.

79. Szittya, *Antifraternal Tradition*, 111.

80. For a detailed account of the conflict, see David Knowles, "The Censured Opinions of Uthred of Boldon," *David Knowles, The Historian and Character: And Other Essays* (Cambridge: Cambridge University Press, 1963, reprinted 2008), 129–70. See also D.H. Farmer, "New Light on Uthred of Boldon," *Benedictines in Oxford*, Henry Wansbrough and Anthony Marett-Crosby, eds. (London: Darton, Longman and Todd, 1997), 116–32, and Geoffrey L. Dipple, "Uthred and the Friars: Apostolic Poverty and Clerical Dominion between Fitzralph and Wyclif," *Traditio* 49 (1994): 235–258. See also Szittya, *Antifraternal Tradition*, 108–111.

81. Szittya, *Antifraternal Tradition*, 68 and 112. He offers a detailed analysis of the manuscript's contents at 67–99. The manuscript is British Library MS Royal 6 E. VI and 6 E. VII. More recently, Szittya has written an article about the manuscript with some splendid examples of the artwork from the manuscript, see Szittya, "Kicking the Habit: the Campaign against the Friars in a Fourteenth-Century Encyclopedia," *Defenders and Critics of Franciscan Life*, 159–75.

82. Szittya, *Antifraternal Tradition*, 69.

83. For a survey of Jean's work in *Omne Bonum*, see ibid., 81–93, especially 91–92, for his solution to the Franciscan problem. For an early study of Jean, see Henry Martin, "La diatribe de Jean d'Anneaux," *Mélanges offerts à M. Émile Picot II* (Paris: Librarie Damascène Morgand, 1913) 225–40.

84. Szittya, *Antifraternal Tradition*, 93–99.

85. Ibid., 62–63 and 121–22. For an edition of the text, see *The Register of John de Grandisson, Bishop of Exeter (A.D. 1327–69)*, F.C. Hingeston-Randolph, ed. (London: George Bill, 1894–99), II, 1197–98. See also Clopper, *Songes of Rechelesnesse*, 44.

86. The definitive biography of FitzRalph, including much on his quarrel with the friars is Katherine Walsh, *A Fourteenth-Century Scholar and Primate: Richard FitzRalph in Oxford, Avignon, and Armagh*. This work is indispensable in the study of FitzRalph, and while detailed and scholarly, still serves as the best thorough introduction, hindered only by a slight tendency to limited and confusing citation. See also her "Archbishop FitzRalph and the Friars at the Papal Court in Avignon, 1357–60," *Traditio* 31 (1975): 223–245. A recent useful collection of essays on various topics is *Richard FitzRalph: His Life, Times and Thought*, Michael W. Dunne and Simon Nolan, eds. (Dublin: Four Courts Press, 2013). For studies of his conflicts with the friars, see Michael J. Haren, "Richard FitzRalph and the Friars: The Intellectual Itinerary of a Curial Controversialist," *Roma, magistra mundi. Itineraria culturae medievalis. Mélanges offerts au Père L.E. Boyle à l'occasion de son 75e anniversaire*, 3 vols., Jacqueline Hamesse, ed. (Louvain-la-Neuve: Fédération des Instituts d'Etudes Médiévales, 1998), I, 349–367; James Doyne Dawson, "Richard FitzRalph and the Fourteenth-Century Poverty Controversies," *Journal of Ecclesiastical History* 34, 3 (1983): 315–44; and L.L. Hammerich, "The Beginning of the Strife between Richard FitzRalph and the Mendicants, with an edition of his autobiographical prayer and his proposition Unusquisque," *Det Kgl. Danske Viderskabernes Selskab / Historisk-filologiske Meddelelser* 26 (Copenhagen: Levin and Munksgaard, 1938), 3–85. For a detailed survey of mendicant responses to his charges, see Walsh, "The 'De Vita Evangelica' of Geoffrey Hardeby, O.E.S.A. (c. 1320-c. 1385). A Study in the Mendicant Controversies of the Fourteenth Century," *Analecta Augustiniana* 33 (1970): 151–261, and 34 (1971): 5–83. See also Szittya, *Antifraternal Tradition*, 123–151, for a useful summary of his main points of attack. FitzRalph's writings are surprisingly not well served in modern editions, either in Latin or in translation. His opening shot at the friars, the *Unusquisque*, is available in Hammerich, "The Beginning of the Strife," 53–73. The first four books of his *De Pauperie Salvatoris* (there were eight in total) are in John Wycliff, *De dominio divino*, R. L. Poole, ed. (London: Trübner for the Wyclif Society, 1890), 257–476. The next three books (which deal more with the friars) are available in Russell O. Brock, Jr., "An Edition of Richard FitzRalph's *De Pauperie Salvatoris*, Books V, VI, and VII," Ph.D. dissertation, University of Colorado, 1953. Walsh provides a comprehensive listing of manuscripts in *A Fourteenth-Century Scholar*, 476–79. See also her Appendix, 469–75, for a study on how FitzRalph's writings circulated in the 14th and 15th centuries. I have not had the opportunity to view these manuscripts, and so am relying on Walsh and Szittya for their excellent summaries.

87. Walsh notes, with sarcasm, in *Fourteenth-Century Scholar*, "Then as now, original spirits in an academic community were rarely to be found in high administrative positions, and we may take the election as chancellor in 1335 of the powerfully-connected Robert de Stratford while still a student of theology as an indication that qualifications other than seniority in the academic hierarchy were regarded as necessary for the position," 71.

88. See ibid., 72–84, for a detailed study of the issues.

89. Ibid., 108.

90. For an early study of the Sermon Diary, see Aubrey Gwynn, "The Sermon-Diary of Richard Fitzralph, Archbishop of Armagh," *Proceedings of the Royal Irish Academy. Section C: Archaeology, Celtic Studies, History, Linguistics, Literature* 44 (1937/1938): 1–57. See also Walsh, *Fourteenth-Century Scholar*, 182–87 for an overview of the sermon diary, and the contents.

91. Szittya, *Antifraternal Tradition*, 124.

92. Based on I Cor., 7:24, *Vulgata*, 1112: "Unusquisque in quo vocatus est, fratres in hoc maneat apud Deum," "In whatever condition each was called, brothers, let him remain there with God."

93. Szittya, *Antifraternal Tradition*, 124. See also Hammerich, "The Beginning of the Strife."

94. Szittya, *Antifraternal Tradition*, 125. See also Walsh, *Fourteenth-Century Scholar*, 358–59.

95. Walsh, *Fourteenth-Century Scholar*, 349.

96. Walsh examines the subject in detail in *ibid.*, 349–65. She notes at 365 that by 1345, he probably had serious concerns about certain of the friars' practices, having seen first-hand issues about confession and absolution (as well as possible abuses of privilege) in Ireland and elsewhere.

97. On questions about the dating of this commission, see ibid., 365–66, and 386. It had been previously thought that the commission only came after FitzRalph's antifraternal sermon of 1350, but Walsh argues convincingly that it was indeed in 1349, and was one of the causes of, rather than a result of, his appeal.

98. ibid., 359–60. See also Knowles, *Religious Orders in England*, 11–12, for examples of the depopulation in England. See Erickson, "Fourteenth-Century Franciscans," *Franciscan Studies* 35, 115, *n*29, for observations about Franciscan losses during the plague and the foundation of new houses afterward. See also Szittya, *Antifraternal Tradition*, 223–24 for actual numbers of losses.

99. Walsh, *Fourteenth-Century Scholar*, 8 and 360. These include FitzRalph, a Cistercian monk named Henry Crumpe, John Whitehead (who opposed both Wyclif and the friars), and Philip Norreys, the Dean of St. Patrick's Cathedral in Dublin. See also *A Biographical Register of the University of Oxford to A.D. 1500*, Alfred B. Emden, ed., 3 vols. (Oxford: Clarendon Press, 1957–59), 524–25, III, 2037.

100. Clopper, *Songes of Rechelesnesse*, 58–59.

101. Walsh, *Fourteenth-Century Scholar*, 350–53.

102. Ibid., 364. See also 401.

103. Ibid., 372–74, including a specific example at 374.

104. Hammerich, "The Beginning of the Strife," 57, ll. 110–12. See also Walsh, *A Fourteenth Century Scholar*, 369.

105. Hammerich, "The Beginning of the Strife," 58, ll. 129–31.

106. Ibid., 59, ll. 147–57. However, see also Walsh, *Fourteenth-Century Scholar*, 370, and *n*67, as well as 371, *n*68.

107. Walsh, *Fourteenth-Century Scholar*, 371.

108. Recalling an incident in *Piers Plowman*, wherein the friar offers Lady Lucre absolution in exchange for some wheat, though

saying that she would have done even better if she had donated a beautiful stained glass window, see chapter 7, and Walsh, *Fourteenth-Century Scholar*, 371, n69.

109. Ibid., 375.

110. Ibid., 394.

111. Ibid., 394.

112. For an edition, see *Aegidius Romanus, De ecclesiatica potestate*, Richard Scholz, ed. (Weimar: Hermann Bölaus, 1929). For a modern English edition, see *Giles of Rome on ecclesiastical power: The De ecclesiastica potestate of Aegidius Romanus*, R.W. Dyson, trans. (Woodbridge: Boydell, 1986).

113. For detailed study, see Aubrey Gwynn, *The English Austin Friars at the Time of Wyclif* (Oxford: Oxford University Press, 1940), 35–73, particularly 66–67. See also Walsh, *Fourteenth-Century Scholar*, 381–84.

114. Ibid., 385.

115. For a summary of the works books see ibid., 390–406. FitzRalph went to some length to distinguish between such concepts as dominion, property, possession, right of use, etc. See 391.

116. Walsh, *Fourteenth-Century Scholar*, 395, and 397–98.

117. Evans, *John Wyclif*, 155.

118. Ibid., 395–96, and 398, "He [FitzRalph] considered the position of the prelates in the Church, who had possessions without being personally wealthy, as they held these goods in their capacity as ministers of the Church for the benefit of the poor. Consequently, these goods were intended only as a means of fulfilling their obligations in charity."

119. James Doyne Dawson, "Richard FitzRalph and the Fourteenth-Century Poverty Controversies," 333.

120. Ibid., 399.

121. Ibid., 403.

122. Ibid., 404–05.

123. The sermons are recorded in manuscripts held at Sidney Sussex College, Cambridge, as well as the British Library and Lambeth Palace, among others. See Szittya, *Antifraternal Tradition*, 127, n15, for a complete list. I have relied on Szittya's excellent summaries, as I have not had the opportunity to view these manuscripts.

124. Walsh, *Fourteenth-Century Scholar*, 388.

125. Szittya provides more detailed summaries of these three sermons in *Antifraternal Tradition*, 127–28.

126. Ibid., 128.

127. Drawn from Eph. 5:6, *Vulgata*, 1136: "Nemo vos seducat inanibus verbis propter haec enim venit ira Dei in filios diffidentiae,"

128. Szittya, *Antifraternal Tradition*, 129. See also Terence Dolan, "The Rhetoric of Richard FitzRalph's *Defensio curatorum*," *Richard FitzRalph: His Life, Times and Thought*, 100.

129. Ibid., 129, drawing from Walsh, *Fourteenth-Century Scholar*, 469, who identified 84 copies. She also notes that it was translated into English by John of Trevisa (1326–1402), and also circulated in printed form during the Reformation. For an edition of the Middle English text, see *Dialogus inter Militem et Clericum. Richard FitzRalph's Sermon: "Defensio Curatorum," and Methodius: "þe Bygynnyng of þe World and þe End of Worldes" by John Trevisa*, Aaron Jenkins Perry, ed. (London: Early English text Society, Oxford University Press, 1925). Though printed in the 17th century, in Melchior Goldast's *Monarchia sacri Romani imperii*, 3 vols. (Hanover and Frankfurt, 1612–1614), there is as yet no modern edition. For a biography, see David C. Fowler, *The Life and Times of John Trevisa* (Seattle: University of Washington Press, 1995).

130. Walsh, *Fourteenth-Century Scholar*, 406.

131. Szittya, *Antifraternal Tradition*, 129–30.

132. Terence Dolan, "The Rhetoric of Richard FitzRalph's *Defensio curatorum*," 99.

133. Szittya, *Antifraternal Tradition*, 130.

134. Walsh, in *Fourteenth-Century Scholar*, offers a detailed analysis of the Avignon debates at 406–51.

135. See ibid., 449–50, for some consideration. The friars by then were a part of the Church, even if not an original part of it. Their abolition was thus highly unlikely.

136. Szittya provides an excellent summary of the biblical content of some of his sermons in *Antifraternal Tradition*, 131–51.

137. Evans, *John Wyclif, Myth and Reality*, 15. This is a good study, serving as an introduction to the man and his times. As with so many of these topics, Wyclif studies are numerous. A useful short introduction is Anthony Kenny, *Wyclif* (Oxford: Oxford University Press, 1985), as well as *Wyclif in his Times*, Kenny, ed. (Oxford: Clarendon Press, 1986). See also J.I. Catto, "Wyclif and Wycliffism in Oxford, 1356–1430," *The History of the University of Oxford II: Late Medieval England*, Catto and Ralph Evans, eds. (Oxford: Clarendon Press, 1992), 175–261. A good collection of essays is *A Companion to John Wyclif, Late Medieval Theologian*, Ian Christopher Levy, ed. (Leiden, Boston: Brill, 2006). For Wyclif's philosophy, see Stephen E. Lahey, *John Wyclif* (Oxford: Oxford University Press, 2009), as well as Lahey, *Philosophy and Politics in the Thought of John Wyclif* (Cambridge: Cambridge University Press, 2003). For Wyclif's writings on the concept of dominion, see Elemér Boreczky, *John Wyclif's Discourse on Dominion in Community* (Leiden and Boston: Brill, 2008), and Michael Wilks, "Predestination, Property, and Power: Wyclif's Theory of Dominion and Grace," *Studies in Church History* 2 (1965): 220–36. For the charges of heresy, see Kantik Ghosh, *The Wycliffite Heresy: Authority and the Interpretation of Texts* (Cambridge: Cambridge University Press, 2004), and Gordon Leff, *Heresy in the Later Middle Ages*, 494–573. For a study of Wyclif as a precursor to later religious thought in England, see Anne Hudson, *The Premature Reformation: Wycliffite Texts and Lollard History* (Oxford: Clarendon Press, 1988). For a study of Wyclif's views on sin in his sermons, both among the laity, as well as in the Church and among the friars, see Katherine C. Little, "Catechesis and Castigation: Sin in the Wycliffite Sermon Cycle," *Traditio* 54 (1999): 213–244. For his negative views on war, and the role of the friars in preaching the crusades, see Ian Christopher Levy, "John Wyclif: Christian Patience in a Time of War," *Theological Studies* 66 (2005): 330–57. For details of Wyclif's conflicts with the Church, see K.B. McFarlane, *John Wycliffe and the Beginnings of English Nonconformity* (New York: Macmillan, 1953), republished as *The Origins of Religious Dissent in England* (New York: Collier Books, 1966); Joseph H. Dahmus, *The Prosecution of John Wyclif* (New Haven: Yale University Press, 1952); and J.A. Robson, *Wyclif and the Oxford Schools: The Relation of the "Summa de Ente" to Scholastic Debates at Oxford in the Later Fourteenth Century* (Cambridge: Cambridge University Press, 1961). For a comprehensive online bibliography and summary of his teachings, see the Stanford Encyclopedia of Philosophy entry at: http://plato.stanford.edu/entries/wyclif/, accessed January 9, 2014. For a more general study of the seculars and friars during Wyclif's time, see Arnold Williams, "Relations between the Mendicant Friars and the Regular Clergy in England in the Later Four-

teenth Century," *Annuale mediaevale* 1 (1960): 22–95.

138. One is tempted to ask: "What else is new?"

139. Evans, *John Wyclif*, 25–26. A more detailed account can be read online by Carol M. Miller, "The St. Scholastica Day Riot Oxford after the Black Death": http://organizations.ju.edu/fch/1993miller.htm, accessed January 9, 2014. See also W. A. Pantin, "The St. Scholastics Day's Riot," *Oxford Life in Oxford Archives* (Oxford: Clarendon Press, 1972), 99–106.

140. Evans summarizes in *John Wyclif*, 92–95. His time there was not without some controversy. See also Kenny, *Wyclif*, 42–43.

141. Evans, *John Wyclif*, 104–06.

142. For a detailed summary of Ockhamism, see Leff, *Paris and Oxford Universities*, 240–55.

143. For a summary, see Anthony Kenny, *Wyclif*, 8–17. For a more detailed study, including Wyclif's time at the university, see Robson, *Wyclif and the Oxford Schools*, available from 2008 as a print-on-demand book: http://www.cambridge.org/us/academic/subjects/history/british-history-general-interest/wyclif-and-oxford-schools-relation-summa-de-ente-scholastic-debates-oxford-later-fourteenth-century.

144. Evans, *John Wyclif*, 135.

145. Kenny, *Wyclif*, 43–45. See also Evans, *John Wyclif*, 156–57. For an edition, see *De civili dominio*, R. L. Poole, J. Loserth, and F. D. Matthew, eds., 4 vols. (London: Trübner, 1895–1904). For select translations, see *The Cambridge Translation of Medieval Philosophical Texts*, A. S. McGrade, J. Kilcullen, and M. Kemoshail, eds., vol. 2: Ethics and Political Philosophy, (Cambridge: Cambridge University Press, 2000).

146. Kenny, *Wyclif*, 46. See also Evans, *John Wyclif*, 157.

147. *De civili dominio*, 96: "Ergo omnis homo debet esse dominus universitatis: quod non staret cum multitudine hominum, nisi omnes illi deberent habere omnia in communi; ergo omnia debent esse communia."

148. Kenny, *Wyclif*, 48–49.

149. Ibid., 49. See also 69–71 for a discussion of grace as it relates to his ideas of predestination.

150. *De civili dominio*, 265–66: "Ex istis videtur correlarie plane sequi quod quacunque communitate vel persona ecclesiastica habitualiter abutente diviciis, reges, principes, et domini temporales possunt legitime et valde meritorie ipsas auferre, eciam quantumcunque tradicionibis humanis eis fuerint confirmate."

151. *De civili dominio*, 340: "Et laycis vel cuicunque communitati que hoc opus perfeccius perficeret, committeretur procuratorium ad recipiendum, conservandum, et distribuendum bona pauperum de decimis et oblacionibus laicorum."

152. *De ecclesia*, J. Loserth and F. D. Matthew, eds. (London: Trübner, 1886), 31–31: "Ex quibus videtur mihi quod nullus Romanus pontifex cui non sit facta specialis revelacio assereret vel opinaretur quod subesse sibi sit de necessitate salutis cuiuslibet christiani.... Item, stat christianum habere graciam a Deo cum hoc quod non credat esse aliquem talem papam, eo quod non oportet Deum uti eo ut ministro, dando quamcunque graciam. Et per idem, stat ipsum cum aliis paribus mori in gracia sine tali recognita; quo facto foret salus facta christiano sine subieccione huiusmodi." See also Kenny, *Wyclif*, 71–72.

153. *De civili dominio*, 384: "et sic de multis blasphemiis inpossibilibus in quas possibile est ipsos incidere, declinando a religione Christi et preparando ad blasphemiam Antichristi." See also Kenny, *Wyclif*, 51–52.

154. Evans, *John Wyclif*, 227. See also Walsh, *A Fourteenth-Century Scholar*, 394.

155. Kenny, *Wyclif*, 53.

156. Ibid., 54.

157. As cardinal, Robert was hardly a saint. When the commune of Cesena rebelled against Pope Gregory XI in 1377, Robert commanded the troops to massacre its civilians, probably more than 3,000 and perhaps more than 5,000. This was an appalling action even by the standards of the time, comparable to the atrocities of the Albigensian Crusade, and it earned Robert the nickname "the butcher of Cesena."

158. Kenny, *Wyclif*, 56.

159. For studies of the Avignon papacy and the schism, see *A Companion to the Great Western Schism (1378–1417)*, Joëlle Rollo-Koster and Thomas M. Izbicki, eds.; Joëlle Rollo-Koster, *Raiding Saint Peter: Empty Sees, Violence, and the Initiation of the Great Western Schism, 1378* (Leiden: Brill, 2008); John Holland Smith, *The Great Schism, 1378* (New York: Weybright and Talley, 1970); Yves Renouard, *The Avignon Papacy, 1305–1403*, trans. Dennis Bethell (Hamden, CT: Archon Books, 1970); and Walter Ullmann, *The Origins of the Great Schism*.

160. Lawrence, *The Friars*, 223.

161. *De ecclesia*, 290: "Unde illud magnum scisma factum per Sergium monachum sicut et illud scisma quod hodie pullulat per duos pseudomonoachos cum aliis particularibus divisionibus in ecclesia causata sunt ex insaciabili affeccione cleri ad temporalia, quam nisi occasione dotacionis cesaree versimiliter non haberent."

162. Margaret Aston discusses this in "Caim's Castles: Poverty, Politics, and Disendowment," in Aston, *Faith and Fire: Popular and Unpopular Religion, 1350–1600* (London: Hambledon Press, 1993), 95–132.

163. For editions, see *De ecclesia*, cited above, *De officio regis*, R. A. Pollard and C. E. Sayle, eds. (London: Trübner, 1887); and *De potestate papae*, J. Loserth, ed. (London: Trübner, 1907). For a short summary, see Kenny, *Wyclif*, 68–79.

164. Szittya, *Antifraternal Tradition*, 155–56, and Kenny, *Wyclif*, 68.

165. *De ecclesia*, 366: "Et stat quod aliquis solempnitate, ritu et reputacione humana sit reputatus Christi vicarius, cum hoc quod sit horrendus dyabolus, ut non est incredibile de Gregorio XI. et multis ei similibus. Nam si maritavit Raymundum nepotem suum cum herede Bolonie mediantibus decimis et bonis pauperum ecclesie Anglicane, si sustentavit iuxta fastum seculi multas parentum suorum familias, si redemit dignam captivitatem fratris sui et fecerit occidi multa millia hominum pocius propter secularem questum quam propter salutem eorum per patrimonium crucifixi, si insuper catholicaverit quod secundum potestates clavium errare non poterit, nec finaliter fructuose penituerit, quis dubitat quin fuit perpetuus hereticus, nunquam caput vel membrum sancte matris ecclesie, quia secundum Augustinum in libello De Decem Cordis vir finaliter infidelis non est caput mulieris membri ecclesie?... Et in hoc iacet periculum humane dotacionis perpetue, cum sepe occasione illius cadit distribucio fertilior bonorum pauperum super membra diaboli."

166. *De potestate papae*, 149: "Ideo videtur salubris doctrina Christi, quod neque nudis verbis dicencium, quod nunc papa sit Rome, nunc quod papa sit Avinione, debemus credere, sed ipsis operibus Christo conformibus." See also Kenny, *Wyclif*, 75–76.

167. Evans, *John Wyclif*, 221 and 225.

168. Ibid., 222, and see 223.

169. Szittya, *Antifraternal Tradition*, 156. For a further summary,

see Evans, *John Wyclif*, 185–88, and Kenny, *Wyclif*, 88–89.

170. *De apostasia*, Michael Henry Dziewicki, ed. (London: Trübner, 1889), 155: "Unde, quia quilibet habet istius erroris opinionem propriam de sacramento quod ut sic est signum sensibile, signanter dicitur quod 'posuerunt signa *sua*,' non signa ecclesie"; See also Szittya, *Antifraternal Tradition*, 156–57, and for a more thorough summary, see Kenny, *Wyclif*, 80–90.

171. Szittya, *Antifraternal Tradition*, 156. Recently, however, Stephen Lahey has questioned whether realism was at the heart of Wyclif's issues with the Eucharist, see his *John Wyclif*, 102–34.

172. Szittya, *Antifraternal Tradition*, 165. See also Margaret Aston, *Faith and Fire*, 68–69. For an edition of *Cum Marthe*, see *Corpus juris canonici*, E. Friedberg, ed. (Leipzing: Tauchnitz, 1879–81), II, cols. 636–39.

173. Szittya, *Antifraternal Tradition*, 164–65. See Wyclif's *Cruciata, Polemical Works in Latin*, Rudolf Buddenseig, ed., 2 vols. (London: Trübner, 1883), II, 623–24: "Tempore autem Innocencii tercii, circa quod tempus sathanas est solutus et fratres intraverant, modificata fuit confessio ab illo Innocencio, quod foret auricularis et abscondita, facta solidarie proprio sacerdoti, ut patet in lege super hoc edita, 'de Penitenciis et Remissionibus'capitulo 'Omnis utriusque sexus'; et tales circumstancie genuflexionis, solitudinis, auricularis taciturnitatis cum limitacione sacerdotis, quem papa voluerit, et forma imposicionis manus in capite cum multis simnilibus non sunt necessaria generaliter ad salutem, eum cordis contricio sine confessione huiusmodi sepe delet peccatum."

174. *De apostasia*, 4–5: "In oppositum videtur quod omnis vera religio consistit in animo, et per consequens est cuicunque habitui corporali inpertinens. Quis, inquam, dubitat, quin habitus mentis non dependet ab habitu corporali? Item, ut logici arguunt, aliter consumpta et inveterata foret proporcionaliter talis religio, ut contingit pannorum consumpcio; et, abiectis pannis, gracia mutacionis vel balnei, sic mutans in apostasiam incideret! Ymo cum religio servatur in pannis, moveretur cum illis; et laicus ydiota vel asinus, habitum talem indutus, fieret ut sic illius religionis vel ordinis."

175. Szittya, *Antifraternal Tradition*, 152. For additional information on Adam, see Gwynn, *English Austin Friars*, 235–39 and 253–54.

176. Kenny, *Wyclif*, 91. See also Lahey, *John Wyclif*, 226, and Szittya, *Antifraternal Tradition*, 152. For a longer summary, see Evans, *John Wyclif*, 181–92.

177. Evans, *John Wyclif*, 188. *Tractatus de blasphemia*, Michael Henry Dziewicki, ed. (London: Trübner, 1893), 89: "Sed inventa est quedam ars nova diaboli quod, displicente tractatu cuiuscunque materie fidei, et deficientibus argumentis, procuretur excommunicacio ferenda in omnes illam materiam pertractantes. Et ut factum sit coloracius, adducuntur 6 vel 7tem veritatis emuli in conclavi, et ipsi hereticant veritatem que eis displicet."

178. Kenny, *Wyclif*, 92.

179. See Boreczky, *John Wyclif's Discourse*, 286–87, for observations on how Wyclif's complicity in inciting the revolt cannot be proven, but that his increasing fame may have been detrimental to him.

180. The full text of the letter can be found in *Fasciculi Zizaniorum Magistri Johannis Wyclif cum Tritico*, Walter W. Shirley, ed. (London: Longman, Brown, Green, Longmans, and Roberts, 1858), 292–95. See also Evens, *John Wyclif*, 193.

181. Lahey, *Philosophy and Politics*, 195 and *n*80.

182. Szittya, *Antifraternal Tradition*, 152, and see 157–58 for the controversies surrounding his belief in the mysterious double nature of the sacrament. See also Kenny, *Wyclif*, 95–96.

183. Lahey, *John Wyclif*, 26. See also Leff, *Heresy in the Later Middle Ages*, 497–98, and McFarlane, *John Wycliffe and the Beginnings of English Nonconformity* (New York: Macmillan, 1952), republished as *The Origins of Religious Dissent in England* (New York: Collier Books, 1966), 97–98 and 105–08.

184. Kenny, *Wyclif*, 95–96.

185. Lahey, *John Wyclif*, 21, noting that he continued his duties as a parish priest.

186. *The English Works of John Wycliffe Hitherto Unprinted*, P.D. Matthew, ed. (London: Trübner, 1880), 8–9: "3if þei studien on þe holy day aboute experymentis or wiche craft or veyn songis and knackynge and harpynge, gyternynge & daunsynge & oþere veyn triflis to geten þe stynkyng loue of damyselis, and stere hem to worldely vanyte and synnes."

187. See chapter 7.

188. Evans, *John Wyclif*, 201.

189. Janetta Rebold Benton, *Holy Terrors: Gargoyles on Medieval Buildings* (New York: Abbeville Press, 1997), 83. For a thorough study of these fascinating carvings in English churches, see Paul Hardwick, *English Medieval Misericords: The Margins of Meaning* (Woodbridge: Boydell, 2011). See also the website "Misericords of the World": http://www.misericords.co.uk, which contains numerous color photographs, accessed January 15, 2014.

190. On Wyclif's death, see Evans, *John Wyclif*, 210–14.

191. Ibid., 200–02.

192. The *Tractatus de blasphemia*.

193. Ibid., x.

194. Kenny, *Wyclif*, 93.

195. *De blasphemia*, xix and 65.

196. Ibid.

197. Wyclif, *Trialogus cum supplemento trialogi*, G. Lechler, ed. (Oxford: Clarendon Press, 1869), 361–62. 362: "Et in testimonium istorum, quattuor literae hujus nominis *Caim* inchoant hos quattuor ordines, secundum ordinem temporis, quo finguntur a fratribus incepisse, ita quod C. Carmelitas, A. Augustinenses, J. Jacobitas et M. Minores significat, secundum ordinem temporis quem mendaciter sibi fingunt. Sed aggregando suas nequitias videtur mihi, quod licet originaliter in Caim inceperant, tamen post solutionem Sathanae et per ejus cautelam sub figura sanctitatis isti hypocritae sunt excussi."

198. *De blasphemia*, a summary is at xxxv ti xxxvii, and the full text is at 203–54.

199. *Polemical Works in Latin*, II, 409: "Pseudofrater degens in seculo est dyabolus incarnatus cum adinventis suis signis sensibilibus, desponsatus ad seminandum discordias in militante ecclesia ex summa cautela sathane machinatus."

200. Szittya, *Antifraternal Tradition*, 176. The work is found in his *Opera Minora*, Johann Loserth and F. D. Matthew, eds., Wyclif's Latin Works 9 (New York: Johnson Reprint, 1966), 15–18. See Clopper, *Songes of Rechelesnesse*, 65, for a short summary of some of Wyclif's main objections and accusations.

201. *De ordinatione fratrum*, in *Polemical Works in Latin*, I, 92: "Et idem facit Willelmus de Sancto Amore cum multis aliis, postquam fratres inceperant." See also Szittya, *Antifraternal Tradition*, 179.

202. Szittya, *Antifraternal Tradition*, 167. He summarizes Wyclif's apocalypticism in detail at 167–82.

203. Wyclif also seems to indicate that the four sects can refer to the four orders of friars; he uses the term interchangeably. See ibid., 180, *n*175. See also Evans, *John Wyclif*, 225.

204. Stephen Lahey, "Richard FitzRalph and John Wyclif: untangling Armachanus from the Wycliffites," *Richard FitzRalph: His Life, Times and Thought*, 181–84, for example, at 183, where he notes that Wyclif "is not simply antifraternal. He is antisectarian, rejecting monks, nuns and anchorites as well as the friars." For Wyclif's detailed denunciations of the sects, see his *Polemical Works in Latin*, I, 1–384.

205. Szittya, *Antifraternal Tradition*, 153, notes that Wyclif, unlike his predecessors, was not a part of the interests of the monastic orders or the secular clergy.

206. Lahey, "Richard FitzRalph and John Wyclif," 159–85. See, for example, 166–67.

207. Ibid., 159–60. See also Walsh, *Fourteenth-Century Scholar*, 378–380

208. Evans, *John Wyclif*, 27–28. See also William J. Courtenay, "The Effect of the Black Death on English Higher Education," *Speculum* 55, 4 (1980): 696–714. See also Erickson, "Fourteenth-Century Franciscans," *Franciscan Studies* 35, 115, *n*29.

209. Lahey, "Richard FitzRalph and John Wyclif," 167–68.

210. Ibid., 168.

211. Ibid., 171–72, and see *n*33, 171–72, for a useful excerpt from FitzRalph's *Defensio curatorum* regarding this issue.

212. Ibid., 172.

213. Kenny, *Wyclif*, 59, and 63–65.

214. Lahey, "Richard FitzRalph and John Wyclif," 183.

215. Ibid., 173–74.

216. Aston, *Faith and Fire*, 68, *n*105. See also the main text of 67–69.

217. For a detailed survey of the council, see Philip Stump, *The Reforms of the Council of Constance (1414–1418)* (Leiden: Brill, 1994). See also Edith C. Tatnall, "The Condemnation of John Wyclif at the Council of Constance," *Councils and Assemblies: Papers Read at the Eighth Summer Meeting and the Ninth Winter Meeting of the Ecclesiastical History Society*, G. J. Cuming and Derek Baker, eds. Studies in Church History 7 (Cambridge: Cambridge University Press, 1971), 209–18. For detailed excerpts from the council's proceedings in English, see "Council of Constance": http://www.ewtn.com/library/COUNCILS/CONSTANC.HTM, accessed January 13, 2014. The Hussites in Bohemia held similar views to the Lollards, and were a more direct influence on Luther and the Reformation.

218. *Wyclif: Trialogus*, Stephen E. Lahey, trans. (Cambridge: Cambridge University Press, 2013), 11. Thomas Gascoigne, chancellor of Oxford University, recorded the incident in 1441. An English account is in Lewis Sergeant, *John Wyclif: Last of the Schoolmen and First of the English Reformers* (New York: Putnam, 1893), 335–36. For a detailed study of Wyclif's opposition, see Mishtooni Bose, "The Opponents of John Wyclif," *A Companion to John Wyclif*, 407–55. Note the useful chronology at 419.

219. Ian Christopher Levy, "Wyclif and the Christian Life," *Companion to John Wyclif*, 295–96. See also Lawrence M. Clopper, "Franciscans, Lollards, and Reform," *Lollards and Their Influence in Late Medieval England*, Fiona Somerset, Jill C. Havens, and Derrick G. Pitard, eds. (Woodbridge: Boydell, 2003), 177–96.

220. Lahey, "Richard FitzRalph and John Wyclif," 184–85, suggests this possibility. See also Lahey, *John Wyclif*, 165–68. For a counter-argument, see Evans, *John Wyclif*, 250–54. She also discusses the uncertainty of Wyclif's relations to these preachers and the Lollards at 197. See also Michael Wilks, "Wyclif and Hus as Leaders of Religious Protest Movements," *Studies in Church History* 9 (1972): 62–84.

221. Lahey, "Richard FitzRalph and John Wyclif," 178.

222. Ibid., 184.

223. Indeed, Lollards developed a more anti-intellectual and anti-academic stance in their sermons, see Ghosh, *The Wycliffite Heresy*, 138–39.

224. For a discussion of Nicholas and Wyclif's enduring legacy at Oxford, see Catto, "Wyclif and Wycliffism," 214–21. See also Kenny, Wyclif, 95–96. Additionally, see Simon Forde, "New Sermon Evidence for the Spread of Wycliffism," *De Ore Domini: Preacher and Word in the Middle Ages*, Studies in Medieval Culture 27, Thomas L. Amos, Eugene A. Green, and Beverly Mayne Kienzle, eds. (Kalamazoo: Medieval Institute Publications, 1989), 169–83.

225. Kenny, *Wyclif*, 101.

226. For a brief summary, see Cole, *Literature and Heresy in the Age of Chaucer*, 72–74. However, see also Lahey, *Philosophy and Politics*, 209–210, and Lahey, *John Wyclif*, 165.

227. Cole, *Literature and Heresy*, 55–60.

228. For studies of the Lollards and the spread of Wyclif's ideas, see *Wycliffite Controversies*, Mishtooni C.A. Bose and J. Patrick Hornbeck, eds., Medieval Church Studies 23 (Turnhout: Brepols, 2012); and Anne Hudson, *Studies in the Transmission of Wyclif's Writings* (Aldershot: Ashgate Variorum, 2008). Maureen Jurkowski, "Lollardy and Social Status in East Anglia," *Speculum* 82 (2007): 120–152, discusses why these beliefs had appeal in this region. See also Robert Lutton, *Lollardy and Orthodox Religion in Pre-Reformation England* (Woodbridge: Boydell, 2006); *Lollards and Their Influence in Late Medieval England*, Fiona Somerset, Jill Havens, and Derrick Pitard, eds. (Woodbridge: Boydell, 2003); Richard Rex, *The Lollards: Social History in Perspective* (New York: Palgrave Macmillan: 2002); *Lollardy and the Gentry in the Later Middle Ages* (New York: St. Martin's, 1997), Margaret Aston and Colin Richmond, eds.; Anne Hudson, *Lollards and their Books* (London: Hambledon, 1985); Margaret Aston, *Lollards and Reformers: Images and Literacy in Late Medieval Religion* (London: Hambledon Press, 1984); and Anne Hudson, "Lollardy: The English Heresy?" *Studies in Church History* 18 (1982): 261–83.

For an English translation of the "Twelve Conclusions of the Lollards," see the "Geoffrey Chaucer Page" at Harvard: http://sites.fas.harvard.edu/~chaucer/special/varia/lollards/lollconc.htm, accessed January 13, 2014, taken from H.S. Cronin, ed., "The Twelve Conclusions of the Lollards," *English Historical Review* 22 (1907): 292–304. For a collection of later 14th-century English poems (some Lollard and Wycliffite) see James M. Dean, "Anticlerical Poems and Documents," *Medieval English Political Writings*, now available online from the University of Rochester at: http://d.lib.rochester.edu/teams/publication/dean-medieval-english-political-writings, accessed February 16, 2014.

229. For an edition, see *Documents Illustrative of Church history Compiled from Original Sources*, Henry Gee and William John Hardy, eds. (London: Macmillan, 1914), 133–37. For an English translation, see the Rhode Island College website: www.ric.edu/faculty/rpotter/heretico.html, accessed January 14, 2014.

230. Charles W. Brockwell Jr., "Answering 'The Known Men': Bishop Reginald Pecock and Mr. Richard Hooker," *Church History* 49, 2 (1980): 133. Certain heretics, such as the Anabaptists, could still suffer terrible fates. Two were burned at the stake in 1575 in London, see J.B. Black, *The Reign of Elizabeth 1558–*

1603, 2nd ed. (Oxford: Clarendon Press, 1959, reprinted 2004), 205.

231. See Leff, *Paris and Oxford Universities*, 96–97. However, from 1412, degree candidates had to swear not to hold or propagate Wycliffism or Lollardy, see 159.

232. Though Shakespeare used Oldcastle's name in his original drafts, he changed the name in the printed version to derive from that of John Fastolf, it is said, due to concerns from one of Oldcastle's descendants. See Stephen Cooper, *The Real Falstaff: Sir John Fastolf and the Hundred Years' War* (Barnsley: Pen and Sword, 2010).

233. For Oldcastle's life, see *The Oldcastle Controversy: Sir John Oldcastle, Part I and The Famous Victories of Henry V*, Peter Corbin, Douglas Sedge, eds. (Manchester: Manchester University Press, 1991), 1–8, which also has useful notes for further study.

234. For recent studies of Netter and his works, see *Thomas Netter of Walden: Carmelite, Diplomat and Theologian (c.1372–1430)*, Johan Bergström-Allen, and Richard Copsey, eds., Carmel in Britain 4 (Faversham and Rome: Saint Albert's Press and Edizioni Carmelitane, 2009); and Kevin J. Alban, *The Teaching and "Doctrinale" of Thomas Netter of Walden (c. 1374–1430)* (Turnhout: Brepols, 2010). See also Stephen Lahey, "Richard FitzRalph and John Wyclif," 163–67, for a useful summary. The 18th-century edition of the *Doctrinale* is still useful, *Thomae Waldensis Carmelitae anglici Doctrinale antiquitatum fidei catholicae Ecclesiae*, Bonaventura Blancotti, ed., 3 vols. (Venice: Typis Antonii Bassanesii ad S. Cantianum, 1757–59), available in a facsimile reprint (Farnborough, UK: Gregg Press, 1967).

235. For a survey of Lollard "literature," see Rita Copeland, "Lollard Writings," *The Cambridge Companion to Medieval English Literature 1100–150*, Larry Scanlon, ed. (Cambridge: Cambridge University Press, 2009), 111–22, and Steven Justice, "Lollardy," *Cambridge History of Medieval English Literature*, David Wallace, ed. (Cambridge: Cambridge University Press, 2002), 662–89.

236. For some details on the Lollard work on the English Bible and glosses, see Catto, "Wyclif and Wycliffism," 221–24. See also Kenny, *Wyclif*, 65–67.

237. Evans, *John Wyclif*, 232.
238. Ibid., 228–30.
239. The so-called "Wycliffite Sermons," of which there are 294 extant. See ibid., 233–36.

240. For editions and a study of these works, see P.L. Heyworth, *Jack Upland, Friar Daw's Reply, and Upland's Rejoinder* (Oxford: Oxford University Press, 1968). See also Heyworth, "The Earliest Black-Letter Editions of Jack Upland," *Huntington Library Quarterly* 30 (1967): 307–14; and Heyworth, "Jack Upland's Rejoinder, a Lollard Interpolator, and Piers Plowman B.X. 249f," *Medium Aevum* 36 (1967): 242–48. See also Szittya, *Antifraternal Tradition*, 196–97. It may also be significant to Clopper's thesis about Langland's Franciscan identity that *Jack Upland* is written in prose, while *Friar Daw's Reply* is poetic, just as *Piers Plowman* is a poem, see Clopper, *Songes of Rechelesnesse*, 77.

241. James M. Dean, *Six Ecclesiastical Satires* (Kalamazoo: Medieval Institute Publications, 1991), 3, an excellent study that also contains editions of the *Jack Upland* poems and other works. The book is available online at the University of Rochester: http://d.lib.rochester.edu/teams/publication/dean-six-ecclesiastical-satires#sixecc, accessed January 14, 2014. For additional studies, see Christina von Nolcken, "Piers Plowman, the Wycliffites, and Pierce the Plowman's Creed," *The Yearbook of Langland Studies* 2 (1988): 71–102; and David Lampe, "The Satiric Strategy of Peres the Ploughmans Crede," *The Alliterative Tradition in the Fourteenth Century*, Bernard S. Levy and Paul E. Szarmach, eds. (Kent: Kent State University Press, 1981): 69–80. For further discussion of *Pierce* in relation to the antifraternal and anti-intellectual wing of Lollardy, see John Scattergood, "Pierce the Plowman's Crede: Lollardy and Texts," *Lollardy and the Gentry in the Later Middle Ages*, Margaret Aston and Colin Richmond, eds. (New York, St. Martin's Press, 1997), 77–94.

242. James M. Dean, *Six Ecclesiastical Satires*, 51–52. A complete edition with notes is at 58–114. For some work on the relationship between the Lollards and *Piers Plowman*, see David Lawton, "Lollardy and the *Piers Plowman* Tradition," *Modern Language Review* 76 (1981): 780–93.

243. James M. Dean, *Six Ecclesiastical Satires*, 53.

244. Ibid., 52–53.

Conclusion

1. A complete version of four separate editions, from 1560, 1570, 1576, and 1583, can be found online at: http://www.johnfoxe.org/index.php, accessed February 18, 2014. A link to the three later editions is at: http://www.johnfoxe.org/index.php?realm=more&gototype=modern...8&type=commentary&book=4, under the heading, "Opponents of the Papacy." Foxe lauds Guillaume for his attack on mendicancy: "Consquently in this order and number, foloweth the worthie and valiant champion of Christ and aduersary of Antichrist Gulielmus de S. Amore, a master of Paris, and a chief ruler then of that vniuersitie. This Gulielmus in his tyme had no small a do writyng agaynst the friers, and their hypocrisie. But especially agaynst the beggyng friers, both condemnyng their whole order, & also accusing them as those þᵗ did disturbe & trouble all the churches of Christe by their preachyng in churches agaynst the will of the ordinaries and pastors, by theyr hearyng of confessions, and executyng the charges of curates and pastors in their churches. All the testimonies of Scripture that make agaynst Antichrist, he applyeth them agaynst the clergy of prelates, and the Popes spiritualtie. The same Gulielmus is thought to be the autor of the booke, whiche is attributed to the schole of Paris, and intituled: De periculis ecclesiæ. Where he proueth by xxxix. argumentes, that friers be false Apostles."

2. *Guillielmi de S. Amore Opera omnia quae reperiri potuerunt* (Coûtances: Alitophilos, 1632, repr. Hildesheim and New York: G. Olms, 1997). The later edition is in Ortwinus Gratius, *Fasciculus rerum expetendarum et fugiendarum*, Edward Brown, ed., 2 vols. (London: Chiswell, 1690), II, 18–41. This is a reprint of the earlier version, and a copy is in the Brotherton Collection, University of Leeds, UK, where I was able to consult it some years ago.

3. Geltner, *De periculis*, 22.

4. For the state of the friars during the Tudor period, see Richard Rex, "Friars in the English Reformation," *The Beginnings of English Protestantism*, Peter Marshall and Alec Ryrie, eds. (Cambridge: Cambridge University Press, 2002), 38–59. See also Susan Wabuda, *Preaching during the English Reformation* (Cambridge: Cambridge University Press, 2002), 107–46.

5. For a short survey of the French Revolution and its aftermath, and the effect on the Dominicans, see the classic study by William Hinnebusch, O.P., *The Dominicans: A Short History*, available online at:

http://opcentral.org/blog/the-order-from-1789-to-1872/, accessed February 18, 2014.

6. William Hinnebusch, "How the Dominican Order Faced Crises," *Review for Religious* 32 (1973/6): 1307–1321, available online at: http://opcentral.org/blog/how-the-dominican-order-faced-crises/, accessed February 18, 2014, where he notes: "From 1789 to 1850 a series of calamities disrupted the order's government, destroyed or weakened priories, monasteries, and provinces, closed foreign missions, scattered the religious, and brought the order close to extinction. No general chapter convened between 1777 and 1832. Between 1790 and 1819 the houses of France, Belgium, and Germany were closed. After 1808 wars of independence destroyed most of the Latin-American provinces. Suppression of Spanish and Portuguese priories followed in 1834 and 1837, respectively. Russia gradually smothered the Lithuanian, Russian, and Polish houses under its dominion following 1842. After repeated suppressions in Italy during the Risorgimento, only 105 of 750 priories survived."

7. Geltner, *Making of Medieval Antifraternalism*, 137.

Bibliography

Manuscripts

Biblia Sacra cum Glossa Ordinaria primum quidem a Strabo Fuldensi monacho Benedictino collecta. Antwerp: apud Ioannem meursium, 1634, 6 vols. Brotherton Collection, University of Leeds, UK.

Chaucer, Geoffrey. *The workes of our Antient and learned English Poet, Geffrey Chaucer*. London: George Bishop, 1598.

Gratius, Ortwinus. *Fasciculus rerum expetendarum et fugiendarum*, edited by Edward Brown. London: Chiswell, 1690, 2 vols. Brotherton Collection, University of Leeds (Contains Guillaume de Saint-Amour's *De Periculis* and other writings).

Guillaume de Saint-Amour. *Guillielmi de S. Amore Opera omnia quae reperiri potuerunt*. Coûtances: Alitophilos, 1632, reprinted by Hildesheim and New York: G. Olms, 1997.

Omne bonum. British Library MS Royal 6 E. VI and 6 E. VII.

Unum Sanctam. Vatican Archives, "Reg. Vatic.," L, fol. 387.

Primary References

Adam de la Halle. *Adam de la Halle: Œuvres completes*, edited and translated by Pierre-Yves Badel. Lettres gothiques. Paris: Librairie générale française, 1995.

———. *The Broken Pot Restored*, edited and translated with commentary by Gordon Douglas McGregor. Nicholasville, KY: The French Forum, 1991.

———. *The Play of Madness*, edited and translated by Guy Mermier. Studies in the Humanities 22. New York: Peter Lang, 1997.

Aelfric of Eynsham. *Aelfric's Lives of Saints*, edited by Walter William Skeat. Early English Text Society. London: Trübner, 1900.

Alfred, King of Wessex. *King Alfred's Old English version of Boethius De consolatione philosophiae*, edited by Walter J. Sedgefield. Oxford: Clarendon Press, 1899.

Ambrose. *Opera Omnia, Patrologia Latina* 15, edited by J.-P. Migne. Paris: Garnier, 1845.

Arnald of Sarrant. *Chronica XXIV Generalium Ordinis Fratrum Minorum (1209–1374)*, Analecta Franciscana 3. Florence: Frati Editori di Quaracchi, 1897.

———. *The Chronicle of the Twenty-Four Generals of the Order of Friars Minor*, translated by Noel Muscat. Malta: TAU Franciscan Communications, 2010.

Augustine of Hippo. *The City of God against the Pagans*, translated by various, 7 vols. London: William Heineman Limited, 1960.

Bartholomaeus Anglicus. *Medieval Lore*, edited and translated by Robert Steele. London: King's Classics, 1907.

Bartholomew Cotton. *Historia Anglicana (449–1298)*, edited by Henry Richards Luard. Rolls Series 16. London: Longman, Green, Longman, and Roberts, 1859.

Bernard of Clairvaux. *Sancti Bernardi Sermones super Canitca canticorum*, edited by Jean Leclercq, C.H. Talbot, and H.M. Rochais. Sancti Bernardi Opera, I-II. Rome: Edizioni Cisterciensi, 1957–58.

Bestiary, translated by Richard Barber. London: Folio Society, 1992.

Biblia Sacra Juxta Vulgatam Clementinam. 7th edition. Madrid: La Editorial Catolica, 1985.

Bonaventure. *Opera Omnia*, 10 vols. Quaracchi: Colegium S. Bonaventurae, 1882–1902.

Bullarium franciscanum, edited by H. Sbaralea and C. Eubel, 7 vols. Rome: Vatican, 1759–68, and 1898–1904.

Caesar of Heisterbach. *Dialogus magnus visionum atque miraculorum*, edited by Joseph Strange, 12 vols. Köln, Bonn, and Brussels: J.M. Heberle, 1851.

Chartularium Universitatis Parisiensis, edited by Heinrich Denifle, O.P., and Émile Chatelain, 4 vols. Paris: Ex Typis Fratrum Delalain via a Sorbone Dicta, 1889–97.

Chaucer, Geoffrey. *The Riverside Chaucer*, 3rd edition. Larry D. Benson, general editor. Oxford: Oxford University Press, 2008.

———. *A Variorum Edition of the Works of Geoffrey Chaucer, 2: The Canterbury Tales, 7: The Summoner's Tale*, edited by

John F. Plummer. Norman: University of Oklahoma Press, 1995.

Clare of Assisi. *Clare of Assisi—The Lady: Early Documents*, edited and translated by Regis J. Armstrong. New York: New City Press, 2006.

Clasen, S. "Tractatus Geraldi de Abbatisvilla 'Contra adversarium perfectionis Christianae.'" *Archivum Franciscanum Historicum* 31 (1938): 284–329, and 32 (1939): 89–200.

Corpus juris canonici 2, edited by A.L. Richteri. Leipzig: Tauchnitz, 1879.

De magistro studentium. "Die Constitutionen des Prediger-Ordens vom J. 1228." In *Archiv für Litteratur- und Kirchengeschichte des Mittelalters*, edited by Heinrich Denifle and Franz Ehrle, 222, no. 28. Berlin: Weidmannschen Buchhandlung, 1885.

Documents Illustrative of Church history Compiled from Original Sources, edited by Henry Gee and William John Hardy. London: Macmillan, 1914.

Dominic, St. *Monumenta diplomatica S. Dominici*, edited by Vladimir Koudelka and Raymondo Loenertz. Monumenta ordinis fratrum praedicatorum historica 25. Rome: Institutum historicum fratrum praedicatorum, 1966.

Ecbasis Cuiusdam Captive Per Tropologiam: An Eleventh-Century Latin Beast Epic, edited and translated by Edwin H. Zeydel. University of North Carolina Studies in the Germanic Languages and Literatures. Chapel Hill: University of North Carolina Press, 1964.

Epistolae in Monumenta Franciscana in Rerum Brittanicarum medii aevi scriptores, edited by J. S. Brewer. London: Rolls Series, 1858.

The Fabliaux, translated by Nathaniel E. Dubin, introduction by R. Howard Bloch. New York: Liveright/Norton, 2013.

Fasciculi Zizaniorum Magistri Johannis Wyclif cum Tritico, edited by Walter W. Shirley. London: Longman, Brown, Green, Longmans, and Roberts, 1858.

FitzRalph, Richard. "Defensio Curatorum." In *Monarchia sacri Romani imperii*, edited by Melchior Goldast, 3 vols. Hanover and Frankfurt, 1612–1614.

———. "An Edition of Richard FitzRalph's *De Pauperie Salvatoris*, Books V, VI, and VII," edited by Russell O. Brock, Jr., Ph.D. dissertation. University of Colorado, 1953.

Francis of Assisi. *Die opuskula des hl. Franziskus von Assisi*, edited by K. Esser, O.F.M. Editiones Collegii S. Bonaventurae ad Claras aquas. Rome: Grottaferrata, 1976.

———. *Francis of Assisi: The Saint*, 3 vols. 1: Early Documents, edited by Regis J. Armstrong, J. A. Wayne Hellmann, and William J. Short. New York: New City Press, 1999.

———. *Opuscula sancti patris Francisci assisiensis*, 3rd edition. Quaracchi: Collegium S. Bonaventure, 1949.

———. *Speculum perfectionis seu: S. Francisci Assisiensis*, edited by Paul Sabatier. Paris: Fischbacher, 1898.

The French Fabliau B. N. MS. 837, edited and translated by Raymond Eichmann and John DuVal. Garland Library of Medieval Literature, Series A, 16–17, 2 vols. New York: Garland, 1984–1985.

Giles of Rome. *Aegidius Romanus, De ecclesiatica potestate*, edited by Richard Scholz. Weimar: Hermann Bölaus, 1929.

———. *Giles of Rome on ecclesiastical power: The De ecclesiastica potestate of Aegidius Romanus*, translated by R.W. Dysons. Woodbridge: Boydell, 1986.

Gower, John. *The Complete Works of John Gower*, edited by George Campbell Macaulay. The English Works. Oxford: Clarendon Press, 1901.

———. *The Complete Works of John Gower*, edited by George Campbell Macaulay. The French Works. Oxford: Clarendon Press, 1899.

———. *The Complete Works of John Gower*, edited by George Campbell Macaulay. The Latin Works. Oxford: Clarendon Press, 1902.

———. *The Latin Verses in the Confessio Amantis: An Annotated Translation*, translated by Sian Echard and Claire Fanger. East Lansing: Colleagues Press, 1991.

———. *Miroir de l'omme - The Mirror of Mankind, by John Gower*, edited and translated by William Burton Wilson, and revised by Nancy Wilson Van Baak. East Lansing: Colleagues Press, 1992.

Gregory the Great, Pope. *Opera Omnia, Patrologia Latina* 76, edited by J.-P. Migne. Paris: Garnier, 1857.

Gui de Mori. *Le remaniement du "Roman de la Rose" par Gui de Mori. Étude et édition des interpolations d'après le manuscrit Tournai, Bibliothèque de la Ville 101*, edited by Andrea Valentini. Collection des Anciens auteurs belges. Collection in–8°, nouvelle série 14. Brussels: Académie royale de Belgique, 2007.

Guillaume de Deguileville. *Le Pèlerinage de la Vie Humaine*, edited by J.J. Stürzinger. London: Nichols & Sons, 1893.

Guillaume de Lorris, and Jean de Meun. *Roman de la Rose*, edited by Ernest Langlois, 5 vols. Paris: Librairie Ancienne Honoré Champion, 1914–24.

———. *Roman de la Rose*, edited by Félix Lecoy, 3 vols. Paris: Librairie Honoré Champion, 1965–70.

———. *Roman de la Rose*, edited by Armand Strubel. Paris: La Librairie générale française, 1992.

———. *The Romance of the Rose*. Trans. Charles Dahlberg. Hanover, NH: University Press of New England, reprinted 1983.

Guillaume de Puylaurens. *Guillaume de Puylaurens, Chronique 1145–1275: Chronica magistri Guillelmi de Podio Laurentii*, edited by Jean Duvernoy. Paris: CNRS, 1976.

———. *The Chronicle of William of Puylaurens: The Albigensian Crusade and Its Aftermath*, edited by W. A. Sibly and M. D. Sibly. Woodbridge: Boydell, 2003.

Guillaume de Saint-Amour. *De periculis novissimorum temporum*. Edition, translation, and introduction by G. Geltner. Dallas Medieval Texts and Translations 8. Louvain and Paris: Peeters, 2008.

Guillaume de Saint-Pathus. "Vie de saint Louis." In *Recueil des historiens des Gaules et de la France* 20, edited by Martin Bourquet. Paris: V. Palmé, 1840, 58–121.

Guiot de Provins. *Les oeuvres de Guiot de Provins, poète lyrique et satirique*, edited by John Orr. Manchester: Manchester University Press, 1915.

Hugh Primas and the Archpoet, edited by Fleur Adcock. Cambridge: Cambridge University Press, 1994.

Innocent III, Pope. "Cum Marthe." *Corpus juris canonici*, edited by E. Friedberg, II, cols. 636–39. Leipzing: Tauchnitz, 1879–81.

Isadore of Seville. *Isidori Hispalensis episcopi Etymologiarum sive Originvm libri XX*, edited by W. M. Lindsay, 2 vols. Oxford: Oxford University Press, 1911.

Jacquemart Gielee. *Renart le Nouvel*, edited by Henri Roussel. Paris: SATF, 1961.

John Grandisson, *The Register of John de Grandisson, Bishop of Exeter (A.D. 1327–69)*, edited by F.C. Hingeston-Randolph. London: George Bill, 1894–99.

John of Reading. *Chronica Johannis de Reading et Anonymi Cantuariensis 1346–1367*, edited by James Tait. Manchester: Manchester University Press, 1914.

John of Trevisa. *Dialogus inter Militem et Clericum. Richard FitzRalph's Sermon: "Defensio Curatorum," and Methodius: "þe Bygynnyng of þe World and þe End of Worldes" by John Trevisa*, edited by Aaron Jenkins Perry. London: Early English Text Society and Oxford University Press, 1925.

Jordan of Saxony. *Chronica Fratris Jordani 5*, edited by H. Boehmer. Paris: Libraries Fischbacher, 1908.

———. *Libellus Iordani de Saxonia*, edited by H.C. Sheeban. Monumenta Ordinis Fratrum Praedicatorum Historica 16. Rome: Institutum Historicum Fratrum Praedicatorum, 1935.

Langland, William. *Piers Plowman: The A Version*, edited by George Kane. London: Athlone, 1988.

———. *Piers Plowman: The A Version*, edited by Míċeál F. Vaughan. Baltimore: Johns Hopkins University Press, 2011.

———. *Piers Plowman: The B Version*, edited by George Kane and E. Talbot Donaldson. London: Athlone, 1988.

———. *Piers Plowman: The C Version*, edited by George Russell and George Kane. London: Athlone, 1997.

———. *Piers Plowman: A New Annotated Edition of the C-Text*, edited by Derek Pearsall. Exeter Medieval Texts and Studies. Exeter, UK: University of Exeter Press, 2008.

———. *Piers Plowman: A Parallel-Text Edition of the A, B, C, and Z Versions*, edited by A. V. C. Schmidt, 2 vols. Kalamazoo: Medieval Institute, 2011.

———. *Piers Plowman: A Facsimile of the Z-Text in Bodleian Library, Oxford, MS Bodley 85*, edited by A.G. Rigg and Charlotte Brewer. Woodbridge: Boydell, 1994.

———. *The Vision of William Concerning Piers Plowman*, edited by Walter William Skeat. London: Trübner, 1867–73.

Liber exemplorum ad usum praedicantium, edited by A.G. Little. Aberdoniae: Typis academicis, 1908.

Lucas Wadding. *Annales Minorum*, 3rd ed., 25 vols. Frati Editori di Quaracchi, 1931–34.

Matthew Paris. *Matthæi Parisiensis: Monachi Santi Albani, Chronica Majora*, edited by Henry Richards Luard. Rolls Series, 7 vols. London: Longmans & Co., 1872–83.

———. *Matthaei Parisiensis, Monachi Sancti Albani, Historia Anglorum, sive, ut Vulgo Dictur, Historia Minor. Item Ejusdem Abbreviatio Chronicorum Angliae*, edited by Frederic Madden. Rolls Series, No. 44, 3 vols. London: Longmans & Co., 1866–69.

———. *Matthew Paris's English History. From the Year 1235 to 1273*, translated by John Allen Giles, 3 vols. London: Henry G. Bohn, 1852–53.

Mechthild of Madeburg. *The Flowing Light of the Godhead*, edited and translated by Frank Tobin. Classics of Western Spirituality Series. New York and Mahwah, NJ: Paulist Press, 1998.

Nicolas of Lisieux. "Liber de Antichristi," *Veterum scriptorium et monumentorum historicum* IX, edited by Edmond Martène and Ursin Durand, cols. 1271–1446. Paris: Montalant, 1733. Reprinted in Burt Franklin: *Research & Source Works Series* 276. New York: Burt Franklin, 1968.

Nicolaus Minorita. *Nicolaus Minorita: Chronica, Documentation on Pope John XXII, Michael of Cesena and the Poverty of Christ with Summaries in English*, edited by Gedeon Gal and David Flood. St. Bonaventure, NY: Franciscan Institute Publications, 1996.

Nouveau recueil complet des fabliaux, edited by Willem Noomen and Nico van den Boogaard (NRCF), 10 vols. Assen and Maastricht: Van Gorcum, 1983–98.

Odo of Cheriton. *The Fables of Odo of Cheriton*, edited and translated by John C. Jacobs. Syracuse: Syracuse University Press, 1985.

Of Reynaert the Fox, translated by Thea Summerfield, edited by André Bouwman and Bart Besamuscas. Amsterdam: Amsterdam University Press, 2009.

Passio Sanctorum Martyrum, Frairum Beraldi, Analecta Franciscana 3, 579–596. Florence: Frati Editori di Quaracchi, 1897.

Peter Lombard. *Magistri Petri Lombardi, Sententiae in IV libris distinctae*, edited by Ignatius Brady, O.F.M., 2 vols. Spicilegium Bonaventurianum 4 and 5. Grottaferrata (Rome): Editiones Collegii S. Bonaventurae ad Claras Aquas, 1971–1981.

———. *The Sentences*, translated by Giulio Silano, 4 vols. Mediaeval Sources in Translation 42–43, 45, and 48. Toronto: Pontifical Institute of Medieval Studies, 2007–2010.

Peter Olivi. *De usus pauper, the quaestio and the Tractatus*, edited by David Burr. Firenze-Perth: Leo S. Olschki, University of Western Australia Press, 1992.

Peter the Venerable. *Contra Petrobrusianos hereticos*, edited by James Fearns. Corpus Christianorum Continuatio Mediaevalis 10. Turnhout: Brepols, 1968.

Renart le contrefait, edited by Gaston Reynaud and H. Lemaitre. Paris: Champion, 1914, reprinted Genève: Slatkine, 1975.

Robert Grosseteste. *The Letters of Robert Grosseteste, Bishop of Lincoln*, edited and translated by Frank Anthony Carl Mantello and Joseph Goering. Toronto: University of Toronto Press, 2010.

Robert Henryson. *Robert Henryson: The Testament of Cresseid & Seven Fables*, translated by Seamus Heaney. New York: Farrar, Straus, and Giroux, 2009.

Roger Bacon. *Opus majus*, edited by John Henry Bridges, 3 vols. London: Williams and Norgate, 1897–1990.

_____. *Roger Bacon and the Origins of Perspectiva in the Middle Ages: A Critical Edition and English Translation of Bacon's Perspectiva with Introduction and Notes*, edited and translated by David C. Lindberg. Oxford: Oxford University Press, 1996.

Roger of Hoveden. *Chronica Magistri Rogeri de Hoveden*, edited by William Stubbs, 4 vols. Rolls Series 51. London: Longmans & Co., 1871.

Le Roman de Fauvel, edited and translated by Armand Strubel. Lettres Gothiques. Paris: Librarie Général Française, 2012.

Le Roman de Fauvel de Gervais du Bus, édition d'après tous les manuscrits existants, edited by Arthur Långfors. Paris: Firmin Didot, Société des anciens textes français, 1914–1919.

Le Roman de Fauvel in the Edition of Messire Chaillou de Pestain: A Reproduction of the Complete Manuscript Paris, Bibliothèque Nationale, fonds francais 146. Introduction by Edward H. Roesner, Francois Avril, and Nancy Freeman Regalado. New York: Broude Brothers, 1990.

Le roman de Renart, edited by Jean Dufournet and Andrèe Méline, 2 vols. Paris: Flammarion, 1985.

Le roman de Renart, edited by Ernest Martin. Strasbourg: Trübner, 1882.

Le roman de Renart, edited by Armand Strubel, with Roger Bellon, Dominique Boutet, and Sylvie Lefèvre, Bibliothèque de la Pléiade 445. Paris: Gallimard, 1998.

The Romance of Reynard the Fox, translated by D. D. R. Owen. Oxford: Oxford University Press, 1994.

Rutebeuf. *Œuvres Complètes de Rutebeuf*, edited by Admond Faral and Julia Bastin, 2 vols. Paris: Picard, 1959–60.

_____. *Œuvres complètes de Rutebeuf, trouvère du XIIIᵉ siècle*, edited by Achille Jubinal. Paris: Paul Daffis, 1874.

_____. *Œuvres completes de Rutebeuf*, edited and translated by Michel Zink, 2 vols. Paris: Bordas, 1989–90.

_____. *Poémes concernant l'Universitie de Paris*. Edited with commentary by H.H. Lucas. Paris: Libraire Nizet, 1952.

_____. *Rutebeuf et les frères mendiants: Poèmes satiriques*, translated by Jean Dufournet. Paris: H. Champion, 1991.

The St Albans Chronicle, Volume I 1376–1394: The Chronica Maiora of Thomas Walsingham, edited and translated by John Taylor, Wendy R. Childs, and Leslie Watkiss. Oxford: Clarendon Press, 2003.

Salimbene de Adam. *Cronica*, edited by Giuseppe Scalia. Corpus Christianorum Continuatio Mediaevalis, 2 vols., 125 and 125A. Turnhout: Brepols, 1998–99.

_____. *Cronica Fratris Salimbene de Adam*, edited by Oswald Holder-Egger. Monumenta Germaniae Historica Scriptores 32. Hannover: Verlag, 1905–13.

_____. *Chronicle of Salimbene De Adam*, edited and translated by Joseph L. Baird, B. Guiseppe, and J. R. Kane. Binghamton, NY: Medieval & Renaissance Texts & Studies, 1986.

Scripta Leonis, Rufini et Angeli, Sociorum S. Francisci, edited by Rosalind B. Brooke. Oxford: Clarendon Press, 1970, reprinted 1990.

Seneca. *L. Annaeus Seneca, Minor Dialogs Together with the Dialog "On Clemency,"* translated by Aubrey Stewart. Bohn's Classical Library Edition. London: George Bell and Sons, 1900.

Speculum Stultorum, edited by John H. Mozley and Robert R. Raymo. Berkeley: University of California Press, 1960.

Thibaut de Champagne. *Les Chansons de Thibaut de Champagne*, edited by Axel Wallensköld. Paris: Édouard Champion, 1925.

Thomas de Celano. *St. Francis of Assisi According to Brother Thomas of Celano: His Descriptions of the Seraphic Father. A.D. 1229–1257*, edited by H.G. Rosedale. London: J.M. Dent, 1904.

Thomas Netter, *Thomae Waldensis Carmelitae anglici Doctrinale antiquitatum fidei catholicae Ecclesiae*, edited by Bonaventura Blancotti, 3 vols. Venice: Typis Antonii Bassanesii ad S. Cantianum, 1757–59. Facsimile reprint: Farnborough, UK: Gregg Press, 1967.

Walafrid Strabo. *Glossa Ordinaria* (ascribed), *Patrologia Latina*, edited Jacques Paul Migne, vols. 113 and 114. Paris: Imprimerie Catholique, 1852.

Walter Map. *The Latin Poems Commonly Attributed to Walter Mapes*, edited by Thomas Wright. London: Camden Society, 1841, reprinted New York: AMS Press, 1968.

William Caxton. *The History of Reynard the Fox: William Caxton's English Translation of 1481*, edited by Henry Morley, Early Prose Romances. London: Routledge, 1889.

William of Ockham. *William of Ockham: A Letter to the Friars Minor and Other Writings*, edited by Arthur Stephen McGrade, and translated by John Kilcullen. Cambridge: Cambridge University Press, 1995.

Wycliff, John. *De apostasia*, edited by Michael Henry Dziewicki. London: Trübner, 1889.

_____. *De civili dominio*, edited by R. L. Poole, J. Loserth, and F. D. Matthew, 4 vols. London: Trübner, 1895–1904.

_____. *De dominio divino*, edited by R. L. Poole. London: Trübner, 1890.

_____. *De officio regis*, edited by R. A. Pollard and C. E. Sayle. London: Trübner, 1887.

_____. *De potestate papae*, edited by J. Loserth. London: Trübner, 1907.

_____. *The English Works of John Wycliffe Hitherto Unprinted*, edited by P.D. Matthew. London: Trübner, 1880.

_____. *Opera Minora*, edited by Johann Loserth and F. D. Matthew. Wyclif's Latin Works 9. New York: Johnson Reprint, 1966.

_____. *Polemical Works in Latin*, edited by Rudolf Buddenseig, 2 vols. London: Trübner, 1883.

_____. *Tractatus de blasphemia*, edited by Michael Henry

Dziewicki. London: Trübner, 1893.

———. *Trialogus cum supplemento trialogi*, edited by G. Lechler. Oxford: Clarendon Press, 1869.

———. *Wyclif: Trialogus*, translated by Stephen E. Lahey. Cambridge: Cambridge University Press, 2013.

Ysengrimus, edited by Ernst Voigt. Halle: Verlag der Buchhandlung des Waisenhauses, 1884.

Ysengrimus: Text with Translation, Commentary, and Introduction, edited and translated by Jill Mann. Leiden: Brill, 1987. Revised in *Ysengrimus*. Cambridge, MA: Harvard University Press, Dumbarton Oaks Medieval Library, 2013.

Secondary References

Aberth, John. *From the Brink of the Apocalypse: Confronting Famine, Plague, War and Death in the Later Middle Ages*. London: Routledge, 2000.

Ackroyd, Peter. *Chaucer: Ackroyd's Brief Lives*. New York: Doubleday/Nan A. Talese, 2005.

Aers, David. "*Vox Populi* and the Literature of 1381." In *The Cambridge History of Medieval English Literature*, edited by David Wallace, 432–53. Cambridge: Cambridge University Press, 1999.

Akehurst, F.R.P., and Judith M. Davis, eds. *A Handbook of the Troubadours*. Berkeley: University of California, Press, 1995.

Alban, Kevin J. *The Teaching and "Doctrinale" of Thomas Netter of Walden (c. 1374–1430)*. Turnhout: Brepols, 2010.

Alberzoni, Maria Pia. *Clare of Assisi and the Poor Sisters in the Thirteenth Century*, translated by William Short and Nancy Celaschi. St. Bonaventure, NY: Franciscan Institute Publications, 2004.

Allen, Valerie. *On Farting: Language and Laughter in the Middle Ages*. New York: Palgrave Macmillan, 2010.

Ames, Christine Caldwell. *Righteous Persecution: Inquisition, Dominicans, and Christianity in the Middle Ages*. Philadelphia: University of Pennsylvania Press, 2009.

Anderson, Marjorie. "Alice Chaucer and Her Husbands." *PMLA* 60, 1 (1945): 24–47.

Andrews, Frances. *The Early Humiliati*. Cambridge: Cambridge University Press, 1999.

———. *The Other Friars: The Carmelite, Augustinian, Sack and Pied Friars in the Middle Ages*. Woodbridge: Boydell, 2006.

Arden, Heather. *The Roman de la Rose: An Annotated Bibliography*, Garland Medieval Bibliographies. New York: Garland, 1993.

———. *The Romance of the Rose*. Boston: Twayne Publishers, 1987.

———. "The Slings and Arrows of Outrageous Love in the Roman de la Rose." In *The Medieval City Under Siege*, edited by Ivy A. Corfis, Michael Wolfe, 191–206. Woodbridge: Boydell, 1995.

Arnold, John H. *Inquisition and Power: Catharism and the Confessing Subject in Medieval Languedoc*. Philadelphia: University of Pennsylvania Press, 2001.

Aston, Margaret. "Caim's Castles: Poverty, Politics, and Disendowment." In Aston, *Faith and Fire: Popular and Unpopular Religion, 1350–1600*, 95–132. London: Hambledon Press, 1993.

———. *Lollards and Reformers: Images and Literacy in Late Medieval Religion*. London: Hambledon Press, 1984.

———. and Colin Richmond, eds., *Lollardy and the Gentry in the Later Middle Ages*. New York: St. Martin's, 1997.

Aubrey, Elizabeth. *The Music of the Troubadours*. Bloomington: Indiana University Press, 1996.

Audisio, Gabriel. *The Waldensian Dissent: Persecution and Survival, c.1170–c.1570*. Cambridge Medieval Textbooks. Cambridge: Cambridge University Press, 1999.

d'Avray, D. L. *The Preaching of the Friars: Sermons diffused from Paris before 1300*. Oxford: Clarendon Press, 1985.

Bagliani, Agostino Paravicini. *Boniface VIII: Un pape hérétique?* Paris: Payot, 2003.

Baika, Gabriella I. "'Double-Talk' (*Bilinguium*) in Faus Semblant's Discourse in the Roman de la Rose." *Medievalia et Humanistica* 35 (2009): 15–32.

Baldwin, Anna. *A Guidebook to Piers Plowman*. Basingstoke: Palgrave Macmillan, 2007.

Baldwin, John W. *The Scholastic Culture of the Middle Ages, 1000–1300*. Prospect Heights, IL: Waveland Press, 1971, reissued 1997.

Barber, Malcolm. *The Cathars: Dualist Heretics in Languedoc in the High Middle Ages*. Harlow, UK: Longman, 2000.

———. *The Trial of the Templars*. Cambridge: Cambridge University Press, 2nd Edition, 2006.

Barre, Aurélie. "Le renard de Rutebeuf." *Cahiers de recherches médiévales et humanists* 14 (2007): 253–66.

Batany, Jean. *Approches du Roman de la Rose*. Paris: Bordas, 1972.

———. "L'image des franciscains dans les 'Revues d'États' du XIIIe au XVIe siècle." In *Mouvements franciscains et société française XIIe-XXe siècles*, edited by André Vauchez, 61–74. Paris: Beauchesne, 1984.

Bate, A.K. "Narrative Techniques in the Ecbasis Captivi." *Canadian Journal of Netherlandic Studies* IV, 1 (1983): 3–8.

Beckmann, Jan. *Ockham-Bibliographie, 1900–1990*. Hamburg: Verlag, 1992.

Bédier, Joseph. *Les fabliaux: Études de littérature populaire et d'histoire littéraire du moyen âge*. Paris: E. Bouillon, 1895.

BeDuhn, Jason David. *The Manichaean Body: In Discipline and Ritual*. Baltimore: Johns Hopkins University Press, 2000, republished 2002.

Bellon, Roger. "Du temps que les bestes parloient. À propos de la création des animaux dans *Le roman de Renart*." In *Recherches et travaux* 3, 21–33. Grenoble: Université Stendhal–Grenoble, 1989.

Bennett, Ralph Francis. *The Early Dominicans: Studies in Thirteenth-century Dominican History*. Cambridge: Cambridge University Press, 1937.

Benson, C. David. "The Langland Myth." In *William Langland's Piers Plowman: A Book of Essays*, edited by Kathleen M. Hewett-Smith, 83–99. New York: Routledge, 2001.

———. *Public Piers Plowman: Modern Scholarship and Late Medieval English*. University

Park: Pennsylvania State University Press, 2005.
Benson. Larry D., and Theodore M. Andersson. *The Literary Context of Chaucer's Fabliaux.* Indianapolis and New York: Bobbs-Merrill, 1971.
Bent, Margaret, and Andrew Wathey, eds. *Fauvel Studies: Allegory, Chronicle, Music, and Image in Paris, Bibliotèque Nationale de France, MS Français 146.* Oxford: Oxford University Press, 1998.
Bercovitch, Sacvan. "Clerical Satire in 'þe Vox and þe Wolf.'" *The Journal of English and Germanic Philology* 65, 2 (1966): 287–294.
Bergström-Allen, Johan, and Richard Copsey, eds. *Thomas Netter of Walden: Carmelite, Diplomat and Theologian (c.1372–1430).* Carmel in Britain 4. Faversham and Rome: Saint Albert's Press and Edizioni Carmelitane, 2009.
Bernstein, A. E. "Magisterium and license: Corporative Autonomy against Papal Authority in the Medieval University of Paris." *Viator* 9 (1978): 291–307.
Biller, Peter. "Northern Cathars and Higher Learning." In *The Medieval Church: Universities, Heresy, and Christian Life. Essays in Honour of Gordon Leff*, edited by Peter Biller and Barrie Dobson, 25–53. Studies in Church History: Subsidia 11. Woodbridge: Boydell, 1999.
―――, and Anne Hudson, eds. *Heresy and Literacy, 1000–1530.* Cambridge: Cambridge University Press, 1994.
Binns, L. Elliot. *The History of the Decline and Fall of the Medieval Papacy.* London: Methuen & Co., 1934.
Black, J.B. *The Reign of Elizabeth 1558–1603*, 2nd edition. Oxford: Clarendon Press, 1959, reprinted 2004.
Blake, N.F. *William Caxton and English Literary Culture.* London: Hambledon Press, 1991.
Bloch, R. Howard. *The Scandal of the Fabliaux.* Chicago: University of Chicago Press, 1986.
Blumenfeld-Kosinski, Renate. "Satirical Views of the Beguines in Northern French Literature." In *New Trends in Feminine Spirituality: The Holy Women of Liège and their Impact*, edited by Juliette Dor, Lesley Johnson, and Jocelyn Wogan-Browne, 237–49. Turnhout: Brepols, 1999.
Boase, T.S.R. *Boniface VIII.* London: Constable & Co., 1933.
Bocquet, Damien. "Un idéal de théocratie monastique au XIIIe siècle: Mathieu Paris, Chronica Majora, 1235–1259." *Revue Mabillon* NS 6 (1995): 83–100.
Bogin, Meg. *The Women Troubadours.* New York: Norton, 1980.
Borroff, Marie. *Traditions and Renewals: Chaucer, the Gawain Poet, and Beyond.* New Haven: Yale University Press, 2003.
Bose, Mishtooni. "The Opponents of John Wyclif." In *Companion to John Wyclif, Late Medieval Theologian*, Brill's Companions to the Christian Tradition 4, edited by Ian Christopher Levy, 407–55. Leiden: Brill, 2006.
Bose, Mishtooni, and J. Patrick Hornbeck, eds. *Wycliffite Controversies.* Medieval Church Studies 23. Turnhout: Brepols, 2012.
Boreczky, Elemér. *John Wyclif's Discourse on Dominion in Community.* Leiden and Boston: Brill, 2008.
Bowers, John. *Chaucer and Langland: The Antagonistic Tradition.* Notre Dame: University of Notre Dame Press, 2007.
Brasher, Sally Mayall. *Women of the Humiliati: Lay Religious Order in Medieval Civic Life.* New York: Routledge, 2003.
Brenon, Anne. *Le Vrai Visage du catharsime.* Reprinted Cahors: La Louve éditions, 2008.
Brett, Edward Tracy. *Humbert of Romans: His Life and Views of Thirteenth-century Society.* Toronto: Pontifical Institute of Mediaeval Studies, 1984.
Breul, Karl. *The Cambridge Songs: A Goliard's Songbook of the Eleventh Century.* Cambridge: Cambridge University Press, 1915, reissued by Cambridge University Press, 2009.
Brewer, Derek. *Chaucer and His World.* New York: Dodd, Mead, 1977.
Brians, Paul, ed. and trans. *Bawdy Tales from the Courts of Medieval France.* New York: Harper and Row, 1972.
Brockwell Jr., Charles W. "Answering 'The Known Men': Bishop Reginald Pecock and Mr. Richard Hooker." *Church History* 49, 2 (1980): 133–146.
Brown, Christopher. *Aquinas and the Ship of Theseus: Solving Puzzles about Material Objects.* London: Continuum, 2005.
Brown, E.A.R. "The Prince is Father of the King: The Character and Childhood of Philip the Fair of France." *Medieval Studies* 49 (1987): 282–334.
Brown, Peter. *Geoffrey Chaucer.* Authors in Context. Oxford: Oxford University Press, 2011.
Brownlee, Kevin. "Machaut's Motet 15 and the 'Roman de la rose': The Literary Context of 'Amours qui a le pouoir/Faus Samblant m'a deceu/Vidi Dominum.'" *Early Music History* 10 (1991): 1–14.
―――. "The Problem of Faux Semblant: Language, History, and Truth in the Roman de la Rose." In *The New Medievalism*, edited by Marina S. Brownlee, Kevin Brownlee, and Stephen G. Nichols, 253–71. Baltimore: Johns Hopkins University Press, 1991.
―――, and Sylvia Huot. *Rethinking the Romance of the Rose: Text, Image, Reception.* Philadelphia: University of Pennsylvania Press, 1992.
Brunner, Melanie. "Papal Interventions in Mendicant Organisation: Pope John XXII and the Franciscans." In *Franciscan Organisation in the Mendicant Context: Formal and Informal Structures of the Friars' Lives and Ministry in the Middle Ages*, edited by Michael Robson, Jens Röhrkasten, 353–75. Berlin: LIT Verlag, 2010.
Burr, David. *Olivi and Franciscan Poverty: The Origins of the Usus Pauper Controversy*, Middle Ages Series. Philadelphia: University of Pennsylvania Press, 1989.
―――. *The Spiritual Franciscans: From Protest to Persecution in the Century After Saint Francis.* University Park: Pennsylvania State University Press, 2001.
―――, and David Flood. "Peter Olivi: On Poverty and Revenue." *Franciscan Studies* 40 (1980), 18–58.
Burr, Kristin L., John F. Moran, and Norris J. Lacy, eds. *The Old French Fabliaux: Essays on Comedy and Context.* Jefferson, NC: McFarland, 2008.
Burrows, Daron. "*Le chastiement des clercs*: a *dit* Concerning

the Nations of the University of Paris, edited from Paris, Bibliothèque nationale MS f. Fr 837." *Medium Aevum* 69 (2000): 211–26.

———. *The Stereotype of the Priest in the Old French Fabliaux: Anticlerical Satire and Lay Identity*. Bern: Peter Lang, 2005.

Busby, Keith. "The Respectable *fabliau*: Jean Bodel, Rutebeuf, and Jean de Condé." *Reinardus* 9 (1996): 15–31.

Buschinger, Danielle, and André Crépin, eds. *Comique, satire et parodie dans la tradition renardienne et les fabliaux*. Göppingen, Kümmerle: Göppinger Arbeiten zur Germanistik 391, 1983.

Butterfield, Ardis. *Chaucer: A London Life*. London: I.B.Tauris, 2013.

———. *Poetry and Music in Medieval France from Jean Renart to Guillaume de Machaut*. Cambridge Studies in Medieval Literature, 49. Cambridge: Cambridge University Press, 2002.

Calker, Marvin, ed. "Contra Religionis Simulatores." In *Analecta Dublinensa*. Cambridge, Mass.: Medieval Academy, 1975.

Callus, D. A., ed. *Robert Grosseteste: Scholar and Bishop, Essays in Commemoration of the Seventh Centenary of his Death*. Oxford: Clarendon Press, 1955.

Carney, Margaret. *The First Franciscan Woman: Clare of Assisi and her Form of Life*. Quincy: Franciscan Press, 1993.

———. "Francis and Clare: A Critical Examination of the Sources." *Laurentianum* 30 (1987): 25–60.

Catto, J.I. "Wyclif and Wycliffism in Oxford, 1356–1430." In *The History of the University of Oxford II: Late Medieval England*, edited by Catto and Ralph Evans, 175–261. Oxford: Clarendon Press, 1992.

Chadwick, Joan V. "The Fox: A Medieval View, and Its Legacy in Modern Children's Literature." *Between the Species* (Winter/Spring 1994), 71–75.

Chamberlin, E.R. *The Bad Popes*. New York: Dorset Press, 1986.

Chamberlin, John. *Medieval Arts Doctrines on Ambiguity and Their Places in Langland's Poetics*. Montreal: McGill-Queen's University Press, 2000.

Chenu, Marie-Dominique. *Nature, Man, and Society in the Twelfth Century*. Chicago: Chicago University Press, 1968.

du Chesnay, C. Berthelot. "Anticlericalism." *New Catholic Encyclopedia* (New York: McGraw-Hill, 1967), I, 618–20.

Clark, Roy Peter. "Doubting Thomas in Chaucer's 'Summoner's Tale.'" *The Chaucer Review* 11, No. 2 (1976): 164–178.

———. "Wit and Whitsunday in Chaucer's *Summoner's Tale*." *Annuale Mediaevale* 17 (1976): 48–57.

Clegg, Brian. *The First Scientist: A Life of Roger Bacon*. New York: Carroll & Graf, 2003.

Clopper, Lawrence M. "Franciscans, Lollards, and Reform." In *Lollards and Their Influence in Late Medieval England*, edited by Fiona Somerset, Jill C. Havens, and Derrick G. Pitard, 177–96. Woodbridge: Boydell, 2003.

———. "Langland's Franciscanism." *The Chaucer Review* 25, 1 (1990): 54–75.

———. "Langland's Persona: An Anatomy of the Mendicant Orders." In *Written Work: Langland, Labor, and Authorship*, edited by Steven Justice and Kathryn Kerby-Fulton, 144–84. Philadelphia: University of Pennsylvania Press, 1997.

———. "*Songes of Rechelesnesse*," *Langland and the Franciscans*. Ann Arbor: University of Michigan Press, 1997.

Cobby, Anne Elizabeth. "L'anticléricalisme des fabliaux." *Reinardus* 7 (1994): 17–29.

———. "The *Fabliau of Le Prestre et le Chevalier*: Aspects of Illumination and Reflection." *Reinardus* 2 (1989): 42–68.

———. *The Old French Fabliaux*. Research Bibliographies and Checklists, New Series, 9. Woodbridge, Tamesis, 2009.

Cohn, Norman. *The World-View of a Thirteenth-Century Intellectual*. Newcastle upon Tyne, UK: University of Durham Press, 1961.

Cole, Andrew. *Literature and Heresy in the Age of Chaucer*. Cambridge: Cambridge University Press, 2008.

Congar, Yves -M. "Aspects ecclésiologiques de la querelle entre mendiants et séculiers dans la seconde moitié du XIIIe siècle et le debut de XIVe." *Archives d'histoire doctrinale et litteraire du moyen âge* 25 (1961): 45–50.

Constable, Giles. *Three Studies in Medieval Religious and Social Thought: The Interpretation of Mary and Martha, the Ideal of the Imitation of Christ, the Orders of Society*. Cambridge: Cambridge University Press, reprinted 1998.

Cooper, Stephen. *The Real Falstaff: Sir John Fastolf and the Hundred Years' War*. Barnsley: Pen and Sword, 2010.

Copeland, Rita. "Lollard Writings," In *The Cambridge Companion to Medieval English Literature 1100–150*, edited Larry Scanlon, 111–22. Cambridge: Cambridge University Press, 2009.

Corbin, Peter, and Douglas Sedge, eds. *The Oldcastle Controversy: Sir John Oldcastle, Part I and The Famous Victories of Henry V*. Manchester: Manchester University Press, 1991.

Corfis, Ivy A., and Michael Wolfe, eds. *The Medieval City Under Siege*. Woodbridge: Boydell, 1995.

Cornelius, Roberta D. "Piers Plowman and the Roman de Fauvel." *PMLA* 47, 2 (1932): 363–367.

Coste, Jean, ed. *Boniface VIII en procès: Articles d'accusation et dépositions des témoins*. Pubblicazioni della Fondazione Camillo Caetani, Studi e Documenti d'Archivio 5. Rome: L'Erma di Bretschneider, 1995.

Coulton, George Gordon. *Five Centuries of Religion*, vol. 2. Cambridge: Cambridge University Press Archive, 1927.

Courtenay, William J. "The Effect of the Black Death on English Higher Education." *Speculum* 55, 4 (1980): 696–714.

———. "Inquiry and Inquisition: Academic Freedom in Medieval Universities," *Church History* 58, 2 (1989): 168–181.

———. *Parisian Scholars in the Early Fourteenth Century: A Social Portrait*. Cambridge: Cambridge University Press, 2004.

Cowdrey, H.E.J. *Pope Gregory VII, 1073–1085*. Oxford: Oxford University Press, 1998.

Crescini, Vicenzo. *Manuale per l'avviamento agli studi provenzali*. Milano: Hoepli, 1926.

Crow, Martin M. and Clair C. Olson, eds. *Chaucer Life-Records*. Oxford: Oxford University Press, and Austin: University of Texas Press, 1966.
Cuthbert (O.S.F.C.), Father. *Life of St. Francis of Assisi*. London: Longmans, Green and Co. 1914.
Dahlberg, Charles. "Chaucer's Cock and Fox." *The Journal of English and Germanic Philology*, 53, 3 (1954): 277–290.
Dahmus, Joseph H. *The Prosecution of John Wyclif*. New Haven: Yale University Press, 1952.
Dahnk, Emilie. *L'Hérésie de Fauvel*. Leipziger romanistische Studien, Literaturwissenschaftliche Reihe 4. Leipzig-Paris: C. & E. Vogel, 1935.
Daly, Lowrie J. *The Medieval University, 1200–1400*. New York: Sheed & Ward, 1961.
Daniel, E. Randolph. "The Double Procession of the Holy Spirit in Joachim of Fiore's Understanding of History." *Speculum* 55, 3 (1980): 469–483.
Dawson, James Doyne. "Richard FitzRalph and the Fourteenth-Century Poverty Controversies." *Journal of Ecclesiastical History* 34, 3 (1983): 315–44.
———. "William of St. Amour and the Apostolic Tradition." *Mediaeval Studies* 40 (1978): 223–38.
Dean, James M., ed. *Medieval English Political Writings*. Kalamazoo MI: Medieval Institute Publications, 1996. Also available online.
———, ed. *Six Ecclesiastical Satires*. Kalamazoo: Medieval Institute Publications, 1991. Also available online.
Denton, Jeffrey. "The attempted trial of Boniface VIII for heresy," In *Judicial Tribunals in England and Europe, 1200–1700: The Trial in History I*, edited by Maureen Mulholland and Brian Pullan, with Anne Pullan, 117–28. Manchester: Manchester University Press, 2003.
Devlin, Dennis. "Feminine Lay Piety in the High Middle Ages: The Beguines." In *Medieval Religious Women, Vol. 1: Distant Echoes*, edited by John A. Nichols and Lillian Thomas Shank, 183–97. Kalamazoo: Cistercian Publications, 1984.
Dillon, Emma. *Medieval Music-Making and the Roman de Fauvel*. Cambridge: Cambridge University Press, 2002.
Dipple, Geoffrey L. "Uthred and the Friars: Apostolic Poverty and Clerical Dominion between Fitzralph and Wyclif." *Traditio* 49 (1994): 235–258.
de Dmitrewski, Michel. "*Fr. Bernard Délicieux, O.F.M. Sa lutte contre l'inquisition de Carcassonne et d'Albi, son procès, 1297–1319.*" *Archivum Franciscanum Historicum* 17 (1924): 183–214, 313–37; 18 (1925): 3–32.
Doane, A.N., and Carol Braun Pasternack, eds. *Vox intexta: Orality and textuality in the Middle Ages*. Madison: University of Wisconsin Press, 1991.
Dobson, R. B. *The Peasants' Revolt of 1381*, 2nd edition. London: Macmillan, 1983.
Dolan, Terence. "The Rhetoric of Richard FitzRalph's Defensio curatorum." In *Richard FitzRalph: His Life, Times and Thought*, edited by Michael Dunne and Simon Nolan, 99–102. Dublin, Ireland and Portland, OR: Four Courts Press, 2013.
Donovan, L.G. "Ysengrimus and the Early Roman de Renard." *Canadian Journal of Netherlandic Studies* IV, 1 (1983): 33–38.
Douais, Célestin, ed. *Les sources de l'histoire de l'inquisition dans le midi de la France, aus XII-I^e et XIVe siècles*. Paris: Victor Palmé, 1881.
Douie, Decima L. *The Conflict between the Seculars and the Mendicants at the University of Paris in the Thirteenth Century*. Aquinas Paper no. 23. London: Blackfriars, 1954.
———. *The Nature and the Effect of the Heresy of the Fraticelli*. Manchester: Manchester University Press, 1932.
Dronke, Peter. *The Medieval Lyric*. Woodbridge: D.S. Brewer, 1968, reprinted 1996.
———. "The Rise of the Medieval Fabliau: Latin and Vernacular Evidence." *Romanische Forschungen* 85, Bd., H. 3 (1973): 275–297.
Dufeil, Michel-Marie. *Guillaume de Saint-Amour et la polémique universitaire parisienne, 1250–1259*. Paris: A. et J. Picard, 1972.
———. *Saint Thomas et l'histoire*. Aix-en-Provence: C.U.E.R.M.A., 1991.
Dufournet, Jean. *Fabliaux de Moyen Âge*. Paris: Flammarion, 1998.
———. *Du Roman de Renart à Rutebeuf*. Caen: Paradigme, 1993.
———. "Rutebeuf et les moines mendicants." *Neuphilologische Mitteilungen* 85 (1984): 152–68.
———. "Rutebeuf et le *Roman de Renart*." *L'information Littéraire* 30 (1978): 7–15; reprinted in *L'univers de Rutebeuf*, 41–60. Medievalia 56. Orléans: Paradigme, 2005.
———. "Sur trois poèmes de Rutebeuf: La Complainte Rutebeuf, Renart le Bestourné, et La Pauvreté Rutebeuf." *Hommage à Gérard Moignet*, Travaux de Linguistique et de Littérature 18, 1 (1980): 413–28.
Dunn, Alastair. *The Great Rising of 1381: The Peasants' Revolt and England's Failed Revolution*. Stroud: Tempus, 2002.
Dunn, Charles W., and Edward T. Byrnes, eds. *Middle English Literature*. New York: Routledge, 1990.
Dunne, Michael W., and Simon Nolan, eds. *Richard FitzRalph: His Life, Times and Thought*. Dublin: Four Courts Press, 2013.
Dutton, Elizabeth, John Hines, and R. F. Yeager, eds. *John Gower, Trilingual Poet: Language, Translation, Tradition*. Cambridge: D. S. Brewer, 2010.
Jean Duvernoy. *Cathares, Vaudois et Beguins, dissidents du pays d'Oc, Domaine Cathare*. Toulouse: Privat, 1994.
———. *Le Catharisme*, Vol. 1: *La Religion des cathares*. Toulouse: Privat, 1976.
———. *Le Catharisme*, Vol. 2: *L'Histoire des cathares*. Toulouse: Privat, 1979.
———. *Le Procès de Bernard Délicieux 1319*. Toulouse: Pérégrinateur, 2001.
Dykema, Peter A., and Heiko A. Oberman, eds. *Anticlericalism in Late Medieval Europe*. Leiden: E.J. Brill, 1993.
Eco, Umberto. *The Name of the Rose*, translated by William Weaver. New York: Harcourt Brace Jovanovich, 1983.
Emden, Alfred B., ed. *A Biographical Register of the University of Oxford to A.D. 1500*, 3 vols. Oxford: Clarendon Press, 1957–59.
Emmerson, Richard K. *Antichrist in the Middle Ages*. Seattle:

University of Washington Press, 1975.

———, and Ronald B. Herzman. "The Apocalyptic Age of Hypocrisy: Faus Semblant and Amant in the Roman de la Rose." *Speculum* 62 (1987): 612–34.

———, and Bernard McGinn, eds. *The Apocalypse in the Middle Ages*. Ithaca: Cornell University Press, 1993.

Erickson, Carolly. "The Fourteenth-Century Franciscans and their Critics," *Franciscan Studies* 35 (1975): 107–35; and 36 (1976): 108–47.

Evans, G.R. *John Wyclif, Myth and Reality*. Downers Grove, IL: IVP Academic, 2005.

———. *Philosophy and Theology in the Middle Ages*. London: Routledge, 1993.

———. *The University of Oxford: A New History*. London and New York: I.B. Taurus, 2010.

Farmer, D.H. "New Light on Uthred of Boldon." In *Benedictines in Oxford*, edited by Henry Wansbrough and Anthony Marett-Crosby, 116–32. London: Darton, Longman and Todd, 1997.

Favier, Jean. *Un conseiller de Philippe le Bel: Enguerran de Marigny*. Mémoires et documents publiés par la Société de l'école des Chartes 16. Paris: Presses Universitaires de France, 1963.

Fenley, G. Ward. "Faus Semblent, Fauvel and Renart le Contrefait: A Study in Kinship." *Romanic Review* 23 (1932): 323–31.

Fennessy, Ignatius. "The Chapter at Cork 1291: A Gory Franciscan Story," *Irish Theological Quarterly* 70 (2005): 283–85.

Ferruolo, Stephen C. *The Origins of the University: The Schools of Paris and their Critics, 1100–1215*. Stanford: Stanford University Press, 1985.

Fichtenau, Heinrich. *Heretics and Scholars in the High Middle Ages, 1000–1200*, translated by Denise. A. Kaiser. University Park, PA: Pennsylvania State University Press, 1998.

Finlayson, John. "Chaucer's *Summoner's Tale*: Flatulence, Blasphemy, and the Emperor's Clothes." *Studies in Philology* 104, 4 (2007): 455–470.

Finn, Thomas M. "The Sacramental World in the Sentences of Peter Lombard." *Theological Studies* 68 (2008): 557–82.

Fisher, John H. *John Gower, Moral Philosopher and Friend of Chaucer*. New York: New York University Press, 1964.

Fleming, John V. "Anticlerical Satire as Theological Essay: Chaucer's *Summoner's Tale*," *Thalia* 6 (1983): 5–21.

———. "The Antifraternalism of the *Summoner's Tale*," *Journal of English and Germanic Philology* 65 (1966): 688–700.

———. "The *Collationes* of William of Saint-Amour against S. Thomas." *Recherches de théologie ancienne et médiévale* 32 (1965 b): 132–38.

———. "The Moral Reputation of the Roman de la Rose before 1400." *Romance Philology* 18, 4 (1965): 430–35.

———. *The Roman de la Rose: A Study in Allegory and Iconography*. Princeton: University Press, 1969.

———. "The Summoner's Prologue: An Iconographic Adjustment." *The Chaucer Review* 2, 2 (1967): 95–107.

Flinn, John. *Le Roman de Renart dans la littérature française et dans les littératures étrangères du Moyen Âge*. Toronto: University of Toronto Press, 1963.

Forde, Simon. "New Sermon Evidence for the Spread of Wyclifism." In *De Ore Domini: Preacher and Word in the Middle Ages*, edited by Thomas L. Amos, Eugene A. Green, and Beverly Mayne Kienzle, 169–83. Studies in Medieval Culture 27 Kalamazoo: Medieval Institute Publications, 1989.

Fowler, David C. *The Life and Times of John Trevisa*. Seattle: University of Washington Press, 1995.

Frassetto, Michael. *Heretic Lives: Medieval Heresy from Bogomil and the Cathars to Wyclif and Hus*. London: Profile, 2007.

Friedlander, Alan. "Bernard Délicieux, le 'marteau des inquisiteurs.'" Heresis 34 (2001): 9–34.

———. *The Hammer of the Inquisitors: Brother Bernard Délicieux and the Struggle against the Inquisition in Fourteenth-Century France*. Cultures, Beliefs, and Traditions 9. Leiden: Brill, 2000.

Fyler, John. *Language and the Declining World in Chaucer, Dante, and Jean de Meun*. Cambridge and New York: Cambridge University Press, 2007.

Gabriel, Astrick L. *Garlandia: Studies in the History of the Mediaeval University*. Notre Dame, IN: The Mediaeval Institute, University of Notre Dame, 1969.

Gál O.F.M., Gedeon. "William of Ockham Died Impenitent in April 1347." *Franciscan Studies* 42 (1982): 90–95.

Galloway, Penelope "'Discreet and Devout Maidens': Women's Involvement in Beguine Communities in Northern France, 1200–1500." In *Medieval Women in Their Communities*, edited by Diane Watt, 92–115. Toronto: University of Toronto Press, 1997.

Gardner, Iain, and Samuel N. C. Lieu. *Manichaean Texts from the Roman Empire*. Cambridge: Cambridge University Press, 2004.

Gasse, Rosanne. "Dowel, Dobet, and Dobest in Middle English Literature." *Florilegium* 14 (1995–96): 171–95.

Geltner, G. "Brethren Behaving Badly: A Deviant Approach to Medieval Antifraternalism." *Speculum* 85 (2010): 47–64.

———. "Faux Semblants. Antifraternalism Reconsidered in Jean de Meun and Chaucer." *Studies in Philology* 101 (2004): 357–80.

———. *The Making of Medieval Antifraternalism: Polemic, Violence, Deviance, & Remembrance*. Oxford: Oxford University Press, 2012.

———. "Mendicants as Victims: Scale, Scope, and the Idiom of Violence." *Journal of Medieval History* 36 (2010): 126–41.

———. "William of St. Amour's *De periculis novissimorum temporum*: A False Start to Medieval Antifraternalism?" In *Defenders and Critics of Franciscan Life Essays in Honor of John V. Fleming*, edited by Michael F. Cusato and G. Geltner, 105–18. Leiden: Brill, 2009.

George, Leonard. *The Encyclopedia of Heresies and Heretics*. London: Robson, 1995.

Ghosh, Kantik. *The Wycliffite Heresy: Authority and the Interpretation of Texts*. Cambridge: Cambridge University Press, 2004.

Gies, Joseph and Frances. *Life in a Medieval City*. New York: Harper Perennial, 1981.

Gilchrist, J. "Laity in the Middle

Ages." *New Catholic Encyclopedia* (New York: McGraw-Hill, 1967), VIII, 331–5.

Given, James Buchanan. *Inquisition and Medieval Society: Power, Discipline, and Resistance in Languedoc.* Ithaca: Cornell University Press, 1997.

Glorieux, Palémon. "Le conflit de 1252–1257 á la lumière du Mémoire de Guillaume de Saint-Amour." *Recherches de théologie ancienne et medievale* 24 (1957): 364–72.

———. "'Contra Geraldinos': L'énchaînement des polèmiques." *Recherches* 7 (1935): 129–55.

———. *La Faculté des arts et ses maitres au XIIIe siècle.* Paris: J. Vrin, 1971.

———. "Une offensive de Nicolas de Lisieux contre sainte Thomas d'Aquin." *Bulletin de Littérature Ecclésiastique* 39 (1938): 121–29.

———. "Les polèmiques 'contra Geraldinos.'" *Recherches* 6 (1934): 5–41.

———. *Repertoire des maitres en théologie de Paris au XIIIe siècle.* 2 vols. Paris: J. Vrin, 1933–34.

Gounet, Jean, and Amédée Molnar. *Les Vaudois au moyen-âge.* Turin: Claudiana, 1974.

Gravdal, Kathryn. *Vilain and Courtois: Transgressive Parody in French Literature of the Twelfth and Thirteenth Centuries.* Lincoln: University of Nebraska Press, 1989.

Greatrex, Joan. "Monks and Mendicants in English Cathedral Cities: Signs of a Mutual Benefit Society?" In *The Friars in Medieval Britain: Proceedings of the 2007 Harlaxton Symposium*, edited by Nicholas Rogers, 97–106. Harlaxton Medieval Studies 19. Donington, UK: Shaun Tyas, 2010.

Greico, Holly J. "Franciscan Inquisition and Mendicant Rivalry in Mid-Thirteenth-Century Marseille." *Journal of Medieval History* 34 (2008): 275–90.

Grundmann, Herbert. "Die Bulle Quo elongati Papst Gregors IX." *Archivum Fratrum Historicum* 54 (1961): 1–25.

Gunn, Alan M.F. *The Mirror of Love.* Lubbock, TX: Texas Tech Press, 1952.

Gwynn, Aubrey. *The English Austin Friars in the Time of Wyclif.* Oxford: Oxford University Press, 1940.

———. "The Sermon-Diary of Richard Fitzralph, Archbishop of Armagh." *Proceedings of the Royal Irish Academy.* Section C: Archaeology, Celtic Studies, History, Linguistics, Literature 44 (1937/1938): 1–57.

Hackett, Jeremiah, ed. *Roger Bacon and the Sciences: Commemorative Essays,* Studien und Texte zur Geistesgeschichte des Mittelalters 57. Leiden: Brill, 1997.

Hackett, M.B. "The University as a Corporate Body." In *The History of the University of Oxford: Vol. 1, The Early Oxford Schools*, edited by J.I. Catto, 1–36. Oxford: Oxford University Press, 1984.

Hagen, Karl T. "A Frere Ther Was, A Wantowne and a Meryee." In *Chaucer's Pilgrims: An Historical Guide to the Pilgrims in The Canterbury Tales*, edited by Laura C. Lambdin and Robert T. Lambdin, 80–92. Westport, CT: Prager, 1996, reprinted 1999.

Haines, John. *Satire in the Songs of Renart le Nouvel.* Publications Romanes et Franaises 247. Geneva: Droz, 2010.

Halphen, Louis. "Les Origines de l'Université de Paris." *Aspects de l'Université de Paris.* Paris: Éditions Albin Michel, 1949.

Ham, Edward Billings. *Rutebeuf and Louis IX.* University of North Carolina Studies in the Romance Languages and Literature 42. Chapel Hill: University of North Carolina Press, 1962.

Hamilton, Bernard. *The Medieval Inquisition.* Teaneck, NJ: Holmes & Meier, 1981.

Hammerich, L.L. "The Beginning of the Strife between Richard FitzRalph and the Mendicants, with an edition of his autobiographical prayer and his proposition Unusquisque." In *Det Kgl. Danske Viderskabernes Selskab / Historiskfilologiske Meddelelser* 26. Copenhagen: Levin and Munksgaard, 1938.

Hammond, Jay M. "Dating Bonaventure's Inception as Regent Master." *Franciscan Studies* 67 (2009): 179–226.

Hanley, Catherine. *War and Combat, 1150–1270: The Evidence from Old French Literature.* Woodbridge: DS Brewer, 2003.

Hanna, Ralph, and Sarah Wood. "Mendicants and the Economies of Piers Plowman," In *The Friars in Medieval Britain: Proceedings of the 2007 Harlaxton Symposium.* Harlaxton Medieval Studies 19, edited by Nicholas Rogers, 218–38. Donington, UK: Shaun Tyas, 2010.

Hannam, James. *God's Philosophers.* London: Icon Books, 2010.

Hardick, L. "Francis of Assisi." *The New Catholic Encyclopedia* (New York: McGraw-Hill, 1967), VI, 28–31.

Hardwick, Paul. *Raising Unruly Voices: The Laity, the Vernacular and the Church in Late Medieval England*, D.Phil. dissertation. University of York, 1997.

Haren, Michael J. "Friars as Confessors: The Canonist Background to the Fourteenth-Century Controversy." *Peritia* 3 (1984): 503–16.

———. "Richard FitzRalph and the Friars: The Intellectual Itinerary of a Curial Controversialist." In *Roma, magistra mundi. Itineraria culturae medievalis. Mélanges offerts au Père L.E. Boyle à l'occasion de son 75e anniversaire*, edited by Jacqueline Hamesse, 3 vols., I, 349–367. Louvain-la-Neuve: Fédération des Instituts d'Etudes Médiévales, 1998.

Harrison, Robert. *Gallic Salt: Eighteen Fabliaux Translated from the Old French.* Berkeley: University of California Press, 1974.

Haskins, Charles H. *The Rise of Universities.* Ithaca: Cornell Great Seal Books, 1957.

———. "Robert Le Bougre and the Beginnings of the Inquisition in Northern France." *The American Historical Review* 7, 4 (1902): 631–652.

Havely, N R. "White Words, False World: Chaucer's Pandarus and the Antifraternal Tradition in *Troilus*, Books I-III." *Medium Aevum* 61, 2 (1992): 250–60.

Healey, J.E. "The Medieval University." *CCHA Report* 17 (1950): 65–77.

Heiman, A.J. "William of St. Amour." *New Catholic Encyclopedia* (New York: McGraw-Hill, 1967), XIV, 936–7.

Heller-Roazen, Daniel. *Fortune's Faces: The Roman de la Rose and the Poetics of Contingency.* Baltimore: Johns

Hopkins University Press, 2003.
Hellman, Robert, and Richard O'Gorman, ed. and trans., *Fabliaux: Ribald Tales from the Old French*. New York: Crowell, 1965.
Henderson, Arnold Clayton. "Animal Fables as Vehicles of Social Protest and Satire: Twelfth Century to Henryson." In *Third International Beast Epic, Fable and Fabliau Colloquium*, edited by Jan Goossens and Timothy Sodmann, 160–73. Münster: Böhlau Verlag Köln Wien, 1979.
———. "Foolish foxes and comic Cistercians: the Roman de Renart, branch IV." *Épopée animale, fable et fabliau, Mediaevalia* 78, Marche romane, 28, 3–4 (1978): 49–57.
———. "Of Heigh or Lough Estat": Medieval Fabulists as Social Critics." *Viator* 9 (1978): 265–90.
Herkless, John. *Francis and Dominic and the Mendicant Orders*. Edinburgh: T. & T. Clark, 1901.
Heyworth, P.L., ed. "The Earliest Black-Letter Editions of Jack Upland." *Huntington Library Quarterly* 30 (1967): 307–14.
———. *Jack Upland, Friar Daw's Reply, and Upland's Rejoinder*. Oxford: Oxford University Press, 1968.
———. "Jack Upland's Rejoinder, a Lollard Interpolator, and Piers Plowman B.X. 249f." *Medium Aevum* 36 (1967): 242–48.
Hilton, Rodney. *Bondmen Made Free: Medieval Peasant Movements and the English Rising of 1381*. London: Routledge, 1995.
Hinnebusch, O.P., William. *The Early English Friars Preachers*. Rome: Ad S. Sabinae, 1951.
———. *The History of the Dominican Order: Origins and Growth to 1500*, 2 vols. New York: Alba House, 1966 and 1972.
House, Adrian. *Francis of Assisi: A Revolutionary Life*. Mahwah, NJ: Hidden Spring, Paulist Press, 2001.
Howard, Donald R. *Chaucer: His Life, His World, His Works*. New York: Dutton, 1987.
Huber, Raphael M. "Elias of Cortona (c. 1180–1253): Minister General of the Friars Minor." *The Catholic Historical Review* 22, 4 (1937): 395–408.
Hudson, Anne. "Lollardy: The English Heresy?" *Studies in Church History* 18 (1982): 261–83.
———. *Lollards and their Books*. London: Hambledon, 1985.
———. *The Premature Reformation: Wycliffite Texts and Lollard History*. Oxford: Clarendon Press, 1988.
———. *Studies in the Transmission of Wyclif's Writings*. Aldershot: Ashgate, 2008.
Hult, David F. *Self-Fulfilling Prophecies: Readership and Authority in the first Roman de la Rose*. Cambridge: Cambridge University Press, 1986.
Huot, Sylvia. *The Romance of the Rose and Its Medieval Readers: Interpretation, Reception, Manuscript Transmission*. Cambridge: Cambridge University Press, 1993.
Hussey, S. S. "Langland the Outsider." In *Middle English Poetry: Texts and Traditions: Essays in Honour of Derek Pearsall*, edited by Alastair J. Minnis, 129–37. Woodbridge: Boydell and York Medieval Press, 2001.
Iogna-Pratt, Dominique. *Order and Exclusion: Cluny and Christendom Face Heresy, Judaism, and Islam (1000–1150)*, translated by Graham Robert Edwards. Ithaca: Cornell University Press, 2002.
Jaeger, C. Stephen. *Ennobling Love: In Search of a Lost Sensibility The Middle Ages*. Philadelphia: University of Pennsylvania Press, 1999.
Jodogne, Omer. "L'anticléricalisme de Rutebeuf." *Lettres Romanes* 23 (1969): 219–44.
Johnson, Timothy J. "Preaching Precedes Theology: Roger Bacon on the Failure of Mendicant Education." *Franciscan Studies* 68 (2010): 83–95.
Jones, Dan. *Summer of Blood: The Peasants' Revolt of 1381*. London: Harper Press, 2010.
Jones, David. *Friar's Tales: Thirteenth-Century Exempla from the British Isles*. Manchester: Manchester University Press, 2011.
Jones, Terry. *Who Murdered Chaucer? A Medieval Mystery*. New York: Thomas Dunne, 2004.
Jordan, William Chester. "The Anger of the Abbots in the Thirteenth Century." *The Catholic Historical Review* 96, 2 (2010): 219–233.
———. "The Case of Saint Louis." *Viator* 19 (1988): 209–17.
———. *Louis IX and the Challenge of the Crusade: A Study in Rulership*. Princeton: Princeton University Press, 1979.
———. "Louis IX: Preaching to Franciscan and Dominican Brothers and Nuns." In *Defenders and Critics of Franciscan Life Essays in Honor of John V. Fleming*, edited by Michael F. Cusato and G. Geltner, 219–35. Leiden: Brill, 2009.
Jurkowski, Maureen. "Lollardy and Social Status in East Anglia." *Speculum* 82 (2007): 120–152.
Justice, Steven. "Lollardy." In *Cambridge History of Medieval English Literature*, edited by David Wallace, 662–89. Cambridge: Cambridge University Press, 2002.
Kaeuper, Richard W. "The King and the Fox: Reactions to the Role of Kingship in the Tales of Reynard the Fox." In *Expectations of the Law in the Middle Ages*, edited by Anthony Musson, 9–21. Woodbridge: Boydell, 2001.
Kamath, Stephanie A. Viereck Gibbs. "Naming the Pilgrim: Authorship and Allegory in Guillaume de Deguileville's *Pèlerinage de la vie humaine*." *Studies in the Age of Chaucer* 32 (2010): 179–21.
Kane, George. "The 'Z Version' of Piers Plowman." *Speculum* 60, 4 (1985): 910–930.
Karras, Ruth Mazo. *Common Women: Prostitution and Sexuality in Medieval England*. New York: Oxford University Press, 1996.
———. "Sharing Wine, Women, and Song: Masculine Identity Formation in Medieval Europe." In *Becoming Male in the Middle Ages*, edited by Jeffrey Jerome Cohen, Bonnie G. Wheeler, 187–202. New York, Garland, 1997.
Katritzky, Linde. *Johnson and the Letters of Junius; New Perspectives on an Old Enigma*. New York: Peter Lang Publishing, 1996.
Keele, Rondo. *Ockham Explained: From Razor to Rebellion*. Chicago and La Salle: Open Court Publishing, 2010.
Kelly, Douglas. *Internal Difference and Meanings in the Roman de la Rose*. Madison: Uni-

versity of Wisconsin Press, 1995.
Kendrick, Laura. "Medieval Satire." In *A Companion to Satire: Ancient and Modern*, edited by Ruben Quintero, 52–69. Oxford: Wiley, 2007.
Kenny, Anthony. *Wyclif*. Oxford: Oxford University Press, 1985.
———, ed. *Wyclif in his Times*. Oxford: Clarendon Press, 1986.
Kerby-Fulton, Kathryn. "Hildegard of Bingen and Anti-mendicant Propaganda." *Traditio* 43 (1987): 386–99.
———. *Reformist Apocalypticism and Piers Plowman*. Cambridge: Cambridge University Press, 1990.
Kibre, Pearl. *The Nations in the Medieval Universities*. Cambridge: Mediaeval Academy of America, 1948.
———. *Scholarly Privileges in the Middle Ages*. London: William Clowes and Sons, 1961.
Kienzle, Beverly Mayne. *Cistercians, Heresy, and Crusade in Occitania, 1145–1229*. Woodbridge: Boydell and York Medieval Press, 2001.
Klein, Karen. *The Partisan Voice: A Study of the Political Lyric in France and Germany, 1180–1230*. The Hague: Mouton, 1971.
Knapp, Fritz Peter. "In Search of the Lost French 'Ur-Renart.'" *Reinardus* 2 (2010): 65–75.
Knowles, David. "The Censured Opinions of Uthred of Boldon." In *David Knowles, The Historian and Character: And Other Essays*, 129–70. Cambridge: Cambridge University Press, 1963, reprinted 2008.
———. *The Religious Orders in England*, 2 vols. Cambridge: Cambridge University Press, 1955.
Knox, Lezlie. "Clare of Assisi: Foundress of an Order?" *Spirit and Life* 11 (2004): 11–29.
Knysh, G. "Biographical Rectifications in Ockham's Avignon Period." *Franciscan Studies* 46 (1986): 61–91.
Kolve, V.A. "Chaucer's Wheel of False Religion: Theology and Obscenity in The Summoner's Tale." In *The Center and Its Compass: Studies in Medieval Literature in Honor of Professor John Leyerle*, edited by Robert A. Taylor, et al., 265–96. Studies in Medieval Culture 33. Kalamazoo: Western Michigan University Press, 1993.
Lahey, Stephen E. *John Wyclif*. Oxford: Oxford University Press, 2009.
———. *Philosophy and Politics in the Thought of John Wyclif*. Cambridge: Cambridge University Press, 2003.
———. "Richard FitzRalph and John Wyclif: untangling Armachanus from the Wycliffites." In *Richard FitzRalph: His Life, Times and Thought*, edited by Michael W. Dunne and Simon Nolan. Dublin: Four Courts Press, 2013.
Lambert, Malcom. *The Cathars*. Oxford: Blackwell, 1998.
———. *Franciscan Poverty: The Doctrine of the Absolute Poverty of Christ and the Apostles in the Franciscan Order, 1210–1323*. London: S.P.C.K., 1961, revised edition, St. Bonaventure, NY: Franciscan Institute Publications, 1998.
———. *Medieval Heresy: Popular Movements from the Gregorian Reform to the Reformation*. Oxford and Cambridge, MA: Blackwell, 1992.
Lampe, David. "The Satiric Strategy of Peres the Ploughmans Crede." *The Alliterative Tradition in the Fourteenth Century*, edited by Bernard S. Levy and Paul E. Szarmach, 69–80. Kent: Kent State University Press, 1981.
Langley, Frederick W. "Community drama and community politics in thirteenth-century Arras: Adam de la Halle's Jeu de la feuillée." In *Drama and Community: People and Plays in Medieval Europe*, edited by Alan Hindley, 57–77. Turnhout: Brepols, 1999.
Larsen, Andrew. "The Oxford 'School of Heretics': the Unexamined Case of Friar John." *Vivarium* 37, 2 (1999): 168–77.
Lawrence, C.H. *The Friars: The Impact of the Early Mendicant Movement on Western Society*. New York: Longman, 1994, reprinted as *The Friars: The Impact of the Mendicant Orders on Medieval Society*, Longman/I.B.Tauris, 2013.
Lawton, David. "Lollardy and the Piers Plowman Tradition." *Modern Language Review* 76 (1981): 780–93.
Leclerq, Jean. *The Love of learning and the Desire for God*. New York: Mentor, 1962.
Lecoy, Félix. "Sur la date du *Roman de la Rose*." *Romania* 89 (1968): 554–55.
Leech, Mary E. "Dressing the Undressed: Clothing and Social Structure in Old French Fabliaux." In *Comic Provocations: Exposing The Corpus of Old French Fabliaux*, edited by Holly A. Crocker, 83–96. New York: Palgrave Macmillan, 2006.
Leff, Gordon. "Christian Thought." In *The Medieval World*, edited by David Daiches and Anthony Thorby, 191–284. London: Aldus Books, 1973.
———. *Heresy in the Later Middle Ages; the Relation of Heterodoxy to Dissent*, 2 vols. Manchester: Manchester University Press, 1967, revised 1999.
———. *Paris and Oxford Universities in the Thirteenth and Fourteenth Centuries: An Institutional and Intellectual History*. New York: John Wiley & Sons, 1968.
Léglu, Catherine, Rebecca Rist, and Claire Taylor, eds. *The Cathars and the Albigensian Crusade: A Sourcebook*. Abingdon: Routledge, 2014.
Le Goff, Jacques. *Intellectuals in the Middle Ages*, translated by Teresa Lavender Fagan. Oxford: Blackwell, 1993.
Lehmijoki-Gardner, Maiju. "Dominican Order," In *Women and Gender in Medieval Europe*, edited by Margaret Schaus, 223–24. New York: Routledge, 2006.
Lehner, C. ed. *St. Dominic: Biographical Documents*. Washington, D.C.: Thomist Press, 1964.
Lerner, Robert. "Refreshment of the Saints: The Time after Antichrist as a Station for Earthly Progress in Medieval Thought." *Traditio* 32 (1976): 99–144.
de Lespinasse, René, ed. *Vie et vertus de Saint Louis*, Petits Mémoires sur l'histoire de France I. Paris: Société bibliographique, 1877, reprinted in facsimile by Elibron Classics, 2001.
Levitan, Alan. "The Parody of Pentecost in Chaucer's Summoner's Tale." *University of Toronto Quarterly* 40 (1970–1): 236–46.
Levy, Bernard S. "Biblical Parody in the Summoner's Tale." *Tennessee Studies in Literature* 11 (1966): 45–60.

Levy, Brian J. "Performing Fabliaux." In *Performing Medieval Narrative*, edited by Evelyn Birge Vitz, Nancy Freeman Regalado, and Marilyn Lawrence, 123–40. Woodbridge: Boydell, 2005.

Levy, Ian Christopher. "John Wyclif: Christian Patience in a Time of War." *Theological Studies* 66 (2005): 330–57.

———. "Wyclif and the Christian Life." In *Companion to John Wyclif, Late Medieval Theologian*, edited by Ian Christopher Levy, 293–363. Brill's Companions to the Christian Tradition 4. Leiden: Brill, 2006.

Lewis, C. S. *The Allegory of Love: A Study in Medieval Tradition*. London: Oxford University Press, 1938.

Lewis, Robert E. "The English Fabliau Tradition and Chaucer's 'Miller's Tale.'" *Modern Philology*, 79, 3 (1982): 241–55.

Lindberg, D.C. "Medieval Science and Its Religious Context." *Osiris* 10, Constructing Knowledge in the History of Science (1995): 60–79.

Little, Andrew. G. "The Franciscan School at Oxford in the Thirteenth Century." *Archivum Franciscanum Historicum* 19 (1926): 803–74.

———. "The Friars v. The University of Cambridge." *The English Historical Review* 50, 200 (1935): 686–96.

———. *The Grey Friars in Oxford: Part I: A History of Convent*, and *Part II: Biographical Notices of the Friars*. Oxford: Clarendon, 1892.

Little, Katherine C. "Catechesis and Castigation: Sin in the Wycliffite Sermon Cycle." *Traditio* 54 (1999): 213–244.

———. "Chaucer's Parson and the Specter of Wycliffism." *Studies in the Age of Chaucer* 23 (2001): 223–243.

Little, Lester K. "Saint Louis' Involvement with the Friars." *Church History* 33 (1964): 125–148.

Livingston, Charles Harold. *Le Jongleur Gautier Le Leu: Étude Sur Les Fabliaux*. Harvard Studies in Romance Languages. Cambridge: Harvard University Press, 1951; New York: Kraus Reprint, 1969.

Logan, Donald F. *Runaway Religious in Medieval England, c.1240–1540*, Cambridge Studies in Medieval Life and Thought, 4th ser., 32. Cambridge: Cambridge University Press, 1996.

Lodge, Anthony R. and Kenneth Varty. *The Earliest Branches of the Roman de Renart*. Synthema 1. Louvain, Belgium: Peeters, 2001.

Lower, Michael. "The Burning at Mont-Aimé: Thibaut of Champagne's Preparations for the Barons' Crusade of 1239." *Journal of Medieval History* 29 (2003): 95–108.

Luria, Maxwell. *A Reader's Guide to the Romance of the Rose*. Hamden, CT: Archon Books, 1982.

———, and Richard Hoffman, eds., *Middle English Lyrics*. New York: Norton, 1974.

Lutton, Robert. *Lollardy and Orthodox Religion in Pre-Reformation England*. Woodbridge: Boydell, 2006.

Mäkinen, Virpi. *Property Rights in the Late Medieval Discussion on Franciscan Poverty*. Leuven, Belgium: Peeters, 2001.

Mann, Jill. "Beast epic and fable." In *Medieval Latin, an Introduction and Bibliographical Guide*, edited by Frank A. C. Mantello and Arthur G. Rigg, 556–61. Washington, D.C.: Catholic University of America, 1996.

———. *Chaucer and Medieval Estates Satire*. Cambridge: Cambridge University Press, 1973.

———. "The Satiric Fiction of the Ysengrimus." In *Reynard the Fox: Cultural Metamorphoses and Social Engagement in the Beast Epic from the Middle Ages to the Present*, edited by Kenneth Varty, 1–16. Berghahn Series, Polygons: Cultural Diversities and Intersections Series, vol. 1. New York: Berghahn Books, 2003.

———. "Satiric Subject and Satiric Object in Goliardic Literature." *Mittellateinisches Jahrbruch*, Band 15 (1980): 63–86.

———. "The 'Speculum Stultorum' and the 'Nun's Priest's Tale.'" *The Chaucer Review* 9, 3 (1975): 262–282.

Marrone, J.T. "The Ecclesiology of the Parisian Secular Masters." Unpublished Doctoral Thesis, Cornell University, 1972.

Martin, Henry. "La diatribe de Jean d'Anneaux." In *Mélanges offerts à M. Émile Picot II*, 225–40. Paris: Librarie Damascène Morgand, 1913.

McDonnell, Ernest W. *The Beguines and Beghards in Medieval Culture*. New Brunswick: Rutgers University Press, 1954, reprinted 1969.

McEvoy, James. *The Philosophy of Robert Grosseteste*. Oxford: Clarendon Press, 1992.

———. *Robert Grosseteste*. Oxford: Oxford University Press, 2000.

McFarlane, K.B. *John Wycliffe and the Beginnings of English Nonconformity*. New York: Macmillan, 1952, republished as *The Origins of Religious Dissent in England*. New York: Collier Books, 1966.

McGinn, Bernard. *The Calabrian Abbot: Joachim of Fiore in the History of Western Thought*. New York: Macmillan, 1985.

———. *The Flowering of Mysticism: Men and Women in the New Mysticism (1200–1350)*. New York: Crossroad Herder, 1998.

———. *Visions of the End: Apocalyptic Traditions in the Middle Ages*. New York: Columbia University Press, revised 1998.

McGrade, A.S. "William of Ockham and Augustinus de Ancona on the Righteousness of Dissent." *Franciscan Studies* 54 (1994): 143–65.

McGrade, A. S., J. Kilcullen, and M. Kemoshail, eds. *The Cambridge Translation of Medieval Philosophical Texts*, vol. 2: Ethics and Political Philosophy. Cambridge: Cambridge University Press, 2000.

McKeon, Peter R. "The Status of the University of Paris as *Parens scientiarum*: An Episode in the Development of its Autonomy." *Speculum* 39 (1964): 651–75.

McKnight, George H., ed. *Middle English Humorous Tales in Verse*. Boston: D.C. Heath, 1913.

———. "The Middle English Vox and Wolf." *PMLA* 23, 3 (1908): 497–509.

McLaughlin, Mary M. *Intellectual Freedom and its Limitations in the University of Paris in the Thirteenth and Fourteenth Centuries*. New York: Arno, 1977.

McMunn, Meredith T. "Animal Imagery in the Text and Illustrations of the *Roman de la*

Rose." *Reinardus* 9 (1996): 87–108.
McPeek, James A. S. "Chaucer and the Goliards." *Speculum* 26, 2 (1951): 332–336.
McWebb, Christine. "Heresy and Debate: Reading the *Roman de la Rose*." *Aevum* 77 (2003): 545–56.
Les Mendiants en Pays D'oc au XIIIe siècle, Cahiers de Fanjeaux 8. Toulouse: Éditions Privat, 1973.
Mews, Constant J. "The Council of Sens (1141): Abelard, Bernard, and the Fear of Social Upheaval." *Speculum* 77 (2002): 342–82.
Moore, R.I. *The Formation of a Persecuting Society*. New York: Blackwell, 1987.
_____, ed. *The Birth of Popular Heresy*, Medieval Academy of America Reprints. Toronto: University of Toronto Press, 1975, reprinted 1995.
Moorman, John. *A History of the Franciscan Order from its Origin to the Year 1517*. Oxford: Clarendon Press, 1968.
Morrison, Karl F. "The Gregorian Reform." In *Christian Spirituality—Origins to the Twelfth Century*, edited by Bernard McGinn, John Myendorf, and Jean Leclercq, 177–93. London: SCM, 1989.
Mortier, Antonin. *Histoire des maîtres généraux de l'Ordre des Frères Prêcheurs*. Paris: A. Picara, 1903–20.
Mühlethaler, Jean-Claude. *Fauvel au pouvoir: Lire la Satire médiévale*, Nouvelle bibliothèque du Moyen Âge, 26. Paris: H. Champion; Genève: Slatkine, 1994.
_____. "Le dévoilement satirique. Texte et image dans le Roman de Fauvel." *Poétique* 146 (2006): 165–179.
Mulchahey, M. Michèle, *"First the Bow is Bent in Study...": Dominican Education before 1350*. Toronto: Pontifical Institute of Mediaeval Studies, 1998.
Mullins, Edwin. *The Popes of Avignon: A Century in Exile*. Katonah, NY: BlueBridge, 2008.
Mundy, John H. *The Repression of Catharism at Toulouse*, Studies and Texts 74. Toronto: Pontifical Institute of Medieval Studies, 1985.
Murk-Jansen, Saskia. *Brides in the Desert: The Spirituality of the Beguines*. Maryknoll, NY: Orbis Books, 1998.
Muscatine, Charles. *Chaucer and the French Tradition: A Study in Style and Meaning*. Berkeley: University of California Press, 1957.
_____. *The Old French Fabliaux*. New Haven: Yale University Press, 1986.
Neel, Carol. "Origins of the Beguines," *Signs* 14 (1989): 321–41.
Nelli, René. "Le Catharisme vu à travers les troubadours." In *Cathares en Languedoc*, 177–97. Cahiers de Fanjeaux 3. Toulouse: Privat, 1968.
Nimmo, Duncan. *Reform and Division in the Medieval Franciscan Order*. Rome: Capuchin Historical Institute, 1987.
Nold, Patrick. *Pope John XXII and his Franciscan Cardinal: Bertrand de la Tour and the Apostolic Poverty Controversy*. Oxford: Oxford University Press, 2003.
_____. "Two Views of John XXII as a Heretical Pope." In *Defenders and Critics of Franciscan Life: Essays in Honor of John V. Fleming*, edited by Michael F. Cusato and G. Geltner, 139–58. Leiden: Brill, 2009.
Nykrog, Per. *Les fabliaux*, Étude d'histoire littéraire et de stylistique médiévale. Copenhagen: Munksgaard, 1957.
O'Gorman, Richard, ed. *Les Braise au Cordelier*. Birmingham, AL: Summa, 1983.
Olson, Glending. "The End of the *Summoner's Tale* and the Uses of Pentecost." *Studies in the Age of Chaucer* 21 (1999): 209–45.
_____. "Measuring the Immeasurable: Farting, Geometry, and Theology in the 'Summoner's Tale.'" *The Chaucer Review* 43, 4 (2009): 414–27.
O'Meara, O.P., Thomas F. "The Theology and Times of William of Tripoli, O.P.: A Different View of Islam." *Theological Studies* 69 (2008): 80–98.
O'Shea, Stephen. *The Friar of Carcassonne*. New York: Walker & Co., 2011.
_____. *The Perfect Heresy*. New York: Walker & Co., 2000.
Otto, Beatrice K. *Fools Are Everywhere: The Court Jester around the World*. Chicago: University of Chicago Press, 2001.
Page, William, ed. *The Victoria History of the County of Oxford*, vol. 2. London: Archibald Constable, 1907.
Painter, Sidney. "The Crusade of Theobald of Champagne and Richard of Cornwall." In *A History of the Crusades*, edited by Kenneth Setton, 3 vols., II, 463–85. Philadelphia: University of Pennsylvania Press, 1962.
Pantin, William Abel. *The English Church in the Fourteenth Century, Based on the Birkbeck Lectures, 1948*. Cambridge: Cambridge University Press, 1955, reprinted 2010.
_____. *Oxford Life in Oxford Archives*. Oxford: Clarendon Press, 1972.
Paterson, Linda M. *The World of the Troubadours: Medieval Occitan Society, c. 1100–1300*. Cambridge: Cambridge University Press, 1993.
Patterson, Lee. *Chaucer and the Subject of History*. Madison: University of Wisconsin Press, 1991.
Payne, Ann. *Medieval Beasts*. New York: New Amsterdam Books, 1990.
Pearsall, Derek. *The Life of Geoffrey Chaucer*, Blackwell Critical Biographies 1. Oxford and Cambridge, MA: Blackwell, 1992.
Pedersen, Olaf. *The First Universities: Studium Generale and the Origins of University Education in Europe*. Cambridge: Cambridge University Press, 1997.
Pegg, Mark Gregory. *The Corruption of Angels: The Great Inquisition of 1245–1246*. Princeton: Princeton University Press, 2001.
_____. *A Most Holy War: The Albigensian Crusade and the Battle for Christendom*. New York: Oxford University Press, 2009.
_____. "On Cathars, Albigenses, and Good Men of Languedoc." *Journal of Medieval History* 27 (2001): 181–190.
Pennington, Kenneth. *Popes and Bishops: The Papal Monarchy in the Twelfth and Thirteenth Centuries*. Philadelphia: University of Pennsylvania Press, 1984.
Pernoud, Regine. *Couleurs du moyen âge*. Genève-Paris: Editions Clairefontaine, 1987.
Perrod, Maurice. *Maître Guillaume de Saint-Amour, l'Université de Paris et les ordres mendiants au XIIIe siècle*. Paris: Firmin-Didot, 1895.

Peters, Edward. *Inquisition.* Berkeley: University of California Press, 1989.

Peuchmard, M. "Le prêtre ministre de la parole dans la théologie du XIIe siècle (canonistes moines, et chanoines)." *Recherches de théologie ancienne et médiévale* 29 (1962): 52-76.

Phillips, Helen. "The French Background." In *Chaucer: An Oxford Guide,* edited by Steve Ellis, 292–312. Oxford: Oxford University Press, 2005.

Piron, Sylvain. "Censures et condamnation de Pierre de Jean Olivi: enquête dans les marges du Vatican, Mélanges de l'Ecole française de Rome." *Moyen Age* 118, 2 (2006): 313–73.

Pitard, Derrick G. "Greed and Anti-Fraternalism in Chaucer's "Summoner's Tale."" In *The Seven Deadly Sins: From Communities to Individuals,* edited by Richard Newhauser, 207–27. Leiden: Brill, 2007.

Pixton, Paul B. "Conrad of Marburg," *Medieval Germany: An Encyclopedia,* edited by John M. Jeep. 230–31. New York: Garland, 2001.

Poirion, Daniel. "Jean de Meun et la querelle de l'Université de Paris: Du libelle au livre." In *Traditions polémiques* 2, edited by Nicole Gazauran and Jean Mesnard, 9–19. Paris: Ecole Normale Supérior des Jeunes Filles, 1985.

Post, Charles H. "The Paradox of Humor and Satire in the Poems of Rutebeuf." *The French Review* 25, 5 (1952), 364–68.

Post, Gaines. "Parisian Masters as a Corporation 1200–1246." *Speculum* 9 (1934): 421–45.

Pratt, R.A. "Chaucer and the Hand That Fed Him." *Speculum* 41 (1966): 621–642.

Prudlo, Donald. "The Assassin-Saint: The Life and Cult of Carino of Balsamo." *Catholic Historical Review* 94 (2008): 1–21.

———. *The Martyred Inquisitor: The Life and Cult of Peter of Verona (+1252).* Aldershot: Ashgate, 2008.

Pulsiano, Phillip. "The Twelve-Spoked Wheel of the Summoner's Tale." *Chaucer Review* 29 (1995): 382–89.

Quicherat, Jules. "Jean de Meung et sa maison à Paris." *Bibliotèque de l'Ecole des chartes* 41 (1880): 46–52

Rashdall, Hastings. "The Friars Preachers and the University." In *Collectanea* II, edited by M. Burrows, 217–273. Oxford: Oxford Historical Society, 1890.

———. *The Universities of Europe in the Middle Ages,* edited by A.B. Emden and Sir Frederick Maurice Powicke, 3 vols. London: Oxford University Press, 1936.

Rastall, Richard. *Secular Musicians in Late Medieval England.* Ph.D. thesis. Victoria University of Manchester, 1968.

Rayborn, Tim. "The Crusade Songs of Thibaut IV." In *Series Intendere: In Celebration of the Twenty-Fifth Anniversary of the Centre for Medieval Studies at Leeds University,* edited by Sharon Hanen, 45–51. Leeds: Centre for Medieval Studies, 1994.

———. *The Violent Pilgrimage: Christians, Muslims and Holy Conflicts, 850–1150.* Jefferson, NC: McFarland, 2013.

Raynaud, Gaston. "Renart le Contrefait et ses deux redactions." *Romania* 37 (1908): 245–283.

Reeves, Marjorie. *The Influence of Prophecy in the Later Middle Ages: A Study in Joachimism.* Oxford: Clarendon Press, 1969.

———. *Joachim of Fiore and the Prophetic Future.* London: SPCK, 1976.

Regalado, Nancy Freeman. "Allegories of power. The Tournament of Vices and Virtues in the *Roman de Fauvel* (BN MS Fr. 146)." *Gesta* 32 (1993): 135–146.

———. "The *Chronique métrique* and Moral Design of BN fr. 146: Feasts of Good and Evil," *Fauvel Studies: Allegory, Chronicle, Music, and Image in Paris, Bibliotèque Nationale de France, MS Français 146,* edited by Margaret Bent and Andrew Wathey, 467–94. Oxford: Oxford University Press, 1998.

———. *Poetic Patterns in Rutebeuf: A Study in Noncourtly Poetic Modes of the Thirteenth Century.* New Haven: Yale University Press, 1970.

———. "Rutebeuf." In *Key Figures in Medieval Europe: An Encyclopedia,* edited by Richard Kenneth Emmerson and Sandra Clayton-Emmerson, 581–83. Routledge Encyclopedias of the Middle Ages. New York: Routledge, 2006.

———. "Rutebeuf." In *Medieval France: An Encyclopedia,* edited by William W. Kibler, 830–31. Abingdon: Routledge, 1995.

Renouard, Yves. *The Avignon Papacy, 1305–1403,* translated by Dennis Bethell. Hamden, CT: Archon Books, 1970.

Rex, Richard. "Friars in the English Reformation." In *The Beginnings of English Protestantism,* edited by Peter Marshall and Alec Ryrie, 38–59. Cambridge: Cambridge University Press, 2002.

———. *The Lollards: Social History in Perspective.* New York: Palgrave Macmillan, 2002.

Richard, Jean. *Saint Louis: Crusader King of France.* Cambridge: Cambridge University Press, 1992.

Richardson, Janette. "Friar and Summoner, the Art of Balance." *The Chaucer Review* 9, 3 (1975): 227–36.

Richardson-Hay, Christine. "The Summoner's Prologue and Tale." In *Sources and Analogues of the Canterbury Tales,* edited by Robert M. Correale and Mary Hamel, vol. 2, 449–77. Woodbridge: Boydell, 2005.

de Ridder-Symoens, Hilde, ed. *A History of the University in Europe. Vol. I: Universities in the Middle Ages.* Cambridge: Cambridge University Press, 1992.

Rigg, A.G. *A History of Anglo-Latin Literature, 1066–1422.* Cambridge: Cambridge University Press, 1992.

———. "Two Latin Poems Against the Friars." *Mediaeval Studies* 30 (1968): 106–18.

Roberts, John G. "Renart Le Nouvel—Date and Successive Editions." *Speculum* 11, 4 (1936): 472–477.

Robertson Jr., D.W. *A Preface to Chaucer: Studies in Medieval Perspectives.* Princeton: Princeton University Press, 1962.

Robertson, Sharon Short. "Those Beastly People: a Study of Human Beings in Animal Epics." *Canadian Journal of Netherlandic Studies* IV, 1 (1983): 63–68.

Robinson, I.S. *The Papacy 1073–1198: Continuity and Innovation.* Cambridge: Cambridge University Press, 1990.

Robinson, Jonathan, "Qui praedicat periculum in illo peribit: William of St-Amour's Anti-Mendicant Sermons." In *Weapons of Mass Instruction: Secular and Religious Institutions Teaching the World, Proceedings of a St. Michael's College Symposium* (25–26 November 2005), edited by Joseph Goering, Francesco Guardiani, and Giulio Silano, 51–63. Ottawa: Legas, 2008.

Robson, J.A. *Wyclif and the Oxford Schools: The Relation of the "Summa de Ente" to Scholastic Debates at Oxford in the Later Fourteenth Century.* Cambridge: Cambridge University Press, 1961.

Robson, Michael J.P. *The Franciscans in the Middle Ages.* London: Boydell, 2007.

———, ed. *The Cambridge Companion to Francis of Assisi.* Cambridge: Cambridge University Press, 2012.

Roesner, Edward H. "Labouring in the Midst of Wolves: Reading a Group of Fauvel Motets." *Early Music History* 22 (2003): 169–245.

Roest, Bert. *A History of Franciscan Education (c. 1210–1517).* Leiden, Brill, 2000.

Rollo-Koster, Joëlle, and Thomas M. Izbicki, eds. *A Companion to the Great Western Schism (1378–1417).* Brill's Companions to the Christian Tradition, 17. Leiden: Brill, 2009.

———. *Raiding Saint Peter: Empty Sees, Violence, and the Initiation of the Great Western Schism, 1378.* Leiden: Brill, 2008.

Rosemann, Philipp W. *The Story of a Great Medieval Book: Peter Lombard's "Sentences."* Toronto: University of Toronto Press, 2007.

Roussel, Henri, ed. *Renart le Nouvel de Jacquemart Gielée.* Lille: Étude littéraire, 1984.

Roux, Simone. *Paris in the Middle Ages,* translated by Jo Ann McNamara. Philadelphia: University of Pennsylvania Press, 2009.

Rowling, Marjorie. *Life in Medieval Times.* New York: Perigree, 1973.

Runciman, Steven. *The Medieval Manichee.* Cambridge: Cambridge University Press, 1991.

Ryding, William W. "Faus Semblant: Hero or Hypocrite?" *Romanic Review* 60 (1969): 163.

Saint Dominique en Languedoc, Cahiers de Fanjeaux 1. Toulouse: Éditions Privat, 1966.

St. John, Jonathan Robin. *The Conflict of Authority Between Peter Abelard and Bernard of Clairvaux: Theological and Historical Issues Reconsidered.* Portland: Reed College, 1996.

Samuels, Michael. "Dialect and Grammar." In *A Companion to Piers Plowman,* edited by John Alford, 201–22. Berkeley: University of California Press, 1988.

de Saulnier, Chantal. "Le clerc auteur et personnage dans Renart le contrefait." In *Le clerc au Moyen Âge,* 515–528. Senefiance 37. Aix: CUERMA, 1995.

Sayers, Jane. "Violence in the Medieval Cloister." *Journal of Ecclesiastical History* 41(1994): 533–42.

Scase, Wendy. *Piers Plowman and the New Anticlericalism.* Cambridge Studies in Medieval Literature 4. Cambridge: Cambridge University Press, 1989.

Scattergood, John. "Pierce the Plowman's Crede: Lollardy and Texts." In *Lollardy and the Gentry in the Later Middle Ages,* edited by Margaret Aston and Colin Richmond, 77–94. New York, St. Martin's Press, 1997.

Schlosser, Marianne. "Bonaventure: Life and Works" In *A Companion to Bonaventure,* edited by Jay M. Hammond, Wayne Hellmann, and Jared Goff, 9–59. Leiden: Brill, 2013.

Schulman, N. M. *Where Troubadours were Bishops: The Occitania of Folc of Marseille (1150–1231).* New York. Routledge, 2001.

Schutter, Lilian. *Misconceptions about Beast Fables and Beast Tales, and the Role of the Fox in All of It.* M.A. dissertation. Rijksuniversiteit Groningen, 2008.

Şenocak, Neslihan. "The Making of Franciscan Poverty." *Revue Mabillon,* New Series 24 (2013): 5–26.

———. *The Poor and the Perfect: The Rise of Learning in the Franciscan Order, 1209–1310.* Ithaca: Cornell University Press, 2012.

Sergeant, Lewis. *John Wyclif: Last of the Schoolmen and First of the English Reformers.* New York: Putnam, 1893.

Serper, Ari. "L'Influence de Guillaume de Saint-Amour sur Rutebeuf." *Romance Philology* 17 (1963): 391–402.

Shank, Michael H. "Myth 2: That the Medieval Christian Church Suppressed the Growth of Science." In *Galileo Goes to Jail, and Other Myths about Science and Religion,* edited by Ronald L. Numbers, 19–27. Cambridge, MA: Harvard University Press, 2009.

Sikes, J.G. "Jean de Pouilly and Peter de la Palu." *English Historical Review* 49 (1934): 219–40.

Simons, Walter. "Beguines." In *Women and Gender in Medieval Europe,* edited by Margaret Schaus, 66–69. New York: Routledge, 2006.

———. *Cities of Ladies: Beguine Communities in the Medieval Low Countries, 1200–1565.* Philadelphia: University of Pennsylvania Press, 2001.

Simpson, J.R. *Animal Body, Literary Corpus: The Old French Roman de Renart.* Amsterdam: Rodopi, 1996.

Smalley, Beryl. *The Study of the Bible in the Middle Ages.* Oxford: Blackwell, 1952.

Smith, Damian J. *Crusade, Heresy and Inquisition in the Lands of the Crown of Aragon: (c. 1167–1276).* Leiden: Brill, 2010.

Smith, John Holland. *The Great Schism, 1378.* New York: Weybright and Talley, 1970.

Smith, Lesley. *The Glossa Ordinaria: The Making of a Medieval Bible Commentary.* Leiden: Brill, 2009.

Snyder, Susan Taylor. "Orthodox Fears: Anti-Inquisitorial Violence and Defining Heresy." In *Fear and Its Representations in the Middle Ages and Renaissance,* edited by Anne Scott and Cynthia Kosso, 92–104. Turnhout: Brepols, 2002.

Solterer, Helen. "Theater and Theatricality." In *The Cambridge Companion to Medieval French Literature,* edited by Simon Gaunt and Sarah Kay, 181–94. Cambridge: Cambridge University Press, 2008.

Somerset, Fiona, Jill Havens, and Derrick Pitard, eds. *Lollards and Their Influence in Late Medieval England.* Woodbridge: Boydell, 2003.

Southern, R.W. "From Schools to University." *The History of the*

University of Oxford: Vol. 1, The Early Oxford Schools, edited by J.I. Catto, 1–36. Oxford: Oxford University Press, 1984.

———. *Robert Grosseteste: The Growth of an English Mind in Medieval Europe.* Oxford: Clarendon Press, 1986.

Southworth, John. *The English Medieval Minstrel.* Woodbridge: Boydell, 1989.

Spade, Paul, ed. *The Cambridge Companion to Ockham.* Cambridge: Cambridge University Press, 1999.

Stakel, Susan. *False Roses: Structures of Duality and Deceit in Jean de Meun's "Roman de la Rose."* Stanford: ANMA Libri, 1991.

Steiner, Emily. *Reading Piers Plowman.* Cambridge: Cambridge University Press, 2013.

Stinson, Timothy L. "Illumination and Interpretation: The Depiction and Reception of Faus Semblant in Roman de la Rose Manuscripts." *Speculum* 87, 2 (2012): 469–498.

Stoyanov, Yuri. *The Other God: Dualist Religions from Antiquity to the Cathar Heresy.* New Haven: Yale Nota Bene, 2000.

Strayer, Joseph. *The Albigensian Crusades.* Ann Arbor: University of Michigan Press, 1992.

———. *The Reign of Philip the Fair.* Princeton: Princeton University Press, 1980.

Strong, David. "The Questions Asked, the Answers Given: Langland, Scotus, and Ockham." *The Chaucer Review* 38, 3 (2004): 255–275.

Stump, Philip. *The Reforms of the Council of Constance (1414–1418).* Leiden: Brill, 1994.

Subrenat, Jean. "Fabliau et satire cléricale: la specificité de Frère Denise par Rutebeuf." In *Risus Mediaevalis: Laughter in Medieval Literature and Art*, edited by Herman Braet, Guido Latré, and Werner Verbeke, 143–53. Leuven: University of Leuven Press, 2000.

Sullivan, Thomas. "Benedictine Masters of the University of Paris in the Late Middle Ages: Patterns of Recruitment." *Vivarium* 31 (1993): 226–40.

Sunderland, Luke. "Le Cycle de Renart: from the Enfances to the Jugement in a Cyclical Roman de Renart Manuscript." *French Studies*, 62, 1 (2008): 1–12.

Swanson, Robert N. "The 'Mendicant Problem' in the Later Middle Ages." In *The Medieval Church: Universities, Heresy, and Christian Life. Essays in Honour of Gordon Leff*, edited by Peter Biller and Barrie Dobson, 217–38. Studies in Church History: Subsidia 11. Woodbridge: Boydell, 1999.

Symes, Carol. *A Common Stage: Theater and Public Life in Medieval Arras.* Ithaca: Cornell University Press, 2007.

Symonds, John Addington. *Wine, Women, and Song.* London: Chatto and Windus, 1907, reprinted from 1884.

Szittya, Penn R. *The Antifraternal Tradition in Medieval Literature.* Princeton: Princeton University Press, 1986.

———. "The Antifraternal Tradition in Middle English Literature." *Speculum* 52 (1977): 287–313.

Tatnall, Edith C. "The Condemnation of John Wyclif at the Council of Constance." In *Councils and Assemblies: Papers Read at the Eighth Summer Meeting and the Ninth Winter Meeting of the Ecclesiastical History Society*, edited by G. J. Cuming and Derek Baker, 209–18. Studies in Church History 7. Cambridge: Cambridge University Press, 1971.

Taylor, Henry Osborn. *The Medieval Mind*, 4th edition. Cambridge: Harvard University Press, 1949.

Tierney, Brian. *Origins of Papal Infallibility, 1150–1350: A Study on the Concepts of Infallibility, Sovereignty and Tradition in the Middle Ages.* Leiden: Brill, 1972.

Thijssen, Johannes. *Censure and Heresy at the University of Paris, 1200–1400.* Philadelphia: University of Pennsylvania Press, 1998.

Thomson, Williel R. "The Image of the Mendicants in the Chronicles of Matthew Paris." *Archivum Franciscanum Historicum* 70 (1977): 3–34.

Thompson, O.P., Augustine. *Francis of Assisi: A New Biography.* Ithaca: Cornell University Press, 2012.

Thorndike, Lynn. *University Records and Life in the Middle Ages.* New York: Columbia University Press, 1949.

Thouzellier, Christine. "La place du De Periculis de Guillaume de Saint-Amour dans les polèmiques universitaires du XIIIe siècle." *Revue Historique* 156 (1927): 69–83.

Thurot, Charles. *De l'Organisation de l'enseignement dans l'Universitie de Paris au Moyen Âge*, Thèse présentée la Facult des Lettres de Paris, Paris, 1850. Frankfurt/Main: Minerva G.M.B.H., Unveräderter Nachdruck, 1967.

Tierney, Brian. *Religion, Law, and the Growth of Constitutional Thought, 1150–1650.* Cambridge: Cambridge University Press, 1982.

Tolan, John. *St. Francis and the Sultan: The Curious History of a Christian-Muslim Encounter.* Oxford: Oxford University Press, 2009.

Tracy, Larissa. *Torture and Brutality in Medieval Literature: Negotiations of National Identity.* Woodbridge: Boydell, 2012.

———. "The Uses of Torture and Violence in the Fabliaux: When Comedy Crosses the Line." *Florilegium* 23, 2 (2006): 143–68.

Traver, Andrew G. *The Identification of the vita apostolica with a Life of Itinerant Preaching and Mendicancy: Its Origins, Adherents, and Critics ca. 1050–1266.* Ph.D. thesis. University of Toronto, 1996.

———. "The Liber de Antichristo and the Failure of Joachite Expectations," *Florensia* 14 (2001): 1–12.

———. *The Opuscula of William of Saint-Amour: The Minor Works of 1255–1256.* Beiträge zur Geschichte der Philosophie und Theologie des Mittelalters vol. 63. Münster: Aschendorff Verlag, 2003.

———. "Rewriting History? The Parisian Secular Masters' Apologia of 1254." In *History of Universities, Volume XV: 1997–1999*, edited by Peter Denley, 9–45. Oxford: University Press, 2000.

———. "Secular and Mendicant Masters of the Faculty of Theology at the University of Paris, 1505–23." *The Sixteenth Century Journal* 26 (1995): 137–155.

———. "Thomas of York's Role in the Conflict between Mendicants and Seculars at Paris." *Franciscan Studies* 57 (1999): 179–202.

———. "William of Saint-Amour's Two Disputed Questions *De quantitate eleemosynae* and *De valido mendicante*." *Archives d'histoire doctrinale et littéraire du moyen âge* 62 (1995): 295–342.

Travis, Peter W. "Thirteen Ways of Listening to a Fart: Noise in Chaucer's *Summoner's Tale*." *Exemplaria* 16, 2 (2004): 323–48.

Troncarelli, Fabio. "Early Joachimism and Early Franciscanism: Manuscript Evidence of a Common Destiny." *Franciscan Studies* 69 (2011): 141–151.

Tugwell, Simon, ed. *Early Dominicans: Selected Writings*. Classics of Western Spirituality. New York: Paulist Press, 1982.

Turberville, Arthur Stanley. *Medieval Heresy & the Inquisition*. London: Lockwood, 1920.

Ullmann, Walter. *The Origins of the Great Schism: A Study in Fourteenth-Century Ecclesiastical History*. Hamden, CT: Archon Books, 1967.

Van der Werf, Hendrik. *The Extant Troubadour Melodies: Transcriptions and Essays for Performers and Scholars*, texts edited by Gerald A. Bond. Rochester, NY: the author, 1984.

Van Dijk, Conrad. *John Gower and the Limits of the Law*. Publications of the John Gower Society. Woodbridge: D.S. Brewer, 2013.

Vargas, Michael. *Taming a Brood of Vipers: Conflict and Change in Fourteenth-Century Dominican Convents*. Leiden: Brill, 2011.

———. "Weak Obedience, Undisciplined Friars, and Failed Reforms in the Medieval Order of Preachers." *Viator* 42, 1 (2011): 283–308.

Varty, Kenneth. "Reynard in England: from Caxton to Present." In *Reynard the Fox: Social Engagement and Cultural Metamorphoses in the Beast Epic from the Middle Ages to the Present*, edited by Kenneth Varty, 163–74. New York: Berghahn Books, 2000.

———. *The Roman de Renart: A Guide to Scholarly Work*. Lanham, MD: Scarecrow Press, 1998.

Vaughan, Richard. *Matthew Paris*. Cambridge: Cambridge University Press, 1958.

———, trans. *The Illustrated Chronicles of Matthew Paris*. Stroud, Gloucestershire, UK: Alan Sutton, 1993.

Verger, Jacques. "The First French Universities and the Institutionalization of Learning: Faculties, Curricula, Degrees." In *Learning Institutionalized*, edited by John Engen, 5–20. Notre Dame: Notre Dame University Press, 2000.

———. *Histoire des universités en France*. Paris: Privat, 1987.

Vicaire, Marie-Humbert. "Dominic." *New Catholic Encyclopedia*. New York: McGraw-Hill, 1967.

———. *Histoire de Saint Dominique*, 2 vols. Paris: Les Éditions de Cerf, 1957, translated by Kathleen Pond as *Saint Dominic and His Times*. Green Bay, WI: Alt Publishing, 1964.

———. "L'ordre de Saint Dominique en 1215." *Archivum Fratrum Praedicatorum* 54 (1984): 5–38.

———. "La prédication nouvelle de prêcheurs méridionaux au XIIIe siècle." In *Le Credo, la morale et l'inquisition en Languedoc au XIIIe siècle*, 21–64. Cahiers de Fanjeaux 6. Toulouse: Éditions Privat, 1971.

———. *Saint Dominique de Caleruega: D'après les documents du XIIIe siècle*. Paris: Éditions du Cerf, 1955.

Vidal, Jean-Marie. *Un inquisitor jugé par ses victimes: Jean Galand et les Carcassonnaise (1285–1286)*. Paris: Picard, 1903.

Vitz, Evelyn Birge. "La liturgie, Le Roman de Renart, et le problème du blasphème dans la vie littéraire au Moyan Age, ou les bêtes peuvent-elles blasphèmer?" *Reinardus* 12 (1999): 205–25.

Von Nolcken, Christina. "Piers Plowman, the Wycliffites, and Pierce the Plowman's Creed." *The Yearbook of Langland Studies* 2 (1988): 71–102.

Wabuda, Susan. *Preaching during the English Reformation*. Cambridge: Cambridge University Press, 2002.

Wackers, Paul. "Medieval French and Dutch Renardian Epics: Between Literature and Society." In *Reynard the Fox: Social Engagement and Cultural Metamorphoses*, edited by Elaine C. Block and Kenneth Varty, 55–72. New York: Berghan Books, 2000.

Waddell, Helen. *The Wandering Scholars*. London: Constable & Robinson, 1927, reprinted by Dover, 2000.

Wailes, Stephen L. "Vagantes and the Fabliaux." In *The Humor of the Fabliaux: A Collection of Critical Essays*, edited by Thomas D. Cooke and Benjamin L. Honeycutt, 43–58. Columbia: University of Missouri Press, 1974.

Wakefield, Walter L. *Heresy, Crusade, and Inquisition in Southern France, 1100–1250*. New York: Allen and Unwin, 1974.

———, and Austin P. Evans, eds. *Heresies of the High Middle Ages*. New York: Columbia University Press, 1991.

Walsh, Katherine. "Archbishop FitzRalph and the Friars at the Papal Court in Avignon, 1357–60." *Traditio* 31 (1975): 223–245.

———. "The 'De vita evangelica' of Geoffrey Hardeby, OESA (c. 1320–c.1385). A Study in Mendicant Controversies of the Fourteenth Century." *Analecta Augustiniana* 33 (1970): 151-261, 34 (1971): 5–83.

———. *A Fourteenth-Century Scholar and Primate: Richard FitzRalph in Oxford, Avignon and Armagh*. Oxford: Clarendon Press, 1981.

Walters, Lori. "Gui de Mori and the Rewriting of Faux Semblant in the Tournai *Roman de la Rose*." In *The Medieval Opus: Imitation, Rewriting and Transmission in the French Tradition*, edited by Douglass Kelly, 261–76. Proceedings of the Colloquium held at the Institute for Research in the Humanities, October 5–7, 1995. Amsterdam: Rodopi, 1996.

Walton, Thomas. "Staging 'Le Jeu de la Feuillée.'" *The Modern Language Review* 36, 3 (1941): 344–350.

Walz, Angelus Maria. *Compendium historiae Ordinis Praedicatorum*. Rome: Herder, 2nd edition. 1948.

Warner, Lawrence. *The Lost History of "Piers Plowman": The Earliest Transmission of Langland's Work*. Philadelphia:

University of Pennsylvania Press, 2011.
Wei, Ian P. "The Self-Image of the Masters of Theology at the University of Paris in the Late 13th and Early 14th Centuries." *Journal of Ecclesiastical History* 46 (1995): 397–431.
Weiler, Björn. "Matthew Paris in Norway." *Revue Bénédictine* 122 (2012): 153–81.
———. "Matthew Paris on the Writing of History," *Journal of Medieval History* 35 (2009): 254–78.
Weis, René. *The Yellow Cross: The Story of the Last Cathars, 1290–1329*. New York: Random House, 2001.
Wheatley, Edward. "The Nun's Priest's Tale." In *Sources and Analogues of the Canterbury Tales*, edited by Robert M. Correale and Mary Hamel, vol. 1, 449–90. Woodbridge: Boydell, 2002.
Whicher, George F., trans. *The Goliard Poets*. Cambridge: Cambridge University Press, 1949, reprinted by Greenwood Press, 1979.
Wickstrom, John B. "The Humiliati: Liturgy and Identity." *Archivum Fratrum Praedicatorum* 4 (1992): 1–32.
Widengren, Geo. *Mani and Manichaeism*. London: Weidenfeld and Nicholson, 1965.
Wieruszowski, Helene. *The Medieval University*. Princeton: Van Nostrand Anvil Original, 1966.
Wilks, Michael. "Predestination, Property, and Power: Wyclif's Theory of Dominion and Grace." *Studies in Church History* 2 (1965): 220–36.
———. "Wyclif and Hus as Leaders of Religious Protest Movements." *Studies in Church History* 9 (1972): 62–84.
Williams, Arnold. "Chaucer and the Friars," *Speculum* 28 (1953): 499–513.
———. "Relations between the Mendicant Friars and the Regular Clergy in England in the Later Fourteenth Century." *Annuale Mediaevale* 1 (1960): 22–95.
Wilshire, Leland Edward. "The Condemnations of 1277 and the Intellectual Climate of the Medieval University." In *The Intellectual Climate of the Early University: Essays in Honor of Otto Gründler*, edited by Nancy van Deusen, 151–93. Kalamzaoo: Western Michigan University, 1997.
———. "Where the Oxford Condemnations of 1277 directed against Aquinas?" *The New Scholasticism* 48 (1964): 125–32.
Wippel, J.F. "The Condemnations of 1270 and 1277 at Paris." *The Journal of Medieval and Renaissance Studies* 7, 2 (1977): 169–201.
Wolf, Kenneth Baxter. *The Poverty of Riches: St. Francis of Assisi Reconsidered*. Oxford: Oxford University Press, 2003.
Wood, Charles, T. *Phillip the Fair and Boniface VIII: State vs Papacy*. New York: Holt, Rhinehart, and Winston, 1967.
Wood, Diana, ed. *The Church and Sovereignty, c. 580*. Oxford: Blackwell, 1991.
Wright, H.G. "Thomas Speght as a Lexicographer and Annotator of Chaucer's Works." *English Studies* 40 (1959): 194–208.
Wright, Thomas, ed. *Political Poems and Songs Relating to English History, Composed During the Period from the Accession of Edward III to that of Richard III*, 2 vols. London: Longman, Green, Longman, and Roberts, 1859.
———, ed. *The Political Songs of England: From the Reign of John to that of Edward II*. London: Camden Society, 1839.
Young, Spencer. "'Consilio hominum nostrorum': A Comparative Study of Royal Responses to Crisis at the University of Paris, 1200–1231." In *History of Universities* 22, edited by Mordechai Feingold, vol. 1, 1–20. Oxford: Oxford University Press, 2007.
Yunck, John A. *The Lineage of Lady Meed: The Development of Mediaeval Venality Satire*. Notre Dame: Notre Dame University Press, 1963.
Ziegler, Philip. *The Black Death*. New York: Penguin Books, 1969, reprinted 1982.
Zink, Gaston. "Le vocabulaire de la ruse et de la tromperie dans les branches X et XI du *Roman de Renart*." *L'information grammaticale* 43 (1989): 15–19.
Ziolkowski, Jan. "Archpoet." In *Medieval Germany: An Encyclopedia*, edited by John M. Jeep, 21–22. Routledge Encyclopedias of the Middle Ages. New York: Routledge, 2001.
———. *Talking Animals: Medieval Latin Beast Poetry, 750–1150*. Philadelphia: University of Pennsylvania Press, 1993.
Zutshi, Patrick. "Letters of Pope Honorius III Concerning the Order of Preachers." In *Pope, Church and City: Essays in Honour of Brenda M. Bolton*, edited by Frances Andrews, Christoph Egger, and Constance M. Rousseau, 269–86. Leiden and Boston: Brill, 2004.

Websites

Ad conditorem canonum, translated by John Kilcullen and John Scott. Macquarie University, accessed January 3, 2014: http://www.mq.edu.au/about_us/faculties_and_departments/faculty_of_arts/mhpir/politics_and_international_relations/staff/john_kilcullen/john_xxii_ad_conditorem_canonum.

"Adam de la Halle." Bibliography at Les Archives de littérature du Moyen Âge (ARLIMA), accessed November 17, 2013: http://www.arlima.net/ad/adam_de_la_halle.html.

Bartholomaeus Anglicus. *De proprietatibus rerum*, Internet Archive, accessed November 10, 2013: https://archive.org/details/deproprietatibu00angl goog.

"Carmina Burana." *Bibliotheca Augustana*, accessed February 2, 2014: http://www.hs-augsburg.de/~harsch/Chronologia/Lspost13/CarminaBurana/bur_car0.html.

Clement V, Pope. *Exivi de paradiso*, Papal Encyclicals Online, accessed February 2, 2014: http://www.papalencyclicals.net/Clem05/exivi-l.htm. For an English translation, see the Franciscan Archive: http://www.franciscan-archive.org/bullarium/exivi-e.html.

"Corpus of Middle English Prose and Verse," accessed January 20, 2014: http://quod.lib.umich.edu/c/cme/AGD2855.0001.001/1:4?rgn=div1;view=fulltext.

"Council of Constance," accessed January 13, 2014: http://www.ewtn.com/library/COUNCILS/CONSTANC.HTM.

"Council of Lyons, 1274." *Papal Encyclicals Online*, accessed

November 13, 2013: http://www.papalencyclicals.net/Councils/ecum14.htm.

De heretico comburendo. The Rhode Island College, accessed January 14, 2014: www.ric.edu/faculty/rpotter/heretico.html.

Dean, James M. "Anticlerical Poems and Documents." In *Medieval English Political Writings*, the University of Rochester, accessed February 16, 2014: http://d.lib.rochester.edu/teams/publication/dean-medieval-english-political-writings.

———. *Six Ecclesiastical Satires*. The University of Rochester, accessed January 14, 2014: http://d.lib.rochester.edu/teams/publication/dean-six-ecclesiastical-satires#sixecc.

Deane, Jennifer. "'Beguines' Reconsidered: Historiographical Problems and New Directions," *Monastic Matrix*, 2008. *Commentaria* 3461, accessed December 29, 2013: http://monasticmatrix.org/commentaria/beguines-reconsidered-historiographical-problems-and-new-directions.

Donavin, Georgiana, and Meghan Hekker Nestel. "Bibliography of Gower Studies, 2005 to 2011," *The Gower Project*, accessed October 26, 2013: http://www.gowerproject.org/bibliography.htm.

Dowd, Matthew F. *Astronomy and Compotus at Oxford University in the Early Thirteenth Century: The Works of Robert Grosseteste*, Ph.D. thesis. University of Notre Dame, 2003, accessed January 4, 2014: http://www3.nd.edu/~mdowd1/dowddissertation.html.

"Fabliaux." Bibliography at Les Archives de littérature du Moyen Âge (ARLIMA), accessed November 26, 2013: http://www.arlima.net/eh/fabliau.html#biblio.

Fansler, Dean Spruill. *Chaucer and the Roman de la Rose*. New York: Columbia University Press, 1914, accessed January 7, 2014: http://books.google.com/books/about/Chaucer_and_the_Roman_de_La_Rose.html?id=rrYLAAAAYAAJ.

"14th Century Oxford Theology Online," project director Stephen E. Lahey. University of Nebraska at Lincoln, accessed March 14, 2014: http://theology.unl.edu/works.html.

The Fox and the Wolf. "Medieval Forum" at San Francisco State, accessed January 20, 2014: http://www.sfsu.edu/~medieval/complaintlit/fox_wolf.html.

"Francis and Clare of Assisi, Early Documents," accessed December 27, 2013: http://franciscantradition.org:8080/FAED/index.jsp?workNum=043&p=570.

Friar Bacon, His Discovery of the Miracles of Art, Nature, and Magick, accessed December 30, 2013: http://www.sacred-texts.com/aor/bacon/miracle.htm. A modern translation by Michael S. Mahoney, accessed December 30, 2013: http://www.princeton.edu/~hos/h392/bacon.html.

"Glosses and Commentaries on the Bible in the Middle Ages," accessed December 22, 2013: http://www.glossae.net.

Harley MS 978. British Library Manuscript Display, accessed November 3, 2013: http://www.bl.uk/manuscripts/FullDisplay.aspx?ref=Harley_MS_978.

Higginbotham, Susan. "The Indomitable Duchess: Alice Chaucer, Duchess of Suffolk," accessed October 27, 2013: http://susanhigginbotham.com/blog/posts/the-indomitable-duchess-alice-chaucer-duchess-of-suffolk/.

Hinnebusch, O.P., William. *The Dominicans: A Short History*, accessed February 18, 2014: http://opcentral.org/blog/the-dominicans-a-short-history/.

———. "How the Dominican Order Faced Crises." *Review for Religious* 32 (19/3/6): 1307–1321, accessed February 18, 2014: http://opcentral.org/blog/how-the-dominican-order-faced-crises/.

"The History of English," accessed February 25, 2014: http://www.thehistoryofenglish.com/index.html.

Innocent IV, Pope. *Ordinem vestrum*, translated by Jonathan Robinson, accessed December 27, 2013: http://individual.utoronto.ca/jwrobinson/translations/innocent4_lat-eng_ordinem-vestrum.pdf.

International John Gower Society. Western Carolina University, accessed October 26, 2013: http://www.wcu.edu/johngower/index.html

"Jean de Meun." Bibliography at Les Archives de littérature du Moyen Âge (ARLIMA), accessed January 22, 2014: http://www.arlima.net/il/jean_de_meun.html.

John XXII, Pope. *Ad conditorem canonum*, translated by John Kilcullen and John Scott, Macquarie University, accessed January 3, 2014: http://www.mq.edu.au/about_us/faculties_and_departments/faculty_of_arts/mhpir/politics_and_international_relations/staff/john_kilcullen/john_xxii_ad_conditorem_canonum.

John Foxe. *Acts and Monuments*, accessed February 18, 2014: http://www.johnfoxe.org/index.php.

"John Wyclif." *Stanford Encyclopedia of Philosophy*, accessed January 9, 2014: http://plato.stanford.edu/entries/wyclif/.

Kindrick, Robert L. "The Morall Fabillis: Introduction," accessed January 20, 2014: http://d.lib.rochester.edu/teams/text/kindrick-poems-of-robert-henryson-morall-fabillis-introduction.

Langland, William. *The Vision of Piers Plowman*. Corpus of Middle English Prose and Verse, University of Michigan/Oxford Text Archive, accessed January 3, 2014: http://quod.lib.umich.edu/c/cme/ppllan.

Leach, Elizabeth Eva. "Renart le Nouvel: Beast Satire with Songs," accessed January 20, 2014: http://eeleach.wordpress.com/2013/05/06/renart-le-nouvel.

Lehner, Francis C., ed. *St. Dominic: Biographical Documents*, accessed December 28, 2013: http://domcentral.org/blog/st-dominic-biographical-documents.

"Meed and Greed." San Francisco State Medieval Forum, accessed February 25, 2014: https://www.sfsu.edu/~medieval/complaintlit/meed_intro.html.

Miller, Carol M. "The St. Scholastica Day Riot Oxford after the Black Death," accessed January 9, 2014: http://organizations.ju.edu/fch/1993miller.htm.

O'Brien, Juliet. "The Paradoxical

Heroism of Rutebeuf's Antimendicant Poems, Jean de Meun's *Roman de la Rose* and Chaucer's *Summoner's Tale*. Three Approaches to the Problem of Truth." (2002), accessed February 16, 2014: http://blogs.ubc.ca/mdvl302/files/2012/01/comm-sample-rose2.pdf.

Papal Encyclicals Online, accessed November 13, 2013: http://www.papalencyclicals.net.

"*Patrologia Latina* Database," accessed December 15, 2013: http://pld.chadwyck.com.

Peire Cardenal. Selected poems, "Rialto," accessed February 2, 2014: http://www.rialto.unina.it/BdT.htm.

"The Piers Plowman Electronic Archive." University of Virginia, accessed February 25, 2014: http://piers.iath.virginia.edu/index.html.

Plumb, Gordon. "Robert Grosseteste and the Early English Franciscans," accessed January 4, 2014: http://www.tssf.org.uk/study-and-prayer-papers/study-week-papers/302-robert-grosseteste-and-the-early-english-franciscans.

"The Premonstratensians." accessed December 30, 2013: http://www.premontre.org.

Robinson, Jonathan. Texts in translation page, accessed November 11, 2013: http://individual.utoronto.ca/jwrobinson/#Translations.

Roger Bacon. *Epistola de Secretis Operibus Artis*, accessed December 30, 2013: http://www.sacred-texts.com/aor/bacon/miracle.htm.

"Roger Bacon." Stanford Encyclopedia of Philosophy, accessed March 2, 2014: http://plato.stanford.edu/entries/roger-bacon.

"Le Roman de Fauvel." Bibliography at Les Archives de littérature du Moyen Âge (ARLIMA), accessed December 3, 2013: http://www.arlima.net/eh/fauvel.html.

"*Roman de la Rose* Digital Library," accessed January 21, 2014: http://romandelarose.org.

"Roman de Renart." Bibliography at Les Archives de littérature du Moyen Âge (ARLIMA), accessed November 4, 2013: http://www.arlima.net/qt/renart_roman.html, last updated in May 2011.

"*Roman de Renart*." Bibliothèque Nationale de France, accessed February 24, 2014: http://classes.bnf.fr/renart/index.htm.

"Rutebeuf." Bibliography at Les Archives de littérature du Moyen Âge (ARLIMA), accessed November 10, 2013: http://www.arlima.net/qt/rutebeuf.html.

Stoner, Abby. "Sisters Between: Gender and the Medieval Beguines." *Ex Post Facto* IV, 2 (Spring 1995), accessed December 29, 2013: http://userwww.sfsu.edu/epf/journal_archive/volume_IV,_no._2_-_sp._1995/.

Tugwell, Simon. "Robert Kilwardby." In *Oxford Dictionary of National Biography*, accessed January 5, 2014: http://www.oxforddnb.com/view/printable/15546.

"Twelve Conclusions of the Lollards," The "Geoffrey Chaucer Page" at Harvard University, accessed January 13, 2014: http://sites.fas.harvard.edu/~chaucer/special/varia/lollards/lollconc.htm. Drawn from H.S. Cronin, ed., "The Twelve Conclusions of the Lollards." *English Historical Review* 22 (1907): 292–304.

Wathey, Andrew. *Roman de Fauvel*, accessed February 16, 2014: http://musicologicus.blogspot.com/2007/05/roman-de-fauvel.html.

Weiler, Björn. "Matthew Paris and Europe," accessed December 1, 2013: http://aber.academia.edu/BjörnWeiler.

"William of Ockham." *Stanford Encyclopedia of Philosophy*, accessed January 5, 2014: www.plato.stanford.edu/entries/ockham.

Index

Abelard, Pierre (Peter) 33, 93, 94
Adam de la Halle 71–72, 88–90, 96, 114; *Jeu de la feuillée* 88–89, 96, 114
Adam Stockton 154
Ælfric of Eynsham 118
Albigensian Crusade 6, 13–14, 19–20, 21, 51, 91, 174*n*26, 192*n*4, 192*n*5
Alexander III, Pope 36; *Quanto Gallicana ecclesia* 36
Alexander IV, Pope 46, 47, 49, 58, 69, 78, 85, 87, 184*n*116; *Nec insolitum* 47; *Quasi Lignum Vitae* 47
Alexander V, antipope 152
Alexander of Hales 39–40
Alfred the Great, King of Wessex 119
Alice, Duchess of Suffolk (granddaughter of Chaucer) 119
Alice Perrers, mistress of Edward III 138
alms *see* mendicancy
Ambrose, St. 59, 96
Antichrist 6, 44, 45, 46, 49, 50, 52, 53, 55, 57, 59, 61, 70, 72, 74–75, 78, 79, 80, 86, 112, 126, 128, 129, 134, 143, 151, 153, 160, 222*n*1
anticlericalism 4–5, 68, 72, 78, 90–91, 98–101, 102–6, 109, 112–13, 154, 155, 156, 160, 162, 166, 198*n*17, 202*n*116
apocalyptic literature 5, 45, 49, 51, 57, 58, 65, 70, 71, 72–75, 78–79, 81, 128–29, 143, 148, 156, 160, 183*n*96, 190*n*55
Aquinas, Thomas 7, 40, 49, 50, 54, 85, 121, 140, 153, 183*n*59; *Summa Theologiae* 140
Archpoet 93, 196*n*99
Aristotle 50, 202*n*109, 215*n*55
Arnaud-Amaury, Abbot of Cîteaux 13
Arnold Catalan 23
Arras 83, 88–89, 90
Augustine of Hippo, St. 12, 20, 59, 73–74, 125, 156
Augustinian order 6, 40, 51, 118, 125, 146, 148, 154, 156, 173*n*15
Avignon 133, 143, 148, 152, 153; papacy at 109, 141, 152; *see also* Western Schism

Baldwin II, Emperor of the Latin Empire of Constantinople 41
Bartholomaeus Anglicus 96
begging *see* mendicancy
Beghards 28
Beguines 24, 26, 27–28, 57, 69, 70–71, 92, 137
Benedict, St. 121, 137
Benedict XI, Pope 26
Benedict Gaetani *see* Boniface VIII
Benedictine order 4, 7, 9, 17, 31, 33, 81, 88, 90, 100, 101, 110, 118, 134, 135, 136, 137, 142, 199*n*25
Benedictine Rule 9, 15, 19, 93, 136, 137
Bernard Delicieux 25–27
Bernard of Clairvaux 33, 93, 98, 121, 156, 176*n*63, 196*n*92
Bernard the donkey 97, 102, 198*n*17
The Bible 5, 11, 15, 45, 48, 52, 54, 58, 59, 70, 74, 86, 88, 93, 96, 124, 133, 134, 140, 153, 157, 159, 209*n*75
Bible of Guiot de Provins 88
Black Death 23, 46, 117, 119, 131, 142, 144, 157, 164
Blanche of Castile, Queen of France 17, 39, 41, 91, 182*n*50
Boccaccio, Giovanni 58, 103, 120, 121
Boethius 76, 119
Bonaventure 7, 15, 40, 41, 49, 50, 51, 54, 56, 59, 60–61, 121, 130, 162; *De mendicitate* 56, 60, 61; *De paupertate quoad abrenuntiationem* 59, 60; *Replicatio adversus objectiones postea factas* 61
Boniface VIII, Pope 41, 51, 109, 110–12, 144; *Super cathedram* 51, 111, 144; *Unum sanctum* 111
Bruys, Peter of 9–11, 173*n*12
Burnellus the donkey 103, 112

Cambridge Songs 103
Canterbury Tales 63, 102–3, 119, 120, 121–22, 126, 127, 132, 160; *see also* Chaucer, Geoffrey
Carcassonne 13, 25, 26
Carmelite order 6, 40, 51, 124, 125, 137, 155, 156, 159, 160, 172*n*15
Carmina Burana 93–95
Castle of Jealousy, in the *Roman de la Rose* 65, 66–67, 71, 74, 75, 79
Cathars 6, 10, 11, 12–14, 19, 20, 21–23, 25, 45, 91, 146, 174*n*27, 176*n*62, 176*n*63

Caxton, William *see The Historie of Reynart the Foxe*
Chaillou de Pesstain 109; *see also Roman de Fauvel*
chancellor, at the University of Paris 33, 36, 37, 42, 47, 72, 138, 139
charivari, in the *Roman de Fauvel* 114
Charles de Valois 110, 114
Chaucer, Geoffrey 5, 7, 58, 81, 102–3, 116, 118, 119, 120–26, 129, 130, 131, 132, 155, 160, 161, 163; General Prologue to the *Canterbury Tales* 119, 122, 155; *Legend of Good Women* 126; Nun's Priests' Tale 97, 103; Summoner's Tale 120, 122–26, 128; *see also Canterbury Tales*
Cistercian order 4, 9, 19, 33, 40, 68, 81, 90, 93, 94, 98, 100, 101, 124, 142, 176*n*63
Clare of Assisi 27
Clement IV, Pope 30, 50, 140
Clement V, Pope 112, 141, 144; *Exivi de paradiso* 141
Clement VII, antipope 152
Cluniacs 9, 68
collegium 35
conductus 113, 114, 204*n*169
confession 11, 78, 81, 100–1, 131, 132, 153, 158; and the friars 46, 47, 53, 57, 69, 71, 108, 111, 130, 141, 142, 145–46, 147, 148, 154, 164, 217*n*96, 222*n*1; *see also* Boniface VIII; Innocent III, *Omnis utriusque sexus*
Confrérie des jongleurs et bourgeois d'Arras 90; *see also* Arras; jongleurs
Constrained Abstinence 65, 66, 67, 69, 71, 72, 74–75, 76, 78, 79
cordeliers 16, 84, 192*n*11
Council of Constance 157
Council of Lyon 50–51, 88, 188*n*3, 196*n*88
Council of Vienne 112
Cruciferi 137

De heretico comburendo 159, 160
De Periculis Novissimorum Temporum 48, 49, 52–59, 61, 62, 67, 69, 74, 85, 141–42, 163; *see also* Guillaume de Saint-Amour
Dee, Dr. John 180*n*152
Li Dis de le vescie à prestre 124
dit 83; *see also* Rutebuef
Doctrinale antiquitatum fidei eccleaisæ catholicæ see Thomas Netter

Dominic of Caleruega, St. 14, 19–20, 22, 32, 37, 57, 95, 113, 121, 128, 136, 140, 158, 160, 176*n*62
Dominican order 3, 4, 6, 14, 17, 19–27, 29, 32, 37, 39, 41–44, 46–47, 49, 51, 64, 69, 86, 87, 88, 90, 91, 92, 94, 102, 104, 109, 115, 125, 136–38, 139–40, 141, 152, 153, 158, 160, 162, 163, 164, 172*n*11, 172*n*15, 174*n*36, 177*n*101, 183*n*59, 215*n*55, 223*n*6; *see also* Inquisition; Jacobins
dominion 145, 146, 147, 150–51, 188*n*12
dominium 146

Earthquake Synod 154–55
Ecbasis captivi, Latin poem 98
Edward I, King of England 31, 140
Edward II, King of England 204*n*87
Edward III, King of England 120, 129, 138, 142, 150
Eleanor of Aquitaine 13, 174*n*26
Elias of Cortona 18
Elizabeth I, Queen of England 159
Elizabethan era 119, 121, 180*n*152
Enguerran de Marigny 109–10, 114, 115
estates satire 118–20, 122, 131
Eternal Gospel 44–45, 46, 53, 55, 61, 70, 75
Eucharist, controversies surrounding 10, 12, 94, 152, 153–54, 158
Evesque de Troyes *see Renart le Contrefait*

fabliaux 5, 7, 71, 84, 92, 95, 98, 103–9, 121, 123, 124, 201*n*80, 208*n*53; *Les Braies au Cordelier* 106–7; *De la Crote* 104; Gautier le Leu 105; *Le Prestre crucifé* 105; *Sacristain* (Rutebeuf) 109; *see also Freire Denise*; Rutebeuf
faculties, at the University of Paris 32, 33, 35, 36, 39–40, 42, 43, 47, 49, 77
Fair Welcome, in the *Roman de la Rose* 64–65, 66, 67, 77
false prophets 53, 54–55, 56, 57, 75, 76, 78, 113, 118; *see also De Periculis*
False Seeming 6, 62, 65–66, 67–72, 74–75, 77–78, 79–82, 86, 92, 102, 112, 113, 115, 121, 122, 126; as a Cretan liar 81

farting: in the *Roman de Renard* 100, 199*n*45; in the Summoner's Tale 123, 124, 125–26
Faus Semblant see False Seeming
Fauvel 109–10, 112–14, 115–16, 154; *see also Roman de Fauvel*
Ferran, Prince of Majorca 26
FitzRalph, Richard 7, 117, 121, 142, 143–49, 150, 152, 156–57, 159, 161, 163, 188*n*12, 217*n*97; *De audientia confessionem* 148; *De pauperie Salvatoris* 144, 146–47, 156; *Defensio curatorum* 147, 148; Diary (sermons) 143, 147–48; *Libellus* 148; *Objectiones et responsiones* 148; *Unusquisque* 144, 145
Flagellants 46, 117
Fortune, in the *Roman de Fauvel* 112, 113–14, 116
Foul Mouth 65, 66, 71, 72
fountain of Narcissus, in the *Roman de la Rose* 64, 75–76, 78
Fourth Lateran Council 19, 20, 45, 51, 153
the fox, in medieval thought 96–97
Foxe, John 163; *Foxe's Book of Martyrs* 163
Francis of Assisi, St. 3, 4, 11, 14–17, 18, 19, 27, 29, 32, 37, 40, 56–57, 61, 113, 121, 122, 124, 125, 128, 129, 136, 140, 143, 158, 160, 174*n*36, 211*n*114
Franciscan order 3–4, 6, 12, 14–19, 20, 22, 23, 25–27, 28–32, 37, 39–40, 41, 43, 44–45, 47, 51, 56, 59, 61, 62, 69, 84, 85, 90, 102, 104, 106, 107–9, 110, 115, 122, 124–26, 129–30, 136, 137, 138, 139, 140, 141, 142, 143, 144–48, 150, 153, 156, 160, 162, 163, 164, 172*n*15, 174*n*36, 177*n*101, 184*n*110, 187*n*47, 192*n*11, 202*n*93, 211*n*115, 211*n*118; as *ioculatores Domini* 122, 129, 211*n*114; *see also* confession
Fraticelli see Spiritual Franciscans
Fraud, in the *Roman de la Rose* 70
Frederick II, Holy Roman Emperor 18, 24, 45–46
French Revolution 163
Friar Daw's Reply 160; *see also Jack Upland*; Lollards
Friar Tuck 3

Friend, in the *Roman de la Rose* 65, 66, 75, 77
Fulk, Bishop of Toulouse 19–20

Gabriel, Archangel 114
Genius, in the *Roman de la Rose* 66, 78; in the *Confessio Amantis* 132
Geoffroy de Saint-Léger 115
Gerard of Abbeville 50, 52
Gerard of Borgo San Donnino 44–45, 46, 70, 75; *see also* Eternal Gospel
Gervais de Bus 109; *see also* Roman de Fauvel
Giles of Rome 146
Glossa Ordinaria 52, 58, 74
God of Love: in the *Legend of Good Women* 126; in the *Roman de la Rose* 64, 65–66, 68, 71, 76, 78, 80, 81
goliards 7, 92–95, 98, 103, 125
Gower, John 58, 81, 116, 118, 119, 130–33, 211n130; *Confessio Amantis* 81, 130–31, 132, 133; *Mirour de l'Omme* 131, 132; *Speculum Meditantis* 131; *Vox Clamantis* 131, 132
Great Dispersion 37, 39
Great Schism *see* Western Schism
Gregory I (the Great), Pope 96
Gregory VII, Pope 9
Gregory IX, Pope 15, 16, 21, 31, 39, 136, 137
Gregory X, Pope 88
Gregory XI, Pope 151–52, 153, 219n157
Grosseteste, Robert 135, 136
Gui, Bernard 26
Gui de Mori 80; *Le Remaniement du Roman de la Rose* 80–81
Guilhabert of Castres, Cathar Bishop of Toulouse 22
Guilhem Figueira 24
Guillaume IX, Duke of Aquitaine 13, 174n26
Guillaume de Deguilleville 81; *Pèlerinage de la vie humaine* 81
Guillaume de Lorris 62, 63, 75, 76, 77, 87, 190n65, 191n79, 202n106
Guillaume de Machaut 81, 120, 191n94, 192n4
Guillaume de Nogaret 111
Guillaume de Saint-Amour 5, 6, 7, 44, 46, 48–50, 51–62, 63, 67, 68, 69, 70, 72, 74, 75, 80, 85, 86–87, 94, 113, 118, 121, 128, 139, 141, 142, 143, 147, 156, 162, 163, 184n116, 190n65; *Collectiones catholi-*
cae et canonical scriptural 49–50; questions 53, 59–60; sermons 48, 53, 56, 59, 61–62, 70, 187n45, 188n76; *see also De Periculis Novissimorum Temporum*
Guiot de Provins 88
gyrovagi 93, 137

Hellequin 88, 114, 194n51
Henry II, Count of Sayn 21
Henry II, King of England 94
Henry III, King of England 39, 45, 48, 135, 136, 140, 183n66
Henry IV, King of England 120–21, 159, 206n19
Henry V, King of England 159
Henry VII, Holy Roman Emperor 110, 113
Henry VIII, King of England 159, 163
Henry of Lausanne 10–11, 173n13, 176n63
Henry Percy, Earl of Northumberland 151
Henryson, Robert *see Morall Fabillis of Esope the Phrygian*
heresy 4, 5, 6, 7, 9–14, 17, 19, 20–23, 24, 25, 26, 27, 28–29, 30, 44–46, 49, 54, 55, 58, 61, 68, 70, 74, 91, 96, 110, 111–12, 113, 133, 136, 141, 142, 146, 147, 150, 153, 154–55, 156, 157, 159–62, 164, 173n7, 173n8, 173n22, 179n141, 179n148, 195n79, 202n115, 222n230; *see also* Bruys, Peter of; Cathars; Gui, Bernard; Humiliati; Inquisition; inquisitors; Konrad von Marburg; Lollards; Petrobrusians; Robert le Bougre; Spiritual Franciscans; Waldensians
Heresy, character in the *Roman de Fauvel* 114
Hermeline 97
Hersent 97, 100, 101
Hildegard of Bingen 49–50, 185n128
The Historie of Reynart the Foxe 103
Honorius III, Pope 19, 37
Hubert, Sir, Reynard's confessor 100–1
Hubert, the friar (*Canterbury Tales* Prologue) 122
Hugh of St. Cher 40
Humbert of Romans 21, 22, 23, 44, 47
Humiliati 11–12, 15
Hus, Jan 146, 157, 159, 221n219
Hypocrisy, as an allegorical figure: in the *Mirour de l'Omme*
132; in the *Montpellier Codex* motets 92; in the *Roman de Fauvel* 115; in the *Roman de la Rose* 64, 69, 70, 74, 75, 77; in the works of Rutebeuf 67, 86, 87

Innocent III, Pope 11, 13, 15, 20, 37, 139, 153; *Cum Marthe* 153; *Omnis utriusque sexus* 153
Innocent IV, Pope 17, 22, 23, 35, 40, 42, 43–44, 46–47, 136, 139; *Etsi animarum* 46–47
Innocent VI, Pope 141
Inquisition 3, 6, 8, 13–14, 21–23, 24–27, 29, 31, 53, 91, 137–38, 159, 163
Inquisitors 3, 21–23, 25–27, 87, 136
Introductorius ad Evangelium Aeternum see Eternal Gospel
Isidore of Seville 96

Jack Upland 160
Jacobins 19, 71, 86, 88, 92, 163; *see also* Dominican order
Jacquemart Gielée *see Renart le Nouvel*
Jacques de Vitry 104
Jaume II, King of Majorca 26
Jealousy, in the Roman de la Rose 65; *see also* Castle of Jealousy
Jean d'Anneux 51, 142
Jean de Meun 6, 28, 44, 57, 62, 63–64, 65, 66, 67, 68, 71, 72, 75, 76, 77, 79–82, 86, 87, 92, 94, 99, 106–7, 118, 122, 162, 192n14, 193n25
Jean de Pouilly 51, 141
Jews 10, 54, 56, 73, 117, 132, 146, 162, 173n8
Joachim of Fiore 45, 46, 74, 183n89
John XXII, Pope 26, 29, 130, 141, 145, 147; *Quorundum exigit* 141
John Ball 154; *see also* Peasants' Revolt
John of Arderne 148
John of Gaunt 131, 150, 151, 154, 159
John of Reading 118
John of St. Giles 39
jongleurs 83, 84, 85, 90, 92, 95, 103, 104, 129, 191n2, 193n27
Jordan of Saxony 19, 20, 138, 142
Junius 87, 194n37

Konrad von Marburg 21–22

Lambert le Bègue 27
Langland, William 7, 81, 116,

118, 119, 126–27, 129–30, 132, 155, 161, 162, 210n94, 210n97, 211n115, 211n118
Latin Quarter *see* University of Paris
Li Dis de le vescie à prestre 124
Lollards 7, 58, 126, 133, 155, 158–61, 221n219, 221n223; *see also Jack Upland*; *Pierce the Plowman's Crede*; *The Plowman's Tale*; Twelve Conclusions of the Lollards; *Upland's Rejoinder*
London 120, 122, 127, 130, 131, 134, 135, 138, 139, 142, 143, 147, 148, 151, 155, 159
Louis IV of Bavaria, Holy Roman Emperor 141
Louis VIII, King of France 17, 91
Louis IX, King of France 6, 17, 31, 40–42, 45, 48, 49, 52, 59, 61–62, 69, 84, 91, 101, 103, 137, 182n50
Louis X, King of France 110
Louis of Navarre *see* Louis X
The Lover, in the *Roman de la Rose* 64–65, 66, 67, 74–76, 77–79, 80
Lucius III, Pope 11

Macrocosm 113
Magna Carta 45, 164
Map, Walter 94
Marsilius of Padua 141
Martin IV, Pope 51, 81; *Ad fructus uberes* 51, 81
Martin V, Pope 158
Matthew Paris 7, 37, 134–38; *Chronica Majora* 134, 135, 137; *Flores Historiarum* 134–35, 137; *Historia Anglorum* 134
Mechthild of Madeburg 28, 179n140
mendicancy 4, 11, 16, 18, 19, 27, 29, 31, 32, 43, 48, 50, 53–54, 57, 59–61, 61, 68, 69, 81, 84, 85, 86, 90, 122, 123, 128, 129, 130, 142, 143, 144, 146–47, 156, 157, 158, 160, 211n118, 222n1
Metamorphosis Goliae Episcopi 94; *see also* goliards
Michael of Cesena 141
minstrels 84, 92, 104, 108, 122, 128, 129, 155, 174n26, 210n107, 220n186
Moneta of Cremona 22; *see also* inquisitors
Montpellier Codex see motet
Morall Fabillis of Esope the Phrygian 103
motet, French 92, 110, 113, 115
Muhammad 74, 98, 174n36

Muslims 10, 45, 46, 50, 54, 74, 91, 146, 162, 174n36

Nature, in the *Roman de la Rose* 66, 78, 80
Nicholas V, antipope 141
Nicholas d'Abbeville 25
Nicholas of Hereford 158
Nicolas of Lisieux 50, 52
Nigel de Longchamps *see* Burnellus
Noble the lion 97, 101, 102, 110
nominalism 150, 153
nuntius 16, 124–25, 156; *see also* poverty

Ockham (Occam), William of 141, 150, 153, 158, 216n73
Old Woman, in the *Roman de la Rose* 65, 66, 74
Oldcastle, Sir John 159, 222n232
Omne Bonum 142–43

Papal Curia 15, 24, 40, 49, 51, 87, 110, 111, 113, 135, 136, 141, 143, 148, 155
papelards 77, 91
Paris 5, 13, 19, 20, 26, 30, 32, 33–34, 35, 36, 40, 43, 44, 48, 49, 50, 51, 53, 59, 62, 64, 68, 69, 83, 84, 85, 86, 88, 89, 90, 92, 99, 100, 103, 111, 114, 139
parody, as a literary form 4, 79, 80, 98, 99–100, 103, 104, 114, 125, 183n89
Peasants' Revolt 119, 130, 131, 154, 164
Peire Cardenal 24
Penetrans Domos, friar in *Piers Plowman* 128
penetrant domos 52, 57–58; *see also De periculis*
Pentecost 48; in the Summoner's Tale 125–26
Peter Lombard 141, 216n66
Peter of Verona 23
Peter Olivi 29, 179n145
Peter the Venerable, Abbot of Cluny 10
Peter Waldes 11
Petrobrusians 9–10
Pharisees 52, 56, 62, 70, 86, 155, 160; *see also De Periculis*
Philip IV (the Fair), King of France 25, 68, 76, 109–112
Philip Augustus, King of France 34, 35
Philip the Chancellor 95, 196n99
Pied Friars 196n88
Pierce the Plowman's Crede 160
Pierre de Saint-Cloud 98

Piers Plowman 81, 119, 126–30, 133, 160, 218n108
The Plowman's Tale 160
poverty, as a religious ideal 4, 11–12, 15–16, 18, 24, 26, 27, 28–29, 37, 56, 59, 68, 69, 130, 132, 134, 137, 138, 140, 141, 142, 144, 145–47, 152, 162, 163, 187n47; *see also* mendicancy; *nuntius*
Pride, in *Piers Plowman* 128
Priest of La Croix-en-Brie 98
privilegium canonis 34, 38
privilegium fori 34, 38–39
Pygmalion 67, 76

Raymond VI, Count of Toulouse 20
Raymond du Fauga 22
realism 150, 153, 220n171
Reformation 5, 7, 10, 58, 133, 146, 149, 158, 161, 163, 221n219
Renart le Contrefait 102
Renart le Nouvel 102
Revelation, book of 73, 74, 102
Reynard the Fox 6, 67, 84, 96–103, 107, 110, 115, 116, 154, 155, 198n17, 199n25, 201n78, 202n123
Richard II, King of England 120, 131, 132
Richard de Lison 98
Richard Flemming, Bishop of Lincoln 157–58
Robert Kilwardby 140
Robert le Bougre 21, 91, 136
Roger Bacon 29–30, 121, 138, 150, 162, 180n162
Roger Conway 148
Roger of Wendover 135; *see also* Matthew Paris
Roland of Cremona 39, 46, 77
Roman de Fauvel 7, 88, 95, 102, 109–10, 112–16, 128
Roman de la Rose 5, 6–7, 28, 57, 62–73, 74–82, 86, 87, 102, 109, 112, 115, 126, 127, 132, 191n79
Roman de Renart 7, 96, 84–85, 90, 92, 96–101, 104, 107, 112, 162; *see also* Reynard the Fox
rose, in the *Roman de la Rose* 64–65, 66, 67, 75, 76, 77–78, 79, 80
Rutebeuf 7, 62, 63, 67, 69, 70, 72, 75, 83–88, 91, 92, 94, 95, 97, 99, 101–2, 106, 107–9, 113, 118, 162, 163, 192n3, 192n14, 193n25; *La Bataille des Vices contre les Vertus* 86; *Complainte de Guillaume* 86, 87; *Des règles* 87; *La Discorde de l'Université et des Jacobins* 86; *Dit de Guillaume de*

Saint-Amour 86; *Dit de l'université* 84; *Dit de Sainte Eglise* 87; *Dit des Cordeliers* 84; *Dit d'Hypocrisie* 87; *Du Pharisien* 86; *Freire Denise* (fabliau) 106, 107–9; *Le Mariage Rutebeuf* 84; *Les Ordres de Paris* 87; *Renart le Bestourné* 101–2

Sack Friars 64, 196n88
St. Alban's, Benedictine monastery 134, 135, 136, 137, 138
St. Scholastica's Day riot 149
Saladin 74
Salimbene di Adam 17
satire, as a literary form 4, 14, 85, 88, 89, 94, 95, 98, 99–100, 102, 103, 106, 109, 110, 112, 114, 118–19, 121–122, 125–26, 127, 128, 161, 162, 164; *see also* estates satire
secular masters, at the University of Oxford 138, 139, 140, 142, 149; at the University of Paris 5, 6, 7, 16, 17, 23, 24, 30, 31–37, 38–40, 42–44, 46–51, 53, 56, 58, 59, 65, 67, 68, 70, 71–72, 74, 79, 85, 86–87, 89, 102, 141, 142–43, 181n1, 182n50, 184n102, 185n132, 185n134, 215n56, 222n1
seipsos amantes 55, 76; *see also De periculis*
sermons 4, 30, 39, 41, 48, 53, 56, 59, 61–62, 66, 70, 71, 78, 85, 91, 99, 101, 104, 123, 125, 126, 129, 140, 143, 145, 147–48, 151, 155, 159, 176n63, 206n21, 207n49; *see also* Guillaume de Saint-Amour; John Wyclif; Richard FitzRalph; Wycliffite sermons
sex 12, 28, 38; and the friars 36, 57, 71; in the fabliaux 105, 106–7, 108; in the *Roman de Fauvel* 115–16; in the *Roman de la Rose* 64, 66, 78–79; in the *Roman de Renart* 98, 100–1
Shakespeare, William 88, 132, 159, 194n51, 195n56
Shepherds' Crusade 41
Simon de Montfort 13, 20
Simon Islip, Archbishop of Canterbury 149–50
Simon Sudbury, Archbishop of Canterbury 154
"The Simonie," English poem 120
Speculum Stultorum see Burnellus

Spiritual Franciscans 26, 28–29, 30, 125, 141, 142, 145, 147, 162, 177n101, 179n148, 180n162, 216n72; *see also* Peter Olivi, *zelanti*
statutum de promovendis 42
Stephen of St. Thibéry 23
students, as goliards 93–94; at the University of Oxford 139, 140, 141, 143, 149–50, 157, 217n87; at the University of Paris 14, 20, 32–33, 34–40, 43, 60, 84, 85, 181n6
studia generalia 35, 39, 44, 139, 182n24
studium universal 35
Summoner's Tale 123–26; *see also Canterbury Tales*; Chaucer, Geoffrey

Tale of the Priest's Bladder see *Li Dis de le vescie à prestre*
þe vox and þe wolf 102
Thibaut IV, King of Navarre and Count of Champagne 91, 136; crusade of 91; and heretics 91, 136
Thomas Arundel, Archbishop of Canterbury 159
Thomas de Wilton 142–43
Thomas Netter of Walden 159
Thomas of Celano 15
Thomas of York 139; *Manus quae contra omnipotentem tenditur* 139
Thomas Speght 121
Thomas Walsingham 138
Tournament of Virtues and Vices, in the *Roman de Fauvel* 114; *see also* Rutebeuf, *La Bataille des Vices contre les Vertus*
troubadours 13, 19, 24, 83, 174n26, 192n4, 192n5
trouvères 7, 62, 67, 71, 83, 88, 90–91, 92, 95, 98, 136, 174n26, 192n4, 192n5, 194n43
Twelve Conclusions of the Lollards 158–59

universitas 35, 37, 47
University of Bologna 20, 33, 49, 181n6
University of Cambridge 39, 154, 216n65, 218n123
University of Oxford 7, 29, 30, 39, 138–41, 142, 143, 149–50, 151, 154–55, 157, 158, 159, 180n154, 208n64, 215n54
University of Paris 5, 6, 16, 17, 18, 20, 23, 24, 30, 31–37, 39–40, 41–44, 46–47, 49–51, 52–53, 54, 55, 56, 58, 63, 65, 67, 68, 69, 70, 72, 75, 79, 83, 84–85, 86, 88, 94, 101, 109, 111, 112, 117, 123, 134, 139, 140, 141, 143, 181n2, 182n51, 192n14
Upland's Rejoinder 160
Urban IV, Pope 50, 87
Urban VI, Pope 152
usus pauper controversy 29, 179n145
Uthred (Uhtred) of Boldon 142

Vainglory, in Rutebeuf's work 87; in the *Roman de Fauvel* 114
Van den vos Reynaerde 103
Venus, in the *Confessio Amantis* 131, 132; in the *Roman de la Rose* 66–67, 79
violence 10, 12, 24, 34–35, 36, 38–39, 72, 89, 98, 100, 101, 102, 105–6, 139, 143, 149, 163; in response to the Inquisition 23–25; toward the friars 1, 23–24, 25, 30–31, 41, 44, 177n104, 180n163, 184n99, 206n21

Waldensians 11, 12, 15, 21
The Wall, in Carcassonne 25, 26
Wat Tyler 131, 133; *see also* Peasants' Revolt
Wealth, in the *Roman de la Rose* 65
Western Schism 119, 133, 152, 157, 212n141
Willem die Madocke maecte see *Van den vos Reynaerde*
William Arnald 23
William Barton 154
William Courtenay, Archbishop of Canterbury 151, 154–55
William of Pelhisson 21, 22–23
Wyclif, John 7, 10, 58, 117, 126, 129, 133, 142, 146, 148–61, 163, 188n12, 221n203; *De blasphemia* 154, 156; *De civili dominio* 150–51; *De ecclesia* 151, 152; *De fratribus* 156; *De potestate papae* 153; *Descriptio fratris* 156; *Summa de Ente* 150
Wycliffite sermons 155

Ysengrimus, Latin poem 98, 199n21
Ysengrin the wolf 24, 97, 99, 100, 102, 116, 199n25

zelanti 18, 29; *see also* Spiritual Franciscans

www.ingramcontent.com/pod-product-compliance
Lightning Source LLC
Chambersburg PA
CBHW081550300426
44116CB00015B/2819